PEARSON CUSTOM LIBRARY

ENGLISH
MERCURY READER

ENGLISH COMPOSITION
FRCC ENG121 ONLINE CLASSES

PEARSON

V092
ISBN 10: 1-256-56596-2
ISBN 13: 978-1-256-56596-3

General Editors

Janice Neuleib
Illinois State University

Kathleen Shine Cain
Merrimack College

Stephen Ruffus
Salt Lake Community College

Table of Contents

WRITING AS INQUIRY

Writing as inquiry
is an invitation to
wonder and
discover again.

WRITING AS INQUIRY

Just the other night I was writing a card to my old friend Linda, someone I went to college with and haven't seen in twenty-five years. As I wrote, my words scribbled in a heavy black pen, she began to appear before me again. I saw her in geology class, a few rows up, wearing a black raincoat and rubber boots, carefully putting her straight black hair behind an ear so she could see her notes. I hadn't seen her so clearly in years, and the writing brought her back. Most of us have had this experience—the power of words to summon images, memories, and feelings—which is why we sometimes indulge, often with pleasure, in writing letters, cards, and e-mails to friends and family.

Yet many of us admit that we really don't like to write, particularly when forced to do it, or we clearly prefer certain kinds of writing and dislike others: "I just like to write funny stories," or "I like writing for myself, and not for other people," or "I hate writing research papers." I can understand this, because for years I felt much the same way. I saw virtually no similarities between my note to Linda and the paper I wrote for my philosophy class in college. Words that had power in one context seemed flimsy and vacant in another. One kind of writing was fairly easy; the other was sweating blood. How could my experience as a writer be so fundamentally different? In other words,

What You'll Learn in This Chapter

- Why it pays to spend time thinking about your writing process.
- Why learning to write well often involves *unlearning* things you already believe.
- How understanding rhetoric will help you analyze writing situations.
- What it means to be a writer who is motivated by a spirit of inquiry.
- How to harness both creative and critical ways of thinking to come up with new ideas.

what's the secret of writing well in a range of contexts *and* enjoying it more? Here's what I had to learn:

1. All writing can offer the joy of discovery, the opportunity to speak and be heard, and the satisfaction of earned insight.
2. A key to writing well is understanding the *process* of doing it.

They're not particularly novel ideas, but both were a revelation to me when I finally figured them out late in my academic career, and they changed the way I wrote for good. These two insights—that the pleasures of writing can span genres and situations, and that thinking about *how* we write matters—are guiding principles. I won't guarantee that haters of writing will come to love it, or that lovers of writing won't find writing to be hard work. But I hope that by the end of your class you'll experience some of the same pleasures I found writing to my friend Linda in most writing situations, and that you'll be able to adapt your own writing process to meet the demands of whatever situation you encounter.

The process of becoming a more flexible and insightful writer must begin by exploring what you already believe it means to write well and learning a bit about how we can talk about writing as a process. In this chapter, I'll also introduce you to an idea that will be at the heart of every activity and assignment I will introduce: the habits of mind and practices that will encourage you to adopt the "spirit of inquiry" as a motive for writing. This may sound a bit lofty and abstract. But by chapter's end I hope you'll recognize some practical implications of this approach that will help you with any writing assignment.

MOTIVES FOR WRITING

Why write? You could probably build a long list of reasons in a minute or two, perhaps beginning facetiously: "Because I *have* to!" But as you consider the many situations that call for writing and the purposes for doing it, I suspect that most will fall under a broad and obvious category: to say something to someone else. I'm less confident that you will see another broad motive for writing, partly because it gets less attention: we write to *discover* what we want to say.

These two motives for writing—to *share* ideas with others and to *discover* what the writer thinks and feels—are equally important.

But both these motives may arise from a still deeper spring: a sense of wonder and curiosity or even confusion and doubt, a desire to touch other people, or an urge to solve a problem. These feelings can inspire what I call the *spirit of inquiry,* a kind of perspective toward the world that invites questions, accepts uncertainty, and makes each of us feel some responsibility for what we say. This inquiring spirit should be familiar to you. It's the feeling you had when you discovered that the sun and a simple magnifying glass could be used to burn a hole in an oak leaf. It's wondering what a teacher meant when he said that World War II was a "good" war and Vietnam was a "bad" war. It's the questions that haunted you yesterday as you listened to a good friend describe her struggles with anorexia. The inquiring spirit even drives your quest to find the best DVD player, an effort that inspires you to read about the technology and visit consumerreports.org.

BELIEFS ABOUT WRITING

Most of us have been taught about writing since the first grade. We usually enter college with beliefs about how best to write a paper, which rules govern school writing, and even how to improve at composing. As I mentioned earlier, I've learned a lot about writing since my first years in college, and a big part of that learning involved unraveling some of my prior beliefs about writing. In fact, initially, I'd say that my development as a writer had more to do with *unlearning* some of what I already knew than it did with discovering new ways to write. What do you believe about how people get better at writing? You have theories that arise from all those years of school writing. Take a moment to find out what they are and whether they still make sense.

EXERCISE 1

What Do You Believe?

STEP ONE: From the following list, identify *the one belief* about writing that you agree with most strongly, and *one* that you're convinced isn't true.

1. Writing proficiency begins with learning the basics and then building on them, working from words to sentences to paragraphs to compositions.

2. The best way to develop as a writer is to imitate the writing of the people you want to write like.

3. People are born writers. Either you can do it or you can't.

4. The best way to develop as a writer is to develop good reading skills.

5. Practice is the key to a writer's development. The more a writer writes, the more he or she will improve.

6. Developing writers need to learn the modes of writing (argument, exposition, description, narration) and the genres (essays, research papers, position papers, and so on).

RULES FOR FASTWRITING

1. There are no rules.

2. Don't try to write badly, but give yourself permission to do so.

3. To the extent you can, think through writing rather than before it.

4. Keep your pen moving.

5. If you run out of things to say, write about how weird it is to run out of things to say until new thoughts arrive.

6. Silence your internal critic to suspend judgment.

7. Don't censor yourself.

---

7. Developing writers should start with simple writing tasks, such as telling stories, and move to harder writing tasks, such as writing a research paper.

8. The most important thing that influences a writer's growth is believing that he or she can learn to write well.

9. The key to becoming a better writer is finding your voice.

STEP TWO: Spend five minutes writing in your notebook or journal about *why* you agree with the one belief and disagree with the other. This is an open-ended "fastwrite." You should write fast and without stopping, letting your thoughts flow in whatever direction they go.

Journal Prompts

- *When* did you first start agreeing or disagreeing with the belief? Can you remember a particular moment or experience as a student learning to write that drove this home?

- *What* do you mean, exactly, when you say you agree or disagree with the belief? Can you explain more fully why you think the belief is true or false?

- *Who* was most influential in convincing you of the truth or falsity of the belief?

ONE STUDENT'S RESPONSE

Bernice's Journal

EXERCISE 1
STEP TWO

I used to be a firm believer in the idea of born writers—it was a genetic thing. People were gifted with the gold pen genes, or they weren't. Writing as a process involved a muse, inspiration, and luck. Things uncontrollable by the writer. Then I started writing, mostly for my 101 class, and I started to feel powerful when I put words on paper. In control. The idea of my voice, my words just being on the page and other people reading it and maybe liking it was a rush. I was always the girl who specialized in the art of being unnoticed, unseen, blending in. My Comp 101 prof. liked my writing and pushed really hard to work on my basics, to think about my process, to prewrite and revise. I started to see a clear distinction between how to write and what to write. How is all mixed up with the process, with discipline, with practice and perseverance.... The how isn't something you are born with; its something you develop, something you practice, a skill you hone.... Becoming a good writer takes learning how to write, figuring out a process that works for you, and then letting your voice be heard on the page.

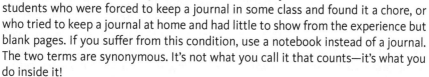

INQUIRING INTO THE DETAILS

Journals

Throughout *The Curious Writer*, I invite you to write in a journal. Some people hate journals. These are usually students who were forced to keep a journal in some class and found it a chore, or who tried to keep a journal at home and had little to show from the experience but blank pages. If you suffer from this condition, use a notebook instead of a journal. The two terms are synonymous. It's not what you call it that counts—it's what you do inside it!

Why do I want you to use a journal? One reason is that it is easier to write freely in this medium than it is when confronting the first page of a rough draft. Also, it's okay to write badly in journals and, as you will see later in this chapter, that's a good thing.

What kind of journal should you use? That's up to you. Some students just use the ubiquitous spiral notebook, which works just fine. Others find the digital journal best. They may be able to write faster and with more ease using a keyboard instead of a pen; keeping a journal on the computer might even be required if you're taking your class in a computer lab.

Unlearning Unhelpful Beliefs

You shouldn't be surprised when I say that I have a lot of theories about writing development; after all, I'm supposedly the expert. But we are *all* writing theorists, with beliefs that grow out of our successes and failures as students who write. Because you don't think much about them, these beliefs often shape your response to writing instruction without your even knowing it. For example, I've had a number of students who believe that people are born writers. This belief, of course, would make any kind of writing course a waste of time because writing ability would be a genetic problem.

A much more common belief is that learning to write is a process of building on basics, beginning with words, and then working up to sentences, paragraphs, and perhaps whole compositions. This belief was very common when I was taught writing. I remember slogging my way through Warriner's *English Grammar and Composition* in the seventh and eighth grade, dutifully working through chapter after chapter, beginning with parts of speech, parts of sentences, sentences, and then paragraphs.

Along with a lot of experts on writing instruction, I don't think that this foundational approach to writing development is very effective. I know it didn't help me become a better writer, and while I can still diagram a sentence, that's never a skill I call on when I'm composing. As a matter of fact, fifty years of research confirms that teaching formal grammar separately from writing essays is largely a waste of time. Despite this, formal grammar instruction persists, testimony to the subversive power of common sense. (Isn't it common sense that we should always learn the basics first?)

> Unlearning involves rejecting common sense if it conflicts with what actually works.

Unlearning involves rejecting common sense *if it conflicts with what actually works*. I hope you'll constantly test your beliefs about writing against the experiences you're having with it. Pay attention to what seems to work for you and what doesn't; mostly, I'd like you at least initially to play what one writing instructor calls the believing game. Ask yourself, *What do I have to gain as a writer if I try believing this is true?*

The Beliefs of This Text

One of the metaphors I very much like about writing development is offered by writing theorist Ann E. Berthoff. She said learning to write is like learning to ride a bike. You don't start by practicing handlebar skills, move on to pedaling practice, and then finally learn balancing techniques. You get on the bike and fall off, get up, and try again, doing all of those separate things at once. At some point, you don't fall and you pedal off down the street. Berthoff said writing is a process that involves *allatonceness* (all-at-once-ness), and it's simply not helpful to try to practice the subskills separately. This is one belief about writing development shared by this author.

Any number of beliefs—the importance of critical thinking, the connection between reading and writing, the power of voice and fluency, and the need to listen to voices other than your own—all guide the way you learn writing. One belief, though, undergirds them all: *The most important thing that influences a writer's growth is believing that he or she can learn to write well*. Faith in your ability to become a better writer is key. From it grows the motivation to learn how to write well.

Faith isn't easy to come by. I didn't have it as a writer through most of my school career because I assumed that being placed in the English class for underachievers meant that writing was simply another thing, like track, that I was mediocre at. For a long time, I was a captive to this attitude. But then, as a college freshman, I wrote a paper I cared about and the writing started to matter, not because I wanted to impress my instructor but because I discovered something I really wanted to say, and say well. I didn't settle for mediocrity after that.

As someone who wasn't too keen on writing for a very long time, I know how difficult it is to develop compelling reasons to write, particularly when the writing is required. I had to learn, among other things, that my teacher wasn't responsible for supplying the motivation (though I acknowledge that deadlines can help). I had to find a way to approach a writing assignment that made it seem like an opportunity to learn something.

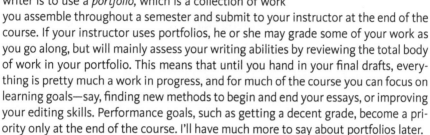

INQUIRING INTO THE DETAILS

Portfolios

One method for evaluating your development as a writer is to use a *portfolio*, which is a collection of work you assemble throughout a semester and submit to your instructor at the end of the course. If your instructor uses portfolios, he or she may grade some of your work as you go along, but will mainly assess your writing abilities by reviewing the total body of work in your portfolio. This means that until you hand in your final drafts, everything is pretty much a work in progress, and for much of the course you can focus on learning goals—say, finding new methods to begin and end your essays, or improving your editing skills. Performance goals, such as getting a decent grade, become a priority only at the end of the course. I'll have much more to say about portfolios later.

WRITING SITUATIONS AND RHETORICAL CHOICES

Good writing is good writing, right? Well, it depends on the situation. For instance, here's what a friend of my daughter wrote as a comment on her blog the other day:

> im happy to be back w/ u guys it was a too long of a weekend- dancing friday then? u hailey and i runnin tomorrow- sounds fun 2 me

This isn't necessarily bad writing for Facebook and sites like it. The message uses online conventions that most of us are familiar with—text messaging abbreviations like "u" for *you* and "2" for *to*—and it possesses a level of informality and intimacy that seems appropriate for its context. Would it be good writing for a college essay? Obviously not.

Part of learning to write well, then, isn't simply learning how to craft transitions, organize information, and follow grammatical rules; it's learning to recognize that each writing situation asks you for something different. Actually, you know this already. You know, for example, that composing a letter to a landlord who refuses to return your security deposit will be fundamentally different from a letter to your sister describing your problem with the landlord. What you may not know is what to call this kind of knowledge: rhetoric.

One way of analyzing any writing situation is by using *the rhetorical triangle,* which reveals the dynamic relationships among the writer, the subject, and the reader (see Figure 1).

What the triangle implies is pretty straightforward—to write effectively, you must simultaneously address three main factors: your own perspective as the writer, the topic you are writing about, and the people you are writing for. The

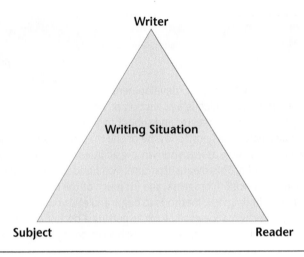

Figure 1 The rhetorical triangle

word *rhetorical,* of course, comes from *rhetoric*, the classical term for the study and practice of written and verbal communication. In fact, the rhetorical triangle has its origins in ancient Greece and the thinking of Aristotle, who first set down the principles of effective communication more than 2,000 years ago.

The three legs of the rhetorical triangle come together to shape the writing situation. The particularities of each leg—the writer, the subject, and the reader—determine the context of the writing situation. Consider again the security deposit problem. In that scenario, one thing is clear: Both of the proposed letters have a distinct—and different—*audience*. While the writer and the subject would seem to be the same for both letters, given the different audiences, the approach will be fundamentally different. In the letter to the landlord, the writer might adopt a formal, even legalistic, tone. The letter would be specific about what the writer is asking and when. The letter to the writer's sister would likely be informal, possibly more emotional. Its purpose would be to enlist a sibling's emotional support, not to persuade a landlord to return $500.

I'm pretty sure this is intuitively obvious to you. What may not be apparent is that you can use the same rhetorical knowledge to understand all kinds of writing situations, including academic ones. For example, consider next the opening two paragraphs from a writing assignment in Political Science 141: Contemporary Political Ideologies.

> This assignment aims to encourage students to connect the arguments being made by the thinkers in class to the issues and themes of our politics today. It aims to help students understand the relevance of political thinking for our political practice. Students are encouraged to share their judgments about the authors, only after they have shown that they understand the authors as the authors would understand themselves.

Use one of the following questions as the basis for a short essay. Your essay should be lucid and concise, and your argument should be thoroughly supported by relevant citations and allusions from the texts at hand. Grammar, spelling, punctuation, and syntax should be perfect.... Your paper is to be three to five pages in length, double-spaced, typed, and stapled in the upper left-hand corner. Please number your pages. A title page with an appropriate title must also be included, and all title pages should show what question the student is answering.

Using your own instincts about the rhetorical situation in this example, answer the following questions:

1. How would you characterize the instructor, and, based on that characterization, what kind of reader do you think he might be?

2. If you were in this class, how might your analysis of the rhetorical situation influence your approach to the writing assignment?

Writing well involves evaluating situations like these using your rhetorical knowledge.

HABITS OF MIND

When I first started teaching writing, I noticed a strange thing in my classes. What students learned about writing through the early assignments in the class didn't seem to transfer to later assignments, particularly research papers. What was I doing wrong, I wondered? Among other things, what I failed to make clear to my students was how certain "essential acts of mind" were present in every assignment, from the very first to the very last. What bound the writing course together was the idea of academic inquiry and the habits of mind—or *dispositions*, as one writer describes them—that lead students to see how writing can be a process of discovery.

Start with Questions, Not Answers

A lot of people think that writing is about recording what you already know, which accounts for those who choose familiar topics to write on when given the choice. "I think I'll write about _____," the thinking goes, "because I know that topic really well and already have an idea what I can say." Unfortunately, the result of writing about what you already know is too often an uninspired draft full of generalizations and clichés.

What do you do about this problem? *Make the familiar strange.* This means finding new ways to see what you've seen before. For years, I've asked some of my writing students to take photographs of any subject they want. Predictably, most students choose to take pictures of familiar things—their rooms or apartments, the trees outside the window, campus buildings, local landscapes—and they almost always take one picture of each subject. The result is that these photographs are rarely surprising. They see these familiar subjects in very familiar ways. But when I ask them to return to a single subject and take multiple pictures of it, there are almost always surprises and fresh ways of seeing the subject.

It's apparent that there are multiple ways of seeing the same thing, and of course this is one thing that we often admire about good writing—it offers a perspective on something familiar that we hadn't considered before. One of the ways writers accomplish this is by using questions. Questions shift a writer's perspective on a subject much as distance, angle, and light alter a photographer's ways of seeing. A shell is just a shell if you only look at it once and in one way. But if you want to see what you've seen before in a way you haven't seen it, you look again and again (see Figure 2). Questions are one way to keep shifting your gaze on any subject.

Therefore, in an inquiry-based approach to writing, you'll choose a writing topic that raises questions about how you think or feel over one that you have all figured out. Almost any topic can raise interesting questions. *There are no boring topics, only boring questions.* The key is to approach any topic with a sense of wonder and curiosity: *Why are houseflies so hard to kill? What distinguishes the cultures of skaters and snowboarders? When do most marriages fail and what can be done about it? Why do young people join gangs?*

Suspend Judgment

What's one of the most common problems I see in student writers? Poor grammar? Lack of organization? A missing thesis? Nope. *It's the tendency to judge too soon and too harshly.* A great majority of my students, including really smart, capable writers, have powerful internal critics, or as the novelist Gail Godwin once called them, "Watchers at the Gates." This is the voice you may hear when you're starting to write a paper, the one that has you crossing out that first sentence or that first paragraph over and over until you "get it perfect."

> It's okay to write badly. Resist the tendency to judge too soon and too harshly.

The only way to overcome this problem is to suspend judgment. In doing so, you essentially tell your Watchers this: *It's okay to write badly.*

I never try to write badly, of course, but whenever I'm stuck in the middle of something, or can't figure out what to say or where to begin, or even when I don't have a clue about my subject, I simply start writing. Sometimes it's absolutely horrible. But just as often, there's a glint of an idea, or direction, or topic, and away I go, trying to keep up with the vein of thought branching in all directions. The British novelist E. M. Forster once said, "How do I know what I think until I see what I say?" I've come to have a lot of faith in this idea. Rather than trying to use my journal the way I used to—to try to write beautiful, eloquent prose—I use the journal simply to think things through; that the prose sometimes stinks doesn't bother me anymore.

Kim Taylor © Dorling Kindersley

Chad Ehlers/Stock Connection

Andreas Von Einsiedel ©
Dorling Kindersley

Figure 2   Good writing makes the familiar strange by offering multiple ways of seeing the same thing.

> ### CONDITIONS THAT MAKE "BAD" WRITING POSSIBLE
>
> 1. Willingness to suspend judgment
> 2. Ability to write fast enough to out-run your internal critic
> 3. Belief that confusion, uncertainty, and ambiguity help thought rather than hinder it
> 4. Interest in writing about "risky" subjects, or those that you don't know what you want to say about until you say it

We know how powerful our internal critics can be, insisting that every word be spelled right, and every thought sharp. Our Watchers can't abide bad writing. One of the conditions that makes bad writing possible for me is that my Watchers are not voices I honor in my journal, at least not when I want to use my journal to think something through.

Now I know it must seem odd that a chapter on writing would talk about the virtues of writing badly, but it can be a useful tool for solving all kinds of writing problems. I encourage you to use this approach. I've seen bad writing turn slow writers into faster ones, procrastinators into initiators. I've seen bad writing help students who always wrote short papers begin to generate longer, more thoughtful essays. Best of all, I've seen bad writing transform students who once hated writing into people who see writing as a useful tool for thinking, and even a source of pleasure.

Search for Surprise

One of the key benefits of writing badly is *surprise*. This was a revelation for me when I first discovered the virtues of bad writing in graduate school. I was convinced that you never pick up the pen unless you know what you want to say, which may account for my struggles with journal writing. Suddenly I stumbled on a new way to use writing—not to *record* what I already knew about a subject, but to *discover* what I actually thought. This way of writing promised a feast of surprises that made me hunger to put words on the page.

EXERCISE 2

A Roomful of Details

STEP ONE: Spend ten minutes brainstorming a list of details based on the following prompt. Write down whatever comes into your mind, no matter how silly. Be specific and don't censor yourself.

> Try to remember a room you spent a lot of time in as a child. It may be your bedroom in the back of the house at the edge of the field, or the kitchen where your grandmother kneaded bread or made thick red pasta sauce. Put yourself back in that room. Now look around you. What do you see? What do you hear? What do you smell?

STEP TWO: Examine your list. If things went well, you will have a fairly long list of details. As you review the list, identify one detail that surprises you the most, a detail that seems somehow to carry an unexpected charge. This might be a detail that seems connected to a feeling or story. You might be drawn to a detail that confuses you a little. Whatever its particular appeal, circle the detail.

> ### BRAINSTORMING
>
> - Anything goes.
> - Don't censor yourself.
> - Write everything down.
> - Be playful but stay focused.

STEP THREE: Use the circled detail as a prompt for a seven-minute fastwrite. Begin by focusing on the detail: What does it make you think of? And then what? And then? Alternatively, begin by simply describing the detail more fully: What does it look like? Where did it come from? What stories are attached to it? How does it make you feel? Avoid writing in generalities. Write about specifics—that is, particular times, places, moments, and people. Write fast, and chase after the words to see where they want to go. Give yourself permission to write badly.

ONE STUDENT'S RESPONSE

Bernice's Journal

EXERCISE 2
STEP THREE

DETAIL: STAINLESS STEEL COUNTERS

When I was five or six my father and I made cookies for the first time. I don't remember what prompted him to bake cookies, he liked to cook but he didn't very well so he didn't like to use cook books. I remember sitting on the cold stainless steel, the big red and white cook book splayed over my lap. I was reading it out loud to my dad. The kitchen was warm but everything gleamed; it was industrial and functional. It was the only room in our house that still looked like it belonged to the "Old Pioneer School." My dad and uncles had renovated every other room into bedrooms, playrooms, family rooms. The place was huge but cozy, it was home. I remember reading off ingredients until I got to the sugar. It called for $\frac{3}{4}$ cup and I didn't understand the fraction. I thought it meant three or four cups. We poured so much sugar into the bowl. The cookies were terrible. Hard and glassy, too sweet and brittle. It wasn't until years later that I understood that my dad didn't understand the measurement either. He was persistent though. We pulled down every cook book in the house until we found one that described the measuring cups and what they meant. We started all over and our second batch was perfect. My dad is one of the smartest people I know, inventive, imaginative

(continued)

One Student's Response (*continued*)

but he only has a rudimentary education. He can read and write enough to get by, he's gifted with numbers, but I can't help looking back and wondering what he could have been, what he could have done for the world if just one person had taken him by the hand and showed him what he showed me. If just one person had told him not to give up, to keep trying, that in the end it will be worth all the work, I wonder who he could have been if one person had seen his curiosity and imagination and fostered it instead of seeing his muscles and capable hands and putting him to work. If just one person had told him that his mind was the greatest tool he possessed. If just one person baked cookies with him.

You may experience at least three kinds of surprise after completing a fast-writing exercise like the preceding one:

1. Surprise about *how much* writing you did in such a short time
2. Surprise about discovering a topic you didn't expect to find
3. Surprise about discovering a *new way of understanding or seeing a familiar topic*

The kind of surprises you encounter doing this sort of writing may not always be profound. They may not even provide you with obvious essay topics. With any luck, though, by hunting for surprises in your own work you will begin to experience the pleasure of writing *to learn*. That's no small thing, particularly if you've always believed that writers should have it all figured out before they pick up the pen.

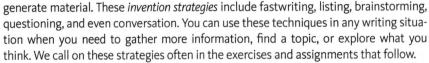

INQUIRING INTO THE DETAILS

Invention Strategies

Perhaps without knowing it, you have already practiced some writing techniques designed to help you generate material. These *invention strategies* include fastwriting, listing, brainstorming, questioning, and even conversation. You can use these techniques in any writing situation when you need to gather more information, find a topic, or explore what you think. We call on these strategies often in the exercises and assignments that follow.

At first, spending time doing all this writing and thinking before you actually begin a draft may seem like a waste of time. After all, your goal is to finish the assignment. But if you want to find a focused topic that means something to you and write it with enough information, then invention strategies such as fastwriting will prove invaluable. They produce the raw material that can be shaped, like clay on a potter's wheel, into something with form and meaning. But really the best thing about invention strategies is that they often generate material that is ripe with surprise.

INVENTION STRATEGIES

- *Fastwriting:* The emphasis is on speed, not correctness. Don't compose, don't think about what you want to say before you say it. Instead, let the writing lead, helping you discover what you think.

- *Listing:* Fast lists can help you generate lots of information quickly. They are often in code, with words and phrases that have meaning only for you. Let your lists grow in waves—think of two or three items and then pause until the next few items rush in.

- *Clustering:* This nonlinear method of generating information, also called *mapping,* relies on *webs* and often free association of ideas or information. Begin with a core word, phrase, or concept at the center of a page, and build branches off it. Follow each branch until it dies out, return to the core, and build another.

- *Questioning:* Questions are to ideas what knives are to onions. They help you cut through to the less obvious insights and perspectives, revealing layers of possible meanings, interpretations, and ways of understanding. Asking questions complicates things but rewards you with new discoveries.

- *Conversing:* Conversing is fastwriting with the mouth. When we talk, especially to someone we trust, we work out what we think and feel about things. We listen to what we say, but we also invite a response, which leads us to new insights.

- *Researching:* This is a kind of conversation, too. We listen and respond to other voices that have said something or will say something if asked about topics that interest us. Reading and interviewing are not simply things you do when you write a research paper but activities to use whenever you have questions you can't answer on your own.

- *Observing:* When we look closely at anything, we see what we didn't notice at first. Careful observation of people, objects, experiments, images, and so on generates specific information that leads to informed judgments.

WRITING AS A PROCESS

There is a process for doing almost anything—fixing a broken washing machine, learning how to play tennis, studying for the SAT, and, of course, writing. It might be hard to imagine, therefore, why some English teachers seem to make such a big deal out of the writing process. Here's why:

- The process of writing, like anything that we do frequently, is not something that we think about.

- When we focus, as we often do in writing, on *what* rather that *how,* on the product rather than the process, then when problems arise we don't see many options for solving them. We get stuck and we get frustrated.

- As we start to pay attention to how we write in a variety of situations, two things happen: We become aware of our old habits that don't always help, and that may actually hurt our success with writing. Second—and this is most important—we begin to understand that there are actually *choices* we can make when problems arise, and we become aware of what some of those are.

- The result of all of this is a simple yet powerful thing: The more we understand writing processes, the more control we get over them. Getting control of the process means the product gets better.[1]

Here's an example of what I mean. Chauntain summarized her process this way: "Do one and be done." She always wrote her essays at the last minute and only wrote a single draft. She approached nearly every writing assignment the same way: Start with a thesis and then develop five topic sentences that support the thesis with three supporting details under each. This structure was a container into which she poured all her prose. Chauntain deliberated over every sentence, trying to make each one perfect, and as a result she spent considerable time staring off into space searching for the right word or phrase. It was agony. The papers were almost always dull—she thought so, too—and just as often she struggled to reach the required page length. Chauntain had no idea of any other way to write a school essay. As a matter of fact, she thought it was really the *only* way. So when she got an assignment in her economics class to write an essay in which she was to use economic principles to analyze a question that arose from a personal observation, Chauntain was bewildered. How should she start? Could she rely on her old standby structure—thesis, topic sentences, supporting details? She felt stuck.

Not only did she fail to see that she had choices in this writing situation, she had no clue what those choices were.

That's why we study process. It helps us to solve problems like these. This must begin with a self-study of your own habits as a writer, identifying not just how you tend to do things but the patterns of problems that might arise when you do them.

EXERCISE 3

What Is Your Process?

Take a moment and analyze your own writing challenges. The following questions might help you develop a profile of your writing process in certain situations, and help you identify problems you might want to address by altering your process.

STEP ONE: Complete the Self-Evaluation Survey.

---

[1]There is considerable research in learning theory that confirms these conclusions; in particular, so-called "metacognitive thinking"—the awareness of how you do things—increases the transfer of relevant knowledge from one situation to another. In other words, what you learn about how to do something in one situation gets more easily activated in another.

Self-Evaluation Survey

1. When you're given a school writing assignment, do you wait until the last minute to get it done?

    Always———Often———Sometimes———Rarely———Never

2. How often have you had the experience of learning something you didn't expect through writing about it?

    Very often———Fairly often———Sometimes———Rarely———Never

3. Do you generally plan out what you're going to write before you write it?

    Always———Often———Sometimes———Rarely———Never

4. *Prewriting* describes activities that some writers engage in before they begin a first draft. Prewriting might include freewriting or fastwriting, making lists, brainstorming or mapping, collecting information, talking to someone about the essay topic, reading up on it, or jotting down ideas in a notebook or journal. How much prewriting do you tend to do for the following types of assignments? Circle the appropriate answer.

    - A personal essay:

        A great deal———Some———Very little———None———Haven't written one

    - A critical essay about a short story, novel, or poem:

        A great deal———Some———Very little———None———Haven't written one

    - A research paper:

        A great deal———Some———Very little———None———Haven't written one

    - An essay exam:

        A great deal———Some———Very little———None———Haven't written one

5. At what point in writing an academic paper do you usually get stuck? Check all that apply.
    - ❑ Getting started
    - ❑ In the middle
    - ❑ Finishing
    - ❑ I never get stuck (go on to Question 9)
    - ❑ Other _____

6. If you usually have problems getting started on an academic paper or essay, which of the following do you often find hardest to do? Check

all that apply. (If you don't have trouble getting started, go on to Question 7.)

❑ Deciding on a topic

❑ Writing an introduction

❑ Finding a good place to write

❑ Figuring out exactly what I'm supposed to do for the assignment

❑ Finding a purpose or focus for the paper

❑ Finding the right tone

❑ Other_____

7. If you usually get stuck in the middle of a paper, which of the following causes the most problems? (If writing in the middle of a paper isn't a problem for you, go on to Question 8.)

❑ Keeping focused on the topic

❑ Finding enough information to meet page length requirements

❑ Following my plan for how I want to write the paper

❑ Bringing in other research or points of view

❑ Organizing all my information

❑ Trying to avoid plagiarism

❑ Worrying about whether the paper meets the requirements of the assignment

❑ Worrying that the paper just isn't any good

❑ Messing with citations

❑ Other_____

8. If you have difficulty finishing an essay or paper, which of the following difficulties are typical for you? Check all that apply.

❑ Composing a last paragraph or conclusion

❑ Worrying that the paper doesn't meet the requirements of the assignment

❑ Worrying that the paper just isn't any good

❑ Trying to keep focused on the main idea or thesis

❑ Trying to avoid repeating myself

❑ Realizing I don't have enough information

❑ Dealing with the bibliography or citations

❑ Other_____

9. Rank the following list of approaches to revision so that it reflects the strategies you use *most often to least often* when rewriting academic

papers. Rank the items 1–6, with the strategy you use most often as a 1 and least often as a 6.

_____ I usually just tidy things up—editing sentences, checking spelling, looking for grammatical errors, and performing other proofreading activities.

_____ I mostly look for ways to reorganize existing information in the draft to make it more effective.

_____ I generally try to fill holes by adding more information.

_____ I do more research.

_____ I often completely change the focus or even the main idea in the revision, rewriting sections, adding or removing information, and rearranging the order of things.

_____ I rarely do any rewriting at all.

10. Finally, do you tend to impose a lot of conditions on when, where, or how you think you write most effectively? For example, do you need a certain pen, do you always have to write on a computer, must it be quiet or noisy, or do you often write best under pressure? Do you need to be in certain kinds of places to write effectively? Or can you write under a range of circumstances, with few or no conditions? Circle one.

Lots of conditions———Some———A few———No conditions

If you do impose conditions on when, where, or how you write, list some of those conditions here:

1.

2.

3.

4.

STEP TWO: In small groups, discuss the results of the survey. Begin by picking someone to tally the answers to each question. Post these on the board or a sheet of newsprint so they can be added to the class totals. Analyze the results for your group. In particular, discuss the following questions:

- Are there patterns in the responses? Do most group members seem to answer certain questions in similar or different ways? Are there interesting contradictions?
- Based on these results, what "typical" habits or challenges do writers in your class seem to share?
- What struck you most?

Thinking About Your Process

The survey you completed is the beginning of reflection on your own writing process. You will do this kind of reflection again and again throughout this text so that by the end you will have written a narrative of thought that tells the story of your reading and writing processes, and how you change those processes to produce better writing more efficiently. The reflective letter in your portfolio might be where you finally tell that story in full, perhaps beginning with your own habits, rituals, and challenges.

However, now is a good time to begin telling yourself that story.

What do you remember about your own journey as a writer both inside and outside of school? One of my earliest, most pleasant memories of writing is listening to the sound of the clacking of my father's old Royal typewriter in the room down the hall as I was going to sleep. I imagine him there now, in the small study that we called the "blue room," enveloped in a cloud of pipe smoke. It is likely that he was writing advertising copy back then, or perhaps a script for a commercial in which my mother, an actress, would appear. I loved the idea of writing then. The steady hammering of typewriter keys down the hall sounded effortless, yet at the same time solid, significant. This all changed, I think, in the eighth grade when it seemed that writing was much more about following rules than tapping along to a lively dance of words.

Spend some time telling your own story about how your relationship to writing evolved.

EXERCISE 4

Literacy Narrative Collage

Generating Ideas

When you get a writing assignment, your habit is probably to sit down and simply write it, composing on the computer. This time, however, we'll begin by generating ideas (classical rhetoricians call this "invention").

To begin working toward a draft essay on your personal writing history, we'll start in your journal with a collage of moments, memories, or reflections. *For each prompt, write fast for about four minutes. Keep your pen moving and give yourself permission to write badly.* After you've responded to one prompt, skip a line and move on to the next one. Set aside about twenty minutes for this generating activity.

1. What is your earliest memory of writing? Tell the story.
2. We usually divide our experiences as writers into private writing and school writing, or writing we do by choice and writing we are required to do for a grade. Let's focus on school writing. Tell the story of a teacher, a class, an essay, an exam, or other moment that you consider a *turning*

point in your understanding of yourself as a writer or your understanding of writing.

3. Writing is part of the fabric of everyday life in the United States, and this is truer than ever with Internet communication. Describe a typical day for you in which writing plays a part, and think about how this has changed in your lifetime so far.

4. What is the most successful (or least successful) thing you've ever written in or out of school? Tell the story.

Congratulations. You've made a mess. But I hope this collage of your experiences as a writer is an interesting mess, one that brought some little surprises. As you look at these four fragments of fastwriting, you might sense a pattern between them. Is there a certain idea about yourself as a writer that seems to emerge in these various contexts for thinking about it? It's more likely that one or perhaps two of the prompts really took off for you, presenting trails you'd like to continue following. Or maybe nothing happened. For now, set your journal aside. We'll return to this material soon.

Writing Creatively, Writing Critically: A Process of Writing

Here was my writing process when I was in school:

1. Get the assignment. Find out when it was due and how long it was supposed to be.
2. Wait until the night before it was due and get started.
3. Stare off into space.
4. Eat ice cream.
5. Write a sketchy outline.
6. Write a sentence; then cross it out.
7. Stare off into space.
8. Write another sentence, and then squeeze out a few more.
9. Think about Lori Jo Flink, and then stare off into space.
10. Write a paragraph. Feel relief and disgust.

I would get the work done eventually, but the process was agonizing and the product mediocre. What did I conclude from this back then? That I wasn't good at writing, which was no big surprise because I pretty much hated it. Something happened to me to change that view, of course, because you hold my writing in your hands. Among other things, I came to understand that the processes I was using for writing were really just habits I applied without thought no matter what the situation. I also was dedicated to the idea that I needed to know exactly what I was trying to say before I said it.

But more than anything, I thought writing was a process like this:

When itís really like this:

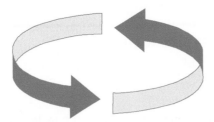

In other words, I had always thought that writing was a straight march forward from beginning to end; I had to wait for something to come into my head and then tried to get it down. At all costs, I avoided things like new ideas or other ways of seeing a topic—anything that might get in the way of the drive to the conclusion. If I thought about anything, it was trying to find the "perfect" way of saying things or worrying about whether I was faithfully following a certain structure. I rarely learned anything from my writing. I certainly never expected I should.

But this isn't the way experienced writers work at all. The writing process isn't a linear trajectory, but a looping, recursive process—one that encourages *thinking,* not simply recording the thoughts that you already have. Writing doesn't involve a series of steps that you must follow in every situation but is a much messier zigzag between collecting information and focusing on it, exploring things and thinking about them, writing and rewriting, reviewing and rearranging, and so on. The process is always influenced by the writing situation. For instance, experienced writers approach the process of writing an essay exam quite differently than they would a lab report. Some writers learn this flexibility slowly through experience. A faster way is to combine experience writing for all kinds of situations *and* monitoring the processes you use for each one and applying your knowledge of what works.

While there isn't a single writing process, I do think there are certain kinds of thinking that we can apply to most writing situations. Rather than read my explanation of it now, try the exercise that follows and maybe you'll see what I mean.

EXERCISE 5

Alternating Currents of Thought: Generating and Judging

Let's return to the subject you began writing about in Exercise 4—your experiences as a writer—but let's spend more time thinking about the third prompt in that exercise: your experience with writing technology.

Generating

STEP ONE: What are your earliest memories of using a computer for writing? Begin by telling the story and then let the writing lead from there. Keep your pen moving and allow yourself to write badly.

STEP TWO: Brainstorm a list of words or phrases that you associate with the word "literate" or "literacy."

Reread what you just wrote in your notebook or journal, underlining things that surprised you or that seem significant or interesting to you. Skip a line and respond in writing to the next set of prompts.

Judging

STEP THREE: Choose one of the following sentences as a starting point, and then write a paragraph about it. This time, compose each sentence thinking about what you want to say before you say it and trying to say it as well as you can.

> *What I understand now about my experiences with writing on computers that I didn't understand when I started out is _____.*
>
> *When they think about writing with computers, most people think _____, but my experience was _____.*
>
> *The most important thing I had to discover before I considered myself "computer literate" was _____.*

Reflecting

If you're like most people, then the parts of this exercise that involved generating felt different than the part where you judged what you had written. But *how* were they different? How would you distinguish between the experience of generating and judging? Talk about this or write about it in your journal.

Thinking and Writing Dialectically

At the heart of the strategy of inquiry, which is at the heart of *The Curious Writer* (see Figure A in the Preface), is the following model:

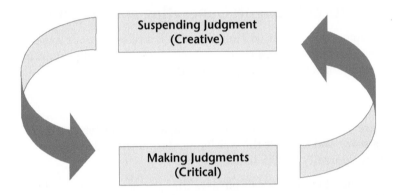

The two parts of Exercise 5, generating and judging, were designed to simulate this shift from suspending judgments and making judgments as you wrote about your early experiences using a computer for writing. In the first two steps, you spent some time fastwriting without much critical interference, trying to generate some information from your own experience. In the third step, which began with "seed" sentences that forced you into a more reflective, analytical mode, you were encouraged to look for patterns of meaning in what you generated.

> Suspending judgment feels freer, exploratory.... Making judgments shifts the writer into an analytical mode.

For many writers, these are two distinct ways of thinking. *Suspending judgment* feels freer, is exploratory, and may spark emotion. *Making judgments* shifts the writer into an analytical mode, one that might lower the temperature, allowing writers to see their initial explorations with less feeling and more understanding. Another way of distinguishing between these two modes of thought is to label the open-ended thinking we often associate with fastwriting as "creative" and the more closed-ended thinking we associate with judging or analyzing as "critical."

INQUIRING INTO THE DETAILS

Organizing Your Computer Files

In a writing class, you typically have lots of documents and frequently multiple versions of the same document. How do you make sure that you can find them? Take a little time to establish conventions for naming your files. Start by establishing a folder for your class, and then decide on what might be helpful naming categories to apply to each document. For example,

- Genre (e.g., essay, exercise, letter, response, and so on)
- Title of document
- Version number
- Date

Using the underscore key, separate each element when naming your document. For example, *essay_importanceofwritingbadly_v2_2008-December-12.* It takes a little more time to compose a more elaborate file name than *doc.1* but it ultimately saves time by helping you locate documents more easily.

Combining these two modes of thinking gives both thinking and writing more range and depth. Creative thinking creates the conditions for discovery—new insights or ways of seeing—while critical thinking helps writers refine their discoveries and focus on the most significant of them.

Figure 3 lists other ways you can visualize creative and critical thinking. In narrative writing, for instance (the kind of writing you likely did in the previous exercise), creative thinking helps you generate information about *what happened,* while critical thinking may lead you to insights about *what happens.* Likewise, in research writing, investigators often move back and forth between their *observations of* things and their *ideas about* them. More broadly speaking, when we think creatively we collect, and when we think critically we evaluate what we have collected.

Note that in Figure 3 double-ended arrows link the items in each pair. The process is *dialectical;* it consists of a back-and-forth movement between the two opposing modes of thought. Many writers do this instinctively. As they compose, they constantly shift between contrasting modes of thought, from collecting to focusing, from generating to criticizing, from showing to telling, from exploring to reflecting, from believing to doubting, from playing to judging.

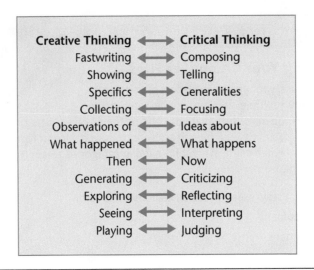

Figure 3 When writers use dialectical thinking, they move back and forth between two opposing modes of thought—the creative and the critical. One seems playful and the other judgmental; one feels open ended and the other more closed. Certain activities such as fastwriting or brainstorming promote one mode of thought, and careful composing or reflection promotes another.

Certain activities—such as fastwriting and composing—encourage one way of thinking or the other. Learning to balance these opposing forces is what dialectical thinking is all about. In practice, however, many beginning writers give too much emphasis to either one mode of thinking or the other, a tendency that accounts for many of the challenges these writers face within their own writing processes.

Spend too much time locked in the critical mode of thinking and your internal critic takes over. This voice pinches off the flow of material generated by creative thinking. The writing then comes slowly and painfully, and it rarely yields surprise. Topics are abandoned before the writer has fully explored their potential. Working from scarcity, the writer is compelled to use all the material he or she has at hand, often resulting in writing that feels forced, incomplete, or obvious.

On the other hand, give too much free rein to creative thinking and the artist runs wild. The problem here isn't scarcity but rather overabundance. It's a poverty of riches, for without a critical eye to provide shape and direction, the writer cannot present all of his or her material in a coherent and meaningful fashion.

Other challenges result when writers fail to move back and forth between creative and critical modes. One excursion into creative thinking followed by a second into critical thinking is rarely enough to produce good writing.

Writers need to move back and forth between the two modes until they come to see their topics in interesting ways that differ from what they might have creatively or critically thought about the topic when they started the writing process.

Put simply, the goal of this dialectical thinking is to address a question that ultimately all writing must answer:

So what?

So what? can be a pretty harsh question, and I find that some students tend to ask it too soon in the writing process, before they've fully explored their topic or collected enough information. That may have been your experience when you suddenly found yourself high and dry, forced to reflect on possible meanings of a moment you've written about for only eight minutes. When you can't come up with an answer to *So what?,* the solution is usually to generate more information.

There's another danger, too. In their enthusiasm to answer *So what?,* some writers seize on the first convenient idea or thesis that comes along. This abruptly ends the process of inquiry before they've had a chance to explore their subjects. These writers squander the opportunity to be surprised by what they discover.

Opening Questions

Using the dialectical thinking process is all well and good, but first you've got to have something to think about. The inquiry approach promoted by *The Curious Writer* is grounded in the idea that the writing process depends, more than anything else, on finding the right questions. What makes a question "right"? First and foremost, you must find it interesting enough to want to think and write about it for awhile.

I recently visited teachers in Laredo, Texas, and I told them that a good question can make even the most boring topic interesting. I would prove it, I said, and picked up a lemon that was sitting on a table and asked everyone, in turn, to ask a question about the lemon or about lemons. Twenty minutes later, we generated sixty questions, and in the process began to wonder how the scent of lemons came to be associated with cleanliness. We wondered why lemons appeared so often in wartime British literature. We wondered why the lime and not the lemon is celebrated in local Hispanic culture. We wondered a lot of interesting things that we never expected to wonder about because a lemon is ordinary. Questions can make the familiar world we inhabit yield to wonder.

The point is this: *There are no boring topics—just poor questions.*

Writing as inquiry, therefore, begins with questions and not answers. We pursue a subject because we want to find out what we think about it, and certain kinds of questions are much more likely to sustain our investigation than others. For example, I had a student once who really, really wanted to know whether Elvis was really dead. Yep, the King is gone. End of story. A better question for writing and thinking would have been to ask *why* we keep asking whether Elvis is dead. What is it about him that seems to sustain such a blind hope in his existence among certain people?

Learning to find the right question, one that will be worth spending time with, is an essential skill, and there are certain qualities that most good questions seem to share. Here are a few of them:

- The writer is genuinely interested in the question and the answers.
- People other than the writer have a stake in the answers to the question.
- It raises more questions; there isn't a simple answer.
- Something has been said already about the question. There's information out there.
- The question is a manageable size. It's isn't too broad ("What is the meaning of lemons?") or too specific ("What is the meaning of that lemon?").

QUESTIONS, CREATIVITY, AND CRITICAL THINKING: A STRATEGY FOR INQUIRY

If you combine the power of good questions with the back-and-forth process of writing creatively and critically discussed earlier in the chapter, you have a model for a strategy of inquiry that you can use for many assignments (see Figure 4). Typically you begin exploring a subject, sometimes generating some initial thoughts through fastwriting, listing, or other invention methods. Subjects are like landscape shots in photography—they cover a huge amount of ground. You need to find a narrower topic, or some *part* of the landscape to look at more closely. Take popular music, for example. That's a huge subject. But as you write and read about it a little, you begin to see that the topic that interests you most is the blues, and maybe something about its influence on American popular music. Here's how it works:

- You start with a *subject* that makes you curious—music—and then work toward a *topic*—the influence of blues—that is beginning to focus your attention for a closer look.

Ultimately you are searching for a few questions about your topic that both interest you and will sustain your project. These are the questions that will help you focus your topic, that guide your research into yourself or other sources of

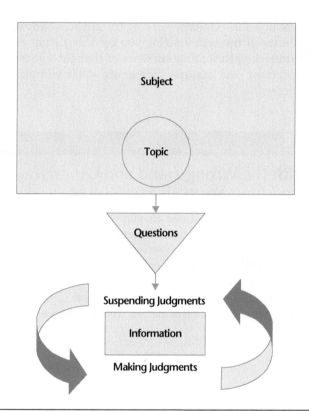

Figure 4   The process of inquiry first involves finding a topic in a larger subject that raises interesting questions, refining those questions, and then using them to collect information. Investigate the significance of what you've found by thinking creatively and critically—withholding judgments and then making judgments—working toward fresh understandings and new discoveries that lead you to what you want to say.

information, and that may eventually become the heart of an essay draft on your topic. For example, you might arrive at a question like this one:

- Beginning with a topic—the influence of the blues on pop music—you work toward questions that might power your writing project—questions, say, like this: *What was the influence of Mississippi delta blues on white performers like Elvis who were popular in the fifties and sixties?*

An inquiry question may be no more than a train station in a longer journey. As you continue to write, you may find another, better question around which to build your project. But a good opening question will keep you on the tracks. This is enormously helpful as you collect information, either from research or from your own experiences and observations, working toward some answers to the questions you pose. And some of the best insights you get about what those answers might be will come from the alternating currents of thought—generating and judging, suspending judgment and making judgments—that energize your writing and thinking processes.

EXERCISE 6

Writing with the Wrong Hand and Other Ways of Thinking About Yourself as a Writer

Though you may not have noticed it, you've already begun using this inquiry strategy in this chapter. In Exercise 4 (Literacy Narrative Collage) you started exploring your own background as a writer, first generating material about your past experiences and then stepping back and judging their significance. I provided most of the questions. So far, everything you've written about your literacy narrative is in your journal. Let's use the inquiry process to shape the material into a three- to five-page essay draft. But before we do that, we'll continue with a little more journal work.

Generating

STEP ONE: This four-minute fastwrite begins strangely. If you're right-handed, put your pen in your left hand. If you're left-handed, put it in your right. Write the following phrase in your journal with your "wrong" hand: *Writing with my wrong hand reminds me of*...Now switch the pen to your writing hand, and in a fastwrite explore the connections you can make, if any, with the experience of writing with the wrong hand. Let the writing lead, especially to stories, particular people, specific memories, or times in your life.

Judging

STEP TWO: Based on what you wrote in step one, compose a brief answer to one or more of the following questions:

- What's the thing that surprised you most when you wrote about writing wrong-handed?
- If you were going to explain the significance of this experience to someone else, what would you say?
- If you were going to do this experiment with a friend, what would you ask him or her about it afterward?

Generating

STEP THREE: The information we generate from our experiences and observations is only one kind of information we can generate for writing. Reading is another. The passage that follows is the opening of an essay by David Bartholomae, a writing theorist, which begins his look at how students in their first years of college must adjust to writing in academic discourses. Carefully read the passage, and in your journal *copy at least three passages* from the Bartholomae excerpt that struck you. Maybe you agreed or disagreed with them, or you found them interesting or confusing, or they spoke in some way to your own experiences so far in college.

From "Inventing the University"
David Bartholomae

Every time a student sits down to write for us, he has to invent the university for the occasion—invent the university, that is, or a branch of it, like history or anthropology or economics or English. The student has to learn to speak our language, to speak as we do, to try on the peculiar ways of knowing, selecting, evaluating, reporting, concluding, and arguing that define the discourse of our community. Or perhaps I should say the *various* discourses of our community, since it is in the nature of a liberal arts education that a student, after the first year or two, must learn to try on a variety of voices and interpretive schemes—to write, for example, as a literary critic one day and as an experimental psychologist the next; to work within fields where the rules governing the presentation of examples or the development of an argument are both distinct and, even to the professional, mysterious.

The student has to appropriate (or be appropriated by) a specialized discourse, and he has to do this as though he were easily and comfortably one with his audience, as though he were a member of the academy or an historian or an anthropologist or an economist; he has to invent the university by assembling and mimicking its language while finding some compromise between idiosyncrasy, a personal history, on the one hand, and the requirements of convention, the history of a discipline, on the other hand. He must learn to speak our language. Or he must dare to speak it or to carry off the bluff, since speaking and writing will most certainly be required long before the skill is "learned." And this, understandably, causes problems.

From "Inventing the University" by David Bartholomae in *When a Writer Can't Write: Studies in Writer's Block and Other Composing-Process Problems*, ed. Mike Rose, The Guilford Press, 1985, pp. 134–65.

STEP FOUR: Now fastwrite for four or five minutes about the Bartholomae excerpt, and begin by exploring your reactions to the passages you selected. This time, tell the story of your thinking as it develops in your bad writing by beginning with your first thoughts: *The first thing I think when I consider what Bartholomae is saying is…And then I think…And then.* Follow the writing.

Judging

STEP FIVE: Reread your fastwriting from the preceding step, and spend a full minute generating a list of questions, either about the Bartholomae excerpt or about your response to it.

STEP SIX: Finally, craft one or two strong sentences that might begin an essay you write in response to "Inventing the University." A strong first sentence is one that would make a reader want to read the next sentence and the one after that.

Writers are almost always better off when they work from abundance rather than scarcity. That makes choosing what to put in and what to leave out of a draft much easier and makes it much more likely that the resulting piece will have a strong focus. That's also why we've spent so much time in this chapter beginning to generate and shape material about your own experiences as a writer. If you go over your journal work on this topic, you should see some or all of the following, depending on what your instructor assigned:

- Your earliest memory of writing
- The story of a turning point in your sense of yourself as a writer or your understanding of writing
- Writing you do on a typical day
- The story of the most or least successful thing you've ever written
- Your earliest memory of writing with a computer
- Your definitions of the word "literate"
- Your exploration of the experience of writing with the wrong hand
- A response to an excerpt on how college students must "learn to speak the language" of the university by "compromising" their "personal history" as writers

That's a fair amount of writing, and most of it probably isn't very good. But now you're ready to try and shape some of that material into a first draft, writing that might make sense to someone other than you.

THE WRITING PROCESS

INQUIRY PROJECT: THE WRITING LITERACY MEMOIR

Drawing on the writing you've done on the topic so far and the writing you will continue to generate, compose a three- to five-page essay that is a memoir of your history as a writer. Like all inquiry projects, this essay should investigate some question about your writing experiences, and this question should be behind the stories you tell. To start with, look for a question that explores a relationship between two things in your writing life. For example, "What is the relationship between my success with online writing and my struggles with school writing?" Or something like this: "What is the relationship between my memories of earning praise about my writing from teachers and the lack of confidence in writing I've always felt, and still feel?"

For additional reading, writing, and research resources, go to www.mycomplab.com

---

Obviously, you've already started this assignment, and you have pages of writing in your journal from which to work. Let the inquiry question you come up with help you decide what to put in and what to leave out. As you are drafting, also consider opportunities to generate new information that will help to develop your essay. For example, there might be a key moment in your narrative that deserves particular emphasis because of its relevance to your question or its importance in developing what it is you might be trying to say.

As you compose your writing history, consider the following:

- Don't just tell one story. Tell several from different parts of your life that might illuminate your question.

- Does it make sense to tell your story out of order, in a structure that doesn't strictly follow chronology?

- Incorporate other sources. Nonfiction writers, no matter what the genre, can turn to four sources of information: personal experience, observation, interview, and reading. While this assignment will mine your personal experience most heavily, would it be useful to talk to a parent about your writing? Can you use any of the Bartholomae excerpt we read in Exercise 6? Might you find a relevant fact online?

■ SAMPLE STUDENT ESSAY

For the last thirty or so pages of this chapter, you've watched a student, Bernice Olivas, work alongside you, doing the exercises, generating material and then judging what she came up with. Here is her writing memoir draft:

Writing a New Path

Bernice Olivas

1   It's getting cold. The leaves have turned from green to gold and orange. A few weeks ago an unexpected snowstorm turned the world white for a few hours. Winter is coming, and with it the holiday season. As a child I lived for this time of year because it brought out the kid in my father. He decorated a tree, hung stockings, and the house was filled with the people we loved. In last five years that celebration has crumbled around us. My sisters treat each other like spun glass, afraid to reignite old fires over old arguments, afraid of what they might say if they speak, afraid of what they can't say out loud. My little brothers swagger in and out of my mother's house as if they owned the place, their young wives and children underfoot. They play house while my mother works herself haggard and my father slips in and out of the house, never staying at home for long.

2   We talk to each other in a way we'd never speak to a stranger, our voice filled with scorn, anger, and indifference. We disrespect each other, we belittle each other, and it's as if we've forgotten how much we love each other. The little ones, my boys, my nieces and nephews run around taking it all in as if such pain was normal. To them it is. I've perfected excuse after excuse to avoid the drive to Jerome because it hurts too much to watch.

3   We've grown up, we've grown apart, or maybe I've just lost the rose colored glasses that let me see a warm, loving home in a household scarred by poverty, and haunted by all the harsh realities of life for a Mexican American family trying to make it up north. Most days I console myself with the fact that my brothers are young, they'll grow up. I tell myself my sisters will come around, after all we're family. Occasionally things slip back into what they used to be and I tell myself time will heal the wounds but come Christmas time I find myself hard pressed to believe myself. I miss them. I miss who we used to be. I let myself wallow in just how much I miss them. Last year three little nieces and nephews joined the family and I couldn't stand the idea that these babies would never know the family the way we used to be.

4   I needed to get it all out of my head so I started writing short stories, memories really, of my siblings, my childhood. As I lost myself in retelling these family stories I recaptured something, a feeling, a sense of self and family I haven't felt in a long time. I wrote for days and finally when I was done I felt closer to my family than I had in years. I decided to make copies of these stories, have them bound, and give them as gifts to my family. As each of my siblings read them, and my mother cried over them, we shared a moment of just being together. It was quick, almost invisible, but for a moment, we were laughing together, leaning into each other, our bodies relaxed. It was good.

5   There were no spoken words that could have given us that little moment because our spoken language is heavy with years of family baggage. Putting it on paper lets each of us experience the camping trips, the smell of baking cookies, the inside jokes all over again. Such is the power of the written word. And it's a power that I had no idea existed until I was twenty-four, married, and the mother of two and going back to college.

I planned to get my teaching degree, work at a high school, and earn a little stability for my children. It simply never occurred to me to want more. Just being at college was more than I'd ever expected to achieve because people like me don't go to college. People like me, and my family, work with our hands, and there is a deep sense of pride, almost a reverence, attached to the conceptualization of ourselves as a strong, working class family.

My classes were amazing. I was learning so much and I loved the buzz and energy of campus, but it was so hard. I'd been out of school for a long time, and even when I was in high school no one ever asked me to write the way they were asking me to write in my college classes. My spelling sucked, my grammar was worse, and I was sure I'd fail my Comp 101 class. My Composition 101 teacher was ruthless, going over and over my drafts, pushing me to think on the page, to ask questions, to push myself past simply reporting information. I hated him for the first semester but found myself signing up for his early morning class in the spring. Somewhere along the way I'd fallen in love with writing.

I'd found my voice and it felt good to write. I loved being able to write out all the noise in my head; it was messy but once it was on the page I could work through it slowly, carefully, untangling it until it was something new and exciting and all my own. The written word is a language unto itself, a form of expression that opens up the world to be explored and navigated in a way that is entirely unique. It was a language I wasn't fluent in. Like the rest of my family, I could write enough to get by, in the same sense a beginning Spanish speaker gets by in Latin America, and I had no idea how much of the conversation I was missing.

My grades improved and that nasty little voice that snuck up on me in the middle of the night and whispered that I didn't belong, that there was no place amid all these intellectuals for someone like me, disappeared. Four years later I'm a writing major, and I'm headed to graduate school where I'll earn my PhD. After that I plan to write books, and teach writing at a university. Finding my voice did more than just help me through a few classes. It gave me a sense of power over my own life, a way to communicate with the world at large. These days I go online and discuss politics with people in Australia, London, and Quebec. I write my opinions to the school editor and occasionally they print them. I'm slowly writing my way through my childhood and seeing it, myself, my family, my people, and history in a whole new way. I'm writing a new path for my own children.

Whenever I go to a family gathering someone asks me why I want to be a writer, why I want to teach writing. They ask me why I don't do something more productive, more useful. Nothing I say seems to make them understand. Nothing I can say satisfies them, and they go away, still confused, reassuring themselves that I was always a little weird, a little off. They remind each other that I was born left handed and my mom had to train me to use my right hand. They remind themselves that I didn't start talking till I was almost four, and then there was that nasty bump on the head that landed me in the hospital when I was six.

After all nobody else in the family writes. In fact Grandpa Domingo was illiterate, could barely sign his own name, until the day he died. He did all right, built a trucking company right up out of the ground and left Grandma the house, the land, and a healthy savings account, and he never wrote a word.

(continued)

(continued)

12   How can I tell them that I write because it makes me more me, in a way I wasn't before. How can I tell them that being voiceless in the written word is dehumanizing in a way I cannot articulate verbally. How can I tell them how much I hurt to think of my grandfather navigating in this world, voiceless? How I can tell them that as a family, as a community, we are powerless without a voice on the page.

13   How can I make them feel the elation I feel when I write, when I learn something new? How can I tell them that writing is a powerful tool, which gave me the courage to step up and take on the responsibility of changing my life, the courage to offer my sons a life of more than backbreaking labor, and the audacity to dream of contributing on a wider scale to the world around me?

14   I can't; I have no words to tell them any of those things. They wouldn't understand if I tried. I don't have the right words to speak, but I can write them, explore them until they're filled with a power of their own, until I find truth within them. Then maybe my family can read them and understand me just a little better. Such is the power of the written word.

EXERCISE 7

Taking a Reflective Turn

After you've finished drafting your writing memoir, back away from the experience and think about how it went. Sadly, reflecting like this about something we've written is rare. But as I said earlier, this focus on *how* instead of *what* will do for you as a writer what a tennis coach can do for a player: help her to see that she's making often unconscious choices that affect her play. As a writer, you can see that in any writing situation you have a range of choices, not just one—but you can see this only if you make time to reflect on the choices you've made.

Let's do that with your writing memoir. In your notebook, use one or more of the following prompts for a fastwrite:

- What was different about how you approached the process of writing this essay from the way you approach other writing for school?

- Where did you run into problems? How might you have solved them if you had the chance to repeat the process of writing this essay?

- What did your writing memoir reveal to you about your writing habits, beliefs, and hopes? What do you see more clearly now that you didn't see before you wrote it?

You'll also have the chance to try out dialectical thinking, a process that may seem a little dizzying. In a way, it should, because both the writing process and dialectical thinking involve a great deal of back-and-forth movement, the sort of mental gymnastics you perform with the pen in your hand or your fingers on the keyboard.

Does it feel natural? Probably not. At least not yet. But I hope you'll find that your understanding of the writing process becomes more intuitive as you progress. You may modify your writing process, add a step here or skip one there, prolong the process, or cut it short, depending on the writing situation and your rhetorical concerns. Whatever you do, though, you need to make choices based on an understanding of how they will influence your process. This is the key to making you a productive, confident writer.

USING WHAT YOU HAVE LEARNED

When I was in college I used to say this to anyone who asked how I felt about writing: *I don't like writing but I love having written.* What I meant, of course, is that I often felt satisfaction with the product of writing—the paper or essay—but didn't like the work that it took to produce it. This belief didn't help me improve as a writer because it prevented me from finding things about the process that could actually be okay, and even pleasurable: things like discovery. I never imagined surprise was possible. I hope this chapter initiated a reexamination of your own beliefs about writing. I hardly expect a revolution in your thinking, but maybe one or two things you once thought were true of writing may at least be in doubt, particularly if you think those beliefs get in the way of your progress. Carry that openness to revise your thinking into every assignment and you may be surprised at what you can do.

You now know more about your writing process. You've identified what seems to go well and when you get into trouble. The habit of reflecting on your process will be invaluable as you face each new writing situation because each one presents different problems and choices. Understanding the basic rhetorical principles—considering how to present yourself to particular audiences on particular subjects—will help. You already know more than you think about rhetoric.

READING AS INQUIRY

From Chapter 2 of *The Curious Writer*, Third Edition. Bruce Ballenger. Copyright © 2011 by Pearson Education, Inc. Published by Pearson Longman. All rights reserved.

Reading to inquire opens a conversation with a text in which the words on the page are only part of the dialogue between the author and the reader.

READING AS INQUIRY

Here's what you might be thinking as you read this sentence: *This is a chapter about reading (in a textbook about writing) and I'm really hungry and could eat some potato chips and I already know about reading; I've been reading for years; this guy has a strange way of opening a textbook chapter, how does he know what I'm thinking, he probably doesn't want to know....*Okay, so I don't know exactly what you're thinking. But I do know that you're not simply sitting there decoding the meaning of each word I've written. For one thing, you're reading faster than that, looking at chunks of language. However, a lot of what is going on in your head isn't directly related to the words here. You're thinking about what kind of book you're reading—the textbook genre—and making mental predictions about what is going to come next. You're thinking about the subject—"reading as inquiry"—and considering what you may already know about it. And you're thinking about your purpose in reading these sentences or this text, trying to use that purpose as a guide to help you navigate my meaning and its relevance to you. However, I'm probably wrong about the potato chips.

I hope the image you get from reading this account is that what *you* bring to the reading situation is much more powerful than the words on the page. Experienced readers are aware of this, and like experienced writers, they can bring this knowledge to a range of reading situations and make choices about *how* to read. This rhetorical knowledge of reading is especially important in

What You'll Learn in This Chapter

- How your existing beliefs about reading might be obstacles to reading rhetorically.
- What connections exist between the writing and reading processes.
- How to use the double-entry journal to encourage dialectical thinking.
- How to apply some of the same strategies to reading pictures that you do to reading texts.
- How to understand the unique grammar of images.
- How to design the "look" of your writing.

college. First, you'll be reading a lot, and you'll be introduced, in classes across campus, to new genres and specialized writing that are entirely new to you. Sometimes you might feel as if you're in a wrestling match with texts whose moves are so novel that they threaten to pin you every time you confront them. But you can learn the moves, and in many cases you already know them.

My students fret about writing. But they don't seem to get very worked up about the challenges of reading. As you've seen, however, reading is complex, and in this chapter I'll show you how the writing process involves some of the same mental activities and even similar rhetorical choices used in reading. I'll also show you how writing can help you read better.

When we think of reading we usually associate the act exclusively with written texts, but so many of the images we encounter are, like written texts, crafted to communicate and persuade and so, whether we recognize it or not, we read images, too. In this chapter we'll use images as a metaphor to talk about all kinds of reading strategies, but we'll also focus on the unique grammar of visual literacy and how images work to influence a "reader."

MOTIVES FOR READING

Why read? In the case of best-selling popular fiction such as *The Da Vinci Code* or the Harry Potter books, the answer seems pretty clear: These are entertaining books. But pleasure is not a motive that seems to apply to most academic reading—we usually regard such reading as something we have to do to study for the test or write the paper. However, reading to inquire, while not always a source of pleasure, can offer the satisfaction of surprise and discovery, just as writing to inquire can. This is because what's behind an encounter with a text can be a desire to answer a question that interests you. Reading to inquire is, like writing to inquire, an open-ended process in which you set out to discover what you think, and along the way welcome confusion and ambiguity as a natural condition of the search. In other words, you never read just to collect information; you read to have a conversation with the information. You go back and forth between what an author says and what you think about what he or she says. *Does this help answer a question I've posed? Does it inspire me to see things differently? Does it complicate what I already believe?*

> Reading with the spirit of inquiry turns books, essays, and articles into one side of a dialog that you're having with yourself and an author.

Reading with the spirit of inquiry turns books, essays, and articles into one side of a dialog that you're having with yourself and an author. The meaning of a text (or an image) isn't fixed forever—engraved in stone tablets like a message from above—but worked out between the two of you, the author and the reader. This turns reading into a much more complicated intellectual activity, but it also makes reading more interesting because you create the conditions for surprise, for learning, and for discovery.

BELIEFS ABOUT READING

Most of us aren't very aware of our reading strategies and habits. Why should we be? After all, isn't reading just reading? How many ways can you do it? The way we go about learning how to read, however, is similar to the way we learn how to write. We start at an early age, perhaps even before we go to school. Along with the learning, we acquire beliefs that inform our response to *how* we read. These beliefs, though, can help or hinder our progress as readers. Once again, then, we need to assess our beliefs. Only by understanding *how* we read in certain situations can we acquire more control over what we get out of the reading experience.

EXERCISE 1

What Do You Believe?

STEP ONE: In your journal, draft a brief definition of a "good" reader. What exactly is a good reader able to do?

STEP TWO: Answer the following questions in your journal.

- Do you think you're a good reader? Why or why not?
- How would you describe your own reading habits and methods?

STEP THREE: It's helpful to think about the characteristics of a "good" reader in certain contexts. For example, what should a good reader be able to do when

- taking computerized exams like the ACT and the SAT?
- researching a paper for school?
- reading a textbook for an exam?
- analyzing a poem or short story?
- reading a text message?
- reading a friend's Facebook page?
- reading instructions on how to set up a new computer?
- reading a novel for pleasure?

Choose two of these reading situations (or two others that you can imagine), and in your journal write a definition of what a good reader should be able to do in each situation.

ONE STUDENT'S RESPONSE

Briana's Journal

STEP ONE:

Good readers read with an open mind and an open heart but cannot be too malleable. They have to be able to empathize and still be able to judge with some sense. They have to immerse themselves in the literature. I love when I read something and I feel something. Good readers have to be able to pick up a variety of materials at any given time and be able to have the skill to immerse themselves into that piece. They need to be able to get the full scope of the writing and see the big picture through the small details.

STEP THREE:

Reading a text message: Inflection is absent in this form of communication. And because it is a casual type of communication, we tend to text like we talk. You have to be able to recall the sender's personality and look at the words he or she has chosen and the order in which he or she has placed them; this takes a high level of analysis.

Most reading instruction seems to focus on comprehension—you know, the SAT- or ACT-inspired kind of situation in which you are asked to read something and then explain what it means. This often becomes an exercise in recall and vocabulary, an analytical challenge in only the most general way. Essentially, you train yourself to distinguish between specifics and generalities and to loosely follow the author's reasoning. In English classes, sometimes we are asked to perform a similar exercise with stories or poems—what is the theme or what does it mean?

> Only by understanding how we read in certain situations can we acquire more control over what we get out of the reading experience.

Questions such as these send students off on what is essentially an archaeological expedition where they must dig for hidden meaning. The "right" answers to the questions are in the text, like a buried bone; you just have to find them. Sometimes the expedition is successful, sometimes not. The trouble with this type of exercise has less to do with its success rate than with the belief that it tends to foster, which is that *all meaning resides in the text and the reader's job is merely to find it*. This belief limits the reader's interaction with the text. If meaning is fixed within the text, embedded like a bone in antediluvian mud, then all the reader has to do is dig to find that meaning. Digging isn't a bad thing, but reading can be so much more than laboring at the shovel and sifting through dirt.

READING SITUATIONS AND RHETORICAL CHOICES

You know those elaborate machines at the eye doctor's office that you look through while the optometrist tries various combinations of lenses, asking which make the fuzzy letters on the wall seem sharper? These devices are called phoropters (see Figure 1) and they immediately come to mind when I think about how we read. When we read anything—writing, images, graphics—we are looking through lenses. In a given situation, the right combination of lenses will help us to read better, and when we do we have found the right "prescription" for seeing a particular text for a particular purpose.

However, unlike the optometrist's phoropter, we can exercise more control over which lenses we use. Skillful readers are in command of the machine. This control comes from the same skill that gives writers more control: awareness of their own process and recognition of what each reading situation might demand. In Exercise 1 you began to think about both of these things, particularly in

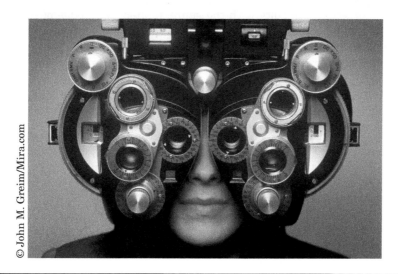

© John M. Greim/Mira.com

Figure 1   Reading is like looking through an optometrist's phoropter: The right combination of lenses will help us read better. Skillful readers are in command of the machine.

Step 3, when you began to think about different contexts for reading, from SAT tests to text messages. Each situation demands different lenses that bring certain things—and not others—into sharper focus. The five most important types of lenses that influence how you see a text include the following:

- **Purpose:** Why are you reading?
- **Genre:** What do you know about this kind of text and what do you therefore expect?
- **Self-perception:** How good do you think you are at this kind of reading?
- **Knowledge:** What do you already know about the subject of the reading?
- **Rhetorical awareness:** What might be the purposes behind the text? What is it trying to do?

Imagine, for example, that you just purchased an iPhone and you're reading a page of instructions on how to use the video feature. Your purpose in reading in this case is entirely informational. You're motivated to learn how to use your new phone. You also probably have some experience with this genre—the instruction manual—because you've been buying electronics much of your life. Maybe you think you're a pretty good reader of the genre as a result. I know I'm not. I misread or misinterpret instructions, or ignore them altogether. I've also got a cell phone, but I've never used an iPhone, so I bring very little knowledge to my reading about how it works. If I were looking through the metaphorical phoropter, I'd start out with a pretty poor combination of lenses: difficulty with the genre, limited knowledge of the subject, and poor self-perception. If you were in my situation—or if you were advising me about how to be a better reader of this text—what would you do or say?

Let's look at an example of another kind of text. Last night I was reading a challenging piece on curiosity by two philosophers. It was published in the journal *Educational Theory*. The piece exemplifies a type of academic discourse that would be fairly typical in the discipline of philosophy. Here's an excerpt from the concluding paragraph of the article:

> In this article, we have characterized curiosity about a topic as attention to the topic giving rise to, and in turn sustained by, a motivationally original desire to know. Curiosity is biased by our practical and epistemic[1] interests. It is tenacious, typically involving a disposition to inquire into topics related to the topic of curiosity. And its motivational originality allows it to be some degree independent of practical and epistemic interests. The value of curiosity depends on these features. Its interest bias and tenacity together lead to deep inquiry than is motivated by practical and epistemic interests.[2]

---

[1]Of or related to knowledge.
[2]Schmitt, Fredrick F. and Reza Lahroodi. "The Epistemic Value of Curiosity." *Educational Theory* 58.2 (2008): 125–148.

This is pretty rough going for most readers. One of the problems has to do with purpose. Why are you reading this excerpt in the first place? I really didn't give you a reason. Now reread the passage once more, but this time your purpose is *to understand it well enough to write a two- or three-sentence summary of what you think the authors are saying.* After you're done, talk in class or in your journal about one or more of the following questions:

1. How competent do you think you are at reading this kind of writing? How did you feel when reading it? How do you often feel when reading difficult material?

2. You're probably not familiar with this genre of academic writing. What do you notice about its conventions: the language, the tone, the manner in which information is presented, and so on?

3. Curiosity is a condition of childhood, so we all bring some knowledge of it to this reading. Does this passage change anything about the way you think about your own curiosity? Does that make you think of a story?

4. What do you infer from reading this passage about the authors' purpose and audience for their article on curiosity? What exactly did you notice that inspired those inferences?

ONE STUDENT'S RESPONSE

Briana's Journal

READING ACADEMIC DISCOURSE

1. I feel like this piece is written for a certain kind of audience and that audience is not me. There are a lot of big words, some I am not sure what they mean and some I do but I have never heard or read them in that combination. As I read on I realize that it is not that difficult and they are really using a lot of words that people learn about that they are curious about. When I read difficult material I usually read the first sentence, then the second, realize that it is difficult and then sigh and then try and dig deeper and understand it and then I find that 4–5 sentences in I am not even paying attention and I usually altogether stop reading it.

2. It is not written plainly or for people that are not extremely knowledgeable in the subject; no one else would bother to read this. The info is presented in what I would consider a highly florid way; they are saying the same thing just in different ways and bringing in a minimum amount of new info.

(continued)

One Student's Response (*continued*)

3. It makes me think that when I find something interesting I will find all the books that I can on the subject and read them. Like I saw the movie *Marie Antoinette* and then I watched the special on the History channel and then I read her auto-biography. Then my curiosity expanded to another queen, Queen Elizabeth. I watched the movies about her, and then I read her biography as well.

4. I am not sure what the authors' purpose is; I will presume it is to inform and I get the feeling that they also want to make others think that they are really smart. Like intellectual showoffs. I was under the assumption that that's what journals were for. But I am finding again that they are not saying a whole lot with all the words. This section is also a conclusion "we have characterized" part, maybe why it doesn't offer a lot of new information.

Figure 2 shows a genre that you might not be able to read very well.

Obviously, the electrical circuit diagram is a very specialized kind of text, and it presents tremendous challenges to novice readers. Even the most difficult academic discourse at least uses recognizable words, a symbol system that we've used most of our lives. But this is written in another language. Assume for a moment, though, that your assignment was to become a good

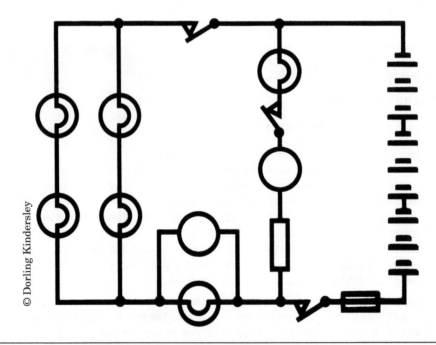

© Dorling Kindersley

Figure 2 An electrical circuit diagram is a specialized kind of text that presents tremendous challenges to novice readers.

enough reader of this kind of text to be able to explain some of what this diagram is saying.

- How would you do that?
- What steps might you take?
- Might you generalize those steps or strategies to apply to any situation in which you're confronted with a difficult text?

Each of these three reading situations—an iPhone instruction manual, an excerpt from an academic journal, and an electrical circuit diagram—make different demands on you as a reader. One way of understanding these demands is to return to the rhetorical triangle (see Figure 3). Reading is a sometimes tricky negotiation between you, what you know, the subject and genre of the text, and the author's purpose behind it.

In the reader's rhetorical triangle, the reader moves to the apex of the triangle and the writer (or text's author, in this case) moves down to one of the lower legs (see Figure 3). The reader's portion of the triangle includes the reader's purpose for reading the text and knowledge of the subject and genre. Readers' self-perceptions—how competent they feel working with a particular text—strongly influence their motivation to wrestle with an unfamiliar work. The subject includes not only the main topic of the reading but the form or genre in which it is presented. The author's purpose shapes the third portion of the triangle. Combined, the three work to determine the context of each reading situation. The verbal SAT exam, for instance, in part involves reading short passages and answering multiple-choice comprehension questions. Speed is important. The significance of the test and the speed required to complete it influence the

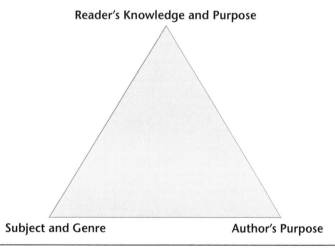

Reader's Knowledge and Purpose

Subject and Genre   **Author's Purpose**

Figure 3   The reader's rhetorical triangle. Reading is a negotiation between you, what you know, the subject and genre of the text, and the author's purpose.

reader's portion of the triangle. So too does the subject, which is presented in the form of multiple-choice questions. The author's intent in composing the questions—to test comprehension—also shapes the reading situation.

Each reading situation, like each writing situation, presents you with a range of choices. Becoming a good reader, like becoming a good writer, involves learning to recognize those situations and being flexible about how you respond to them. The path to becoming a more sophisticated reader, like being a stronger writer, begins with a look at your history and habits dealing with texts.

EXERCISE 2

Reading Autobiography

How do you think of yourself as a reader? Let's explore that self-perception in your journal. You'll be working toward a memoir essay, but this time on yourself as a reader.

Generating

STEP ONE: Think back to an experience with reading—or being read to—that stands out in your memory. I immediately think about my father reading *Lassie Come Home* aloud to me as a child. My head was on his chest and I could feel the words vibrate, and once I caught him weeping. For five or six full minutes, tell your own story with as much detail as you can. This is a fastwrite, so give yourself permission to write badly.

STEP TWO: Skip a line, and then write about another experience with reading. Write for five minutes.

STEP THREE: Imagine that you've been given a reading assignment in a class. You must read the first three chapters in the textbook. There are hints about the material being on an exam. Describe yourself, in the third person, doing this reading. Write this as a scene. For example, *He is sitting at a cluttered desk with his earphones on in an otherwise darkened room staring at the open book before him. His eyes wander…*

Judging

STEP FOUR: Look over the material you generated in the first three steps. In your journal, finish each of the following phrases, follow it until the writing dies out, and then move on to the next one.

1. *The thing that surprised me most about what I wrote is…*
2. *If someone else were to read what I wrote, they would probably see…*
3. *Overall, the one thing my writing seems to say about me as a reader is…*

READING AS A PROCESS

The difference between novice readers and more experienced readers comes down to this: Experienced readers always keep their purposes for reading in mind. Generally, these purposes arise from these three questions:

- Will this give me pleasure?
- What can I *learn* from this?
- What can I *do* with this?

Obviously, an act of reading can involve a combination of these motives, but reading for inquiry is ultimately concerned with the last: How can what I'm reading be used to explore the questions that interest me? Learning and the pleasure that arises from chasing after the answers to questions that interest you is a wonderful byproduct of the inquiry process, but as a writer your reading goal is much more utilitarian: You want to see if you can *use* what you're reading in your writing.

Reading to Write

The process of reading to write is going to be different than, say, reading for pleasure. For example, I'm currently stuck in an odd obsession with reading Lincoln biographies. I just can't get enough of them. My motives are both learning and pleasure, but I really don't plan on writing anything about Lincoln, so I don't bother with things like taking notes, marking passages, mining the bibliography, and other things like that. I certainly think about what I'm reading, and sometimes I even talk about what I've learned and bore everybody to death who isn't a Lincoln fan. I am, in short, a much less active reader when I'm not worrying about what I can do with what I'm reading.

Lately, I've been working on an essay in which I am exploring why certain landscapes—usually the ones we know best from our childhoods—often get under our skins even if we no longer live in those places. My reading for this project has led me to all kinds of sources—articles in anthropology, history, and literary works. This reading is enjoyable, but it's also work. In the back of my mind, I'm always asking, *Does this relate to the questions I'm interested in?* It's a reading process that is much more directed by my goals, my interests, and my desire to use what I'm reading in my own writing.

Reading for inquiry is a process that looks something like Figure 4.

Prereading. Before I read to write, I'm thinking:

- What are my inquiry questions? What do I want to find out?
- How might this text provide new answers, extending or changing what I think now?

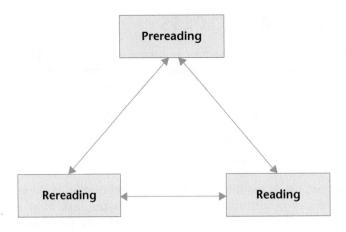

Figure 4 **A process for reading to write.** Reading, like writing, is a recursive process.

- What do I assume about the author's purposes?
- What do I know about how to read this kind of text?

Reading. When I read to write, I'm thinking:

- Is this relevant to what I want to know?
- Is this reliable?
- What does this say that I don't expect?
- What do I *think* about what it says?
- *How* might I use this in my writing?

Rereading. If the text seems relevant, I'll read it again, focused on not just the whole but also the parts, asking myself questions like these:

- What do I understand this to be saying?
- How does this connect with what I already know?
- Does it change the questions I'm asking?
- In my own words, what is the significance of this?
- How might the author's motives influence what this says?
- *Where* might I use this in my writing?

This process, like the writing process, is recursive. What I read may change the questions I'm asking, and every time I reread I'm also rereading my impressions from my first reading. But one thing doesn't change at any point in the process: My reading is always consciously goal-directed.

Goal-Directed Reading

Given a particular goal for reading, more experienced readers tend to agree on what's important. They learn to recognize certain patterns in a text that help them to use it more effectively. For example, I gave the following passage to sixty English majors. It's the concluding paragraphs of an essay by Christine Rosen[3] on the impact of social networking sites like Facebook on friendship. I then asked the students to assume that their purpose in reading the passage was to write a summary of what they understood Rosen to be saying about the effect of virtual relationships on human relationships, and I urged them to underline the words, phrases, or sentences in the excerpt that they thought would help them write it.

I've highlighted the sentences and phrases that my students consistently underlined the most. Keeping the goal of their reading in mind—to write a summary of this passage—what do you notice about the pattern of underlinings? What does this infer about where, in an article like this, readers can often find the most important information?

We should also take note of the trend toward giving up face-to-face for virtual contact—and, in some cases, a preference for the latter. Today, many of our cultural, social, and political interactions take place through eminently convenient technological surrogates—Why go to the bank if you can use the ATM? Why browse in a bookstore when you can simply peruse the personalized selections Amazon.com has made for you? In the same vein, social networking sites are often convenient surrogates for offline friendship and community. In this context it is worth considering an observation that Stanley Milgram made in 1974, regarding his experiments with obedience: "The social psychology of this century reveals a major lesson," he wrote. "Often it is not so much the kind of person a man is as the kind of situation in which he finds himself that determines how he will act." To an increasing degree, we find and form our friendships and communities in the virtual world as well as the real world. These virtual networks greatly expand our opportunities to meet others, but they might also result in our valuing less the capacity for genuine connection.

(continued)

---

[3]Rosen, Christine. "Virtual Friendship and the New Narcissism." *The New Atlantis* 2007 (Summer): 15–31.

(continued)

As the young woman writing in the *Times* admitted, "I consistently trade actual human contact for the more reliable high of smiles on MySpace, winks on Match.com, and pokes on Facebook." That she finds these online relationships more *reliable* is telling: it shows a desire to avoid the vulnerability and uncertainty that true friendship entails. Real intimacy requires risk—the risk of disapproval, of heartache, of being thought a fool. Social networking websites may make relationships more reliable, but whether those relationships can be humanly satisfying remains to be seen.

Sometimes we can learn the most about ourselves as readers by watching ourselves deal with a genre with which we're unfamiliar. Our knowledge about how the text works is limited so we're not quite sure where to direct our attention. We don't really trust ourselves to read the text "correctly." This may be exactly how you feel when you try to "read" a work of abstract art like the one by the artist Bridget Riley titled *Hesitate* (1964), shown in Figure 5. Riley was one of the most prominent artists in the short-lived Optical Art movement that began in the United States in the sixties.

Suppose you were asked by your art history professor to write a persuasive interpretation of *Hesitate*. Where would you begin? I would hope your instructor would have prepared your "reading" by helping you to understand how a painting like this one might be analyzed. What parts of this visual text should you pay attention to? How might you interpret the language of abstract art like this? One of the most important aspects of prereading is

© Tate London/Art Resource

Figure 5   Where would you begin if you were asked to write a persuasive interpretation of a piece of abstract art like *Hesitate* (1964), by Bridget Riley?

tapping the knowledge you have about the subject, genre, and conventions of the text you're working with. If you don't have that knowledge, you're likely to read it pretty poorly. If you've never really read a painting or know little about "optical art," then you'll probably be at a loss when pressed to say anything insightful about *Hesitate*.

EXERCISE 3

What Do You Know and When Did You Know It?

What *do* you know about how to read certain kinds of texts?

Generating

STEP ONE: Think for a moment about what you *believe you read pretty well* and perhaps what you've always liked to read: science fiction, auto repair manuals, blogs, short stories, song lyrics, poetry, newspapers, recipes, comic books? In your journal, begin by telling yourself the story of how you came to enjoy that genre. What moments or situations come to mind? What were particularly influential encounters with that type of text? Write fast for at least three minutes.

Judging

STEP TWO: Reflect on the genre you wrote about in step one and finish the following sentence in your journal at least four times:

One of the things I learned about how to read_____ is that you should_____.

Our knowledge about reading comes to us accidentally, unexpectedly, and often unconsciously. We just do it, and eventually, if we're lucky, we get better at it. Eventually, we work tacitly from a series of assumptions about what it means to read something well, and we measure our success or failure against those assumptions. Perhaps several of those assumptions surfaced in this exercise. Examine them if they did. Do they still make sense? If you were going to teach someone else about how to read a recipe book, a comic book, or a poem, would these be the suggestions you might make?

Obviously, one way to become a more sophisticated reader is to expand this genre knowledge to other forms that you encounter with which you're less familiar, especially those you want to learn how to use in your writing.

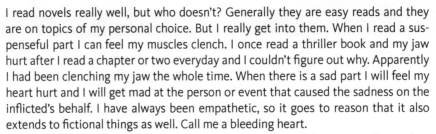

ONE STUDENT'S RESPONSE

Briana's Journal

EXERCISE 3

STEP ONE: Generating

I read novels really well, but who doesn't? Generally they are easy reads and they are on topics of my personal choice. But I really get into them. When I read a suspenseful part I can feel my muscles clench. I once read a thriller book and my jaw hurt after I read a chapter or two everyday and I couldn't figure out why. Apparently I had been clenching my jaw the whole time. When there is a sad part I will feel my heart hurt and I will get mad at the person or event that caused the sadness on the inflicted's behalf. I have always been empathetic, so it goes to reason that it also extends to fictional things as well. Call me a bleeding heart.

I also love to read textbooks and nonfiction books. In between college when I was taking my seven-year break, I would find textbooks somewhere and appropriate them or buy them online; and read them from cover to cover. I think that it is really important to keep learning and growing as a human; don't let your brain be idle. Of course all the books I chose were on subjects that I was interested in: physics, history, biographies on infamous queens, music theory, Che Guevara, or Eastern European culture. I will get "stuck" on a subject and then have to learn everything about it. I want to know, so I pay close attention and will have great retention of the information.

STEP TWO: Judging

- ■ *One of the things that I learned about how to read* textbooks *is that you should* really be interested in the subject that you are reading about.

- ■ *One of the things that I learned about how to read* a novel *is that you can* skip the boring parts that you don't like and fill in the blanks (I pretty much skipped all of the Elvish poetry in *The Two Towers*).

- ■ *One of the things that I learned about how to read* either novels or textbooks *is that you should* be interested in the subject, and if it is an area that you are not interested in and you have to read it, say for an assignment, then try and stay open-minded and try and find something that interests or intrigues you about it.

Inquiry Questions for Reading to Write

Writing to inquire, as you learned in the chapter, begins with questions, not answers, and learning to craft a good question—one that will sustain your writing and thinking for some weeks—is an essential skill. Questions can also crack open a text and lead to new discoveries. To begin with, questions give you an initial reason for reading. I can imagine many kinds of questions that might

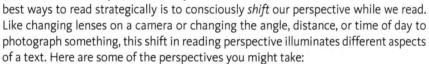

INQUIRING INTO THE DETAILS

Reading Perspectives

When we read, we always adopt certain perspectives toward a text, usually unconsciously. But one of the best ways to read strategically is to consciously *shift* our perspective while we read. Like changing lenses on a camera or changing the angle, distance, or time of day to photograph something, this shift in reading perspective illuminates different aspects of a text. Here are some of the perspectives you might take:

- *Believing:* What the author says is probably true. Which ideas can I relate to? What information should I use? What seems especially sound about the argument?

- *Doubting:* What are the text's weaknesses? What ideas don't jibe with my own experience? What are the gaps in the information or the argument? What isn't believable about this?

- *Updating:* What does this add to what I already know about the subject?

- *Hunting and gathering:* What can I collect from the text that I might be able to use?

- *Interpreting:* What might be the meaning of this?

- *Pleasure seeking:* I just want to enjoy the text and be entertained by it.

- *Connecting:* How does this information relate to my own experiences? What is its relationship to other things I've read? Does it verify, extend, or contradict what other authors have said?

- *Reflecting:* How was this written? What makes it particularly effective or ineffective?

- *Resisting:* This doesn't interest me. Why do I have to read it? Isn't *Survivor* on television right now?

guide your reading (also see "Inquiring into the Details: Reading Perspectives," above), but when you're reading to write, the following four categories of questions are the most common:

- Exploring questions
- Explaining questions
- Evaluating questions
- Reflecting questions

Questions in all four of these categories shift the way we see something. Years ago, I spent an afternoon taking photographs of an old wagon on a rolling New Hampshire hillside. I got up early on a September morning, hoping to take advantage of the slanting light and the shreds of mist that hung on the hayfield. I resolved to shoot an entire roll of film of the wagon, and I literally circled it, clicking away. By the fourth or fifth shot, I started to see the wagon in ways I'd never seen it, even though I had driven by it on my way to work for years. I saw how the beads of dew covered the bleached wood of the wagon's wheel. I saw how the ironwork of the driver's bench created a shadow on the grass that was a tangle of geometric shapes.

What I'm describing is the process of revision. But the anecdote also comes to mind now because it illustrates how different questions can shift your gaze on a topic. They help you to circle the wagon, changing your angle and revealing certain aspects of the subject. Behind each question is a different perspective on the subject. For example, take this finding from studies on computer literacy:

Boys generally outperform girls in knowledge and use of computers.

Suppose that you want to think about this. If you want to tap the power of questions, here are some that you might start with that fall into each of the four categories:

1. Do my own experiences and observations with computers tell me anything about what I think about this proposition? (Exploration)
2. How would I define "computer knowledge" in this context? (Explanation)
3. What have I seen, read, or experienced that provides support—or opposing evidence—for this idea? (Evaluation)
4. What do I notice about how each of the preceding questions shifts my way of seeing the claim about gender and computer use? (Reflection)

Can you see how each of these questions shifts your relationship to the topic and triggers different ways of thinking about it? Obviously, these aren't the only categories into which questions can be put, but they are very useful ones for reading to write.

You'll find exploring, explaining, evaluating, and reflecting questions (Figure 6) following readings throughout *The Curious Writer*. These form a launching point for your inquiry into the texts.

Exploration. To explore is to see a topic with wide-eyed wonder. *What might this mean to me? What do I feel or think about this?* Through questions like these, writers can openly investigate the things they read and there can be a big pay-off: You *discover* what you think. Obviously, exploratory questions about texts and the writing they inspire are most useful when you're writing about a topic that's relatively new to you. But you can also explore your existing beliefs, feelings, or ideas and you might also be surprised by what you find.

Here are some opening questions that might put you in an exploratory mode about any reading:

- What does this mean to me, or how do I think or feel about it?
- What are my first thoughts about this? And then what? And then?

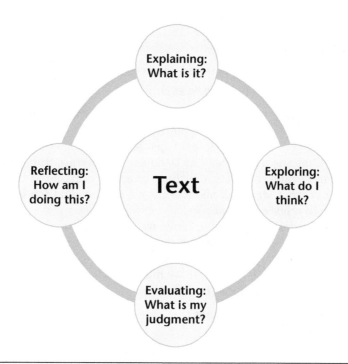

Figure 6 The four question categories—exploring, explaining, evaluating, and reflecting—will shift your gaze as a reader, encouraging you to see different things.

- What interests me most about this? What additional questions does it raise?
- What is the relationship between _____ and _____?
- How do my personal experiences and knowledge affect the way I feel and what I see?
- What surprises me about the way I see or think about this?

Explanation. We explain things all the time. Just a minute ago, Jim, the plumber who is working on our bedroom remodel, explained to me how the boiling water tap works on our sink. We use it for making tea, and it was sputtering and coughing and generally looking like it had symptoms of influenza. When we explain things, we usually have a particular audience in mind. We want audience members to *understand* something, but we are not merely reporting information. We're thinking about it too, trying to clarify in our own minds what we know or see and what we want to say about it.

Some of the most common types of explanations involve defining, describing, categorizing, and comparing, often inspired by questions like these:

- What kind of text is this?
- What is its purpose?

- How is it put together?
- What is the text trying to do?
- How does it compare to something someone else has said?
- What do I understand this to be saying?

Evaluation. To evaluate something is to judge it or form an opinion about it. Evaluating things—restaurants, the quality of play in the NBA, the religious motives of Islamic extremists, the latest rap offering—is something we do all the time. These evaluations tend to lead us to do and say certain things and then to offer reasons and evidence that make them sound reasonable. If exploration is about *finding out* what we think about what we read, evaluation is often about using a reading to *prove our ideas.*

Don't misunderstand me, though. While we often have opinions about a topic, reading inquiry questions that move us to evaluate often inspire us to do more than simply find support for those opinions in what we read. We also evaluate the opinions themselves, and in the process we may begin to think differently.

Evaluation questions include the following:

- What's my opinion about what this reading seems to be saying, and what are my reasons?
- What is most convincing here? What is least convincing?
- What does the text assume to be true that might not be?
- What do I agree with? What do I disagree with?
- What does the author fail to see? How might it be seen differently?
- Who do I believe?

Reflection. If you did Exercise 3, you might have reflected on what you know about *how to read* the kinds of things you like to read. We often develop this kind of knowledge—knowledge about how to do things—slowly over time. But you can speed up the process by making time to ask yourself questions that encourage reflection.

You probably already have experience with this. We reflect on all kinds of processes that we want to get better at—things like playing golf, learning to act, and, of course, reading and writing. How am I executing that back swing? How might I do it differently? What new technique can I try that will deepen the emotional response of the character I'm playing? When we reflect like this on golf or acting, we discover other choices we can make that will help us perform better. The same is true when we reflect on how we think or write. The benefit of doing this is significant for everyone, but it's huge when you have problems with a process or you want to get better at it.

Inquiry questions that prompt reflection about how you read include:

- What do I notice about how I'm reading this?
- What assumptions do I bring to the reading that might influence what I think or how I feel about what it says?

- How do I compare how I approach this task with how I approach another one?
- When did I have the most problems with the text? What were they?
- How did this add to my knowledge about how to become a better reader?

READING DIALECTICALLY

Opening questions will give us goals for reading, as they do for writing, and we can also use the method of combining creative and critical thinking to help us get more out of what we read (see Figure 7).

You have already used this process extensively in the writing exercises so far, moving from suspending judgment when you generate ideas to making judgments when you analyze what you've generated. When we read to write, we can also use these alternate modes of thinking to ultimately answer the same question that all writing must answer: *So what?* What are you trying to say to others about what you've read that they might care to know? On the way to answering the "so what" question, we're trying to figure out what *we* think and, in particular, how a text helps us to think about the questions that moved us to look at it

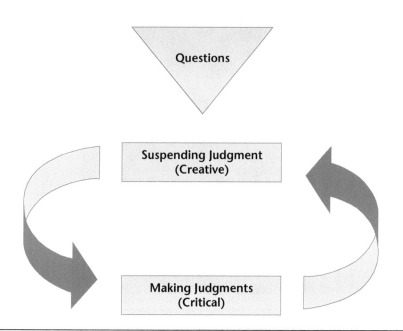

Figure 7 The inquiry process combines creative and critical thinking.

in the first place. Let's see how this might work with a visual text and then, later, a print text.

Suppose you were asked to *explain* the image in Figure 8, by famed American photographer Edward Weston, in a short response, offering your own idea about what it means based on particular things you see in the photograph.

You could approach this in two ways:

1. You could just make something up without thinking about it much and leave it at that. "Gee, this looks like, um, a bull's nostril."

2. You could withhold judgment and spend a little more time figuring out what you think.

The first option is a closed, cursory reading. It starts with answers rather than questions, and sidesteps any genuine inquiry into the text. The second option is more open-ended, and it requires that you look more closely at the text and *then* develop ideas about it. Reading dialectically is a method that can encourage that kind of inquiry.

When we read to write, we work from a question that gives our reading a goal. In the case of the photograph, we're asking an explaining question: "What is this image trying to do?" As you know, knowledge of *how* to read a kind of text with which we may not be familiar will really help us work toward a good reading

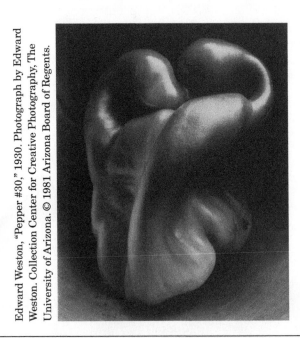

Edward Weston, "Pepper #30," 1930. Photograph by Edward Weston. Collection Center for Creative Photography, The University of Arizona. © 1981 Arizona Board of Regents.

Figure 8   How would you explain this photograph?

(see "Inquiring into the Details: Visual Literacy: Reading Photographs). With this background knowledge, here's one way of finding an answer to our question:

- Start with two blank, opposing pages in a journal. Beginning on the left page, note your observations of the photograph. Writing fast, use your knowledge of how to read a photograph and explore what exactly you see in the image, describing this as specifically as you can.

- On the right page, compose your initial thoughts in response to the question, looking at the information you collected on the left page to help you think about what you are trying to say.

For example:

Observations of	Ideas about
What's interesting is that the setting of the image is stripped down and bare so that the green pepper is without question the most important visual subject here. The framing is so simple, really. All we need to know is before us. It's realistic and it's abstract at the same time. I can see the pepper, particularly the bruise in the bottom and the curving ribs of the thing, but the light seems to emphasize not the structure of the green pepper but the skin. The skin is amazing. The light has this amazing range reflecting on the skin—very dark at the top where the pepper turns into itself in contrast with the sheen on the edges. . . .	By stripping away any context and filling the frame with the image of a single green pepper, Weston's photograph emphasizes its abstract qualities. And yet, though we know it's a pepper, it's impossible to avoid seeing the play of the light on its skin as incredibly suggestive. It's sensuous and has some of the qualities of flesh, especially the curves and the muscular ridges.

Reading dialectically like this mimics the process of moving back and forth from creative and critical, collecting and focusing, observations and ideas, specifics and generalizations. On the left page you are withholding judgment, trying to think through writing about what you see. On the right, you work toward making some kind of judgments about what you see. Obviously, this method—what writing theorist Ann Berthoff called the "dialogue journal" or double-entry journal—takes more time than just making a pronouncement like "It's a pepper!" or "It looks like two wrestling dinosaurs!" But by postponing the rush to a conclusion, you use the inquiry process to come up with better, more insightful, more informed ideas.

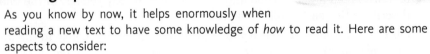

INQUIRING INTO THE DETAILS

Visual Literacy: Reading Photographs

As you know by now, it helps enormously when reading a new text to have some knowledge of *how* to read it. Here are some aspects to consider:

- **Framing:** As in writing, what the photographer chooses to leave in an image and what she chooses to leave out profoundly affect the story, idea, or feeling a photograph communicates.

- **Angle:** A front-on view of a subject creates a different effect than looking up—or down—at it.

- **Setting:** While good photographs emphasize certain visual elements and not others, some try, directly or indirectly, to communicate other information about where and when the photograph was taken. It's also significant when setting or context is missing.

- **Arrangement:** In writing, we give certain information emphasis by where we place it in a sentence, in a paragraph, or in the whole composition. Visual information also uses the physical arrangement of objects for emphasis, making some things larger or smaller, in the foreground or background, to one side or the other. Focus, or what is clear and what is fuzzy, is one way to manage visual arrangement.

- **Light:** What is most illuminated and what is in shadows—and everything in between—also influences what is emphasized and what is not. But since light is something we strongly associate with time and place, it also has an emotional impact.

EXERCISE 4

Reading Creatively, Reading Critically

Now that you've seen how the dialectical thinking approach can help analyze an image, let's try it with a more familiar kind of text. I published the essay "The Importance of Writing Badly" some years ago, but I think it still expresses several of the main ideas behind this text. I'd like you to read the piece critically, though, using the double-entry journal method we used when interpreting the pepper photograph.

As before, you'll use opposing pages of your journal. At the top of the left page write the word "Collecting," and at the top of the right page write the word "Focusing."

STEP ONE: Read the essay once through, and then once again. The second time through, carefully *copy* lines of passages from the essay on the left page of your notebook that:

- Connected with your own experience and observations
- Raised questions for you
- Puzzled you
- You thought seemed a key point
- You disagreed or agreed with or you think about differently
- You found surprising or unexpected

The Importance of Writing Badly
Bruce Ballenger

I was grading papers in the waiting room of my doctor's office the other day, and he said, "It must be pretty eye-opening reading that stuff. Can you believe those students had four years of high school and still can't write?" 1

I've heard that before. I hear it almost every time I tell a stranger that I teach writing at a university. 2

I also hear it from colleagues brandishing red pens who hover over their students' papers like Huey helicopters waiting to flush the enemy from the tall grass, waiting for a comma splice or a vague pronoun reference or a misspelled word to break cover. 3

And I heard it this morning from the commentator on my public radio station who publishes snickering books about how students abuse the sacred language. 4

I have another problem: getting my students to write badly. 5

Most of us have lurking in our past some high priest of good grammar whose angry scribbling occupied the margins of our papers. Mine was Mrs. O'Neill, an eighth-grade teacher with a good heart but no patience for the bad sentence. Her favorite comment on my writing was "awk," which now sounds to me like the grunt of a large bird, but back then meant "awkward." She didn't think much of my sentences. 6

I find some people who reminisce fondly about their own Mrs. O'Neill, usually an English teacher who terrorized them into worshipping the error-free sentence. In some cases that terror paid off when it was finally transformed into an appreciation for the music a well-made sentence can make. 7

But it didn't work that way with me. I was driven into silence, losing faith that I could ever pick up the pen without breaking the rules or drawing another "awk" from a doubting reader. For years I wrote only when forced to, and when I did it was never good enough. 8

(continued)

(continued)

9   Many of my students come to me similarly voiceless, dreading the first writing assignment because they mistakenly believe that how they say it matters more than discovering what they have to say.

10   The night before the essay is due they pace their rooms like expectant fathers, waiting to deliver the perfect beginning. They wait and they wait and they wait. It's no wonder the waiting often turns to hating what they have written when they finally get it down. Many pledge to steer clear of English classes, or any class that demands much writing.

11   My doctor would say my students' failure to make words march down the page with military precision is another example of a failed education system. The criticism sometimes takes on political overtones. On my campus, for example, the right-wing student newspaper demanded that an entire semester of Freshman English be devoted to teaching students the rules of punctuation.

12   There is, I think, a hint of elitism among those who are so quick to decry the sorry state of the sentence in the hands of student writers. A colleague of mine, an Ivy League graduate, is among the self-appointed grammar police, complaining often about the dumb mistakes his students make in their papers. I don't remember him ever talking about what his students are trying to say in those papers. I have a feeling he's really not that interested.

13   Concise, clear writing matters, of course, and I have a responsibility to demand it from students. But first I am far more interested in encouraging thinking than error-free sentences. That's where bad writing comes in.

14   When I give my students permission to write badly, to suspend their compulsive need to find the "perfect way of saying it," often something miraculous happens: Words that used to trickle forth come gushing to the page. The students quickly find their voices again, and even more important, they are surprised by what they have to say. They can worry later about fixing awkward sentences. First, they need to make a mess.

15   It's harder to write badly than you might think. Haunted by their Mrs. O'Neill, some students can't overlook the sloppiness of their sentences or their lack of eloquence, and quickly stall out and stop writing. When the writing stops, so does the thinking.

16   The greatest reward in allowing students to write badly is that they learn that language can lead them to meaning, that words can be a means for finding out what they didn't know they knew. It usually happens when the words rush to the page, however awkwardly.

17   I don't mean to excuse bad grammar. But I cringe at conservative educational reformers who believe writing instruction should return to primarily teaching how to punctuate a sentence and use *Roget's Thesaurus*. If policing student papers for mistakes means alienating young writers from the language we expect them to master, then the exercise is self-defeating.

18   It is more important to allow students to first experience how language can be a vehicle for discovering how they see the world. And what matters in this journey—at least initially—is not what kind of car you're driving, but where you end up.

STEP TWO: Now use the right page of your notebook to think further about what you wrote down on the left page. Remember these inquiry questions that can guide your thinking and writing:

- *Exploring:* What do I first notice about notes I took on "The Importance of Writing Badly?" And then what do I notice or think? And then?
- *Explaining:* What is it that I understand this to be saying?
- *Evaluating:* What is most convincing here? What is least convincing?

Write for five or six minutes without stopping.

STEP THREE: Reread what you've written. Again, on the right page of your notebook write your half of the dialog below with someone who is asking you about the idea of "bad writing."

Q: I don't understand how bad writing can help anyone write better. Can you explain it to me?

A:

Q: Okay, but is it an idea that makes sense to you?

A:

Q: What exactly (i.e., quotation) does Ballenger say that makes you feel that way?

A:

STEP FOUR: Finish the exercise by reflecting in your journal for five minutes on what, if anything, you noticed about this method of reading. In particular:

- How did it change the way you usually read an article like this?
- How might you adapt it for other situations in which you have to read to write?
- What worked well? What didn't?
- Do you think the method encouraged you to think more deeply about what you read?

ONE STUDENT'S RESPONSE

Briana's Journal

EXERCISE 4 READING CREATIVELY, READING CRITICALLY

STEP TWO:

I took pieces of the sentences, not necessarily writing down the whole sentence but the parts that were the most poignant. I mostly chose sentences that I found to be clever, amusing, or just liked the way they sounded…I also created a dichotomy,

(continued)

One Student's Response (*continued*)

focusing on two things: 1) the "proper" way of writing, which is English elitism, and is focusing on grammatical perfection and 2) the "artsy" way of writing, which focuses on writing as a thought process to help create understanding and growth. While I was writing down my notes and sentences, I was thinking that I have never had a Mrs. O'Neil. This has not been my experience. I write to write, and mostly to amuse myself or as a form of cheap therapy (also cheaper than cable). I also think that sometimes "grammatical imperfection" can add to the style and the voice of a piece. I also value voice and style over perfection…I see this piece as saying that writing is like a thinking process, like thinking out loud but you have an invaluable record of your thoughts. I also get that you need to write and write a lot. The more the better; it gives you more to work with. I also think that it helps you write better and enjoy it because you are getting a lot of experience. It's not so much about how you wrote it as it is about what you write about.

STEP THREE

Q: I don't understand how bad writing can help anyone write better. Can you explain it to me?
A: What you have to say is just as important as how you write it. Writing is a way of thinking, sort of like thinking out loud—a way of thinking through things and reflecting more deeply on things. It feels awesome to write with reckless abandon and show no concern for punctuation or grammar. It helps you think unhindered, to find out how you truly think and feel. Thoughts and feelings have little concern for these things. Looking back at your thoughts that you have written you can see your thoughts. Then you can look at how you have written. Being observant and introspective of your own writing will help you develop better writing skills.

Q: Okay, but is it an idea that makes sense to you?
A: Definitely, I prefer to write badly. I believe that it's a better expression of my actual thoughts, flaws and all. When I write on my computer my spellcheck goes crazy with "fragment sentences." But who cares? That's what I want to say and that is how it comes out and how it sounds in its natural state. I don't change it. Give me all your green squiggly underlinings, Windows Vista. It has been driven into so many students that we have to write perfectly—use correct punctuation, no vague pronouns, correct verb tense, good sentence syntax, and structure. I think that writing should be more than that. I think that it should be more of a form of expression.

Q: What exactly (i.e., quotation) does Ballenger say that makes you feel that way?
A: "Many of my students come to me similarly voiceless, because they mistakenly believe that how they say it matters more than discovering what they have to say."

I have never actually used the "double-entry" journal method before. I think it gave me a more articulate and clear idea of what I thought and how I came to think that. It became a map of my thought process. I usually have trouble pulling my thoughts in my writing together, but this gave me my thoughts more concisely. I also liked that

I had a record of my thoughts and that regardless of the quality of writing, it was an accurate record because we all know that memory is not all that reliable. I think that method would be good when you have to opine on a subject at length. I liked the explore, explain, evaluate, and reflect structure because when you are writing off the top of your head it is easy to lose focus. So this helps keep you on track.

Read to Write and Write to Read

In this chapter I'm making a case for an approach to reading that is probably unfamiliar to you. It includes the following:

1. **When you read to write, do it with certain goals in mind**. For many of us this isn't new—we often do read with purpose—but these goals are often limited to two things: comprehending and cherry-picking. The lesson of the SAT is that comprehension is what reading is all about since that is what you get tested on. Similarly, the five-paragraph theme and other formulaic forms of writing, which are so popular in school, teach us that reading to write is no more than plucking information from sources to plug into paragraphs to support topic sentences. But reading can also be a kind of conversation in which we talk with others with an open mind.

2. **Questions shift your perspective on what you read**. When we read to write we may have only one question in mind: What do I understand this to be saying? That's a good question, of course, but it's not the only one that can guide your thinking. Photographers consciously change lenses, angles, and distances on their subjects to see them in new ways. Questions have the same effect when you read—especially those that *explore, explain, evaluate*, and *reflect*.

3. **When you read to write you can write *and* read**. Some of us underline, highlight, and even make marginal notes when we read to write. But I'm encouraging you to do much more writing than that as you read, and after you read. If writing about your personal experiences can be a process of discovery, then you can use the same method to explore anything else you want to think about. In other words, if you're trying to figure out what you think about what you're reading, then you can *write* your way to new understandings.

4. **Good readers develop *rhetorical knowledge***. You already have more of this kind of knowledge than you think. You know, for example, to read a text message differently than a textbook. But the best readers pay a lot of attention to learning explicitly about this. They remember what different reading situations demand from them. For example, they learn to distinguish goals for reading to write about a short story from goals for reading to write about marketing. They also develop knowledge about genre. Good readers, for instance, know that Web pages are often designed to put the most important information across the top and down the left side.

THE WRITING PROCESS

INQUIRY PROJECT: THE READING LITERACY MEMOIR

This time your three- to five-page essay will focus on your experiences as a reader. You've already started writing and thinking about this in Exercises 1 and 2. If you can, draw on some of that material and draft a personal essay that does two things:

- Tells stories about some of your reading experiences, in school and out
- Reflects on what you understand about those experiences now, as you look back on them

For your reflection, exploit, if you can, some of the information in this chapter, particularly ideas about what the differences might be between a "good" reader and a novice reader and where you see yourself as a reader now, what you think you need to learn, and why it matters.

For additional reading, writing, and research resources, go to www.mycomplab.com

Unfortunately, schooling can brand us and give us ideas about ourselves that are hard to change. I was told in subtle and unsubtle ways that I was not good at English. When it comes to reading—the major focus of language arts classes—one moment stands out that affected the way I thought about myself as a reader for a long time. My memoir, for example, might start like this:

In 1965, I moved from green to orange in the SRA reading packet but never moved again. In those days, orangeness was a sign of mediocrity. The shame of never busting through orange to blue, the color Jeff Brickman, Mark Levy, and Betsy Cochran seemed to achieve with such ease quite naturally made it easy to convince me that reading was just not my thing. From then on I hated English (a feeling I freely shared on the inside covers of my class yearbooks), except the time we studied the lyrics of Simon and Garfunkel's "The Sounds of Silence." I was a high school sophomore, and while I would sometimes, in my own way, think deeply on things, I was attached more to *the idea* of thinking deeply on things, usually expressed in the ponderous and self-consciously deep lyrics of early Simon and Garfunkel's. To *feel* deep, I thought, was to *be* deep.

■ STUDENT ESSAY

Reading Literacy Memoir
Briana Duquette-Shackley

I was born into a very blue-collar family, almost anti-intellectual. You read recipes, you read car repair manuals, you read the TV guide or on occasion you read those novels that they sell on the shelf at the checkout aisle. There was very little emphasis on learning or intellect. Instead you were told to be who you are and do what you like best. There was never anyone pushing me to be a doctor and when I said I wanted to be one, my parents said "OK." I said I wanted to be a racecar driver and they said "if that's what you want to do." I said that I wanted to be a fashion designer and they said "that's a fine idea."

Under this intellectual neutrality I just went with what interested me and I blossomed in the reading and language department. I could speak and read at an early age and was reading at a college freshman level in the fifth grade. If I wanted a book, my parents bought it; so when I asked for *The Scarlet Letter* at an early age, they didn't seem concerned about the content or the level of reading. I read it. There were some things that I had to reread, but I read it. I was a good student and consistently on the honor roll.

It was not that my parents didn't praise me for my academics, but they just didn't push me in any one direction. I found a love of reading, and once I started to read I didn't want to stop. I would read anything that I could get my hands on, and I continue to be like that to this day. I read *People*, *Us Weekly*, and *Good Housekeeping*, not because they are what I love to read but because it's the only thing to read at work. I could spend days in Barnes and Noble and not buy anything. And all the librarians at my local library know me by name.

In kindergarten I remember reading the books that they have that teach you how to read, the same "decodable" books I read to my own daughter, and I loved them. I would read aloud at the kitchen counter as my mom cooked dinner. I now find myself with a compulsion to read anything that is in front of me no matter how lame: cereal boxes, random pamphlets, those weird quips in the phonebook. I love the communication and the nuances between words, their meanings, and their usage. It's like how I look at fashion magazines for ideas on how to dress, I look to literature to show me examples of how to speak and write, and even to try out who I might want to be.

I have gone through phases where I want to explore an area of myself or life and I will turn to literature for information about it. During my punk rock phase in high school, I read books and periodicals about revolution and anarchy and became very politically savvy. I went through an artistic phase where I wanted to learn about the great artists and how to revolutionize the art world. I went to the library and checked out art book after art book. I went through an indie rock, intellectual phase and read exclusively books by the beat writers. Then I went through a Che Guevara phase and read *The Motorcycle Diaries* and his lengthy autobiography. I noticed toward the end of the bio that I didn't even want to read it; I really couldn't

(continued)

73

(continued)

care less about the flawed bureaucracy of the new Cuban government. I was mostly in love with the romantic ideal of the revolutionist, no matter how misguided. But I read it all, to have the sense of accomplishment and for fear that I might miss out on something.

6   Reading is something less that I do because I want to; it seems more like a compulsion. It's part pleasure and part practicality. I read for information, but I only read about things that I want to know about. I always have at least one book by my bed that I am reading. When I was a child, my parents read to me every night before bed. Even when I could read they would still read to me. But this wasn't about learning; it was about enjoyment. It was something that they shared with me; they liked doing it and I like being read to. So through the two—information and enjoyment—this compulsion arose.

7   Unfortunately, this passion for reading did not always help me in school. In elementary school, I struggled with reading comprehension. I guess I equated reading really fast with being a good reader. I didn't think about what the words were saying. When we would have a test I would read the piece and then not be able to answer any of the questions about what I had just read. When I would get my test back I would have A's in everything but reading comprehension. Working with my teacher after school, I learned to slow down to understand the words instead of merely repeating them.

8   Even now I will find myself "just trying to make it through" texts that I am not really all that into. And then I will look back and think that I have gotten absolutely nothing out of what I have just read and then have to reread it. I read extremely slowly when I am really trying to read and comprehend something that I don't really want to read. Yet when I am reading something that I really like, the same slow reading makes all else in my environment fade. When I read what I want and what I enjoy, comprehension is totally effortless. I have to give the piece value, and then I can enjoy it; I have to try to find one thing that I can derive pleasure from, and then I can get into it.

9   I think that my love of reading comes from the fact that I come from a blue-collar background. And herein lies the irony. Blue-collar people, from my observations, tend to be more rebellious. I guess reading and becoming more literate was my way of rebelling, too. And maybe that was what asking for *The Scarlet Letter* was all about. Reading a book that was considered a "great" or a "classic" was my equivalent to getting a facial piercing or a tattoo. Also, it is just in my nature to be curious and want to know about things. Since I always hated to ask anyone, for whatever reason, going and reading a book seemed like a much better and more direct route. I have a friend who told me that there is this Jewish philosophy that says that the only thing that you can take with you when you die is knowledge. Now I don't necessarily agree with this, but I think that knowledge can and will make the life that you are currently living much more rich and fulfilling. And the best place to get information is to read it. There are countless books and other sources of text, literature, prose, and everything in between. Thanks to the Internet you can read about anything at the touch of your fingertips, and you don't even have to get up. Reading to get information just makes good sense in my world.

10   At the moment, I am going through an, as of yet, unnamed phase, but I am reading Aleister Crowley. Someday, I hope to look back and see the story of myself in what I was reading and hope that what I was reading made my life better in some way.

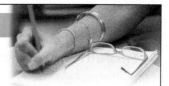

INQUIRING INTO THE DETAILS

The Double-Entry Journal

A double-entry journal is essentially a written dialog between a reader and a text. As a reader you ask questions, make connections, and note memories and associations.

Here's how it works: You can either draw a line down the middle of a page to make two columns, or you can use the spine of your notebook for the line and use two opposing pages.

What the Text Says	What I Think
In the left column, write out the passages from the reading that confuse you, surprise you, make you think of other ideas, seem key to your understanding of what it says, and so on.	In the right column, write out your response to those passages. Sometimes you'll do a fastwrite; other times you may simply jot down quick thoughts.
■ Jot down direct quotes, paraphrases, summaries, facts, claims.	Play the doubting game, questioning the source; play the believing game, trying to find its virtues, even if you disagree.
■ Note page numbers next to each passage or summary/paraphrase. Put them in the far right margin next to the borrowed material or ideas.	■ Shift to other reading perspectives.
	■ Tell the story of your thinking about what you're reading: *My initial reaction to this is… but now I think…and now I think…*
	■ List questions you have about the source's ideas, your emotional responses, other ideas or readings it connects to.

Continue this process for the entire reading, moving back and forth across the columns. Remember that you want to explore your response to a text, make connections to other works and your own writing, and analyze the writer's choices in terms of language, style, detail, and so forth. *Be sure to note all the bibliographic information from the source at the top of the page.*

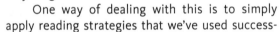

INQUIRING INTO THE DETAILS

Encountering Unfamiliar Genres

The only time most of us ever really pay attention to genre is when we encounter one that defies our expectations. When the low-budget film *Memento* was released several years ago, its puzzling narrative structure (beginning at the end of the story and proceeding to the beginning), its use of an unreliable narrator, and its alternation between black-and-white and color took audiences by surprise and generated lots of print by movie critics. Ultimately, the film became a phenomenal success, partly because its approach was so unexpected. *Memento* got people talking about a completely different way to think about filmmaking.

The response to the movie was so significant because we are a nation of moviegoers who are quite familiar with the genre, and *Memento* made us wonder how much we really know about film. These kinds of *Memento* movements happen to readers all the time, especially when we're in an academic setting and aren't familiar with the genres we're asked to read—a poem, a lab report, an academic argument, a minimalist painting. Our first response might be to question how well we can read, even though we've all been reading for a very long time.

An ad for the film *Memento*

Photofest NYC

One way of dealing with this is to simply apply reading strategies that we've used successfully in other genres. For example, because your verbal score on the reading comprehension portion of the SAT was so high, why not approach reading the essay on the need for a new immigration policy the same way, and try to decode exactly what the writer must have meant and leave it at that? Well, your instructor will likely say, "Fine, but I want to know what you think about his argument."

A better approach when you encounter types of readings that are new to you is to let the reading situation be your guide.

- Ask yourself, *Why am I reading this? How is it relevant to my inquiry question?* or *What exactly is my instructor asking me to do with this text?*

- Are there clues in the text about how it might be efficiently read? For instance, do subheadings provide guidance? Is there a preface that reviews the argument? Does the concluding section have the most weight?

- Who is the intended audience for this text and what clues does that provide about the writer's purpose? Might that explain not only how she composed the text—its language, organization, and so on—but also what she hoped to accomplish with it?

- Whenever possible, "frontload" before you read something challenging; that is, learn as much as you can about the subject and even the writer's relationship to the subject. This knowledge will make a big difference in how much you understand.

USING WHAT YOU HAVE LEARNED

Inquiry-based writing and reading begins with an open-eyed sense of wonder. Instead of initially asking, *What should I say?* you ask, *What do I think?* You begin by trying to find questions that interest you, knowing that there isn't necessarily a single right answer. At the same time, you know that just as you open up possible meanings, at some point you need to narrow them. You are both creative *and* critical, moving back and forth between collecting and focusing, exploring and evaluating, narrating and reflecting.

I encourage you to apply this process to nearly every assignment. Before long, it will become second nature to you; you'll find yourself naturally shifting back and forth between the creative and the critical, whether you're exploring a topic for an assignment, reading an essay that you'll discuss in class, or analyzing an advertisement. Techniques that you've already practiced such as fastwriting and listing, the double-entry journal, and generating questions will help this along.

WRITING A PERSONAL ESSAY

From Chapter 3 of *The Curious Writer*, Third Edition. Bruce Ballenger. Copyright © 2011 by Pearson Education, Inc. Published by Pearson Longman. All rights reserved.

Writing a personal essay is like seeing an old picture of yourself. This publicity photograph of my mother, my brother, and me in the 1950s returns me to that world—a time when fathers were often missing from the picture.

Bruce Ballenger

WRITING A PERSONAL ESSAY

WRITING ABOUT EXPERIENCE

Most us were taught and still believe that we need to know what we are going to write before we actually pick up the pen or sit in front of the computer. My student Lynn was typical.

"I think I'll write about my experience organizing the street fair," she told me the other day. "That would be a good topic for a personal essay, right?"

"Do you think so?" I said.

"Well, yes, because I already know a lot about it. I'll have a lot to write about."

"Okay, but is there anything about this experience that you want to understand better?" I said. "Anything about it that makes you curious?"

"Curious? It was just a street fair," she said.

"Sure, but is there something about what happened that makes you want to look at the experience again? Is there a chance that you might learn something about yourself, or about street fairs, or about the community, or about people, or...?"

Lynn was clearly sorry she asked. What I should have said was much more to the point: The best essay topics are those that are an itch you need to scratch. These tend not to be topics you have already figured out. While the topics can be familiar to you, the results of your inquiry are usually much better if you don't yet know what you think about your topics and you're interested to learn more about them.

> ### What You'll Learn in This Chapter
>
> - How personal essays can help you with academic writing.
> - What distinguishes a personal essay from other forms.
> - How to write a sketch.
> - Why a confusing topic may be better than one you have all figured out.
> - Questions for revising personal essays.

The best topics ask to be written about because they make you wonder *Why did I do that? What does that mean? Why did that happen? How did I really feel? What do I really think?*

Unlike most other forms of inquiry, the personal essay invites an initial display of confusion or uncertainty from writers regarding their subjects. In other words, writers do not have to have their subjects figured out when starting a personal essay. This form of inquiry is a vehicle for writers to work through their thinking and feeling on a subject directly in front of their readers.

> The personal essay is a vehicle for writers to work through their thinking and feeling on a subject directly in front of their readers.

As a form, the *personal* essay places the writer at center stage. This doesn't mean that once she's there, her responsibility is to pour out her secrets, share her pain, or confess her sins. Some essays do have these confessional qualities, but more often they do not. Yet a personal essayist, no matter the subject of the essay, is still *exposed*. There is no hiding behind the pronoun "one," as in "one might think" or "one often feels," no lurking in the shadows of the passive voice: "An argument will be made that...." The personal essay is first-person territory.

In this sense, the personal essay is much like a photographic self-portrait. Like a picture, a good personal essay tells the truth, or it tells *a* truth about the writer/subject, and it often captures the writer at a particular moment of time. Therefore, the experience of taking a self-portrait, or confronting an old picture of oneself taken by someone else, can create the feeling of exposure that writing a personal essay often does.

But it does more. When we gaze at ourselves in a photograph we often see it as yanked from a larger story about ourselves, a story that threads its way through our lives and gives us ideas about who we were and who we are. This is what the personal essay demands of us: We must somehow present ourselves truthfully and measure our past against the present. In other words, when we hold a photograph of ourselves we know more than the person we see there knew, and as writers of the personal essay, we must share that knowledge and understanding with readers.

MOTIVES FOR WRITING A PERSONAL ESSAY

Essai was a term first coined by the sixteenth-century French nobleman Michel de Montaigne, a man who had lived through occurrences of the plague, the bloody civil war between French Catholics and Protestants, and his own ill health. These were tumultuous and uncertain times when old social orders and intellectual traditions were under assault, and it proved to be ideal ferment for the essay. The French verb *essaier* means "to attempt" or "to try," and the essay became an opportunity for Montaigne to work out his thoughts about war, the education of children, the evils of doctors, and the importance of pleasure. The personal essay tradition inspired by Montaigne is probably unlike the essays you are familiar with in school. The school essay is often formulaic—a five-paragraph theme, or thesis-example paper—while the personal essay is an open-ended form that allows for uncertainty and inconclusiveness. It is more about the process of coming to know than presenting *what* you know. The personal essay attempts *to find out* rather than *to prove*.

It is an ideal form of inquiry if your purpose is exploratory rather than argumentative, and if you're particularly interested in working out the possible relationships between your subject and yourself. Because the personal essay is openly subjective, the writer can't hide. The intruding *I* confronts the writer with the same questions over and over again: *Why does this matter to me? What do I make of it? How does this change the way I think of myself and the way I see the world?* Because of this, one of the principal dangers of the personal essay is that it can become narcissistic; it can go on and on about what the writer thinks and feels, and the reader can be left with that nagging question—*So what?* The personal essayist must always find some way to hitch the particulars of his or her experience to something larger—an idea, a theme, or even a feeling that readers might share.

On the other hand, one of the prime rhetorical advantages of the personal essay is its subjectivity. Because it is written with openness and honesty, the essay is often a very intimate form, inviting the reader to share in the writer's often concealed world. In the personal essay, we often get to see the face sweating under the mask. Honesty is one of the essay's primary virtues, and because the form allows for uncertainty and confusion, the writer doesn't need to pretend that he has *the* answer, or that he knows more than he lets on about his subject.

THE PERSONAL ESSAY AND ACADEMIC WRITING

In some ways, the personal essay might seem like a dramatic departure from the kind of academic writing you've done in other classes. Openly subjective and sometimes tentative in its conclusions, the personal essay is a relatively open form that is not predictably structured, like much academic writing. Additionally, the tone of the personal essay is conversational, even intimate, rather than impersonal and removed. If your sociology or economics professor will never ask for a personal essay, why bother to write one in your composition class?

It's a fair question. While the pleasures of personal essay writing can be significant, and reason alone to write essays, there are other important reasons to practice the form. The most obvious is that the essay, more than any other form, gives you an opportunity to use exploration as a method of inquiry, and to practice those habits of mind that are so important to academic inquiry: suspending judgment, tolerating ambiguity, and using questions to challenge easy assumptions.

> The essay, more than any other form, gives you an opportunity to use exploration as a method of inquiry.

But the purpose of writing personal essays in your composition class goes beyond this. For one thing, the essay emphasizes the *process* of coming to know about yourself and your subject, exposing your reasoning and the ways you use knowledge to get at the truth of things. Reflecting on these things in a personal essay can tell you a lot about how you think. The *dialectical thinking* required by the personal essay—the movement back and forth between critical and creative thinking—is a useful mental exercise for a range of academic situations. Finally, much of what you are asked to write in college depends on your willingness to step forward and express a belief, make an assertion, or pose a relevant question. The personal essay is a form that puts the writer in the spotlight. You can't hide in the wings, concealed in the shadow of other people's opinions or someone else's findings. What *you* think is what the essay is all about.

FEATURES OF THE FORM

There are many different kinds of personal essays, of course, but certain conventions are present in most of them. Keep these in mind as you read the professional essays that follow. Which of the conventions listed here seem to be present? Can you detect any others?

- *Personal essays are usually written in the first person.* There is no pretense of scientific objectivity in personal essays.

- *The subject of the essay is often commonplace.* Although essayists sometimes write about dramatic things, they most often are interested in the drama of everyday life.

- *Narrative is often the primary method of development.* Personal essays often tell two kinds of stories—they relate narratives of the writer's experiences and observations, and they tell the story of the writer's thinking about what those experiences and observations might mean.

- *The thesis can be implicit, and it frequently emerges late, rather than at the beginning, of the essay.*

- *Of the four sources of information, the personal essay relies on memory and observation most of all.* Because of the subjectivity of the essay, the writer often reports *what has happened* to her as a means to account for *what happens*.

- *The essay often mimics the dialectical process that helped the writer compose it, shifting back and forth from the then and now, what happened to what happens, and showing and telling.*

READINGS

■ PERSONAL ESSAY 1

The essayist Scott Russell Sanders once observed that an essay "scatters a bunch of rabbits that go bounding in all directions....If you refuse to chase any of them, and keep plodding along in a straight line, you and your reader will have a dull outing. If you chase too many, you will soon wind up lost in a thicket of confusion...." In "Buckeye," Sanders flushes a few rabbits of his own, chasing down ideas about coping with grief, the life in a piece of wood, and learning to love land that doesn't yield easily to such affection. In this sense, it's a complicated essay; in another, it's as simple as an Ohio buckeye, rubbed shiny from handling. The essay that follows exemplifies one of the most appealing features of the personal essay: Its subject is often ordinary, familiar. In "Buckeye," Sanders is doing no more than telling stories about his father, a handmade wooden box, and a November afternoon. Yet the piece is anything but ordinary in its language, and especially in what it comes to say about how to "dwell in our place with a full heart."

BUCKEYE

Scott Russell Sanders

Years after my father's heart quit, I keep in a wooden box on my desk the two buckeyes that were in his pocket when he died. Once the size of plums, the brown seeds are shriveled now, hollow, hard as pebbles, yet they still gleam from the polish of his hands. He used to reach for them in his overalls or suit pants and click them together, or he would draw them out, cupped in his palm, and twirl them with his blunt carpenter's fingers, all the while humming snatches of old tunes. 1

"Do you really believe buckeyes keep off arthritis?" I asked him more than once. 2

He would flex his hands and say, "I do so far." 3

My father never paid much heed to pain. Near the end, when his worn knee often slipped out of joint, he would pound it back in place with a rubber mallet. If a splinter worked into his flesh beyond the reach of tweezers, he would heat the blade of his knife over a cigarette lighter and slice through the skin. He sought to ward off arthritis not because he feared pain but because he lived through his hands, and he dreaded the swelling of knuckles, the stiffening of fingers. What use would he be if he could no longer hold a hammer or guide a plow? When he was a boy he had known farmers not yet forty years old whose hands had curled into claws, men so crippled up they could not tie their own shoes, could not sign their names. 4

"I mean to tickle my grandchildren when they come along," he told me, "and I mean to build doll houses and turn spindles for tiny chairs on my lathe." 5

(continued)

(continued)

6   So he fondled those buckeyes as if they were charms, carrying them with him when our family moved from Ohio at the end of my childhood, bearing them to new homes in Louisiana, then Oklahoma, Ontario, and Mississippi, carrying them still on his final day when pain a thousand times fiercer than arthritis gripped his heart.

7   The box where I keep the buckeyes also comes from Ohio, made by father from a walnut plank he bought at a farm auction. I remember the auction, remember the sagging face of the widow whose home was being sold, remember my father telling her he would prize that walnut as if he had watched the tree grow from a sapling on his own land. He did not care for pewter of silver or gold, but he cherished wood. On the rare occasions when my mother coaxed him into a museum, he ignored the paintings or porcelain and studied the exhibit cases, the banisters, the moldings, the parquet floors.

8   I remember him planing that walnut board, sawing it, sanding it, joining piece to piece to make foot stools, picture frames, jewelry boxes. My own box, a bit larger than a soap dish, lined with red corduroy, was meant to hold earrings and pins, not buckeyes. The top is inlaid with pieces fitted so as to bring out the grain, four diagonal joints converging from the corners toward the center. If I stare long enough at those converging lines, they float free of the box and point to a center deeper than wood.

9   I learned to recognize buckeyes and beeches, sugar maples and shagbark hickories, wild cherries, walnuts, and dozens of other trees while tramping through the Ohio woods with my father. To his eyes, their leaves, their bark, their winter buds were as distinctive as the set of a friend's shoulders. As with friends, he was partial to some, craving their company, so he would go out of his way to visit particular trees, walking in a circle around the splayed roots of a sycamore, laying his hand against the trunk of a white oak, ruffling the feathery green boughs of a cedar.

10   "Trees breathe," he told me. "Listen."

11   I listened, and heard the stir of breath.

12   He was no botanist; the names and uses he taught me were those he had learned from country folks, not from books. Latin never crossed his lips. Only much later would I discover that the tree he called ironwood, its branches like muscular arms, good for axe handles, is known in the books as hophombeam; what he called tuliptree or canoewood, ideal for log cabins, is officially the yellow poplar; what he called hoop ash, good for barrels and fence posts, appears in books as hackberry.

13   When he introduced me to the buckeye, he broke off a chunk of the gray bark and held it to my nose. I gagged.

14   "That's why the old-timers called it stinking buckeye," he told me. "They used it for cradles and feed troughs and peg legs."

15   "Why for peg legs?" I asked.

16   "Because it's light and hard to split, so it won't shatter when you're clumping around."

He showed me this tree in late summer, when the fruits had fallen and the ground was littered with prickly brown pods. He picked up one, as fat as a lemon, and peeled away the husk to reveal the shiny seed. He laid it in my palm and closed my fist around it so the seed peeped out from the circle formed by my index finger and thumb. "You see where it got the name?" he asked.   17

I saw: what gleamed in my hand was the eye of a deer, bright with life, "It's beautiful," I said.   18

"It's beautiful," my father agreed, "but also poisonous. Nobody eats buckeyes, except maybe a fool squirrel."   19

I knew the gaze of deer from living in the Ravenna Arsenal, in Portage County, up in the northeastern corner of Ohio. After supper we often drove the Arsenal's gravel roads, past the munitions bunkers, past acres of rusting tanks and wrecked bombers, into the far fields where we counted deer. One June evening, while mist rose from the ponds, we counted three hundred and eleven, our family record. We found the deer in herds, in bunches, in amorous pairs. We came upon lone bucks, their antlers lifted against the sky like the bare branches of dogwood. If you were quiet, if your hands were empty, if you moved slowly, you could leave the car and steal to within a few paces of a grazing deer, close enough to see the delicate lips, the twitching nostrils, the glossy fathomless eyes.   20

The wooden box on my desk holds these grazing deer, as it holds the buckeyes and the walnut plank and the farm auction and the munitions bunkers and the breathing forests and my father's hands. I could lose the box, I could lose the polished seeds, but if I were to lose the memories I would become a bush without roots, and every new breeze would toss me about. All those memories lead back to the northeastern corner of Ohio, the place where I came to consciousness, where I learned to connect feelings with words, where I fell in love with the earth.   21

It was a troubled love, for much of the land I knew as a child had been ravaged. The ponds in the Arsenal teemed with bluegill and beaver, but they were also laced with TNT from the making of bombs. Because the wolves and coyotes had long since been killed, some of the deer, so plump in the June grass, collapsed on the January snow, whittled by hunger to racks of bones. Outside the Arsenal's high barbed fences, many of the farms had failed, their barns carving in, their topsoil gone. Ravines were choked with swollen couches and junked washing machines and cars. Crossing fields, you had to be careful not to slice your feet on tin cans or shards of glass. Most of the rivers had been dammed, turning fertile valleys into scummy playgrounds for boats.   22

One free-flowing river, the Mahoning, ran past the small farm near the Arsenal where our family lived during my later years in Ohio. We owned just enough land to pasture three ponies and to grow vegetables for our table, but those few acres opened onto miles of woods and creeks and secret meadows. I walked that land in   23

(continued)

(continued)

every season, every weather, following animal trails. But then the Mahoning, too, was doomed by a government decision; we were forced to sell our land, and a dam began to rise across the river.

24   If enough people had spoken for the river, we might have saved it. If enough people had believed that our scarred country was worth defending, we might have dug in our heels and fought. Our attachments to the land were all private. We had no shared lore, no literature, no art to root us there, to give us courage, to help us stand our ground. The only maps we had were those issued by the state, showing a maze of numbered lines stretched over emptiness. The Ohio landscape never showed up on postcards or posters, never unfurled like tapestry in films, rarely filled even a paragraph in books. There were no mountains in that place, no waterfalls, no rocky gorges, no vistas. It was a country of low hills, cut over woods, scoured fields, villages that had lost their purpose, roads that had lost their way.

25   "Let us love the country of here below," Simone Weil urged. "It is real; it offers resistance to love. It is this country that God has given us to love. He has willed that it should be difficult yet possible to love it." Which is the deeper truth about buckeyes, their poison or their beauty? I hold with the beauty; or rather, I am held by the beauty, without forgetting the poison. In my corner of Ohio the gullies were choked with trash, yet cedars flickered up like green flames from cracks in stone; in the evening bombs exploded at the ammunition dump, yet from the darkness came the mating cries of owls. I was saved from despair by knowing a few men and women who cared enough about the land to clean up trash, who planted walnuts and oaks that would long outlive them, who imagined a world that would have no call for bombs.

26   How could our hearts be large enough for heaven if they are not large enough for earth? The only country I am certain of is the one here below. The only country I am certain of is the one here below. The only paradise I know is the one lit by our everyday sun, this land of difficult love, shot through with shadow. The place where we learn this love, if we learn it at all, shimmers behind every new place we inhabit.

27   A family move carried me away from Ohio thirty years ago; my schooling and marriage and job have kept me away ever since, except for visits in memory and in flesh. I returned to the site of our farm one cold November day, when the trees were skeletons and the ground shone with the yellow of fallen leaves. From a previous trip I knew that our house had been bulldozed, our yard and pasture had grown up in thickets, and the reservoir had flooded the woods. On my earlier visit I had merely gazed from the car, too numb with loss to climb out. But on this November day, I parked the car, drew on my hat and gloves, opened the door, and walked.

28   I was looking for some sign that we had lived there, some token of our affection for the place. All that I recognized, aside from the contours of the land, were two weeping willows that my father and I had planted near the road. They had been slips the length of my forearm when we set them out, and now their crowns rose higher

than the telephone poles. When I touched them last, their trunks had been smooth and supple, as thin as my wrist, and now they were furrowed and stout. I took off my gloves and laid my hands against the rough bark. Immediately I felt the wince of tears. Without knowing why, I said hello to my father, quietly at first, then louder, as if only shouts could reach him through the bark miles and years.

Surprised by sobs, I turned from the willows and stumbled away toward the drowned woods, calling to my father. I sensed that he was nearby. Even as I called, I was wary of grief's deceptions. I had never seen his body after he died. By the time I reached the place of his death, a furnace had reduced him to ashes. The need to see him, to let go of this land and time, was powerful enough to summon mirages; I knew that. But I also knew, stumbling toward the woods, that my father was here.   29

At the bottom of a slope where the creek used to run, I came to an expanse of gray stumps and withered grass. It was a bay of the reservoir from which the water had retreated, the level drawn down by engineers or drought. I stood at the edge of this desolate ground, willing it back to life, trying to recall the woods where my father had taught me the names of trees. No green shoots rose. I walked out among the stumps. The grass crackled under my boots, breath rasped in my throat, but otherwise the world was silent.   30

Then a cry broke overhead and I looked up to see a red-tailed hawk launching out from the top of an oak. I recognized the bird from its band of dark feathers across the creamy breast and the tail splayed like rosy fingers against the sun. It was a red-tailed hawk for sure; and it was also my father. Not a symbol of my father, not a reminder, not a ghost, but the man himself, right there, circling in the air above me. I knew this as clearly as I knew the sun burned in the sky. A calm poured through me. My chest quit heaving. My eyes dried.   31

Hawk and father wheeled above me, circle upon circle, wings barely moving, head still. My own head was still, looking up, knowing and being known. Time scattered like fog. At length, father and hawk stroked the air with those powerful wings, three beats, then vanished over a ridge.   32

The voice of my education told me then and tells me now that I did not meet my father, that I merely projected my longing onto a bird. My education I've read, no lesson reached by logic has ever convinced me as utterly or stirred me as deeply as did that red-tailed hawk. Nothing in my education prepared me to love a piece of the earth, least of all a humble, battered country like northeastern Ohio; I learned from the land itself.   33

Before leaving the drowned woods, I looked around at the ashen stumps, the wilted grass, and for the first time since moving from this place I was able to let it go. This ground was lost; the flood would reclaim it. But other ground could be saved, must be saved, in every watershed, every neighborhood. For each home ground we need new maps, living maps, stories and poems, photographs and paintings, essays and songs. We need to know where we are, so that we may dwell in our place with a full heart.   34

Inquiring into the Essay

I invite you to respond to readings such as "Buckeye," using questions based on the four methods of inquiry. The following questions, therefore, encourage you to explore, explain, evaluate, and reflect to discover and shape what you think about the reading. If you're using a double-entry journal, use these questions to prompt writing on the right page of your notebook. Use the opposing left page to collect passages, details, and quotations from the reading that you think might be important.

1. Sanders handles a pair of buckeyes that once belonged to his father, and this triggers stories that allow him to look into ideas about grief and love of the land. It's a powerful thing, this recognition that the same ordinary objects hold a "deeper center," a meaning we don't often recognize unless we stop to look. In your journal, brainstorm a list of objects that hold significance for you. Choose one, and spend seven full minutes fastwriting in your journal about the stories it inspires. If the writing stalls, choose another. Keep your pen moving. Finally, skip a line and finish this sentence: *What surprised me most about what I just wrote is…*

2. Personal essays often tell two stories: the story of what happened, and the story of what the writer came to understand about the meaning of what happened. Explain your understanding of that second story in "Buckeye."

3. Though we rarely link the personal narrative and the argument, personal essays often make at least implicit arguments. "Buckeye" does. For example, Sanders writes that the steady destruction of the Ohio landscape has to do with the absence of a "shared lore" or art or literature that celebrates the land in the Midwest. "The Ohio landscape never showed up on postcards or posters," writes Sanders, "never unfurled like tapestry in films, rarely filled even a paragraph in books." What does Sanders assume to be true for this claim to be believable? Do you agree?

4. While "Buckeye" is not a confessional essay, it is quite personal. Reflect on how comfortable you are writing, as Sanders did, about the details of your life.

■ PERSONAL ESSAY 2

Try this exercise: Think about things, ordinary objects, that you have held onto all these years because you simply can't throw them away. They *mean* something to you. They are reminders of another time, or a turning point in your life, or a particular moment of joy, or sadness, or perhaps fear. Consider a few of mine: a green plaster Buddha, handmade; a glow-in-the-dark crucifix; an old pair of 7 × 50 Nikon binoculars; a 1969 Martin D 28 guitar; a brown-handled flathead screwdriver with a touch of red nail polish on the handle; a homemade lamp made from a wooden wallpaper roller; a red dog's collar. While they are meaning-less to you, naturally, to me each of these objects carry a charge; they remind me of a story, a moment, a feeling. The personal essay makes space for writers to explore the meanings of such ordinary things.

Taking Things Seriously: 75 Objects with Unexpected Meanings, the book from which the following short essay was taken, is a gallery of objects—a bottle of dirt, a Velveeta Cheese box, a bear lamp, a pair of shells, and more—that are displayed along with the meditations on their significance by the writers who have carefully kept them as reminders on a shelf, in a closet, by their beside. Laura Zazulak's short essay focuses on a doll that she snatched from a neighbor's trash can. Just telling a story about what happened is not enough in an essay. The essay must have something to say to someone else. As you read Zazulak's brief piece, consider what that might be.

Every Morning for Five Years

Laura Zazulak

Every morning for five years, I was not so welcomingly greeted by my middle-aged, developmentally disabled neighbor across the street. Scotty never smiled and seemed to hate everyone. He never left the perimeter of his mother's lawn and apparently didn't know how to do anything but rake, shovel, take out the trash, and yell in a high-pitched voice. I'd pull out of my driveway and see him there, wearing a neon orange hunting cap, raking absolutely nothing at the same spot that he'd raked the day before. I'd think to myself, "Don't make eye contact!" But I always did. He'd stare at me and neither of us would blink.

Near the end of my fifth year on the street, Scotty stopped coming out of his house. At first, I was thankful. But as time passed, I began to worry. Then one Saturday morning in the middle of January I noticed that his window was wide open. Later that day, a police car showed up. Maybe Scotty and his mother got into one of their screaming matches again? Then a funeral-home van pulled up and they brought out Scotty's body. Although it came as a surprise to me to discover that he knew how miserable his life was, he had killed himself.

The next day Scotty's uncle came over and began furiously carting things off to the dump. He left behind a garbage can in the driveway piled with all of Scotty's earthly possessions. I noticed two little pink feet sticking up into the air.

After dark, I crept across the street to the garbage can, armed with a travel-sized bottle of hand sanitizer. I looked left, then right. I dashed forward, tugged at the feet, and then ran as fast as I could back into my own backyard with my prize. Only then did I look at what I'd rescued. I would like you to meet Mabel.

1

2

3

4

"Every Morning for Five Years" by Laura Zazulak. Reprinted by permission of the author.

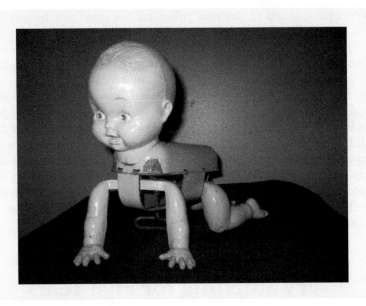

Craig Lupien/Laura Zazulak

Inquiring into the Essay

Use the four methods of seeing what you've read—exploring, explaining, evaluating, and reflecting—to find out what you think about "Every Morning for Five Years."

1. All of the essays in the book *Taking Things Seriously*, from which the piece you just read was taken, have this to say: It is remarkable how much meaning we can invest in the ordinary when we take the time to notice. This is an idea you can explore. Brainstorm a list of objects that might have "unexpected significance" for you. Choose one and fastwrite about it for four minutes. Then skip a line, choose another, and write for another four minutes. If this is interesting to you, repeat this over a few days and create a collage of brief stories that four or five objects inspired. Are there any themes that seem to run through all of them? Do they speak to each other in any way?

2. Read together, explain how the photograph and the essay work together to create meanings that might not be apparent if read separately.

3. Evaluate the effectiveness of the last line, which is arguably one of the most important in any essay.

4. Okay, so you have this object that means something to you—say a bobby pin with a hand-stitched white daisy attached to it. How do you make it mean something to someone else? And, especially, what is the process you might use for figuring that out?

■ PERSONAL ESSAY 3

America is a nation of immigrants, and their stories often haunt their children. Judith Ortiz Cofer moved from Puerto Rico as a child with her family in the mid-1950s to a barrio in Paterson, New Jersey. There she became both part of and witness to a familiar narrative, that of the outsider who finds herself wedged between two worlds, two cultures, and two longings: the desire to return "home" and the desire to feel at home in the new place. While this is a story most immigrants know well, it is also a deeply personal one, shaded by particular places, prejudices, and patterns.

In "One More Lesson," Cofer describes both the places that competed for her sense of self—the Puerto Rico of her childhood, where she spent time as a child while her Navy father was away at sea, and an apartment in New Jersey where she would go when he returned.

One More Lesson
Judith Ortiz Cofer

I remember Christmas on the Island by the way it felt on my skin. The temperature dropped into the ideal seventies and even lower after midnight when some of the more devout Catholics—mostly older women—got up to go to church, *misa del gallo* they called it; mass at the hour when the rooster crowed for Christ. They would drape shawls over their heads and shoulders and move slowly toward town. The birth of Our Savior was a serious affair in our *pueblo*.

At Mamá's house, food was the focal point of *Navidad*. There were banana leaves brought in bunches by the boys, spread on the table, where the women would pour coconut candy steaming hot, and the leaves would wilt around the sticky lumps, adding an extra tang of flavor to the already irresistible treat. Someone had to watch the candy while it cooled, or it would begin to disappear as the children risked life and limb for a stolen piece of heaven. The banana leaves were also used to wrap the traditional food of holidays in Puerto Rico: *pasteles*, the meat pies made from grated yucca and plantain and stuffed with spiced meats.

Every afternoon during the week before Christmas Day, we would come home from school to find the women sitting around in the parlor with bowls on their laps, grating pieces of coconut, yuccas, plantains, cheeses—all the ingredients that would make up our Christmas Eve feast. The smells that filled Mamá's house at that time have come to mean anticipation and a sensual joy during a time in my life, the last days of my early childhood, when I could still absorb joy through my pores—*when I had not yet learned that light is followed by darkness, that all*

(continued)

1

2

3

(continued)

of creation is based on that simple concept, and maturity is a discovery of that natural law.

4   It was in those days that the Americans sent baskets of fruit to our barrio—apples, oranges, grapes flown in from the States. And at night, if you dared to walk up to the hill where the mango tree stood in the dark, you could see a wonderful sight: a Christmas tree, a real pine, decorated with lights of many colors. It was the blurry outline of this tree you saw, for it was inside a screened-in-porch, but we had heard a thorough description of it from the boy who delivered the fruit, a nephew of Mamá's, as it had turned out. Only, I was not impressed, since just the previous year we had put up a tree ourselves in our apartment in Paterson.

5   Packages arrived for us in the mail from our father. I got dolls dressed in the national costumes of Spain, Italy, and Greece (at first we could not decide which of the Greek dolls was the male, since they both wore skirts); my brother got picture books; and my mother, jewelry that she would not wear, because it was too much like showing off and might attract the Evil Eye.

6   Evil Eye or not, the three of us were the envy of the pueblo. Everything about us set us apart, and I put away my dolls quickly when I discovered that my playmates would not be getting any gifts until *Los Reyes*—the Day of the Three Kings, when Christ received His gifts—and that even then it was more likely that the gifts they found under their beds would be practical things like clothes. Still, it was fun to find fresh grass for the camels the night the Kings were expected, tie it in bundles with string, and put it under our beds along with a bowl of fresh water.

7   The year went by fast after Christmas, and in the spring we received a telegram from Father. His ship had arrived in Brooklyn Yard. He gave us a date for our trip back to the States. I remember Mother's frantic packing, and the trips to Mayagüez for new clothes; the inspections of my brother's and my bodies for cuts, scrapes, mosquito bites, and other "damage" she would have to explain to Father. And I remember begging Mamá to tell me stories in the afternoons, although it was not summer yet and the trips to the mango tree had not begun. In looking back I realize that Mamá's stories were what I packed—my winter store.

8   Father had succeeded in finding an apartment outside Paterson's "vertical barrio," the tenement Puerto Ricans called *El Building*. He had talked a Jewish candy store owner into renting us the apartment above his establishment, which he and his wife had just vacated after buying a house in West Paterson, an affluent suburb. Mr. Schultz was a nice man whose melancholy face I was familiar with from trips I had made often with my father to his store for cigarettes. Apparently, my father had convinced him and his brother, a look-alike of Mr. Schultz who helped in the store, that we were not the usual Puerto Rican family. My father's fair skin, his ultra-correct English, and his Navy uniform were a good argument. Later it occurred to me that my father had been displaying me as a model child when he took me to that store with him. I was always dressed as if for church and held firmly by the hand. I imagine he did the same with my brother. As for my mother,

her Latin beauty, her thick black hair that hung to her waist, her voluptuous body which even the winter clothes could not disguise, would have been nothing but a hindrance to my father's plans. But everyone knew that a Puerto Rican woman is her husband's satellite; she reflects both his light and his dark sides. If my father was respectable, then his family would be respectable. We got the apartment on Park Avenue.

Unlike El Building, where we had lived on our first trip to Paterson, our new home was truly in exile. There were Puerto Ricans by the hundreds only one block away, but we heard no Spanish, no loud music, no mothers yelling at children, nor the familiar *¡Ay Bendito!*, that catch-all phrase of our people. Mother lapsed into silence herself, suffering from *La Tristeza*, the sadness that only place induces and only place cures. But Father relished silence, and we were taught that silence was something to be cultivated and practiced.

9

Since our apartment was situated directly above where the Schultzes worked all day, our father instructed us to remove our shoes at the door and walk in our socks. We were going to prove how respectable we were by being the opposite of what our ethnic group was known to be—we would be quiet and inconspicuous.

10

I was escorted each day to school by my nervous mother. It was a long walk in the cooling air of fall in Paterson and we had to pass by El Building where the children poured out of the front door of the dilapidated tenement still answering their mothers in a mixture of Spanish and English: "Sí, Mami, I'll come straight home from school." At the corner we were halted by the crossing guard, a strict woman who only gestured her instructions, never spoke directly to the children, and only ordered us to "halt" or "cross" while holding her white-gloved hand up at face level or swinging her arm sharply across her chest if the light was green.

11

The school building was not a welcoming sight for someone used to the bright colors and airiness of tropical architecture. The building looked functional. It could have been a prison, an asylum, or just what it was: an urban school for the children of immigrants, built to withstand waves of change, generation by generation. Its red brick sides rose to four solid stories. The black steel fire escapes snaked up its back like an exposed vertebra. A chain-link fence surrounded its concrete playground. Members of the elite safety patrol, older kids, sixth graders mainly, stood at each of its entrances, wearing their fluorescent white belts that criss-crossed their chests and their metal badges. No one was allowed in the building until the bell rang, not even on rainy or bitter-cold days. Only the safety-patrol stayed warm.

12

My mother stood in front of the main entrance with me and a growing crowd of noisy children. She looked like one of us, being no taller than the sixth-grade girls. She held my hand so tightly that my fingers cramped. When the bell rang, she walked me into the building and kissed my cheek. Apparently my father had done all the paperwork for my enrollment, because the next thing I remember was being led to my third-grade classroom by a black girl who had emerged from the principal's office.

13

Though I had learned some English at home during my first years in Paterson, I had let it recede deep into my memory while learning Spanish in Puerto Rico. Once again I

14

(continued)

95

(continued)

was the child in the cloud of silence, the one who had to be spoken to in sign language as if she were a deaf-mute. Some of the children even raised their voices when they spoke to me, as if I had trouble hearing. Since it was a large troublesome class composed mainly of black and Puerto Rican children, with a few working-class Italian children interspersed, the teacher paid little attention to me. I re-learned the language quickly by the immersion method. I remember one day, soon after I joined the rowdy class when our regular teacher was absent and Mrs. D., the sixth-grade teacher from across the hall, attempted to monitor both classes. She scribbled something on the chalkboard and went to her own room. I felt a pressing need to use the bathroom and asked Julio, the Puerto Rican boy who sat behind me, what I had to do to be excused. He said that Mrs. D. had written on the board that we could be excused by simply writing our names under the sign. I got up from my desk and started for the front of the room when I was struck on the head hard with a book. Startled and hurt, I turned around expecting to find one of the bad boys in my class, but it was Mrs. D. I faced. I remember her angry face, her fingers on my arms pulling me back to my desk, and her voice saying incomprehensible things to me in a hissing tone. Someone finally explained to her that I was new, that I did not speak English. I also remember how suddenly her face changed from anger to anxiety. But I did not forgive her for hitting me with that hard-cover spelling book. Yes, I would recognize that book even now. It was not until years later that I stopped hating that teacher for not understanding that I had been betrayed by a classmate, and by my inability to read her warning on the board. *I instinctively understood then that language is the only weapon a child has against the absolute power of adults.*

15   I quickly built up my arsenal of words by becoming an insatiable reader of books.

"One More Lesson" is reprinted with permission from the publisher of *Silent Dancing: A Partial Remembrance of a Puerto Rican Childhood* by Judith Ortiz Cofer (© 1990 Arte Público Press–University of Houston).

Inquiring into the Essay

Explore, explain, evaluate, and reflect on Cofer's "One More Lesson."

1. In the 1950s and 1960s, many saw America as a "melting pot." The idea then was that although we may have many different immigrant backgrounds, we should strive toward some common "Americanism." For some, this is still a powerful idea, but for others the melting pot is a metaphor for cultural hegemony or even racial prejudice, a demand that differences be ignored and erased rather than celebrated. In your journal, write about your own feelings on this controversy. Tell the story of a friend, a relative, a neighbor who was an outsider. Tell about your own experience. What did it mean to assimilate, and at what cost?

2. Personal essays, like short fiction, rely heavily on narrative. But unlike fiction, essays both *show* and *tell*; that is, they use story to reveal meaning (*show*) and they also explain that meaning to the reader (*tell*). Identify

several places in the essay where Cofer "tells." What do you notice about the placement of these moments of reflection?

3. Does this essay make an evaluation, and, if so, what is it asserting about cultural assimilation in America during the 1950s and 1960s? Is Cofer's evaluation still relevant?

4. One of the most common reasons students cite for liking a story is that "they could relate to it." Does that criterion apply here? Reflect on whether it's a standard you often use as a reader to judge the value of something. What exactly does it mean to "relate to" a text?

SEEING THE FORM

Nautilus Shell

© Roderick Chen/Alamy

We think of most forms of writing as linear—beginning to end, thesis to supporting evidence, claims to reasons—in a steady march to a conclusion. And yes, much writing is like that. The essay is not. Or at least that's true of the essay inspired by the first essayist Montaigne, a sixteenth-century French nobleman who coined the term "essai," which in its verb form means to attempt, to try. A better analogy for the essay is the spiral rather than the line. It is the uncoiling of thought. The essay begins, much like a nautilus shell, when writers make tight spirals around a particular moment, object, observation, or fact that

(continued)

Seeing the Form (*continued*)

makes them wonder. The personal essay is an inductive form, working from the small things to larger ideas about them, with larger turns of thought. The work challenges writers to move outward from small, private chambers of experience to finally emerge into the more open spaces that others can share, meanings that others can understand even though they don't share exactly the same experience.

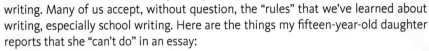

WRITING IN THE DISCIPLINES

The Personal Academic Essay

"You can't use 'I' in an academic essay," one of my students insisted. "It's just not done."

This is always the beginning of a great discussion about academic conventions, objectivity, and personal writing. Many of us accept, without question, the "rules" that we've learned about writing, especially school writing. Here are the things my fifteen-year-old daughter reports that she "can't do" in an essay:

1. Use first person.

2. Put a thesis anywhere but the first paragraph.

3. Write a paragraph without a topic sentence.

Anything that violates these rules is something called "creative" writing. Where do these ideas come from? The injunction against using "I" in academic writing, probably the most common assumption, isn't without support. After all, a great deal of academic writing avoids any reference to the author, or if it must, uses the more neutral pronoun "one." The question that is rarely asked is, Why is this so?

One reason is that scholars believe that "objectivity"—or at least the appearance of objectivity—gives their research more authority. In addition, in some disciplines, especially the sciences, the attention needs to be on the data and not the author. For these reasons, among others, avoiding first person in academic writing became a tacit tradition.

And yet, there are a surprising number of academic articles published in the first person, and not just in the humanities where you might expect authors to be more likely to acknowledge bias. While "autobiographical criticism" has been around for some time in literature, there is personal scholarship in many disciplines, including business, anthropology, education, nursing, and even geology. This first-person writing often tells a story, sometimes through a case study, a narrative of the writer's experiences, or an account of his or her intellectual journey.

WRITING IN YOUR LIFE

Essaying "This I Believe"

The essay genre, which has been around for about 500 years, is a vibrant and increasingly common form of writing on the radio and online audio. Why? One reason might be that the intimacy of the essay—the sense of a writer speaking directly to a reader without the masks we often wear when we write—seems particularly powerful when we *hear* the voice of writing embodied in speech. Certainly, the ease with which we can "publish" essays as podcasts accounts for the explosion of online essayists.

"This I Believe," a program on National Public Radio, is typical of the radio programs (which are then subsequently published as podcasts) that actively seek student writing. The program began in the 1950s by famed journalist Edward R. Murrow, who invited radio listeners and public figures to submit very brief (350–500 word) essays that stated some core belief that guides the writers' "daily lives." The program, which was revived several years ago, is enormously popular on NPR and features work from people from all walks of life, including college students who may have written a "This I Believe" essay in their writing courses.

The program's Web site offers this advice to essayists:

1. Find a way to succinctly and clearly state your belief.

2. If possible, anchor it to stories.

3. Write in your own voice.

4. "Be positive," and avoid lecturing the listener.

THE WRITING PROCESS

INQUIRY PROJECT: WRITING A PERSONAL ESSAY

Write a 1,000-word personal essay that explores some aspect of your experience. Your instructor may provide additional details. Choose your topic carefully. Because of the essay's exploratory methods, the best topics are those that you want to write about *not* because you know what you think, but because you want to *discover* what you think. The essay should have the following qualities:

- It must do more than tell a story; there must be a *purpose* behind telling the story that speaks in some way to someone else.
- It should, ultimately, answer the *So what?* question.
- Your essay should include some reflection to explain or speculate about what you understand *now* about something that you didn't understand *then*.
- It should be richly detailed. Seize opportunities to *show* what you mean, rather than simply explain it.

For additional reading, writing, and research resources, go to www.mycomplab.com

Thinking About Subjects

When you are assigned a personal essay, it's essential to embrace uncertainty and be willing to suspend judgment. This is risky. Obviously, one of the risks when you start out with uncertainty is that you also might end up that way; your draft may just seem to go nowhere. The key to writing strong personal essays is accepting that first drafts might be real stinkers. But there's a payoff to this risk—the personal essay frequently yields surprise and discovery.

Generating Ideas

Begin exploring possible subjects by generating material in your notebook. This should be an open-ended process, a chance to use your creative side, not worrying too much about making sense or trying to prejudge the value of the writing or the subjects you generate. In a sense, this is an invitation to play around.

ONE STUDENT'S RESPONSE

Margaret's Journal: Listing Questions

Is my cat extremely unusual or can any cat be taught to walk and be as needy and attached as her?

Does testosterone really make one more confident? Is there a correlation between high T and aggressiveness?

How did I once find Dr. Laura so compelling?

Why are women seldom loyal to each other? How are female friendships different from male ones? Can women and men be friends without an underlying sexual tension?

Listing Prompts. Lists can be rich sources of triggering topics. Let them grow freely, and when you're ready, use an item as the focus of another list or an episode of fastwriting. The following prompts should get you started.

1. Make a fast list of experiences you've had that you can't forget. Reach into all parts and times of your life.

2. Make a list of questions that have always nagged you about some of the following: school, men or women, fast food, hair, television, public restrooms, shoes, and sports.

Fastwriting Prompts. In the early stages of generating possible topics for an essay, fastwriting can be invaluable, *if* you allow yourself to write "badly." Once you've tentatively settled on something, use a more focused fastwrite, trying to generate information and ideas within the loose boundaries of your chosen topic.

1. Choose an item from any one of the preceding lists as a prompt. Just start fastwriting about the item; perhaps start with a story, a scene, a situation, a description. Follow the writing to see where it leads.

2. Most of us quietly harbor dreams—we hope to be a professional dancer, a good father, an activist, an Olympic luger, or a novelist. Begin a fastwrite in which you explore your dreams. When the writing stalls, ask yourself questions: *Where did this dream come from? Do I still believe in it? In what moments did it seem within reach? In what moments did it fade?* Plunge into those moments.

3. What was the most confusing time in your life? Choose a moment or scene that stands out in your memory from that time, and, writing in the present tense, describe what you see, hear, and do. After five

minutes, skip a line and choose another moment. Then another. Make a collage.

4. What do you consider "turning points" in your life, times when you could see the end of one thing and the beginning of something else? Fastwrite about one of these for seven minutes.

Visual Prompts. Sometimes the best way to generate material is to see what we think in something other than sentences. Boxes, lines, arrows, charts, and even sketches can help us see more of the landscape of a subject, especially connections between fragments of information that aren't as obvious in prose. The clustering or mapping method is useful to many writers early in the writing process as they try to discover a topic. (See the "Inquiring into the Details" box for more details on how to create a cluster.) Figure 1 shows my cluster from the first prompt listed here.

1. What objects would you most regret losing in a house fire? Choose a most-treasured object as the core for a cluster. Build a web of associations from

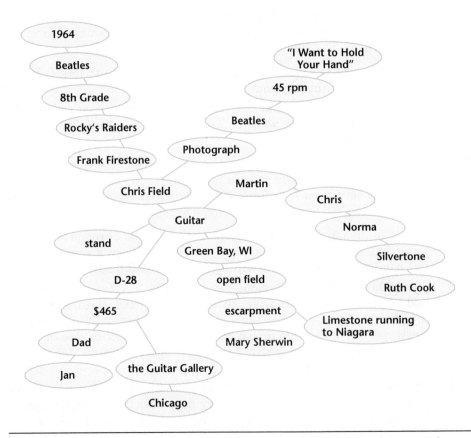

Figure 1 A cluster built around the one object I would most regret losing in a house fire: my Martin guitar

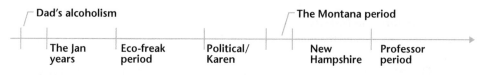

Figure 2 A sample timeline from my own life

it, returning to the detail in the core whenever a strand dies out. One of the wonderful complexities of being human is that we are sometimes deeply conflicted (I'm not suggesting this is always fun). Pair two opposed attributes that you consider typical of yourself. For example, *ambivalence/commitment, fear/risk taking, lonely/sociable, beautiful/ugly, composed/flaky,* and so on. Use these paired words as a core for a cluster.

2. Draw a long line on a piece of paper in your journal. This is your life. Divide the line into segments that seem to describe what feels like distinct times in your life. These may not necessarily correspond to familiar age categories like adolescence or childhood. More likely, the periods in your life will be associated with a place, a relationship, a dilemma, a job, a personal challenge, and so on, but because this is a timeline, these periods will be chronological. Examine your timeline and, as a fastwrite prompt, put two of these periods in your life together. Explore what they had in common, particularly how the earlier period might have shaped the later one. See Figure 2 for a sample timeline.

Research Prompts. Things we hear, see, or read can be powerful prompts for personal essays. It's tempting to believe that personal essays are always about the past, but just as often essayists are firmly rooted in the present, commenting and pondering on the confusions of contemporary life. In that sense, personal

INQUIRING INTO THE DETAILS

Clustering or Mapping

One of the virtues of clustering as a method of generating information is that it defies the more linear nature of writing, putting one sentence after another in a chain of thought. When you make a cluster, there are multiple chains, each growing from a core word, phrase, or idea. In Figure 1, I clustered the word *guitar*. I'm not just thinking of any guitar, of course, but my 1969 Martin D-28 with

(continued)

Inquiring into the Details (*continued*)

Brazilian rosewood and the ding on the front. This is the one object I'd rescue from a fire.

Clusters are in code; each item in the web says more than it says, at least to me, because I'm familiar with its meaning. You don't have that kind of knowledge, obviously, so my cluster wouldn't say much to you. Each strand suggests a story, an idea, or a feeling that I might explore.

Typically, clustering is most useful at the beginning of the writing process as you test a possible subject and want to see its landscape of possibilities. I can see, for example, possible essays about not only the significance of this guitar, but essays on the eighth grade, my old friend Chris Field, and the natural history of limestone. The best clusters are richly suggestive that way, but they're only starting places for more writing. How do you cluster?

1. Begin with a blank page in your journal. Choose a core word, phrase, name, idea, detail, or question; write it in the middle of the page and circle it.

2. Relax and focus on the core word or phrase, and when you feel moved to do so, build a strand of associations from the core, circling and connecting each item. Write other details, names, dates, place names, phrases, and so on—whatever comes to mind.

3. When a strand dies out, return to the core and begin another. Keep clustering until the page looks like a web of associations. Doodle, darkening lines and circles, if that helps you relax and focus.

4. When you feel the urge to write, stop clustering and use one of the strands as a prompt for journal work.

---

essayists are researchers, always on the lookout for material. Train your eye with one or more of the following prompts.

1. Return to the list of questions you made in the "Listing Prompts" section. Choose one nagging question about any of the subjects you were asked to consider and set aside time to explore it by carefully *observing* them. Write down exactly what you see...and what you think about it. (The double-entry notebook method is particularly useful for this.)

2. Newspaper "filler"—short stories, often about odd or unusual things—can be a wonderful source of inspiration for personal essays. Read your local paper for a few days, clipping these brief articles. Paste them in your journal and use them as prompts for fastwriting.

3. Although the Internet offers infinite opportunities for procrastination, with some focus it can also be a great source for jump-starting ideas. What happened to your best friend from kindergarten? Type her name into the Google search engine and find out. Think about your favorite vacation—a search for "Grand Canyon" might help jog your memory.

Judging What You Have

Generating may produce messy, incoherent writing that would earn you bad grades in most classes. If this material is going to go anywhere, it must be judged, shaped, and evaluated; the writer must emerge from particulars of his/her experience and find a vantage point to see what, if anything, those particulars add up to.

The initial challenge in producing a first draft is clarifying your topic: What are you really writing about? Suspend judgment for a bit and work through the following questions as you scrutinize the material you've collected so far in your journal.

What's Promising Material and What Isn't? A good topic for a personal essay need not be dramatic or profound; in fact, some of the most compelling essays are about quite ordinary things. But as you examine your journal writing so far, consider the following:

- **Abundance.** What subject generated the most writing? Do you sense that there is much more to write about?
- **Surprise.** What material did you find most confusing in interesting ways?
- **Confusion.** What subject raises questions you're not sure you can answer easily?
- **Honesty.** What subjects are you willing to write honestly about?

Questions About Purpose and Audience. Obviously, why you're writing and for whom will profoundly influence your approach. That's a fundamental principle of rhetoric, one that you applied when you jotted that note to your teacher explaining the late assignment or texted your friend about your new bicycle. With many types of writing, it's wise to consider your purpose and audience very early on—like, say, for an essay exam or an e-mail requesting information about a job. Sometimes, however, thinking too soon about purpose and audience will squeeze off your writing.

To begin with, then, embrace the open-ended process of "trying out" possible subjects. Initially, don't rule out anything because you think other people might find the topic boring. For now, you're the most important audience, and what you want to know from your writing is this:

- What topics raise questions about your experiences that you find puzzling or intriguing?
- What did you say that you didn't expect to say?

Choose a topic for your essay not because you know what you think but because you want to find out what you think.

Questions for Reflection. After you've generated enough material on your topic, seize opportunities to reflect. Remember that this move to reflect is an essential part of the dialectical thinking that helps writers make sense of things, going back and forth between *what happened* and *what happens*, between *showing* and *telling*, and *observations of* and *ideas about*. If you need help finding reflective distance, questions are the best way to do it. Use one or more of the following questions as prompts for thinking or writing in your journal.

- What do you understand now about this topic that you didn't fully understand when you began writing about it?
- What has surprised you most? Why?
- What seems to be the most important thing you're trying to say so far?
- Focus on how your thinking has changed about your topic. Finish this seed sentence as many times as you can in your notebook: Once I thought _____, and now I think _____.
- Quickly write a narrative of thought about your topic: When I began writing about my father's alcoholism, I thought I felt relieved when he died. Then I decided that when he died some part of me died with him, and then I realized that the real truth is…
- Finish this sentence in your journal: As I look back on this, I realize that…Follow that sentence with another, and another, until you feel there's nothing more to say.

Writing the Sketch

It's hard to say when it's time to begin composing the draft, particularly with open-ended forms such as the personal essay. But bear in mind that working from abundance is particularly important when you're using writing to discover, the essayist's main motive.

Before you write a full draft, you'll compose a *sketch* or two of what seems to be the most promising material. A sketch is a brief treatment—probably no more than 300 words—that is composed with a sense of audience but not necessarily a clear sense of a thesis, theme, or controlling idea. Later, you'll revise a sketch into a draft personal essay.

Your instructor may ask you to write several sketches using the most promising material you've developed from the prompts. *The following guidelines apply to all sketches.*

- *The sketch should have a tentative title*. This is crucial because a title can hint at a possible focus for the revision.
- *The sketch should be approximately 300 to 500 words*. The sketch is a brief look at a topic that may later be developed into a longer essay.
- *The sketch should be a relatively fast draft*. Avoid the temptation to spend a lot of time crafting your sketch. Fast drafts are easier to revise.

- *The sketch may not have a clear purpose or theme.* That's what you hope to discover by writing the sketch.

- *The sketch should have a sense of audience.* You're writing your sketch to be read by someone other than you. That means you need to explain what may not be apparent to someone who doesn't know you or hasn't had your experiences.

- *The sketch should be richly detailed.* Personal essays, especially, rely on detail to help the writer and, later, the reader see the possible meanings of events or observations. Essayists are inductive, working from particulars to ideas. In early drafts especially, it's important to get down the details by drawing on all your senses: What exactly was the color of the wallpaper? How exactly did the beach smell at low tide? How exactly did the old man's hand feel in yours? What exactly did the immigration officer say?

■ STUDENT SKETCH

Amanda Stewart's sketch, "Earning a Sense of Place," faintly bears the outlines of what might be a great personal essay. When they succeed, sketches are suggestive; it is what they're not quite saying that yields promise. On the surface, "Earning a Sense of Place" is simply a piece about Amanda Stewart's passion for skiing. So what? And yet, there are lines here that point to larger ideas and unanswered questions. For example, Amanda writes that the "mental reel" of her swishing down a mountain on skis is "the image that sustains me when things are hard, and when I want to stop doing what is right and start doing what is easy." Why is it that such a mental image can be sustaining in hard times? How well does this work? The end of the sketch is even more suggestive. This really might be a piece about trying to find a "sense of place" that doesn't rely on such images; in a sense, the sketch seems to be trying to say that joy on the mountain isn't enough.

The pleasure of writing and reading a sketch is looking for what it might teach you, learning what you didn't know you knew.

Earning a Sense of Place
Amanda Stewart

The strings to my earflaps stream behind me, mixing with my hair as a rooster-tail flowing behind my neck. Little ice crystals cling to the bottom of my braid and sparkle in the sunlight. The pompom on top of my hat bobs up and down as I arc out, turning cleanly across the snow. I suck in the air, biting with cold as it hits my hot lungs, and breathe deep as I push down the run.

1

(continued)

(continued)

2   This is what I see when I picture who I want to be. It's the image that sustains me when things are hard, and when I want to stop doing what is right and start doing what is easy. I have made so many terrible decisions in the past that I know how far astray they lead me; I don't want that. I want the girl in the mental reel in her quilted magenta jacket and huge smile. She's what I grasp at when I need help getting through the day.

3   She's an amalgam of moments from the past mixed with my hopes for the future. I love to ski, and have since my parents strapped little plastic skis onto my galoshes when I was a year and a half old. From that day I flopped around our snow-covered yard, I've been in love with skiing. It's the only time I feel truly comfortable. Day to day I often feel so awkward. I wonder if my hair is right, or if my clothes fit. Last night, my roommate had a boy over, and as he sat on the couch talking to me, all I felt was discomfort and awkwardness. I didn't know what to say, felt judged, felt out of place. I never feel that way on skis. Even floundering in heavy, deep snow, or after a fall that has packed my goggles with snow and ripped the mittens off my hands I know exactly what to do. I'm a snow mermaid, only comfortable in my medium. I often wish I could trade in my walking legs for something like a tail that is more truly me.

4   My dad's coffee cup at home says, "I only work so I can ski," and for him, it's true. Sometimes I feel like I only push through my daily life so I can get to the next mountain and zip up my pants and go. I don't want to live like that though: it's too much time looking forward to something, and not enough looking at what I'm living in. I need to appreciate my life as it is, snowy cold or sunny warm. That sense of place I have on skis can probably be earned here on the flat expanses of campus just as easily as I got it pushing myself down the bunny slopes so long ago. I just have to earn it.

Moving from Sketch to Draft

A sketch is often sketchy. It's generally underdeveloped, sometimes giving the writer just the barest outline of his or her subject. But as an early draft, a sketch can be invaluable. A sketch might suggest a focus for the next draft, or simply a better lead. Learning to read your sketches for such clues takes practice.

Evaluating Your Own Sketch. Initially, you're the most important reader of your own sketches. It's likely that you're in the best position to sense the material's promise because you understand the context from which it sprang better than any reader can. What are the clues you should look for in a sketch?

1. What surprised you? Might this discovery be the focus of the draft? Chances are, if it surprised you, it will surprise your readers.

2. What is the most important line in the sketch? What makes it important? Might this line be a beginning for more fastwriting? Might it be the theme or controlling idea of the draft?

3. What scene, moment, or situation is key to the story you're telling? Could this be the lead in the draft?

4. What's your favorite part of the sketch? What would happen if you cut it?

Questions for Peer Review. If you'll be sharing your sketch with one or more of your classmates, you'll likely need the most help with clarifying your purpose and focus for a draft. Here are some useful questions that might guide peer responses to your personal essay sketches.

- What does the writer seem to want to say but doesn't quite say in the sketch?

- What line appears most important to the meaning of the sketch, as you understand it?

- What was most surprising about what the writer said or showed?

- What part of the story seems most important? What part might need to be told and isn't?

Reflecting on What You've Learned. Before you begin working on the draft of your personal essay, take a few minutes in your journal to think about your thinking. Finish the following sentence, and follow it in a fastwrite for at least five minutes. *The thing that struck me most about writing and sharing my sketch on _____ was....* When you finish, quickly complete the following sentences:

1. The *real* story I seem to be trying to tell is _____.

2. So what? I'd answer that question by saying _____.

3. The main thing I'm planning to do in the draft is _____.

Research and Other Strategies: Gathering More Information

> **METHODS FOR PEER REVIEW OF SKETCHES**
>
> 1. Choose a partner, exchange sketches, read, and comment both in writing and through conversation.
>
> 2. Create a pile of sketches in the middle of the classroom. Everyone takes one (not his or her own, obviously), provides written comments, returns it to the pile, and takes another. Repeat this until everyone has read and commented on at least four sketches.
>
> 3. Share sketches online on the class Web site.

If everything has gone well so far, then your sketch has already given you a sense of direction and some ideas about how to develop your topic. But remember the importance of that dialectical movement between sea and mountain, or collecting and composing. Now that you have a topic and a tentative sense of purpose for your personal essay, journal work can be even more valuable because it can be *more focused*. Before you begin composing the draft—or during that process—consider using the following prompts to generate more information in your notebook:

- *Explode a moment.* Choose a scene or moment in the story or stories you're telling that seems particularly important to the meaning of the essay. Re-enter that moment and fastwrite for a full seven minutes, using all your senses and as much detail as you can muster.

- *Make lists.* Brainstorm a list of details, facts, or specifics about a moment, scene, or observation. List other experiences that seem connected to this one (see the "*Cluster*" point below).

- *Research.* Do some quick-and-dirty research that might bring in other voices or more information that will deepen your consideration of the topic.

- *Cluster.* In your journal, try to move beyond narrating a single experience and discover other experiences, moments, or scenes that might help you see important patterns. Use the preceding list of related experiences or observations and fastwrite about those, or develop a cluster that uses a key word, phrase, or theme as its core, and build a web of associations. For example, let's say your sketch is about your experience working with the poor in Chile. Have you had other encounters with extreme wealth or extreme poverty? Can you describe them? What do they reveal about your feelings or attitudes about poverty or your reactions to what happened in Chile? See Figure 3.

Composing the Draft

Some of my students get annoyed at all the "stuff" I encourage them to do before they begin a first draft of a personal essay. In some cases, all the journal work isn't necessary; the writer very quickly gets a strong sense of direction and feels

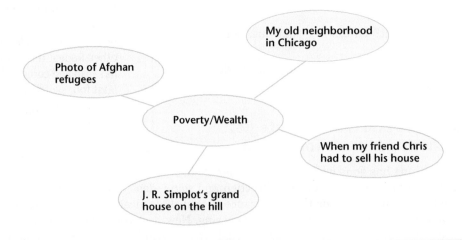

Figure 3 The start of a cluster built around poverty/wealth

ready to begin composing. But from the beginning I've encouraged you to gravitate toward topics that you find confusing, and with that kind of material exploratory writing is time well spent. Remember, too, that journal writing counts as writing. It not only offers the pleasures of surprise, but it can ultimately make the drafting process more efficient by generating material that you won't have to conjure up during those long, painful periods of staring at the computer screen wondering what to say next. This front-end work may also help abbreviate the end of the writing process—essentially, all this work in your journal and sketches is revision.

As you begin drafting, keep in mind what you've learned from your writing so far. For example:

- What is the question(s) behind your exploration of this topic?
- What do you understand now that you didn't understand fully when you started writing about it?
- How can you show *and* explain how you came to this understanding?
- Have you already written a strong first line for the draft? Can you find it somewhere in all your journal writing?

INQUIRING INTO THE DETAILS

More Than One Way to Tell a Story

This is my daughter Julia telling a story:
"And she was like…"
"And then I was like…"
"And then she was like…"

Generally there are two structures for organizing information: reason and experience. Sometimes writing will combine both, but much academic writing is logically organized rather than experientially organized. Of course, when we think about organizing experiences—something that personal essays try to do—we immediately think of narrative, and then, naturally, we consider the most common narrative structure of all: chronology. This is Julia's method of oral storytelling, as it is for most of us.

Yet in essay writing, strict chronology—this happened and then this and then this—may not be the best way to tell a story. Once locked into a strictly chronological narrative, you may feel compelled to tell the *whole* story. It's a misconception that because it "happened that way" you have to tell the whole story in a personal essay. What you need to do is to tell those *parts* of the story (or stories) that are relevant to the question you're exploring or the thing you're trying to say.

(continued)

111

Inquiring into the Details (*continued*)

While chronological storytelling might be a good way to remember what happened as you explore your experiences in your journal or in early drafts, it isn't the only choice for structuring your essay. Structure in the personal essay, as in all writing, must be a servant to purpose. Simply put, purpose is how you might answer a potential reader who wants to know this: *So what*? Why should I read this?

Organize a narrative essay with the *So what*? question in mind. That means, first and foremost, that you start a narrative essay in that part of the story that illuminates the dilemma you're trying to solve, the question you're exploring, or the idea you're trying to understand. Typically, the beginning of the story ("The alarm clock went off at 6 AM, and I was groggy from sleep") isn't the best place to emphasize your dilemma, question, or idea. Sometimes, the middle or even the end is better for that.

Notice, for example, that Scott Sanders's essay "Buckeye" begins in the present, not the past, and in doing so he not only sidesteps the problem of telling his story from beginning to end, but he begins the essay reflectively. The most important part of organizing a personal narrative is not how you tell what happened. It is what you *now* think about the significance of what happened. It is this shift from past to present, from what you remember and what you understand about it now that you didn't then, that is the most important structure of all.

Methods of Development. How might you use some of the typical forms of development to develop your subject?

Narrative. The backbone of the personal essay is often, but not always, narrative. Remember, however, that narrative can work in an essay in at least three ways: (1) you tell an extended story of what happened, (2) you tell one or more anecdotes or brief stories, or (3) you tell the story of your thinking as you've come to understand something you didn't understand before. Often a single essay uses all three types of narrative.

Consider beginning your draft with an anecdote or the part of the story you want to tell that best establishes your purpose in the essay (see "Inquiring into the Details: More Than One Way to Tell a Story"). If you're writing about the needless destruction of a childhood haunt by developers, then consider opening with the way the place looked *after* the bulldozers were done with it.

A personal essay can stitch together not just one narrative but several stories, all of which are connected by the essay's theme or question. Time in writing is nothing like real time. You can write pages about something that happened in seven minutes or cover twenty years in a paragraph. You can ignore chronology, if it serves your purpose, too. The key is to tell your story or stories in ways that emphasize what's important. Ask yourself, *What does the reader most need to know to understand my thinking and feelings about this topic? What should I show about what happened that gives the reader a clear sense of what happened?*

Using Evidence. How do you make your essay convincing, and even moving, to an audience? It's in the details. This form thrives, like most literary genres, on particularity: What exactly did it look like? What exactly did she say? What exactly did it sound and smell like at that moment? Evidence that gives a personal essay authority are details that make a reader believe the writer can be trusted to observe keenly and to remember accurately. All of the professional essays in this chapter are rich in detail. There are the buckeyes, "as fat as a lemon," in Scott Russell Sanders' essay, and Laura Zazulak's neighbor with the "neon orange hunting cap" who rakes the same spot every day, and wilting banana leaves that curl around the coconut candy in Judith Ortiz Cofer's "One More Lesson." This focus on the particular—what it *exactly* looked like, smelled like, felt like, sounded like—makes an essay come alive for both writer and reader.

As you draft your essay, remember the subtle power of details. Tell, but always show, too.

Workshopping the Draft

If your draft is subject to peer review, think carefully about the kind of responses you need from readers at this point in the process. In general, you should encourage comments that make you want to write again.

Reflecting on the Draft. To prepare for the workshop, make an entry in your journal that explores your feelings about the draft:

- What do you think worked?
- What do you think needs work?

Following the workshop session, do a follow-up entry in your notebook that summarizes what you heard, what made sense and what didn't, and how you plan to approach the next draft. Your instructor may ask you to share this information in a cover letter submitted with the revision.

Questions for Readers. A writer can structure responses to a draft in many ways. The key is to find a way to get what you need *at this stage in the writing process* that will be most helpful as you revise.

There are a few questions, however, that you might pose to your group that are particularly relevant to the personal essay:

1. Is there a story I'm telling that I need to develop more? Is there a story I'm not telling that I should?

2. What do you think is the *real* story? In other words, what idea or theme lurks beneath the accounts of my experiences and observations?

3. What seems the most important detail, the one that seems to say more than it says, that *reveals* some important feeling, attitude, or idea? What detail seems less important, less revealing?

4. Do my reflective observations seem obvious or overly abstract and general? If so, what questions do you have about what I say that might direct back into the essay's details, where I'm more likely to have better insights?

5. Do I explain things that are unnecessary to explain, that are better told through *showing* rather than *telling*?

Revising the Draft

Revision is a continual process—not a last step. You've been revising—literally "re-seeing" your subject—from the first messy fastwriting in your journal. But the things that get your attention during revision vary depending on where you are in the writing process. You've generated material, chosen a topic, done some research, and written both a sketch and a draft. Most students think that the only thing left to do is "fix things." Check for misspellings. Correct an awkward sentence or two. Come up with a better title. This is editing, not revision, and while editing is important, to focus solely on smaller "fixes" after writing a first draft squanders an opportunity to really *learn* from what the draft is telling you, or perhaps not quite telling you.

The questions you can ask a draft fall into five categories: purpose, idea, information, development, and editing. Use the following chart to find the revision strategies that might help you re-see what you've written so far.

GUIDE TO REVISION STRATEGIES

Problems in the Draft

Unclear purpose
- Not sure what the essay is about? Fails to answer the *So what?* question?

Unclear thesis, theme, or main idea
- Not sure what you're trying to say?

Lack of information or development
- Needs more details; more showing and less telling?

Disorganized
- Doesn't move logically or smoothly from paragraph to paragraph?

Unclear or awkward at the level of sentences and paragraphs
- Seems choppy or hard to follow at the level of sentences or paragraphs?

Personal essay drafts typically have some of the following problems:

- They don't answer the *So what?* question. Are you telling a story but don't help your readers understand *why* you're telling it?

- There is too much showing and not enough telling. In other words, do you *reflect* sufficiently in the draft, contributing your new understandings of what happened?

- There isn't enough detail. Because personal essays often rely heavily on narrative, they should show as well as tell. That is, help readers not only understand the significance of your experiences but in some small way experience those significant moments themselves.

Polishing the Draft

After you've dealt with the big issues in your draft—is it sufficiently focused, does it answer the *So what?* question, is it organized, and so on—you must deal with the smaller problems. You've carved the stone into an appealing figure but now you need to polish it. Are your paragraphs coherent? How do you manage transitions? Are your sentences fluent and concise? Are there any errors in spelling or syntax?

Before you finish your draft, work through the following checklist:

- ✓ Every paragraph is about one thing.
- ✓ The transitions between paragraphs aren't abrupt.
- ✓ The length of sentences varies in each paragraph.
- ✓ Each sentence is concise. There are no unnecessary words or phrases.
- ✓ You've checked grammar, particularly for verb agreement, run-on sentences, unclear pronouns, and misused words (*there/their, where/were,* and so on). (See the handbook at the end of the text for help with these grammar issues.)
- ✓ You've run your spellchecker and proofed your paper for misspelled words.

▪ STUDENT ESSAY

In my part of the country, the seasonal migration of field workers occurs quietly; most of us rarely notice the cars parked on the country roads and the children sitting in the shade waiting near them. We don't notice the bent backs in the fields, moving methodically from row to row. We are dimly aware, of course, that seasonal workers are key to the beet and potato harvests, but these men and women are largely invisible to us.

Julia Arredondo's essay, "Beet Field Dreams," provides a glimpse of this life. She migrated from Texas to Idaho with her family for nearly fourteen years, where they worked the fields from May to October. For many years, when assigned the ubiquitous topic "What I Did on My Summer Vacation" in school, Julia made up stories about another Julia, one with a "normal" life of picnics, barbecues, and days spent at amusement parks. In this personal essay, the Julia who migrated "like a goose" comes to terms with the truth of those summers, and what they have come to mean.

Beet Field Dreams
Julia C. Arredondo

1   I was born in Welsaco, Texas, and for my entire childhood I considered myself Tejana—a Texan. It was true that I didn't live my entire life—or even my childhood—in the Rio Grande Valley of Southern Texas, but El Valle was my home, where my family and I lived on our own, where I went to school, where we celebrated the major holidays—Thanksgiving, Christmas, New Year's, and everyone's birthdays. Yet the Mini-Cassia, Magic Valley, area of Southern Idaho was also my home—and in a way, not my home—as a child. My father's parents—and their parents before them—were all migrant, seasonal farm workers. This was more than a kind of tradition; it was a way of life, a way of survival, and after a time, it began to feel that it was what my family was meant to do in this world.

2   Every year from late May to August my parents worked alongside my extended family hoeing sugar beets in the fields of Burley, Rupert, Heyburn, Paul, Oakley, and Twin Falls, Idaho. It was either thinning and chopping down beets to make room for more or searching for weeds to eliminate and protect the beets. From September to late October they worked in the spud harvest. Twelve to fourteen hour days picking clots out of the clusters of potatoes that flashed before their eyes, and they worked on combines, as if that's what God had put them here to do. And so we migrated. And migrated. And migrated.

* * *

3   School usually started in early September, but by the time we returned to Texas, Alamo public schools had been running for at least a couple of months. I hated being the new kid in school every year and I especially hated it when people started asking where I'd been, why I was coming into the semester late.

4   It was the infamous "How I spent my summer vacation" essay assignment that would always make me lie like Pinocchio. When the essay topic was assigned, I would panic and begin to feel my heart beat faster. I couldn't tell them what I had really been doing all five months of summer. I could not help it; I'd write about a stranger's summer: picnics, vacations, amusement parks, barbecues. A family trip to Fiesta Texas was the biggest, fictional vacation my elementary mind could conjure up and I think I believed the trip myself. I raved in my essay about how we'd spent an entire week in the

San Antonio amusement park, how the rides were awesome and how much fun I had had—all the while hoping, praying that no one would uncover the lies, and wishing that the teacher would never really read it. After all, they were only dreams that would never come true. I never told about the car. About the fields. Instead, I continued with the grand fabrications.

* * *

We slept in the car, of course. No hotels. Abandoned parking lots. Grocery store parking lots. My Dad liked to park the car somewhere where there was always a lot of light shining. One year in Moab, Utah, we had a really hard time finding a resting spot. First we stopped at a store on the main road that ran through the small town; but then a police officer came around and asked us to keep on moving. He said it was illegal for people driving through to just park anywhere to sleep and pointed us toward a rest area just on the edge of Moab. We went there. Dad parked the car under the only light post in the middle of the dirt parking lot. Then, he got off the car and walked to the pay phone just out of reach of the glowing light. Only a few minutes later, a large truck roared into the empty parking lot. Men's voices shouted and hollered from within as they circled our car, picking up speed, raising up dust clouds, tying a knot in my throat. And then just like that, they were gone. My dad came back to the car, got in, and we drove off.

After that, we mostly slept in truck stops. They were always lit, always alive. They were twenty-four-hour oases for travelers on the go. We had bathrooms available—no matter what time my bladder decided I needed to pee. We had hot food within reach. Hot coffee. So whenever Pa wanted to wake up and drive his family on, he could have a cup. It was almost as convenient as a hotel except that we slept amongst the trucks, their thunderous vibrations never really let me sleep. We'd put towels up as curtains, to block out some of the light—noise. But sometimes when I woke up in the middle of the night, and everyone in the car was asleep, I would look out and wonder where these monsters were going and whether they were as driven as we were to move.

* * *

As a kid I'd wake up on most summer mornings to the sound of doors slamming shut and cool breezes of fresh morning wind sweeping into the car, making me shiver. I could feel the weight of the car shift as the grown-ups pulled their hoes from the trunk. Their voices lingered outside the vehicle for minutes as they prepared for the day's work, waiting for the first light of day to guide their strokes. I'd lay still and listen as their voices became distant, then I would slowly drift back to my dreams.

Some mornings, when the sun wasn't quite strong enough to warm us up, my sister Debra and I would stay inside the car. I'd lounge around in the front seat—a place I hardly ever got to ride in—and impatiently wait for the adults to return to the *caheceras*. From the car they looked miniature as they moved at a hurried pace along the mile long rows. Debra and I would guess which one was Ma and which one was Pa. Sometimes we

(continued)

(continued)

were right. Sometimes I'd drift back to sleep and miss them reaching our end of the field. I'd awake to find they were already halfway back across the field and feel my heart weigh down.

9   I was always looking for a reason to join them in their hard labor; years later when I would have to really start working I knew exactly how hard it was. Still, I'd mention to my parents how I could work too, how we'd make more money that way. I'd ask them to break a hoe in half and let me have it. They only laughed and said when the time came for me to work I wasn't going to want to, so for me to just enjoy this time.

10   Sometimes near the field there would be a farmhouse from which laughter floated down towards us. Sometimes we could spot kids that looked our age jumping on their trampoline, swimming in their pool and I'd find myself longing to be them. Normal. Playing on a lawn, instead of a field. Waking in a bed, instead of a car's backseat. Eating lunch at a table, instead of from tin foil while I sat in the dirt on the shady side of the car to avoid the hot sun.

* * *

11   When I was fourteen we finally stopped moving. Field work continued being our main source of income, but we made Idaho our permanent home. And as the years passed, returning to Texas became preposterous; we were always too afraid to fall back into the old migrating lifestyle. Yet, even today I am a migrant. And it's not merely the fact that I've spent more than half my life migrating—like a goose—according to the seasons, but because it was a lifestyle that penetrates and becomes part of who I am for the rest of my life. As I grew older, I began to slowly acknowledge to others the kind of lifestyle my family lived during my childhood. Though no longer on the move, I will always be a migrant and sugar beet dreams will always haunt my sleep.

Evaluating the Essay

Discuss or write about your response to Julia Arredondo's essay using some or all of the following questions.

1. What is the essay's greatest strength? Is this something you've noticed in your own work, or the drafts of classmates?

2. Is the balance between exposition and narration, showing and telling, handled well in "Beet Field Dreams"? Does it read fairly quickly or does it drag at points?

3. The essay uses line breaks between sections. What do you think of this technique? What are its advantages and disadvantages?

4. What would you recommend to Arredondo if she were to revise "Beet Field Dreams"?

USING WHAT YOU HAVE LEARNED

My students often love writing personal essays. At its best, the genre is a rare opportunity to reexamine our lives and better understand our experiences. The insights we earn are often reward enough, but what have you learned in this assignment that you might apply in other writing situations?

1. The personal essay you wrote relies heavily on narrative and personal experience. How might an ability to tell a good story, using your experiences or the experiences of others, be a useful academic skill? How might you use it to write a paper for another class?

2. The personal essay is a deeply subjective form, seeming to put it at odds with formal academic writing, which strives for "objectivity." Are they at odds?

3. Based on your experience writing a personal essay, what do you think are its most important qualities? If you were to write more personal essays, what would you strive to do next time?

120

WRITING AN ARGUMENT

Arguing is a civic duty. It is an essential activity in any democratic culture and a major element of academic discourse. Academic argument is one of the key means of making new knowledge.

Christinne Muschi/CORBIS–NY

WRITING AN ARGUMENT

WRITING TO PERSUADE PEOPLE

Where I live, public arguments about wolf reintroduction, saving salmon, growing property taxes, and the need for a local community college are waged on the editorial pages of the local newspaper, *The Idaho Statesman*. The paper's editorials and so-called op-ed articles (short persuasive essays that are literally on the opposite page from editorials) present usually well-reasoned arguments of 250 to 600 words, but the real slugfest takes place in the letters to the editor. Reading letters to the editor is a form of recreation here. One correspondent complained a few years ago that the song "Rain, Rain, Go Away" was objectionable because it made her children dislike precipitation. Another letter writer, an angry animal rights activist, is a regular who always generates heated rebuttals here in cattle country. Last week, she railed about the evils of "Rocky Mountain oysters" (fried cattle testicles), which were served up at the Eagle Fire Department fundraiser. I can't wait to see the responses to that one.

Letters to the editor, while an important opinion forum, frequently feature great examples of flawed arguments, including logical fallacies, poor reasoning, and a pitiful lack of audience awareness. In the hands of a good writer, however, a short persuasive essay like the op-ed can move people to think and act. It is a genre that attracts some of the best nonfiction writers in the country—Ellen Goodman, George Will, Bob Greene, Anna Quindlen, and others—but op-ed essays are also written by anyone with an idea about a public problem. Across the

What You'll Learn in This Chapter

- New ways to understand the purpose of argument.
- Some differences between formal and informal arguments.
- The basic argument strategies most writers use.
- How to map an argument.
- How to avoid common logical fallacies.
- Revision strategies to fine-tune your argument.

United States, newspapers and magazines publish the opinion pieces of ordinary citizens, and these essays are among our liveliest forums for public debate.

While we often think of persuasive writing as stiff and formal, the op-ed essay is usually lively and engaging. Here's a sample of some opening lines from published op-ed pieces:

> Many of the hundreds of thousands of Hispanic demonstrators who poured out into the streets on Monday may not know much English, but they've learned the language of American politics: Flags. Tons of flags. And make them American.
>
> —"Immigrants Must Choose," Charles Krauthammer

> Maybe it was at the moment I found myself on my knees in my bathrobe, carefully prying tiny shards of paper out of the immobilized teeth of the shredder, that it finally hit me: The shredder had a paper jam. I had an info jam.
>
> —"C'mon, America, Fire Up Those Shredders," Lisa Johnston

> On the premise that spring is too beautiful for a depressing topic like Iraq, I thought I'd take up a fun subject—global warming.
>
> —"Global Warming: What, Me Worry?" Molly Ivins

Persuasive essays like the op-ed are a great way to participate in public debates that affect your campus and community, and even your nation.

While these essays are often informal, they are still persuasive forms, and as you'll see later, they often employ the same methods of more formal arguments. However, unlike formal arguments—the kind you might write in a logic or philosophy course—persuasive essays of this kind have a much larger audience, and they are a great way to participate in public debates that affect your campus and community, and even your nation. In this chapter, you'll learn how to use some principles of argument to write persuasive essays like the op-ed that will give voice to things you care about, and that will increase the likelihood that voice will be heard.

What Is Argument?

Argument is not war.

When I was growing up, argument meant only one thing: indigestion. My father loved to argue at the dinner table, hotly pursuing any stray comment that would give him the chance to demonstrate his superior knowledge and logic. What I remember about these "arguments" was the hot-faced humiliation and anger I felt back then, and later, the feeling that I would prefer to avoid an argument at any cost. When I mention argumentative writing to my students, I think I recognize in the slumped shoulders and distant looks of some of them that they might have similar feelings.

Some of us think argument is impolite. It means uncomfortable conflict. It is the verbal equivalent of war.

And yet, we engage in argument every day when we attempt to persuade an instructor to extend the deadline on a paper, try to convince our spouse to help more around the apartment, or seek a loan from a bank.

Arguments *can* involve conflict, but they are rarely combat—despite the war metaphors like "finding ammunition" or "attacking a position." Far more often, the motives for arguing are more benign. We want others to consider seeing the world the way we see it. Or we want to encourage them to *do* something we believe is in their interests as well as ours. These are the motives behind the attempts at persuasion of several of the assignments you may have completed earlier in *The Curious Writer:* the review, the proposal, and the critical essay.

In a sense, all writing is persuasive. *See the world my way*, we ask of readers, *at least for a moment.*

There aren't just two sides.

Two Sides to Every Argument?

TV talk shows stage "discussions" between proponents of diametrically opposed positions. Academic debating teams pit those for and those against. We are nurtured on language like *win* or *lose, right* and *wrong,* and *either/or*. It's tempting to see the world this way, as neatly divided into truth and falsehood, light and dark. Reducing issues to two sides simplifies the choices. But one of the things that literature—and all art—teaches us is the delightful and nagging complexity of things. By inclination and upbringing, Huck Finn is a racist, and there's plenty of evidence in *Huckleberry Finn* that his treatment of Jim confirms it. Yet there are moments in the novel when we see a transcendent humanity in Huck, and we can see that he may be a racist, *but.* . . . It is this qualification—this modest word *but*—that trips us up in the steady march toward certainty. Rather than *either/or,* can it be *both/and?* Instead of two sides to every issue, might there be thirteen?

Here's an example:

One side: General education requirements are a waste of time because they are often irrelevant to students' major goal in getting a college education—getting a good job.

The other side: General education requirements are invaluable because they prepare students to be enlightened citizens, more fully prepared to participate in democratic culture.

It's easy to imagine a debate between people who hold these positions, and it wouldn't be uninteresting. But it *would* be misleading to think that these are the only two possible positions on general education requirements in American universities. One of the reasons why people are drawn to arguing is that it can be a method of discovery, and one of the most useful discoveries is some side to the story that doesn't fall neatly into the usual opposed positions. The route to these discoveries is twofold: *initially withholding judgment* and *asking questions.*

For instance, what might be goals of a university education other than helping students get a good job and making them enlightened citizens? Is it possible that a university can do both? Are general education courses the only route to enlightenment? Are there certain situations in which the vocational motives of students are inappropriate? Are there certain contexts—say, certain students at particular schools at a particular point in their education—when general education requirements might be waived or modified?

All of these questions, and more, tend to unravel the two sides of the argument and expose them for what they often are: *starting points* for an inquiry into the question, *What good are general education requirements?*

Premises are what hold up claims.

I actually asked my first-year students recently what they thought of general education or "core" classes at our university. It provoked a lively debate. Here's what one of them said:

> "I am all for the rant about higher education costing a fortune. The core classes are a joke, to be quite honest. Who hasn't had math, science, and history in high school?"

What interests me here is not the claim that "core classes are a joke" but a key assumption behind the claim that the writer assumes her readers agree with. Are high school math, science, and history classes equivalent to university core classes in the same subjects? It's a premise that isn't addressed, yet her argument fundamentally depends on our consent that it is true. In logical persuasion, not all premises need explanation because the audience may grant their truth without it—racism is bad, depression is a treatable condition, citizens in a democracy have a right to vote. But when writers ignore controversial premises, the argument is a house of cards, vulnerable to the slightest push back.

In argument, premises or assumptions are reasons that we believe something is true, and one way to find the path back from a claim to a reason is to use the word "because." *Core classes are a joke because their content is similar to what most students learn in high school.*

Arguments prove claims with appropriate evidence.

"I have a headache" is a statement, not a claim, because no one is likely to disagree with it. "Headaches can be caused by secondhand smoke" is a statement that is a claim because reasonable people might agree or disagree with it. Claims are at the heart of argument, and if you think about it, you already know this. Every time you make a judgment, interpretation, or evaluation, you make a claim. We do this daily: "Macs are better than PCs." "The food in this place sucks." "This town needs more buses."

However, unlike these often-offhand comments, argumentative writing is organized around convincing someone else that the claim is true. This means not only establishing the reasons behind why we think so, but providing evidence that seems convincing. For example, a comparison between the syllabi for my high school history course and my college core course in history shows that 60 percent of the time they cover the same material. Hmmm. Maybe core classes can be a "joke."

Not just any evidence will do, of course. It depends on the situation. For example, statistical data are appropriate evidence in a environmental health paper on the effect of inversions and not personal experience. An opinion essay on

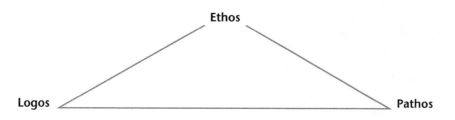

Figure 1   Aristotle's rhetorical triangle

the need to act on air inversions might use statistics but is just as likely to use the writer's personal experience.

There is an artful balance between persona, emotion, and logic.

Persuasion, as Aristotle reminded us a few thousand yeas ago, depends not just on good reasoning (*logos*), but on moving an audience (*pathos*) and making it believe the speaker is someone worth listening to on the subject (*ethos*). Figure 1 shows Aristotle's famous rhetorical triangle, a visual presentation of this idea.

What may be a little misleading about Aristotle's graphic is the idea that the recipe for good argument is equal measures of ethos, pathos, and logos. Not at all. These are blended in varying amounts depending on the situation. One factor, for example, is the disposition of an audience toward your claim.

Figure 2 broadly describes the balance between Aristotle's three categories of appeals in the three most common rhetorical situations: when an audience is resistant to what you're trying to say, neutral about it, or receptive. For instance, direct-mail marketers, particularly those trying to raise money for nonprofit groups and political causes, make a living buying and cultivating lists of people who might be receptive to their messages. Direct-mail letters, therefore, are strong on emotional appeals (*pathos*): The humane society will include photographs of a sad-looking abandoned puppy, a conservative political action group will raise fears about threats to "family values," and so on. There's no need to spend a great deal reasoning (*logos*) with an audience that already agrees with your message. Move them with emotion!

In contrast, resistant audiences immediately suspect the credibility of speakers or writers (*ethos*), and so their challenge is to establish some common

Disposition of Audience	*Ethos*	*Pathos*	*Logos*
Resistant	Most important	Least important	Most important
Neutral	Important	Important	Important
Receptive	Least important	Most important	Least important

Figure 2   Audience and the balance of ethos, logos, and pathos

ground with their audiences. Emotional appeals will be unlikely to move this audience, at least initially.

Neutral audiences may be difficult to gauge. Sometimes an emotional appeal will spark its members' interest. Sometimes a well-reasoned argument (*logos*) will move them, and sometimes a neutral audience will be persuaded by the credibility of the speaker. Frequently, a careful combination of all three of Aristotle's appeals transforms a neutral audience into one that is receptive to what you have to say.

For many of us, then, argument in civic and private discourse is bound by our *feelings* about argument—how comfortable we are with conflict, how confident we are in our ability to say what we think, and how strongly we feel about our opinions. These feelings are complicated by our beliefs about the purpose of argument. Sorting through these beliefs can help us discover new, perhaps more productive ways of approaching argument. Does argument make you uncomfortable? What do you consider a "good" argument? What is a "bad" argument?

Argument and Inquiry

Like all inquiry projects, the process of writing an argument involves both suspending judgment and making judgments (see Figures 3 and 4). Directly or indirectly, arguments address some kind of problem that needs to be solved—global warming, lack of funding for local preschool education, online music piracy, or whatever issue is complex and interesting.

Suspending Judgment. When you suspend judgment you openly explore a problem, including your own initial assumptions about it, if you have any. This is your chance to discover what you think by looking at the evidence and arguments others have already put forward. One of the things this might inspire is clarifying what the problem really is that most needs a solution.

Making Judgments. Since all arguments are organized around a claim, clarifying the problem will help you determine what that might be. This is the most important judgment you'll make. From there, the process is a more familiar one of establishing the reasons behind your claim and then finding and organizing the relevant evidence that will make them convincing to someone else.

Inquiry arguments work best under the following conditions:

1. You choose a topic that you find confusing in interesting ways, which may not yield easily to obvious solutions.

2. You may have tentative ideas about what you think, but you're willing to change your mind.

3. You're willing to wrestle with viewpoints other than your own, even after you've decided on the claim you want to prove.

Suspending Judgment

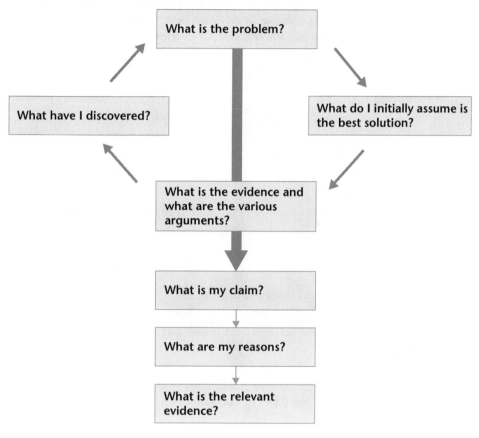

Making Judgments

Figure 3   An inquiry argument. Rather than rushing to judgment, inquiry-based arguments begin with an open exploration of the problem. The aim, as always, is discovery. These discoveries are the basis for clarifying the problem and then making a claim about what should be done about it. (See Figure 4 for an example of how this might work.)

Analyzing Argument

How might you analyze this letter writer's argument?

Dear editor,

As part of my required humanities class, I was forced to see the art exhibit "Home of the Brave" at the university gallery. As a combat veteran, what I saw there deeply offended me. I saw so-called "art" that showed great American military leaders like General Petraeus with skulls superimposed on their faces, and a photo of a man with an American flag wrapped around his head and lashed with a plastic tie at his neck. It's popular to say these days that we should support the troops. Apparently, a group of artists who haven't defended our freedom feel free to use that freedom to be unpatriotic. I wonder if they would feel differently if they had to pay the real cost for freedom of speech.

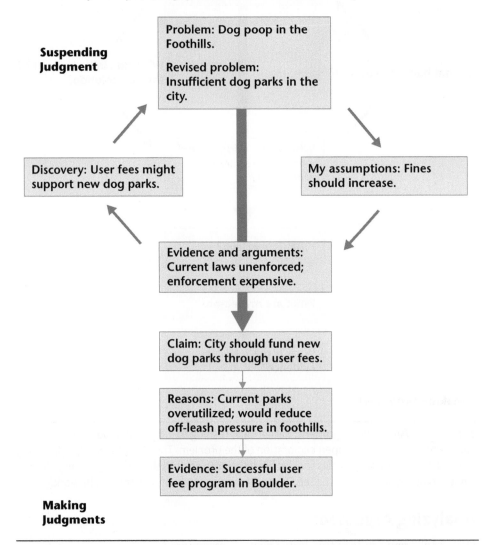

Suspending Judgment

Problem: Dog poop in the Foothills.

Revised problem: Insufficient dog parks in the city.

Discovery: User fees might support new dog parks.

My assumptions: Fines should increase.

Evidence and arguments: Current laws unenforced; enforcement expensive.

Claim: City should fund new dog parks through user fees.

Reasons: Current parks overutilized; would reduce off-leash pressure in foothills.

Evidence: Successful user fee program in Boulder.

Making Judgments

Figure 4   An inquiry argument: Example. Here's how you might apply the inquiry process to discovering an argument. In Boise, Idaho, where I live, there are more dogs per capita than nearly every other city in the U.S. That's a lot of dog poop, particularly on trails in the surrounding foothills. When you don't rush the claim and suspend judgment for a bit you're more likely to find a more insightful—and more focused—argument. For instance, instead of simply declaring, "There are too many dog piles on hiking paths!" you might discover a more interesting and useful claim: "Boise needs more off-leash dog parks."

Most arguments like this don't provoke an analytical response at first. We react emotionally: "This guy is so full of it!" or perhaps, "It's about time someone spoke up about the cost of freedom!" This letter, like many that raise controversial issues, triggers a whole set of deeply held beliefs about things like patriotism, freedom of speech, and the purpose of art. These are things that *should* provoke discussion—and inevitably trigger feelings. But without involving the head as well as the heart, it's impossible to have a civil discussion—one that will lead to new understanding. We need to understand not only what we ourselves believe but also what the other guy believes.

Using Toulmin. Fortunately, there are tools to help with this analysis. For example, Stephen Toulmin, an English philosopher, argued that arguments about any subject have features that include:

- claims
- evidence (grounds)
- warrants (reasons)
- backing

The most penetrating aspect of Toulmin's approach is the idea that *warrants*—or assumptions about the way things are—are key to the logical relationship between evidence and claims. For example, my colleague Dr. Michelle Payne does an exercise with her students in which she empties her purse and asks, "What claim might you make about what kind of person I am based on the evidence before you?" Michelle's students once inferred, for example, that the fact she carries three credit cards meant that she had a lot of money (she doesn't). Others claimed that the cards suggested she carried a lot of debt (actually, no). How might these opposing claims be evaluated? That's where warrants come in. "What do you need to believe is true," Michelle asked, "if your claims from the evidence are valid?" The backers of the high-debt claim agreed they would have to believe that there is a relationship between the number of credit cards one has and the amount of debt one carries. That's the warrant, and there actually is some factual backing for it. The success of any argument, Toulmin believed, depends on the validity of its warrants.

Earlier in the chapter, we talked about warrants as assumptions or premises, and they're pretty much the same things, except that Toulmin's model highlights a more formal relationship between evidence, claims, warrants, and backing. Figure 5 shows how we might use Toulmin to chart the claim Michelle's students made about the contents of her purse.

As you can see, arguing well isn't simply a matter of lining up ducks. The task isn't to make a claim and then hunt up evidence to support it. Toulmin reminds us that wedged between evidence and claims are warrants—things the writers assume must be true for their claims to be believable. These warrants may be implicit or explicit, and one of the best ways to analyze an argument is to figure out what the warrants are and to decide if they have enough backing to be believable.

Evidence		Claim
If Michelle has 3 credit cards in her purse...		...Michelle must carry too much debt.

Warrants

There is a relationship between the number of credit cards and personal debt.

Backing

Kim and Devaney (2001) cite a positive relationship between the number of credit cards and a consumer's debt.

Figure 5 Toulmin's model shows how to analyze the claim that carrying three credit cards means that one is also carrying too much debt.

Let's apply Toulmin's approach to the letter to the editor that began this section. What's the claim? What are its warrants? Here's one take:

Evidence and Claim: If artists subject "great American military figures" to ridicule in a time of war, they are being unpatriotic.
Warrant #1: During wartime, Americans should temper their criticism of the military.
Warrant #2: Those who haven't seen military service don't fully appreciate the costs associated with protecting freedom.
Warrant #3: Art can be unpatriotic.

These are not the only warrants implied by the letter writer's claim, and it's certainly debatable if I've actually got the claim right. But if someone asked me to go beyond an emotional reaction to the letter and offer a reasoned response, then these warrants might be the ideas I would start with. Do I agree with them? Why or why not? What backing might support or refute a particular warrant?

Using Logical Fallacies. Toulmin's method is just one of many ways to analyze the arguments that we encounter in our reading.

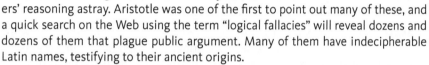

INQUIRING INTO THE DETAILS

Common Logical Fallacies

An important way to evaluate the soundness of an argument is to examine its logic and, in particular, look for so-called logical fallacies that may lead writers' reasoning astray. Aristotle was one of the first to point out many of these, and a quick search on the Web using the term "logical fallacies" will reveal dozens and dozens of them that plague public argument. Many of them have indecipherable Latin names, testifying to their ancient origins.

Here are ten of the most common logical fallacies. I think they cover about 90 percent of the ways in which writers stumble when making an argument.

1. *Hasty generalization:* We're naturally judgmental creatures. For example, we frequently make a judgment about someone after just meeting him or her. Or we conclude that a class is useless after attending a single session. These are generalizations based on insufficient evidence. Hasty generalizations *might* be true—the class might turn out to be useless—but you should always be wary of them.

2. *Ad hominem:* When arguments turn into shouting matches, they almost inevitably get personal. Shifting away from the substance of an argument to attack the person making it, either subtly or explicitly, is another common logical fallacy. It's also, at times, hard to resist.

3. *Appeal to authority:* We all know that finding support for a claim from an expert is a smart move in many arguments. But sometimes it's a faulty move because the authority we cite isn't really an expert on the subject. A more common fallacy, however, is when we cite an expert to support a claim without acknowledging that many experts disagree on the point.

4. *Straw man:* One of the sneakiest ways to sidetrack reason in an argument is to misrepresent or ignore the actual position of an opponent. Unfortunately, the "straw-man" fallacy thrives in many political debates: "I can't support this proposal for universal health care," says politician A. "It's clear that politician A doesn't really take the problem in American health care seriously," says politician B. Huh?

5. *False analogy:* Analogies can be powerful comparisons in argument. But they can also lead us astray when the analogy simply doesn't hold. Are A and B *really* similar situations? For example, when a critic of higher education argues that a public university is like a business and should be run like one, are the two really analogous? Fundamentally, one is nonprofit and the other is designed to make money. Is this really a useful comparison?

(continued)

Inquiring into the Details (*continued*)

6. ***Post hoc or false cause:*** Just because one thing follows another doesn't necessarily mean one *causes* the other. It might be coincidence, or the cause might be something else entirely. For example, if you're really keen on arguing that losing the football coach was the cause of the team's losing record, you might link the two. And it's possible that you're right, but it's also just as possible that the injury to the quarterback was one of the real reasons.

7. ***Appeal to popularity:*** In a country obsessed by polls and rankings, it's not hard to understand the appeal of reasoning that argues that because it's popular it must be good or true. Advertisers are particularly fond of this fallacy, arguing that because their brand is most popular it must be the best. In fact, this might not be the case at all. The majority can be wrong.

8. ***Slippery slope:*** I love the name of this one because it so aptly describes what can happen when reasoning loses its footing. You might start out reasonably enough, arguing, for example, that a gun control law restricts the rights of some citizens to have access to certain weapons, but pretty soon you start sliding toward conclusions that simply don't follow, such as that a gun control law is the beginning of the end of gun ownership in the country. Now you might really believe this, but logic isn't the route to get there.

9. ***Either/or fallacy:*** In a black-and-white world, something is right or wrong, true or false, good or bad. But ours is a colorful world with many shades. For instance, while it might be emotionally satisfying to say that opponents of the war in Iraq must not support the troops there, it is also possible that the war's opponents are against the war *because* they're concerned about the lives of American service people. Rather than *either/or* it might be *both/and*. We see this fallacy often in arguments that suggest that there are only two choices and each are opposites.

10. ***Begging the question:*** This one is also called circular reasoning because it assumes the truth of the arguer's conclusion without bothering to prove it. An obvious example of this would be to say that a law protecting people from Internet spam is good because it's a law, and laws should be obeyed. But *why* is it a good law?

MOTIVES FOR WRITING AN ARGUMENT

Argument, obviously, is a part of everyday life, though as I noted before, it doesn't always go well. I'm constantly trying to persuade my wife Karen that it would be a good thing if I added another guitar to my acoustic collection. I was thinking a new Martin with mahogany back and sides and onboard Fishman electronics would be good.

"You've already got seven guitars," she said. "How many more do you need?"

We argue to get something we want but these are often the least interesting arguments to make.

Classical rhetoricians like Plato, Aristotle, and Cicero had a great deal to say about how to argue well, and while their focus was largely on public speaking, their ideas are foundational for a modern understanding of argument. For

Aristotle, there were three arenas for persuasion—before the courts, before legislators and others who make public policy, and at social occasions.

Of course, there are plenty of other reasons to argue. In academic writing, the purpose of argument is usually to establish the truth of something. Modern advertising, the most common medium of modern persuasion, attempts to influence people's behaviors. Generally speaking, you can distinguish between these two purposes—to establish the validity of a certain way of seeing things and the desire to move people to action—but because the persuasive essay you will be writing in this chapter can do both, we won't make much of the distinction between these two purposes here.

Arguing is a civic duty. In fact, it is an essential activity in any democratic culture, and it's certainly a major element of academic discourse; academic argument is one of the key means of making new knowledge.

Knowing how to argue well has practical value, even if you don't become a lawyer. It might help you make the best case to a local legislator to support the bill providing tuition relief to students, or even bargaining with the used-car dealer for a better price on that black convertible Mazda Miata. Understanding argument helps you find the flaws in *other people's* arguments as well. Knowing how to analyze an argument gives me a language to talk about the flawed arguments in the letters to the editor in *The Idaho Statesman,* and it also helps me thoughtfully and critically read articles and essays that make claims.

Finally, the most important motive behind writing and studying argument is that you care about something. Throughout this text, I've argued that the personal motive for writing is the most powerful one of all; in this case, you're passionate about a question or an issue, and building a written argument channels that passion into prose that can make a difference.

THE ARGUMENT AND ACADEMIC WRITING

Argumentative writing is one of the most common of all academic forms. One reason for this is that the ability to argue well requires some command of subject matter. There is another motive for mastering argument in academic settings, however, and it has less to do with proving that you know your stuff. Argument is really about trying to get at the truth.

> Argument is one of the key means of making new knowledge.

In college, the audiences for your arguments are often your instructors. As experts in a particular discipline, professors argue all the time. They're not simply trying to be contrary but trying to get at the truth. Arguing is the main way that the academic community makes knowledge.

Notice I used the word *make*. While it often seems that the facts we take for granted are immutable truths—as enduring as the granite peaks I can see through my office window—things aren't often that way at all. Our knowledge of things—how the planet was formed, the best ways to save endangered species, the meaning of a classic novel, how to avoid athletic injuries—is entirely made up of ideas that are *contested*. They are less mountains than the glaciers that carved them, and in some cases the sudden earthquakes that bring them down. The primary tool for shaping and even changing what we know is argument.

FEATURES OF THE FORM

Generally speaking, persuasive writing can take many forms. Indeed, reviews and proposals both represent different types of persuasive writing. The argument essay we are covering in this chapter, however, more obviously embodies persuasive writing than either of these two other forms. This essay typically makes explicit claims and backs them up with hard evidence. It also employs the well-established rhetorical devices and the reasoning of formal argumentation in the effort to sway readers to its point of view. However, unlike more formal academic papers, the argument you'll be writing in this chapter is intended for a more general audience. It's what we might call a *public argument*. It's the kind of piece you might see in your local newspaper, or in a magazine. *Newsweek*'s "My Turn" column is an excellent example. (See Figure 6 for a comparison of argument essays.)

Here are some of the features of the public argument essay:

- *Public arguments are often relatively brief treatments of a topic.* Readers of newspapers and many magazines read fast. They want to quickly get the gist

Rhetorical Context	Academic Argument Essay	Public Argument Essay
Audience	Academic discourse community	Publication's readers
Speaker	You as a member of above	You as an authority on subject
Purpose	To demonstrate your authority	To make something happen
Subject	Of academic interest	Of community interest
Voice	Conventional, academic	Personal, informed
Research	Always	Usually
Citations	Yes	No
Length	Varies, usually 8–25 pages	Varies, usually 500–1,000 words
How to read	Slowly, thoughtfully	Rapidly, mining for meaning

Figure 6 A comparison of academic and informal argument (Devan Cook, Boise State University)

of an essay or article and move on to the next story. In addition, space is often limited, particularly in newspapers. As a result, the op-ed or opinion piece rarely exceeds 1,000 words, or about four double-spaced manuscript pages.

■ *Subject matter often focuses on issues of public concern.* The magazines and newspapers that publish argument essays typically report on news, events, or issues that might affect a lot of people. Not surprisingly, then, writers of these essays are keen observers of public debates and controversies.

■ *A public argument has a central claim or proposition.* Sometimes we also call this a *thesis,* a term that's a holdover from the scientific terminology that dominated American scholarship from the end of the nineteenth century. Classical arguments, the kind many of us wrote in high school, usually state this central claim or thesis in the introduction. But many arguments, particularly essays that rely on narrative structure or explore the answer to a question or problem, may feature the thesis in the middle or at the end of the essay.

■ *The central claim is based on one or more premises or assumptions.* You already know something about this from the discussion earlier in the chapter. Basically, a premise suggests that something is true *because* of something else; it expresses the relationship between *what* you claim and *why* you believe that claim to be true. This is discussed at greater length later in the chapter.

■ *The public argument relies on evidence that a general audience will believe.* All arguments should use evidence appropriate for a particular audience. Academic writers in marine biology, for example, rely on data collected in the field and analyzed statistically because this kind of evidence is most persuasive to other marine biologists. Anecdotes or personal observation alone simply won't cut it in the *Journal of Marine Biology.* But the persuasive essay's more general audience finds a greater range of evidence convincing, including personal experience and observation. Writers of persuasive essays are likely to do the kind of research you use to write research papers—digging up statistics, facts, and quotations on a topic.

■ *They sometimes invite or encourage a response.* Earlier I noted a broad distinction between the purposes of argument: (1) to establish the validity of a writer's way of seeing what's true and (2) to move or persuade an audience to act a certain way. The second purpose is most obvious in the advertisement, which is a visual argument that asks viewers to *do* something—buy a Jeep or change toilet bowl cleaners. But public arguments sometimes ask for or imply a course of action readers should take. An op-ed piece might attempt to change the views and behaviors of political leaders, or influence how people vote for them. It might urge support for a school bond issue, or encourage fellow students to protest against the elimination of an academic program.

■ *Readers won't respond unless they know what's at stake.* An essential element of argument is establishing why a certain action, policy, or idea *matters.* How will opposition to the administration's strip-mining policies in West Virginia and Kentucky make a difference in the quality of life in those states, but even more important, why should someone in Boise, Idaho, care? The best arguments are built to carefully establish, sometimes in quite practical terms, how a certain action, belief, or idea might make a difference in the lives of those who are the argument's audience.

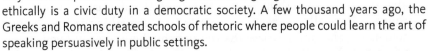

WRITING IN YOUR LIFE

Public Argument in a Digital Age

Winning an argument with Northwest Airlines over whether they owe you a lunch voucher after your flight was cancelled is typical of the way persuasion is an everyday concern. But in a larger sense—and probably more important one—arguing well and arguing ethically is a civic duty in a democratic society. A few thousand years ago, the Greeks and Romans created schools of rhetoric where people could learn the art of speaking persuasively in public settings.

These days, probably more than ever, argument is a vibrant part of civic life in the United States, particularly on the Internet. Here are a few of the many genres of public argument available to you for moving people to think or do something you consider important:

- *Op-ed essays:* These are possibly the most common brief argumentative essays for a general audience. The term "op-ed" refers to the editorial essays that are published opposite of the editorial page, a ubiquitous feature in most American newspapers.

- *Editorials:* Brief statements of opinion, often 500 words or less, represent the institutional judgment about a policy issue of a newspaper, radio or TV station, online publication, and so on.

- *Blogs:* One of the newest forms of public argument is the blog. Hosted by online sites like Google's "Blogger," the so-called blogosphere is sixty times larger than it was three years ago.

- *Photo essay:* Over 100 years ago, Jacob Riis used photographs of immigrants' squalid conditions in New York City tenements to incite a public outcry—and policy change—on how we treat the poor.

- *Letters to the editor:* These appear in print or online and, unlike editorials, people read them.

- *YouTube:* It's not just a forum for published videos on weird cat tricks.

- *PowerPoint:* Former Vice President Al Gore's slide presentation, "An Inconvenient Truth," made the point that there really is power in PowerPoint. Of course, more often these presentations are really awful.

READINGS

■ ARGUMENT 1

It's hard to imagine that one of the chief planners of the September 11, 2001, attacks on New York and Washington, D.C., might invoke George Washington as his hero. In the excerpt that follows, Kahlid Sheikh Mohammed, a commander for al Queda, who has been in custody since 2003, argues that Islamic extremists, like Washington, are just fighting for their independence. The language of war, says Mohammed, is universal, and that language is killing.

This partial transcript of Mohammed discussing his role in the 9/11 attacks, the murder of journalist Daniel Pearl, and the hotel bombings in Bali, was released by the U.S. Department of Defense and later appeared in *Harper's Magazine*.

The Language of War Is Killing
Khalid Sheikh Mohammed

I'm not making myself a hero when I said I was responsible for this or that. You   1
know very well there is a language for any war. If America wants to invade Iraq, they will not send Saddam roses or kisses. They send bombardment. I admit I'm America's enemy. For sure, I'm America's enemy. So when we make war against America, we are like jackals fighting in the night. We consider George Washington a hero. Muslims, many of them, believe Osama bin Laden is doing the same thing. He is just fighting. He needs his independence. Many Muslims think that, not only me. They have been oppressed by America. So when we say we are enemy combatants, that's right, we are. But I'm asking you to be fair with many detainees who are not enemy combatants. Because many of them have been unjustly arrested. You know very well, for any country waging war against their enemy, the language of the war is killing. If man and woman are together as a marriage, the others are kids, children. But if you and me, two nations, are together in war, the others are victims. This is the way of the language. You know forty million people were killed in World War I. Many people are oppressed. Because there is war, for sure, there will be victims. I'm not happy that three thousand have been killed in America. I feel sorry even. Islam never gives me the green light to kill people. Killing, in Christianity, Judaism, and Islam, is prohibited. But there are exceptions to the rule. When you are killing people in Iraq, you say, We have to do it. We don't like Saddam. But this is the way to deal with Saddam. Same language you use I use. When you are invading two thirds of Mexico, you call your war "manifest destiny."

(continued)

(continued)

It's up to you to call it what you want. But the other side is calling you oppressors. If now we were living in the Revolutionary War, George Washington would be arrested by Britain. For sure, they would consider him an enemy combatant. But in America they consider him a hero. In any revolutionary war one side will be either George Washington or Britain. So we considered American Army bases in Saudi Arabia, Kuwait, Qatar, and Bahrain. This is a kind of invasion, but I'm not here to convince you. I don't have to say that I'm not your enemy. This is why the language of any war in the world is killing. The language of war is victims. I don't like to kill people. I feel very sorry kids were killed in 9/11. What will I do? I want to make a great awakening in America to stop foreign policy in our land. I know Americans have been torturing us since the seventies. I know they are talking about human rights. And I know it is against the American Constitution, against American laws. But they said, Every law has exceptions. This is your bad luck—you've been part of the exception to our laws. So, for me, I have patience. The Americans have human rights, but enemy combatant is a flexible word. What is an enemy combatant in my language? The Ten Commandments are shared between all of us. We are all serving one God. But we also share the language of War. War started when Cain killed Abel. It's never gonna stop killing people. America starts the Revolutionary War, and then the Mexican, then the Spanish, then World War I, World War II. You read the history. This is life. You have to kill.

Inquiring into the Essay

Explore, explain, evaluate, and reflect on "The Language of War."

1. Does Mohammed have a point when he compares Islamic extremists who fight for "freedom" to American revolutionaries like George Washington who fought for independence? Fastwrite on this question in your journal for five minutes, exploring what you think. When you're done, skip a line and compose a one-sentence answer to this question: *What surprised you most about what you said in your fastwrite?*

2. Summarize in your own words what you think is Mohammed's main claim.

3. Make a list of reasons that he states in (or you infer from) the transcript that are meant to support Mohammed's main claim. Remember that reasons are ideas that can be attached to a claim using the word "because." For example, "Because most professors are liberals (reason), an open and balanced political discussion in the college classroom is unlikely (claim)." Choose one or more of these reasons, and evaluate whether they are convincing. If not, why not?

4. The September 11 attacks have, understandably, made many Americans very emotional about terrorism and terrorists. What did you notice about

your emotional reaction to Mohammed's argument in "The Language of War"? Did you find it difficult to read the transcript analytically, as the previous questions asked you to do? If so, is this a problem?

INQUIRING INTO THE DETAILS

Some Basic Argument Strategies

- *Argument from generalization:* What I've seen or observed of a particular group is true of the group as a whole. *Risk: Are you sure that what you've observed is typical of the larger population?*

- *Argument from analogy:* If it is true in one situation, it's likely true in another similar situation. *Risk: Are the situations really similar?*

- *Argument from cause:* If one thing always seems present with something else, then one probably causes the other. *Risk: Is cause and effect really the relationship between the two things?*

- *Argument from authority:* If an expert said it, it's true. *Risk: Is the expertise of the authority really relevant to the question at issue?*

- *Argument from principle:* This general principle (which most of us agree with) applies in this case. *Risk: Is there really agreement on the rightness of the principle, and does it actually apply in this specific context?*

Adapted from Richard Fulkerson, *Teaching the Argument in Writing.* Urbana, IL: National Council of Teachers of English, 1996.

ARGUMENT 2

Faith and reason don't have to clash. In his encyclical on the subject, Pope John Paul II wrote that "faith and reason are like two wings on which the human spirit rises to the contemplation of truth." Before the modern era of science, any conflict between the two could be easily resolved by simply accepting that any proposition can, at the same time, be true by reason and false by faith. But these days, such a contradiction is hard to swallow. Take evolution. Darwin's scientific argument intensified the clash between faith and reason, and it still produces pitched battles between school boards and teachers, preachers and scientists, and believers and nonbelievers of all types.

One answer to the conflict is simple. Choose one or the other:

1. When science and scripture collide, scripture wins.
2. When science and scripture collide, science wins.

In the op-ed essay that follows, *Boston Globe* columnist Jeff Jacoby seems to offer another alternative. Using the intellectual success—and deep religious commitment—of one great figure, Jacoby argues that faith and reason aren't necessarily incompatible.

A Teacher with Faith and Reason

Jeff Jacoby

1   Did you hear about the religious fundamentalist who wanted to teach physics at Cambridge University? This would-be instructor wasn't simply a Christian; he was so preoccupied with biblical prophecy that he wrote a book titled *Observations on the Prophecies of Daniel and the Apocalypse of St. John.* Based on his reading of Daniel, in fact, he forecast the date of the Apocalypse: no earlier than 2060. He also calculated the year the world was created. When Genesis 1:1 says "In the beginning," he determined, it means 3988 BC.

2   Not many modern universities are prepared to employ a science professor who espouses not merely "intelligent design" but out-and-out divine creation. This applicant's writings on astronomy, for example, include these thoughts on the solar system: "This most beautiful system of sun, planets, and comets could only proceed from the counsel and domination of an intelligent and powerful Being…He governs all things, and knows all things that are or can be done."

3   Hire somebody with such views to teach physics? At a Baptist junior college deep in the Bible Belt, maybe, but the faculty would erupt if you tried it just about anywhere else. Many of them would echo Oxford's Richard Dawkins, the prominent evolutionary biologist, who writes in "The God Delusion" that he is "hostile to fundamentalist religion because it actively debauches the scientific enterprise.…It subverts science and saps the intellect."

4   Equally blunt is Sam Harris, a PhD candidate in neuroscience and another unsparing foe of religion. "The conflict between religion and science is inherent and (very nearly) zero-sum," he has written. "The success of science often comes at the expense of religious dogma; the maintenance of religious dogma always comes at the expense of science." Less elegant but more influential, the National Science Education Standards issued by the National Academy of Sciences in 1995 classified religion with "myths," "mystical inspiration," and "superstition"—all of them quite incompatible with scientific study. Michael Dini, a biologist at Texas Tech University in Lubbock, made headlines in 2003 over his policy of denying letters of recommendation for any graduate student who could not "truthfully and forthrightly affirm a scientific answer" to the question of mankind's origin. Science and religion, he said in an interview at the time, "shouldn't overlap."

5   But such considerations didn't keep Cambridge from hiring the theology- and Bible-drenched individual described above. Indeed, it named him to the prestigious

Lucasian Chair of Mathematics—in 1668. A good thing too, since Isaac Newton—notwithstanding his religious fervor and intense interest in Biblical interpretation—went on to become the most renowned scientist of his age, and arguably the most influential in history.

Newton's consuming interest in theology, eschatology, and the secrets of the Bible is the subject of a new exhibit at Hebrew University in Jerusalem (online at jnul.huji.ac.il/dl/mss/Newton). His vast religious output—an estimated 3 million words—ranged from the dimensions of Solomon's Temple to a method of reckoning the date of Easter to the elucidation of Biblical symbols. "Newton was one of the last great Renaissance men," the curators observe, "a thinker who worked in mathematics, physics, optics, alchemy, history, theology, and the interpretation of prophecy and saw connections between them all." The 21st-century prejudice that religion invariably "subverts science" is refuted by the extraordinary figure who managed to discover the composition of light, deduce the laws of motion, invent calculus, compute the speed of sound, and define universal gravitation, all while believing deeply in the "domination of an intelligent and powerful Being." Far from subverting his scientific integrity, the exhibition notes, "Newton's piety served as one of his inspirations to study nature and what we today call science."

For Newton, it was axiomatic that religious inquiry and scientific investigation complemented each other. There were truths to be found in both of the "books" authored by God, the Book of Scripture and the Book of Nature—or as Francis Bacon called them, the "book of God's word" and the "book of God's works." To study the world empirically did not mean abandoning religious faith. On the contrary: The more deeply the workings of Creation were understood, the closer one might come to the Creator. In the language of the 19th Psalm, "The heavens declare the glory of God, and the sky above proclaims his handiwork."

To be sure, religious dogma can be a blindfold, blocking truths from those who refuse to see them. Scientific dogma can have the same effect. Neither faith nor reason can answer every question. As Newton knew, the surer path to wisdom is the one that has room for both.

6

7

8

"A Teacher with Faith and Reason" by Jeff Jacoby, *The Boston Globe*, July 22, 2007. Reprinted by permission of The New York Times Company.

Inquiring into the Essay

Explore, explain, evaluate, and reflect on "A Teacher with Faith and Reason."

1. Perhaps the central claim of this essay appears, as it often does in an op-ed essay, two thirds of the way into the piece, when Jacoby writes,

> The 21st-century prejudice that religion invariably "subverts science" is refuted by the extraordinary figure who managed to discover the composition of light, deduce the laws of motion, invent calculus, compute the speed of

sound, and define universal gravitation, all while believing deeply in the "domination of an intelligent and powerful Being."

When you analyze an argument, it's often helpful to first explore—in a relatively open-ended way—what you think about the central claim. Do that now in a four-minute fastwrite in your journal. Do you agree or disagree that Isaac Newton's legacy "refutes" the current "prejudice" that religion undercuts scientific inquiry? Try writing a narrative of thought, beginning with "The first thing I think about this is...And then I think...And then..." Allow yourself to digress if that's where your writing takes you.

2. Define the two key terms in this debate—reason and faith—in your own words.

3. An argument about potential conflicts between faith and reason can easily become too abstract to evaluate well. So consider the case Jacoby mentions in his essay: A Texas Tech biology professor routinely refused to write recommendations for any graduate student who didn't provide a "scientific answer" to explain the beginnings of humankind. Do you find Jacoby's argument helpful in developing your own response to that particular situation?

4. This is one of those social issues that trigger strong feeling which, at times, can cloud reasoning. Reflect on your own response to issues like this one. When you have an emotional response to a public argument, how do you get past it?

■ ARGUMENT 3

During the fall semester, 2008, Laredo businessman Loye Young agreed to teach a business management class at nearby Texas A&M International University (TAMIU). Like many instructors, he toiled over his syllabus, trying to make sure his course policies were clear, especially a section on the consequences of plagiarism in his class. Young warned that plagiarists would not only flunk the course, they would be reported to university officials. That's fairly standard punishment at most universities. What got critics' attention was Young's warning that he would publicly humiliate any student caught cheating.

True to his word, when he caught six students plagiarizing a paper, Young published their names on his blog, and soon after, TAMIU officials fired him, arguing that he violated the Family Educational and Privacy Act, a policy designed to protect the confidentiality of certain student information. Young, a former attorney, strongly disagreed.

The firing ignited a national controversy and a wild debate in the blogosphere over whether Loye Young's decision to out students he suspected of academic dishonesty was effective, ethical, and fair. In response to one of his critics, Loye posted the following defense of his approach on his blog.

Is Humiliation an Ethically Appropriate Response to Plagiarism?

Loye Young

I'm a business owner in Laredo, Texas. I had never taught a college course before, and I never asked to teach. The department asked me to teach this course. I accepted because of my commitment to Laredo's future.

1

I worked hard on the syllabus, and everything in the syllabus was deliberate. Specifically, the language about dishonesty was based on moral and pedagogical principles. The department chairman, Dr. Balaji Janamanchi, reviewed the syllabus with me line-by-line, and I made a few changes in response to his comments.

2

I was surprised by how common and blatant plagiarism turned out to be. Six students in one class is an extraordinarily high number. I thought and prayed about what to do for about a week before following through on my promise. I decided I had only one moral choice. I am certain it was right.

3

My decision was guided by two factors: What is good for the students themselves? and What is good for other students?

4

What is good for the students themselves?

5

I am cognizant of the extraordinary moral difficulty involved when deciding what is in another's best interests. Nonetheless, I am convinced that public disclosure, including the concomitant humiliation, is in the interests of the student because it is the best way to teach the student about the consequences of dishonesty and discourage the student from plagiarizing again. Humiliation is inextricably part of a well-formed conscience.

6

The Vice President-elect, Senator Joseph Biden, is perhaps the most well-known plagiarizer in recent history. Biden was caught plagiarizing while at Syracuse Law School. The school gave him an F, required him to retake the course, and subsequently treated the incident as confidential.

7

Unfortunately, Biden didn't learn his lesson at law school. He continued to plagiarize for another 20 years. During the 1988 presidential campaign, Senator Biden's career of plagiarizing came to light, and he was forced to end his presidential bid.

8

It is my belief that the Syracuse incident left a subtle and subliminal message in Biden's mind: plagiarism is not a deal breaker. Consequently, he continued to plagiarize. Unfortunately for the Senator, the facts came to public light at the worst possible time: when he was running for President.

9

I believe that had the Syracuse incident been available publicly, Mr. Biden would have actually learned his lesson and would not have plagiarized later. Twenty years later, if the incident had come up at all, the Senator would have plausibly and convincingly maintained that the incident was a youthful mistake.

10

There is yet another reason for publicity in such cases: unjustly accused students are protected, for two reasons. One, a professor will be more careful before blowing

11

(continued)

(continued)

the whistle. I myself knew that posting the students' names would be appropriately subject to intense public scrutiny. Therefore, I construed every ambiguity in the students' favor. Two, public disclosure ensures that subsequent determinations by the university are founded on evidence and dispensed fairly.

12   What is good for other students?

13   On the second question, four reasons convince me: deterrents, fairness, predictability, and preparedness for life.

14   Deterrents—Only if everyone knows that violations of plagiarism will be exposed and punished will the penalties for plagiarism be an effective deterrent. (As a lawyer once told me after hearing of another lawyer's disbarment, "I'm damn sure not going to do THAT again!") In fact, one of the six students had not plagiarized (to my knowledge) until the week before I announced my findings. Had I announced the plagiarism earlier, it is possible that student would not have plagiarized at all.

15   Fairness—Honest students should have, in fairness, the knowledge that their legitimate work is valued more than a plagiarizer's illegitimate work. In my course, the students were required to post their essays on a public website for all to see. Thus, anyone in the world could have detected the plagiarism. Had another student noticed the plagiarism but saw no action, the honest student would reasonably believe that the process is unfair.

16   Predictability—By failing publicly to follow through on ubiquitous warnings about plagiarism, universities have convinced students that the purported indignation against deceit is itself deceitful and that the entire process is capricious. TAMIU's actions in this case have confirmed my suspicions that such a perception is entirely justified.

17   Preparedness for life—In the real world, deceitful actions have consequences, and those consequences are often public. Borrowers lose credit ratings, employees get fired, spouses divorce, businesses fail, political careers end, and professionals go to jail. Acts of moral turpitude rightly carry public and humiliating consequences in real life, and students need to be prepared.

18   In closing, I submit that education died when educators came to believe that greater self-esteem leads to greater learning. In fact, the causality is backwards: self-esteem is the result of learning, not the cause.

"Is Humiliation an Ethically Appropriate Response to Plagiarism," Blog post by Loye Young on http://www.adjunctnation.com/archive/magazine/article/715/, Reprinted by permission of Adjunct Advocate Magazine.

Inquiring into the Essay

Explore, explain, evaluate, and reflect on "Is Humiliation an Ethically Appropriate Response to Plagiarism?"

1.   If you accept that plagiarism is a problem, then what should an instructor do about it? What would you consider not just an ethical policy but one that you think might be an effective deterrent? Fastwrite about this question in your journal for four minutes, exploring what you think.

2. How would *you* define plagiarism? Is it possible that some students might be understandably confused about what it means?

3. Loye Young writes, "Humiliation is inextricably part of a well-formed conscience." How would you evaluate that claim? Can you imagine the *reasons* that Young believes it's true? (Try filling in the blank in this sentence: *Because _____, humiliation is inextricably part of a well-formed conscience.*) Do you agree with them?

4. Reflect on the blog as a genre of public argument. How would you distinguish it from, say, an op-ed essay or a letter to the editor?

SEEING THE FORM

The "Imagetext" as Argument

While model Kate Moss is likely disturbed by the appropriation of her image by advocates in the pro-anorexia ("pro-ana") movement, Moss's picture along with those of other celebrities such as Calista Flockhart, Mary-Kate Olsen, and Keira Knightley appear as "thinspiration" on Web sites that argue that eating disorders are a "lifestyle choice," not a disease. Some of these images (though not this one) are digitally altered to make the models seem even thinner than they really are. In a recent article on the "imagetexts" used by these controversial Web sites, Robin Jensen observes that images rarely argue in isolation, a phenomenon that is particularly relevant to the Web, which often combines pictures and verbal texts. Jensen notes that when pictures like this one of Kate Moss are given a new "visual frame," quite different from the one originally intended, the meaning of the picture can be manipulated. Imagine, for instance, that the Kate Moss photograph appeared in a "thinspiration" gallery of celebrity photographs on a "pro-ana" Web site, and included the following caption: "Maintaining a weight that is 15 percent below your expected body weight fits the criteria for anorexia, so most models, according to medical standards, fit into the categeory of being anorexic." Analyze this "imagetext" rhetorically. How does this picture of Moss combined with the caption serve the purpose of the "pro-ana" movement? What message is it meant to convey and is it persuasive to its intended audience?

Kate Moss in ultra-thin pose.

THE WRITING PROCESS

INQUIRY PROJECT: WRITING A PUBLIC ARGUMENT

Now that you've explored various approaches to persuasion and argument, try your hand at writing an argument essay. Remember that these are brief (700- to 1,000-word) essays meant for a general audience. Imagine, for example, that you're writing an op-ed piece for the campus newspaper, the local daily, or the *New York Times*. Your essay should be lively and logical, with a strong personal voice, and also have the following features:

- It focuses implicitly or explicitly on a question. This is always the starting point for inquiry in any genre. In an argumentative essay, you are providing evidence to support a particular answer to this question.

- The essay makes clear premises and claims, including one central claim around which the draft is organized. In other words, *the essay should be clear about what it is asking its readers to do or to believe.*

- It provides specific and appropriate evidence in support of the claims, including research when relevant.

- The essay should address one or more of the counterarguments offered by those who take a different position from yours.

Thinking About Subjects

Gun control, abortion rights, and other hot-button public controversies often make the list of banned topics for student essays. This is not because they aren't important public debates. Instead, the problem is much more that the writer has likely already made up his mind and sees the chance to ascend a soapbox.

> The best argument essays make a clear claim, but they do it by bowing respectfully to the complexity of the subject, examining it from a variety of perspectives, not just two opposing poles.

Now, I have my own favorite soapboxes; people with strong convictions do. But as you think about subjects for your essay, consider that the soapbox may not be the best vantage point for practicing inquiry. If you've already made up your mind, will you be open to discovery? If you just want to line up ducks—assembling evidence to support an unwavering belief—will you be encouraged to think deeply or differently? Will you be inclined to filter the voices you hear rather than consider a range of points of view?

The best persuasive essays often emerge from the kind of open-ended inquiry that you might have used writing the personal essay. What do you want to understand better? What issue or question makes you wonder? What controversies are you and your friends talking about? Be alert to possible subjects that you might write about *not* because you already know what you think, but because you want to find out. Or consider a subject that you might have feelings about but feel uninformed, lacking the knowledge to know exactly what you think.

Generating Ideas

Play around with some ideas first by using some of the following triggers for thinking-through-writing in your journal. Suspend judgment. Don't reject anything. Explore.

Listing Prompts. Lists can be rich sources of triggering topics. Let them grow freely, and when you're ready, use an item as the focus of another list or an episode of fastwriting. The following prompts should get you started.

1. In your journal, make a quick list of issues that have provoked disagreements between groups of people in your hometown or local community.

2. Make a quick list of issues that have provoked disagreements on your college's campus.

3. Make another list of issues that have created controversy between groups of people in your state.

4. Think about issues—local, statewide, regional, national, or even international—that have touched your life, or could affect you in some way in the following areas: environmental, health care, civil rights, business, education, crime, or sports. Make a quick list of questions within these areas you wonder about. For example, *Will there be enough drinking water in my well if the valley continues to develop at this rate?* Or *Will I be able to afford to send my children to the state college in twelve years?* Or *Do new domestic antiterrorism rules threaten my privacy when I'm online?* Or *Will I benefit from affirmative action laws when I apply to law school?*

5. Jot down a list of the classes you're taking this semester. Then make a quick list of topics that prompt disagreements among people in the field that you're studying. For example, in your political science class, did you learn that there are debates about the usefulness of the electoral college? In your biology class, have you discussed global warming? In your women's studies class, did you read about Title 9 and how it affects female athletes?

Fastwriting Prompts. Remember, fastwriting is a great way to stimulate creative thinking. Turn off your critical side and let yourself write "badly." Don't worry too much about what you're going to say before you say it. Write fast, letting language lead for a change.

1. Write for five minutes beginning with one of the questions you raised in Question 4 in the "Listing Prompts" section. Think through writing about when you first began to be concerned about the question, how you think it might affect you, and what you currently understand are the key questions this issue raises. Do you have tentative feelings or beliefs about it?

2. In a seven-minute fastwrite, explore the differences between your beliefs and the beliefs of your parents. Tell yourself the story of how your own beliefs about some question evolved, perhaps moving away from your parents' positions. Can you imagine the argument you might make to help them understand your point of view?

3. Choose an item from any of the lists you generated in the "Listing Prompts" section as a starting place for a fastwrite. Explore what you understand about the issue, what the key questions are, and how you feel about the issue at the moment.

Visual Prompts. In your journal, cluster one or more of the following phrases:

"Things that seem unfair"

"Things that bug me the most"

"There oughta be a law about…"

"Problems that must be solved"

"The worst thing about living here"

Let your cluster grow as many branches as possible; when one dies out start another. Focus on ideas, people, places, facts, observations, questions, experiences,

ONE STUDENT'S RESPONSE

Ben's Journal

FASTWRITE
WHY DO STUDENTS SEEM SO APATHETIC ABOUT POLITICS?

We're in the midst of presidential elections and I can't seem to get anyone interested in talking about it. I wonder why that is? Are college students more cynical about politics and politicians than other groups? It seems like it to me. I can think of a few reasons right off the bat. First, college students are mostly young (though certainly not all at this school) so they don't have the habit of going to the polls. Whenever a generation loses the habit of voting, I'll bet the next generation is even more likely to be apathetic. I also think my generation has seen so few effective politicians. My dad talks about being inspired by the likes of JFK but I can't think of too many national politicians who have inspired me as much as JFK inspired him. I also wonder if there is that basic sense of powerlessness. We just don't feel like much of anything makes a difference. I wonder if that is also reflected in volunteerism. Do students volunteer less than they used to? Have to check on that. I guess I just find politics kind of interesting. I wonder why? Hmmm…I think it had something to do with my Dad. But I guess I also have this basic belief in voting as an important part of being a citizen. Seems like one of the best ways to be patriotic…

and details that pop into your mind when you focus on the pair of words at the center of your cluster. Look for interesting argument topics when you're done. See Figure 7 for an example.

Research Prompts. By definition, argument essays deal with subjects in which people beyond the writer have a stake. And one of the best ways to collect ideas about such issues is to do a little quick and dirty research. Try some of the following research prompts:

1. Spend a few days reading the letters to the editor in your local paper. What issue has people riled up locally? Is there one that you find particularly interesting?

2. Do a Web search to find op-ed essays written by one or more of the following national columnists: Ellen Goodman, Cal Thomas, George Will, David Broder, Nat Hentoff, Mary McGrory, Molly Ivins, Bob Herbert, or Clarence Page. Read their work with an eye toward topics that interest you.

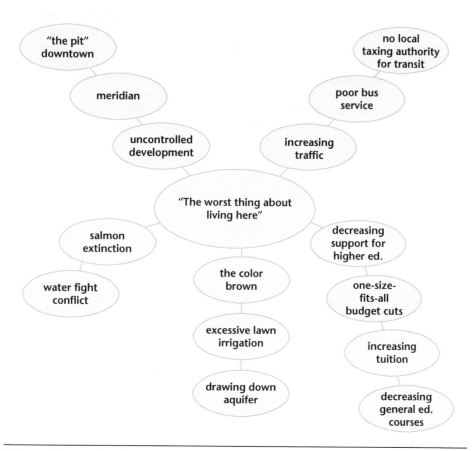

Figure 7 Sample cluster

3. Do a Google search for terms or phrases on an issue that interests you, such as "global warming Greenland glaciers" or "pro-anorexia Web sites." Did you produce any results that make you curious or make you feel something about the issue, one way or another?

4. Interview people you know—on or off campus—about the public issues that they care about most.

Judging What You Have

Shift back to your more critical mind and sift through the material you generated. Did you discover a topic that might be interesting for your argument essay? Did you stumble over some interesting questions you'd like to explore further? Did anything you wrote or read make you *feel* something? Evaluate the raw material in your journal and keep the following things in mind as you zero in on a topic for your argument essay.

What's Promising Material and What Isn't? Let's take a critical look at the subjects you've generated so far. What promising topics might be lurking there for an argumentative essay? Consider some of the following as you make your choice.

- *Interest.* This almost goes without saying. But you were warned earlier about seizing on a topic if you already have strong convictions about it. Do you already know what you think? If so, why not choose a topic that initially invites more open-ended inquiry? On the other hand, it matters a lot whether you *care*. What topic might touch your life in some way? Do you have some kind of stake in how the questions are answered?

- *Focus.* One of the most common flaws of student drafts in all genres is that they attempt to cover too much territory. A more *limited* look at a larger landscape is always best. Because these argument essays are brief, consider topics that you can do justice to in less than a thousand words. As you review potential topics for your essay, can you see how some aspect of a larger question can be addressed by asking a smaller question? You can't write a short piece about the negative impact of affirmative action policies on the nation's colleges and universities, but you can write a brief op-ed about the specific impacts on your school.

- *Disagreement.* A topic lends itself to argumentative writing if it leads to disagreement among reasonable people. *Is smoking bad for your health?* was once a question that was debatable, but now pretty much everyone concedes that this question has been answered. *Did the Holocaust really happen?* is a question that only blockheads debate. But the question, *What are the motives of people who deny the Holocaust?* is a question that would generate a range of views.

- *Information.* Is sufficient information available on the topic for you to make a reasonable judgment about what is true? Is it accessible? One great advantage of choosing a local question as the focus for an argumentative essay is that often the people are close by and the relevant information can easily be had. It's also essential that you can obtain information from more than just a single viewpoint on the question.

- *Question.* What makes a topic arguable is that it raises questions to which there are multiple answers. Which of them makes the most sense is at issue. But some questions are merely informational. For example, *How do greenhouse gases contribute to global warming?* is a question that will likely lead to explanations rather than argument. On the other hand, *Is the U.S. rejection of the Kyoto accords on global warming a responsible policy?* is an arguable, rather than informational, question.

Questions About Audience and Purpose. Persuasive writing is a very audience-oriented form. *To whom* you make your case in an argument matters a lot in *how* you make it, but audience also matters in *whether* one topic is a better choice for an essay than another topic. The public argument is written for a more general audience. Your readers are unlikely to be experts on your topic, and they are likely to read your essay quickly rather than slowly and thoughtfully. What does this imply about the best subjects?

- *Do your readers have a stake in the question you're answering?* The word *stake* can be broadly considered. For example, a topic may directly affect the readers of your essay; say you're writing for fellow college students on your campus, all of whom pay tuition, and your topic addresses whether a 12 percent hike in fees is justified. Sometimes, however, you choose a topic because readers need to know that they *do* have a stake in how a question is answered. For instance, the argument that new antiterrorist rules threaten online privacy is something you believe your readers, most of whom surf the Web, should consider.

- *Can you identify what your readers might already believe?* One of the key strategies of persuasion is to find ways to link the values and attitudes of your audience with the position you're encouraging them to believe. Does your potential topic lend itself to this kind of analysis?

- *Is your purpose not only to inform readers but also to encourage them to believe or do something?* As you know by now, one of the things that distinguishes argument essays such as the op-ed piece from other forms of writing is the writer's intention to change his or her audience.

Research Considerations. While writing this argument essay does involve some research, it isn't exactly a research paper. A research paper is a much more extended treatment of a topic that relies on more detailed and scholarly information than is usually needed for an argument essay.

To develop a working knowledge of the topic for your public argument essay, focus your research on the following:

1. *The back-story:* What is the history of the controversy? When did it begin, who was involved, how was the issue addressed, what were the problems?

2. *Popular assumptions:* What do most people currently believe is true about the issue?

3. *The evidence:* Who has said what that seems to support your claim or provide backing for your assumptions?

4. *Opposing arguments:* Who offers a counterargument that you might need to consider?

Consider working through some of the following research strategies to find this information.

Researching on the Web

- Google (for relevant Web sites, online periodicals, and some newspapers)
- Google Scholar (if your topic is discussed by scholars)
- Google Blog Search (to get the gist of the public discussion of your topic)
- GPO Access (go to http://www.gpoaccess.gov/ to search for relevant federal documents)
- Online version of local newspaper (if your topic has a local angle)
- State and Local Government on the Net (go to http://www.statelocalgov.net/ if your topic is an issue of policy)

Researching in the Library

- General subject databases (these cover a wide range of subjects, and many include nonacademic publications as well)
- Newspaper databases (for example National Newspaper Index or Newspaper Source)
- Newspapers on microfilm (your university library might archive copies of the local paper on microfilm, going back for many years)

While both the Web and the university library are great sources of information on your topic, often the best way to learn about it—and get some good quotes for your essay—is to find someone to talk to. Your reading will probably give you the best clues about who to contact. Who is often quoted in news stories? Who has been writing or blogging about the issue? You might also be able to find someone on your own campus. If you're writing, say, about measures that attempt to protect students from date rape on your campus, someone in the Criminal Justice department or in Student Affairs can tell you more about the issue in a few minutes than you might learn in a couple hours online.

Narrowing the Question. I've been vaguely aware of the crisis in Medicaid funding—federal health care support for the poor—but the issue really came home when officials told Dorothy Misner, a ninety-two-year-old woman in nearby Nampa, that she would have to gum her food because the state refused to pay for dentures. Probably the best way to make a larger controversy a manageable writing topic is to find a local angle. In this case, for example, the larger question—*Should the national Medicaid program do more to support the poor without health insurance?*—becomes a much narrower question: *Is the state's Medicaid program failing people like Dorothy Misner?* Whenever possible, make big issues smaller by finding some connection to the local.

That isn't always possible, however. Unless you live in Alaska, for instance, the debate over development of the Arctic National Wildlife Refuge is hard to cut as a local issue. Then it becomes important to find a narrower question, something that may not be possible until after you've done a little research. For example, the question, *Should the Arctic National Wildlife Refuge be open to oil development?* could be narrowed by asking, *Are oil company claims about the potential of recoverable oil in the refuge reasonable?*

Another way to narrow the focus of an argument is to find a useful case study, anecdote, or example that somehow typifies some aspect of the issue you want to examine. Finally, do what journalists do: Peg your essay to a recent event related to the issue you're writing about. George Will's approach to many of his op-ed essays is to use a newly released study, report, academic article, or interview with an expert as the anchor for his piece. He then takes off on his own from there. Other events might include a relevant hearing, a protest, a court decision, a crime, an accident, and so on.

Writing the Sketch

Now draft a sketch of roughly 500 to 600 words with the following elements:

- It has a tentative title.
- It makes at least one claim and offers several reasons that support the claim.
- It presents and analyzes at least one contrasting point of view.
- The sketch includes specific evidence to support (or possibly complicate) the reasons offered in support of the claim, including *at least* several of the following: an anecdote or story, a personal observation, data, an analogy, a case study, expert testimony, other relevant quotations from people involved, or a precedent.

STUDENT SKETCH

Inspiring young voters isn't easy. In my own classes, I almost never hear younger students talk casually about elections. On the rare occasions that I actually see a button on a backpack for one candidate or another, I'm always a little surprised. Are young voters apathetic? And if they are, what should be done about it? Those were Ben Bloom's questions, both of which arose from a fastwrite. Here is his sketch on the topic. Where should he go from here? What should he research before the next draft? What should he consider that he doesn't consider here?

How to Really Rock the Vote
Ben Bloom

1   MTV sponsors "Rock the Vote." Presidential candidates swing through college campuses wearing blue jeans and going tieless. There's even an organization called "Kid's Vote" that tries to get high school students involved in the political process. It's pretty clear that student vote matters but are these efforts paying off?

2   It doesn't seem so. On my own campus, fewer than a few hundred students vote in the annual elections for the Student Senate. I can't even get my roommate to talk about the Presidential election, much less who's running for student body president.

3   What seems typical is the following comment from a college-age columnist: "On the issue of voter apathy, I look at myself first. I'm not even registered to vote, which is as apathetic as it gets. I do, however, educate myself about presidential candidates and their proposed policies—I just never have thought my one, lonesome vote could matter. I've neglected registering because it has never seemed logical to inconvenience myself, through the registration process, only to give another drop of water to an ocean (to add one vote to millions)."

4   "Never seemed logical to inconvenience" yourself to participate in the most basic part of the democratic process? Has it gotten this bad?

5   The student journalist above was responding to a survey that came out two years ago from a group called Project Vote Smart. It found what I suspected from my own experiences: young voters are staying away from the polls.

6   According to the study, there has been a decline in the numbers of 18- to 25-year-olds voting by 13% over the last twenty-five years. Actually, I think the situation is worse than that. The main reason they cite is that young people don't think their votes make a difference.

7   What should be done about this? How can we convince young voters to believe in the power of their vote? Are organizations like "Rock the Vote" or "Project Vote Smart" going to convince students like the guy who finds voting "inconvenient" that it's worth the effort?

8   In my opinion, celebrities and rock stars won't make a difference. The key is for political candidates to find a way to talk about issues so that young voters overcome their apathy and actually *feel* something. In the sixties, it was the draft. I'm not sure what the issues with emotional impact are these days. But the people who want students to vote have got to find them.

Moving from Sketch to Draft

A sketch is often sketchy. It's generally underdeveloped, sometimes giving the writer just the barest outline of his subject. But as an early draft, a sketch can be invaluable. It might hint at what the real subject is, or what questions seem to be behind your inquiry into the subject. A sketch might suggest a focus for the next draft, or simply a better lead. Here are some tips for finding clues in your sketch about directions you might go in the next draft.

Evaluating Your Own Sketch. You've read and written about an issue you care about. Now for the really hard part: getting out of your own head and into the heads of your potential readers, who may not care as much as you do. At least not yet. Successful persuasion fundamentally depends on giving an audience the right reasons to agree with you, and these are likely both logical and emotional, involving both *logos* and *pathos,* as you learned earlier in this chapter.

Another element of argument is the way the writer comes across to readers—his or her *ethos.* What's the ethos of your sketch? How might you be perceived by a stranger reading the sketch? Is your tone appealing, or might it be slightly off-putting? Do you successfully establish your authority to speak on this issue, or do you sense that the persona you project in the sketch is unconvincing, perhaps too emotional or not appearing fair?

As we develop convictions about an issue, one of the hardest things to manage in early argument drafts is creating a persuasive persona (*ethos*). Another is finding ways to establish connections with our audience; this does not merely involve connecting writers and readers but includes creating some common ground between readers and *the topic.* There are many ways to do this, including the following:

1. Connecting your readers' prior beliefs or values with your position on the topic.
2. Establishing that readers have a *stake,* perhaps even a personal one, in how the question you've raised is answered; this may be self-interest, but it may also be emotional (remember the advertiser's strategy).
3. Highlighting the common experiences readers may have had with the topic and offering your claim as a useful way of understanding that experience.

As you look over your sketch, evaluate how well you create this common ground between your topic and your intended audience. Might you revise it by exploiting one or more of the strategies listed here?

Finally, is there enough evidence to support the reasons you've provided to support your claims? Initial drafts commonly lack enough specifics. Do you see places in the sketch that could be developed with specific information in the next draft?

Questions for Peer Review. Because the argument essay is such an audience-oriented form, these initial peer reviews of your sketch are invaluable in helping you get your bearings. Much of what you might have felt about how you managed the ethos and connections with readers can be confirmed or challenged by this first public reading. Ask your workshop group some of the following questions:

- How is the *ethos* of the sketch? Do I come across in the sketch as an advocate for my position? For example, am I *passionate, preachy, reasonable, one-sided, sympathetic, overbearing, intimate, detached, objective, subjective, uncaring, empathetic, humorous, serious, angry, mellow, contemptuous, approachable, patronizing, respectful, thoughtful, presumptuous, fair*, or *judgmental*?

- In your own words, what do you think was my central claim?

- Which reasons did you find most convincing? Which were least convincing?

- What do you think was the best evidence I offered in support of my reasons? Where exactly did you feel that you needed more evidence?

- What were the stated or unstated "warrants" or assumptions behind the claims? What do you need to assume is true to believe in their validity?

Reflecting on What You've Learned. Spend a few minutes following your peer review workshop to generate a list of everything you heard, and then begin a five-minute fastwrite that explores your reaction to these suggestions and your tentative plan for revision. In particular, what will you change? What will you add, and what will you cut in the next draft? What problems were raised that you don't yet know how to solve? What problems *weren't* raised that you expected might be? Do you still need to worry about them? End your fastwrite by writing about what you understand now about your topic, and your initial beliefs about it, that you didn't fully understand when you began writing about it.

Research and Other Strategies: Gathering More Information

Here's a mortifying thought: You've completely changed your mind about what you think about your topic and what you want to say in your argument. That's unsettling, but it's also a sign that you're willing to allow things to get a bit messy before they get sorted out. This is good because it's much more likely to result in an essay that gets at the truth of what you feel than if you doggedly stick to a particular point of view, come what may. If you *have* changed your mind, you have a lot of collecting to do. Return to the Web sites of current publications and search for information that might be relevant to your emerging idea.

Another research strategy can be helpful whether you change your mind or not: the interview. People who are somehow involved in your topic are among the best sources of new information and lively material. An interview can provide ideas about what else you should read or who else you might talk to, and it can be a source of quotations, anecdotes, and even case studies that will make the next draft of your argument essay much more interesting. After all, what makes an issue matter is how it affects people. Have you sufficiently dramatized those effects?

When appropriate, you can also add images to dramatize your claims or your evidence. They're easier than ever to find on nearly any subject using on-line services like Google Image Search. But they must be relevant. Figure 8, for example, is an ad by the National Eating Disorders Association that focuses on the relationship between our genetic disposition to be a certain body size.

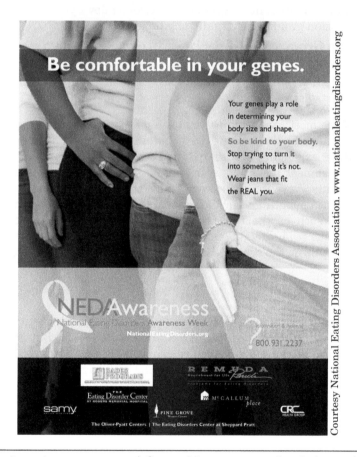

Figure 8   Sometimes your research for a public argument will include visual sources. This poster for National Eating Disorders Awareness Week reads, "Be comfortable in your genes. Your genes play a role in determining your body size and shape. So be kind to your body. Stop trying to turn it into something it's not. Wear jeans that fit the REAL you."
Source: http://www.gurze.com/productdetails.cfm?PC=1588 National Eating Disorders Association, http://www.nationaleatingdisorders.org/index.php

Imagine if the image was dropped into an argument essay—or a PowerPoint presentation—that argued for the strong influence of an "obesity gene."

The Internet can also be a source for interview material. Look for e-mail links to the authors of useful documents you find on the Web and write to them with a few questions. Interest groups, newsgroups, or electronic mailing lists on the Web can also provide the voices and perspectives of people with something to say on your topic. Remember to ask permission to quote them if you decide to use something in your draft. For leads on finding Web discussion groups on your topic, visit the following sites:

- **Google Groups,** http://groups.google.com, allows you to search for online discussion groups on virtually any topic.
- **Yahoo Groups** offers a similar service, allowing you to search for groups by keyword. Find it at http://groups.yahoo.com.
- **Catalist,** the official catalog of electronic mailing lists, http://www.lsoft. com/lists/listref.html, has a database of about 15,000 discussion groups.

One of the most useful things you can do to prepare for the draft is to spend forty-five minutes at the campus library searching for new information on your topic. Consider expanding your search from current newspapers and periodicals to books or government publications. In addition, you can refer to almanacs such as *Infoplease* (http://www.infoplease.com) and the *CIA World Factbook* (http:// www.odci.gov/cia/publications/factbook/) as well as statistical information available from sources such as the U.S. Census Bureau's *American Fact Finder* (http:// factfinder.census.gov/home/saff/main.html?_lang=en), which is a wonderful resource that draws on the agency's massive database of information on U.S. trends.

Composing the Draft

As always, it's best to work from abundance rather than scarcity. If you don't have enough evidence to support your argument, find more. But if you're feeling reasonably well prepared to develop your argument essay from a sketch (or proposal) to a longer draft, then begin by crafting a strong lead. There are so many ways to begin an essay like this one; which is best? As always, think of a beginning that might not only interest your readers in your topic but also hints at or states your purpose in writing about it. Through tone, your beginning also establishes your relationship with your readers. Here's instructor Andrew Merton's lead in "The Guys Are Dumbing Down," a piece that argues that students' baseball caps in class indicate something other than studiousness.

> Here is the big social note from the campus of the University of New Hampshire, where I teach: Dumbing down is in. For guys.

Merton's tone is a strong element of this lead. He begins casually—"Here is the big social note..."—suggesting some friendly, almost chatty relationship with his readers. This lead also does what many argument essay beginnings do: It states the writer's main claim. You may assume it is always required to state your thesis in your introduction, but this isn't true at all. Some argument essays, especially op-ed pieces, have a delayed thesis, in which the writer works methodically toward his or her point. Which approach should you use in your draft? In part, that depends on your method of development.

Methods of Development. What are some of the ways you might organize the next draft?

Narrative. Telling a story is an underrated way of developing an argument. Can you imagine a way to turn your topic into an extended story, perhaps by focusing on the experience of a particular person or group of people, in a particular place, at a particular time? Somehow the story must be logically linked to your claim; obviously, just any old story won't do.

There are other ways to use narrative, too. Anecdotes, or brief stories used to illustrate an idea or a problem, are frequently used in argument essays. One effective way to begin your essay might be to tell a story that highlights the problem you're writing about or the question you're posing.

Question to Answer. Almost all writing is an attempt to answer a question. In the personal essay and other open forms of inquiry, the writer may never arrive at a definite answer, but an argument essay usually offers an answer. An obvious method of development, therefore, is to begin your essay by raising the question and end it by offering your answer.

Are there several key questions around which you might organize your draft, leading to your central claim at the end?

Problem to Solution. This is a variation on the question-to-answer structure. But it might be a particularly useful organization strategy if you're writing about a topic readers may know very little about. In that case, you might need to spend as much time establishing what exactly the problem is—explaining what makes it a problem and why the reader should care about it—as you do offering your particular solution.

Effect to Cause or Cause to Effect. At the heart of some arguments is the *relationship* between two things, and often what is at issue is pinpointing the real causes for certain undesirable effects. Once these causes are identified, then the best solutions can be offered. Sadly, we know the effects of terrorism, but what are its causes? If you argue, as some do, that Islamic radicalism arose in response to U.S. policies toward Israel and the Palestinians, then the solution offered might be a shift in foreign policy. The international debate over global warming, for some participants, is really an argument about causes and effects. If you don't believe, for example, that U.S. contributions to atmospheric carbon dioxide in the next ten years will match contributions from the developing world, then the U.S. refusal to sign the Kyoto treaty—one proposed solution—may not matter that much. Some arguments like these can be organized simply around an examination of causes and effects.

Combining Approaches. As you think about how you might organize your first draft, you don't necessarily have to choose between narrative, problem-to-solution, or cause-to-effect structures. In fact, most often they work well together.

Using Evidence. All writing relies on evidence, usually some specific information in relationships with general ideas (see the "Inquiring into the Details: What Evidence Can Do" box). Evidence in an argumentative essay often has a *particular* relationship to ideas; most often it is offered to support ideas the writer wants the reader to believe. What *kind* of evidence to include is a rhetorical question. To whom are you writing, and what kind of evidence will they be more likely to believe? Generally speaking, the narrower and more specialized the audience, the more particular they will be about the types of evidence they'll find convincing.

For example, as you write more academic papers in your chosen major, the types of evidence that will help you make a persuasive argument will be more and more prescribed by the field. In the natural sciences, the results of quantitative studies count more than case studies; in the humanities, primary texts count more than secondary ones. The important thing for this argument essay, which you're writing for a more general audience, is that you attempt to *vary* your evidence. Rather than relying exclusively on anecdotes, include some quotes from an expert as well.

INQUIRING INTO THE DETAILS

What Evidence Can Do

Usually we think of using evidence only to support an idea or claim we're making. But evidence can be used in other ways, too. For example, it can do the following:

- *support* an idea, observation, or assertion
- *refute* or challenge a claim with which you disagree
- *show* that a seemingly simple assertion, problem, or idea is really more complex
- *complicate* or even contradict an earlier point you've made
- *contrast* two or more ways of seeing the same thing
- *test* an idea, hypothesis, or theory

Workshopping the Draft

If your draft is subject to peer review, you may want to organize workshop groups and decide on how your group can help you. The following journal activities and questions should help you make the most of your opportunity to get peer feedback on your work in progress.

Reflecting on the Draft. After you've finished the draft, prepare for peer review by making a journal entry that explores your experience writing the essay.

- What proved hardest?
- What most surprised you about the process?
- What did you find particularly gratifying? What was especially frustrating?
- How did your process for writing this type of essay differ from writing the personal essay or some other form?
- If you were going to start all over again, what would you do differently?

Discuss the insights that might have emerged from this open-ended writing in class or in your workshop group. After your draft has been discussed, make some notes in your journal in response to the following questions:

- What most surprised you about your group's response to your essay?
- What did you hear that most made you want to write again?
- What specifically do you think you need to do in the next draft?

Questions for Readers. Here are some questions that might prompt members of your workshop group to offer helpful advice on your argument draft.

1. What was the most interesting part of the draft? What was the least interesting?
2. What did you believe about my topic before you read the draft? What did you believe after you read it?
3. What reason most strongly supported my main point? What reason seemed the weakest?
4. What was the most convincing evidence I offered? What was the least convincing?

Revising the Draft

Revision is a continual process—not a last step. You've been revising—literally "re-seeing" your subject—from the first messy fastwriting in your journal. But the things that get your attention during revision vary depending on where you are in the writing process. You've generated material, chosen a topic, done some research, and written both a sketch and draft. Most students think that the only thing left to do is "fix things." Check for misspellings. Correct an awkward

WRITING IN THE DISCIPLINES

Argument in Academic Disciplines

Arguing is the main way that academic communities make knowledge. While the process for developing and making an argument can be applied in any discipline, the types of evidence and the forms of arguments can vary widely from one discipline to another. Knowing what kind of knowledge is valued in a particular discipline can help you to shape effective academic arguments as you move from subject to subject throughout your college career.

Discipline	Common Types of Argument	Valued Evidence
humanities	interpretive essays textual analyses reviews formal arguments	textual details personal observations and experience historical background personal insights biographical evidence about authors and creators ethnographic (small-scale) studies
social sciences	causal analyses historical trends projections about effects of policies	demographics and statistics research data large-scale studies interviews
natural sciences	lab reports experimental studies	experimental data quantitative data visual information
applied sciences	feasibility reports recommendations and proposals	quantitative data research data field research findings firsthand observations
business	proposals	case studies survey data

sentence or two. Come up with a better title. This is editing, not revision, and while editing is important, to focus solely on smaller "fixes" after writing a first draft squanders an opportunity to really *learn* from what the draft is telling you, or perhaps not quite telling you.

GUIDE TO REVISION STRATEGIES

Problems in the Draft

Unclear purpose
- Not sure what the paper is about?

Unclear thesis, theme, or main idea
- Not sure what you're trying to say?

Lack of information or development
- Need more convincing evidence? Need to check for logical fallacies?

Disorganized
- Doesn't move logically or smoothly from paragraph to paragraph?

Unclear or awkward at the level of sentences and paragraphs
- Seems choppy or hard to follow at the level of sentences or paragraphs?

The questions you can ask about a draft fall into five categories: purpose, idea, information, development, and editing. Use the Guide to Revision Strategies chart above to find revision strategies that might help you re-see what you've written so far.

Draft argument essays have some typical problems at this stage in the process. Do any of these apply to yours?

- Is your central claim or thesis stated clearly?
- Do you employ any logical fallacies? See "Inquiring into the Details: Common Logical Fallacies."
- Do you have sufficient evidence or information to make your assertions convincing? Do you need to gather more facts?
- Have you considered any counterarguments in your essay? This is especially important if you think the audience for your essay might not be inclined to initially agree with your position.
- Have you clearly established what stake your readers have in the issue you're writing about?
- Does the draft use *pathos, logos*, and *ethos* effectively? (See Figure 1.)

Polishing the Draft

After you've dealt with the big issues in your draft—is it sufficiently focused, does it answer the *So what?* question, is it well organized, and so on—you must deal with the smaller problems. You've carved the stone into an appealing figure, but now you need to polish it. Are your paragraphs coherent? How do you manage transitions? Are your sentences fluent and concise? Are there any errors in spelling or syntax?

Before you finish your draft, work through the following checklist:

- ✓ Every paragraph is about one thing.
- ✓ The transitions between paragraphs aren't abrupt.
- ✓ The length of sentences varies in each paragraph.
- ✓ Each sentence is concise. There are no unnecessary words or phrases.
- ✓ You've checked grammar, particularly verb agreement, run-on sentences, unclear pronouns, and misused words (*there/their, where/were,* and so on). (See the handbook at the back of the text for help with these grammar issues.)
- ✓ You've run your spellchecker and proofed your paper for misspelled words.

STUDENT ESSAY

Many Americans are fond of talking about our country's native people in the past tense. We admire the tribal cultures as they existed a century or two ago, and borrow freely from them, engaging in "vision quests" and drumming circles. We feel the tug of nostalgia for these lost tribes, and yes, guilt for the sad history of relations between the mostly white immigrants who dispossessed the tribes and the Indian people who were confined to reservations. It's convenient to assume that the problems were in the past because contemporary Native Americans are largely invisible to us—except if you happen to drive through a reservation as Kelly Sundberg would on her way to visit friends at a nearby university.

Confronting Native Americans in the present tense forced Kelly to examine her own prejudices, and in the essay that follows she argues that the route to understanding begins at school.

I Am Not a Savage

Kelly Sundberg

1   Salmon, Idaho, is named after the river that runs through it, a river that is filled with turbulent whitewater punctuated by deep and calm pools and shallow riffles. In the spring, I have looked into these riffles and seen waves of silver and red moving gently just underneath the surface of the water.

2   We call them "reds"—spawning salmon. Nowadays, they are diminished in numbers, but at one time the river was full of them, and full of abundance as well for the

Lemhi Indians who once lived on the banks. For the Lemhi, the salmon was not solely for sustenance, but also an integral part of their culture and spirituality.

Today there are few "reds" and almost no Lemhi left in the valley. 3

The initial influx of Mormon settlers followed by migrations of Californians and 4 Midwesterners forced Native Americans out of the valley. Still, upon entering the Salmon city limits from Highway 28, a large sign proclaims, "Welcome to Salmon, Idaho. Birthplace of Sacagawea!" In a time when anything related to Lewis and Clark means profit, the city of Salmon, my hometown, has now chosen to capitalize on this marketable heritage, even though they once ignored it or treated it derisively.

My high school mascot is the "Salmon Savage." The marquee in front of the school has 5 a picture with an Indian warrior on it, and when the football team scores a touchdown a white girl wearing war paint and a "made in China" headdress will ride a horse around the track in celebration.

I never questioned the integrity or intent of these symbols until I was a sophomore at 6 the school. For Civil Rights Day, the school invited Rosa Abrahamson, a Lemhi Indian, to speak to the students. She cried as she spoke about the injustice of the name "savage." "My people are not savages," she said. "We are peaceful and do not take pride in that name." When she finished speaking the applause was polite but subdued.

The next speaker was a rancher named Bud, who lit into a tirade about the govern- 7 ment subsidizing "lazy Indians." As he finished with fists raised into the air, he was greeted by a standing ovation. For the first time in my life, I felt ashamed to be a part of the community.

It wasn't that those of us in the gym had consciously made the decision to be racist. It 8 was simply ignorance. Despite the history of the Lemhi in the valley, our ideas of their culture are shaped from drives through the reservation on the way to campus visits at the University of Idaho. Our perceptions were safely gleaned from inside of an automobile and never involved real interaction with Native Americans.

Once, when asked to write our opinions about reservations in a U.S. government class, 9 I wrote that I thought the government was making it "too easy on the Native Americans and they had become apathetic and unmotivated because of subsidies."

I got a better glimpse at my Lemhi neighbors recently reading Sherman Alexie's 10 novel *The Lone Ranger and Tonto Fistfight in Heaven*. Alexie, a member of the Spokane/ Coeur d'Alene tribes, conveys the opposition between contemporary and traditional Native American culture. His characters are torn and struggle to reconcile the two: "At the halfway point of any drunken night, there is a moment when an Indian realizes he cannot turn back toward tradition and that he has no map to guide him toward the future."

My own community struggles to reconcile two conflicting ideas as well—we embrace 11 the symbols of savagery to inspire the football team, yet in order to make a profit we proudly claim Sacagawea as one of our own. Still, when the Lemhi wanted to build a school near Sacagawea's birthplace, the county refused to sell them the land, claiming it would become a "mini-reservation."

(continued)

(continued)

12   Ironically, Salmon shares more than it cares to admit with its neighbors on the reservation. Poverty, alcoholism, and depression are a way of life for many Salmon residents. Yet the perception in the community is that an alcoholic white man is somehow superior to a "drunk Indian."

13   In Salmon, all students are required to take an Idaho history class, yet this class makes almost no mention of Native American history in the valley. None of the readings in Advanced Placement English classes are by Native American authors, and government classes don't address Native American issues at all.

14   Is it any wonder that racism persists?

15   The local school system needs to lead. English teachers should require readings by authors like Alexie, they should provide field trips to local and national archeological sites, and they should bring in Native American interpreters to speak about local history. By letting go of negative and outdated ideas, the city of Salmon and the Lemhi can take the first step toward healing.

Evaluating the Essay

Discuss or write about your response to Kelly Sundberg's essay using some or all of the following questions:

1. What is the thesis of the essay? Where in the piece is it most clearly stated?

2. Refer to the box that lists ten common logical fallacies and reread Sundberg's essay. Do you suspect there are any logical fallacies in "I Am Not a Savage"?

3. Consider the *ethos* of this essay. How does the writer come across? Is her persona effective?

4. What do you think is the most effective paragraph in the essay? Why? What is the least effective?

USING WHAT YOU HAVE LEARNED

You've read published op-ed essays and a student draft. You've also worked on your own argument essay, a genre that may be new to you. Take a moment to consider how you might use what you've learned.

1. Reflect on how your thinking about argument and argumentative writing may have changed because of the reading and writing in this chapter by finishing the following sentence in your journal at least four times: Before I began this chapter I thought _____, but now I think _____.

2. The personal essay and the argument essay might seem at first to be fundamentally different kinds of writing. Do you see any connections between the two genres now?

3. Examine the letters to the editor or the editorials in your local newspaper. How do you read these pages differently after studying and writing an argument? Clip a letter or editorial that might best demonstrate what you've learned.

WRITING A RESEARCH ESSAY

From Chapter 10 of *The Curious Writer*, Third Edition. Bruce Ballenger. Copyright © 2011 by Pearson Education, Inc. Published by Pearson Longman.

Mill

What is the relationship between jazz and African music? How is jazz related to hymns and spirituals? Is there a connection between jazz and the history of slavery? Questions like these motivate effective research projects. The best reason to investigate something is because you genuinely wonder about it.

Viesti Associates, Inc.

WRITING A RESEARCH ESSAY

WRITING WITH RESEARCH

Let's be honest. Most students hate writing research papers. There are exceptions, of course, and these are invariably students who see in a research-based essay the same thing they see in other writing they enjoy: an opportunity to discover something new and share it with someone else. In contrast, students who dislike research-based writing usually share the following assumptions:

- Whenever "facts" are required in a paper, the writing is generally boring.

- The research paper is a unique genre of writing, different from other forms, with its own special rules.

- No matter what the instructor says, the student's own opinions aren't really very important in a research paper.

With these assumptions in mind, I should clarify a few things now about the research essay. The most important is this: *The research essay shares qualities with all of the inquiry projects you've written to this point, whether it's a profile, a proposal, or a personal essay. In fact, the research essay is a natural extension of all of these other essays.* Research is something writers naturally do whenever they have questions they can't answer on their own. Every inquiry project in this text emphasizes the importance of research *throughout* the writing process.

What You'll Learn in This Chapter

- How to apply what you've learned about writing shorter inquiry-based papers to an extended research project.
- Which beliefs about research you may want to "unlearn."
- How to distinguish between academic research genres.
- Techniques for reading academic articles.
- How to discover a "researchable" question.
- How to focus your essay.

However, the research essay does present a few differences: First, the research essay may be the most thoroughly documented of the essays you've written so far, and it may be the one that is most likely to require scholarly sources such as journal articles and academic books. It's also likely to be a project that takes more time to do, and may be the longest essay you're assigned, ranging from eight to twenty pages. A writing project with such an extended process of inquiry is more complicated to manage—it has more steps, you have more information to organize, and it's often harder to figure out what you want to say. For all of these reasons, the research essay is a form of inquiry that deserves special attention.

> Research is something writers naturally do whenever they have questions they can't answer on their own.

Still, research is hardly something alien to you. You've written research essays before, and although you probably don't consider yourself a researcher, for most of us research is a daily affair, whether looking up the details on new laptop computers in order to buy the right one or hunting for a new apartment in a highly competitive real estate market. Finally, research need not be boring at all. On the contrary, reading, observing, and interviewing can crack open worlds of study you never imagined.

RESEARCH ESSAYS, RESEARCH PAPERS, AND RESEARCH REPORTS

While any piece of writing can be researched—including things like short stories, blogs, and personal essays—academic research assignments typically fall into one of three categories: research reports, research papers, and research essays (see Figure 1). The least common of these in college is the research

	Research Report	Research Paper	Research Essay
Purpose	To explain	To prove	To discover
Thesis	None	Up front	Delayed
Documentation	Yes	Yes	Usually
Organization	Summary-explanation	Thesis-support	Question-answer
Use of "I"	No	Sometimes	Usually
Inquiry	Low	High	Highest

Figure 1   Three genres of academic research

report. This is the familiar paper many of us wrote in high school that simply explains—Wikipedia-like—what is known about some topic. The writer of a research report isn't trying to *use* the information to make a point or investigate a question.

A far more common (and useful) college writing assignment is the research paper, a term that is loosely used to describe an essay that is an extended argument on some topic. It's like an essay you might have tackled previously—the public argument—except that the research paper leans much more heavily on outside sources and is intended for a more academic audience. Its goal is to prove a thesis using the evidence the writer gathers.

The research essay is the most inquiry-based of the three genres. While the research paper certainly can involve an open-ended investigation, the paper itself usually reports conclusions rather than the questions that gave rise to them. Both the research paper and research essay have a thesis, but in the essay it might appear late in the work, as the writer works through questions and evidence to arrive at an understanding of the topic. While it may be a less common assignment than the argumentative research paper, the research essay is much more likely to encourage the habits of mind that encourage genuine inquiry. It invites writers to begin with questions rather than answers, to suspend judgment, and accept that ambiguity—even confusion—is a natural part of the research process.

> The research essay is likely to encourage the habits of mind that encourage genuine inquiry and accepting ambiguity as a natural part of the process.

In the three professional readings that follow in this chapter, you'll get a chance to see the range of approaches to research writing, from the informal and undocumented researched essay to the formal research paper. Most of these readings focus on a single subject—courtship and sexuality on the American college campus—which will help you appreciate how the different forms of research writing offer different ways of examining a subject.

MOTIVES FOR WRITING A RESEARCH ESSAY

I was in the market for a new guitar, and for several weeks I'd been studying back issues of an acoustic guitar magazine, searching the Web for guitar makers, and talking to people who play. My process was driven by particular questions I had: What are the best tone woods for a classical guitar? *What are the various models and how much do they cost? What are the sound qualities to consider when selecting an instrument?* While I probably would never write an essay using my research, the stakes were rather high. I was likely to spend a lot of money on a guitar and I didn't want to make a mistake.

Although everyday research may not be as methodical as academic research, both approaches employ many of the same skills and share the same motive: curiosity. Sometimes this curiosity is intellectual interest—What are the origins of radical Islam?—and sometimes it's in response to a need for information: What is the best-quality acoustic guitar? Either way, the process begins as all inquiry projects do, with a question.

Not just any question will do. It has to be one that will drive the process for the few weeks it takes for you to learn about your topic and know enough to discover your own ideas about it. For example, the question, "Is Elvis dead?" will take about a second to answer: Yes, the King is dead. Why people keep asking that particular question is much more interesting and a more researchable question that just might work for an extended investigation. But whatever question you ask, it must be interesting to *you*.

Academic researchers *always* ask questions that interest them; curiosity is the most important motive. It should be for you, too. The essential thing you must learn about research writing is how to craft a good question that makes you wonder enough to live with the question long enough for you to write on it. This takes more skill than you might imagine, but once you know how to ask researchable questions, you'll be much more likely to see research writing the way your professors do—an opportunity for discovery.

THE RESEARCH ESSAY AND ACADEMIC WRITING

The research paper is a fixture in high school courses, usually lodged in the junior or senior English class and advertised as preparation for The College Research Paper. (Even my nine-year-old daughter wrote research papers.) Research-based writing assignments are probably among the most common in college, across the curriculum. In fact, at my own university almost three-quarters of the faculty surveyed said they assign an "academic paper that requires research." That's one reason you're writing a research essay in your composition class—to help prepare you to write papers in other courses.

These writing assignments can take a number of forms, including term papers, proposals, literature reviews, abstracts, and reports. But they all demand facility with finding information in the library, on the Web, or in the field; the skills to evaluate the information you have uncovered; and the ability to *use* that information appropriately and purposefully. Because research writing involves dealing with all of these things—something like a novice juggler trying to keep five balls in the air—even talented writers can see their prose fall apart when trying to communicate their findings. Additionally, the writers' beliefs and assumptions may make it harder to get the work done, and their beliefs and assumptions may even be misleading, if not downright wrong.

Some years ago, I surveyed about 250 first-year writing students about the research paper assignment, and at least 60 percent of them shared the following beliefs:

- "I have to be objective."
- "I have to know my thesis before I start."
- "I need to follow a formal structure."
- "I can't use 'I'."

There is an element of truth to each of these, but each of these beliefs *works against* a genuine understanding of what it means to do academic research. Then what *is* the nature of academic research and the research essay?

FEATURES OF THE FORM

There's quite a range of research-based writing. Nearly every assignment you've done so far in *The Curious Writer* might be considered research based; reading, interviewing, and observing could be elements of any of the inquiry projects you've attempted. But the research essay has a few distinctive features:

- *Academic research is driven by questions, not answers.* Most scholarship begins with a question about something: What is the impact of congressional redistricting on representation of minorities? What are the various ways the river might be understood symbolically in *Huckleberry Finn*? What is the distribution of bracken fern in a mature upland forest? What are the rhetorical strategies of pro-anorexia groups on the Web? Researchers begin with a question, not an answer, and although they may hypothesize, researchers are always prepared to be proved wrong. Framing the question is a crucial and often difficult part of the process.

- *The question is put in the context of what has already been said.* You're interested in whether so-called relational aggression between girls might be present in your niece's second-grade classroom. That's a great research question. What have others already said about it? How might the answers to your question contribute to the ongoing conversation about how young girls treat each other? This often means that you will need to become familiar with the published conversation about your topic, a step in the research process called a literature review.

- *Source material is used in the service of what writers are trying to say about their topics.* Research essays are not like encyclopedia entries or the research reports you may have written in high school. They do not merely present information gathered from source material. Instead, they actively *use* the information to explore or answer questions or to test the truth of an idea or thesis. In this sense, the research essay is very much like the other kinds of essays you have written so far.

- *Sources that contributed to a writer's thinking are formally given credit.* The larger purpose of academic inquiry is to make new knowledge, to contribute in some way to what people understand about how the world works. This always involves standing on the shoulders of others who have already said something about your topic, and this is something that you acknowledge explicitly through citation. While citation has all sorts of conventions, and yes, it can be a pain, the acknowledgment of your sources is both a gracious gesture and a source of authority for you—it indicates that you're party to the ongoing conversation about your topic. Accurately acknowledging your sources is also an ethical obligation that all good researchers take seriously.

- *Most research essays have a clearly stated thesis.* Like a long train, research essays carry a lot of freight and they must stay on track. One way to do this is to clearly organize the information you gather around an explicit focusing question. This question should lead readers to some answers, particularly one main idea, claim, or thesis that seems most persuasive to the writer. While some formal research papers state this thesis in the introduction, research essays typically have a "delayed" thesis that may be stated somewhere near the end.

- *Research essays typically use four sources of information.* Nonfiction writing draws on four sources of information: memory or experience, observation, interviews, and reading. It's not unusual to read a personal essay that relies solely on the writer's memory of an experience as a source of information. A profile might use two or three sources, including observation and interview. But a research essay may draw information from *all four* sources. Writers cast as wide a net as possible to discover the answers to their questions.

READINGS

■ UNDOCUMENTED RESEARCH ESSAY

You will read Brian Doyle's essay "Joyas Voladoras" and will think, "Surely, this is not a research paper," and you would be partly right. The reading that follows was not written for specialists, and does not have the ambition of much academic writing to contribute to an ongoing conversation in a discipline. For this reason, it doesn't have citations. But "Joyas Voladoras" is an essay that relies on research, and a lot of it. The great wonder is how such a lovely, moving essay isn't ruined by facts, as we might expect. Consider that as you read Doyle's essay.

Whenever we write about a subject as large as the human capacity for love—what Doyle calls the "house of the heart"—it's easy to lose our footing in the specific and the concrete and drift, like people in a hot air balloon, up into the thin air of abstraction or generalization. This is particularly easy to do in research writing. There is so much terrain, so much to cover, and so much to know! Doyle's essay demonstrates how to avoid this. He finds a focus in the particulars of a hummingbird's "racecar heart," which becomes the tiniest window into his meditation on love and connection. Doyle helps us to see big things *through* small ones. This is the goal of much research as well, whether it's sampling invertebrates to make a judgment on the health of a creek or sorting through information and claims about how Facebook might affect friendship.

Mostly, though, it's inspiring to encounter researched writing like "Joyas Voladoras" that reminds us that what we learn from others can help us discover more about ourselves.

Joyas Voladoras

Brian Doyle

Consider the hummingbird for a long moment. A hummingbird's heart beats ten times a second. A hummingbird's heart is the size of the pencil eraser. A hummingbird's heart is a lot of the hummingbird. *Joyas voladoras,* flying jewels, the first white explorers in the Americas called them, and the white men had never seen such creatures, for hummingbirds came into the world only in the Americas, nowhere else in the universe, more than three hundred species of them whirring and zooming and nectaring in hummer time zones nine times removed from ours, their hearts hammering faster than we could clearly hear if we pressed our elephantine ears to their infinitesimal chests.

Each one visits a thousand flowers a day. They can dive at sixty miles an hour. They can fly backward. They can fly more than five hundred miles without pausing to

(continued)

(continued)

rest. But when they rest they come close to death: on frigid nights, or when they are starving, they retreat into torpor, their metabolic rate slowing to a fifteenth of their normal sleep rate, their hearts sludging nearly to a halt, barely beating, and if they are not soon warmed, if they do not soon find that which is sweet, their hearts grow cold, and they cease to be. Consider for a moment those hummingbirds who did not open their eyes again today, this very day, in the Americas: bearded helmeterests and booted racket-tails, voilet-tailed sylphs and violet-capped woodnymphs, crimson topazes and purple-crowned fairies, red-tailed comets and amethyst woodstars, rainbow-bearded thornbills and glittering-bellied emeralds, velvet-purple coronets and golden-bellied star-frontlets, fiery-tailed awlbills and Andean hillstars, spatuletails and pufflegs, each the most amazing thing you have never seen, each thundcrous wild heart the size of an infant's fingernail, each mad heart silent, a brilliant music stilled.

3   Hummingbirds, like all flying birds but more so, have incredible enormous immense ferocious metabolisms. To drive those metabolisms they have racecar hearts that eat oxygen at an eye-popping rate. Their hearts are built of thinner, leaner fibers than ours. Their arteries are stiffer and more taut. They have more mitochondria in their heart muscles—anything to gulp more oxygen. Their hearts are stripped to the skin for the war against gravity and inertia, the mad search for food, the insane idea of flight. The price of their ambition is a life closer to death; they suffer more heart attacks and aneurysms and ruptures than any other living creature. It's expensive to fly. You burn out. You fry the machine. You melt the engine. Every creature on earth has approximately two billion heartbeats to spend in a lifetime. You can spend them slowly, like a tortoise, and live to be two hundred years old, or you can spend them fast, like a hummingbird, and live to be two years old.

4   The biggest heart in the word is inside the blue whale. It weighs more than seven tons. It's as big as a room. It *is* a room, with four chambers. A child could walk around in it, head high, bending only to step through the valves. The valves are as big as the swinging doors in a saloon. This house of a heart drives a creature a hundred feet long. When this creature is born it is twenty feet long and weighs four tons. It is waaaaay bigger than your car. It drinks a hundred gallons of milk from its mama every day and gains two hundred pounds a day, and when it is seven or eight years old it endures an unimaginable puberty and then it essentially disappears from human ken, for next to nothing is known of the mating habits, travel patterns, diet, social life, language, social structure, diseases, spirituality, wars, stories, despairs, and arts of the blue whale. There are perhaps ten thousand blue whales in the world, living in every ocean on earth, and of the largest mammal who ever lived we know nearly nothing. But we know this: the animals with the largest hearts in the world generally travel in pairs, and their penetrating moaning cries, their piercing yearning tongue, can be heard underwater for miles and miles.

5   Mammals and birds have hearts with four chambers. Reptiles and turtles have hearts with three chambers. Fish have hearts with two chambers. Insects and mollusks have hearts with one chamber. Worms have hearts with one chamber, although they

may have as many as eleven single-chambered hearts. Unicellular bacteria have no hearts at all; but even they have fluid eternally in motion, washing from one side of the cell to the other, swirling and whirling. No living being is without interior liquid motion. *We all churn inside.*

So much held in a heart in a lifetime. So much held in a heart in a day, an hour, a moment. We are utterly open with no one, in the end—not mother and father, not wife or husband, not lover, not child, not friend. *We open windows to each but we live alone in the house of the* heart. Perhaps we must. Perhaps we could not bear to be so naked, for fear of a constantly harrowed heart. When young we think there will come one person who will savor and sustain us always; when we are older we know this is the dream of a child, that all hearts finally are bruised and scarred, scored and torn, repaired by time and will, patched by force of character, yet fragile and rickety forevermore, no matter how ferocious the defense and how many bricks you bring to the wall. You can brick up your heart as stout and tight and hard and cold and impregnable as you possibly can and down it comes in an instant, felled by a woman's second glance, a child's apple breath, the shatter of glass in the road, the words "I have something to tell you," a cat with a broken spine dragging itself into the forest to die, the brush of your mother's papery ancient hand in the thicket of your hair, the memory of your father's voice early in the morning echoing from the kitchen where he is making pancakes for his children.

6

"Joyas Voladoras" by Brian Doyle. Reprinted by permission of the author.

Inquiring into the Essay

Explore, explain, evaluate, and reflect on "Joyas Voladoras."

1. At the end of his essay, Doyle writes, "We open windows to each but we live alone in the house of the heart." Does this ring true for you? In your journal, tell yourself a story about a time when you tried to do more than open windows and invited someone into the "house of your heart." Write fast for five full minutes. Now skip a line, and write a text message to Doyle that responds to his sentence based on what you've learned from your own fastwriting.

2. Make a list of at least four methods or techniques that Doyle uses to keep the many facts in "Joyas Voladoras" from making it dull reading. Or if you think it *is* dull, explain why using two relevant passages from the essay.

3. What is the implicit argument in this essay? Do you agree with it?

4. Like many research essays, the thesis in "Joyas Voladoras" comes toward the end of the piece rather than at the beginning. Reflect on other ways in which you might distinguish this piece from more conventional research papers. What can you learn from Doyle's essay that might apply to academic research writing?

■ DOCUMENTED RESEARCH ESSAY

When I went to college in the seventies, dating was dead but "hooking up," at least in its current meaning, was not all that common. Though the "sexual revolution" of the sixties still resonated on campuses thirty years ago, people generally were still interested in commitment when they sought intimacy. However, I dated in high school, as did most of my friends. There were dances, dinners, movies, and concerts, all occasions that demanded dates. I imagine that it's hard for my younger students today to picture the dating scene, which is why the following academic essay, excerpted from the book *From Front Porch to Back Seat: Courtship in the Twentieth Century,* is so illuminating.

Using the popular magazines of the day as sources, Beth Bailey describes the rise of dating as a social ritual in the 1940s and 1950s. This historical context is useful when considering the argument in the preceding reading, "Courting Confusion," that we need new rituals like dating that stop way short of "hooking up."

While "The Worth of a Date," unlike some research essays, makes an argument from the outset, it is a less formal treatment of its subject and taps largely popular sources rather than academic ones. Notice, however, that it is a scholarly essay that includes citations and references. Unlike the preceding essay, "The Worth of a Date" is intended for other academics, but it's written to be accessible to nonspecialists, too.

The Worth of a Date

Beth Bailey

1 Before the sexual revolution of the 1960s provided juicier material, *Esquire* was fond of running cartoons featuring a short, elderly, and paunchy millionaire escorting a tall, enormous-breasted young showgirl through opulent settings. The captions didn't really matter. The cartoons worked best subtextually, and all contained variations on the same theme: money and sex; the coupling of wallet and bosom.

2 It is easy, today, to center on the objectification of woman represented by the showgirl, a caricature stripped to her essentials: legs, breasts, and greed. She is clearly a commodity, purchased by man's wealth. But the man, too, is objectified. His value to her lies only in what he can buy. He is interchangeable with any other well-stuffed wallet. Their relationship is obviously mutually exploitative: the man is as much a commodity to the woman as she is a commodity to him.

3 The millionaire and the showgirl are a long way from our image of young love, but this mass-produced image can illustrate some of the values inherent in the American dating system. In courtship, no less than in the culture at large, we find America's "culture of consumption"—a way of seeing that encourages the paired acts of consumption and commodification.

The culture of consumption, as Jackson Lears and Richard Wrightman Fox describe it in a book of that title, is not simply the system of values underlying a consumer economy or a society "saturated by mass-produced and mass-marketed goods." It is also "an ethic, a standard of living, and a power structure" that centers on consumption, in which "individuals have been invited to seek commodities as keys to personal welfare...even to conceive of their own selves as commodities" (Wrightman and Lears ix–xvii). And, I might add, to transform personal relationships into commodities.

4

In dating, American young people sought their "personal welfare" through dates (and later through steadies), as commodities that afforded public validation of popularity, of belonging, of success. Whether or not one liked the date (person), the date (event) was valuable, a necessary commodity in youth culture. As commodities, dates (events) were valued differentially by the level of consumption they entailed—in short, by their cost. The date (person) could also become a commodity. In this system, men and women often defined themselves and each other as commodities, the woman valued by the level of consumption she could demand (how much she was "worth"), and the man by the level of consumption he could provide.

5

The particular form the American dating system took as it emerged in the early twentieth century was determined, in large part, by the new centrality of money in the act of courtship. As "going somewhere" became the thing to do, the man had to spend money to provide entertainment, refreshments, and transportation for the couple. Gradually, as dating became the dominant form of courtship, participants and observers recognized how important money had become. In general, dates had come to be defined by the fact that they cost money. Over and over in the national media, women and men, girls and boys, advisers and experts insisted on this definition of dating. Money was central: a date took place when a couple "went out" and spent money.

6

All the polls and columns and books on dating in the second third of the twentieth century made abundantly clear that American youth did not consider spending time with a member of the opposite sex the same as dating. In almost all instances, a date centered around an act of consumption: going out for dinner or a Coke, seeing a movie, buying access to some form of entertainment. Of course, the emphasis was not on unbridled consumption. The act had to take place within certain limits and according to many conventions, one of the most important being that the man pay the woman's way.

7

The "sub-deb" adviser for the *Ladies' Home Journal* shows the extent of these implicit definitions of a date in a 1944 column. She tells the story of a young girl—about fourteen—who is "fed up" because she can't get a date. The girl, as the author describes her, has a good social life—lots of friends, including boys who like her well enough to meet her and sit beside her at the movies. The adviser does not give the obvious moral. Instead of pointing out that this sub-deb should concentrate on enjoying the movie and the boy's company, she approvingly recounts the girl's "plan": she

8

(continued)

(continued)

will concentrate on "Pete," the "likeliest one" (note that she does not say "the one she likes best"). "When he sits by me in the movies," the girl says, "I'm going to pretend he paid my way in. I'm going to play-act it's a real date" (Woodward 8). The only thing lacking, evidently, is knowledge that the boy *paid* for her.

9   A real girl, Margaret Graves of St. Louis, had a similar opinion on the subject. Writing to *Senior Scholastic* in 1951, she said, "If a girl has to pay her own way [on a date], she might as well go alone or with girl friends" (Head 24). To her, the date was not the event, was not the companionship, was not even being *seen* with the boy. A date meant being paid for. And boys agreed. A *Senior Scholastic* poll on dating found that while 90 percent of the girls questioned would agree to "occasionally," if reluctantly, share expenses, 50 percent of the boys strenuously objected to the idea. "If a boy is financially embarrassed," one boy wrote, "he shouldn't date" (Head 24)....

10   This concern with being seen is crucial, for it relates to the role of the date in youth culture...[D]ates often functioned in youth culture as tools for acquiring popularity—much as did clothes, cars, and other consumer goods. But a date that had no independent content, that was only a marker for popularity, had no meaning if no one knew about it. The date had to be public.

11   The boy who longed for a date, as Margaret Mead noted in the 1940s, was not longing for a girl, much less for a relationship with a particular girl (Mead 145). He desired to be in the public situation that defined a date: he desired to *have* a date, and he desired for others to see that he had a date. This sort of date, "had" and displayed, is itself a commodity....

12   Of course, some dates were prized more than others. Teen advice books warned girls to be understanding and hospitable to the boy who was occasionally low on funds, but not to let him get in the habit of hanging around their living rooms with no "real" dates in exchange. And real dates, the public culture of dating constantly emphasized, were expensive and flamboyant. While most polls discovered that teens' usual dates were for a movie and a snack, the magazines that conducted these polls frequently described the unusual dates—the "ideal" dates—in loving detail....

13   The high school prom, the biggest social event of the year, represented the "ideal" date to most students. Proms were, of course, something more than special dates. They were a kind of rite of passage that transformed boys and girls into young men and women; they were occasions for magical extravagance. They required elegant evening attire and transportation, and included postprom entertainment at the fanciest night spot the area offered....

14   Proms offered high school students not only a taste of the "ideal" extravagant dates otherwise largely denied them (at least until they were older) but also a forum for social competition. The first level of competition was simply rating a bid or getting a date; the next was getting the "right" date. Beyond these basics, proms stressed competition through material goods. With all (who qualified) brought

together, it was easy to compare dresses, to see who rated an orchid and who just a gardenia, to rank postprom destinations and modes of transportation. The pressure could be intense, and during the Depression years of the 1930s, Chicago high school principals frequently cancelled school proms because they feared the many students who couldn't afford them would be "psychologically wounded" by that failure (Gutowski 256)....

In college, the pressure was more consistent. College students didn't have to contend with only one prom or ideal date a year, but with a whole succession of extravagant events. College football weekends were glamorized by a wide range of national magazines as one dizzy succession of brunches and lunches and dances and dinners—at a cost to men, *Good Housekeeping* estimated in 1953, of about $83 a weekend (Frey 225). *Mademoiselle,* in its 1954 college issue, showed the pressure for expensive dates by defining "Quiet Evening" as "Any nocturnal date that results in a heightened feeling of well being and costs less than $5" (Frey 309). The previous year *Good Housekeeping* had published results of an informal survey of the cost of college "big" dates. Average outlays for one date ranged from a low of $25 in Boston and Dallas to a high of $35 in St. Louis. Paducah, Kentucky, with a population of 35,000, came in just about average at $30 (Frey 224)....

Flowers, both in college and outside, exemplify the dating system's emphasis on competing through consumption. Almost every description of a "big date," from the 1920s through the 1950s, features the kind of corsage the girl or woman wears, and sample budgets for major dates allot anywhere from $2 to $10 for corsages (Frey 225). These flowers were not private gifts—cut flowers for the woman's dressing table—but public symbols. They said, for the man, "See what I can afford," and for the woman, "See how much I'm worth." The girl who said she could buy her own Cokes understood that in the dating competition the companionship of a Coke date couldn't match the symbolic importance of flowers on a big date....

In quite literal terms, women gauged their own value in dating by how much money men spent on them....In this system, that the man pay for the date was crucial. Beyond that, the more he spent—publicly—the better.

15

16

17

Works Cited

Frey, Richard L. "The High Cost of Dating." *Good Housekeeping* Aug. 1953: 224–309. Print.

Gutowski, Thomas. "The High School as Adolescent-Raising Institution: An Inner History of Chicago Public Secondary Education, 1856–1940." Diss. of Chicago, 1978. Print.

Head, Gay. "Boy Dates Girl Jam Session." Senior Scholastic 11 Apr. 1951: 24. Print.

Mead, Margaret. "The Male and Female." *Ladies' Home Journal* Sept. 1949: 145. Print.

Woodward, Elizabeth. "The Sub-Deb: I'm Fed Up." *Ladies' Home Journal* Jan. 1944: 2. Print.

Wrightman, Richard Fox, and T. J. Jackson Lears, eds. *The Culture of Consumption.* New York: Pantheon, 1983. Print.

Inquiring into the Essay

Use the ways of inquiring—exploring, explaining, evaluating, and reflecting—to discover what you think about "The Worth of a Date."

1. Historical research such as "The Worth of a Date" is a frame through which we can see the present, in this case specifically the ways that social rituals such as dating have changed. As soon as you finish the essay, try to use the frame that Bailey provides as a way to look at your own experience. In your journal, write for five full minutes, using the reading as a prompt. Begin by exploring what struck you most by this description of dating in the 1930s through the 1950s, especially when compared with your own experiences in the present.

2. Using the window into fifties dating that "The Worth of a Date" provides, how would you contrast the social rituals then and now? Could you make an argument that they haven't really changed much despite the current era of texting, Twitter, and Facebook?

3. The argument in "The Worth of a Date" is implied by its title. Do you find the idea that dating was "commodified" persuasive? Even more important, is such a claim relevant?

4. Some years ago, a writer used the term *presentism* to describe how modern readers often unfairly apply contemporary moral standards and values to historical events. It wouldn't be hard to do the same thing here. Reflect on how a modern researcher can avoid being blinded by presentism.

INQUIRING INTO THE DETAILS

Reading Academic Research Essays

Just as reading a poem demands some different reading strategies than reading an essay, making sense of academic writing presents its own peculiar challenges. Here are some tips for picking your way through an academic journal article.

- Pay particular attention to the *justification* for why this research question is worthy of study. Do you understand how it extends existing scholarship on the topic?

- Imagine an artichoke. You have to work your way through the leaves to get to the heart, the best part. In a journal article, this is the main argument, thesis, finding, or claim. You will find this in a range of locations—sometimes it's stated in an "abstract" (if there is one), at the end of an introduction or literature review, or even at the very end of the article.

- You don't have to understand all the jargon, just enough that you understand the research question and the conclusions.

- You're probably not in a position to evaluate the methods used, but make an effort to identify and understand them.
- When doing your own research, pay attention to names of people who are cited often. These are often people who have said the most in the ongoing conversation about the topic.
- Carefully consider how the author qualifies his or her conclusions. This often mutes the significance of the findings and helps you understand how seriously to take them.

▪ DOCUMENTED RESEARCH PAPER

Though the following academic paper, published in the *Journal of Sex Research*, was originally written as an undergraduate honors thesis, chances are that, unless you're going on to graduate school, you won't write a paper that will end up in a scholarly journal. But depending on the field you choose, you will be expected to think and write like the author of this essay. That means that you must learn to ask researchable questions that somehow extend or challenge what has already been said by others on your topic. It also means that you will collect and analyze evidence of some kind to test your hunches. And above all, being an academic researcher means you explore topics that genuinely interest you and might make a difference to others.

"Pluralistic Ignorance and Hooking Up" does all of these things. Tracy Lambert and her coauthors take an idea that has been around for a while and wonder whether it might apply to hooking up behaviors on her college campus. She suspects that something called "pluralistic ignorance," or the sense that what makes you feel uncomfortable probably doesn't bother other people nearly as much, strongly operates among men and women who hook up. With the help of her professors, Tracy designs a study to test the hypothesis.

Like most social-science research, this paper follows a prescribed format: introduction (literature review and purpose of the study), methods, results, and discussion. At first, these conventions might seem alien to you (see "Inquiring into the Details: Reading Academic Research Essays"), but once you get used to navigating academic discourse, a whole new world of information opens.

Pluralistic Ignorance and Hooking Up

Tracy Lambert, Arnold Kahn, and Kevin Apple

"Hooking up"—when two people agree to engage in sexual behavior for which there is no future commitment—has become popular on college campuses. In this study we examined the extent to which pluralistic ignorance affects hooking up. One hundred

(continued)

(continued)

thirty-six female and 128 male college students answered questions regarding their own comfort and their perceived peers' comfort in engaging in a variety of sexual behaviors while hooking up. We hypothesized and found that both women and men rated their peers as being more comfortable engaging in these behaviors than they rated themselves. Men expressed more comfort than did women in engaging in these behaviors, and both sexes overestimated the other gender's comfort with hooking up behaviors. Pluralistic ignorance appears to apply to hooking up on college campuses, and we explore some potential consequences of pluralistic ignorance in this context.

1   Although one-night stands and uncommitted sexual behaviors are not a recent phenomenon, past research has focused on personality traits, attitudes, and individual differences in willingness to engage in such behaviors (e.g., Gerrard, 1980; Gerrard & Gibbons, 1982; Simpson & Gangestad, 1991; Snyder, Simpson, & Gangestad, 1986). The tacit assumption in this past research was that sexual behaviors within a committed and loving relationship were unproblematic, but that unloving, uncommitted sexual relations had to be explained. However, today on college campuses across the United States what was once viewed as problematic has now become normative, and students refer to this process as "hooking up."

2   Hooking up occurs when two people who are casual acquaintances or who have just met that evening at a bar or party agree to engage in some forms of sexual behavior for which there will likely be no future commitment (Boswell & Spade, 1996; Kahn et al., 2000; Paul, McManus, & Hayes, 2000). The couple typically does not communicate what sexual behaviors they will or will not engage in, and frequently both parties have been drinking alcohol (Kahn et al., 2000; Paul et al., 2000). Paul et al. (2000) found that 78% of women and men on the campus being studied had engaged in hooking up at least once. In the Kahn et al. (2000) sample of college students, 86% of the women and 88% of the men indicated they had hooked up. Almost one half (47%) of the men and one third of the women in the Paul et al. sample engaged in sexual intercourse during the hookup, and Kahn et al. found that their sample believed petting below the waist, oral sex, and sexual intercourse occurred with some regularity in the process of hooking up.

3   *Pluralistic ignorance,* a concept first coined by Floyd Allport (1924, 1933), exists when, within a group of individuals, each person believes his or her private attitudes, beliefs, or judgments are discrepant from the norm displayed by the public behavior of others. Therefore, each group member, wishing to be seen as a desirable member of the group, publicly conforms to the norm, each believing he or she is the only one in the group experiencing conflict between his or her private attitude and his or her public behavior. Group members believe that most others in their group, especially those who are popular and opinion leaders (Katz & Lazarsfeld, 1955), actually endorse the norm and want to behave that way, while they themselves privately feel they are going along with the norm because of a desire to fit in with the group and exemplify the norm (Prentice & Miller, 1993, 1996). In this study we examined the extent to which pluralistic ignorance might be related to U.S. college students' comfort

levels with sexual behaviors involved in hooking up. Consistent with the premise of pluralistic ignorance, we hypothesized that college students would perceive others as having a greater comfort level engaging in a variety of sexual behaviors than they themselves would have.

Prentice and Miller (1993) demonstrated pluralistic ignorance among college students in the area of alcohol consumption. On a campus where heavy alcohol use was the perceived norm, Prentice and Miller found that students estimated both the average student and their friends to have less discomfort with the level of alcohol consumption on campus than they reported for themselves. Furthermore, for male but not female students, they found greater consistency between respondents' comfort levels with alcohol consumption and the perceived norm and between respondents' reported drinking levels and the perceived norm at the end of the semester than at the beginning of the semester. Although correlational in nature, these results suggest that over time, male students may have changed their attitudes and behaviors to bring them more in line with the perceived norm. Perkins and Berkowitz (1986) reported similar findings with regard to the discrepancy between college students' own comfort with the amount of drinking at the university and what they estimated to be the general campus attitude.

Although pluralistic ignorance was originally conceptualized as a discrepancy between public behavior and private beliefs (Miller & McFarland, 1987), others have used the concept to refer to situations in which there is not direct evidence of behavioral similarity (e.g., Fields & Schuman, 1976; O'Gorman & Garry, 1976). More recently, Cohen and Shotland (1996) invoked the concept of pluralistic ignorance in a variety of dating situations for which public scrutiny was absent. They found that both men and women believed that the average other person of their sex had more liberal sexual expectations than they set for themselves, both sexes believing the average other person of their sex would expect sexual intercourse much sooner in a relationship than they themselves would expect it. When asked whether a same-sex peer would expect to have sexual intercourse with a person with whom they were emotionally involved but for whom they felt no physical attraction, both men and women believed the average man and woman would expect sexual intercourse, while only approximately 50% of the participants would expect sex themselves in such a relationship, and an even smaller percentage reported having had sex in such a relationship. Finally, when there was neither emotional nor physical attraction to a partner, few women or men expected that they would have sexual intercourse with the partner, but believed the average man and woman would indeed expect sexual intercourse.

Pluralistic ignorance might have consequences when beliefs about the norm condone intimate sexual behaviors. In the process of hooking up, pluralistic ignorance may lead one or both sexual partners to act according to the perceived norm rather than to their own convictions. There is a large literature showing that men have more liberal attitudes towards sexual behaviors and expect sexual intercourse sooner in a

(continued)

(continued)

relationship than do women (Cohen & Shotland, 1996; Knox & Wilson, 1981; Oliver & Hyde, 1993) and that men are much more receptive than are women to offers of sexual intercourse (Clark & Hatfield, 1989). Byers and Lewis (1988) found that disagreements among dating partners on the desired level of sexual behavior was almost always in the direction of the male partner wanting a higher level of sexual intimacy than that desired by the female partner. Thus, it is possible that many men go into hooking-up situations hoping to engage in more intimate sexual behaviors than are desired by their female partners. Because men are expected to initiate sexual activity (DeLamater, 1987; Peplau & Gordon, 1985), it is possible that in the process of hooking up, some women will experience unwanted sexual advances and possibly even sexual assault or rape.

7   In their research on hooking up, Kahn et al. (2000) asked 92 female and 50 male college students if they had ever had a "really terrible hooking up experience." Nearly one half of the women (42%) and the men (46%) indicated they had had such an experience. A "terrible experience" for the men was usually due to the women wanting a relationship or to the use of too much alcohol or drugs; none mentioned pressure to go further than they desired. However, nearly one half of the women (48.3%) who reported having a terrible hooking-up experience indicated that they were pressured to go further than they had wanted to go. They gave responses such as "I hooked up with a guy who didn't understand the meaning of 'no'" and "I didn't want to—he did—he wouldn't back off." These women may have experienced sexual assault during a hook up but did not label their experiences as such because they believed the behaviors to be normative. In addition, 10.3% of the women and 11.1% of the men in this sample said the hook up was terrible because they had gone too far without mentioning pressure from their partner. Going too far might have been the consequence of pluralistic ignorance, conforming to a presumed norm.

8   The present study sought to extend the findings of Cohen and Shotland (1996), which were restricted to expectations of sexual intercourse in dating situations, to the area of hooking up. Further, we wanted to examine whether pluralistic ignorance occurred with other sexual behaviors besides sexual intercourse. Based on the research on pluralistic ignorance and gender differences in expected sexual behaviors, we hypothesized that both male and female students would see other students as more comfortable with various hooking-up behaviors than they were themselves. Although we expected individuals would vary in their own comfort levels with various hooking-up behaviors, we expected they would believe other students to be uniformly more comfortable engaging in those behaviors than they were themselves. Furthermore, consistent with previous literature, we hypothesized that men would be significantly more comfortable than women with engaging in all hooking-up behaviors. Finally, we hypothesized that due to pluralistic ignorance, both women and men would overestimate the other gender's comfort with all hooking-up behaviors.

Method

Participants

One hundred seventy-five female and 152 male undergraduate students from a mid-sized residential southeastern public university that has few nontraditional students served as participants for the study. The convenience sample represented a moderately even distribution of years in school: for first years, $n = 79$ (41 females, 38 males); for sophomores, $n = 70$ (37 females, 33 males); for juniors, $n = 84$ (45 females, 39 males); and for seniors, n = 93 (52 females, 41 males). A female experimenter approached students as they entered the university library and asked them to volunteer to answer some questions about hooking up and sexual behaviors as part of her senior honors project. She approached other students in their residence halls. No differences appeared between these two samples for any of the dependent measures. Analyses concerning pluralistic ignorance and comfort with hooking up are based on the data from 136 women (77.7%) and 128 men (84.2%) who indicated that they had hooked up.

Materials and Procedure

The questionnaire consisted of questions developed by the authors to examine student attitudes toward hooking up. On the first page, students read that the investigator was interested in "students' attitudes and behaviors with regard to dating and 'hooking up,'" and hooking up was defined as "a sexual encounter between two people who may or may not know each other well, but who usually are *not* seriously dating." Participants also signed an informed consent form, which indicated all information would be anonymous and confidential. To insure anonymity and encourage honest responding, the only demographic information obtained was the participants' year in school. We made no attempt to determine sexual orientation or marital status: however, on this residential campus the overwhelming majority of students come to the university directly from high school, identify themselves as heterosexual, and have never been married (James Madison University Office of Institutional Research, 2001–2002). Participants were told they were not required to complete the survey if they became uncomfortable.

Students who said they had hooked up were instructed to continue to the next page. We constructed 11-point scales modeled after those used by Prentice and Miller (1993) on which 3 points were labeled: 1 = not at all comfortable, 6 = *neutral*, and 11 = *very comfortable*. Participants responded to the question "How comfortable are you with the amount of hooking up that goes on at [school name]?" They then responded to the question "How comfortable are you with engaging in the following activities during a hook up?" with regard to "petting above the waist," "petting below the waist," "oral sex," and "sexual intercourse." Participants used the same scales in response to the questions "How comfortable do you think the *average female* student is with the amount of hooking up that goes on at [school name]?" and "How comfortable do you think the *average female* student is with engaging in the following activities during a hook up?" Finally, they responded to the questions "How comfortable do you think the *average male* student is

(continued)

9

10

11

(continued)

with the amount of hooking up that goes on at [school name]?" and "How comfortable do you think the *average male* student is with engaging in the following activities during a hook up?"

12   Students who indicated that they had never hooked up were asked to skip to a different page of the survey, which contained questions regarding why they did not hook up and whether or not they believed that there was a relationship between hooking up and sexual assault. This part of the questionnaire was included so that all participants would work on the survey for approximately the same amount of time without knowing who had or had not hooked up.

13   Participants completed the questionnaire privately, usually within a short distance of the researcher. Those participating at the library placed their completed questionnaires in a large box, and those participating in their residence hall placed completed questionaires in a large envelope. When they were finished, participants were encouraged to ask questions and discuss the questionnaire with the researcher, who provided them with a debriefing statement and a list of campus resources for sexual assault.

Results

14   We tested the hypothesis that students would experience pluralistic ignorance regarding hooking up with a 2 (Gender) X 2 (Target: self or other) ANOVA, with target as a within-subjects variable. As hypothesized, participants demonstrated pluralistic ignorance by evaluating their own comfort level with the amount of hooking up. $M = 7.08$, $SD = 2.31$, significantly lower than their estimate of a same-sex peer's comfort level, $M = 7.75$, $SD = 2.08$, $F(1.262) = 24.24$, $p < .0001$, partial $\eta^2 = .085$. Participants believed that other college students were more comfortable with the amount of hooking up than were they. This main effect of target was qualified by a significant gender by target interaction, $F(1.262) = 7.55$, partial $\eta^2 = .028$, $p < .01$. Both men and women showed the same pattern of overestimating their peers' comfort levels: however, the pattern was more pronounced among the male students (9.01_{peer} vs. 7.95_{self}), $t(127) = 4.68$, $p < .0001$, $d = .502$, than among the female students (6.57_{peer} vs. 6.26_{self}), $t(135) = 1.85$, $p < .05$, one-tailed, $d = .185$. Table 1 presents these means and standard deviations.

15   A dependent *t* test for equality of variances revealed that participants showed significantly less variability in their ratings of peer comfort level in hooking up than in their

Table 1   Ratings of Own and Average Same-Sex Student's Comfort with Hooking Up

Measure	Self: *M (SD)*	Average student: *M (SD)*
Women	6.26 (1.79)	6.57 (1.63)
Men	7.95 (2.48)	9.01 (1.74)

Note. Ratings were made on 11-point scales (1 = *not at all comfortable* and 11 = *very comfortable*).

Table 2 Ratings of Men's and Women's Own Comfort with Hooking-Up Behaviors

	Men: M (SD)	Women: M (SD)
Petting above the waist	9.12 (2.47)	7.29 (2.68)
Petting below the waist	8.42 (2.60)	5.13 (2.73)
Oral sex	7.56 (3.05)	3.49 (2.63)
Sexual intercourse	5.65 (3.57)	2.15 (2.31)

self-ratings: t (262) = 1.96, p < .05, one-tailed. When rating their own comfort levels, the standard deviation in participants' responses was 2.31. However, the standard deviation significantly decreased to 2.08 when participants estimated their peers' comfort with hooking up. This decrease in variability when estimating others' comfort provides some evidence for an illusion of universality. That is, participants showed greater uniformity in their beliefs about others' comfort levels compared to their own actual comfort levels.

We used multivariate analysis of variance (MANOVA) to examine the hypothesis regarding men's and women's own comfort levels with various sexual behaviors, with participant gender as the between-subjects variable. Men reported significantly greater comfort with these behaviors than did women. F (4.259) = 35.17, p < .0001, partial η^2 = .352. Table 2 shows that men's greater comfort occurred with all four hooking-up behaviors.

We tested the hypothesis that both men and women would overestimate the other gender's comfort with hooking-up behaviors using two separate MANOVAS. The first examined the men's estimates of the average woman's comfort, and the second examined the women's estimates of the average man's comfort. To evaluate the accuracy of these estimates, the comfort estimates were compared with the means of the actual comfort ratings of these hooking-up behaviors. Both the men, F (4, 259) = 7.82, p < .0001, partial η^2 = .108, and the women, F (4, 259) = 16.25, p < .0001, partial η^2 = .201, significantly overestimated the other gender's actual comfort levels with various hooking-up behaviors. As shown in Table 3, this overestimation occurred for both sexes on each of the four hooking-up behaviors.

Discussion

Cohen and Shotland (1996) found evidence of pluralistic ignorance regarding expectations of sexual intercourse on a date. The current research extended these findings to other sexual behaviors, and did so in the context of hooking up. We found that both women and men reported less comfort with their perceived norm of hooking up than they believed was experienced by their same-sex peers, with men showing a greater difference between self- and peer-ratings than women. In addition, both men and women believed members of the other gender experienced greater comfort with hooking-up behaviors than members of the other gender actually reported. Men were less comfortable with engaging in hooking-up behaviors than women believed them to be, and women

(continued)

16

17

18

(continued)

Table 3 Differences Between Each Gender's Own Comfort Level with Hooking-Up Behaviors and Estimates of the Other Gender's Comfort Levels

	Women's estimate of men: M (SD)	Men's actual comfort level: M (SD)	Men's estimate of women: M (SD)	Women's actual comfort level: M (SD)
Petting above the waist	9.80 (1.45)	9.12 (2.47)	7.73 (1.92)	7.29 (2.68)
Petting below the waist	9.30 (1.67)	8.42 (2.60)	6.38 (2.07)	5.13 (2.73)
Oral sex	8.61 (1.93)	7.56 (3.04)	5.49 (2.19)	3.49 (2.62)
Sexual intercourse	7.62 (2.24)	5.65 (3.57)	4.28 (2.36)	2.15 (2.31)

were less comfortable with engaging in hooking-up behaviors than men believed them to be. These findings appear to be due to pluralistic ignorance: Hooking up has become the norm for heterosexual sexual relationships on this campus, and since the great majority of students do in fact hook up, it appears that most students believe that others are comfortable—more comfortable than they are themselves—with engaging in a variety of uncommitted sexual behaviors. It is likely that most students believe others engage in these hooking-up behaviors primarily because they enjoy doing so, while they see themselves engaging in these behaviors primarily due to peer pressure.

19   Consistent with other pluralistic ignorance research (e.g., Prentice & Miller, 1993), this study showed evidence of an illusion of universality. The students failed to appreciate the extent to which others have different comfort levels with hooking-up behaviors. That is, students wrongly assumed that the attitudes of others about hooking up were more homogenous than they actually were.

20   Similar to other researchers (Cohen & Shotland, 1996; Knox & Wilson, 1981; Oliver & Hyde, 1993), we found that men expressed greater comfort than did women with sexually intimate hooking-up behaviors. In the context of hooking up, this could lead to serious consequences. Our study suggests that men believe women are more comfortable engaging in these behaviors than in fact they are, and also that women believe other women are more comfortable engaging in these behaviors than they are themselves. As a consequence, some men may pressure women to engage in intimate sexual behaviors, and some women may engage in these behaviors or resist only weakly because they believe they are unique in feeling discomfort about engaging in them. In this context it is possible for a woman to experience sexual assault but not interpret the behavior as such, believing it to be normative behavior with which her peers are comfortable.

21   "Most of Us" is a campaign implemented on many college campuses in an attempt to reveal pluralistic ignorance about alcohol consumption among college students (DeJong & Langford, 2002; Haines, 1998). The campaign is based on providing students with statistical evidence about actual student attitudes and behaviors regarding alcohol consumption. The goal of the campaign is to show that pluralistic ignorance exists regarding college students'

heavy alcohol consumption, and that most students prefer to drink less than what is commonly perceived to be the norm. Considering the results of this study, we propose that a similar campaign highlighting students' beliefs about and comfort levels with sexual behaviors while hooking up might help reduce pluralistic ignorance about hooking up.

Tracy A. Lambert is now at the University of Georgia.

This paper is based on an honors thesis by the first author under the direction of the second author. We wish to thank Steven Wise for his statistical assistance.

Address correspondence to Arnold S. Kahn, School of Psychology, MSC 7401, James Madison University, Harrisonburg, VA 22807: e-mail: kahnas@jmu.edu.

References

Allport, F. H. (1924). *Social psychology*. Boston: Houghton Mifflin.

Allport, F. H. (1933). *Institutional behavior*. Chapel Hill: University of North Carolina Press.

Boswell, A., & Spade, J. (1996). Fraternities and collegiate rape culture. *Gender and Society, 10*, 133–147.

Byers, S., & Lewis, K. (1988). Dating couples' disagreements over the desired level of sexual intimacy. *The Journal of Sex Research, 24*, 15–29.

Clark, R. D., & Hatfield, E. (1989). Gender differences in receptivity to sexual offers. *Journal of Psychology and Human Sexuality, 2*, 39–55.

Cohen, L. L., & Shotland, R. L. (1996). Timing of first sexual intercourse in a relationship: Expectation, experiences, and perceptions of others. *The Journal of Sex Research, 33*, 291–299.

DeJong, W., & Langford, L. A. (2002). Typology for campus-based alcohol prevention: Moving toward environmental management strategies. *Journal of Studies on Alcohol Supplement, 14*, 140–147.

DeLamater, J. (1987). Gender differences in sexual scenarios. In K. Kelley (Ed.), *Females, males, and sexuality* (pp. 127–139). Albany, NY: SUNY Press.

Fields, J. M., & Schuman, H. (1976). Public beliefs and the beliefs of the public. *Public Opinion Quarterly, 40*, 427–448.

Gerrard, M. (1980). Sex guilt and attitudes towards sex in sexually active and inactive female college students. *Journal of Personality Assessment, 44*, 258–261.

Gerrard, M., & Gibbons, F. X. (1982). Sexual experience, sex guilt, and sexual moral reasoning. *Journal of Personality, 50*, 345–359.

Haines, M. (1998). Social norms: A wellness model for health promotion in higher education. *Wellness Management, 14*(4), 1–8.

James Madison University Office of Institutional Research. (2001–2002). Retrieved February 22, 2003, from http://www.jmu.edu/instresrch/statsum/2001_02/2001-02toc.htm

Kahn, A. S., Fricker, K., Hoffman, J., Lambert, T., Tripp, M., Childress. K., et al. (2000, August). Hooking up: Dangerous new dating methods? In A. S. Kahn (Chair), *Sex, unwanted sex, and sexual assault on college campuses*. Symposium conducted at the annual meeting of the American Psychological Association, Washington, DC.

(continued)

(continued)

Katz, E., & Lazarsfeld, P. F. (1955). *Personal influence: The part played by people in the flow of mass communication.* Glencoe, IL: Free Press.

Knox, D., & Wilson, K. (1981). Dating behaviors of university students. *Family Relations, 30,* 255–258.

Miller, T. D., & McFarland, C. (1987). Pluralistic ignorance: When similarity is interpreted as dissimilarity. *Journal of Personality and Social Psychology, 53,* 298–305.

O'Gorman, H. J., & Garry, S. L. (1976). Pluralistic ignorance: A replication and extension, *Public Opinion Quarterly,* 40, 449–458.

Oliver, M. B., & Hyde, J. S. (1993). Gender differences in sexuality: A meta-analysis. *Psychological Bulletin,* 114, 129–151.

Paul, E. L., McManus, B., & Hayes, A. (2000). "Hookups": Characteristics and correlates of college students' spontaneous and anonymous sexual experiences. *The Journal of Sex Research, 37,* 76–88.

Peplau, L. A., & Gordon, S. L. (1985). Women and men in love: Gender differences in close heterosexual relationships. In V. E. O'Leary, R. K. Unger, & B. S. Wallston (Eds.), *Women, gender, and social psychology* (pp. 257–292). Hillsdale, NJ: Lawrence Erlbaum Associates.

Perkins, H. W., & Berkowitz, A. D. (1986). Perceiving the community norms of alcohol use among students: Some research implications for campus alcohol education programming. *International Journal of the Addictions, 21,* 961–976.

Prentice, D. A., & Miller, D. T. (1993). Pluralistic ignorance and alcohol use on campus: Some consequences of misperceiving the social norm. *Journal of Personality and Social Psychology,* 64, 243–256.

Prentice, D. A., & Miller, D. T. (1996). Pluralistic ignorance and the perpetuation of social norms by unwitting actors. In M. P. Zanna (Ed.), *Advances in experimental social psychology* (Vol. 28, pp. 161–209). San Diego, CA: Academic Press.

Simpson, J. A., & Gangestad, S. W. (1991). Individual differences sociosexuality: Evidence for convergent and discriminant validity. *Journal of Personality and Social Psychology,* 60, 870–883.

Snyder, M., Simpson, J. A., & Gangestad, S. (1986). Personality and sexual relations. *Journal of Personality and Social Psychology, 51,* 181–190.

Manuscript accepted August 21, 2002

Inquiring into the Essay

Use all four ways of inquiring to think about your reaction to this essay.

1. If true, the idea of "pluralistic ignorance"—that we consistently behave in ways that make us uncomfortable because we want to conform to the norm—is pretty disturbing because it implies that we internalize a certain kind of social control over our behavior that may not be in response to something real. For instance, this study suggests that for women especially, hooking up

might not feel right, but they do it anyway because they don't think others feel as they do. Explore this in your own life. Fastwrite about whether "pluralistic ignorance" makes sense to you, and bend the writing, if you can, toward a story that might reveal your own experience with the idea.

2. Using different color highlighters or pens, identify some of the following elements of an academic paper: review of the literature, hypothesis, purpose of the study, interpretation of data, and assertion about the significance of the findings.

3. Are the findings of this study credible? Based on your own experience and observations, how would you evaluate them? If you were going to suggest an area for further research, what might that be?

4. A common and perfectly understandable response to an initial encounter with academic discourse like this is to find it utterly boring. Why is this so? If it is important to learn to get past this initial response to do serious research, what strategies would you use?

SEEING THE FORM

Idaho State Penitentiary, Women's Prison

(continued)

Seeing the Form (*continued*)

I took the picture on page 415 on a ridge overlooking the valley where I live. It includes a lot of visual information: long shots of the city of Boise, the university, the state penitentiary, and in the far distance, the Owyhee Range, which was recently designated as a federal wilderness. But do you really get a good look at any of these subjects? I don't think so, which is why I don't think much of the photograph. My brother, a professional photographer, would probably consider this shot a throwaway—a kind of photographic "prewriting" activity that might help him discover the visual subject he *really* wants to work with.

At the bottom middle of the photograph is a small building surrounded by high stone walls. This was the women's prison, which was built in the 1920s. It's a fascinating place both visually and historically, and so I "revised" my photographic project to focus on the women's prison rather than attempting to capture the valley. I took a slew of shots of the women's prison, including the two pictures shown above—one of a small cell with the light streaming through the tiny window and another of a rusting iron door. They are hardly masterpieces, but I do like them a lot better than the landscape shot. Do you agree? If so, why?

If the process of taking these pictures is a good analogy for the process of writing research essays, what do the comparisons between the landscape shot and the women's prison photographs suggest to you about the qualities of a good paper? What do they imply about the research process?

THE WRITING PROCESS

INQUIRY PROJECT: WRITE A RESEARCH ESSAY

Develop a 2,000- to 3,000-word research essay on a topic of your choice. (Your instructor may present some broad subjects or other limitations on topic choice.) The most important quality of this research essay is that it be organized around your own questions or ideas about the topic; it should be an *essay*, not a *report*. The research question should also have a sufficiently narrow focus. Don't look at the entire landscape of a topic but focus instead on a specific feature in that landscape. Your essay should also do the following:

- Be based on a "researchable" question.
- Have a central thesis or claim that represents your answer to the question you pose, even if it's tentative.
- Use appropriate and relevant sources based on your own experiences, observations, interviews, and reading, or all four sources of information.
- Be cited using the conventions recommended by your instructor.
- Be written for an audience of peers rather than experts on the topic.

For additional reading, writing, and research resources, go to www.mycomplab.com

Thinking About Subjects

What are you going to write about? This choice may be wide open, or your instructor might ask you to focus on a broad theme, perhaps one on which your class is focused. Either way, the same principle applies:

There are no boring topics, only poor questions.

There is no topic—dust mites, fruit cake, Elvis, nuclear fusion, or basketballs—that won't yield to the right question. (We'll take up the characteristics of a good question later.) But there's another condition upon which the success of your research project depends: Your curiosity. Whatever the question that eventually becomes a focus for inquiry, it must be one that you find interesting. Typically, this means that you choose a topic because it holds the promise of discovery.

Ask yourself this: *What have I seen, read, experienced, or heard about that raises interesting questions that research might help answer?*

Approaching your research project this way is exactly the impulse that might have motivated you to write a personal essay on growing up with an autistic sibling or a persuasive essay on the downside of recruiting NCAA athletes at your school. It's the same motive that inspires all genuine inquiry: *How do I feel about this? What do I think about this? What do I want to know?*

Generating Ideas

Use your notebook to generate some material. As in previous inquiry projects, at this stage don't prejudge anything you come up with. Let yourself play around with possibilities.

Listing Prompts. Lists can be rich sources of triggering topics. Let them grow freely, and when you're ready, use an item as the focus of another list or an episode of fastwriting. The following prompts should get you started.

1. Inventory your interests by creating five separate lists on a page of your notebook. Choose among the following words as a general category for each of the five lists you will create: Places, Trends, Things, Technologies, People, Controversies, History, Jobs, Habits, Hobbies. In each of the five categories you choose, brainstorm a list of words or phrases that come to mind when you think about *what you know and what you might want to know.* For example, under Places I would put "pigeons in Florence" because I want to know more about their impact on Renaissance buildings. Under Hobbies, I would put "fly fishing" because that's something I know about. Spend about fifteen minutes building these lists.

2. Look over your lists and ask yourself, *Are there research topics implied by a few of the items on these lists?* In other words, what here raises questions that more research might answer? What is it about this item that I wonder about?

3. Finally, choose a promising item from one of the lists and generate questions about it that you'd love to have answered. Perhaps you already know something about the topic but would like to learn more. Don't worry yet whether all the questions are great.

Fastwriting Prompts. Remember, fastwriting is a great way to stimulate creative thinking. Turn off your critical side and let yourself write "badly."

1. Choose an item from your lists and use it as a prompt for a seven-minute fastwrite. Begin by telling yourself the story of when, where, and why you first got interested in the subject. When the writing stalls, write the following phrase, and follow it for as long as you can: Among the things I most want to learn about this are...

2. Get a copy of the daily newspaper. Read it quickly and then clip any articles that make you think or feel something, even if you can't quite say much more about your reaction. Choose one article and glue it into your notebook. Just below, use the article as a prompt for a "narrative of thought" response. Begin this way: When I first read this article, I thought (or felt)...And then I thought...And then...If the writing takes off in another direction, let it. End by finishing the following sentence: When I first started thinking about this I thought _____, but now I think _____.

ONE STUDENT'S RESPONSE

Julian's Journal

TOPIC: JAZZ

My dad was into jazz. Would listen to it all night long after working all day long. He listened to all kinds of jazz—Bird, Miles Davis, Billy Holiday, Monk. It took me years to really appreciate the music but now it's my favorite kind. **Among the things I most want to learn about** jazz is its connection to African music and slave songs. It makes me wonder whether the uniqueness of jazz, its spontaneity especially, has something to do with the hymns and spirituals of the slaves. **Among the other things I want to learn** is whether jazz was accepted in the early days. I seem to remember my dad saying that the...

Visual Prompts. Sometimes the best way to generate material is to see what we think represented in something other than sentences. Boxes, lines, webs, clusters, arrows, charts, and even sketches can help us to see more of the landscape of a subject, especially connections among fragments of information that aren't as obvious in prose.

1. Cluster the phrase, *I'm really curious about.*...Put the phrase in the center of a blank page and build a web of associations, each of which might begin with the word *why*. Explore your curiosity about things in your personal life, in the community, in the region, the state, the country, the world.

2. Do an image search using Google on some person, place, thing, or event that interests you (see the accompanying photo). Might one of the pictures you find be the focus of an investigation? Who was that guy? What *was* going on when this happened? Why did it happen?

Research Prompts. Should you do some research before you begin your research? Absolutely. By exploring what others have said or done or wondered about, you might discover an interest in something you wouldn't have otherwise considered.

1. Surf the Net, perhaps beginning with a subject directory such as The Virtual Library (http://vlib.org). Start by clicking on a subject area that interests you. Keep following the links as you branch more deeply into the subcategories and subdisciplines of that area of knowledge. Look for specific subject areas that intrigue you. For example, you might have begun in the broad subject of history, clicked the link for medieval history (maybe you've always wondered what was dark about the Dark Ages), and ended up reading some fascinating articles on the home life of medieval women. Does it raise some questions you'd like to explore?

2. Study the local newspaper. Devote some time to reading the local paper to discover a local controversy that intrigues you. Say there was an article on the impact of Title IX on the university's athletic department, and you wonder, *Is the elimination of the men's wrestling team really the result of shifts in funding to women's sports*? Or perhaps there's a letter to the editor about the condition of housing for migrant workers in the valley. Are things really that bad?

Judging What You Have

The great thing about simply generating material is that you can turn off your critical mind and simply muck about all sorts of possible topics for your essay. But, as always, the process depends on taking a more analytical look at whether you've discovered anything genuinely useful. Remember your goal at this stage: You want

A Google image search on the "Harlem Renaissance" produced this 1936 painting, *Aspiration* by Aaron Douglas. The image depicts one reason for the African American artistic renaissance in many American cities back then—the migration of blacks from the South to places such as New York and Chicago. The image suggests a great focus for an investigation of the Harlem Renaissance: Why did this migration occur?

to identify a possible topic—and maybe, if you're lucky, a research question—that will move your investigation forward in the next few days. The following suggestions should help.

What's Promising Material and What Isn't? Do you have a researchable *question*? The topic itself may not be the problem at all. Wondering whether Elvis is really dead isn't really a very good research question because the answer is pretty simple: Yep. But wondering why certain people keep asking the question in the first place—why there's a need to maintain the fiction that the King is still around—is an excellent opening question for a research project. I've read riveting books on the most common subjects—salt, for example—that succeeded because the writer found interesting questions to ask about them. This, by the way, is the key to writing strong research papers about assigned topics. Virtually any topic can be interesting to you if you find the question that makes you wonder.

Is It a Researchable Question? What is a researchable question? I've already mentioned the most important characteristic: The question interests you. But there are some other things to consider as well:

- *Is it the right size?* As illustrated in the earlier "Seeing the Form" feature, the quickest way to make any research project unmanageable is to ask a really, really big question: What were the causes of the Iraqi War? Why is there racism in America? At the other extreme is the question that is so limited, so small in scope, that it isn't enough to carry the weight of your investigation; but this is rarely a problem. The key is to find an opening question that isn't too broad and isn't too narrow, one that allows you to *exclude* aspects of the topic because they aren't relevant.

- *Has something already been said about it?* In other words, is information available that *is* relevant to the question you're asking? Have experts and others addressed the question in some way, perhaps indirectly or in other contexts? This may be hard to know until you look.

- *Does it raise more questions?* Some questions have pretty simple answers. For example, wondering why the sky is blue might be an interesting question, but it probably won't sustain any kind of extended inquiry because the reasons for blue skies are well known. A better research question raises more questions the more you think about it, or seems to lead to controversies, debates, or disagreements among knowledgeable people.

- *Does it matter?* It might matter to you, and it needs to. But the best research questions should be potentially interesting and relevant to other people, too. Doing research on how to deal with your messy boyfriend, for example, may not matter really to anyone but you. But it really depends on how you frame the research question. Do men and women in this culture see domestic spaces differently, use them for different reasons, and talk about them in different ways? That's probably too big a research question, but it certainly transcends your personal problem to address questions many of us find interesting and relevant to our lives.

Questions About Audience and Purpose. The best motive for writing a research essay about a particular topic is the same reason you might want to write about anything—it makes you curious. It could interest you for any number of reasons. Perphaps you want to research an illness because your mother has it; maybe you're an engineering major and you're interested in the early history of the computer; maybe you're a hunter and want to know the impact of gray wolf reintroduction on the elk herd; or maybe you're a single parent interested in the impact of divorce on very young children.

You already know what a huge difference audience makes in how you write something. This applies to research papers, too. Though it may seem that there's some standard Research Paper, there's actually quite a range of writing that uses research. One way to distinguish between these types of writing is to think about *for whom* they're written. Readers of research who are less knowledgeable about your topic have different expectations than those who know a lot. For one thing, a general audience might welcome a conversational tone and wouldn't necessarily see the absence of, say, MLA documentation as a problem. On the other hand, a research paper you write in an environmental history class for your professor will likely be documented and may not use "I." Your professor might also expect you to use certain types of evidence, maybe drawing heavily on original (or primary) historical documents and avoiding information from Wikipedia, *History Magazine,* and other sources that might be perfectly fine in an essay for less knowledgeable readers. Consequently, the most important question you can ask when you're given a research assignment is about audience. Is this written for more—or less—knowledgeable readers?

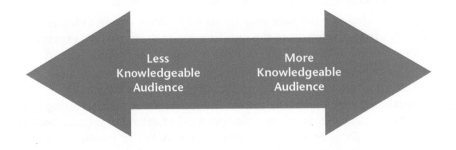

Essay

First person (subjective)

Informal structure

Fewer rules of evidence

No peer review

May document

More conversational

Question-driven

Paper

Third person (objective)

Formal structure

Stricter rules of evidence

Strong peer review

Always documents

More formal

Thesis-driven

For this assignment you'll likely be writing for a larger, less specialized audience—your peers and your instructor in this class. Learning to write about complex or technical subjects for a more general audience is enormously valuable, not only because you have to write papers in future classes. Much of the research-based writing you'll do after college will demand the ability to write clearly for readers who are less knowledgeable than you about a subject.

Practically speaking, then, this means choosing a topic that might interest other nonexperts. It also means choosing a good question to guide your investigation, one that people other than you might want to know the answer to. You can get some direction on this in class; also see the "Inquiring into the Details: Finding the Focusing Question" box below.

INQUIRING INTO THE DETAILS

Finding the Focusing Question

Once you tentatively settle on a topic, you're ready to do this in-class exercise. It should help you find questions that will help you focus your project.

1. Each student will take a piece of paper or a large piece of newsprint and post it on the wall. (In computer labs, students can use a word-processing program and move from station to station in the steps that follow.)

2. Write your topic at the very top of the paper (for instance, "hybrid cars").

3. Take a few minutes to briefly describe why you chose the topic.

4. Spend five minutes to briefly list what you know about your topic already (for instance, any surprising facts or statistics, the extent of the problem, important people or institutions involved, key schools of thought, common misconceptions, important trends, and controversies).

5. Now spend fifteen or twenty minutes brainstorming a list of questions about your topic that you'd love to learn the answers to. Make the list as long as you can.

6. Look around the room. You'll see a gallery of topics and questions on the walls. Now you can help each other. Move around the room, reviewing the topics and questions other students have generated. For each topic posted on the wall, do two things: Check the *one* question on the list you find most interesting, and add a question *you* would like answered about that topic.

7. Now you have long lists of questions about your topic. Is there one that you think might be researchable, using the criteria for such questions? Which questions seem to generate the most interest in the class? Do any of those interest you, too?

8. Pick one question from the list that could be your initial focusing question. Remember, you can change it later.

ONE STUDENT'S RESPONSE

Julian's Journal

FINDING THE FOCUSING QUESTION

1. The Blues

2. Chose this topic because I've listened to jazz and blues since I was a kid, but never really understood its origins.

3. Some famous blues singers: Robert Johnson, Blind Lemon Jefferson...Some qualities of blues: appeals more to the heart than the head, has a characteristic "bluesy" sound, early music in the South...

4. Questions:

   What's the relationship between blues and jazz?

   Who was the most influential blues musician in the early days?

   How is African music part of the blues?

   Did only blacks listen to blues in the beginning?

   How does the blues vary by region?

Writing the Sketch

The sketch for your research essay will be a little different from those you've written earlier. Rather than writing a "sketchy" draft of a possible essay, you'll develop a project narrative, one that summarizes your working knowledge of the topic and how your thinking about it has evolved so far. A working knowledge of your topic, according to William Badke, is achieved when you have enough information to be able to talk about it for five minutes without repeating yourself. You develop a working knowledge by conducting basic research on the Web and at the university library.

Once you are ready, your project narrative should contain the following features:

- The title should be the tentative focusing question you've chosen on your topic.

- The piece itself should tell the story of your thinking about that question and topic from the beginning until now.

- This narrative of thought should discuss the ways in which your working knowledge of the topic has changed the way you think about it.

- The narrative should be about 500 words.

- Information, ideas, or quotations you borrow from outside sources should be cited.

■ STUDENT SKETCH

It was spring and Amy Garrett-Brown began to imagine shorts and bathing suits, but then she took a look at her skin in the mirror. She looked pale and pasty. Wouldn't a nice tan be good about now? But would she be compromising her health for vanity, she wondered? Suddenly, Garrett had a research topic and an opening question. Here's her sketch on the topic.

Why Do People Tan?

Amy Garrett-Brown

This started as a simple question spurred by one of my occasional "people are so stupid" rants. I wondered who was to blame for this, who made it cool for white people to be tan? It seems completely asinine on the surface to waste money and time on a prepaid tan that will only result in prematurely leathered and wrinkled skin and a much higher risk of developing melanoma or other skin cancers. And then I looked down at my arms and noticed that I've managed to build up a decent tan this summer myself, not via lightbulb technology, but the old fashioned way, by playing in the sun. Hmmm...am I a hypocrite? [1]

I wondered about that. As I researched sunbathing and the like I came across an interesting article in *The Atlanta Journal-Constitution* titled "The Rural South These Days Has More Tanning Salons Than John Deeres" by Rheta Grimsley Johnson. Johnson summarizes her point with a quote from E. B. White, "I am fascinated by the anatomy of decline...by the spectacle of people passively accepting a degenerating process which is against their own interests." She then explains, "He was writing about the redesign of the automobile—longer and lower with bigger fenders. He also objected to replacing the car window crank with a lazy push-button. If he could see us now, jumping into our foreign cars and speeding down to the tanning bed and nail art salon. Lost, buffed souls" (M1). [2]

It struck me as I read the last lines of this sardonic critique of society that I don't necessarily wonder why people tan, but why they completely gyp themselves of the pleasures of the sun to be rewarded with a battle with cancer at worst and saggy skin at best. It seems like everyone wants to feel active, even if they aren't. [3]

In a survey conducted by *Seventeen* magazine, "2/3 of the teens say they look better with a tan and feel healthier, more sophisticated and 50% say they looked more athletic" (qtd. in "Sun Tanning"). Somehow it seems that society has missed the forest for the trees. A nice tan once meant you spent your days on the beach playing volleyball and swimming, hiking in the mountains or riding a horse, riding a bike around town or jogging in the afternoons; it was usually accompanied by fit and trim bodies and healthy smiles. Now it means you spent $45 a month building a base tan. [4]

But somehow the message isn't translating. People still feel healthy with a bastardized tan? So there must be something more to it all. Is the fashion industry that powerful? In her fashion column Patricia McLaughlin puts the fascination with a tan into perspective. [5]

(continued)

(continued)

White people have it tough. At least the pale ones, whose skin is really a mottled, un-appetizing grayish-yellowish-pinkish off-white threaded with blue veins. Once, amazing as it may seem, it was actually cool to have skin this color. Then Coco Chanel came home with a tan from a cruise on the Duke of Westminster's yacht, and ever since, white people have preferred to be a biscuity golden color. (2)

6   So maybe that's it, people just like the way it looks to be tan. I know I feel better about putting on a bathing suit if I'm not so starkly white that I worry about blinding young children. I also know that it just feels good to be in the sun. The warm rays beating down on my back and shoulders as I work outdoors or go for a hike seem therapeutic and natural.

7   But the health industry sure doesn't like to condone it. In an article by Alexandra Greeley titled "No Tan Is a Safe Tan," she presents her case against spending time in the sun and especially tanning with facts and statistics, but I couldn't help but wonder if she ever has any fun after reading the closing lines to her article. "In the end, there really is nothing new under the sun, except that perhaps more people are staying out of it, heeding medical warnings such as Bergstresser's: 'Less sun is better. No sun is best of all'" (15).

8   I disagree. But I'm no expert, so I sought proof of my hunch that the sun is really our friend and found it. Of course, I'm not condoning the 1976 "Savage Tan" or complete ignorance of the dangers of a depleted ozone and proof that severe sunburns lead to cancers, but I think there must be some middle ground.

Works Cited

Greeley, Alexandra. "No Tan Is a Safe Tan." *Nutrition Health Review: The Consumer's Medical Journal* 59 (Summer 1991): 14–15. Print.

Johnson, Rheta Grimsley. "The Rural South These Days Has More Tanning Salons Than John Deeres." *The Atlanta Journal-Constitution* 23 Apr. 2000, home ed.: M1. Print.

McLaughlin, Patricia. "Dying for a Tan This Summer?" *St. Louis Post-Dispatch* 15 June 1995: 2.

"Sun Tanning." *Cool Nurse* 2000–2003 18 June 2003. Print.

Moving from Sketch to Draft

Your sketch may not really be an early draft of the essay you'll write later. It's probably more of a record of your thinking about your topic, perhaps leading you to a clearer idea about the best focusing question and perhaps a stronger sense of what you might want to say in the draft. Your sketch also gives you a chance to share what you've discovered so far with others in your class, but not in the usual way. Rather than workshopping your sketch, you'll use it to develop a brief presentation.

Evaluating Your Own Sketch. Follow the road map of the thinking present in your sketch to get a clearer sense of where you want to go in the draft.

1. What seemed to be the turning point in your own thinking about the topic? What caused it?

2. Is the focusing question you wrote at the beginning of the sketch still the right title? Does that question need to be revised or do you need to write a new one?

3. Based on what you know now, how would you answer the question you're asking?

Questions for Peer Review. Rather than workshopping your sketch, you will use it as the basis for a brief class presentation. Following a press conference format, you will speak for about five to ten minutes, highlighting some or all of the following:

- What focusing question did you start with? What question do you want to ask now?
- What is the most surprising thing you've learned so far?
- What do experts on the topic debate about?
- What are the most common misconceptions about the topic?
- What story can you tell about the topic—a case study, a telling event, a profile of the person involved?

Try to make this presentation lively and interesting. Your purpose, in part, is to get a sense of potential reader interest in your topic and the question you're pursuing. Students listening to the presentations should be encouraged to ask questions about what you've said—or haven't said. They also might have some suggestions of questions about your topic you hadn't considered, or tips on where to search for more information. Allow another five to ten minutes for this question-and-answer session.

Reflecting on What You've Learned. Following your presentation, spend a few minutes generating a list of everything you heard, and then begin a five-minute fastwrite that explores your reaction to these questions and suggestions and your tentative plan for revision. Did the class have a lot of questions about your topic following the presentation? What seems to have most piqued their interest? What questions or controversies seem to ignite the most discussion? What did the discussion suggest might be new avenues for research? End your fastwrite by writing about what you understand now about your topic and your initial beliefs about it that you didn't fully understand when you began writing.

Research and Other Strategies: Gathering More Information

Discovery is what drives inquiry-based research. This is why having a good question matters so much, and finding a good question for your project depends on knowing something about your topic. "Working knowledge" seeds this effort.

A working knowledge will give you an encyclopedia-like view of your topic—what is the terrain, what are the controversies or the questions, who is influential—and from this you can frame a question that interests you.

But this is just the beginning. As you explore your research question in the coming weeks, you'll go beyond working knowledge to "focused knowledge," finding information that drills down more deeply into your topic's terrain. Good questions are sharper drills. However, this is an open-ended process and your goal at this stage is to use what you discover to continually shape what you want to see. As you become more informed, you'll revise your approach: refining your question, developing ideas about what you think, and always searching for the answers to this simple question: *So what?*

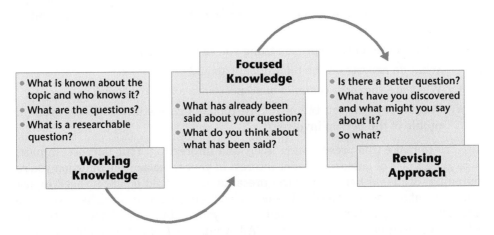

Writing *while you research* will help you figure this all out and even help you get a start on drafting your essay. I'm not talking about simply taking notes on the information that you find in the coming weeks. Writing about what you *think* about what you're reading or hearing is the best incubator of insight. The double-entry journal is one method that encourages this kind of writing.

Composing the Draft

Sara was a compulsive collector of information. She researched and researched, collecting more books and articles and Web sources until the desk in her apartment looked like a miniature version of downtown Chicago—towering piles of paper and books everywhere. She never felt as if she knew enough to begin writing her essay, and would only begin drafting when forced to—the paper was due tomorrow. Neal figured he could find most of what he needed pretty quickly on the Internet. He printed out a few articles and Web pages and felt confident he could write his paper using those. He didn't feel pressured to begin writing until the due date loomed. When Neal started writing and realized that he probably wouldn't be able to get the required page length, he widened the margins.

Sara and Neal obviously use different strategies for getting to the draft. Sara relies on accumulating great quantities of information, trusting that aggressively collecting sources will make the writing easier—the main source of anxiety for her—although she probably doesn't really believe that. On the other hand, Neal suffers from overconfidence. He figures he can make do with a few sources and doesn't look around much. Both Neal and Sara do what research paper writers have done forever: wait until the last minute. Neither of these writers will be happy with the result.

It's easy to avoid this situation if you begin the draft after you've accomplished the following:

- *You've done some writing before you start writing.* In other words, have you exploited the double-entry journal or an alternative notetaking method to both collect useful information and to explore your reaction to what it says?

- *You are working from abundance (but not overabundance).* Neal is much more typical than Sara. He is trying to compose his draft by drawing from a nearly empty well. Almost any writing—and particularly research writing—depends on working from abundance. You need to collect more information than you can use. But not too much. Don't let endless collecting become an avoidance tactic.

- *Your focusing question has helped you* exclude *information.* A good focusing question is a guide. It will help you see the relevance of certain portions of the sources you've collected and give you reason to ignore the rest. If you sense that this is happening consistently as you review your sources, you're probably ready to write.

- *You have a tentative idea about what you think.* By now, you know enough about your topic to have some feelings or ideas about a possible answer to the question behind your investigation. Remember the draft may make you change your mind—that's fine—but begin composing with at least a tentative point of view.

Methods of Development. The research essay is more likely than the previous essays to combine a range of methods of development. You can see that already from the professional essays earlier in this chapter. However, here are some more typical designs for research essays:

Narrative. We don't usually associate narrative structure with research papers, but research-based writing tells stories all the time. Perhaps one of the most common techniques is use of the case study, which can be an excellent way to begin your paper. Case studies or anecdotes about people involved or affected by a topic often bring that topic to life by moving it closer to the everyday *lives* of people. But narrative is also used as the backbone of a research essay. Sometimes an essay tells the story of what the writer wanted to know and what she found out, a kind of narrative of thought. The sketch you wrote earlier is an early project narrative that established your initial focusing question and some tentative clues about where it might lead. This structure could easily be imported into the final draft of your research essay, only it will be more developed and more insightful.

Question to Answer. Because much of the research process is devoted to developing a good question to drive the inquiry, it makes sense to consider organizing your essay around what that question is, where it came from, and what has already been said about it, and then reporting what you've discovered about possible answers to the question that triggered the investigation. A lot of formal academic research is organized this way, although there might be an added section about the methods the investigator chose to try to seek the answers.

Known to Unknown. This is a variation on the question-to-answer structure that might be particularly useful if you're writing about a complex topic about which much remains unknown. Your research might have led to the discovery that the question you're interested in is a question that has very speculative or limited answers. For example, Andy was writing about the use of psychiatric medicine such as antidepressants and antipsychotics on children because his family physician had recommended them for one of his own kids. Andy quickly discovered that this was a relatively new use for such drugs and that much mystery surrounded both the diagnosis and treatment of children with emotional problems. It became clear that the purpose of his essay was not to offer a definitive answer to his question, but to suggest areas that still needed further study.

Using Evidence. While every discipline has its own ideas about what counts as good research evidence, the research essay is a less specialized form with a more general audience. Therefore, the rules of evidence for a research essay aren't nearly as strict as they might be, say, in an academic article in psychology or biology. But that's not to say that anything goes. Research writing obviously depends mainly on sources outside the writer—published materials, interviews with people involved in the topic, and observations in the field—but the writer's personal experience can count if it's relevant. In some cases, you may want to cite your own experience as evidence that either supports or contradicts a claim made by someone else, but your experience alone probably isn't sufficient evidence. Find other voices that confirm it.

> Research writing obviously depends mainly on sources outside the writer…but the writer's personal experience can count if it's relevant.

Not all outside sources are equally convincing either. Figure 2 suggests a hierarchy that is one way of evaluating how "authoritative" a source might be. Notice that, generally speaking, the more specialized a publication's audience, the more likely the information in it will be valued. For example, an article on dream interpretation in the *Journal of American Psychology* is considered more authoritative than an article on the same subject in *Ladies' Home Journal*. The reasons for this are pretty obvious: When you write for experts in the field, you'd better know what you're talking about.

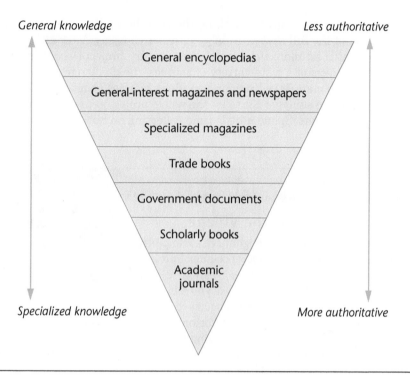

General knowledge   Less authoritative

General encyclopedias

General-interest magazines and newspapers

Specialized magazines

Trade books

Government documents

Scholarly books

Academic journals

Specialized knowledge   More authoritative

Figure 2   A hierarchy of sources places the most credible at the bottom of an inverted pyramid. For academic research, these are usually articles and books that are reviewed by other experts before they're published.

Finally, an important way to write authoritatively using outside sources is not only to use the right sources but to cite them carefully. It's crucial that you acknowledge those whose ideas have helped you see more deeply into your topic. In your draft, acknowledge your sources in two ways:

1. Mention them in your essay using attribution tags, such as *according to Jones*...or *Hill argues that*...or *Baraka said*....

2. Cite borrowed information, quotations, and ideas using MLA or APA conventions.

Workshopping the Draft

Share your research essay in a small group workshop before you begin your final revision. Because of the length of these essays, you might want to allow more time for these discussions, or encourage group members to read the drafts before the group meets. Your instructor might also put you in smaller groups.

Reflecting on the Draft. A draft is a thing the wind blows through. That might be especially true of the full first draft of your research essay. After all, this project involves juggling a lot more than most other inquiry projects—controlling information and the ideas of a wide variety of sources, the challenge of trying to surround that outside material with your own ideas, worries about following citation conventions, and the struggle not to let the whole project get away from your own purposes and questions. Spend a little time reflecting on how all this went.

WRITING IN THE DISCIPLINES

Being a Stranger in the Village

As you do your research you might have some pretty heavy reading. Most things you encounter from the bottom of the pyramid of sources (see Figure 2) is pretty scholarly stuff. This might make you feel like a stranger in a faraway village. What language do these people speak? What are these odd customs? All communities have their own *discourses* or ways of talking and behaving that are familiar to insiders and make everyone else feel like outsiders. That's exactly how I might feel if I hung out with the "dudes" at the skateboard park in town.

Your frustration of trying to understand an article from the *Journal of Artificial Organs* (yes, there is one) when you're not a surgeon isn't that different from a surgeon's frustration at trying to understand an article in the *Journal of Bank Cost and Management Accounting*. In both cases, the readers are the village strangers.

Yet, if you're an undergraduate trying to do research, you've got to try to make sense of unfamiliar academic discourses. What can you do? Well, you can do what a visitor to a foreign land tries to do: Pay attention to the purposes of local customs, try to pick up some of the language, and figure out the minimum you need to know to get what you need.

While there are many different academic discourses, there are a few conventions that articles in many disciplines share. Knowing these will help you get what you need to do your research:

- **Read abstracts.** Journal articles in the social sciences and dissertations often include one-paragraph summaries of the investigator's findings, usually written by the investigator. Start with the abstracts to get a sense of whether it's worth your time to wade through the article.
- **Read conclusions.** The formally structured article in many disciplines has the following parts: abstract, introduction or literature review, methods, results or discussion, and conclusions. Skim the article to get a sense of the purpose of the study and then focus on the conclusion for more careful reading. There you should find the most important findings.

- *Go to the literature review.* For undergraduate research, sometimes the best part of any academic book or article isn't the findings, the claim, or the theory but the literature review. This is the part that appears in or immediately after an introduction where the author updates the reader on the current "conversation" on the topic, including prevailing findings, current theories, and important contributions to think about.
- *Mine the bibliography.* The author of a book or article may have done some of your research for you. Even if you can't use much from a particular source for your paper, the bibliography can be invaluable, directing you to some of the best sources on your topic. The sources in the literature review section (see the preceding bullet point) are usually the best out there on that topic.

In your notebook or on a separate piece of paper you'll attach to the draft when you hand it in, answer the following questions:

- What's the most important thing you learned about your topic after the research and writing you've just completed? Is this important understanding obvious in the draft?
- Choose two paragraphs that incorporate outside sources—one that you think is written pretty well, and another less well. What differences do you notice between the two? Can you identify at least one problem you need to work on in the next draft that will help you improve the way you integrate sources?
- What was your focusing question? How does the draft attempt to answer it?

Questions for Readers. Make sure that you have some specific questions you'd like to ask your workshop group about how the draft is working. Here are some others:

1. In your own words, what do you think is the main thing I'm trying to say in the draft? Where in the draft do you think I say it?
2. What was the most interesting part of the essay? What was the least interesting? Why?
3. After you read the first few paragraphs, did you have a clear sense of what my focusing question was?
4. Did any part of the draft seem to drift away from that focus?
5. Where do I need more information or more evidence?

Revising the Draft

One of the most common misconceptions about revision is that you do it only at the end of the writing process. In fact, up to this point, you should have been revising your work all along, from the first few journal exercises when you chose a topic and played with possible angles on it, to the journal work you might have done to prepare to write the sketch, and then again with your efforts to turn your sketch into a more developed draft. Revision is literally "re-seeing," and every time you create the conditions that allow you to discover something new about how you see or what you think about your subject, you are, in fact, engaged in the act of revision. In a sense, then, each writing assignment you undertake is one long act of revision, from start to finish.

But once you've completed a draft, the revision process becomes more focused. You are mostly working with material that should be somewhat settled, with purposes that might be clearer, and ideas that may have more shape. At this point, the biggest temptation is to tell yourself you are largely done and what revision remains is merely a matter of "fixing things"—tinkering with sentences, correcting typos, and running a spellchecker. In one survey, 70 percent of students admitted as much. "I usually just tidy things up" was ranked first or second by students who were asked what they do most often when they revise an academic paper.

These activities are certainly an element of revision—and an important one—but as the word *revision* implies, it's important to "re-see" both what you are trying to say and how you try to say it, even at this stage in the process. Writers can break the bonds that limit their ability to find new ways of seeing the draft.

As you plan for revision, do any of the following problems typical of research essay drafts apply to yours?

- Is the essay sufficiently focused? Remember the photography metaphor from the "Seeing the Form" feature: you want to take closer pictures rather than landscape shots of your subject. Having too broad a focus is a particularly troublesome issue with research-based writing. You can fix this by refining your question and narrowing the scope of your project.

- Did you collect enough information? Drafts that work from scarcity typically run short, have too broad a focus, or suffer from vagueness. The solution? Go back to the library or the Web and collect more information.

- Is the essay organized around your research question from beginning to end? Do any paragraphs or passages strike off in irrelevant directions?

- Does the draft say too much? Remember that a strong research essay not only asks an interesting question about a topic but explicitly states what the writer thinks is the best answer, even if it's speculative. Is this thesis clear?

It would probably be useful to check your draft for logical fallacies. One of the challenges of a longer essay with sources is organizing all that information. Use the following table to find other appropriate revision strategies. Remember that a draft may present problems in more than one category.

WRITING IN YOUR LIFE

Everyday Research

Because of the Internet, people do everyday research more now than at any time in my lifetime. Online research skills are not only a key to academic success but will help keep you healthy, save money, and solve marital problems. A recent Pew study (2007) found that more people consult the Internet to solve problems than consult professionals who are experts on these problems. More surprising, though, was that people—particularly people aged 18 to 30—still go to libraries for a variety of purposes, including research.

"Information literacy" has long been a hot topic among librarians, but in recent years others—including business leaders—have called it one of "the basic skills sets of the twenty-first century." What exactly are we talking about here? Information literacy isn't just possessing the skills to use a computer to search for information, but knowing how to match appropriate information to solve a particular problem. People who are information literate can evaluate what they find, synthesize the information, and *use* it purposefully.

GUIDE TO REVISION STRATEGIES

Problems in the Draft

Unclear purpose
- Not sure what the paper is about?

Unclear thesis, theme, or main idea
- Not sure what you're trying to say?

Lack of information or development
- Need more convincing evidence? Need to check for logical fallacies?

Disorganized
- Doesn't move logically or smoothly from paragraph to paragraph?

Unclear or awkward at the level of sentences and paragraphs
- Seems choppy or hard to follow at the level of sentences or paragraphs?

Polishing the Draft

After you've addressed the more global problems in your draft, you should focus on more local matters, such as how effectively you integrate and cite sources, how successfully you've organized your paragraphs, and whether you've written the draft in a clear, lively style. Don't forget to use the handbook at the back of the book to help you with any grammatical and stylistic questions you might have; also use guides to MLA or APA citations to check how well you've followed those conventions.

Before you finish your draft, work through the following checklist:

✓ Every paragraph is about one thing.

✓ The transitions between paragraphs aren't abrupt.

✓ The length of sentences varies in each paragraph.

✓ Each sentence is concise. There are no unnecessary words or phrases.

✓ You've checked grammar, particularly verb agreement, run-on sentences, unclear pronouns, and misused words (*there/their, where/were,* and so on).

✓ You've run your spellchecker and proofed your paper for misspelled words.

✓ You've double-checked your citations and Works Cited or References page to ensure that the formatting is correct.

■ STUDENT ESSAY

Gordon Seirup's essay "College Dating," which is formatted according to MLA documentation guidelines, is a great finale to this chapter's readings on the "hooking up" phenomenon on American college campuses. I like this essay because Seirup takes control of the information he gathered in his Web research by finding—and naming—the patterns he sees in college dating and using them to organize his essay. He does a great job of tapping a variety of sources and bringing in the voices of other students and experts who have something relevant to say. Also notice how well these quotations are embedded in Gordon's own prose.

Like any work, "College Dating" could be an even stronger essay. While the essay employs evidence from some of the professional readings in this chapter, most of these sources Seirup cites consist of informal quotations taken from the online versions of college newspapers and lack the authority of formal print sources. Though the research question is clear, Gordon's essay also isn't explicitly organized around a specific claim that arises from his research. What thesis about college romance would you advance after reading the essay?

Seirup 1

Gordon E. Seirup

Professor Ballenger

English 101

6 October 2006

College Dating

First there was the passing notes, hand holding, and name-calling of middle school. Then you survived your first heartbreak when your high school sweetheart decided it would be best to "just be friends." Now swept away in college life you hardly take the time to step back and ask yourself, "What am I doing here? Whose bed did I just wake up in, and how the hell did I get here?!" If you have not yet taken the time to ponder what it is you plan to do with the so-called best four years of your life, besides studying and eating dorm food, perhaps it is about time you did. What do you want to be accomplishing in these prime dating years? More importantly, is that what you are accomplishing? In short, my purpose is to discuss the question: "What role should dating play in college students' lives?"

If you assume that most college students have thought how their dating decisions today might affect them tomorrow, think again. The students I spoke with informally here on the Colorado State University campus all hesitated when asked to simply "define dating." Once done struggling through that answer, they were asked, What is the purpose of dating in college?" These students' answers ranged from "getting laid!" to "discover more about yourself through others" to "find the person you want to marry" to "I have no clue." Are the college masses blissfully unaware of exactly what it is they are doing when they pursue relationships?

First, what is dating? For my purposes, dating is defined as seeing someone socially in a one-on-one setting. Other terms used within the following pages are "hooking up" and "courtship," defined as noncommittal sexual acts

1

2

3

and nonserial exclusive dating with the intention of marriage, respectively. What I mean by "nonserial" dating is that when you choose to date someone, you intend to marry that person. While this may not work out, and might lead you to enter this process again, you sincerely choose each person you date as a potential spouse. While you may court more than one person, it isn't your intention to do so.

4   I have defined five major approaches to college dating based on their common purpose, values, and motivations, in addition to their general line of reasoning: Casual Dating, Exclusive Dating, Courting, Cannot Date, and Hooking Up.

5   Casual dating was popular during the American 1950s, although Beth Bailey notes that "between 1890 and 1925, dating—in practice and in name—had gradually, almost imperceptibly, become a universal custom in America" (19). The emergence of public dating rituals coincided with the emergence of mass media, especially TV and magazines that made dating a feature of the typical American romance (Bailey 9). Casual dating was modeled on popular TV shows, and analyzed in mostly women's magazines—where to go, how much to spend, when to allow a first kiss. A major motive for dating was, according to Bailey, public competition to spend the most, choose the best partner, and so on.

6   However, dating these days is much less ritualized. Rather than focusing on public display, these days casual daters value meeting new people, discovering and/or reinventing who you are as a person, and enjoying yourself. The original scenario for casual dating typically went something like this: Guy meets Girl, decides he would like to see her socially, and asks her to join him at the diner for hamburgers and a shared milkshake. If this date goes well, they may see each other again. After about three dates there is a good chance Guy would be graced with a goodnight kiss.

These dates did not imply exclusivity or any concrete commitment at all. 7
While social enjoyment is the driving force behind the Casual Dating approach,
there are two other important aspects: meeting new people and discovering yourself. By the simple act of participating in these dates, each party naturally learns
more about himself and herself through their interaction. "Dating one-on-one
gives you a chance to become comfortable with new people," says Julie Baugher,
Georgetown University's premier relationship columnist (Baugher, "'Rules'").

The key to developing sufficient attachment for a couple to want to date 8
multiple times is that elusive quality called "chemistry." One study that
attempted to pin down exactly what college students mean by chemistry suggested that it involves similarity of interests and backgrounds, as well as
"reciprocity," or the feeling that both partners are giving something to each
other (Peretti and Abplanalp 5).

But chemistry isn't necessarily a scarce phenomenon, and it's possible to 9
find it with more than one person. According to Lee Ann Hamilton, a health
educator at the University of Arizona, "College is the time to re-invent yourself
and try new things; many people don't want to be tied down" (qtd. in Hill). It
is very important to keep in mind that not being "tied down," as Ms. Hamilton
put it, is a fundamental aspect of the Casual Dating approach.

Columnist Julie Baugher has laid out some guidelines helpful to circum- 10
venting our typical defensive maneuvers when it comes to dating. (It may be
useful to remember these next time you are asked out for a date.) "Don't
think about whether you want to Date him with an uppercase 'D' (meaning
exclusive dating). Don't conclude that he isn't 'Your type.' Don't assume this is
the beginning of a long-term relationship that you're not ready for" (Baugher,
"Dating"). Approaching it casually, couples may date as many people as there

Seirup 4

are nights available in the week, so long as all parties involved know the arrangement.

11   Similar to the Casual Dating approach is the Exclusive Dating approach. Both parties value dating as an activity for social enjoyment, as well as self-education. Exclusive dating may be thought of as the "next step" from casual dating, and indeed commonly tends to grow out of casual dating. When exclusively dating, you are not only learning more about yourself, but also consciously aware of what you are learning about your partner. Which characteristics can you see yourself living with for the rest of your life? Which make you want to run away and never date again? "Through several short-term relationships, students can find personalities with which they are most compatible," claims Matt West, a writer at the University of Virginia. "Relationships at this age allow you to explore what you like and don't like in a partner," agrees Mary Anne Knapp, a clinical social worker. Through a series of exclusive relationships, one forms a model of the ideal spouse (qtd. in Pleiss).

12   However, here is the crucial detail for this approach: This flirtation with long-term commitment is solely a mental exercise. Marriage is not a goal of the exclusive dating approach. Exclusively dating college students are aware of their proximity to marriage; however, they are not going to let that detail dominate their lives. The goal is gaining knowledge. This distinction is memorably worded by Jennifer Graham, a senior staff writer at Stanford University: "I think I'm going to put marriage on the backburner and, at least for the time being, refrain from appraising my peers' credentials for parenthood. There's no need to sap all the joy from life." Don't misinterpret Graham as saying she wishes to ignore completely her peers' credentials for parenthood; rather the issue is at which stage in the dating process qualifications for

Seirup 5

marriage become important. When making the choice of whether or not to date someone, these marriage-related thoughts are minimally important. However, while in a relationship, it would be wise to consider these credentials to learn what you are looking for when you are shopping for a spouse.

Expert testimony supports the Exclusive Dating approach. Clinical social worker Mary Anne Knapp says these exclusive relationships are healthy and "serve more of a purpose than just having a permanent date every Friday night," since "having a supportive partner, someone who knows you and is on your side, is good for a positive outlook on life" (qtd. in Pleiss 1).   13

The premise of the Courting approach is that dating should play no role in the lives of college students. Believers in courtship argue for a return to the practice of courtship rather than dating, and hold marriage absolutely paramount. Furthermore, proponents argue that this courtship should take place after college. In general, students who advocate the Courting approach share strong religious backgrounds, and actively use their faith to both justify their opinion and denounce others'. In fact, the approach is as much their adamant opposition to dating as it is their support of courtship, saying casual dating is "a bankrupt convention...a training ground for divorce [and]... a cheap imitation of the love and intimacy of a real marriage (Jensen)". Furthermore, they believe that the practice of casual dating is futile: "If the couple never intends to get married in the first place, then breaking up is a foregone conclusion, and their relationship is doomed" (Jensen).   14

Advocates of this approach value the unique bonds that are formed between husband and wife as well as purity upon entering marriage. Courtship "is the only way to date with true love, respect and honesty because it is rooted in a desire to take the relationship to its complete and glorious fulfillment"   15

(Jensen). Those seeking courtship seek others who seek the same; assuming that if you have kept pure in pursuit of marriage, you should expect the same of your spouse to-be—though today the selection of potential partners may be slim. "It's hard enough to meet somebody who doesn't have a past relationship that is like a skeleton in her closet," says Matt Sweet, finance major at the University of Virginia (qtd. in Jensen). According to those who take the Courting approach, if more college students adopted their strategy, this wouldn't be a problem.

16   Believers in courtship share both a wholehearted commitment to a relationship that will lead to marriage and the best possible education while in college. Value is placed on the concept of college students being just that—students. During college they have neither the time nor energy to responsibly court a spouse. Therefore, it is best for people to engage in courtship only after graduation and they are settled into their careers.

17   Proponents of the Cannot Date approach also believe that dating should play no role in the lives of college students. They don't oppose dating, but these students have tried to date, or at least wanted to, but deemed it to be impossible. Like the Courting approach, these students value their standing as students and hold education as a very high priority. This approach is aptly described by a student at the University of Arizona: "While pursuing a double major, interning, working, maintaining a social life and attending school full time," Danielle Demizjian, a business economics and finance senior, finds "exclusive dating too much of a commitment" (qtd. in Hill). This is a common complaint among college students. Despite their desire to date, exclusively or casually, there just does not seem to be the time, though time alone is not the only issue. For those students advanced in their time management skills, the

Seirup 7

emotional burden may be too great. Jaime Dutton, a sophomore at Johns Hopkins University, says, "It's hard enough to have fun here with all the work you have to do, [and] there's no reason to have the extra drama in your life" (qtd. in Saxe). Nicole Kucewitz, a writer for the *Rocky Mountain Collegian*, agrees: "Relationships take time and patience, and in college, both of these can be very limited."

Finally, there is the Hooking Up approach. This last group has an alternate social structure to replace traditional dating. Their philosophy is this: At the college level, formal dating is unnecessary. For social activities, in contrast with the one-on-one date, groups are ideal. As for sexual needs, noncommittal hooking up is not only acceptable, it's preferred. Common values amongst this group include enjoying yourself socially with friends, casually fulfilling sexual needs, and avoiding commitment. This "new age" form of dating is the solution that has flourished as a result of the gripes of the Cannot Date approach. 18

Many of the students who Hook Up see the dating arena as split into two distinct groups: "People are either single or practically married" (Burney). Hooking Up is the solution for those people who wish to largely retain their single status while still satisfying their social and sexual needs, and avoiding the "marriage-type" exclusive relationship. Dan, a student at Duke University, puts it this way: "In the real world, there is an expectation that after the third date, you might get a hookup. At Duke, there is the expectation that after the third hookup, you might get a date" (qtd. in Beckett). So perhaps once college students reach the "real world" this approach will fade away, but it remains wildly popular on campus. 19

One reason for its popularity is that Hooking Up avoids potential complications of exclusive dating or even casual dating. With this approach, future hookup partners spend time in groups and get to know each other in a friendlier 20 context first, avoiding the awkward chesslike strategies common to the predate period. Or even simpler, the story goes like this: "Now all a guy in a decent fraternity has to do to hookup on a Saturday night is to sit on the couch long enough at a party. It's slow at first, but eventually a girl will plop herself down beside him, they'll sit there drinking, he'll make a joke, she'll laugh, their eyes will meet, sparks will fly, and the mission is accomplished. And you want me to tell this guy to call a girl, spend $100 on dinner and hope for a goodnight kiss" (qtd. in Beckett)? This trend is perpetuated by "the beds [being] short walks from the parties. This increases the likelihood of the drunken hookup, while simultaneously decreasing the frequency of actual dates," according to Tom Burney, a columnist and student at Duke University (qtd. in Beckett).

21   With this tendency to go from partying to hooking up, a critic may be quick to draw the conclusion that sex is the driving force behind this approach. On the contrary, students' motives are often to get to know potential partners as friends (at least superficially) first. David Brunkow, computer science major at Colorado State University, attests to this: "Most of the people I've been with were already my friends . . . It's so much easier that way. You already know they're a good person and that they're not going to screw you over. Also, if things don't work out, you don't lose your friend" (qtd. in Borra).

22   Research seems to confirm Brunkow's contention. According to Paul and Hayes, the best hookups were more likely to be prefaced by hanging out, flirting, mutual attraction, and talking. The worst hookups often resulted from a friend's instigation (Paul and Hayes 648).

23   Of the five categories I've offered to describe college dating, Hooking Up is both the most common and the most controversial. In a recent study, three quarters of students interviewed reported that they had hooked up at least

Seirup 9

once and at least a third said this involved sex with a stranger or a new ac-
quaintance (Paul, McManus, and Hayes 84). Students who choose Hooking Up
may not believe that there are other, socially sanctioned choices, as this paper
suggests. Do participants think Hooking Up is a good thing? One would assume
so since it's so popular these days. But there is some evidence that the practice
is driven by "pluralistic ignorance" or the mistaken assumption that their discomfort with the behavior is unique. This is particularly true of women
(Lambert, Kahn, and Apple 132), a situation which could lead to abuses.

While no one approach is clearly ideal for all students, there seems to be one   24
to suit everyone, despite a wide range of personal beliefs. Casual Dating, Exclusive
Dating, Courting, Cannot Date, and Hooking Up represent distinct alternatives to
college students, difficult choices that add to the complexities—both academic
and non-academic—that college students find themselves caught up in every day.
But it's crucial that students at least be aware that there are choices to make.

Works Cited

Bailey, Beth. "The Worth of a Date." *From Front Porch to Back Seat: Courtship in
Twentieth-Century America*. 1998. Baltimore: Johns Hopkins University
Press. Print.

Baugher, Julia. "Dating with a Lower Case 'd.'" *Hoya* 4 Oct. 2002. Web. 8 Oct.
2003.

Baugher, Julia. "'Rules' Teach Ladies Tricks to Winning Love." *Hoya* 15 Nov. 2002.
Web. 7 Oct. 2003.

Beckett, Whitney. "What Lies Between the Hookup and Marriage?" *Chronicle*
5 Sept. 2003. Web. 13 Oct. 2003.

Borra, Jessup. "The 'He-Said-She-Said' on Dating." *Rocky Mountain Collegian*
17 Oct. 2002. Web. 19 Oct. 2003.

Seirup 10

Burney, T. "Dating Sea Nuggets." *Chronicle* 26 Mar. 2003. Web. 13 Oct. 2003.

Graham, Jennifer. "Graduation Time: Cap and Gown or Wedding Gown?" *Stanford Daily* 17 July 2003. Web. 13 Oct. 2003.

Hill, Tessa. "UA students Have Lost That Lovin' Feeling." *Arizona Daily Wildcat* 30 Jan. 2003. Web. 8 Oct. 2003.

Jensen, Mark. "A Return to Courtship." *Cavalier Daily* 26 Apr. 2002. Web. 19 Oct. 2003.

Kucewicz, Nicole. "Ins and Outs of the College Dating Game: Fun or Forever?" *Rocky Mountain Collegian* 15 Aug. 2001. Web. 19 Oct. 2003.

Lambert, Tracy, Arnold Kahn, and Kevin Apple. "Pluralistic Ignorance and Hooking." *Journal of Sex Research* 40.2 (2003): 129–33. Print.

Paul, Elizabeth, Brian McManus, and Allison Hayes. "Hookups: Characteristics and Correlates of College Students' Spontaneous and Anonymous Sexual Experiences." *Journal of Sex Research* 37.1 (2000): 76–88. Print.

Paul, Elizabeth, and Kristen Hayes. "The Casualities of Casual Sex: A Qualitative Exploration of the Phenomenology of College Student Hookups." *Journal of Social and Personal Relationships* 19 (2002): 639–61. Print.

Peretti, Peter, and Richard Abplanalp, Jr. "Chemistry in the College Dating Process: Structure and Function." *Social Behavior and Personality* 32.2 (2004): 147–54. Print.

Pleiss, Carissa. "Couples Can Offer Support, Comfort." *Collegian* 11 Feb. 2003. Web. 17 Oct. 2003.

Saxe, Lindsay. "Books before Relationships?" *Johns Hopkins News–Letter* 28 Mar. 2003. Web. 8 Oct. 2003.

West, Matt. "Steering clear of marriage until after College." *Cavalier Daily* 26 Apr. 2001. Web. 19 Oct. 2005.

Evaluating the Essay

1. Choose a page of Seirup's research essay and, using a highlighter, mark every line or passage in which he actually *does* something with information rather than simply explain or report what he found. In other words, where does he interpret, argue, analyze, assert, speculate, or evaluate? How much of the page is covered with color when you're done highlighting? Do the same thing with your own essay draft. Do you do more than report? Do you control information as well as Seirup did here?

2. Using Seirup's essay as a model, identify at least one question you have about the proper way to cite sources in a research essay.

3. If you were going to suggest that the writer revise "College Dating" around a particular assertion or thesis, what would it be? After reading the essay, what are your conclusions about the dating scene at American universities?

4. Identify at least two places where you might use other information from the professional reading in this chapter in "College Dating." Exactly what information would you use? How would you cite it?

USING WHAT YOU HAVE LEARNED

You've been involved in writing your own research essay and reading published and student essays that use research. What have you learned about the research process and the research essay that you can apply in other writing situations?

1. Explore how your thinking about research writing might have changed by completing the following sentence at least five times in your journal: *Before I worked through this chapter I thought writing research essays involved _____, but now I think _____.*

2. In this chapter you were introduced to a range of research-based work, from an undocumented essay to a formal academic paper. How will you use your understanding of academic research genres to prepare to write a research paper for another class? What information will you want to know before you start?

3. Writers of any academic essay must come across as authorities of sorts— credible and persuasive voices on whatever topics they choose to write about. This is particularly important in research-based writing. How exactly do you establish this authority?

RESEARCH TECHNIQUES

From Chapter 11 of *The Curious Writer*, Third Edition. Bruce Ballenger. Copyright © 2011 by Pearson Education, Inc. Published by Pearson Longman. All rights reserved.

Where would you start looking for information about wind power? A student architect published a wind power proposal on a blog that got the attention of professional architects. Is a blog a reliable source? A smart researcher knows to use both the library and the Web.

Martin Bond/Photo Researchers, Inc.

RESEARCH TECHNIQUES

METHODS OF COLLECTING

This chapter should tell you everything you need to know about finding what you need in the university library and on the Web. It is particularly useful for collecting information for research essays, but research is a source of information that can make *any* essay stronger. Research also can be an especially useful revision strategy for any essay.

Use this chapter much as you would a toolbox—a handy collection of tips and research tools that you can use for any assignment. Refer to it whenever you discover a topic that raises questions that research can help answer, or whenever it would be helpful to hear what other people say about the things you're thinking about.

RESEARCH IN THE ELECTRONIC AGE

Here's a recipe for research in the digital age:

- Take a Pacific Ocean of information + a fishing trawler named Google + a lawn chair and laptop. Heap on accessibility and then subtract reliability.

What You'll Learn in This Chapter

- How librarians organize knowledge.
- How to use library and Internet sources to develop a working knowledge of your topic.
- How to craft the best search terms for the library and the Internet.
- How to use more advanced research strategies to build on your working knowledge and develop a deep knowledge of your topic.
- How to evaluate sources and decide what you should use in your writing and what you should ignore.
- Methods of notetaking that promote a conversation with sources.
- Techniques for developing surveys and conducting interviews.

Here's a formula for research twenty years ago:

- Take an upscale department store of information + store maps, clearly marked + helpful employees. Whip in reliability and strain out some accessibility.

I'm not that nostalgic about the old days when nearly all research was done in the university library. I will never miss the toil of thumbing through multiple volumes of bound indexes, trying to find a few articles located on another floor. And yet, it was awfully convenient to walk into a library, and like a customer in a big store, know where to find what I needed and get help from a reference librarian if I needed it. Best of all, because library specialists not only organize information but evaluate its quality, I could put some faith in the usefulness of what I found. The good news is that hasn't changed—the library still effectively organizes knowledge (see Figure 1 for how this is done using the Library of Congress system of letters and numbers) and makes the best of it available. What's more, even the online accessibility of information in the library has improved dramatically. The bad news is that Google is irresistibly convenient and can produce immediate results.

But this doesn't have to be bad news. The smart researcher knows that *both* the library and the Web are tremendous resources and always tries to combine them in the hunt for good information. In this chapter, you'll find out how you can do this. Maybe most important, you'll learn that one of the keys to efficient academic research is something most of us don't often think about much: crafting search terms.

LIBRARY OF CONGRESS SYSTEM

Organization of Books by Letter

A	General Works	L	Education
B	Philosophy, Psychology, Religion	M	Music
C	Auxiliary Sciences of History	N	Fine Arts
D	History: General and Europe	P	Language and Literature
E	History: America	Q	Science
F	History: America	R	Medicine
G	Geography, Anthropology, Recreation	S	Agriculture
H	Social Sciences	T	Technology
J	Political Sciences	U	Military Science
K	Law	Y	Naval Science
		Z	Library Science and Reference

Figure 1 Librarians categorize general areas of knowledge by letter, A–Z. These letters, used in combination with other letters and numbers, make up the "call numbers" that will help you locate a book.

Magic Words That Open Doors

One of the key electronic literacies is something that seems so simple you might wonder why I bring it up first: *the words you choose to search for information.* Consider that in 1850 the Harvard library, the first academic library in the nation, had only 84,200 volumes, and many of those were kept behind locked cabinets. To search these stacks, a student would plead with a librarian for a book. Today, my own university's library has more than a half million books and access to millions more through interlibrary loan. In addition, it has tens of thousands of periodicals on microfilm and access to millions more through electronic databases. Then there's the World Wide Web; it's impossible to know its actual size, but the number of pages is certainly in the billions. All this information can make a researcher giddy, except for this: How do you find your needle in that gargantuan haystack?

In 1850, the Harvard librarian was familiar with the books in the stacks and could lead you to what you wanted. Today, librarians must trust in the language systems and codes they've created to organize knowledge; to find anything, you have to know those language systems. And while information on the Web isn't nearly as organized as it is in the library—for one thing, there isn't any librarian in charge, although there are some Internet directories that librarians maintain—the software that searches the Web also uses a language logic. Using it well means the difference between getting 1 million "hits" on a topic search, which you will never be able to read through, or getting 300 hits, many of which will be relevant to your topic.

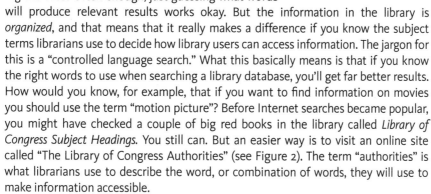

INQUIRING INTO THE DETAILS

The Big Red Books (Online)

We're all addicted to keyword searches when searching the Web. Often enough, just guessing what words will produce relevant results works okay. But the information in the library is *organized*, and that means that it really makes a difference if you know the subject terms librarians use to decide how library users can access information. The jargon for this is a "controlled language search." What this basically means is that if you know the right words to use when searching a library database, you'll get far better results. How would you know, for example, that if you want to find information on movies you should use the term "motion picture"? Before Internet searches became popular, you might have checked a couple of big red books in the library called *Library of Congress Subject Headings.* You still can. But an easier way is to visit an online site called "The Library of Congress Authorities" (see Figure 2). The term "authorities" is what librarians use to describe the word, or combination of words, they will use to make information accessible.

The site has some resources you'll never use. But if you want to know what terms to use in a library database search, something called the "subject authority

(continued)

Inquiring into the Details (*continued*)

headings" search is really useful. It will tell you what the preferred terms are for finding stuff on any subject. Interested in the history of chewing gum in the United States? You'll get better (though not necessarily more) information, says the Library of Congress Authorities site, if you use *chewing gum-America-history* when you do a "subject browse" on the library's book search page.

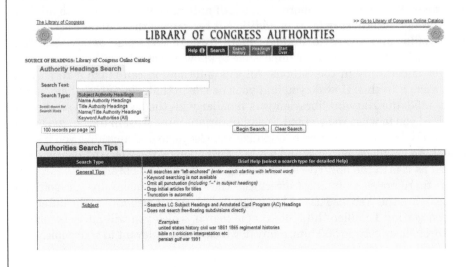

Figure 2   Now you can find the terms librarians use to help people find material on any subject online. The "Library of Congress Authorities" is a Web alternative to the bound *Library of Congress Subject Headings* in the reference room. Especially useful is the "subject authority headings" search.

Google Your Boole

George Boole was the eighteenth-century mathematician who came up with the system for using the words AND, OR, and NOT to help researchers design logical queries. Boole's professional legacy is something every modern college researcher should know. Consider Paul's situation. His grandmother has Alzheimer's disease, and his initial research question was, *What are the best therapies for treating Alzheimer's?* When Paul consulted PsycINFO, a popular database of citations from journals relating to psychology, his instinct was simply to enter the word *Alzheimer's* in the online search form. The result was 13,392 citations, and only a portion of these were relevant. But when Paul put the word AND between two key terms from his research question—*Alzheimer's AND therapy*—he managed to reduce his results to 1,955 more relevant citations (see Figure 3). As he was looking over his results, Paul became interested specifically in music therapies. His next search was even more focused when he typed in the words *Alzheimer's AND therapy AND music*. That produced 74 citations, and nearly all of these seemed promising (see Figure 4).

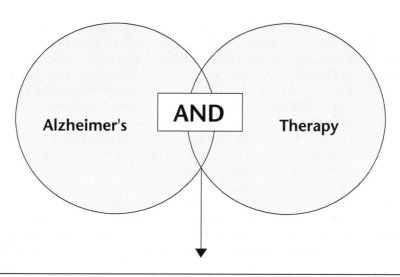

Figure 3 This query searches all documents that contain *both* words in the abstract or title. PsycINFO returned a list of 1,955 citations for *Alzheimer's AND therapy*.

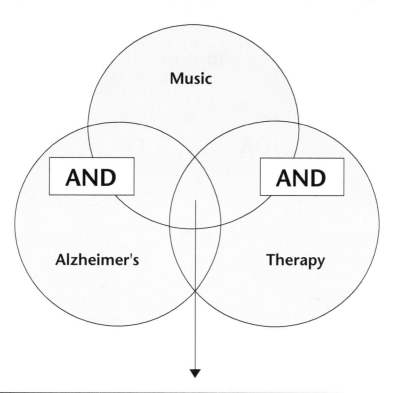

Figure 4 This focused query finds documents that include all the keywords. It generated a list of 74 citations, many of which were relevant and useful, for *Alzheimer's AND therapy AND music*.

The Boolean operator AND helped Paul search the PsycINFO database much more efficiently because it asked the computer to look for documents that had all three words in the title or abstract. What would happen if Paul left the AND operators out and simply searched using the three terms *Alzheimer's music therapy*? The result would have been 184,532 documents because the search software would assume that keywords with no operators in between them imply the Boolean operator OR. In other words, *Alzheimer's music therapy* is interpreted as *Alzheimer's OR music OR therapy* (see Figure 5). That means it would return citations for documents that had only one of the three words in the title or abstract. For a database of psychology publications, that's a lot of documents.

The only other Boolean operator you should know is the word NOT. This simply tells the search software to exclude documents that include a particular keyword. For example, if you were interested in finding information about environmental organizations in Washington State rather than Washington, D.C., you might construct a query like this: *environmental AND organizations AND Washington NOT D.C.*

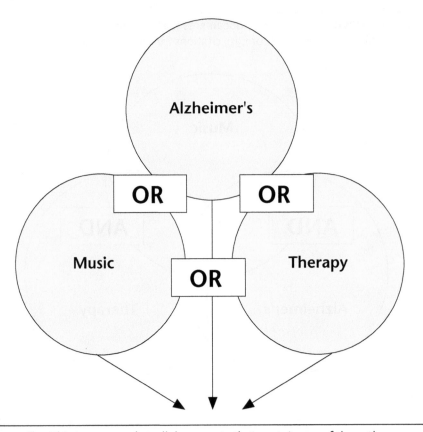

Figure 5   This query searches all documents that contain *any* of these three words in the abstract or title. PsycINFO returned an overwhelming list of 184,532 citations for *Alzheimer's music therapy.*

The real art of designing queries using the Boolean system is combining the operators to refine your search. For example, let's take the last search on environmental groups in Washington State. Suppose the previous query didn't produce enough results. Let's broaden it a bit: *(environmental OR conservation) AND organizations AND Washington NOT D.C.* This search would find documents that use either *environmental* or *conservation* in the title or abstract, probably returning a longer list. The parentheses simply group the keywords *environmental OR conservation* together as an expression that the search software evaluates first. You can use multiple parentheses in a query to control the order in which expressions are evaluated, beginning with the innermost parenthetical expressions. Librarians call the use of parentheses to group keywords in this manner *nesting*.

Increasingly, search pages for databases make it easy to exploit Boolean language in a search. For example, in the accompanying figure you can see how the advanced search page for Academic Search Premier, an EBSCOhost database, allows you to enter search terms and then use drop-down menus to add the Boolean connectors AND, OR, or NOT (see Figure 6). The search page adds even more refinement by allowing you to relate a particular term to a type or source or search. For example, you might want to search for Alzheimer's articles by a particular author whose work is relevant to your project. Using the advanced search page, you could simultaneously use *Alzheimer's* as a subject search, with *Smith* as an author search.

Knowing your Boolean operators will help you search library databases because most of the search software relies on the system. Some Web search

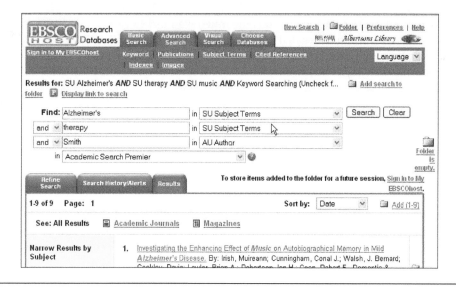

Figure 6   Advanced search pages such as the EBSCOhost database allow you to exploit Boolean terms using drop-down menus. Further refinements allow the researcher to link terms to different kinds of searches or sources.

239

engines do, too. But more often, search engines such as Google use a somewhat different language that accomplishes the same thing.

Today, search engines such as Google have an advanced search option that allows you to simply fill in a form if you want to search for certain keywords or phrases. I've found that, by far, the most useful syntax to use when searching the Web is quotation marks—an exact phrase search—and carefully ordered keywords, if possible more than three. For example, let's return to Paul's topic of Alzheimer's therapy. If he searched the Web using Google and the keywords *Alzheimer's therapy,* a syntax that implies an AND between the two words, Google would return about 9.9 million documents. But because the phrase *Alzheimer's therapy* or *therapies for Alzheimers* would likely appear in many relevant documents, Paul would be better off to try a phrase search. The result? Searching for *Alzheimer's therapy* produced 10,000 sites.

That's better, but Paul could further focus his research by querying Google with multiple terms, listed in order of importance because search engines usually evaluate keywords from left to right in level of importance. For example, Paul could try this: *+ Alzheimer's + research "music therapy,"* and this time focus the search on journal articles using Google Scholar. The results of this search were about 900 sites and a rich list of scholarly sources on his topic. There is much more to know about composing queries, but you now know enough to make a significant difference in the effectiveness of your searches.

DEVELOPING WORKING KNOWLEDGE

Every day we make decisions about how much we need to know about something. Twenty-five years ago, I decided to know enough to tune up my own car. Fifteen years ago I decided I wasn't interested in keeping up with the changes in electronic ignitions and fuel injection, so now I leave car repair to Davey at State Street Auto. A scholar is someone who, like Davey, has committed his or her professional life to keeping up with the knowledge in his or her field. College professors possess *expert knowledge* of their discipline. Five hundred years ago, the French writer Montaigne was a "scholar of the self," proposing that self-knowledge was the most important kind of knowing of all. If you wrote a personal essay previously, you also tapped expert knowledge. Who is more of an authority on your experience than you?

How much we need to know about a subject is, in part, a personal choice, but a college education does at least two things: It challenges you to develop new knowledge about things that will make you a better citizen and more productive professional, and it teaches you *how* to better acquire the new knowledge that you might seek by choice. A research project like this is driven by both goals—you'll be challenged to go beyond superficial knowledge about a meaningful topic, and you'll learn some of the methods for doing that.

You will not end up a scholar on anorexia, college dating, the medical effects of music, or whatever topic you're researching. But you will go way beyond superficial knowledge of your subject, and when you do, it will be like opening a door and entering a crowded room of intelligent strangers, all deep in conversation about your

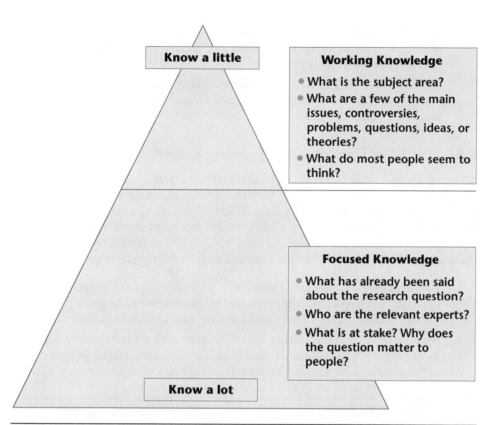

Figure 7 Working and focused knowledge. Inquiry projects often encourage you to choose a research topic you don't know much about. But you must quickly develop at least a *working knowledge* in order to come up with a good question. Guided by that question, you'll later develop a more *focused knowledge* of your topic and then discover what you have to say about it.

topic. At first you simply listen in before you speak, and that begins with a *working knowledge* (see Figure 7).

All of us know how to develop a working knowledge of something, especially when we need to. For example, I recently developed a working knowledge of podcasting software for a course I was teaching. Now I can knowledgeably talk about how to use Audacity to edit digital recordings for a few minutes without repeating myself. An audio expert would be unimpressed, but someone unfamiliar with the software might find it informative. As a researcher, you've got to know enough about your topic in order to come up with a research question. But how much knowledge is enough working knowledge? Here are some questions you need to ask:

■   What are some people currently thinking about the topic? What are the controversies, problems, questions, or theories? (*Example: Some people who are interested in "green architecture" are enthusiastic about the energy savings but think the buildings are ugly. Can anything be done about that?*)

- Who are some of the individuals or groups that have a stake in the topic? *(Example: There's something called the "Sustainable Building Alliance" that seems influential.)*
- Is there a local angle? Are there people or organizations in the community who might have something to say? Are there local examples of the problem or solution? *(Example: There's a "certified" green building on campus.)*

A Strategy for Developing Working Knowledge

It's hard to beat the Internet as a quick-and-dirty way to develop working knowledge about nearly any topic. But the library can play an important role, too. While it's impossible to resist immediately firing up Google and trolling the Web, you are more likely to learn what's really important about your topic if you work systematically from general to more specialized sources. (See examples of these sources in Figure 8.) Here's a research sequence you might try:

1. **General encyclopedias.** These days many of us ignore encyclopedias in our rush to Google. Yet they are still wonderful ways to get a landscape picture of nearly any subject and they are also available online.
2. **Specialized encyclopedias.** But don't stop with a general encyclopedia. Next, search your library's database for the specialized encyclopedia offerings. You'd be amazed by how many there are on nearly any subject

Source	Examples
General Encyclopedias	Encyclopedia.com, Columbia Encyclopedia, Wikipedia, Oxford Reference, Encyclopedia Britannica
Specialized Encyclopedias	Encyclopedia of Psychology, Encyclopedia of World Art, Encyclopedia of Sociology, Encyclopedia of the Environment, Encyclopedia of Women and Sports, Encyclopedia of African-American Culture and History, Encyclopedia of Democracy, Encyclopedia of Science and Technology, Encyclopedia of Children, Adolescents, and the Media
Google (or other search engines)	www.google.com, www.mama.com, www.dogpile.com
Virtual Library or Internet Public Library	vlib.org, ipl.org
Google Scholar	google.scholar.com

Figure 8 Examples of sources that will help you develop a working knowledge of your topic

imaginable. (My favorite is the *Encyclopedia of Hell*). These reference works provide a more focused look at the subject area in which your topic falls. Writing about pigeons? There is an *Encyclopedia of Pigeon Breeds*. Writing something related to Islam? Look at the *Encyclopedia of Islam*.

3. **Google or other general search engines.** Google is, for many of us, the default choice. It's where we always start. There are other search engines, of course, including the so-called "metasearch" portals that will use multiple search engines at once and produce a combined result with the duplicates removed (e.g., www.mama.com and www.dogpile.com). These can complement Google because they increase the territory you cover.

4. **Virtual Library or Internet Public Library.** Fortunately, the Web isn't entirely information anarchy. People who have expertise on a subject may contribute or even manage content on reference sites. The two most popular of these is the Virtual Library (vlib.org) and the Internet Public Library (ipl.org). The Virtual Library is the "oldest catalog on the Web," and includes links on diverse subjects that are maintained by a worldwide network of expert volunteers. The Internet Public Library has more direct links to academic institutions in the United States. Both sites include subject directories that allow you to drill down from larger subjects to related smaller ones, an enormously useful method for discovering a topic or seeing an existing topic in a larger context.

5. **Google Scholar.** The emergence of Google Scholar in recent years has been a boon to academic researchers. While the search engine isn't nearly as good as a search of your university's library databases (a step you will take to develop focused knowledge on your topic), it's a wonderful resource to get a quick glimpse at information written by authorities.

DEVELOPING FOCUSED KNOWLEDGE

If working knowledge equips you to sustain a one-minute monologue on your topic, then focused knowledge is enough for you to make a fifteen-minute presentation to your class and to answer most of their questions. Knowing this much doesn't make you an expert, but it does make you far more informed than most people on your topic. Here are some questions you should be able to answer:

- Who are key people who have influenced the published conversation on your topic? (*Example: Among the key advocates for a playoff system in college football are long-time Penn State coach Joe Paterno and even President Barack Obama.*)

- What has already been said about the topic? Up until now, what are the major themes of the conversation? (*Example: Among the arguments against a playoff system is that student athletes will miss too much class. Others add that such a system will lead to the "NFL-ization" of college football, extending the season and compounding student athletes' academic problems, who already spend as many as 40 hours a week on football.*)

■ What is at stake for people? Why is the research question significant? (*Example: Thousands of student athletes in the United States are wedged between two conflicting goals for college football: the public hunger for big-time entertainment and the athletes' desire to complete a degree.*)

A Strategy for Developing Focused Knowledge

To move to this next level of knowing about your topic, launch your research on three fronts:

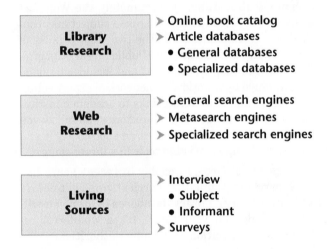

Library Research. While the Web is an intoxicating source of information, academic research still fundamentally depends on library work. Much of this work you can do online. Libraries offer database indexes to magazines, journals, and books that are accessible from your computer at home or at school, and in some cases you can retrieve and print out full-text articles.

But there are still reasons to walk into the university library. Here are six:

1. That's where the books are.
2. Some of the best articles on your topic aren't available as full-text PDFs.
3. Browsing the stacks in your topic's subject area will produce books you won't find any other way.
4. You can read current periodicals not yet online.
5. The reference room has books and other resources that aren't available anywhere else.
6. Reference librarians are irreplaceable.

So you'll want to go to the library—online and on foot—but you won't want to waste your time. The two best ways to avoid this are to have a good research question, one that will allow you to focus your efforts, and to have a handful of good search terms to try. Earlier in this chapter we discussed crafting search terms. Don't forget to use "controlled language searches," or searches that use the terms librarians have chosen to organize access to materials on every subject. As you recall, you discover these terms using the big red books in the reference room, *Library of Congress Subject Headings*, or by going online to the "Library of Congress Authorities," a Web version of the *LCSH*.

> Laying some groundwork in the library at the start of your research will save you time later.

Where should you begin? When you developed working knowledge, you started with more general sources like encyclopedias and then shifted to more specialized sources like Google Scholar, trying to drill down a little ways into your subject. Now it's time to drill more deeply. For focused knowledge, you can start anywhere, really, especially since you've already got some background knowledge on your research question. The key is to cover a lot of ground.

Searching for Books. Every library has an online index for books (also available at computers in the library, naturally), and using the right search terms you'll get an instantaneous list of relevant books on your topic and "call numbers" that will help you find them in the stacks. Your results will also tell you if the book is checked out, missing, or unavailable in your college library. If any of these apply to a book you're really hankering for, don't despair. You've got several options:

- *Recall.* Make an online request that the book is returned (usually in a few weeks) by the person who has checked it out.

- *Interlibrary loan.* This is a wonderful, underutilized service, often provided by campus libraries at no charge to students. You can request, usually online, a call-out to a large network of university libraries for the book (or article) you need. It is delivered to you, sometimes within days.

- *Check another library.* If the campus library doesn't have it, check the community library's index online.

The book search form on your university's Web site, like most search portals, has simple and advanced options. The advanced page is pretty cool because it makes it easy to do a Boolean search on your topic. You can also put "limiters" on the terms, allowing you to control the results for things like author, title, date, and so on. Learning to use the Advanced Search will really pay off after enduring the initial brief learning curve.

Searching for Periodicals and Newspapers. It's hard to imagine a research question or topic that isn't covered by periodicals. You'll want to check those databases, too. These are organized into four broad categories:

1. General subject databases, or indexes to periodicals across disciplines.
2. Specialized databases, or indexes that are discipline-specific.
3. Genre-specific databases like Newspaper Source.
4. Government document databases.

Quite often, general subject databases include periodicals that may not be considered scholarly, including magazines like *Discover, Newsweek,* or *Psychology Today.* These databases are a good place to start. To drill down further, use specialized databases, which are much more likely to produce the most interesting results on your research question because they are written by specialists in the field. They will also produce articles that can be a chore to understand if you don't know the jargon. That's when your working knowledge on your topic will really pay off. Also consider databases that warehouse certain types of content—plays, government documents, dissertations, and so on. You can see examples of all of these databases in the table that follows.

Web Research. "Google" is the new verb for research: "Did you Google it?" The consolidation in the last decade of public confidence in a single company's applications is remarkable, especially when there was once healthy competition between

Database Type	Examples
Interdisciplinary/general subject databases	Academic Search Premier, LexisNexis Academic, JSTOR, ArticleFirst, Project Muse, MasterFILE Premier, WorldCat
Discipline-specific databases	ABI/INFORM (business), AnthroSource, America: History and Life, ArtSTOR, Applied Science and Technology, Biography Index, BioOne, Communication and Mass Media, ERIC (education), MLA Bibliography (languages and literature), Philosopher's Index, PyscINFO, Sociological Abstracts, Worldwide Political Science Abstracts
Genre-specific databases	National Newspapers, Newspaper Source, New York Times Index, Dissertation Abstracts International, Book Review Digest, Literature Criticism Online, Play Index
Government documents	Fed in Print, GPO Monthly Catalog, LexisNexis Government Periodicals Index

companies with popular search portals like AltaVista and Excite. But that's another story. The point is this: Google is the dominant player in everyday research, but academic researchers shouldn't limit themselves to a single search service. Web research for inquiry projects should be motivated by the following principles:

1. Maximize coverage.
2. Maximize relevant results.
3. Find stable sources.
4. Find quality sources.

Later in this chapter, I'll elaborate on what I mean by stable, quality sources, but examples would include Web pages and documents with ".edu," ".gov," or ".org" domains, those that are routinely updated, and those that might include a bibliography of references that document claims.

On the other hand, depending on your topic you might seek a range of types of sources. For instance, suppose you're writing about green design and a blog from an architect in Texas has an interesting proposal for using turbines on a highway in Austin, powered by passing cars (see Figure 9). The proposal is interesting, and

© Piers Cavendish/Impact/HIP/The Image Works

Figure 9   A student architect in Texas published a wind power proposal on a blog that got the attention of professional architects. While a blog isn't a conventional academic source, depending on the quality of its content and the purpose of your essay, it might be a perfectly good source.

Search Type	Examples
General search engines	www.google.com, www.ask.com, www.yahoo.com
Metasearch engines	www.dogpile.com, www.clusty.com, www.surfwax.com, www.mamma.com
Subject directories	www.yahoo.com, www.about.com, directory.google.com, botw.org
Academic search engines or directories	google.scholar.com, infomine.ucr.edu, www.academicinfo.net, www.academicindex.net,
Search engines for particular content	www.videosurf.com, books.google.com, blogsearch.google.com, images.google.com, www.newslink.org, www.internetarchive .org (audio, video, education, etc.), www.usa.org (federal government)

other sites refer to the blogger's idea. While this isn't a conventional academic source, the architect's blog is certainly a relevant and useful one for your essay.

Consider other types of online content as well: images, video, podcasts, discussion boards, and so on. For example, iTunes includes iTunesU, a remarkable collection of lectures, interviews, and video clips on a range of subjects uploaded from universities around the United States.

The challenge is to find this stuff. Google is just the beginning. Try some of the alternative search portals or directories listed in the above table.

INQUIRING INTO THE DETAILS

Full-Text Articles and the Convenience Trap

We're spoiled by full-text articles that are served up by some databases. Not only do you get a citation, there is the huge bonus of actually looking at the article and printing it out. More and more indexes provide this service, and every database will allow you to filter your search so that you only get full-text results. This is all good except for one thing: Many articles still aren't available as instantly downloadable PDF or Web files. It's pretty common, in fact, to discover that the article you really need—the one that seems right on topic— isn't available online. That often means that student researchers ignore the really good article and just go for the one that's instantly available, even if it isn't quite right. Convenience isn't the highest value in academic research.

The commercial owners of periodical databases do not convert citations to include full-text articles on the basis of their significance to the subject. It's much more random than that. So you can't be sure, if you rely only on full-text versions, that you're getting the best information.

Finding those articles that aren't immediately available online requires a trip to the library where, armed with the citation information, you can find the piece in bound volumes of the journal or on microfilm. It might seem a bit old-fashioned, but that's the best way to get good information that isn't available digitally. Alternatively, you can order that article through the library's interlibrary loan service.

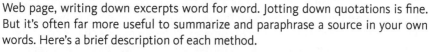

INQUIRING INTO THE DETAILS

Methods of Recording Information

The default mode for many student researchers is to simply quote information from a book, article, or Web page, writing down excerpts word for word. Jotting down quotations is fine. But it's often far more useful to summarize and paraphrase a source in your own words. Here's a brief description of each method.

1. *Summary.* One of the more useful ways of taking notes because it challenges you to condense, in your own words, a longer text, capturing key concepts or claims.

2. *Paraphrase.* This also tests your understanding of what you read, prompting you to translate a passage from a source into your own words; your paraphrase will be roughly the same length as the original.

3. *Quotation.* A perennial favorite approach to notetaking because it's mere transcription, ranging from a few key words to several paragraphs. Remember to always transcribe the words of the original source exactly.

EVALUATING LIBRARY SOURCES

One of the huge advantages of finding what you need at the campus library is that nearly everything there was chosen by librarians whose job it is to make good information available to academic researchers. Now that many of the university library's databases are available online, including full-text articles, there really is no excuse for deciding to exclusively use Web pages you downloaded from the Internet for your essays. But even in the campus library, some sources are more authoritative than others. The "Pyramid of Library Sources" gives you a general idea of the hierarchy of authority for most library sources.

In general, the more specialized the audience for a publication, the more authoritatively scholars view the publication's content. Academic journals are at the bottom of this inverted pyramid because they represent the latest thinking and knowledge in a discipline, and most of the articles are reviewed

---

INQUIRING INTO THE DETAILS

The Working Bibliography

A working bibliography lists sources you've collected that you think will be helpful when you draft your essay. These may include annotations or brief summaries of what the source says that you find relevant to your research question. Consider the following examples:

TOPIC: RELATIONAL AGGRESSION
PRINT SOURCES

Simmons, Rachel. *Odd Girl Out: The Hidden Culture of Aggression in Girls*. New York: Harcourt, 2002.

> Simmons argues that the "secret world of girls' aggression"—the backstabbing, the silent treatment, the bartering of friendship for compliance to a group's "rules"—can be just as bad as the less subtle aggression of boys. Her basic thesis is that girls in American culture are supposed to be "nice," and therefore have no outlet for their anger except for exploiting the one thing they do covet: relationships. Because my essay focuses on the popularity phenomenon in high school—How does it affect girls when they become adults?—Simmons's chapter on parents of these girls seems particularly useful because it shows how the parents' responses are often shaped by their own experiences in school.

WEB SOURCES

"What Is Relational Aggression?" *The Ophelia Project*. 22 Sept. 2003 http://www.opheliaproject.org/issues/issues_RA.shtml.

> The page defines relational aggression by contrasting it with physical aggression. It argues that most research, naturally, has focused on the latter because of need to limit physical injury between children. But girls tend to avoid physical aggression and instead indulge in actions that harm others by disrupting their social relationships, like giving someone the silent treatment. The Ophelia Project is a nonprofit group created in 1997 by parents who wanted to address the problem.

---

by specialists in the field before they are published. At the top of the inverted pyramid are general encyclopedias and general-interest magazines such as *Newsweek* and *Time*. These have broader audiences and feature articles that are written by nonspecialists. They are rarely peer-reviewed. As a rule, then, the lower you draw from this inverted pyramid, the more authoritative the sources are from an academic point of view. Here are some other guidelines to consider:

- *Choose more recent sources over older ones.* This is particularly good advice, obviously, if your subject is topical; the social and natural sciences also put much more emphasis on the currency of sources than humanities disciplines.

- *Look for often-cited authors.* Once you've developed a working knowledge of your topic, you'll start noticing that certain authors seem to be mentioned or cited fairly frequently. These are likely to be the most listened-to authors, and may be considered the most authoritative on your topic.

- *If possible, use primary sources over secondary sources.* In literary research, primary sources are the original words of writers—their speeches, stories, novels, poems, memoirs, letters, interviews, and eyewitness accounts. Secondary sources would be articles that discuss those works. Primary sources in other fields might be original studies or experiments, firsthand newspaper accounts, marketing information, and so on.

EVALUATING WEB SOURCES

One of the more amusing sites on the Web is titled "Feline Reactions to Bearded Men." At first glance, the site appears to be a serious academic study of the physiological responses of cats—heartbeat, respiration, and pupil dilation—to a series of photographs of men with beards. The researchers are listed with their affiliations to respected universities. The article includes an abstract, a methodology, and a results section, as well as a lengthy list of works cited.

The conclusions seem genuine and include the following:

1. Cats do not like men with long beards, especially long dark beards.
2. Cats are indifferent to men with shorter beards.
3. Cats are confused and/or disturbed by men with beards that are incomplete and, to a lesser degree, by men whose beards have missing parts.

The study is a hoax, a fact that is pretty obvious to anyone who critically examines it. For one thing, it was "published" in the *Annals of Improbable Research,* but I can usually fool about a third of my class with the site for five to ten minutes as I discuss the conventions of academic research, some of which are accurately reproduced in the "study."

Everyone knows to be skeptical of what's on the Web. But this is even more crucial when using Web sources for college writing. Because it's dominated by commercial sites, much of the World Wide Web has limited usefulness to the academic researcher, and although very few online authors are out to fool researchers with fake scholarship, many have a persuasive purpose. Despite its "educational" mission, for example, the purpose of the Web site ConsumerFreedom.com is to promote industry views on laws relating to food and beverages. That doesn't make the information it offers useless, but a careful researcher would be wary of the site's claims and critical of its studies. At the very least, the information on ConsumerFreedom.com should be attributed as a pro-industry view.

Imagine, as you're researching on the Web, that you've been dropped off at night in an unfamiliar neighborhood. You're alert. You're vigilant. And you're careful about whom you ask for directions. You can also be systematic about how you approach evaluating online sources. In general, follow these principles:

- *Favor governmental and educational sources over commercial ones.* These sites are more likely to have unbiased information. How can you tell which are institutional sites when it's not obvious? Sometimes the domain name—the abbreviation *.edu, .org,* or *.gov* at the end of an Internet address—provides a strong clue, as does the absence of ads on the site.

- *Favor authored documents over those without authors.* There's a simple reason for this: You can check the credentials of authors if you know who they are. Sometimes sites provide e-mail links so you can write to authors, or you can do a search on the Internet or in the library for other materials they've published.

- *Favor documents that are also available in print over those available only online.* Material that is published in both forms generally undergoes more

Robert Bull Design

A cat reacts to a picture of a bearded man from the study "Feline Reactions to Bearded Men."

scrutiny. An obvious example would be newspaper articles, but also some articles from journals and magazines are available electronically and in print.

- *Favor Web sources that document their claims over those that don't.* This familiar academic convention is strong evidence that the claims an online author is making are supported and verifiable.

- *Favor Web pages that have been recently updated over those that haven't changed in a year or more.* Frequently at the bottom of a Web page there is a line indicating when the information was posted to the Internet and/or when it was last updated. Look for it.

An Evaluation Process for Web Sources

1. **Relevance.** Is this Web source relevant to my research question?
2. **Authors.** Are there any? If so, can I trust them? Are they recognized experts on the subject? Do they have a bias? Do they say sensible things? If there aren't authors, are there other things about the source that make it credible?

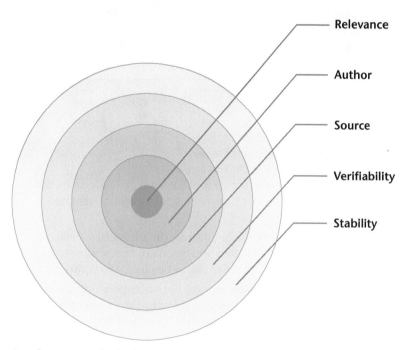

Another way to think about evaluating Web sources is to imagine a series of questions you ask yourself beginning with the relevance of a site or document to your project and then working outward to some judgments about the author, the source, the verifiability of the information, and its stability.

3. **Source.** What's the domain: .edu, .gov, .org.? If it's a commercial site, is the content still useful because of its author, content, or relevance?

4. **Verifiability.** Can you contact the authors? Is there a bibliography of references? Do other credible sites refer to this one?

5. **Stability.** How long has the Web site been around and how often is it updated?

Writing in the Middle: Synthesizing Source Information and Your Own Ideas

It's not news that there is an epidemic of plagiarism, and it's not just a problem on the college campus. Recently, several well-known historians admitted to being a bit sloppy about giving their sources proper credit. Naturally, a lot of people assume that the problem of plagiarism has to do with ethics. Students cheat. They confuse means and ends. And so on. There's some truth to this, but I contend that the real cause of the problem comes not from what students do, but what they don't do—they don't "write in the middle."

The plagiarism problem usually surfaces when writers are rushed, madly composing drafts at the last minute, and they simply haven't made the time to make the information they've collected their own. As a result, they're controlled *by* the information rather than controlling it for their own purposes. "How can I improve on what this guy says?" The thinking goes, "I guess I should just get it

---

INQUIRING INTO THE DETAILS

How to Annotate a Book

The brevity of articles and most Web pages makes them much easier to annotate than a book. You can usually summarize the argument or relevant ideas of such sources fairly easily. But how do you do that with a book that may have hundreds of pages of information and an extended argument? Read strategically.

1. To summarize a book's approach or basic argument, skim the preface and introduction. Sometimes there's a concluding chapter that neatly summarizes things, too. Even the back cover or jacket flap can be helpful for this overview.

2. To explain the relevance of the book to your research question or topic, you may focus on a particular chapter or chapters. Again, at this point you can probably skim the text quickly to discover its relevance. Later, you may do a more careful reading.

3. Evaluate *part* of the author's treatment of your topic rather than the whole book. Search the table of contents for what you suspect are the most relevant chapters, and focus your reading on those.

down in my paper." The result is sometimes unintentional plagiarism—some quotation marks were omitted or the paraphrase was too close to the original—but more often the paper suffers from another problem: the absence of an author. The writer doesn't seem to be in charge of where the essay goes and what it says.

There's a solution to this that is really quite simple. Write about what you're reading *as you collect it*.

Note cards aren't what I have in mind unless you use them to do more than simply jot down what a source says. Instead, I strongly recommend that you keep a double-entry journal or a research log that will serve two purposes: collecting information and exploring your reactions to what you've found. This is merely an extension of what I've been suggesting from the beginning of *The Curious Writer*—that you can move dialectically from creative thinking to critical thinking and back again—but this time you'll be creatively exploring information and then reflecting on how it addresses your research question.

The suggestion that you take time to write about the information you have collected in the middle of the process may come across as needing a pretty tough sell. *Save the writing for the draft*, you're thinking. But you are essentially *beginning* your draft with thoughtful note taking, which will save you time later.

Double-Entry Journal. You already are familiar with the double-entry journal. This approach uses opposing pages of your notebook to encourage dialectical thinking. On the left page take notes—paraphrases, summaries, and quotations—as you might usually do with conventional note taking, and on the opposing right page *explore* your responses, reactions, and questions about the information you've collected on the left page.

Research Log. Another method of note taking that also exploits dialectical thinking is the research log. Rather than using opposing pages, you'll layer your notes and responses, one after another. This is a particularly useful method for those who would prefer to work with a keyboard rather than a pencil. Here's how it works:

1. Begin by taking down the full bibliographic information on the source, something you may already have in your working bibliography.

2. Read the article, book chapter, or Web page, marking up your personal copy as you typically do, perhaps underlining key facts or ideas or information relevant to your research question.

3. Your first entry in your notebook or on the computer will be a fastwrite, an open-ended response to the reading under the heading What Strikes Me Most. As the title implies, you're dealing with first thoughts here. Consider some of the following approaches to this initial response to the source:

   - First play the believing game, exploring how the author's ideas, arguments, or findings seem sensible to you. Then shift to the doubting game, a more critical stance in which you look for gaps, raise questions, or express doubts about what the source says.

- What strikes you as the most important thing the author was trying to say?
- What do you remember best? What surprised you most after reading the source?
- What seemed most convincing? Least convincing?
- How does the source change your thinking on the topic? What do you understand better now than you did before you read the piece?
- How does it compare to other things you've read?
- What seems most relevant to your research question?
- What other research possibilities does it suggest?

4. Next, take notes on the source, jotting down summaries, paraphrases, quotations, and key facts you glean from it. Title this section Source Notes.

5. Finally, follow up with another episode of fastwriting. Title this The Source Reconsidered. This is a *more focused* look at the source; fastwrite about what stands out in the notes you took. Which facts, findings, claims, or arguments shape your thinking now? If the writing stalls, skip a line, take another look at your source notes, and seize on something else to write about.

ONE STUDENT'S RESPONSE

Claude's Research Log

SOURCE

Source Letawsky, Nicole R., et al. "Factors Influencing the College Selection Process of Student Athletes." *College Student Journal* 37.4 (2003): 604–11. *Academic Search Premier.* EBSCOhost Databases. Albertson's Lib. 5 Apr. 2004.

WHAT STRIKES ME MOST

Really interesting article that studied about 130 student athletes at a large 1-A university. Noted that there have been a lot of research studies on why students choose a particular school but not so much on why student-athletes choose a school. Everyone assumes, of course, that student-athletes go somewhere because they're wined and dined and promised national TV exposure. In other words, it all has to do with the glamour of playing 1-A, particularly the so-called revenue sports like basketball and football. But this study had some surprising findings. They found that the number one reason that student-athletes chose a school was the degree options it offers. In other words, the reasons student-athletes choose a school aren't that much different than the reason regular students choose one. The study also found that the glamour stuff—getting awards, getting on TV, and future professional possibilities—mattered the least to the student-athletes. This study challenges some of the myths about student recruiting, and should be read by recruiters especially. If you want to get a blue-ribbon player at your school, tell him or her about the academic opportunities there.

SOURCE NOTES (CUT-AND-PASTE FROM ELECTRONIC VERSION)

"This study found that the most important factor for student-athletes was the degree program options offered by the University. Other important factors were the head coach, academic support services, type of community in which the campus is located, and the school's sports traditions. Two of the top three factors were specifically related to the academic rather than athletic environment. This is a key finding and should be understood as recruiting efforts should be broad based, balancing academics and athletics if they are to be effective."

"A somewhat surprising result of the study concerned relatively low ratings associated with factors considered essential to 'Big-Time College Sports.' Television exposure, perceived opportunity to play immediately, and perceived future professional sporting opportunities were among the lowest-ranked factors. Furthermore, the participants rated athletic rewards (a 5-item survey scale containing these and other reward items) consistently lower than both the campus and athletic environment. These results may be due to the fact that respondents were from each of the sports offered by the University. Many of the sports (e.g., swimming, track), although funded and supported similar to the other sports, do not receive the national attention, large crowds, and television exposure."

SOURCE RECONSIDERED

This article did more than anything I've read so far to make me question my thesis that big-time college sports recruiting is way out of control. It's pretty convincing on the point that athletes care about the academic programs when they're choosing a school. But then the second quotation has an interesting part that I just noticed. This study surveyed athletes in all sports, not just the big-time sports like football and basketball at the university where the study was conducted. It seems to me that that would really skew the findings because someone participating in a sport like tennis that doesn't get a lot of attention and doesn't necessarily lead to professional opportunities after school *would* be more interested in academics. They're not dreaming of making a name for themselves, but getting a scholarship to pay for school. Seems like a better study would focus on the big-time sports...

Whichever note-taking method you choose—the double-entry journal or the research log—what you are doing is taking possession of the information and making it yours by evaluating it for your own purposes. One of the hardest parts of writing with outside sources is doing exactly that—using someone else's ideas or information in the service of your own questions. And that's why taking the time to write in the middle is so important: You're doing the most important intellectual work *as* you encounter the perspectives of others. This will make writing the draft much easier and will also, I believe, lower the risk of unintentional plagiarism, a mistake that often occurs in the mad rush to begin writing the draft the night before it's due.

INTERVIEWS

Tethered as we are these days to the electronic world of the Web and the increasingly digital university library, it's easy to forget an old-fashioned source for research: a living, breathing human being. People are often the best sources of information because you can have a real conversation rather than the imagined one simulated by the double-entry notebook. Some kinds of writing, such as the profile, fundamentally depend on interviews; with other genres, such as the personal essay or the research paper, interviews are one of several sources of information. But they can be central to bringing writing to life because when we put people on the page, abstract ideas or arguments suddenly have a face and a voice. People on the page make ideas matter.

> The principal advantage of doing interviews is that you ask the questions that you are most interested in learning the answers to.

Arranging Interviews

Whom do you interview? Basically, there are two kinds of interviews: (1) the interviewee is the main subject of your piece, as in a profile, and (2) the interviewee is *a source of information* about another subject.

The interviewee as a source of information is the far more common type of interview, and it usually involves finding people who either are experts on the topic you're writing about or have been touched or influenced in some way by it. For example, Tina was writing a research essay on the day-care crisis in her community. Among those affected by this issue were the parents of small children, their day-care teachers, and even the kids themselves; all were good candidates for interviews about the problem. Experts were a little more difficult to think of immediately. The day care teachers might qualify—after all, they're professionals in the area—but Tina also discovered a faculty member in the College of Health and Social Sciences who specialized in policies related to child care. Interviewing both types of people—experts and those influenced by the issue—gave Tina a much richer perspective on the problem.

How do you find experts in your topic? Here are a few strategies for locating potential interviewees:

- *Check the faculty directory on your campus.* Many universities publish an annual directory of faculty and their research interests, which may be online. In addition, your university's public information office might have a similar list of faculty and areas of expertise.

■ *Cull a name from an online discussion group.* Use a specialized search engine like Google's group search (groups.google.com) to search by your topic and find someone interesting who might be willing to do an e-mail interview.

■ *Ask friends and your instructors.* They might know faculty who have a research interest in your topic, or might know someone in the community who is an expert on it.

■ *Check the phone book.* The familiar *Yellow Pages* can be a gold mine. Want to find a biologist who might have something to say about the effort to bring back migrating salmon? Find the number of the regional office of the U.S. Fish and Wildlife Service in the phone book and ask for the public information officer. He or she may help you find the right expert.

■ *Check your sources.* As you begin to collect books, articles, and Internet documents, note their authors and affiliations. I get calls or e-mails from time to time from writers who came across my book on lobsters, posing questions I love to try to answer because no one in Idaho gives a hoot about lobsters. Google searches of authors who are mentioned in your sources may produce e-mail addresses or Web sites with e-mail links that you might query.

■ *Check the* Encyclopedia of Associations. This is another underused book and database in your university's reference room that lists organizations in the United States with interests as varied as promoting tofu and saving salmon.

Conducting the Interview

The kinds of questions you ask fundamentally depend on what type of interview you're conducting. In a profile, your questions will focus on the interview subject. To some extent, this is also true when you interview nonexperts who are *affected* by the topic you're writing about. For example, Tina is certainly interested in what the parents of preschoolers *know* about the day-care crisis in her town, but she's also interested in the feelings and *experiences* of these people. Gathering this kind of information leads to some of the questions you may have used in a profile, but with more focus on the subject's experience with your topic:

■ What was your first experience with _____? What has most surprised you about it?

■ How does _____ make you feel?

■ Tell me about a moment that you consider most typical of your experience with _____.

More often, however, your motive in an interview will be to gather information. Obviously, this will prompt you to ask specific questions about your topic as you try to fill in gaps in your knowledge. But some more general, open-ended questions may be useful to ask. For example:

- What is the most difficult aspect of your work?
- What do you think is the most significant popular misconception about _____?
- What are the significant current trends in _____?
- If you had to summarize the most important thing you've learned about _____, what would that be?
- What is the most important thing other people should know or understand?
- What do you consider the biggest problem?
- Who has the power to do something about it?
- What is your prediction about the future? Ten years from now, what will this problem look like?

Once you have a list of questions in mind, be prepared to ignore them. Good interviews often take turns that you can't predict, and these journeys may lead you to information and understandings you didn't expect. After all, a good interview is like a good conversation; it may meander, speed up or slow down, and reveal things about your topic and your interview subject that you don't expect. But good interviewers also attempt to control an interview when the turns it's taking aren't useful. You do this through questions, of course, but also more subtle tactics. For example, if you stop taking notes most interview subjects notice, and the astute ones quickly understand that what they're saying has less interest to you. A quick glance at your watch can have the same effect.

E-mail interviews produce a ready-made text with both your questions and the subject's answers. This is pretty wonderful. Live interviews, on the other hand, require more skill. It's usually a good idea to use a tape recorder (with your subject's permission), but never rely exclusively on it especially since machines can fail and batteries can expire unexpectedly. *Always take notes.* Your notes, if nothing else, will help you know where on the tape you should concentrate later, transcribing direct quotations or gathering information. Notetaking during interviews is an acquired skill; the more you do it, the better you get, inventing all sorts of shorthand for commonly occurring words. Practice taking notes while watching the evening news.

Most of all, try to enjoy your interview. After all, you and your interview subject have something important in common—you have an interest in your topic—and this usually produces an immediate bond that transforms an interview into an enjoyable conversation.

Using the Interview in Your Writing

Putting people on the page is one of the best ways to bring writing to life. This is exactly what information from interviews can do—give otherwise abstract questions or problems a voice and a face. One of the most common ways to use interview material is to integrate it into the lead or first paragraph of your essay. By focusing on someone involved in the research question or problem you're exploring, you immediately capture reader interest. For example, here's the beginning of a *Chronicle of Higher Education* essay, "What Makes Teachers Great?"[1] Quite naturally, the writer chose to begin by profiling someone who happened to be a great teacher, using evidence from the interviews he conducted.

> When Ralph Lynn retired as a professor of history at Baylor University in 1974, dozens of his former students paid him tribute. One student, Ann Richards, who became the governor of Texas in 1991, wrote that Lynn's classes were like "magical tours into the great minds and movements of history." Another student, Hal Wingo, the editor of *People* magazine, concluded that Lynn offered the best argument he knew for human cloning. "Nothing would give me more hope for the future," the editor explained, "than to think that Ralph Lynn, in all his wisdom and wit, will be around educating new generations from here to eternity."

This is a strong way to begin an essay because the larger idea—the qualities that make a great teacher—is grounded in a name and a face. But information from interviews can be used anywhere in an essay—not just at the beginning—to make an idea come to life.

Information from interviews can also provide strong evidence for a point you're trying to make, especially if your interview subject has expertise on the topic. But interviews can also be a *source* of ideas about what you might want to say in an essay. The essay on great teaching, for instance, offers seven qualities that great teachers embrace in their classrooms, things such as "create a natural critical learning environment" and "help students learn outside of class." All of these claims grew from interviews with sixty professors in a range of disciplines.

The principal advantage of doing interviews is that *you* ask the questions that you're most interested in learning the answers to. Rather than sifting through other sources that may address your research questions briefly or indirectly, interviews generate information that is often relevant and focused on the information needs of your essay. In other words, interviews are a source of data that can also be a *source* of theories or ideas on your topic. And this is often the best way to use interview material in your essay.

---

[1] Ken Bain, "What Makes Teachers Great?" *Chronicle of Higher Education* (April 9, 2004): B7–B9.

SURVEYS

The survey is a fixture in American life. We love surveys. What's the best economical laptop? Should the president be reelected? Who is the sexiest man alive? What movie should win Best Picture? Some of these are scientific surveys with carefully crafted questions, statistically significant sample sizes, and carefully chosen target audiences. In your writing class, you likely won't be conducting such formal research. More likely it will be like Mike's—fairly simple, and although not necessarily statistically reliable, your informal survey will likely be more convincing than anecdotal evidence or your personal observation, particularly if it's thoughtfully developed.

Defining a Survey's Goals and Audience

A survey is a useful source of information when you're making some kind of claim regarding "what people think" about something. Mike observed that his friends all seem to hate pennies, and he wanted to generalize from this anecdotal evidence to suggest that most people probably share that view. But do they? And which people are we really talking about? As we discussed this in his writing group, Mike pointed out that his grandfather grew up during the Great Depression, and that he has a very different perspective on money than Mike. "So your grandfather would probably pick up a penny in the parking lot, right?" I asked. Probably, Mike said.

Quickly, Mike not only had a survey question but began to think about qualifying his claim. Maybe younger adults—Mike's generation—in particular share this attitude about the lowly penny. To confirm this, Mike's survey had both a purpose (to collect information about how people view pennies) and an audience (students on his campus). If he had the time or inclination, Mike could conduct a broader survey of older Americans, but for his purposes the quad survey would be enough.

Types of Survey Questions

You can typically ask two types of questions on a survey: *open-ended questions* and *direct questions*. Open-ended questions often produce unexpected information, while direct questions are easier to analyze. Open-ended questions are like those on the narrative evaluations students might fill out at the end of the semester, such as, "What did you learn in this course?" and "What were the instructor's strengths and weaknesses?" Direct questions are the kind used on quizzes and tests, the kind that have a limited number of answers. The simplest, of course, would be a question or statement that people might agree or disagree with: "Would you pick up a penny if you saw it lying on the street?" Yes? No? You don't know?

How do you decide which types of questions to ask? Here are some things to consider:

- *How much time do you have to analyze the results?* Open-ended questions obviously take more time, while direct questions often involve mere tabulation of responses. The size of your sample is a big factor in this.

- *How good are you at crafting questions?* Direct questions need to be more carefully crafted than open-ended ones because you're offering limited responses. Are the responses appropriate to the question? Have you considered all the alternative ways of responding?

- *Do you want statistical or qualitative information?* Qualitative information—anecdotes, stories, opinions, case studies, observations, individual perspectives—are the stuff of open-ended questions. This can be wonderful information because it is often surprising, and it offers an individual's voice rather than the voiceless results of statistical data. On the other hand, statistical information—percentages, averages, and the like—is easily understood and can be dramatic.

Crafting Survey Questions

To begin, you want to ask questions that your target audience can answer. Don't ask a question about a campus alcohol policy that most students in your survey have never heard of. Second, keep the questions simple and easy to understand. This is crucial because most respondents resist overly long survey questions and won't answer confusing ones. Third, make sure the questions will produce the information you want. This is a particular hazard of open-ended questions. For example, a broad open-ended question such as, "What do you think of the use of animals in the testing of cosmetics?" will probably produce a verbal shrug or an answer of "I don't know." A better question is more focused: "What do you think about the U.S. Food and Drug Administration's claim that animal testing by cosmetic companies is 'often necessary to provide product safety'?"

Such a question could be an open-ended or direct question, depending on the kind of responses you're seeking. Focusing the question also makes it more likely to generate information that will help you compose your essay on the adequacy of current regulations governing animal testing. Also note that the question doesn't necessarily betray the writer's position on the issue, which is essential—a good survey question isn't biased or "loaded." Imagine how a less neutral question might skew the results: "What do you think of the federal bureaucrats' position that animal testing for cosmetics is 'often necessary to provide product safety'?" An even more subtle bias might be introduced by inserting the term *federal government* rather than *Food and Drug Administration* in the original question. In my part of the world, the Rocky Mountain West, the federal government is generally not viewed favorably, no matter what the issue.

Keep your survey questions to a minimum. It shouldn't take long—no more than a few minutes at most—to complete your survey, unless you're lucky enough to have a captive audience such as a class.

Finally, consider beginning your survey with background questions that establish the identity of each respondent. Typical information you might collect includes the gender and age or, with student-oriented surveys, the class ranking of the respondent. Depending on your topic, you might be interested in particular demographic facts, such as whether someone has children or comes from a particular part of the state. All of these questions can help you sort and analyze your results.

INQUIRING INTO THE DETAILS

Types of Survey Questions

These are a few of your options when deciding what type of questions to ask in a survey.

1. Limited choice

Do you believe student fees should be used to support campus religious organizations?

- ☐ Yes
- ☐ No
- ☐ I'm not sure

At what point in the writing process do you usually get stuck?

- ☐ Getting started
- ☐ In the middle
- ☐ Finishing
- ☐ I never get stuck
- ☐ Other_____.

2. Scaled response

The Student Film Board should show more foreign films.

- ☐ Strongly agree
- ☐ Agree
- ☐ Neither agree or disagree
- ☐ Disagree
- ☐ Strongly disagree

3. Ranking

Which of the following do you consider important in designing a classroom to be conducive to learning? Rank them from 1 to 5, with the most important a "1" and the least important a "5."

Comfortable seating	
Natural light from windows	
Carpeting	
Effective soundproofing	
Dimmable lighting	

4. Open-ended

Describe three things you learned in this course.

What steps do you think the university should take to increase attendance at women's soccer games?

Conducting a Survey

People who design surveys for a living always test them first. Invariably this turns up problems: A survey is too long, a question is poorly worded, the response rate to a particular question is low, and so on. You won't be able to test your draft survey nearly as thoroughly as the experts do, but before you put your faith in an untested survey, ask as many people as you can to try it out and describe their experience answering your questions. Was there any confusion? How long did it take? Is the survey generating relevant information?

Once you're confident in the design of your survey, plan how you'll distribute it. How do you reach the audience you've selected for your survey? Professional pollsters have all sorts of methods, including computerized dialing in some regions of the country and purchasing mailing lists. Your project is much more low tech. Begin by asking yourself whether your target audience tends to conveniently gather in a particular location. For example, if you're surveying sports fans, then surveying people by the main gate at the football stadium on Saturday might work. If your target audience is first-year college students and your university requires freshman English composition, then surveying one or more of those classes would be a convenient way to reach them.

In some situations, you can leave your survey forms in a location that might produce responses from your target audience. For example, a student at my university wanted to survey people about which foothill's hiking trails they liked best, and she left an envelope with the forms and a pencil at several trailheads.

A new possibility for tech-savvy students is the online survey. Software for designing online surveys is available now, but unless the survey is linked to a Web site that is visited by the target audience whose opinions you seek, the response rates will most likely be low. Telephone surveys are always a possibility, but they are often time consuming, and unless you can target your calls to a specific audience—say, people living in the dorms on your campus—it's hard to reach the people you most want to query. Postal mail is usually too slow and expensive, although intercampus mail can be an excellent option for distributing surveys. Response rates, however, may not meet your expectations.

Using Survey Results in Your Writing

The best thing about conducting an informal survey is that you're producing original and interesting information about your topic's local relevance. This can be an impressive element of your essay and will certainly make it more interesting.

Because analysis of open-ended questions can be time consuming and complicated, consider the simplest approach: As you go through the surveys, note which responses are worth quoting in your essay because they seem representative. Perhaps the responses are among the most commonly voiced in the entire sample, or they are expressed in significant numbers by a particular group of respondents. You might also quote a response because it is particularly articulate, surprising, or interesting.

In a more detailed analysis, you might try to nail down more specifically the *patterns* of responses. Begin by creating a simple coding system—perhaps numbers or colors—that represents the broadest categories of response. For example, perhaps you initially can divide the survey results into two categories: people who disagree with the university's general-education requirements and those who agree with it, Group 1 and Group 2. The next step might be to further analyze each of these groups, looking for particular patterns. Maybe you notice that freshmen tend to oppose the requirement in larger numbers than seniors and voice similar criticisms. In particular, pay attention to responses you didn't expect, responses that might enlarge your perspective about what people think about your topic.

Direct questions that involve choosing limited responses—true/false, yes/no, multiple choice, and so on—often involve tabulation. This is where knowledge of a spreadsheet program such as Microsoft Excel is invaluable.

Your analysis of the responses to direct questions will usually be pretty simple—probably a breakdown of percentages. What percentage of the sample, for example, checked the box that signaled agreement with the statement that their "main goal for a college education was to get a good job"? In a more sophisticated analysis, you might try to break the sample down, if it's large enough, to certain categories of respondents—men and women, class ranking, respondents with high or low test scores, and so on—and then see if any response patterns correlate to these categories. For example, perhaps a much higher percentage of freshmen than seniors sampled agreed that a good job was the most important reason to go to college.

What might this difference mean? Is it important? How does it influence your thinking about your topic or how does it affect your argument? Each of these questions involves interpretation of the results, and sample size is the factor that most influences the credibility of this kind of evidence. If you surveyed only five freshmen and three seniors about their attitudes toward your school's general-education requirements, then the comparisons you make among what they say are barely better than anecdotal. It's hard to say what the appropriate sample size for your informal survey should be—after all, you aren't conducting a scientific survey, and even a small sample might produce some interesting results—but, in general, the more responses you can gather the better.

USING WHAT YOU HAVE LEARNED

You will have countless opportunities, in school and out, to apply your research skills. But have you learned enough about research techniques to find good information efficiently? Consider the following situations. What would you suggest to the writer as a good research technique?

1. Casey is revising his essay on the effectiveness and accuracy of Internet voting. His workshop group says he needs more information on whether hackers might compromise the accuracy of computers used for voting. Casey says he's relied pretty heavily on Internet sources. Where else would you suggest he search for information? What search terms might he use?

2. Alexandra needs to find some facts on divorce rates in the United States. Where might she find them fairly easily?

3. The university is proposing to build a new parking lot on a natural area near the edge of campus. Sherry wants to investigate the proposal to write a paper on whether the parking lot might be built with minimal environmental damage. What steps might she take to research the topic? Where should she look for information first? And then?

REVISION STRATEGIES

From Chapter 13 of *The Curious Writer*, Third Edition. Bruce Ballenger. Copyright © 2011 by Pearson Education, Inc. Published by Pearson Longman. All rights reserved.

Revision is work. But it's also an opportunity for surprise. The trick is to see what you have written in ways you haven't seen it before.

REVISION STRATEGIES

RE-SEEING YOUR TOPIC

"I don't really revise," Amy told me the other day. "I'm usually pretty happy with my first draft."

Always? I wondered.

"Well, certainly not always," she said. "But I know I work better under pressure, so I usually write my papers right before they're due. There usually isn't much time for revision, even if I wanted to do it, which I don't, really."

Amy is pretty typical. Her first-draft efforts usually aren't too bad, but I often sense tentativeness in her prose, endings that seem much stronger than beginnings, and promises that aren't really kept. Her essay promises to focus on the dangers of genetically engineered foods to teenagers who live on Cheeze-Its and Cheetos, but she never quite gets to saying much about that. The writing is competent—pretty clear and without too many awkward passages—but ultimately it's disappointing to read.

You can guess what I'm getting at here—Amy's work could be much stronger if it were rewritten—but the logic of last-minute writing is pretty powerful: "I really think I need to bump up against a deadline."

The writing process has three phases: prewriting, drafting, and rewriting. Prewriting refers to a range of activities writers might engage in before they attempt to compose a first draft, including fastwriting, listing, clustering, rehearsing lines or passages, preliminary research, conversations, or even the kind of

> ## What You'll Learn in This Chapter
> - How genuine revision involves exactly that: revision, or *re-seeing* your topic.
> - Basic revision strategies for "divorcing the draft."
> - How to become a reader of your own work.
> - The five categories of revision.
> - Advanced revision strategies.

deep thought about a topic that for some of us seems to occur best in the shower. The drafting stage is hardly mysterious. It often involves the much slower, much more focused process of putting words to paper, crafting a draft that presumably grows from some of the prewriting activities. Rewriting is a rethinking of that draft. Although this typically involves tweaking sentences, it's much more than that. Revision, as the name implies, is a *re-seeing* of the paper's topic and the writer's initial approach to it in the draft.

DIVORCING THE DRAFT

Sometimes I ask my students to generalize about how they approach the writing process for most papers by asking them to divide a continuum into three parts

> Revision, as the name implies, is a *re-seeing* of the paper's topic and the writer's initial approach to it in the draft.

corresponding to how much time, roughly, they devote to prewriting, drafting, and rewriting. Then I play "writing doctor" and diagnose their problems, particularly resistance to revision. Figure 1 depicts a typical example for most of my first-year writing students.

The writing process shown in Figure 1 obviously invests lots of time in the drafting stage and very little time in prewriting or rewriting. For most of my students, this means toiling over the first draft, starting and then starting over, carefully hammering every word into place. For students who use this process, strong resistance to revision is a typical symptom. It's easy to imagine why. If you invest all that time in the first draft, trying to make it as good as you can, you'll be either too exhausted to consider a revision, delusional about the paper's quality, or, most likely, so invested in the draft's approach to the topic that revision seems impossible or a waste of time.

There also is another pattern among resistant revisers. Students who tend to spend a relatively long time on the prewriting stage also struggle with revision. My theory is that some of these writers resist revision as a final stage in

Figure 1   How some writers who resist revision typically divide their time between the three elements of the writing process: prewriting, drafting, and rewriting. The most time is devoted to writing the first draft, but not much time is given to prewriting and rewriting.

the process because *they have already practiced some revision at the beginning of the process*. We often talk about revision as occurring only after you've written a draft, which of course is a quite sensible idea. But the process of revision is an effort to *re-see* a subject, to circle it with questions, to view it from fresh angles; and many of the open-ended writing methods we've discussed in *The Curious Writer* certainly involve revision. Fastwriting, clustering, listing, and similar invention techniques all invite the writer to re-see. Armed with these discoveries, some writers may be able to write fairly strong first drafts.

What is essential, however, whether you revise at the beginning of the writing process or, as most writers do, after you craft the draft, is achieving some separation from what you initially thought, what you initially said, and how you said it. To revise well, writers must divorce the draft.

STRATEGIES FOR DIVORCING THE DRAFT

You can do some things to make separation from your work easier, and spending less time on the first draft and more time on the revision process is one of them. But aside from writing fast drafts, what are other strategies for re-seeing a draft that already has a hold on you?

1. **Take some time.** Absolutely the best remedy for revision resistance is setting the draft aside for a week or more. Professional writers, in fact, may set a piece aside for several years and then return to it with a fresh, more critical perspective. Students simply don't have that luxury. But if you can take a week or a month—or even a day—the wait is almost always worth it.

2. **Attack the draft physically.** A cut-and-paste revision that reduces a draft to pieces is often enormously helpful because you're no longer confronted with the familiar full draft, a version that may have cast a spell on you. By dismembering the draft, you can examine the smaller fragments more critically. How does each piece relate to the whole? Might there be alternative structures? What about gaps in information? (See Revision Strategy 18 later in this chapter for a useful cut-and-paste exercise.)

3. **Put it away.** Years ago I wrote a magazine article about alcoholism. It was about twenty-five pages long and it wasn't very good. I read and reread that draft, completely puzzled about how to rewrite it. One morning, I woke up and vowed I would read the draft just once more, then put it away in a drawer and start all over again, trusting that I would remember what was important. The result was much shorter and much better. In fact, I think it's the best essay I've ever written. Getting a troublesome draft out of sight—literally—may be the best way to find new ways to see it.

4. **Ask readers to respond.** Bringing other people's eyes and minds to your work allows you to see your drafts through perspectives other than your own. Other people have a completely different relationship with your writing

than you do. They will see what you don't. They easily achieve the critical distance that you are trying to cultivate when you revise.

5. **Write different leads.** The nonfiction writer John McPhee once talked about beginnings as the hardest thing to write. He described a lead as a "flashlight that shines down into the story," illuminating where the draft is headed. Imagine, then, the value of writing a new beginning, or even several alternative beginnings; each may point the next draft in a slightly different direction, perhaps one that you didn't consider in your first draft.

6. **Conduct research.** One of the central themes of *The Curious Writer* is that research isn't a separate activity but a source of information that can enrich almost any kind of writing. Particularly in genres such as the personal essay, in which the writer's voice, perspective, and experience dominate the draft, listening to the voices and knowledge of others about a topic can deepen and shift the writer's thinking and perspectives.

7. **Read aloud.** I always ask students in workshop groups to read their drafts aloud to each other. I do this for several reasons, but the most important is the effect that *hearing* a draft has on a writer's relationship to it. In a sense, we often hear a draft in our heads as we compose it or reread it, but when we read the words aloud the draft comes alive as something separate from the writer. As the writer listens to herself—or listens to someone else read her prose—she may cringe at an awkward sentence, suddenly notice a leap in logic, or recognize the need for an example. Try reading the work aloud to yourself and the same thing may happen.

8. **Write in your journal.** One of the strategies you can use to divorce the draft is to return to your notebook and fastwrite to yourself about what you might do to improve the piece. You can do this by asking yourself questions about the draft and then—through writing—attempt to answer them. The method can help you see a new idea that may become key to the structure of your next draft. Too often we see the journal exclusively as a prewriting tool, but it can be useful throughout the writing process, particularly when you need to think to yourself about ways to solve a problem in revision.

Later in this chapter, we'll build on some of these basic strategies with specific revision methods that may work with particular kinds of writing and with drafts that have particular problems. All of these methods encourage a separation between the writer and his or her draft or rely on that critical distance to be effective.

PHOTOGRAPHY AS A METAPHOR FOR REVISION

For several years, I taught composition by asking students to bring along a camera. The idea grew out of an experience I had in a graduate seminar with my friend and mentor Donald Murray, in which we were asked to apprentice to a creative activity and then write about how the process seemed to compare to the ways we write. I chose photography. It became clear almost immediately that there were dramatic parallels between the composing processes in each; the most striking was how much taking pictures taught me about revision.

What does it really mean to revise, or put another way, to *re-see*? What might be rewarding about such an effort? For many, revision may involve little more than proofreading a first draft. But when most experienced writers imagine revision, they mean something much less superficial (not that proofreading is unimportant!). Rewriting may involve adding or cutting information, reorganizing the draft, or even rebuilding around a new angle or purpose. This kind of revision grows from the conviction that when we first look at a topic there is much we don't notice, and this is a lesson photography teaches as well.

When I first ask my students to go out and take pictures, the only instruction I provide is that they must shoot an entire roll of film. I don't suggest photographic subjects, and I don't offer tips on technique. "Just go out and take a roll of pictures," I say, "and bring back the slides next week." The results are almost always the same: Every student in the class takes one photograph of every subject, a shot that usually captures it in the most familiar angle and light conditions—the school building from across the street, the roommate or friend squinting into the sun, the long shot down the beach at midday. Rarely were these particularly interesting pictures.

The same might be said of first drafts, especially those written in a rush the night before the paper is due. The writer pretty much goes with the first picture of his topic that he sees, and revision is pretty limited to "fixing" things here and there at the last minute. One common characteristic of these one-draft papers is that they often seize on the most obvious point or idea about their topics. A paper on the accuracy of "smart bombs" argues that they aren't always smart. Or a personal essay on fading friendships concludes that "true friends are hard to find." There isn't anything wrong with stating the obvious in a first draft *if* in a revision you plan to dig more deeply, working toward a fresher argument, a better insight, a less familiar way of seeing.

My students' first roll of film makes this point really well. When you take only one picture of a subject, you're not likely to see beyond what you've already seen. Our first look at almost anything is likely to reveal only what's most obvious about it. If we *really* want to see, if we really want to learn something we don't already know, we have to look and then look again. Speaking photographically, deep revision requires that we take more than one picture.

The value of taking more than one picture becomes apparent to my students when I ask them to complete a second assignment with their cameras. This time, I say, choose only two subjects from the first roll and take twelve shots of each one. Make every shot different by varying distance, angle, and light conditions. By composing multiple "drafts" of their subjects, even novice photographers discover new ways of seeing things they've seen before. They see the pattern of three kinds of stone that come together on the corner of Thompson Hall—something they never really noticed before although they walk by the building every day. They see the way the fire escapes cling like black iron insects to the west side of the building, its bricks bloodied by the setting sun. They see the delicate structure of a tulip or their best friend's hand, roughened by a summer of carpentry. Once my students get past the first few pictures of a subject, they really begin to see it freshly. More often than not, the twelfth picture is much more interesting than the fifth or sixth. The principle is simple: *The more you look, the more you see.*

Although the Greek meaning of the word is "light writing," photography, of course, is *not* writing. It really isn't hard to look through a camera, take a bunch of pictures, and re-see a subject. Doing this in writing is more difficult, because we must "see" through language. Words often get in the way. Yet the motive for revision in writing isn't much different from a photographer's inclination to take more than one shot—both writer and photographer know not to trust their first look at something. They know they won't see it well enough, so both writers and photographers use a process that helps them to see their subjects in new ways. The rewards for doing this are similar, too: the pleasure of surprise and discovery, of learning something new about their subjects and about themselves.

> The motive for revision is like a photographer's inclination to take more than one shot—both writer and photographer know not to trust their first look at something.

FIVE CATEGORIES OF REVISION

The following kinds of writers are typically ones who most need to revise:

1. Writers of fast drafts
2. Writers who compose short drafts
3. Writers who indulge in creative, but not critical, thinking
4. Writers who rarely go past their initial way of seeing things
5. Writers who have a hard time imagining a reader other than themselves
6. Writers who rely on limited sources of information
7. Writers who still aren't sure what they're trying to say
8. Writers who haven't found their own way of saying what they want to say
9. Writers who haven't delivered on their promises
10. Writers who think their draft is "perfect"

These are the usual suspects for revision, but there are many more. In general, if you think there's more to think about, more to learn, more to say, and better ways to say it, then revision is the route to surprise and discovery. Most writers agree that rewriting is a good idea, but where should they start?

Problems in drafts vary enormously. But the diagnosis tends to involve concerns in five general areas: purpose, meaning, information, structure, and clarity and style. Here are some typical reader responses to drafts with each kind of problem:

1. **Problems with Purpose**
   - "I don't know why the writer is writing this paper."
   - "The beginning of the essay seems to be about one thing, and the rest of it is about several others."
   - "I think there are about three different topics in the draft. Which one do you want to write about?"
   - "So what?"

2. **Problems with Meaning**
   - "I can't tell what the writer is trying to say in the draft."
   - "There doesn't seem to be a point behind all of this."
   - "I think there's a main idea, but there isn't much information on it."
   - "I thought the thesis was saying something pretty obvious."

3. **Problems with Information**
   - "Parts of the draft seemed really pretty vague or general."
   - "I couldn't really *see* what you were talking about."
   - "It seemed like you needed some more facts to back up your point."
   - "It needs more detail."

4. **Problems with Structure**
   - "I couldn't quite follow your thinking in the last few pages."
   - "I was confused about when this happened."
   - "I understood your point but I couldn't figure out what this part had to do with it."
   - "The draft doesn't really flow very well."

5. **Problems with Clarity and Style**
   - "This seems a little choppy."
   - "You need to explain this better. I couldn't quite follow what you were saying in this paragraph."
   - "This sentence seems really awkward to me."
   - "This doesn't have a strong voice."

PROBLEMS WITH PURPOSE

A draft that answers the *So what?* question is a draft with a purpose. Often enough, however, writers' intentions aren't all that clear to readers and they don't have a strong reason to keep reading.

It's a little like riding a tandem bike. The writer sits up front and steers while the reader occupies the seat behind, obligated to pedal but with no control over where the bike goes. As soon as the reader senses that the writer isn't steering anywhere in particular, then the reader will get off the bike. Why do all that pedaling if the bike seems to be going nowhere?

Frequently, when you begin writing about something, you don't have any idea where you're headed; that's exactly *why* you're writing about the subject in the first place. When we write such discovery drafts, revision often begins by looking for clues about your purpose. What you learn then becomes a key organizing principle for the next draft, trying to clarify this purpose to your readers. The first question, therefore, is one writers must answer for themselves: "Why am I writing this?" Of course, if it's an assignment it's hard to get past the easy answer—"Because I have to"—but if the work is going to be any good, there must be a better answer than that. Whether your topic is open or assigned, you have to find your own reason to write about it, and what you discover becomes an answer to your bike partner's nagging question, yelled into the wind from the seat behind you: "If I'm going to pedal this hard, you better let me know where we're going."

In general, writers' motives behind writing often involve more than one of these following four purposes.

1. **To explore.** One way to handle complicated questions is to approach the answers in an open-ended way; the writer writes to discover what he thinks or how he feels and reports to the reader on these discoveries.

2. **To explain.** Much of the writing we encounter in daily life is meant simply to provide us with information: This is how the coffeemaker works, or this is the best way to prepare for a trip to New Zealand. Expository writing frequently explains and describes.

3. **To evaluate.** In a sense, all writing is evaluative because it involves making judgments. For instance, when you explain how to plan a New Zealand vacation, you're making judgments about where to go. But when the explicit purpose is to present a judgment about something, the writer encourages readers to see the world the way the writer does. He or she may want the reader to think or behave a certain way: It makes sense to abolish pennies because they're more trouble than they're worth, or you should vote for the bond issue because it's the best way to save the foothills.

4. **To reflect.** Less frequently, we write to stand back from what we're writing about and consider *how* we're thinking about the subject, the methods we're using to write about it, and what we might learn from this writing situation that might apply to others.

Revision Strategy 1: The Motive Statement

It may help to begin a revision by attempting to determine your *primary motive* for the next draft. Do you want to explore your topic, explain something to your readers, offer a persuasive judgment, or step back and reflect on what you're saying or how you're saying it? The genre of writing has a great deal to do with this (see the following table). If you're writing a personal essay, your purpose is likely to be exploratory. If you're writing a review, a proposal, a critical essay, or an argument essay, it's likely your primary motive is to evaluate. One way, then, to get some basic guidance for the next draft is to carefully craft the second half of the following sentence: My primary motive in writing this paper is to explore/evaluate/explain/reflect about _____.

Genre	Primary Motive
Personal essay	Explore
Profile	Explore or explain
Review	Evaluate
Proposal	Evaluate
Argument	Evaluate
Critical essay	Evaluate
Ethnographic essay	Explore or evaluate
Research essay	Explore or evaluate
Reflective essay	Reflect

Of course, any one essay may involve all four motives, but for the purpose of this exercise, choose your *main* purpose in writing the essay. Composing the second half of the sentence may not be so easy because it challenges you to limit your subject. For instance, the following is far too ambitious for, say, a five-page essay: My main motive in writing this paper is to evaluate the steps taken to deal with terrorism and judge whether they're adequate. That's simply too big a subject for a brief persuasive paper. This is more reasonable: My main motive in writing this paper is to evaluate passenger screening procedures in Europe and decide whether they're better than those in the United States.

Since largely exploratory pieces often are motivated by questions, a writer of a personal essay might compose the following sentence: My main motive in writing this essay is to explore why I felt relieved when my father died.

After you craft your motive sentence, put it on a piece of paper or index card and post it where you can see it as you revise the draft. Periodically ask yourself, *What does this paragraph or this section of the draft have to do with my main motive?* The answer will help you decide what to cut and what needs more development in the next draft. Remember, the essay should be organized around this motive from beginning to end.

Revision Strategy 2: What Do You Want to Know About What You Learned?

Because inquiry-based writing is usually driven by questions rather than answers, one way to discover your purpose in a sketch or draft is to generate a list of questions it raises for you. Of course, you hope that one of them might be

ONE STUDENT'S RESPONSE

Julia's Draft

What do I understand about this topic now that I didn't understand before I started writing about it?

After writing this essay, I understand more clearly that there's a relationship between a girl's eating disorders and how her father treats her as a child.

LIST OF QUESTIONS

- Why the father and not the mother?
- What is it about father/daughter relationships that make them so vulnerable to feminine body images?
- Is the father's influence on a girl's body image greater at certain ages or stages in her life?
- How can a father be more informed about his impact on a daughter's body image?

behind your purpose in the next draft. Try the following steps with a draft that needs a stronger sense of purpose.

1. Choose a draft or sketch you'd like to revise, and reread it.

2. On the back of the manuscript, craft an answer to the following question: *What do I understand about this topic now that I didn't understand before I started writing about it?*

3. Next, if you can, build a list of questions—perhaps new ones—that this topic still raises for you. Make this list as long as you can, and don't censor yourself (see "One Student's Response" above).

4. Choose one or more of the questions as a prompt for a fastwrite. Follow your writing to see where it leads and what it might suggest about new directions for the revision.

5. If you can't think of any questions, or find you didn't learn much from writing about the topic (step 2), you may have several options. One is to abandon the draft altogether. Is it possible that this topic simply doesn't interest you anymore? If abandoning the draft isn't possible, then you need to find a new angle. Try Revision Strategy 3.

Revision Strategy 3: Finding the Focusing Question

The best topics, and the most difficult to write about, are those that raise questions for you. In a sketch or first draft, you may not know what these questions are. But if your subsequent drafts are going to be purposeful and focused, then discovering the main question behind your essay is essential. This is particularly important in essays that are research based because the drafts are longer and you're often trying to manage a lot of information. This revision strategy works best when it's a class activity.

1. Begin by simply putting your essay topic on the top of a large piece of paper such as newsprint or butcher paper. If yours is a research topic—say, Alzheimer's disease—jot that down. Post your paper on the classroom wall.

2. Spend a few minutes writing a few sentences explaining why you chose to write about this topic in the first place.

3. Make a quick list of everything you *already know* (if anything) about your topic—for instance, surprising facts or statistics, the extent of the problem, important people or institutions involved, key schools of thought, common misconceptions, familiar clichés that apply to the topic, observations you've made, important trends, and typical perspectives. Spend about five minutes on this.

4. Now spend fifteen or twenty minutes brainstorming a list of questions about your topic that you'd love to learn the answers to. Make this list as long as possible.

5. As you look around the room, you'll see a gallery of topics and questions on the walls. You can help each other. Circulate around the room and do two things: add a question that you're interested in about a particular topic, and check the question (yours or someone else's) that seems most interesting.

When you return to your newsprint or butcher paper, it should be covered with questions. How will you decide which of them might provide the best focus for the next draft? Consider the following criteria as you try to make this decision:

- **What question do you find most intriguing?** After all, it's your essay, and it should be driven by your own interests in the subject.

- **Which question seems most manageable?** This mostly has to do with the level of generality or specificity of the question. You want a focusing question that isn't too general or too specific. For example, a question such as *What causes international terrorism*? is a landscape question—it contains so much possible territory that you'll never get a close look at anything. But a question such as *How effective has the Saudi royal family been in limiting terrorist activities*? is a much more focused, and therefore manageable, question.

- **What question seems most appropriate for the assignment?** For example, if you're assigned a research essay, certain questions are more likely than others to send you to the library. If you're writing a persuasive essay, gravitate toward a question that might point you toward a claim or thesis.

- **What seems most relevant to the information you've already collected?** It would be convenient if information from your research or first draft is relevant to the question that's behind the next draft. While this might make the revision go more quickly, always be open to the possibility that a question that takes you in new directions might simply be more interesting to you.

- **What question is likely to yield answers that interest your readers?** You already have a sense of this from the questions that students in your class added to your newsprint about your topic. The challenge in any piece of writing, of course, is to answer the *So what?* question. Does your focusing question promise to lead you somewhere that readers would care to go?

Revision Strategy 4: What's the Relationship?

One of the more common purposes for all kinds of essays is to explore a relationship between two or more things. We see this in research all the time. What's the relationship between AIDS and IV drug use in China? What's the relationship between gender and styles of collaboration in the workplace? What's the social class relationship between Huck and Tom in *The Adventures of Huckleberry Finn*?

One way, then, to clarify your purpose in revision is to try to identify the relationship that may be at the heart of your inquiry. Relationships between things can be described in a couple different ways.

- **Cause and effect.** What is the relationship between my father's comments about my looks and my eating disorder when I was a teenager? What is the relationship between the second Iraqi war and destabilization in Saudi Arabia? What is the relationship between the decline of the Brazilian rain forest and the extinction of the native eagles? What is the relationship between my moving to Idaho and the failure of my relationship with Kevin?

- **Compare and contrast.** How is jealousy distinguished from envy? How might writing instruction in high school be distinguished from writing instruction in college? What are the differences and similarities between my experiences at the Rolling Stones concert last month and my experiences at the Stones concert fifteen years ago?

Review your sketch or draft to determine whether what you're really trying to write about is the relationship between two (or more) things. In your journal, try to state this relationship in sentences similar to those listed here. With this knowledge, return to the draft and revise from beginning to end with this purpose in mind. What do you need to add to the next draft to both clarify and develop the relationship you're focusing on? What should you cut that is irrelevant to that focus?

PROBLEMS WITH MEANING

Fundamentally, most of us write something in an attempt to say something to someone else. The note my wife Karen left for me yesterday said it in a sentence: "Bruce—could you pick up some virgin olive oil and a loaf of bread?" I had no trouble deciphering the meaning of this note. But it isn't always that easy. Certain poems, for example, may be incredibly ambiguous texts, and readers may puzzle over them for hours, coming up with a range of plausible interpretations of meaning. (See Figure 2.)

Where Does Meaning Come From?

Depending on the writing situation, you may know what you want to say from the start or you may *discover* what you think as you write and research. Inquiry-based projects usually emphasize discovery, while more conventional argument papers may rely on arriving at a thesis earlier in the process. It's something like the difference between sledding with a saucer or a flexible flyer. The saucer is likely to veer off course and you might find yourself somewhere unexpected, yet interesting.

TERMS TO DESCRIBE DOMINANT MEANING

- Thesis
- Main point
- Theme
- Controlling idea
- Central claim or assertion

No matter what you think about a topic when you start writing—even when you begin with a thesis to which you're committed—you can still change your

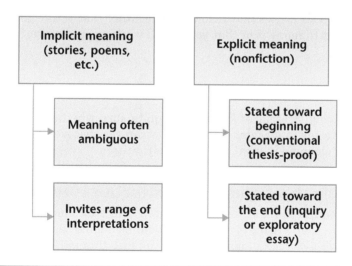

Figure 2   Depending on the genre, writers say it straight or tell it slant. In short stories, for example, the writers' ideas may be ambiguous, inviting interpretation. Nonfiction genres—the kind you will most often write in college and beyond—usually avoid ambiguity. Writers say what they mean as clearly and as persuasively as they can.

mind. You *should* change your mind if the evidence you've gathered leads you away from your original idea. Unfortunately, writers of thesis-driven papers and other deductive forms are far more resistant to any change in their thinking. In some writing situations—say, essay exams—this isn't a problem. But it's often important in academic writing, including arguments, to always be open to new insight.

Ideas about what we want to say on a writing topic grow from the following:

1. **Thesis.** This is a term most of us know from school writing, and it's most often associated with types of writing that work deductively from a main idea. Here's a sample thesis:

   The U.S. Securities and Exchange Commission is incapable of regulating an increasingly complex banking system.

2. **Theory.** We have strong hunches about how things work all the time, but we're not certain we're right. We test our theories and report on the accuracy of our hunches. Here's an example of a theory:

   Certain people just don't have a "head" for math.

3. **Question.** In a question-driven process, the emphasis is on discovery and you might work more inductively. You see or experience something that makes you wonder. Here's a question that led a writer to ideas about girls, advertising, and sexuality.

   Why does my ten-year-old want to dress like a hooker?

The revision strategies that follow assume either that you've got a tentative thesis and want to refine it or that you're still working on discovering what you want to say.

Methods for Discovering Your Thesis

Use the following strategies if you're not quite sure whether you know what you're trying to say in a sketch or draft. How can you discover clues about your main point or meaning in what you've already written?

Revision Strategy 5: Find the "Instructive Line"

It may seem odd to think of reading your own drafts for clues about what you mean. After all, your writing is a product of your own mind. But often a draft can reveal to us what we didn't know we knew—an idea that surfaces unexpectedly, a question that we keep asking, or a moment in a narrative that seems surprisingly significant. Part of the challenge is to recognize these clues to your own meanings, and understand what they suggest about the revision.

This isn't always easy, which is one reason it's often so helpful to share your writing with other readers; they may see the clues that we miss. However, this revision strategy depends on reading your own drafts more systematically for clues about what your point might be. What do you say in this draft that might suggest what you really want to say in the next one?

1. **Find the "instructive line."** Every draft is made up of many sentences. But which of these is *the most important sentence or passage*? What do I mean by *important*? Which line or passage points to a larger idea, theme, or feeling that seems to rise above much of the draft and illuminates the significance or relevance of many other lines and passages? The writer Donald Murray calls this the "instructive line," the sentence that seems to point upward toward the meaning of what you've set down. Underline the instructive line or passage in your draft. It may be subtle, only hinting at larger ideas or feelings, or quite explicitly stated. In a narrative essay, the instructive line might be a moment of stepping back to reflect—"As I look back on this now, I understand that…" In a review or persuasive essay, it might be an assertion of some kind—"American moviegoers are seduced by the 'twist' at the end of a film, and learn to expect it."

2. **Follow the thread of meaning.** If the instructive line is a ball of string, tightly packed with coils of meaning that aren't readily apparent, then to get any guidance for revision you need to try to unravel it. At the top of a journal page, write the line or passage you selected in your draft as most important. Use it as a prompt for five minutes of exploratory writing, perhaps beginning with the following seed sentence: I think/feel this is true because…and also because…and also…and also…

3. **Compose a thesis.** Reread your fastwriting in the preceding step and, keeping your original passage in mind, craft a single sentence that best captures the most important idea or feeling you'd like to bring into the next draft. For example, *Because of the expectation, encouraged by Hollywood, that every good movie has a surprise ending, American moviegoers often find even superior foreign films a disappointment.*

4. **Post it.** Put this thesis on the wall above your computer, or use a Post-it note and place the thesis on your computer screen. Revise with the thesis in mind, from beginning to end. Add information that will *illustrate, extend, exemplify, complicate, clarify, support, show, provide background,* or *prove* the thesis. Cut information from the draft that does none of these things.

Revision Strategy 6: Looping Toward a Thesis

I've argued throughout *The Curious Writer* for a dialectical approach to writing, moving back and forth between creative and critical modes of thinking, from your observations of and your ideas about, from generating and judging, from specifics and generalities. This is how writers can make meaning. The approach can also be used as a revision strategy, this time in a technique called *loop writing*. When you loop write, you move back and forth dialectically between both modes of thought—opening things up and then trying to pin them down. I imagine that this looks like an hourglass.

1. Reread the draft quickly, and then turn it upside down on your desk. You won't look at it again but trust that you'll remember what's important.

2. Begin a three-minute fastwrite on the draft in which you tell yourself the story of your thinking about the essay. When you first started writing it, what did you think you were writing about, and then what, and then...Try to focus on your ideas about what you were trying to say and how it evolved.

3. Sum up what you said in your fastwrite by answering the following question in a sentence: *What seems to be the most important thing I've finally come to understand about my topic?*

4. Begin another three-minute fastwrite. Focus on scenes, situations, case studies, moments, people, conversations, observations, and so on that stand out for you as you think about the draft. Think especially of specifics that come to mind that led to the understanding of your topic that you stated in the preceding step. Some of this information may be in the draft, but some may *not* yet be in the draft.

5. Finish by restating the main point you want to make in the next draft. Begin the revision by thinking about a lead or introduction that dramatizes this point. Consider a suggestive scene, case study, finding, profile, description, comparison, anecdote, conversation, situation, or observation that points the essay toward your main idea (see the "Inquiring into the Details: Types of Leads"). For example, if your point is that your university's program to help second-language learners is inadequate, you could begin the next draft by telling the story of Maria, an immigrant from Guatemala who was a victim of poor placement in a composition course that she was virtually guaranteed to fail. Follow this lead into the draft, always keeping your main point or thesis in mind.

Revision Strategy 7: Reclaiming Your Topic

When you do a lot of research on your topic, you may reach a point when you feel awash in information. It's easy at such moments to feel as if you're losing control of your topic, besieged by the voices of experts, a torrent of statistics and facts, and competing perspectives. Your success in writing the paper depends on making it your own again, gaining control over the information for your own purposes, in the service of your own questions or arguments. This revision strategy, a variation of Revision Strategy 6, should help you gain control of the material you collected for a research-based inquiry project.

1. Spend ten or fifteen minutes reviewing all of the notes you've taken and skimming key articles or passages from books. Glance at your most important sources. If you have a rough draft, reread it. Let your head swim with information.

2. Now clear your desk of everything but your journal. Remove all your notes and materials. If you have a rough draft, put it in the drawer.

3. Now fastwrite about your topic for seven full minutes. Tell the story of how your thinking about the topic has evolved. When you began, what did you think? What were your initial assumptions or preconceptions? Then what happened, and what happened after that? Keep your pen moving.

4. Skip a few lines in your notebook, and write Moments, Stories, People, and Scenes. Now fastwrite for another seven minutes, this time focusing more on specific case studies, situations, people, experiences, observations, facts, and so on that stand out in your mind from the research you've done so far, or perhaps from your own experience with the topic.

5. Skip a few more lines. For another seven minutes, write a dialogue between you and someone else about your topic. Choose someone who you think is typical of the audience you're writing for. If it helps, think of someone specific—an instructor, a fellow student, a friend. Don't plan the dialogue. Just begin with the question most commonly asked about your topic, and take the conversation from there, writing both parts of the dialogue.

6. Finally, skip a few more lines and write these two words in your notebook: So what? Now spend a few minutes trying to summarize the most important thing you think your readers should understand about your topic, based on what you've learned so far. Distill this into a sentence or two.

As you work your way to the last step, you're reviewing what you've learned about your topic without being tyrannized by the many voices, perspectives, and facts in the research you've collected. The final step, Step 6, leads you toward a thesis statement. In the revision, keep this in mind as you reopen your notes, reread your sources, and check on facts. Remember in the rewrite to put all of this information in the service of this main idea, as examples or illustrations, necessary background, evidence or support, counterexamples, and ways of qualifying or extending your main point.

Revision Strategy 8: Believing and Doubting

In persuasive writing such as the argument, review, proposal, or research paper, we often feel that a thesis involves picking sides—"the play was good" or "the play was bad," "the novel was boring" or "the novel was fun to read." Instead of *either/or*, consider *both/and*. This might bring you to a more truthful, more sophisticated understanding of your subject, which rarely is either all bad or all good. One way to do this is to play Peter Elbow's doubting game and believing game.

1. Set aside ten to twelve minutes for two episodes of fastwriting in your journal or on the computer. First, spend a full five minutes playing the "believing game" (see the following prompts), exploring the merits of your subject even

if (and especially if) you don't think it has any. Then switch to the "doubting game." Write fast for another five minutes using a skeptical mind.

THE BELIEVING GAME

Give the author, performer, text, or performance the benefit of the doubt. Suspend criticism.

1. What seems true or truthful about what is said, shown, or argued?

2. How does it confirm your own experiences or observations of the same things?

3. What did you like or agree with?

4. Where is it strongest, most compelling, most persuasive?

5. How does it satisfy your criteria for being good, useful, convincing, or moving?

THE DOUBTING GAME

Adopt a critical stance. Look for holes, weaknesses, omissions, problems.

1. What seems unbelievable or untrue?

2. What does it fail to consider or consider inadequately?

3. Where is the evidence missing or insufficient, or where do the elements not work together effectively?

4. How does it fail to meet your criteria for good in this category of thing?

5. Where is it the least compelling or persuasive? Why?

2. From this work in your notebook, try to construct a sentence—a thesis—that is more than a simple statement of the worth or worthlessness of the thing you're evaluating, but an expression of *both* its strengths and weaknesses: Although _____ succeeds (or fails) in _____, it mostly _____. For example: Although reality television presents viewers with an often interesting glimpse into how ordinary people handle their fifteen minutes of celebrity, it mostly exaggerates life by creating drama where there often is none.

Methods for Refining Your Thesis

You may emerge from writing a draft with a pretty clear sense of what you want to say in the next one. But does this idea seem a little obvious or perhaps too general? Does it fail to adequately express what you really feel and think? Use one or more of the following revision strategies to refine a thesis, theme, or controlling idea.

Revision Strategy 9: Questions as Knives

Imagine that your initial feeling, thesis, or main point is like an onion. Ideas, like onions, have layers, and to get closer to their hearts you need to cut through the most obvious outer layers to reveal what is less obvious, probably more specific, and almost certainly more interesting. Questions are to ideas as knives are to onions: They help you slice past your initial impressions. The most important question—the sharpest knife in the drawer—is simply *Why? Why* was the Orwell essay interesting? *Why* do you hate foreign films? *Why* should the university do more for second-language speakers? *Why* did you feel a sense of loss when the old cornfield was paved over for the mall?

Why may be the sharpest knife in the drawer, but there are other *W* questions with keen blades, too, including *What?, Where?, When?,* and *Who?* In Figure 3 you can see how these questions can cut a broad thesis down to size. The result is a much more specific, more interesting controlling idea for the next draft.

1. Subject your tentative thesis to the same kind of narrowing. Write your theme, thesis, or main point as a single sentence in your notebook.
2. Slice it with questions and restate it each time.
3. Continue this until your point is appropriately sliced; that is, when you feel that you've gone beyond the obvious and stated what you think or feel in a more specific and interesting way.

As before, rewrite the next draft with this new thesis in mind, reorganizing the essay around it from beginning to end. Add new information that supports the idea, provides the necessary background, offers opposing views, or extends it. Cut information that no longer seems relevant to the thesis.

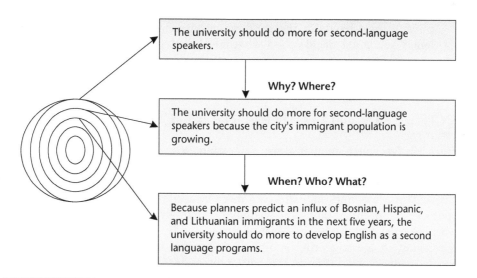

Figure 3   Why? Where? When? Who? and What? Using questions to narrow the focus of a thesis is like using a knife to cut into the heart of an onion.

Revision Strategy 10: Qualifying Your Claim

In your research you discovered that, while 90 percent of Americans think that their fellow citizens are too "fat," only 39 percent would describe themselves that way. This evidence leads you to make the following claim: *Although Americans agree that obesity is a national problem, their response is typical: it's somebody else's problem, an attitude that will cripple efforts to promote healthier lifestyles.* This seems like a logical assertion if the evidence is reliable. But if you're going to try to build an argument around it, a claim should be rigorously examined. Toulmin's approach to analyzing arguments provides a method for doing this.

1. Toulmin observes that sometimes a claim should be *qualified* to be more accurate and persuasive. The initial question is simple: *Is what you're asserting always or universally true?* Essentially, you're being challenged to examine your certainty about what you're saying. This might lead you to add words or phrases to it that acknowledge your sense of certainty: *sometimes, always, mostly, in this case, based on available evidence,* and so on. In this case, the claim is already qualified by specifying that it is limited to Americans, but it is also based on evidence from a single source. The claim, therefore, might be qualified to say this: *Although one survey suggests that Americans agree that obesity is a national problem, their response is typical: it's somebody else's problem, an attitude that will cripple efforts to promote healthier lifestyles.*

2. Imagining how your claim might be rebutted is another way to strengthen it. How might someone take issue with your thesis? What might be the exceptions to what you're saying is true? For example, might someone object to the assertion that Americans "typically" respond by putting their heads in the sand when personally confronted with problems? You must decide then whether this clever aside in your claim is something you're prepared to support. If not, cut it.

PROBLEMS WITH INFORMATION

Writers who've spent enough time generating or collecting information about their topics can work from abundance rather than scarcity. This is an enormous advantage because the ability to throw stuff away means you can be selective about what you use, and the result is a more focused draft. But as we revise, our purpose and point might shift, and we may find ourselves in the unhappy position of working from scarcity again. Most of our research, observation, or fastwriting was relevant to the triggering subject in the initial sketch or draft, not to the generated subject we decide is the better direction for the next draft. In some cases, this might require that you research the new topic or return to the generating activities of listing, fastwriting, clustering, and so on that will help provide information for the next draft.

More often, however, writers don't have to begin from scratch in revision. Frequently, a shift in the focus or refining a thesis in a first draft just means emphasizing different information or perhaps filling in gaps in later drafts. The strategies that follow will help you solve this problem.

Revision Strategy 11: Explode a Moment

The success of personal essays that rely on narratives frequently depends on how well the writer renders an important scene, situation, moment, or description. When you're telling a story from experience, not all parts of the story are equally important. As always, emphasis in a narrative depends on the writer's purpose in the essay. For example, Matt's essay on the irony of the slow poisoning of Butte, Montana, his home town, by a copper mine that once gave the city life would emphasize those parts of the story that best highlight that irony. Or a description of the agonizing death of the snow geese that unwittingly landed on the acid pond—their white beauty set against the deadly dark water—might be an important scene in Matt's next draft; it nicely portrays life and death, beauty and ugliness in much the same way the town and the mine might be contrasted. Matt should "explode that moment" because it's an important part of the story he's trying to tell about his Montana home town.

If you're trying to revise a draft that relies on narratives, this revision strategy will help you first identify moments, scenes, or descriptions that might be important in the next draft, and then develop these as more important parts of your story.

1. Choose a draft that involves a story or stories.
2. Make a list in your journal of the moments (for example, scenes, situations, and turning points) that stand out in the narrative.
3. Circle one that you think is most important to your purpose in the essay. It could be the situation that is most telling, a dramatic turning point, the moment of a key discovery that is central to what you're trying to say, or a scene that illustrates the dilemma or raises the question you're exploring in the draft.
4. Name that moment at the top of a blank journal page (for example, the snow geese on the acid pond, when the ice broke, or when I saw my grandfather in his coffin).
5. Now put yourself back into that moment and fastwrite about it for seven full minutes. Make sure that you write with as much detail as possible, *drawing on all your senses*. Write in the present tense if it helps.
6. Use this same method with other moments in the narrative that might deserve more emphasis in the next draft. Remember that real time means little in writing. An experience that took seven seconds can easily take up three pages of writing if it's detailed enough. Rewrite and incorporate the best of the new information in the next draft.

Revision Strategy 12: Beyond Examples

When we add information to a draft we normally think of adding examples. If you're writing a research essay on living with a sibling who suffers from Down syndrome, you might mention that your brother typically tries to avoid certain cognitive challenges. Members of your workshop group wonder, "Well, what kind of challenges?" In revision, you add an example or two from your own experience to clarify what you mean. This is, of course, a helpful strategy; examples of what you mean by an assertion are a kind of evidence that helps readers more fully understand your work. But also consider other types of information it might be helpful to add to the next draft. Use the following list to review your draft for additions you might not have thought of for revision.

- **Presenting counterarguments.** Typically, persuasive essays include information that represents an opposing view. Say you're arguing that beyond "avoidance" behaviors, there really aren't personality traits that can be attributed to most people with Down syndrome. You include a summary of a study that says otherwise. Why? Because it provides readers with a better understanding of the debate, and enhances the writer's ethos because you appear fair.

- **Providing background.** When you drop in on a conversation between two friends, you initially may be clueless about the subject. Naturally, you ask questions: "Who are you guys talking about? When did this happen? What did she say?" Answers to these questions provide a context that allows you to understand what is being said and to participate in the conversation. Background information like this is often essential in written communication, too. In a personal essay, readers may want to know when and where the event occurred or the relationship between the narrator and a character. In a critical essay, it might be necessary to provide background on the short story because readers may not have read it. In a research essay, it's often useful to provide background information about what has already been said on the topic and the research question.

- **Establishing significance.** Let's say you're writing about the problem of obesity in America, something that most of us are generally aware of these days. But the significance of the problem really strikes home when you add information from research suggesting that 30 percent of American adults are overweight, up from 23 percent just six years ago. It is even more important to establish the significance of a problem about which there is little awareness or consensus. For example, most people don't know that America's national park system is crumbling and in disrepair. Your essay on the problem needs to provide readers with information that establishes the significance of the problem. In a profile, readers need to have a reason to be interested in someone—perhaps your profile subject represents a particular group of people of interest or concern.

- **Giving it a face.** One of the best ways to make an otherwise abstract issue or problem come to life is to show what it means to an individual person. We can't fully appreciate the social impact of deforestation in Brazil without being introduced to someone such as Chico Mendes, a forest defender who was murdered for his activism. Obesity might be an abstract problem until we meet Carl, a 500-pound 22-year-old who is "suffocating in his own fat." Add case studies, anecdotes, profiles, and descriptions that put people on the page to make your essay more interesting and persuasive.

- **Defining it.** If you're writing about a subject your readers know little about, you'll likely use concepts or terms that readers will want you to define. What exactly do you mean, for example, when you say that the Internet is vulnerable to cyberterror? What exactly is cyberterror anyway? In your personal essay on your troubled relationship with your mother, what do you mean when you call her a narcissist? Frequently your workshop group will alert you to things in the draft that need defining, but also go through your own draft and ask yourself, *Will my readers know what I mean?*

Revision Strategy 13: Research

Too often, research is ignored as a revision strategy. We may do research for the first draft of a paper or essay, but never return to the library or search the Web to fill in gaps, answer new questions, or refine the focus of a rewrite. That's crazy, particularly because well-researched information can strengthen a draft of any kind. That has been one of the themes of *The Curious Writer* since the beginning of the book: Research is not a separate activity reserved only for the research paper, but a rich source of information for any type of writing. Try some of these strategies:

1. For quick facts, visit http://www.refdesk.com. This enormously useful Web site is the fastest way to find out the exact height of the Great Wall of China or the number of young women suffering from eating disorders in America today.

2. Return to the *Library of Congress Subject Headings*, the reference mentioned that will help you pinpoint the language you should use to search library databases on your topic. Particularly if the focus of your next draft is shifting, you'll need some fresh information to fill in the gaps. The *LCSH* will help you find more of it, more quickly.

3. To maximize Web coverage, launch a search on at least three different search engines (for example, Google, MSN Search, and Yahoo!), but this time search using terms or phrases from your draft that will lead you to more specific information that will fill gaps in the draft.

4. Interview someone relevant to your topic.

5. To ferret out some new sources on your topic, search library databases under author rather than keyword. Focus on authors that you know have something to say on your topic.

6. Return to any of the steps that involve developing deep knowledge about your topic.

Revision Strategy 14: Backing Up Your Assumptions

Targeted research is particularly important when you're making an argument. In addition to providing evidence that is relevant to your thesis, frequently an argument rests on the assumptions behind that assertion. Stephen Toulmin calls these assumptions *warrants*. For example, suppose your claim is the following: *Although most Americans agree that obesity is a national problem, most don't describe themselves as fat, an attitude that will cripple efforts to promote healthier lifestyles*. Every claim rests on assumptions, or warrants. In other words, what do you have to believe is true to have faith in the accuracy of the claim?

1. Write your claim on the top of a journal page, and then list the assumptions or warrants on which it seems to rest. For example, the claim about obesity includes an assumption that most Americans equate the words *obesity* and *fat*. Also there's an assumption that public attitudes—particularly the view that there is a problem but it isn't my problem—hinder progress on public policy.

2. Which of the warrants behind your claim would be stronger if there were "backing" or evidence to support them? This will give you new direction for research. It might strengthen the argument on the obesity problem, for example, to draw on evidence from the civil rights struggle. Is there any evidence that attitudes toward personal responsibility for racism lagged behind acknowledgment of racial inequality as a national problem? Was progress finally made when this gap narrowed?

PROBLEMS WITH STRUCTURE

When it's working, the structure of a piece of writing is nearly invisible. Readers don't notice how the writer is guiding them from one piece of information to the next. When structure is a problem, the writer asks readers to walk out on a shaky bridge and trust that it will help them get to the other side, but the walkers can think of little else but the shakiness of the bridge. Some professional writers, such as John McPhee, obsess about structure, and for good reason—when you're working with a tremendous amount of information, as McPhee often does in his research-based essays, it helps to have a clear idea about how you'll use it.

It's helpful to distinguish two basic structures for writing. One typically organizes the information of experience, and one organizes our thinking so that it's clear and convincing. Typically, we use narrative, and especially chronology, to organize our experiences, though how we handle time can vary considerably. Writing that presents information based on the writer's reasoning—perhaps making an argument or reporting on an experiment—is logically structured. The most common example is the thesis-example, or thesis-proof, paper. Much formal academic writing relies on logical structures that use deduction or induction.

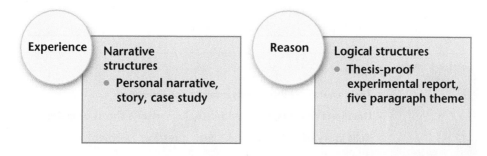

And yet some kinds of writing, like the researched essay or ethnography, may *combine* both patterns, showing how the writer reasoned through to the meaning of an experience, observation, reading, and so on. These essays tell a "narrative of thought."

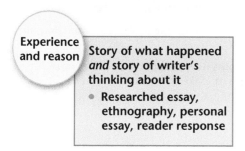

Formal Academic Structures

In some academic writing, the structure is prescribed. Scientific papers often have sections—Introduction, Methodology, Results, Discussion—but within those sections writers must organize their material. Certain writing assignments may also require you to organize your information in a certain way. The most common of these is the thesis/support structure. In such essays you typically establish your thesis in the first paragraph, spend the body of the paper assembling evidence that supports the thesis, and conclude the essay with a summary that restates the thesis in light of what's been said.

Thesis/support is a persuasive form, so it lends itself to arguments, critical essays, reviews, proposals, and similar pieces. In fact, you may have already structured your draft using this approach. If so, the following revision strategy may help you tighten and clarify the draft.

Beginning

- Establishes purpose (answers *So what?* question)
- Introduces question, dilemma, problem, theory, thesis, claim (sometimes dramatically)
- Helps readers understand—and feel—what's at stake for them

Middle

- Tests theory, claim, thesis against the evidence
- Develops reasons, with evidence, for writer's thesis or claim
- Tells story of writer's inquiry into question, problem, or dilemma

End

- Proposes answer, even if tentative, for writer's key question
- Revisits thesis or claim, extending, qualifying, contradicting, or reconfirming initial idea
- Raises new questions, poses new problems, or offers new understanding of what is at stake for readers

Revision Strategy 15: Beginnings, Middles, Ends, and the Work They Do

Stories, we are often told, always have a beginning, middle, and end. This may be the most fundamental structure of all, and it doesn't just apply to narratives. The figure above explains what a beginning, middle, and end might contribute to making nearly any piece of writing coherent and convincing. Apply some of these ideas to your draft.

1. Divide a draft you'd like to revise into three parts—beginning, middle, and end—by drawing lines in the paper to distinguish each section. Where you decide to divide the draft is entirely up to you; there's no formula to this. But you may change your mind as you go along.

2. Now use the figure above to analyze your beginning, middle, and end. Does each section do at least *one* of the listed tasks? If not, revise that section

so that it does. This may involve adding one sentence or possibly para-graphs of new information, perhaps moving some from elsewhere in the draft.

3. Generally speaking, the middle of an essay does the most work, and so proportionally it should have the most information. For example, many essays look like this:

If you find, for example, that your beginning takes three pages of a five-page essay, then you might want to cut away at the first few pages and concen-trate on developing the body of your essay.

Revision Strategy 16: Reorganizing Around Thesis and Support

Because the thesis/support structure is fairly common, it's useful to master. Most drafts, even if they weren't initially organized in that form, can be revised into a thesis/support essay. (Personal essays would be an exception.) The order of information in such an essay generally follows this design:

■ **Lead paragraph:** This paragraph introduces the topic and explicitly states the thesis, usually as the last sentence in the paragraph. For exam-ple, a thesis/support paper on the deterioration of America's national parks system might begin this way:

> Yellowstone National Park, which shares territory with Idaho, Montana, and Wyoming, is the nation's oldest park and, to some, its most revered. Established on March 1, 1872, the park features the Old Faithful geyser, which spouts reli-ably every 76 minutes on average. What isn't nearly as reliable these days is whether school groups will get to see it. Last year 60% of them were turned away because the park simply didn't have the staff. <u>This essay will argue that poor funding of our national parks system is a disgrace that threatens to under-mine the Park Service's mission to preserve the areas "as cumulative expressions of a single national heritage" ("Famous Quotes")</u>.

The thesis (underlined) is the final sentence in the paragraph, for emphasis.

- **Body:** Each succeeding paragraph until the final one attempts to prove or develop the thesis. Often each paragraph is devoted to a single *reason* why the thesis is true, frequently stated as the topic sentence of the paragraph. Specific information then explains, clarifies, and supports the reason. For example, here's a typical paragraph from the body of the national parks essay:

> One aspect of the important national heritage at risk because of poor funding for national parks is the pride many Americans feel about these national treasures. *Newsweek* writer Arthur Frommer calls the national park system among the "crowning glories of our democracy." He adds, "Not to have seen them is to have missed something unique and precious in American life" (12). To see the crumbling roads in Glacier National Park, or the incursion of development in Great Smoky Mountains National Park, or the slow strangulation of the Everglades is not just an ecological issue; it's a sorry statement about a democratic nation's commitment to some of the places that define its identity.

The underlined sentence is the topic sentence of the paragraph and is an assertion that supports and develops the thesis in the lead of the essay. The rest of the paragraph offers supporting evidence of the assertion, in this case a quotation from a *Newsweek* writer who recently visited several parks.

- **Concluding paragraph:** This paragraph reminds the reader of the central argument, not simply by restating the original thesis from the first paragraph but by reemphasizing some of the most important points. This may lead to an elaboration or restatement of the thesis. One common technique is to find a way in the end of the essay to return to the beginning. Here's the concluding paragraph from the essay on national park funding:

> We would never risk our national heritage by allowing the White House to deteriorate or the Liberty Bell to rust away. As the National Park Service's own mission states, the parks are also "expressions" of our "single national heritage," one this paper contends is about preserving not only trees, animals, and habitats, but our national identity. The Old Faithful geyser reminds Americans of their constancy and their enduring spirit. What will it say about us if vandals finally end the regular eruptions of the geyser because Americans didn't support a park ranger to guard it? What will we call Old Faithful then? Old Faithless?

Note that the underlined sentence returns to the original thesis but doesn't simply repeat it word for word. Instead, it amplifies the original thesis, adding a definition of "national heritage" to include national identity. It returns to the opening paragraph by finding a new way to discuss Old Faithful. Revise your draft to conform to this structure, beginning with a strong opening paragraph that explicitly states your thesis and with an ending that somehow returns to the beginning without simply repeating what you've already said.

Revision Strategy 17: Multiple Leads

A single element that may affect a draft more than any other is the beginning. There are many ways into the material, and of course you want to choose a beginning or lead that a reader might find interesting. You also want to choose a beginning that makes some kind of promise, providing readers with a sense of where you intend to take them. But a lead has less obvious effects on both readers and writers. How you begin often establishes the voice of the essay; signals the writer's emotional relationship to the material, the writer's ethos; and might suggest the form the essay will take.

This is, of course, why beginnings are so hard to write. But the critical importance of where and how we begin also suggests that examining alternative leads can give writers more choices and more control over their essays. To borrow John McPhee's metaphor, if a lead is a "flashlight that shines down into the story," then pointing that flashlight in four different directions might reveal four different ways of following the same subject. This can be a powerful revision strategy.

1. Choose a draft that has a weak opening, doesn't have a strong sense of purpose, or needs to be reorganized.

2. Compose four *different* openings to the *same* draft. One way to generate ideas for this is to cluster your topic, and write leads from four different branches. Also consider varying the type of lead you write (see the "Inquiring into the Details: Types of Leads" box on the following page).

3. Bring a typed copy of these four leads (or five if you want to include the original lead from the first draft) to class and share them with a small group. First simply ask your classmates to choose the beginning they like best.

4. Choose the lead *you* prefer. It may or may not be the one your classmates chose. Find a partner who was not in your small group and ask him or her the following questions after sharing the lead you chose:

   ▪ Based on this lead, what do you predict this paper is about?

   ▪ Can you guess the question, problem, or idea I'm writing about in the rest of the essay?

   ▪ Do you have a sense of what my thesis might be?

   ▪ What is the ethos of this beginning? In other words, how do I come across to you as a narrator or author of the essay?

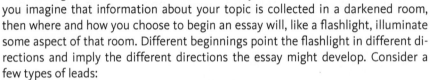

INQUIRING INTO THE DETAILS

Types of Leads

Writer John McPhee says beginnings—or leads—are "like flashlights that shine down into the story." If you imagine that information about your topic is collected in a darkened room, then where and how you choose to begin an essay will, like a flashlight, illuminate some aspect of that room. Different beginnings point the flashlight in different directions and imply the different directions the essay might develop. Consider a few types of leads:

1. *Announcement.* Typical of a thesis/support essay, among others. Explicitly states the purpose and thesis of the essay.

2. *Anecdote.* A brief story that nicely frames the question, dilemma, problem, or idea behind the essay.

3. *Scene.* Describe a situation, place, or image that highlights the question, problem, or idea behind the essay.

4. *Profile.* Begin with a case study or description of a person who is involved in the question, problem, or idea.

5. *Background.* Provide a context through information that establishes the significance of the question, problem, or idea.

6. *Quotation or Dialogue.* Begin with a voice of someone (or several people) involved or whose words are relevant.

7. *Comparison.* Are there two or more things that, when compared or contrasted, point to the question, problem, or idea?

8. *Question.* Frame the question the essay addresses.

If the predictions were fairly accurate using the lead you preferred, this might be a good alternative opening to the next draft. Follow it in a fastwrite in your notebook to see where it leads you. Go ahead and use the other leads elsewhere in the revision, if you like.

If your reader's predictions were off, the lead may not be the best choice for the revision. However, should you consider this new direction an appealing alternative for the next draft? Or should you choose another lead that better reflects your current intentions rather than strike off in new directions? Either way, follow a new lead to see where it goes.

Revision Strategy 18: The Frankenstein Draft

One way to divorce a draft that has you in its clutches is to dismember it; that is, cut it into pieces and play with the parts, looking for new arrangements of information or new gaps to fill. Writing teacher Peter Elbow's cut-and-paste revision can be a useful method, particularly for drafts that don't rely on narrative structures (although sometimes playing with alternatives, particularly if the draft is strictly chronological, can be helpful). Research essays and other pieces that attempt to corral lots of information seem to benefit the most from this strategy.

1. Choose a draft that needs help with organization. Make a one-sided copy.

2. Cut apart the copy, paragraph by paragraph. (You may cut it into smaller pieces later.) Once you have completely disassembled the draft, shuffle the paragraphs to get them wildly out of order so the original draft is just a memory.

3. Now go through the shuffled stack and find the *core paragraph*. This is the paragraph the essay really couldn't do without because it helps answer the *So what?* question. It might be the paragraph that contains your thesis or establishes your focusing question. It should be the paragraph that explains, implicitly or explicitly, what you're trying to say in the draft. Set this aside.

4. With the core paragraph directly in front of you, work your way through the remaining stack of paragraphs and make two new stacks: one of paragraphs that don't seem relevant to your core (such as unnecessary digressions or information) and those that do (they support the main idea, explain or define a key concept, illustrate or exemplify something important, or provide necessary background).

5. Put your reject pile aside for the moment. You may decide to salvage some of those paragraphs later. But for now focus on your relevant pile, including the core paragraph. Now play with order. Try new leads, ends, and middles. Consider trying some new methods of development as a way to organize your next draft (see the "Methods of Development" box). As you spread the paragraphs out before you and consider new arrangements, don't worry about the lack of transitions; you can add those later. Also look for gaps, places where more information might be needed. Consider some of the information in the reject pile as well. Should you splice in *parts* of paragraphs that you initially discarded?

6. As a structure begins to emerge, begin taping together the fragments of paper. Also splice in scraps in appropriate places and note what you might add in the next draft that is currently missing.

> **METHODS OF DEVELOPMENT**
>
> - Narrative
> - Problem to solution
> - Cause to effect, or effect to cause
> - Question to answer
> - Known to unknown, or unknown to known
> - Simple to complex
> - General to specific, or specific to general
> - Comparison and contrast
> - Combinations of any of these

Now you've created a Frankenstein draft. But hopefully this ugly mess of paper and tape and scribbled notes holds much more promise than the monster. On the other hand, if you end up with pretty much the original organization, perhaps your first approach wasn't so bad after all. You may at least find places where more information is needed.

Revision Strategy 19: Make a PowerPoint Outline

While outlines can be a useful tool for planning a formal essay, they can also help writers revise a draft. One of the best tools for doing this is a program such as PowerPoint that challenges you to develop brief slides in sequence. The ease of moving the slides around, the imperative to be brief and to the point, and the visual display of your logic all combine to make the program an ideal medium for playing with the order of information. This is often helpful even if you don't ever make a presentation.

Your goal in creating a PowerPoint outline isn't to transfer all your text to slides and then move it around, though you could do that if you thought it helpful. Your aim is to exploit the software to help you develop a logical outline. You have several options for doing this. One is to title separate slides using some of the conventional structures of academic essays, and then make bulleted lists of the information you might include in each (see the sample slide). For example, these could be slide titles:

- Abstract, Introduction, Literature Review, Thesis/Purpose, Methods, Results, Discussion, Conclusion
- The Problem/Question, Purpose of the Essay, Claim, Reasons and Evidence (separate slide for each reason), Conclusion

Reason #3

Research on the benefits of the sun is routinely ignored.
- Concession that sun can be hazardous
- Quote by Henderson on biological need for sun
- Data on Vitamin D benefits
- Inaccurate warnings to encourage lotion sales

Sample PowerPoint slide outlining a plan for an essay.

- Introduction, Thesis, Example 1, Example 2, Example 3, etc., Conclusion
- Lead/Introduction, Background, Research Question, Significance of the Problem or Question, Other Voices on the Question, Thesis, Conclusion

Alternatively, you might use less formal methods of parsing the information in the draft onto slides. For example, can you label categories of information? In a narrative essay, it might be a particular scene, description, or reflection. In an argument it might be claims, warrants or assumptions, evidence, and counterarguments. A literary essay might be grouped on slides using key passages, the main idea, textual background, information on the author, and so on.

Whichever method you use, once you are able to disassemble your draft onto PowerPoint slides using some logic, don't just play with the order. Consider moving some of the information from slide to slide, too.

PROBLEMS WITH CLARITY AND STYLE

One thing should be made clear immediately: Problems of clarity and style need not have anything to do with grammatical correctness. You can have a sentence that follows all the rules and still lumbers, sputters, and dies like a Volkswagen bug towing a heavy trailer up a steep hill. Take this sentence, for instance:

> Once upon a point in time, a small person named Little Red Riding Hood initiated plans for the preparation, delivery, and transportation of foodstuffs to her grandmother, a senior citizen residing at a place of residence in a wooded area of indeterminate dimension.

Strong writing at the sentence and paragraph levels always begins with clarity.

This beastly sentence opens Russell Baker's essay "Little Red Riding Hood Revisited," a satire about the gassiness of contemporary writing. It's grammatically correct, of course, but it's also pretentious, unnecessarily wordy, and would be annoying to read if it wasn't pretty amusing. This section of the chapter focuses on revision strategies that improve the clarity of your writing and will help you consider the effects you want to create through word choice and arrangement. Your questions about grammar and mechanics can be answered in the handbook at the back of the text.

Maybe because we often think that work with paragraphs, sentences, and words always involves problems of correctness, it may be hard to believe at first that writers can actually manage readers' responses and feelings by using different words or rearranging the parts of a sentence or paragraph. Once you begin to play around with style, however, you will discover that it's much more than cosmetic. In fact, style in writing is a lot like music in movies. Chris Douridas, a Hollywood music supervisor who picked music for *Shrek* and *American Beauty*, said recently that he sees "music as an integral ingredient to the pie. I see it as helping to flavor the pie and not as whipped cream on top." Certainly people don't pick a movie for its music, but we know that the music is central to our experience of a film. Similarly, *how* you say things in a piece of writing powerfully shapes the reader's experience of *what* you say.

But style is a secondary concern. Strong writing at the sentence and paragraph levels always begins with clarity. Do you say what you mean as directly and economically as you can? This can be a real problem, particularly with academic writing, in which it's easy to get the impression that a longer word is always better than a shorter word, and the absence of anything interesting to say can be remedied by sounding smart. Nothing could be further from the truth.

Solving Problems of Clarity

Begin by revising your draft with one or more revision strategies that will make your writing more direct and clear.

Revision Strategy 20: The Three Most Important Sentences

Writers, like car dealers, organize their lots to take advantage of where readers are most likely to look and what they're most likely to remember. In many essays and papers, there are three places to park important information and to craft your very best sentences. These are,

- the very first sentence
- the last line of the first paragraph
- the very last line of the essay

The First Sentence. Obviously, there are many other important places in a piece of writing—and longer essays, especially, have more and different locations for your strongest sentences. But in an informal piece of modest length, the first sentence not only should engage the reader, it should, through strong language and voice, introduce the writer as well. For example, here's the first line of Richard Conniff's researched essay, "Why God Created Flies": "Though I've been killing them for years now, I have never tested the folklore that, with a little cream and sugar, flies taste very much like black raspberries." In more formal writing, the first line is much less about introducing a persona than introducing the subject. Here's the first line of an academic piece I'm reading at the moment: "Much of the international debate about the relationship between research and teaching is characterized by difference." This raises an obvious question—"What is this difference?"—and this is exactly what the author proposes to explore.

The Last Line of the First Paragraph. The so-called "lead" (or "lede" in journalism speak) of an essay or article does three things: It establishes the purpose of the work, raises interesting questions, and creates a register or tone. A lead paragraph in a shorter essay is just that—the first paragraph—while a lead in a longer work may run for paragraphs, even pages. Whatever the length, the last sentence of the lead launches the work and gets it going in a particular direction. In conventional thesis-proof essays, then, this might be the sentence where you state your main claim. In inquiry-based forms like the essay, this might be where you post the key question you're exploring or illuminate the aspect of the problem you want to look at.

The Last Line of the Essay. If it's good, this is the sentence readers are most likely to remember.

Try this revision strategy:

1. Highlight or underline each of these three sentences in your draft.
2. Ask yourself these questions about the first line and, depending on your answers, revise the sentence:
   - Is the language lively?
   - Does it immediately raise questions the reader might want to learn the answers to?
   - Will they want to read the second sentence, and why?
3. Analyze the last sentence of your "lead" paragraph for ideas about revision. Ask yourself this:
   - Is the sentence well-crafted?
   - Does it hint at or explicitly state your motive for asking readers to follow along with you in the paragraphs and pages that follow?
4. Finally, scrutinize your last sentence:
   - Is this one of the best-written sentences in the piece?
   - Does it add something?

Revision Strategy 21: Untangling Paragraphs

One of the things I admire most in my friends David and Margaret is that they both have individual integrity—a deep understanding of who they are and who they want to be—and yet they remain just as profoundly connected to the people close to them. They manage to exude both individuality and connection. I hope my friends will forgive the comparison, but good paragraphs have the same qualities: Alone they have their own identities, yet they are also strongly hitched to the paragraphs that precede and that follow them. This connection happens quite naturally when you're telling a story, but in expository writing the relationship between paragraphs is more related to content than time.

The following passage is the first three paragraphs from Paul de Palma's essay on computers, with the clever title "www.when_is_enough_enough?.com." Notice the integrity of each paragraph—each is a kind of mini-essay—as well as the way each one is linked to the paragraph that precedes it.

A paragraph should be unified, focusing on a single topic, idea, or thing. It's like a mini-essay in that sense.

Note how the first sentence in the new paragraph links with the last sentence in the preceding one.

As before, the first sentence links with the last sentence in the previous paragraph.

The final sentence is the most important one in a paragraph. Craft it carefully.

In the misty past, before Bill Gates joined the company of the world's richest men, before the mass-marketed personal computer, before the metaphor of an information superhighway had been worn down to a cliché, I heard Roger Schank interviewed on National Public Radio. Then a computer science professor at Yale, Schank was already well known in artificial intelligence circles. Because those circles did not include me, a new programmer at Sperry Univac, I hadn't heard of him. Though I've forgotten details of the conversation, I have never forgotten Schank's insistence that most people do not need to own computers.

That view, of course, has not prevailed. Either we own a personal computer and fret about upgrades, or we are scheming to own one and fret about the technical marvel yet to come that will render our purchase obsolete. Well, there are worse ways to spend money, I suppose. For all I know, even Schank owns a personal computer. They're fiendishly clever machines, after all, and they've helped keep the wolf from my door for a long time.

It is not the personal computer itself that I object to. What reasonable person would voluntarily go back to a typewriter? The mischief is not in the computer itself, but in the ideology that surrounds it. If we hope to employ computers for tasks more interesting than word processing, we must devote some attention to how they are actually being used, and beyond that, to the remarkable grip that the idol of computing continues to exert.

Well-crafted paragraphs like these create a fluent progression, all linked together like train cars; they make readers feel confident that this train is going somewhere. This might be information that clarifies, extends, proves, explains, or even contradicts. Do the paragraphs in your draft work well on their own and together?

1. Check the length of every paragraph in your draft. Are any too long, going on and on for a full page or more? Can you create smaller paragraphs by breaking out separate ideas, topics, discussions, or claims?

2. Now examine each paragraph in your draft for integrity. Is it relatively focused and unified? Should it be broken down further into two or more paragraphs because it covers too much territory?

3. In Figure 4, note the order of the most important information in a typical paragraph. Is each of your paragraphs arranged with that order in mind? In particular, how strong is the final sentence in each paragraph? Does it prepare readers to move into the next paragraph? In general, each paragraph adds some kind of new information to the old information in the paragraphs preceding it. This new material may clarify, explain, prove, elaborate on,

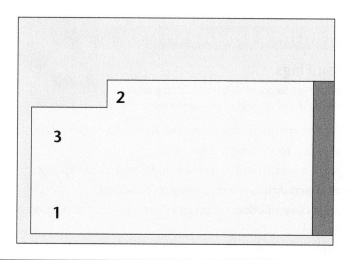

Figure 4 Order of important sentences in a paragraph. Often the first sentence is the second most important sentence in a paragraph. The third most important sentence follows immediately thereafter. The most important sentence usually comes at the end of the paragraph.

contrast, summarize, contradict, or alter time. Sometimes you should signal the nature of this addition using transition words and phrases (see the "Inquiring into the Details: Transition Flags" box). Are there any awkward transitions? Should you smooth them using transition flags?

Revision Strategy 22: Cutting Clutter

Russell Baker's overinflated version of "Little Red Riding Hood" suffered from what writer and professor William Zinsser called "clutter." This disease afflicts much writing, particularly in academic settings. Clutter, simply put, is saying in three or four words what you might say in two, or choosing a longer word when a shorter one will do just as well. It grows from the assumption that simplicity means simplemindedness. This is misguided. Simplicity is a great virtue in writing. It's respectful of the readers, for one thing, who are mostly interested in understanding what you mean without unnecessary detours or obstacles.

In case Russell Baker's tongue-and-cheek example of cluttered writing isn't convincing because it's an invention, here's a brief passage from a memo I received from a fellow faculty member some years ago. I won't make you endure more than a sentence.

> While those of us in the administration are supporting general excellence and consideration of the long-range future of the University, and while the Faculty Senate and Caucus are dealing with more immediate problems, the Executive Committee feels that an ongoing dialogue concerning the particular concerns of faculty is needed to maintain the quality of personal and educational life necessary for continued educational improvement.

INQUIRING INTO THE DETAILS

Transition Flags

One way to connect paragraphs is to signal to a reader with words what the relationship is between them.

- **Clarifying:** *for example, furthermore, specifically, also, to illustrate, similarly*
- **Proving:** *in fact, for example, indeed*
- **Time:** *first…second…finally, subsequently, following, now, recently*
- **Cause or effect:** *therefore, consequently, so, accordingly*
- **Contrast or contradiction:** *on the other hand, in contrast, however, on the contrary, despite, in comparison*
- **Summarizing:** *finally, in the end, in conclusion, summing up, to conclude*

That's a 63-word sentence, and while there is nothing inherently wrong with long sentences, I'm pretty sure that at least half of the words are unnecessary. For the fun of it, see if you can cut at least thirty words from the sentence without compromising the writer's intent. Look for ways to say the same things in fewer words, and look for shorter words that might replace longer ones. What kinds of choices did you make to improve the clarity of the sentence?

Now shift your attention to one of your own drafts and see if you can be as ruthless with your own clutter as you were with the memo writer's.

1. One of the most common kinds of clutter is stock phrases, things we mindlessly say because we've simply gotten in the habit of saying them. *Due to the fact that…* is the one that drives me most crazy. Why not the simpler word *Because*? The following table lists some of the most common stock phrases used in student writing. Read your draft from beginning to end and when you see one of these, cut it down to size.

STOCK PHRASE	SIMPLER VERSION
Due to the fact that…	Because
At the present time…	Now
Until such time as…	Until
I am of the opinion that…	I think
In the event of…	When
This is an appropriate occasion to…	It's time
Proceed with the implementation of…	Begin
Referred to as…	Called
Totally lacked the ability to…	Couldn't
A number of…	Many
In the event of…	If
There is a need for…	Must

2. Another thing to consider is choosing a shorter, simpler word rather than a longer, more complicated word. For example, why not say *many* rather than *numerous*, or *ease* rather than *facilitate*, or *do* rather than *implement*, or *found* rather than *identified*. Go through your draft and look for opportunities such as these to use simpler, more direct words.

3. In his book *Style: Ten Lessons in Clarity and Grace*, Joseph Williams cleverly calls the habit of using meaningless words "verbal tics." These are words, he writes, that "we use unconsciously as we clear our throats." My favorite verbal tic is the phrase *in fact*, which I park at the front of a sentence when I feel like I'm about to clarify something. Mostly I can do without it. In fact, most of us have verbal tics, and we should learn to recognize them. Williams mentions a few common ones, including *kind of, actually, basically, generally, given, various*, and *certain*. For example, *It's generally assumed that certain students have various reasons for being apolitical these days.* A better version would be, *Students have reasons for being apolitical these days.*

Go through your draft and search for words and phrases that you use out of habit, and cut them if they don't add meaning.

Revision Strategy 23: The Actor and the Action Next Door

I live in a relatively urban neighborhood, and so I can hear Kate play her music across the street and Gray powering up his chainsaw to cut wooden pallets next door. I have mixed feelings about this. Kate and I have different taste in music and Gray runs the saw at dusk. But I am never confused about who is doing what. That's less obvious in the following passage:

> A conflict that was greeted at first with much ambivalence by the American public, the war in Iraq, which caused a tentativeness that some experts call the "Vietnam syndrome," sparked protests among Vietnam veterans.

The subject or actor of the sentence (*the war in Iraq*) and the action (*sparked protests*) are separated by a few city blocks. In addition, the subject is buried behind a long introductory clause. As a result, it's a bit hard to remember who is doing what. Putting actor and action next door to each other makes the writing livelier, and bringing the subject up front helps clarify who is doing what.

> The war in Iraq sparked protests among Vietnam veterans even though the conflict was initially greeted with public ambivalence. Some experts call this tentativeness the "Vietnam syndrome."

Review your draft to determine whether the subjects in your sentences are buried or in the same neighborhood as the verbs that modify them. If not, rewrite to bring the actors up front in your sentences and to close the distance between actors and actions.

Improving Style

These revision strategies will improve the style of your writing. In the same way that a John Williams score can make movies such as *Indiana Jones and the Temple of Doom* and *Star Wars* more memorable and moving, style in writing can add to readers' experiences of a text. These are often calculated moves. Writers adopt a style because it serves a purpose, perhaps encouraging a certain feeling that makes a story more powerful, enhancing the writer's ethos to make an essay more convincing, or simply giving certain information particular emphasis. For example, here's the beginning of an article about Douglas Berry, a Marine drill sergeant.

> He is seething, he is rabid, he is wound up tight as a golf ball, with more adrenalin surging through his hypothalamus than a cornered slum rat, he is everything these Marine recruits with their heads shaved to dirty nubs have ever feared or ever hoped a drill sergeant might be.

The style of this opening is calculated to have an obvious effect—the reader is pelted with words, one after another, in a breathless sentence that almost simulates the experience of having Sgt. Douglas Berry in your face. There's no magic to this. It is all about using words that evoke action and feeling, usually verbs or words based on or derived from verbs.

Revision Strategy 24: Actors and Actions

My favorite verb yesterday was *shattered*. I often ask my writing students to come to class and share their favorite verb of the day; last spring, my senior seminar consistently selected *graduate* as their favorite.

As you know, verbs make things happen in writing, and how much energy prose possesses depends on verb power. Academic writing sometimes lacks strong verbs, relying instead on old passive standbys such as *it was concluded by the study* or *it is believed*. Not only are the verbs weak, but the actors, the people or things engaged in the action, are often missing completely from the sentences. *Who* or *what* did the study? *Who* believes?

This is called *passive voice*, and while it's not grammatically incorrect, passive voice can suck the air out of a room. While reasons exist for using passive voice (sometimes, for instance, the writer wants the reader to focus on the action, not the actor), you should avoid it in your own writing. One of the easiest ways to locate passive voice in your drafts is to conduct a *to be* search. Most forms of the verb *to be* (see the Forms of *To Be* box on the next page) usually signal passive voice. For example,

> It is well known that medieval eating habits were unsavory by contemporary health standards. Cups were shared, forks were never used, and the same knives used to clean under fingernails or to gut a chicken were used to cut and eat meat.

What is missing, of course, are the actors. To revise into active voice you simply need to add the actors, whenever possible:

> Medieval diners had unsavory eating habits by contemporary health standards. They shared cups with friends, they never used forks, and they used their knives, the same ones they used to clean under their fingernails or gut a chicken, to cut and eat their meat.

1. Conduct a *to be* search of your own draft. Whenever you find passive construction, try to put the actor into the sentence.

2. Eliminating passive voice is only one strategy for giving your writing more energy. Try to use lively verbs as well. Can you replace weak verbs with stronger ones? How about *discovered* instead of *found*, or *seized* instead of *took, shattered* instead of *broke*. Review every sentence in the draft and, when appropriate, revise with a stronger verb.

FORMS OF *TO BE*

- Is
- Are
- Was
- Were
- Has been
- Have been
- Will be

Revision Strategy 25: Smoothing the Choppiness

Good writing reads like a Mercedes drives—smoothly, suspended by the rhythms of language. One of the most important factors influencing this rhythm is sentence length, or, more precisely, pauses in the prose that vary as the reader travels from sentence to sentence and paragraph to paragraph. We rarely notice either the cause or the effect, but we certainly notice the bumps and lurches. Consider the following sentences, each labeled with the number of syllables:

> When the sun finally rose the next day I felt young again.(15) It was a strange feeling because I wasn't young anymore.(15) I was fifty years old and felt like it.(10) It was the smell of the lake at dawn that thrust me back into adolescence.(19) I remembered the hiss of the waves.(9) They erased my footprints in the sand.(9)

This really isn't awful; it could pass as a bad Hemingway imitation. But do you notice the monotony of the writing, the steady, almost unvarying beat that threatens to dull your mind if it goes on much longer? The cause of the plodding rhythm is the unvarying length of the pauses. The last two sentences in the passage each have 9 syllables, and the first two sentences are nearly identical in length as well (15 and 15 syllables, respectively).

Now notice how this choppiness disappears by varying the lengths of the pauses through combining sentences, inserting other punctuation, and dropping a few unnecessary words.

When the sun finally rose the next day I felt young again,(15) and it was a strange feeling because I wasn't young.(13) I was fifty years old.(6) It was the smell of the lake at dawn that thrust me back into adolescence and remembering the hiss of the waves as they erased my footprints in the sand.(39)

The revision is much more fluent and the reason is simple: The writer varies the pauses and the number of syllables within each of them—15, 13, 6, 39.

1. Choose a draft of your own that doesn't seem to flow or seems choppy in places.

2. Mark the pauses in the problem areas. Put slash marks next to periods, commas, semicolons, dashes, and so on—any punctuation that prompts a reader to pause briefly.

3. If the pauses seem similar in length, revise to vary them, combining sentences, adding punctuation, dropping unnecessary words, or varying long and short words.

Revision Strategy 26: Fresh Ways to Say Things

It goes without saying that a tried-and-true method of getting to the heart of revision problems is to just do or die. Do you know what I mean? Of course you don't, because the opening sentence is laden with clichés and figures of speech that manage to obscure meaning. One of the great challenges of writing well is to find fresh ways to say things rather than relying on hand-me-down phrases that worm their way into our speech and writing. Clichés are familiar examples: *home is where the heart is, hit the nail on the head, the grass is greener,* and all that. But even more common are less figurative expressions: *more than meets the eye, rude awakenings, you only go around once, sigh of relief,* and so on.

Removing clichés and shopworn expressions from your writing will make it sound more as if you are writing from your own voice rather than someone else's. It gives the work a freshness that helps readers believe that you have something interesting to say. In addition, clichés especially tend to close off a writer's thoughts rather than open them to new ideas and different ways of seeing. A cliché often leaves the writer with nothing more to say because someone else has already said it.

1. Reread your draft and circle clichés and hand-me-down expressions. If you're not sure whether a phrase qualifies for either category, share your circled items with a partner and discuss them. Have you heard these things before?

2. Cut clichés and overused expressions and rewrite your sentences, finding your own way to say things. In your own words, what do you really mean by "do or die" or "striking while the iron is hot" or becoming a "true believer"?

USING WHAT YOU HAVE LEARNED

Take a few moments to reflect on what you learned in this chapter and how you can apply it.

1. Which revision strategy has proved most helpful to you so far? Does it address one of your most common problems in your drafts?

2. Here's a common situation: You're assigned a paper for another class and the professor doesn't require you to hand in a draft. She's just interested in your final version. What incentive do you have to work through a draft or two?

3. If revision is rhetorical, then the kinds of revision strategies you need to use depend on the particular situation: to whom you're writing and why, and in what form. The kind of writer you are—and the kinds of problems you have in your drafts—also matters. Consider the following forms: the essay exam, the review, the annotated bibliography, the letter, the formal research paper, and the reading response. Which of the five revision strategies would probably be most important for each form?

THE WRITER'S WORKSHOP

Writers rarely experience the impact their writing has on readers. When they do experience this in a writing workshop, the idea of writing for an audience ceases to be an abstraction.

Dennis MacDonald/PhotoEdit Inc.

THE WRITER'S WORKSHOP

MAKING THE MOST OF PEER REVIEW

Sharing your writing with strangers can be among the most frightening and gratifying social experiences. It can be a key to the success of the next draft or a complete waste of time. One thing sharing your writing can't be, however, is avoided, at least in most composition courses, which these days frequently rely on small and large group workshops to help students revise. This is a good thing, I think, for three reasons:

1. It's useful to experience *being read* by others.
2. Workshops can be among the most effective ways for writers to divorce the draft.
3. The talk about writing in workshops can be enormously instructive.

Being Read

Being read is not the same thing as being read to. As we share our writing, sometimes reading our own work aloud to a group, we are sharing ourselves in a very real way. This is most evident with a personal essay, but virtually any piece of writing bears our authorship—our particular ways of seeing and saying things—and included in this are our feelings about ourselves as writers.

Last semester, Matthew told me that he felt he was the worst writer in the class, and that seemed obvious when I watched him share his writing in his workshop group. Matthew was quiet and compliant, readily accepting suggestions with little comment, and he seemed to rush

> ### What You'll Learn in This Chapter
> - The purpose of peer review.
> - The most common approaches for organizing writing workshops.
> - How to plan to make the most of the chance to share your draft.
> - What can go wrong and how to deal with it.
> - Response formats for guiding how readers evaluate your drafts.

the conversation about his draft as if to make the ordeal end sooner. When Matthew's drafts were discussed, his group always ended in record time, and yet he always claimed that they were "helpful."

Tracy always began presenting her drafts by announcing, "This really sucks. It's the worst thing I've ever written." Of course it wasn't. But this announcement seemed intended to lower the stakes for her, to take some of the pressure off of her performance in front of others, or, quite possibly, it was a hopeful invitation for Tracy's group members to say, "You're too hard on yourself. This is really good."

To *be read* in a workshop group can mean more than a critique of your ideas or sentences; for students like Matthew and Tracy it is an evaluation of *themselves*, particularly their self-worth as writers. Of course, this isn't the purpose of peer review at all, but for those of us with sometimes nagging internal critics, it's pretty hard to avoid feeling that both your writing and your writing self are on trial. This is why it's so helpful to articulate these fears before being read. It's also helpful to imagine the many positive outcomes that might come from the experience of sharing your writing.

While taking workshop comments about your writing personally is always a risk, consider the really rare and unusual opportunity to *see* readers respond to your work. I often compare my published writing to dropping a very heavy stone down a deep well and waiting to hear the splash. And waiting. And waiting. But in a workshop, you can actually hear the murmurs, the sighs, and the laughter of your readers as you read to them; you can also see the smiles, puzzled expressions, nodding heads, and even tears. You can experience your readers' experiences of your writing in ways that most published authors never can.

> In a workshop, you can actually hear the murmurs, the sighs, and the laughter of your readers as you read to them.

What is so valuable about this, I think, is that audience is no longer an abstraction. After your first workshop, it's no stretch to imagine the transaction that most writing involves—a writer's words being received by a reader who thinks and feels something in response. And when you take this back to the many solitary hours of writing, you may feel you have company; that members of your workshop group are interested in what you have to say.

This is a powerful thing. In some ways, it's the most important thing about the workshop experience.

Divorcing the Draft

Our writing relationships include our emotional connection to drafts, and this often has to do with the time we spent writing them. We can get entangled in first drafts that blind us to other ways of seeing a topic. Sometimes we need to divorce a draft, and the best remedy for this is time away from it. But students rarely have that luxury.

Workshops provide an alternative to time away from a draft and are effective for the same reason some people see therapists—group members offer an "outsider's" perspective on your work that may give it new meanings and raise new possibilities. If nothing else, readers offer a preview of whether your current meanings are clear and whether what you assume is apparent *is* apparent to someone other than yourself. It's rare when a workshop doesn't jerk writers away from at least a few of their assumptions about a draft, and the best of these experiences inspire writers to want to write again. This is the outcome we should always hope to attain.

Instructive Talk

Consider a few comments I overheard during workshops recently:

- "I don't think the focus is clear in this essay. In fact, I think there are at least two separate essays here, and it's the one on the futility of antiwar protests I'm most interested in."
- "Do you think that there's a better lead buried on the third page, in the paragraph about your sister's decision to go to the hospital? That was a powerful scene, and it seemed to be important to the overall theme."
- "I was wondering about something. What is it about the idea that we sometimes keep silent not only to protect other people but to protect ourselves that surprised you? I mean, does knowing that change anything about how you feel about yourself as a parent?"
- "I loved this line. Simply loved it."

The talk in workshops is not always about writing. The "underlife" of the classroom often surfaces in workshops, a term one educator uses to describe the idle talk about the class itself. Most writing classes ask students to step out of their usual student roles. Rather than quietly listen to lectures or study a textbook, in a writing course you are asked to make your own meanings and find your own ways of making meaning. Whenever we are asked to assume new roles, some resistance can set in, and workshops can become an occasion for talk about the class, often out of earshot of the instructor. This talk isn't always complaining. Often workshops are opportunities to share understandings or approaches to assignments and especially experiences with them. They can also be a chance for students to try out new identities—"I really liked writing this. Maybe I'm an okay writer after all."

While this kind of talk may not be directly about a draft, it can help you negotiate the new roles you're being asked to assume in your writing class. This is part of becoming better writers who are confident that they can manage the writing process in all kinds of situations. However, the main purpose of workshop groups is to help students revise their drafts. But why seek advice from writers who are clearly less experienced than the instructor?

1. By talking with other students about writing, you get practice using the language you're learning in the writing classroom, language that helps you describe important features of your own work.

2. Because writing is about making choices among a range of solutions to problems in a draft, workshop groups are likely to surface possibilities that never occurred to you (and perhaps wouldn't occur to the instructor, either).

3. Your peers are also student writers and because they come from similar circumstances—demands of other classes, part-time jobs, and perhaps minimal experience with college writing—they are in a position to offer practical and realistic revision suggestions.

4. Finally, in most writing courses, the students in the class are an important audience for your work. Getting firsthand responses makes the rhetorical situation real rather than imagined.

Will you get bad advice in a peer workshop? Of course. Your group members will vary in their experience and ability to read the problems and possibilities in a draft. But in the best writing workshops, you learn together, and as time goes by the feedback gets better and better. Paradoxically, it pays off in your own writing to be generous in your responses to the work of others.

MODELS FOR WRITING WORKSHOPS

The whole idea of peer review workshops in writing classes has been around for years. Collaboration is hardly a novelty in the professional world, but small-group work in academia is a relatively recent alternative to lecture and other teaching methods in which the student listens to a professor, takes notes on what is said, and later takes a test of some kind. You won't learn to write well through lecture, although it may be a perfectly appropriate approach for some subjects. Because collaboration in the writing classroom fits in perfectly with the class's aim of generating knowledge about the many ways to solve writing problems, peer review of drafts in small groups is now fairly common. You'll find workshops in writing classes ranging from first-year composition to advanced nonfiction writing.

What will workshops be like in your course? Your instructor will answer that question, but the workshop groups will likely reflect one or more of the following models.

Full-Class Workshops

Sometimes you may not work in small groups at all. Depending on the size of your class and your instructor's particular purposes for using peer review, you may share your work with everyone in a full-class session. This approach is popular in creative writing classes, and it's typically used in composition classes to introduce students to the process of providing responses to other students' work. It also can work nicely in small classes with ten students or fewer.

In a full-class workshop, you'll choose a draft to share, and you (or your instructor) will provide copies for everyone either a few days before the workshop or at the beginning of the workshop session. On drafts you receive days ahead of the session, you're often expected to read and bring written comments to class with you. If you receive the draft at the beginning of the workshop session, you might make notes while the draft's author reads the piece aloud, or take some time to write some comments either immediately after the draft is read or following the group discussion.

Reading your draft aloud to your workshop group is a common convention in all kinds of workshop groups, large or small. This might be something you resist at first. It will quickly become apparent, however, how useful it is to read your own work aloud. It's an entirely different reading to literally give voice to your words. You'll stumble over passages in your draft that seemed fine when you read them silently, and you may notice gaps you glossed over. You'll hear what your writing voice sounds like in this particular essay, and whether it works for you and your readers.

Your instructor may lead the discussion in a full-class workshop, or she may sit back and wait while students share their responses. There may be guidelines and ground rules for responses as well (for some examples of these, see "The Reader's Responsibilities" section later in the chapter). If your draft is being discussed, your instructor may ask you to simply listen. Sometimes it's best to avoid defending certain choices you made in a draft and simply take in the range of responses you receive to what you have done. In other cases, you may be asked to present the large group with questions to consider. It certainly can be scary sharing your work with twenty or twenty-five people, but imagine the range of perspectives you'll get!

Small-Group Workshops

Far more typical is the workshop group of between three and seven members, either chosen randomly by your instructor or self-selected. These groups may stay together all semester or part of the semester, or you may find yourself working with fresh faces every workshop session. Each of these alternatives has advantages and disadvantages, all of which your instructor has considered in making a choice.

Ideally, your workshop group will meet in a circle, because when everyone, including the writer presenting a draft, is facing each other you'll have more of a conversation and be able to engage each other directly (see Figure 1). Like so many writing group methods, this is a basic principle of teamwork borrowed from the business world.

Some of the methods of distributing drafts apply to the small group as well as to the full-class workshop discussed earlier: Writers will distribute copies of their drafts either a few days before their workshops or at the beginning of the sessions. You will provide written comments to each writer either before or after the workshop.

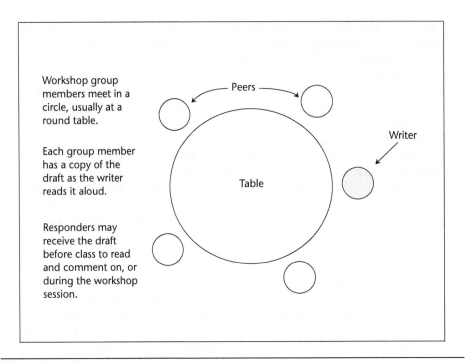

Workshop group members meet in a circle, usually at a round table.

Each group member has a copy of the draft as the writer reads it aloud.

Responders may receive the draft before class to read and comment on, or during the workshop session.

Peers

Writer

Table

Figure 1   The small-group workshop

One-on-One Peer Review

Your instructor also may ask you to work with a partner, exchanging drafts and discussing them with each other. While you lose some of the range and quantity of feedback by working with a single reader, this conversation is often richer because each of you is reading the other's work with particular care and attention. You'll probably also have more time to talk because you'll be discussing only two rather than four or five drafts.

One variation of this kind of one-on-one peer review is the draft exchange. Your instructor will ask you to make a pile of drafts at the front of the room and ask you to take a draft from the pile, comment on it, return it, and then take another. You may return multiple times to collect, comment on, and return a draft, and the result is that each draft may have three or four readers during the class session.

THE WRITER'S RESPONSIBILITIES

No matter what model your instructor chooses, the success of the workshop depends largely on the writers themselves. Sure, it can be harder to get what you need from some groups, but in the end, you can always get *some* help with a draft if you ask the right questions and seek certain kinds of responses.

How should you prepare for a workshop to make the most of it, and what are your responsibilities during the workshop? Here's a list you might find helpful:

- Make sure everyone in the group gets a copy of the draft in a timely way.

- Reread and reflect on the draft before the workshop session. What kinds of responses would be most helpful from your group? What questions do you have about the draft's possible problems?

- Time the discussion so that your draft gets the allotted time and no more, particularly if there are other drafts to discuss.

- Avoid getting defensive. Listen to comments on your work in an open-minded way. Your obligation is simply to listen, not to take all the advice you're offered.

- Take notes. There are two reasons for this. First, it will help you remember other students' comments and, second, it will signal that you take those comments seriously. This increases everyone's engagement with your work.

THE READER'S RESPONSIBILITIES

Tina poured her heart and soul into her personal essay draft, and she was eager to get some response to it. When it was her turn to workshop the piece, however, one of the group's members was absent, and two others failed to write her the required response. "It was so lame," she told me. "It was as if no one cared about my essay. It sure makes me feel less inclined to read their stuff carefully." If this workshop group were at Hewlett-Packard or any of the thousands of businesses that encourage teamwork, the slackers would be in trouble. But teamwork in the writing class depends more on internal motivation—a sense of responsibility to others—than any external reward or punishment. There is some external motivation: It pays to be generous with your responses to others' work because you'll learn more about your own.

You can increase your own learning in a workshop and contribute to a writer's positive experience by taking the following responsibilities seriously:

- Always read and respond to a writer's draft in a timely way. The writer may suggest the type of response that would be most helpful; if so, always keep that in mind.

- Whenever possible, focus your responses on particular parts or passages of the draft but, except in an editorial workshop, avoid a focus on grammar or mechanics.

- Offer suggestions, not directives. The word *could* is usually better than *should*. Remember that the purpose of the workshop is to help identify the range of choices a writer might make to improve a draft. There is almost always more than one.

- Identify strengths in the draft. This is often a good place to begin because it sets writers at ease, but, more important, writers often build on strengths in revision.

■ Consider varying the roles you play in conversation with your group (see the "Inquiring into the Details: Finding a Role" box). It's easy to fall into a rut in group work, pretty much sticking to saying the same kinds of things or developing certain patterns of response. Stay vigilant about this and try deliberately shifting the role you play in the workshop group.

WHAT CAN GO WRONG AND WHAT TO DO ABOUT IT

Lana is not a fan of workshops. In an argument essay, she complained that they "lack quality feedback," and sometimes workshop groups encourage "fault finding" that can hurt the writer and the writing. Things can go wrong in workshops, of course, and when they do students like Lana feel burned. Typically, unsuccessful

---

INQUIRING INTO THE DETAILS

Finding a Role

"Slacker" is a role that's easy to slide into in small-group work. It's completely passive, and it's really pretty self-ish. Active roles ask more of you, but they pay off big because you learn more about your own writing. You might assume any of several active roles in a workshop group. Try them out.

ROLES THAT HELP GROUPS GET THINGS DONE

Initiators: "Here's how we might proceed with this."
Information seekers: "What do we need to know to help the writer?"
Information givers: "This seems to be an important example."
Opinion seekers: "What do you think, Al?"
Opinion givers: "I think this works."
Clarifiers: "We all seem to be saying that the lead doesn't deliver, right?"
Elaborators: "I agree with Tom, and would add…"
Summarizers: "I think we've discussed the thesis problem enough. Should we move on to the evidence?"

ROLES THAT HELP MAINTAIN GROUP HARMONY

Encouragers: "I love that idea, Jen."
Expressivists: "My silence isn't because I'm not moved by the essay, but I'm still trying to figure out why. Is that why you're quiet, Leah?"
Harmonizers: "I think we disagree about this, but that's okay. Let's move on to discussing this next page."
Compromisers: "Maybe both Richard and Joseph are right, particularly if we look at it this way…"
Gatekeepers: "Jon, we haven't heard anything from you yet."

---

workshop groups suffer from two major problems: lack of commitment by group members and lack of clarity about the process of giving feedback. It's like a cold and a runny nose—when a group is afflicted with one problem it usually suffers from the other.

Lack of commitment is easy to see. The writer whose draft is to be discussed forgets to make copies for the rest of her group. Members who were supposed to provide written responses to a writer's draft before class hastily make notes on his manuscript as it's being discussed. The group is supposed to allot fifteen minutes to discuss each draft but finishes in five. Members are frequently absent and make no effort to provide responses to drafts they missed. Discussion is limited to general, not particularly thoughtful, compliments: "This is really good. I wouldn't change a thing," or "Just add a few details."

This lack of commitment is contagious and soon infects nearly every group meeting. Things rarely improve; they frequently get worse. Part of the problem may be that workshop participants are not clear on what is expected of them, a problem that should be minimized if you reviewed the checklists about the writer's and reader's responsibilities in workshop, discussed in the preceding sections. A solution that is beyond your control is that the instructor evaluates or even grades workshop participation, but a group can evaluate itself, too. Questions members should ask when evaluating their group can include: How effectively does your group work together? How would you evaluate the participation of group members? How do you feel about your own performance? How satisfied were you with the responses to your draft?

Groups that work together over a period of time should always monitor how things are going, and the group evaluations can be particularly helpful for this. If problems persist, the instructor may intervene or the group might consider intervention of its own (consider Exercise 1 as one option). Remember, the best workshops have a simple but powerful effect on writers who share their work: *It makes them want to write again.*

EXERCISE 1

Group Problem Solving

If group evaluations reveal persistent problems, devote ten minutes to exploring possible solutions.

STEP ONE: Choose a facilitator and a recorder. The facilitator times each step, directs questions to each participant, and makes sure everyone participates. The recorder takes notes on newsprint.

1. Discuss the patterns of problems identified by group members. Do writers seem dissatisfied? Do readers feel like they're performing poorly?
2. What is behind these problems? Brainstorm a list.

3. What might be done to change the way the group operates? You must come up with *at least* one concrete idea that you agree to try.

STEP TWO: After the next workshop session, set aside five minutes at the end to discuss whether the change improved the group's performance. Is there something else you should try?

ONE STUDENT'S RESPONSE

Amy's Perspective On Workshops

WHEN THINGS GO RIGHT

In both small and large workshops things are most productive when the conversation delves deep into a couple of issues instead of skimming the surface on a broad range of topics. My best experiences have been in small workshops because the groups were willing to get more deeply involved in a piece. It probably helps that there aren't too many ideas in a small group and the ones that get thrown out for debate are well considered. I always appreciate it when the group writes notes on my paper for future reference and my absolute best workshops have been multiple sessions with the same small group. Assessing each other's progress really helps in the revision stages.

WHEN THINGS GO WRONG

Especially in a small workshop people can take things too personally and ruin the objective atmosphere, letting their own agenda take precedence over progression. In one of the worst workshops I've been a part of, we were assessing an essay by a writer who chose to write about her relationship with God. The essay had many problems, she used very vague metaphorical language, and the attempted symbolism didn't really work. It was a bit hard to read because of the overly sentimental tone of the piece. Instead of discussing these points, though, the workshop turned into an argument about outside topics and became pretty vicious. The writer was very open to most of the comments I made about some major changes that needed to happen in the piece, but very defensive (understandably) to the personal attacks. The communication simply broke down due to varying personal beliefs when they could have been a strength of the group.

In a large group a fine balance must be achieved. It is important that the conversation runs deep, but also that it covers more than one topic. Because of the multitude of opinions in a large group, the entire workshop can get stuck on one topic or section of the piece. Not only is it unproductive when the debate gets stuck, but it's also really hard to sit through.

METHODS OF RESPONDING

One thing I don't need with an early draft is someone telling me that I misspelled the word *rhythm*. It is a word I'll never be able to spell, and that fact makes me eternally grateful for spellcheckers. I do like to know whether an early draft delivers on its implied promises to the reader, and especially whether there is another angle or another topic lurking there that I might not have noticed. But I don't want my wife, Karen, to read my stuff until I have a late draft to show her because I sometimes find her comments on early drafts discouraging.

> The kinds of responses we seek to our writing in workshops depend on at least two things: where we are in the writing process and how we feel about the work in progress.

The *kinds* of responses we seek to our writing in workshops depend on at least two things: where we are in the writing process and how we feel about the work in progress. This is not particularly surprising. After all, certain kinds of problems arise during different stages of the writing process, and sometimes what we really need from readers of our work is more emotional than practical. We want to be motivated, encouraged, or validated, or feel any number of things that will help us work well.

Experiential and Directive Responses

It makes sense, then, to invite certain kinds of readings of your work that you'll find timely. In general, these responses range from experiential ("this is how I experienced your draft") to more directive ("this is what you could do to make it better"). Which of these two forms would make reader comments on your work most helpful? For example, depending on who you are and how you work, it may be most helpful to get less directive responses to your work early on. Some people feel that very specific suggestions undermine their sense of ownership of rough drafts. They don't want to know what readers think they should do in the revision but how readers experienced their draft. What parts were interesting? What parts were confusing? On the other hand, other writers feel particularly lost in the early stages of the writing process; they could use all the direction they can get. You decide (or your instructor will make suggestions), choosing from the following menu of workshop response methods. These begin with the most experiential methods of response to those that invite your readers to offer quite specific suggestions about the revision.

Response Formats

The following formats for responding to workshop drafts begin with the least directive, most experiential methods and move to the more directive approaches.

THE ETHICS OF RESPONDING

- Respect the writer.
- Everyone contributes.
- Say "could" rather than "should."
- Say "I" rather than "you," as in "I couldn't follow this" rather than "You weren't very clear."

While many of these formats feature some particular ways of responding to drafts, remember that the writer's and reader's responsibilities described earlier apply to all of them. Participate thoughtfully and ethically (see the box "The Ethics of Responding") and you'll be amazed at what you learn about your own writing from talking with other writers about theirs.

The No-Response Workshop. Sometimes the most useful response to your work comes from simply reading it aloud to your group and asking them to just listen—nothing more. Why? You may not be ready for comments because the work is unformed and you're confident that'll you discover the direction you want to go in the next draft. Comments may confuse or distract you. It's always helpful to read your work aloud to yourself, but it's also valuable to read to an audience even if you don't invite a response. You will read with more attention and awareness. Finally, you may simply feel unprepared for a response because your confidence is low.

The method couldn't be simpler. You read your draft with little or no introduction while your group quietly listens. They will not comment unless they want you to repeat something because it was inaudible. Remember to read slowly and clearly.

The Initial-Response Workshop. Robert Brooke, Ruth Mirtz, and Rick Evans[1] suggest a method that is useful for "maintaining your motivation to write while indirectly learning what to improve in your text." It might also be appropriate for an early draft.

They suggest that you invite three kinds of responses to your work: a "relating" response, a "listening" response, and a "positive" response. These three types of response to a draft could be made in writing, in workshop discussion, or both.

- **Relating response.** As the name implies, group members share what personal associations the writer's topic inspires. Perhaps they've had a similar or a contradictory experience. Maybe they've read something or seen something that is relevant to what the writer is trying to do in the draft.

---

[1]Robert Brooke, Ruth Mirtz, and Rick Evans, *Small Groups in Writing Workshops* (Urbana, IL: NCTE, 1994).

- **Listening response.** This is much like the "say back" method some therapists use with patients. Can you summarize what it is that you hear the writing saying in the draft? Is this something that is helpful to know?

- **Positive response.** What parts of the draft really work well and why? Might these be things the writer could build on in the next draft?

The Narrative-of-Thought Workshop. A writer who hears the story of readers' thinking *as they experienced the draft* can get great insight about how the piece shapes readers' expectations and how well it delivers on its promises. This method borrows a term from Peter Elbow— "movie of the mind"—to describe the creation of such a narrative response to a piece of writing.

The easiest way to create stories of your readers' experiences is to prepare your draft ahead of time to accommodate them. Before you make copies for your workshop group, create 2- to 3-inch white spaces in the manuscript immediately after the lead or beginning paragraph, and then again in the middle of the essay. Also leave at least that much white space after the end of the piece.

You will read your draft episodically, beginning by just reading the lead or introductory paragraph, then allowing three or four minutes for your group's members to respond in writing in the space you provided for some of the following questions. The writer should time this and ask everyone to stop writing when it's time to read the next section of the draft. Repeat the process, stopping at the second patch of white space after you've read roughly half of the essay. Give your group the same amount of time to respond in writing and then finish the essay to prompt the final episode of writing.

- **After hearing the lead:** What are your feelings about the topic or the writer so far? Can you predict what the essay might be about? What questions does the lead raise for you that you expect might be answered later? What has struck you?

- **After hearing half:** Tell the story of what you've been thinking or feeling about what you've heard so far. Has the draft fulfilled your expectations from the lead? What do you expect will happen next?

- **After hearing it all:** Summarize your understanding of what the draft is about, including what it *seems* to be saying (or not quite saying). How well did it deliver on its promises in the beginning? What part of your experience of the draft was most memorable? What part seemed least clear?

Discuss with your group each of the responses—after the lead, after the middle, and at the end of the draft. This conversation, and the written comments you receive when you collect their copies of your draft, should give you strong clues about how well you've established a clear purpose in your essay and sustained it from beginning to end. The responses also might give you ideas about directions to take the next draft that you hadn't considered.

The Instructive-Lines Workshop. Most essays balance on a thesis, theme, question, or idea. Like the point of a spinning top, these claims, ideas, or questions are the things around which everything else revolves. Essay drafts, however, may easily topple over because they lack such balance—there is no clear point, or there are too many, or some of the information is irrelevant. In discovery drafts especially, a writer may be seeking the piece's center of gravity—or *centers* of gravity—and a useful response from a workshop group is to help the writer look for the clues about where that center might be.

This format for a workshop invites the members to try to identify the draft's *most important lines and passages,* by clearly marking them with underlining or highlighting. What makes a line or passage important? *These are places where writers explicitly or implicitly seem to suggest what they're trying to say in a draft,* and they may include the following:

- A line or passage where the writer seems to state his or her thesis.
- A part of a narrative essay when the writer adopts a critical stance and seems to be trying to pose a question or speculate about the meaning of an experience or some information.
- A part of the draft in which the writer seems to make an important claim.
- A scene or comparison or observation that hints at the question the writer is exploring (or could explore).
- A comment in a digression that the writer didn't seem to think was important, but you think might be.

These portions of the text become the subject of discussion in the workshop session. Questions to consider include the following: Why did this particular line seem important? What does it imply about what you think is the meaning of the essay? Do the different underlined passages speak to each other—can they be combined or revised into a controlling idea or question for the next draft—or do they imply separate essays or treatments? Would the writer underline something else? How might the different interpretations of the draft be reconciled?

The Purpose Workshop. Sometimes writers know their purpose in a draft: "I'm trying to argue that the Enron collapse represented the failure of current methods of compensating CEOs," or "I'm proposing that having vegetarian fast-food restaurants would reduce American obesity," or "This essay explores the question of why I was so relieved when my father died." What these writers may need most from their workshop groups is feedback on how well the draft accomplishes particular purposes.

Before the workshop session, the writer crafts a statement of purpose similar to those in the preceding paragraph—a sentence that clearly states what the writer is trying to do in the draft. This statement of purpose should include a verb that implies what action the writer is trying to take—for example, *explore, argue, persuade, propose, review, explain,* or *analyze.* As you probably guessed, these verbs are usually associated with a particular form of inquiry or genre.

The writer should include this sentence *at the end* of the draft. It's important that you make group members aware of your purpose only after they've read the entire piece and not before. Discussion and written responses should then focus on some of the following questions:

- Were you surprised by the stated purpose, or did the essay prepare you for it?
- If the stated purpose did surprise you, what did you think the writer was trying to do in the draft instead?
- Does the lead explicitly state or hint at the stated purpose?
- What parts or paragraphs of the draft seemed clearly relevant to the stated purpose, and which seemed to point in another direction?
- Did the draft seem to succeed in accomplishing the writer's purpose?

If more directive responses would be helpful to you, consider also asking some questions such as whether there might not be a stronger beginning or lead buried elsewhere in the draft, or soliciting suggestions about which parts or paragraphs should be cut or what additional information might be needed. Which parts of the draft seemed to work best in the context of the writer's stated purpose, and which didn't work so well?

The Graphing-Reader-Interest Workshop. What commands readers' attention in a draft and what doesn't? This is useful to know, obviously, because our overall aim is to engage readers from beginning to end—which is difficult to do, particularly in longer drafts, and reader attention often varies from paragraph to paragraph in shorter drafts. But if three or four paragraphs or a couple of pages of your draft drone on, then the piece isn't working well and you need to do something about it in revision.

One way to know this is to ask your workshop group members to graph their response to your essay, paragraph by paragraph, and then discuss what is going on in those sections that drag.

For this workshop, consecutively number all the paragraphs in your draft. You or your instructor will provide each member of your group with a "reader interest chart" (see Figure 2), on which the corresponding paragraph numbers are listed. On the vertical axis is a scale that represents reader interest, with 5 being high interest and 1 being low interest in that particular paragraph. As you slowly read your draft aloud to your group's members, they mark the graph after each paragraph to roughly indicate their interest in what the paragraph says and how it says it.

When you're finished, you'll have a visual representation of how the essay worked, paragraph by paragraph, but the important work is ahead. Next, you need to discuss with your group *why* a paragraph or section of the draft failed to hold some readers' attention. What is going on in those parts of the draft?

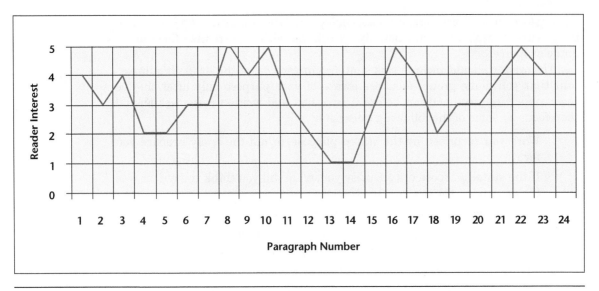

Figure 2   Reader interest chart

- Are they confusing?
- Do they needlessly digress?
- Is the prose awkward?
- Is there too much or too little explanation?
- Are they too loaded with facts and not enough analysis?
- Does the writer seem to lose his voice?

One way to find out what's going on with the weaker parts of your essay is to look at the stronger ones. What do you notice about those paragraphs that were rated 4 or 5 by your group members? What are the particular strengths of these sections? Can you do more of that in other, less lively sections of the draft?

The Sum-of-the-Parts Workshop. Like a watch, a well-written essay moves fluently forward because all of its parts work together. In workshops you can never talk about all those parts; there is too little time, and often it's hard to tease apart all the gears and the springs that make an essay go. But you can try to be as thorough as you can during a workshop, essentially running through a checklist of some of the most important elements, including purpose, theme, structure, information, and style. In this workshop, you attempt to cover as much territory as possible, so the responses you get will have breadth but not depth. You also invite some directive responses from your readers—suggestions for the revision and specific areas of confusion—as well as their interpretation of your purpose and theme.

One of the best ways to solicit this information is to use a worksheet like the one that follows. Typically, this worksheet would be filled out by your group's members outside class and before you workshop the draft. It would then be attached to the copies of your draft and returned to you after the group discusses the work. If your peers respond thoughtfully to the worksheet, it can generate a wealth of information for you about your draft.

The Thesis Workshop. An alternative to the sum-of-all-parts format is to focus on a single element of the draft that you are particularly concerned about, and no part is more important than the thesis. An essay without an implicit theme or an explicit thesis is an essay without meaning. No one is particularly interested in reading a pointless story or research essay, nor are most readers interested in points that seem unrelated to the information in the draft or that are painfully obvious. For example, the idea that the death of your Aunt Trudy was sad for you is a much less compelling theme to build an essay around than the idea that her death—and the deaths of family members generally—upset the family system in ways that helped you to take on new roles, new identities.

A thesis workshop will help you make sure there is a controlling idea or question behind the draft, and help you think more deeply about what you're trying to say. Your workshop members can help with this because they bring a range of perspectives and experiences to a conversation about your theme that might make it richer and more informative for you.

In this workshop, group members receive the drafts ahead of time. Before the workshop session they should underline the thesis, main idea, theme, or question

---

WORKSHOP WORKSHEET

Purpose: In your own words, what is the writer's motive in the draft? Use one of the following verbs to describe this in a sentence: *explore, explain, argue, analyze, review, report, propose, persuade, reflect.*

Theme: State in your own words what you think the thesis, main point, or central question is in this draft. What question does this idea or question raise for you?

Information: Name at least two specific places in the draft where you wanted more information to fully appreciate what the writer was trying to say. What kind of information do you suggest (anecdote, story, fact, detail, background, example, interview, dialogue, opposing perspective, description, case study, etc.)?

Design: Identify *at least* one paragraph or passage that seemed out of place. Any suggestions about where it belongs?

Style: Place brackets [ ] around several sentences or passages in the draft that seemed awkward or confusing to read.

that seems to be behind the draft. This will be the *main thing* the writer seems to be saying or exploring. This isn't particularly difficult in essays with explicit thesis statements, such as arguments or proposals, but in personal essays and other more literary pieces, the theme may not be so explicit. In that type of essay, they should underline the passage that seems central to the meaning of the essay. This may be a reflective passage or it might be a scene or moment.

Second, at the top of a piece of paper, they should write down in a sentence or two—at most—the thesis or theme as they understand it. This may involve simply copying it down from the draft. However, if the thesis or theme is not that clear or explicit, each reader should write it down in his or her own words, trying to capture the main point of the draft.

Then members should fastwrite for five minutes about their own thoughts and experiences about the writer's thesis or theme, constantly hunting for questions it raises for them. Say the draft's thesis is that the university athletic programs have become too powerful and have undermined the university's more important academic mission. In the fastwrite, explore what you've noticed about the football team's impact on the school. Where does the football program get funds? Does it compete with academic programs? Then fastwrite about what you've heard—for instance, that athletics have strong alumni support. Keep the fastwrite focused on the thesis; if it helps, stop and reread it for another prompt.

The workshop session that follows will be a conversation largely focused on what people thought was the point of the draft, and their own thoughts and feelings about it. The writer should facilitate the conversation without comment and make sure the following two things are discussed in this order:

1. What seems to be the thesis, theme, or question behind the essay? Is it clear? Are there alternative ideas about what it might be?

2. What does each group member think or feel about what the writer seems to be saying? How do the reader's experiences and observations relate to the writer's main point or question? And especially, what questions should the writer consider in the next draft?

Although it may be hard to keep quiet if your draft is being discussed, the conversation will probably surprise you. You may discover that several of your group members either failed to understand what you were trying to say in the draft or give you a completely new idea about what you were up to. At its best, the thesis workshop inspires you to think more deeply about your theme or main idea as you consider the range of experiences and questions that other people have about it. Take lots of notes.

The Editing Workshop. In a late draft, the larger issues—for example, having a clear purpose, focus, and point, as well as appropriate information to support it—may be resolved to your satisfaction, or you may feel that you already have some pretty good ideas about how to deal with them. If so, what you may need most from your workshop group is editorial advice: responses to your work at the sentence and paragraph levels.

In the editing workshop, you invite your group members to focus on style and clarity (and perhaps grammar and mechanics). The questions that direct the reading of the draft might include some or all of the following:

- Did you stumble over any awkward passages that seemed to interrupt the fluency of the writing?

- Were there any sentences or passages that you had to read a few times to understand?

- Could any long paragraphs be broken down into smaller ones? Did any paragraphs seem to be about more than one thing?

- Are the first and last lines of the essay well crafted? Are the last lines of paragraphs strong enough?

- Were there any abrupt transitions between paragraphs?

- Was the voice or tone of the draft consistent?

- (Optional) Did you notice any patterns of grammatical problems, including run-on sentences, unclear pronoun references, or lack of subject–verb agreement?

Group members who see any of these problems should bracket [ ] the sentence or passage and refer to it when discussing the editorial issue with the group. The workshop discussion has the following ground rules:

- Be respectful of the writer's feelings. Some of us feel that style is a very personal issue, and that grammar problems are related somehow to our self-worth.

- Don't have arguments about editorial judgments. Group members don't have to agree. In fact, you probably won't agree about a lot of things. Offer your comments on style as suggestions and then move on, although don't hesitate to offer a differing opinion.

- Make sure to identify places in the draft where the writing is working just fine. Editorial workshops need not focus exclusively on problems. Sentences, paragraphs, or passages that work well stylistically can often help the writer see how to revise the less effective parts.

- If readers have some comments about larger issues in the draft, things such as purpose or theme, ask the writer first if he or she welcomes that kind of feedback. Otherwise, keep the workshop focused on editorial matters.

An editing workshop may sound a little harrowing. It really isn't, particularly if the group knows the ground rules. My students often tell me that these conversations about style are some of the best workshops they have had. Everybody learns something—not just the writer—a principle that applies to many workshop formats and another reason that peer review is such a useful practice in the writing classroom.

Reflecting on the Workshop

The real work follows the workshop. Then you have the task of mulling over the things you've heard about your draft and deciding how you're going to rewrite it. This calls for a way of inquiring—reflection—that you've already practiced. As soon as possible after your workshop session, reread your notes and your readers' comments, then go to your journal and fastwrite for five minutes. Choose one of the following prompts to get—and keep—you going.

- What did I hear that seemed most useful? What did I hear that I'm not sure about?
- What responses to my draft do I remember most? Why?
- What did I think I needed to do to revise the draft before the workshop? Did my peer review experience change my mind? Did it reinforce my initial plans?
- What do I plan to do to revise this draft to make it stronger?

USING WHAT YOU HAVE LEARNED

The writing workshop is just one of many forms of collaboration that you'll likely experience both during and after college. Even unsuccessful workshops are instructive because they help you understand how groups work and what roles you can play to make them function better. Consider your experience so far.

1. What is the best workshop group experience you've had in this class? What made it so good? What was the worst experience? What made it so bad?

2. As you reflect on your own performance in groups, what have you learned about yourself as a collaborator? How would you describe yourself as a group member? How would you *like* to describe yourself?

3. If you're currently involved in a group project in another class, how would you compare your writing workshop with that other group project? Can what you've learned in one provide useful guidance for the other?

THINKING RHETORICALLY ABOUT GOOD WRITING

It seems to me, then, that the way to help people become better writers is not to tell them that they must first learn the rules of grammar, that they must develop a four-part outline, that they must consult the experts and collect all the useful information. These things may have their place. But none of them is as crucial as having a good, interesting question.

—*Rodney Kilcup, Historian*

When new students ask us about the rules for good college writing, they are often surprised by history professor Rodney Kilkup's unexpected advice in the epigraph above. To become a better writer, says Kilcup, the most crucial thing is to have "a good, interesting question." We love Professor Kilcup's advice because we'd like you to think of good writers as critical thinkers who pose questions and problems.

Writing is closely allied to critical thinking and to the innate satisfaction you take in exercising your curiosity, creativity, and problem-solving ability. Writing helps you discover and express ideas that you would otherwise never think or say. Unlike speaking, writing gives you time to think deeply and long about an idea. Because you can revise writing, it lets you pursue a problem in stages, with each draft reflecting a deeper, clearer, or more complex level of thought. Moreover, the skills you learn in a writing course are transferable to all majors and to your professional careers. Research has shown that managers, accountants, lawyers, engineers, and other professionals spend, on average, forty-four percent of their professional time writing. In sum, writing has lifelong importance: It stimulates, challenges, and stretches your mental powers while giving you a voice in important academic, civic, and professional conversations.

In this chapter, you will learn three important concepts about writing:

- CONCEPT 1   Good writing can vary from closed to open forms.
- CONCEPT 2   Good writers address problems rather than topics.
- CONCEPT 3   Good writers think rhetorically about purpose, audience, and genre.

From Chapter 1 of *The Allyn & Bacon Guide to Writing*, Sixth Edition. John D. Ramage, John C. Bean, June Johnson. Copyright © 2012 by Pearson Education, Inc. Published by Pearson Allyn & Bacon. All rights reserved.

CONCEPT | Good writing can vary from closed to open forms.

In our experience, beginning college writers are often discomforted by the ambiguity of the rules governing writing. They often wish for some consistent rules: "Never use 'I' in a formal paper" or "Start every paragraph with a topic sentence." The problem is that different kinds of writing have different criteria for effectiveness, leaving the writer with rhetorical choices rather than with hard-and-fast formulas for success. You'll be able to appreciate this insight for yourself through the following exercise.

Read the following short pieces of nonfiction prose. The first is a letter to the editor written by a professional civil engineer in response to a newspaper editorial arguing for the development of wind-generated electricity. The second short piece is entitled "A Festival of Rain." It was written by the American poet and religious writer Thomas Merton, a Trappist monk. After reading the two samples carefully, proceed to the discussion questions that follow.

David Rockwood
A Letter to the Editor

1   Your editorial on November 16, "Get Bullish on Wind Power," is based on fantasy rather than fact. There are several basic reasons why wind-generated power can in no way serve as a reasonable major alternative to other electrical energy supply alternatives for the Pacific Northwest power system.

2   First and foremost, wind power is unreliable. Electric power generation is evaluated not only on the amount of energy provided, but also on its ability to meet system peak load requirements on an hourly, daily, and weekly basis. In other words, an effective power system would have to provide enough electricity to meet peak demands in a situation when the wind energy would be unavailable—either in no wind situations or in severe blizzard conditions, which would shut down the wind generators. Because wind power cannot be relied on at times of peak needs, it would have to be backed up by other power generation resources at great expense and duplication of facilities.

3   Secondly, there are major unsolved problems involved in the design of wind generation facilities, particularly for those located in rugged mountain areas. Ice storms, in particular, can cause sudden dynamic problems for the rotating blades and mechanisms which could well result in breakdown or failure of the generators. Furthermore, the design of the facilities to meet the stresses imposed by high winds in these remote mountain regions, in the order of 125 miles per hour, would indeed escalate the costs.

4   Thirdly, the environmental impact of constructing wind generation facilities amounting to 28 percent of the region's electrical supply system (as proposed in your editorial) would be tremendous. The Northwest Electrical Power system presently has

a capacity of about 37,000 megawatts of hydro power and 10,300 megawatts of thermal, for a total of about 48,000 megawatts. Meeting 28 percent of this capacity by wind power generators would, most optimistically, require about 13,400 wind towers, each with about 1,000 kilowatt (one megawatt) generating capacity. These towers, some 100 to 200 feet high, would have to be located in the mountains of Oregon and Washington. These would encompass hundreds of square miles of pristine mountain area, which, together with interconnecting transmission facilities, control works, and roads, would indeed have major adverse environmental impacts on the region.

5   There are many other lesser problems of control and maintenance of such a system. Let it be said that, from my experience and knowledge as a professional engineer, the use of wind power as a major resource in the Pacific Northwest power system is strictly a pipe dream.

Thomas Merton
A Festival of Rain

1   Let me say this before rain becomes a utility that they can plan and distribute for money. By "they" I mean the people who cannot understand that rain is a festival, who do not appreciate its gratuity, who think that what has no price has no value, that what cannot be sold is not real, so that the only way to make something *actual* is to place it on the market. The time will come when they will sell you even your rain. At the moment it is still free, and I am in it. I celebrate its gratuity and its meaninglessness.

2   The rain I am in is not like the rain of cities. It fills the woods with an immense and confused sound. It covers the flat roof of the cabin and its porch with insistent and controlled rhythms. And I listen, because it reminds me again and again that the whole world runs by rhythms I have not yet learned to recognize, rhythms that are not those of the engineer.

3   I came up here from the monastery last night, sloshing through the corn fields, said Vespers, and put some oatmeal on the Coleman stove for supper. … The night became very dark. The rain surrounded the whole cabin with its enormous virginal myth, a whole world of meaning, of secrecy, of silence, of rumor. Think of it: all that speech pouring down, selling nothing, judging nobody, drenching the thick mulch of dead leaves, soaking the trees, filling the gullies and crannies of the wood with water, washing out the places where men have stripped the hillside! What a thing it is to sit absolutely alone, in a forest, at night, cherished by this wonderful, unintelligible, perfectly innocent speech, the most comforting speech in the world, the talk that rain makes by itself all over the ridges, and the talk of the watercourses everywhere in the hollows!

4   Nobody started it, nobody is going to stop it. It will talk as long as it wants, this rain. As long as it talks I am going to listen.

5   But I am also going to sleep, because here in this wilderness I have learned how to sleep again. Here I am not alien. The trees I know, the night I know, the rain I know. I close my eyes and instantly sink into the whole rainy world of which I am a part, and the world goes on with me in it, for I am not alien to it.

Comparing Rockwood's and Merton's Writing

Working in small groups or as a whole class, try to reach consensus on the following specific tasks:

1. What are the main differences between the two types of writing? If you are working in groups, help your recorder prepare a presentation describing the differences between Rockwood's writing and Merton's writing.
2. Create a metaphor, simile, or analogy that best sums up your feelings about the most important differences between Rockwood's and Merton's writing: "Rockwood's writing is like ..., but Merton's writing is like...."
3. Explain why your metaphors are apt. How do your metaphors help clarify or illuminate the differences between the two pieces of writing?

Now that you have done some thinking on your own about the differences between these two examples, turn to our brief analysis.

Distinctions between Closed and Open Forms of Writing

David Rockwood's letter and Thomas Merton's mini-essay are both examples of nonfiction prose. But as these examples illustrate, nonfiction prose can vary enormously in form and style. From the perspective of structure, we can place nonfiction prose along a continuum that goes from closed to open forms of writing (see Figure 1).

Closed-Form Prose Of our two pieces of prose, Rockwood's letter illustrates tightly closed writing and falls at the far left end of the continuum because it has these elements:

- An explicit thesis in the introduction that informs readers of the point of the whole essay (i.e., wind-generated power isn't a reasonable alternative energy source in the Pacific Northwest)

FIGURE 1
A Continuum of
Essay Types:
Closed to Open
Forms

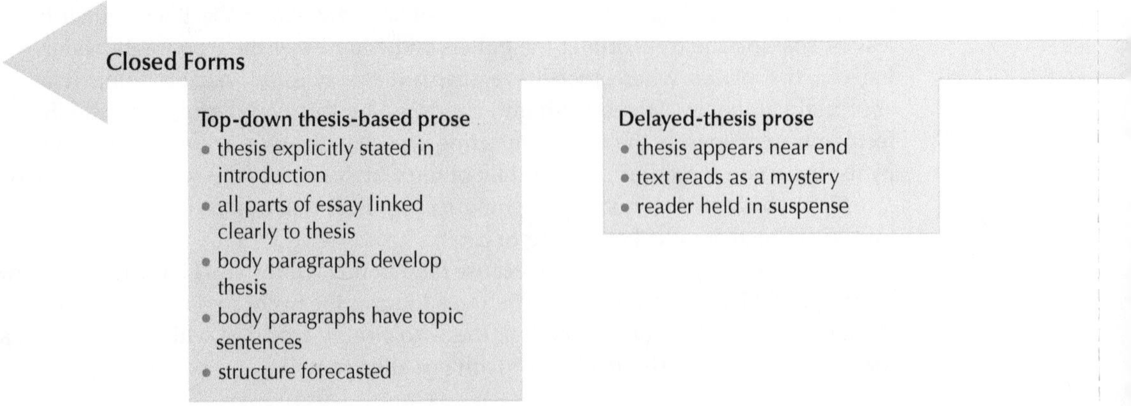

Closed Forms

Top-down thesis-based prose
- thesis explicitly stated in introduction
- all parts of essay linked clearly to thesis
- body paragraphs develop thesis
- body paragraphs have topic sentences
- structure forecasted

Delayed-thesis prose
- thesis appears near end
- text reads as a mystery
- reader held in suspense

- Unified and coherent paragraphs (i.e., "First and foremost, wind power is unreliable. ... Secondly, there are major unsolved problems. ... Thirdly, ...")
- Sustained development of that thesis without digressions

Once the thesis is stated, readers know the point of the essay and can predict its structure. (You might note that the five-paragraph essay sometimes taught in high school is a by-the-numbers way to teach closed-form prose.) Because its structure is transparent and predictable, the success of closed-form prose rests entirely on its ideas, which must "surprise" readers by asserting something new, challenging, doubtful, or controversial. It aims to change readers' view of the subject through the power of reason, logic, and evidence. Closed-form prose is what most college professors write in their scholarly research, what they most often expect from their students, and what is most common in professional and business contexts.

Open-Form Prose In contrast, Merton's "A Festival of Rain" falls toward the right end of the closed-to-open continuum because it exhibits these features:

- No reduction to a single, summarizable thesis (Merton clearly opposes the consumer culture that will try to "sell" you the rain, but what exactly does Merton mean by "festival" or by rain's "gratuity and its meaninglessness"?)
- The use of story or narrative as an organizing principle (i.e., the story of Merton's leaving the monastery to sleep in the rain-drenched cabin) through which a point emerges suggestively

Although open-form prose does not announce its thesis and support it with reasons and evidence, it does have a focus. As Merton's piece illustrates, the focus is more like a theme in fiction that readers might discuss and even dispute than like a thesis in argument.

Consider also the extent to which Merton violates the rules for closed-form prose. Instead of using transitions between paragraphs, Merton juxtaposes passages that tell the story of his camping trip ("I came up here from the monastery last night ...") with passages that make cryptic, interpretive comments about his experience ("The rain I am in is not like the rain of cities"). Unlike paragraphs in

Open Forms

Thesis-seeking prose
- essay organized around a question rather than a thesis
- essay explores the problem or question, looking at it in many ways
- writer may or may not arrive at thesis

Theme-based narrative
- often organized chronologically or has storylike elements
- often used to heighten or deepen a problem, or show its human significance
- often has an implicit theme rather than a thesis
- often violates rules of closed-form prose by using literary techniques

closed-form prose, which typically begin with topic sentences and are developed with supporting details, the paragraphs in Merton's piece have no clear hierarchical structure; paragraph 4, in fact, is only two lines long. These open-form elements often appear in personal essays, in blogs, in newspaper or magazine feature stories or character profiles, or in professional nonfiction.

Flexibility of "Rules" along the Continuum As you can see from the continuum in Figure 1, essays can fall anywhere along the scale. Not all thesis-with-support writing has to be top down, stating its thesis explicitly in the introduction. In some cases writers choose to delay the thesis, creating a more exploratory, open-ended, "let's think through this together" feeling before finally stating the main point late in the essay. In some cases writers explore a problem without *ever* finding a satisfactory thesis, creating an essay that is thesis seeking rather than thesis supporting, an essay aimed at deepening the question, refusing to accept an easy answer. Such essays may replicate their authors' process of exploring a problem and include digressions, speculations, conjectures, multiple perspectives, and occasional invitations to the reader to help solve the problem. When writers reach the far right-hand position on the continuum, they no longer state an explicit thesis. Instead, like novelists or short story writers, they embed their points in plot, imagery, dialogue, and so forth, leaving their readers to *infer* a theme from the text. This kind of writing is often called "literary nonfiction."

Where to Place Your Writing along the Continuum

Clearly, essays at opposite ends of this continuum operate in different ways and obey different rules. Because each position on the continuum has its appropriate uses, the writer's challenge is to determine which sort of writing is most appropriate in a given situation. Most college papers (but not all) and much professional writing are written in closed form. Thus if you were writing a business proposal, a legal brief, or an academic paper for a scholarly audience, you would typically choose a closed-form structure, and your finished product would include elements such as the following:

- An explicit thesis in the introduction
- Forecasting of structure
- Cohesive and unified paragraphs with topic sentences
- Clear transitions between sentences and between parts
- No digressions

But if you were writing to express your conflicted relationship with, say, a parent or friend or to reflect on your first discovery of racism or homophobia, you would probably move toward the open end of the continuum and violate one or more of these conventions. Instead of a thesis-support structure, you might use the power of compelling stories, vivid characterization, dialogue, and evocative language to convey your ideas.

If we return now to the question about good writing posed at the beginning of this chapter, we can see that having a thesis statement, topic sentences, good transitions, and unified and coherent paragraphs are not qualities of "good prose" but simply of "closed-form prose." What makes a piece of closed-form prose "good," as we will see in the next section, is the extent to which it addresses a problem or question that matters to the reader and brings to the reader something new, surprising, or provocative. In contrast, we have seen that open-form prose can be "good" without having a thesis-driven, hierarchical structure. Open-form prose conveys its pleasures and insights through narrative strategies rather than through thesis-with-support strategies.

Thinking Personally about Closed and Open Forms

FOR WRITING AND DISCUSSION

Do you and your classmates most enjoy writing prose at the closed or at the more open end of the continuum?

Individual task: Recall a favorite piece of writing that you have done in the past. Jot down a brief description of the kind of writing this was (a poem, a personal-experience essay, a piece of workplace writing, a research paper, a newspaper story, a persuasive argument). Where would you place this piece of writing on the closed-to-open continuum? Explore why you like this piece of writing. Are you at your best in closed-form writing that calls for an explicit thesis statement and logical support? Or are you at your best in more open and personal forms?

Small-group or whole-class task: Share the results of the individual tasks. Is there a wide range of preferences in your class? If so, how do you account for this variance? If not, how do you account for the narrow range?

CONCEPT 2 Good writers address problems rather than topics.

In the previous section, we explained how the rules for good writing vary along a continuum from closed to open forms. In this section, we return to the close connection between writing and critical thinking. From your previous schooling, you are probably familiar with the term **thesis statement**, which is the main point a writer wants to make in an essay. However, you may not have thought much about the *question* that lies behind the thesis, which is the problem or issue that the writer is wrestling with. Behind every thesis statement is an explicit or implied **thesis question**, which is the problem or issue to which the thesis responds. An essay's thesis statement is actually the writer's proposed answer to this question, and it is this question that has propelled the writer's thinking.

Thus, the problem that matters to engineer David Rockwood is whether wind power can be a viable alternative energy source. Rockwood writes to make his answer ("No!") persuasive to readers. Thomas Merton's question is more complex and subtle, one that leads him to use open-form narrative strategies. His question seems to be: What is the effect of a consumer economy on our understanding of meaning and value? He wants to raise readers' awareness of a problem with corporate capitalism (where corporations want to sell you even the rain), which alienates us from nature and from our deepest selves.

This focus on a writer's motivating problem or question differs somewhat from the common view that writers first choose a topic and then narrow it down. Of course, writers have broad areas of interest (which we might call topics), but what they are seeking isn't the topic itself but a cluster of problems or questions within the topic. Instead of "narrowing a topic," they seek a problem that grips their curiosity and gets them thinking.

Shared Problems Unite Writers and Readers

For college professors, "a good, interesting question" is at the heart of good writing. Professors want students to become gripped by problems because they themselves are gripped by problems. For example, at a workshop for new faculty members, we asked participants to write a brief description of the question or problem that motivated their Ph.D. dissertation or a recent conference paper or article. Here is how a biochemistry professor responded:

> During periods of starvation, the human body makes physiological adaptations to preserve essential protein mass. Unfortunately, these adaptations don't work well during long-term starvation. After the body depletes its carbohydrate storage, it must shift to depleting protein in order to produce glucose. Eventually, this loss of functional protein leads to metabolic dysfunction and death. Interestingly, several animal species are capable of surviving for extensive periods without food and water while conserving protein and maintaining glucose levels. How do the bodies of these animals accomplish this feat? I wanted to investigate the metabolic functioning of these animals, which might lead to insights into the human situation.

As you progress through your college career, you will find yourself increasingly engaged with the kinds of questions that motivate your professors. All around college campuses you'll find clusters of professors and students asking questions about all manner of problems ranging from puzzles in the reproductive cycles of worms and bugs to the use of nanotechnology to fight global warming, from the changing portrayal of race and gender in American films to the impact of digital technology on the dissemination of news. At the heart of all these communities of writers and readers is an interest in common questions and the hope for better or different answers. Writers write because they have something new or surprising or challenging to say in response to a question. Readers read because they share the writer's interest in the problem and want to deepen their understanding.

Where Do Problems Come From?

So where do these problems come from? How does a writer get hooked on a problem? Although this question is complex at a philosophical level, we can offer two relatively simple and helpful answers: Sometimes you encounter a problem that is already "out there" in a conversation already in progress in some human community. Some enduring problems have been sparking conversations that have lasted for thousands of years: Do humans have free will? What constitutes ethical action? What is the origin of the universe? Why do good people have to suffer? Thousands of less sweeping problems are being discussed by human communities all the time. In many of your college courses, you'll be introduced to long-standing problems that you hadn't encountered before and that may hook you and draw you into their spell. In these cases, a problem that is already "out there" initiates your search for a possible answer and invites you to join the conversation.

But sometimes you actually find, pose, or articulate a problem yourself, fresh from your own brain. In this case you start a conversation, rather than join an existing one. (It may turn out later that other people have asked the same question, but you didn't know that at the time.) For example, you find your own problem whenever you see something puzzling in the natural world, note curious or unexplained features in a cultural phenomenon or artifact, or discover conflicts or contradictions within your own way of looking at the world.

In the table below we describe some of the ways that writers can become gripped by a problem that may lead to engaged writing.

TABLE 1   How Writers Become Gripped by a Problem

Occasion That Leads to Problem	Your Interior Mental State	Example
The problem is already "out there." *(You enter a conversation already in progress)*		
You encounter others arguing about a problem, and you don't know where you stand.	• You are equally persuaded by different views or dissatisfied with all the views • Part of you thinks X but another part thinks Y (you feel divided)	I don't know where I stand on the question of whether health care should be rationed. In *To Kill a Mockingbird*, I can't decide whether Atticus Finch is a good father.
You aren't satisfied with a common view of something or you disagree with someone on an issue.	• Your skepticism or intuition pushes against some popular view • You are committed to a view different from someone else's • *Note: You must go beyond simply having an opinion. You aren't gripped by a problem until you have seen the possible strengths of other views and the possible weaknesses of your own.*	My teacher's explanation of the causes for anorexia doesn't seem quite right to me. Shanita says that we should build more nuclear power plants to combat global warming, but I say nuclear power is too dangerous.
Someone gives you a question that you can't yet answer.	• You feel overwhelmed with unknowns • You feel that you can't begin to answer until you do more exploration and research • If you know enough to start proposing hypotheses, you aren't satisfied with any of your approaches	Your boss asks you whether the company should enact the proposed marketing plan. Your history professor asks you, "To what extent does Frederick Jackson Turner's frontier hypothesis reflect a Euro-centric world view?"

(continued)

TABLE I	*continued*	
Occasion That Leads to Problem	**Your Interior Mental State**	**Example**
	You pose the problem yourself. *(You initiate the conversation)*	
You see something puzzling in a natural or cultural phenomenon.	• Something deviates from what you would expect or is otherwise unexplainable • You begin testing possible solutions or answers. (Often you want to talk to someone—to start a conversation about the problem)	Why is this fungus appearing on some of these tomatoes but not on the others? Why is Twitter more popular among middle-aged adults than teenagers?
You see something unexpected, puzzling, or unexplained in a poem, painting, or other human artifact.	• You can't see why the artist/maker did something in such a way • You wonder why this particular artifact is different from other artifacts that you thought would be similar	Why does Merton call rain "meaningless"? If Hamlet really loves Ophelia, then why does he treat her like a whore in the nunnery scene?
You articulate something inconsistent or contradictory in your own view of the world.	• You feel unsettled by your own inconsistent views or values • You probe more deeply into your own identity and place in the world	I agree with Merton's argument against consumerism, but I really want a large plasma TV. Is consumerism really bad? Am I a materialist?

In each of these cases, the problem starts to spark critical thinking.

FOR WRITING AND DISCUSSION

Finding a Problem

This classroom exercise, based on the image in Figure 2, will give you the experience of posing a problem for yourself and then participating in a conversation initiated by shared questions from the class. It is designed to help you think about your own thinking as you ask questions and formulate problems that you might want to explore. Figure 2 is a photograph of a sculpture, called *The Foundling*, by Australian artist Patricia Piccinini. (The photograph is taken in an art museum; note the spectator walking by in the background.) The sculpture, which is made of silicone, fiberglass, human hair, leather, plywood, and clothing, is part of a larger Piccinini exhibit of similar life-size figures. Imagine that you came across this sculpture while visiting a museum. Consider the sculpture's title as well as its appearance and its effect on viewers.

Individual task: Working individually, spend several minutes writing down one or more thought-provoking questions that emerge from your looking

Ennio Leanza/epa/Corbis

FIGURE 2 The Foundling

at the photo of the front view of this sculpture. By "thought-provoking," we mean questions that don't have simple "right answers" but that invite "possible answers" supported by different lines of reasoning, speculation, and argument.

Task for group or whole class discussion: Working in small groups or as a whole class, share your individual questions. Then speculate about possible answers to several of them. The best questions will lead to alternative responses—the feeling of a genuine conversation with different points of view. Each individual should now write down new questions that emerge from the conversation.

Individual reflection: To what extent did the activities provoked by this exercise help you think about where questions come from? How did the questions that you initially posed for yourself evolve as you participated in a conversation about the sculpture? Identify one question that now particularly intrigues you and explain why you find it a good question. (If you would like to find out more about Patricia Piccinini, a quick Web search will yield many results, including statements of her philosophy of art and photographs of her other works.)

CONCEPT 3 Good writers think rhetorically about purpose, audience, and genre.

So far, we have used the term "rhetoric"—as in "A Rhetoric for Writers" or "thinking rhetorically"—without defining it. Now is the time for us to explain what we mean by *rhetoric*.

What Is Rhetoric?

At the broadest level, **rhetoric** is the study of how human beings use language and other symbols to influence the attitudes, beliefs, and actions of others. One prominent twentieth-century rhetorician, Kenneth Burke, calls rhetoric "a symbolic means of inducing cooperation in beings that by nature respond to symbols." To understand what Burke means by "symbols," consider the difference in flirting behavior between peacocks and humans. When male peacocks flirt, they spread their fantastic tail feathers, do mating dances, and screech weirdly to attract females, but the whole process is governed by instinct. Peacocks don't have to choose among different symbolic actions such as buying an Armani tail versus buying a knockoff from Wal-Mart or driving to the mating grounds in the right car. Unlike a peacock, however, a flirting human must make symbolic choices, all of which have meaning. Consider the different flirting messages humans send to each other by their choice of clothes, their method of transportation, their choice of major, their favorite music. Even word choices (for example, academic jargon words versus street slang) or texting behavior give further hints of a person's identity, values, and social groups. Rhetoricians study, among other things, how these symbols arise within a given culture and how they influence others.

In a narrower sense, rhetoric is the art of making messages persuasive. Perhaps the most famous definition of rhetoric comes from the Greek philosopher Aristotle, who defined rhetoric as "the ability to see, in any particular case, all the available means of persuasion." An effective speaker's task, in Aristotle's view, is to persuade listeners to accept the speaker's views on a question of action or belief. But to do so, the speaker must first understand all the arguments on all sides of the question ("all the available means of persuasion"). If we imagine the interaction of several speakers, each proposing different answers to a question, and if we imagine all the speakers listening to each other respectfully and open-mindedly, we can see how productive human conversation could emerge. The study of rhetoric can therefore help people write, speak, read, and listen more effectively.

At an operational level, writers can be said to "think rhetorically" whenever they are consciously aware of writing to an audience for a purpose within a genre. (A *genre*, to be explained in more detail shortly, is a recurring type of writing with distinguishing features and conventions such as a letter to the editor, a scholarly article, a business memo, or a blog.) To think rhetorically, writers consider questions like these:

- *Purpose:* What am I trying to accomplish in this paper? What do I want my readers to know, believe, see, or do?
- *Audience:* Who are my intended readers, and what are their values and assumptions? What do they already know or believe about my subject? How much do they care about it?
- *Genre:* What kind of document am I writing? What are its requirements for structure, style, and document design?

Let's look more closely at each of these components of a writer's rhetorical context.

How Writers Think about Purpose

In this section, we want to help you think more productively about your purpose for writing, which can be examined from several different perspectives: your rhetorical aim, the motivating occasion that gets you going, and your desire to change your reader's view. All three perspectives will help you make your awareness of purpose work for you and increase your savvy as a writer. Let's look at each in turn.

Purpose as Rhetorical Aim One powerful way to think about purpose is through the general concept of "rhetorical aim." We identify six different rhetorical aims of writing: to express, to explore, to inform, to analyze and synthesize, to persuade, and to reflect. Thinking of each piece of writing in terms of one or more of these rhetorical aims can help you understand typical ways that your essay can be structured and developed and can help you clarify your relationship with your audience. Table 2 gives you an overview of each of the six rhetorical

TABLE 2   Purpose as Rhetorical Aim

Rhetorical Aim	Focus of Writing	Relationship to Audience	Forms and Genres
Express or share May also include an artistic aim	Your own life, personal experiences, reflections	You share aspects of your life; you invite readers to walk in your shoes, to experience your insights	**Form:** Has many open-form features **Sample genres:** journal, blog, personal Web site, or online profile; personal essays or literacy narratives, often with artistic features
Explore or inquire	A significant subject-matter problem that puzzles you	You take readers on your own intellectual journey by showing your inquiry process (raising questions, seeking evidence, considering alternative views)	**Form:** Follows open form in being narrative based; is thesis seeking rather than thesis supporting **Sample genres:** freewriting; research logs; articles and books focused on process of discovery
Inform or explain	Factual knowledge addressing a reader's need or curiosity	You provide knowledge that your readers need or want, or you arouse curiosity and provide new, surprising information. You expect readers to trust your authority	**Form:** Usually has a closed-form structure **Sample genres:** encyclopedia articles; instruction booklets; sales reports; technical reports; informative magazine articles; informative Web sites

(continued)

TABLE 2 *continued*

Rhetorical Aim	Focus of Writing	Relationship to Audience	Forms and Genres
Analyze, synthesize, or interpret	Complex subject matter that you can break down into parts and put together in new ways for greater understanding	Using critical thinking and possibly research, you challenge readers with a new way of understanding your subject. Skeptical readers expect you to support your thesis with good particulars.	**Form:** Typically has a closed-form structure **Sample genres:** scholarly articles; experimental reports; many kinds of college research papers; public affairs magazine articles; many kinds of blogs
Persuade	Subject-matter questions that have multiple controversial answers	You try to convince readers, who may not share your values and beliefs, to accept your stance on an issue by providing good reasons and evidence and attending to alternative views.	**Form:** Usually closed form, but may employ many open-form features for persuasive effect **Sample genres:** letters to the editor; op-ed pieces; advocacy pieces in public affairs magazines; advocacy Web sites; researched academic arguments
Reflect	Subject matter closely connected to your interests and experience; often involves self-evaluation of an experience	Writing for yourself as well as for a reader, you seek to find personal meaning and value in an experience or course of study. You assume a sympathetic and interested reader.	**Form:** Anywhere on the closed-to-open-form continuum **Sample genres:** memoirs, workplace self-evaluations; introductory letter for a portfolio; personal essays looking back on an experience

aims and sketches out how the subject matter differs from aim to aim, how the writer's task and relationship to readers differ according to aim, and how a chosen aim affects the writing's genre and its position on the spectrum from open to closed forms.

Purpose as a Response to a Motivating Occasion Another important way to think about purpose is to think about each piece of writing as a response to a particular motivating occasion. Almost all writing is compelled by some sort of motivating occasion or exigency.* This exigency can be external (someone giving you a task and setting a deadline) or internal (your awareness of a problem stimulating your desire to bring about some change in people's views). Thus, when engineer David Rockwood read a newspaper editorial supporting wind-power projects, his own belief in the impracticality of wind power motivated him to write a letter to

*An *exigency* is an urgent or pressing situation requiring immediate attention. Rhetoricians use the term to describe the event or occasion that causes a writer to begin writing.

the editor in rebuttal. But he also knew that he had to write the letter within one or two days or else it stood no chance of being published. His exigency thus included both internal and external factors.

College students' motivations for writing can be equally mixed: In part, you write to meet an assignment deadline; in part, you write to please the teacher and get a good grade. But ideally you also write because you have become engaged with an intellectual problem and want to say something significant about it. Our point here is that your purposes for writing are always more complex than the simple desire to meet an assignment deadline.

Purpose as a Desire to Change Your Reader's View Perhaps the most useful way to think about purpose is to focus on the change you want to bring about in your audience's view of the subject. When you are given a college writing assignment, this view of purpose engages you directly with the intellectual problem specified in the assignment. For most essays, you can write a one-sentence, nutshell statement about your purpose.

> My purpose is to give my readers a vivid picture of my difficult struggle with Graves' disease.
> My purpose is to explain how Thoreau's view of nature differs in important ways from that of contemporary environmentalists.
> My purpose is to persuade the general public that wind-generated electricity is not a practical energy alternative in the Pacific Northwest.

In closed-form academic articles, technical reports, and other business and professional pieces, writers often place explicit purpose statements in their introductions along with the thesis. In most other forms of writing, the writer uses a behind-the-scenes purpose statement to achieve focus and direction but seldom states the purpose explicitly. Writing an explicit purpose statement for a paper is a powerful way to nutshell the kind of change you want to bring about in your reader's view of the subject.

How Writers Think about Audience

In our discussion of purpose, we have already had a lot to say about audience. What you know about your readers—their familiarity with your subject matter, their reasons for reading, their closeness to you, their values and beliefs—affects most of the choices you make as a writer.

In assessing your audience, you must first determine who that audience is—a single reader (for example, your boss), a select group (a scholarship committee; attendees at an undergraduate research conference), or a general audience. If you imagine a general audience, you will need to make some initial assumptions about their views and values. Doing so creates an "implied audience," giving you a stable rather than a moving target so that you can make decisions about your own essay. Once you have identified your audience, you can use the following strategies for analysis.

Strategies for Analyzing Audience	
Questions to Ask about Your Audience	Reasons for Asking the Question
How busy are my readers?	• Helps you decide on length, document design, and open versus closed features • In workplace writing, busy readers often require closed-form prose with headings that allow for skimming
What are my readers' motives for reading?	• If the reader has requested the document, you need only a short introduction • In most cases, your opening must hook your reader's interest
What is my relationship with my readers?	• Helps you decide on a formal or informal style • Helps you select tone—polite and serious or loose and slangy
What do my readers already know about my topic? Do my readers have more or less expertise than I have, or about the same expertise?	• Helps you determine what will be old/familiar information for your audience versus new/unfamiliar information • Helps you decide how much background and context to include • Helps you decide to use or avoid in-group jargon and specialized knowledge
How interested are my readers in my topic? Do my readers already care about it?	• Helps you decide how to write the introduction • Helps you determine how to make the problem you address interesting and significant to your reader
What are my readers' attitudes toward my thesis? Do my readers share my beliefs and values?	• Helps you make numerous decisions about tone, structure, reference to alternative views, and use of evidence • Helps you decide on the voice and persona you want to project

To appreciate the importance of audience, consider how a change in audience can affect the content of a piece. Suppose you want voters to approve a bond issue to build a new baseball stadium. If most voters are baseball fans, you can appeal to their love of the game, the pleasure of a new facility, and so forth. But non-baseball fans won't be moved by these arguments. To reach them, you must tie the new stadium to their values. You can argue that it will bring new tax revenues, clean up a run-down area, revitalize local businesses, or stimulate tourism.

Your purpose remains the same—to persuade taxpayers to fund the stadium—but the content of your argument changes if your audience changes.

In college, you often seem to be writing for an audience of one—your instructor. However, most instructors try to read as a representative of a broader audience. To help college writers imagine these readers, many instructors try to design writing assignments that provide a fuller sense of audience. They may ask you to write for the readers of a particular magazine or journal, or they may create case assignments with built-in audiences (for example, "You are an accountant in the firm of Numbers and Fudge; one day you receive a letter from …"). If your instructor does not specify an audience, you can generally assume the audience to be what we like to call "the generic academic audience"—student peers who have approximately the same level of knowledge and expertise in the field as you do, who are engaged by the question you address, and who want to read your writing and be surprised in some way.

How Writers Think about Genre

The term *genre* refers to categories of writing that follow certain conventions of style, structure, approach to subject matter, and document design. Table 3 shows different kinds of genres.

The concept of genre creates strong reader expectations and places specific demands on writers. How you write any given letter, report, or article is influenced by the structure and style of hundreds of previous letters, reports, or articles written in the same genre. If you wanted to write for *Reader's Digest*, for example, you would have to use the conventions that appeal to its older, conservative readers: simple language, subjects with strong human interest, heavy reliance on anecdotal evidence in arguments, an upbeat and optimistic perspective, and an approach that reinforces the conservative *ethos* of individualism, self-discipline, and family.

TABLE 3   Examples of Genres

Personal Writing	Academic Writing	Popular Culture	Public Affairs, Civic Writing	Professional Writing	Literature
Letter	Scholarly article	Articles for magazines such as *Seventeen*, *Ebony*, or *Vibe*	Letter to the editor	Cover letter for a job application	Short story
Diary/journal	Research paper		Newspaper editorial	Résumé	Novel
Memoir	Scientific report	Advertisements	Op-ed piece	Business memo	Graphic novel
Blog	Abstract or summary	Hip-hop lyrics	Advocacy Web site	Legal brief	Play
Text message	Book review	Fan Web sites	Political blog	Brochure	Sonnet
E-mail	Essay exam	Bumper stickers	Magazine article on civic issue	Technical manual	Epic poem
Facebook profile	Annotated bibliography	Reviews of books, films, plays, music		Instruction booklet	Literary podcast
Personal essay	Textual analysis			Proposal	
Literacy narrative				Report	
				Press release	

If you wanted to write for *Seventeen* or *Rolling Stone*, however, you would need to use quite different conventions.

To illustrate the relationship of a writer to a genre, we sometimes draw an analogy with clothing. Although most people have a variety of different types of clothing in their wardrobes, the genre of activity for which they are dressing (Saturday night movie date, job interview, wedding) severely constrains their choice and expression of individuality. A man dressing for a job interview might express his personality through choice of tie or quality and style of business suit; he probably wouldn't express it by wearing a Hawaiian shirt and sandals. Even when people deviate from a convention, they tend to do so in a conventional way. For example, teenagers who do not want to follow the genre of "teenager admired by adults" form their own genre of purple hair and pierced body parts. The concept of genre raises intriguing and sometimes unsettling questions about the relationship of the unique self to a social convention or tradition.

These same kinds of questions and constraints perplex writers. For example, academic writers usually follow the genre of the closed-form scholarly article. This highly functional form achieves maximum clarity for readers by orienting them quickly to the article's purpose, content, and structure. Readers expect this format, and writers have the greatest chance of being published if they meet these expectations. In some disciplines, however, scholars are beginning to publish more experimental, open-form articles. They may slowly alter the conventions of the scholarly article, just as fashion designers alter styles of dress.

FOR WRITING AND DISCUSSION

Thinking about Purpose, Audience, and Genre

1. This exercise, which is based on Table 2, will help you appreciate how rhetorical aim connects to choices about subject matter as well as to audience and genre. As a class, choose one of the following topic areas or another provided by your instructor. Then imagine six different writing situations in which a hypothetical writer would compose an essay about the selected topic. Let each situation call for a different aim. How might a person write about the selected topic with an expressive aim? An exploratory aim? An informative aim? An analytic aim? A persuasive aim? A reflective aim? How would each essay surprise its readers?

automobiles	animals	hospices or nursing homes
homelessness	music	dating or marriage
advertising	energy crisis	sports injuries

   Working on your own or in small groups, create six realistic scenarios, each of which calls for prose in a different category of aim. Then share your results as a whole class. Here are two examples based on the topic "hospices."

   Expressive Aim   Working one summer as a volunteer in a hospice for dying cancer patients, you befriend a woman whose attitude toward death changes your life. You write an autobiographical essay about your experiences with this remarkable woman.

Analytic Aim	You are a hospice nurse working in a home care setting. You and your colleagues note that sometimes family members cannot adjust psychologically to the burden of living with a dying person. You decide to investigate this phenomenon. You interview "reluctant" family members in an attempt to understand the causes of their psychological discomfort so that you can provide better counseling services as a possible solution. You write a paper for a professional audience analyzing the results of your interviews.

2. Working in small groups or as a whole class, develop a list of the conventions for one or more of the following genres:
   - Cell phone text messages as typically created by teenagers
   - A Facebook profile
   - The home page for a college or university Web site

Chapter Summary

This chapter has introduced you to three transferable rhetorical concepts aimed at deepening your thinking about "good writing" in college.

- ***Concept 1: Good writing can vary from closed to open forms.*** Closed-form prose has an explicit thesis statement, topic sentences, unified and coherent paragraphs, and good transitions. At the other end of the continuum is open-form prose, which often uses narrative techniques such as storytelling, evocative language, surprising juxtapositions, and other features that violate the conventions of closed-form prose. Closed-form prose is "good" only if its ideas bring something new, provocative, or challenging to the reader.
- ***Concept 2: Good writers address problems rather than topics.*** Writers write because they have something surprising or challenging to say in response to a question that matters to the reader. Writers can pose their own problematic questions about a subject or become engaged in controversies or issues that are already "out there."
- ***Concept 3: Good writers think rhetorically about purpose, audience, and genre.*** In thinking about purpose, writers consider their rhetorical aim, their motivating occasion, or their desire to bring about change in their readers' view. They also think about their audience, analyzing how much their readers already know about (and care about) their subject and assessing their readers' values, beliefs, and assumptions. Writers attend to genre by thinking about the conventions of content, structure, and style associated with the kind of document they are writing.

Two Messages for Different Purposes, Audiences, and Genres

BRIEF WRITING PROJECT 1

The purpose of this brief write-to-learn assignment is to let you experience first-hand how rhetorical context influences a writer's choices. The whole assignment, which has three parts, should not be more than two double-spaced pages long.

1. ***A Text Message to a Friend.*** Write a text message to a friend using the abbreviations, capitalization, and punctuation style typically used for text messages. Explain that you are going to miss an upcoming social event (movie, football game, dance, trip to the local diner or coffee house) because you are feeling sick. Then ask your friend to text you during the event to schedule another get-together. (Make up details as you need them.)

2. ***An E-Mail Message to a Professor.*** Compose an e-mail message to your professor explaining that you cannot meet an assignment deadline because you are sick and asking for an extension. (Use the same sickness details from Part 1.) Create a subject line appropriate for this new context.

3. ***Reflection on the Two Messages.*** Using items 1 and 2 as illustrative examples, explain to someone who has not read this chapter why a difference in your rhetorical context caused you to make different choices in these two messages. In your explanation, use the terms "purpose," "audience," and "genre." Your goal is to teach your audience the meanings of these terms.

BRIEF WRITING PROJECT 2

A Letter to Your Professor about What Was New in this Chapter

Write a letter to your instructor in which you reflect on the extent to which the ideas in this chapter are new to you or have caused you to think about writing in new or different ways. Structure your letter in the following way:

- Describe for your instructor a piece of writing you did in high school or elsewhere that represents your most engaged work or about which you are most proud. Explain the context of this piece of writing (class or professional setting, nature of the assignment, length, and so forth) and provide a brief summary of your intentions and argument. Explain why this piece of writing particularly engaged you.
- Then analyze this piece of writing and your own thinking processes in producing it in light of the following three questions from this chapter:
  - Where would you place this piece of writing on the continuum from closed to open forms? Why?
  - To what extent was this piece of writing rooted in a "good, interesting question"? Explain.
  - To what extent did you think about purpose, audience, and genre as you wrote this piece?
- Finally, explain to your instructor the extent to which this chapter caused you to think about writing in any new or different ways.

 For additional help with writing, reading, and research, go to **www.mycomplab.com.**

THINKING RHETORICALLY ABOUT YOUR SUBJECT MATTER

"In management, people don't merely 'write papers,' they solve problems," said [business professor A. Kimbrough Sherman]. . . . He explained that he wanted to construct situations where students would have to **"wallow in complexity"** and work their way out, as managers must.

—*A. Kimbrough Sherman, Management Professor, Quoted by*

Barbara E. Walvoord and Lucille P. McCarthy

The rules for good writing vary along a continuum from closed to open forms, writers become engaged with subject-matter questions, and they think rhetorically about their purpose, audience, and genre. In this chapter we show how writers think rhetorically about their "subject matter"—that is, how they think about what is unknown, puzzling, or controversial in their subject matter and about how their view of the subject might be different from their audience's.

Because this chapter concerns academic writing, we focus on closed-form prose—the kind of thesis-governed writing most often required in college courses and often required in civic and professional life. As we will show, thesis-governed writing requires a behind-the-scenes ability to think rigorously about a problem and then to make a claim* based on your own solution to the problem. This claim should bring something new, interesting, useful, or challenging to readers.

In this chapter, you will learn four concepts of significant explanatory power:

- **CONCEPT 1** To determine their thesis, writers must often "wallow in complexity."
- **CONCEPT 2** A strong thesis surprises readers with something new or challenging.
- **CONCEPT 3** In closed-form prose, a typical introduction starts with the problem, not the thesis.
- **CONCEPT 4** Thesis statements in closed-form prose are supported hierarchically with points and particulars.

*We use the words *claim* and *thesis statement* interchangeably. In courses across the curriculum, instructors typically use one or the other of these terms. Other synonyms for *thesis statement* include *proposition, main point,* or *thesis sentence.*

CONCEPT I To determine their thesis, writers must often "wallow in complexity."

The starting point of academic writing is a "good, interesting question." At the outset, we should say that these questions may lead you toward new and unfamiliar ways of thinking. Beginning college students typically value questions that have right answers. Students ask their professors questions because they are puzzled by confusing parts of a textbook, a lecture, or an assigned reading. They hope their professors will explain the confusing material clearly. Their purpose in asking these questions is to eliminate misunderstandings, not to open up controversy and debate. Although basic comprehension questions are important, they are not the kinds of inquiry questions that lead to strong college-level writing and thinking.

Instead, the kinds of questions that stimulate the writing most valued in college are open-ended questions that focus on unknowns or uncertainties (what educational researcher Ken Bain calls "beautiful problems") rather than factual questions that have single, correct answers.* Good open-ended questions invite multiple points of view or alternative hypotheses; they stimulate critical thinking and research. We don't mean to make this focus on problems sound scary. Indeed, humans pose and solve problems all the time and often take great pleasure in doing so. Psychologists who study critical and creative thinking see problem solving as a productive and positive activity. According to one psychologist, "Critical thinkers are actively engaged with life.... They appreciate creativity, they are innovators, and they exude a sense that life is full of possibilities."** Our way of thinking about problems has been motivated by the South American educator Paulo Freire, who wanted his students (often poor, illiterate villagers) to become *problematizers* instead of memorizers. Freire opposed what he called "the banking method" of education, in which students deposit knowledge in their memory banks and then make withdrawals during exams. The banking method, Freire believed, left third world villagers passive and helpless to improve their situations in life. Using the banking method, students being taught to read and write might learn the word *water* through drill-and-skill workbook sentences such as, "The water is in the well." With Freire's problematizing method, students might learn the word *water* by asking, "Why is the water dirty and who is responsible?" Freire believed that good questions have stakes and that answering them can make a difference in the world.

---

*Cognitive psychologists call these beautiful problems "ill-structured." An ill-structured problem has competing solutions, requiring the thinker to argue for the best solution in the absence of full and complete data or in the presence of stakeholders with different backgrounds, assumptions, beliefs, and values. In contrast, a "well-structured" problem eventually yields a correct answer. Math problems that can be solved by applying the right formulae and processes are well structured. That's why you can have the correct answers in the back of the book.

**Academic writers regularly document their sources. Two standard methods for documenting sources in student papers and in many professional scholarly articles are the MLA and APA citation systems.

Learning to Wallow in Complexity

This focus on important problems explains why college professors want students to go beyond simply understanding course concepts as taught in textbooks and lectures. Such comprehension is important, but it is only a starting point. As management professor A. Kimbrough Sherman explains in the epigraph to this chapter, college instructors expect students to wrestle with problems by applying the concepts, data, and thought processes they learn in a course to new situations. As Sherman puts it, students must learn to "wallow in complexity" and work their way out. To put it another way, college professors want students to "earn" their thesis. (Earning a thesis is very different from simply stating your opinion, which might not be deeply examined at all.) Because college professors value this kind of complex thinking, they often phrase essay exam questions or writing assignments as open-ended problems that can be answered in more than one way. They are looking not for the right answer, but for well-supported arguments that acknowledge alternative views. A C paper and an A paper may have the same "answer" (identical thesis statements), but the C writer may have waded only ankle deep into the mud of complexity, whereas the A writer wallowed in it and worked a way out.

What skills are required for successful wallowing? Specialists in critical thinking have identified the following:

CRITICAL THINKING SKILLS NEEDED FOR "WALLOWING IN COMPLEXITY"

- The ability to pose problematic questions
- The ability to analyze a problem in all its dimensions—to define its key terms, determine its causes, understand its history, appreciate its human dimension and its connection to one's own personal experience, and appreciate what makes it problematic or complex
- The ability (and determination) to find, gather, and interpret facts, data, and other information relevant to the problem (often involving library, Internet, or field research)
- The ability to imagine alternative solutions to the problem, to see different ways in which the question might be answered and different perspectives for viewing it
- The ability to analyze competing approaches and answers, to construct arguments for and against alternatives, and to choose the best solution in light of values, objectives, and other criteria that you determine and articulate
- The ability to write an effective argument justifying your choice while acknowledging counterarguments

We discuss and develop these skills throughout this text.

Seeing Each Academic Discipline as a Field of Inquiry and Argument

In addition to these general thinking abilities, critical thinking requires what psychologists call "domain-specific" skills. Each academic discipline has its own characteristic ways of approaching knowledge and its own specialized habits of mind. The questions asked by psychologists differ from those asked by historians or anthropologists; the evidence and assumptions used to support arguments in literary analysis differ from those in philosophy or sociology. As illustrations, here are some examples of how different disciplines might pose different questions about hip-hop:

- *Psychology:* To what extent do hip-hop lyrics increase misogynistic or homophobic attitudes in male listeners?
- *History:* What was the role of urban housing projects in the early development of hip-hop?
- *Sociology:* How does the level of an individual's appreciation for rap music vary by ethnicity, class, age, geographic region, and gender?
- *Rhetoric/Composition:* What images of urban life do the lyrics of rap songs portray?
- *Marketing and Management:* How did the white media turn a black, urban phenomenon into corporate profits?
- *Women's Studies:* What influence does hip-hop music have on the self-image of African-American women?
- *Global Studies:* How are other countries adapting hip-hop to their cultures?

As these questions suggest, when you study a new discipline, you must learn not only the knowledge that scholars in that discipline have acquired over the years, but also the processes they used to discover that knowledge. It is useful to think of each academic discipline as a network of conversations in which participants exchange information, respond to each other's questions, and express agreement and disagreement. As each discipline evolves and changes, its central questions evolve also, creating a fascinating, dynamic conversation that defines the discipline. Table 1 provides examples of questions that scholars have debated over the years as well as questions they are addressing today.

TABLE 1	**Scholarly Questions in Different Disciplines**	
Field	Examples of Current Cutting-Edge Questions	Examples of Historical Controversies
Anatomy	What is the effect of a pregnant rat's alcohol ingestion on the development of fetal eye tissue?	In 1628, William Harvey produced a treatise arguing that the heart, through repeated contractions, causes blood to circulate through the body. His views were attacked by followers of the Greek physician Galen.
Literature	To what extent does the structure of a work of literature, for example, Conrad's *Heart of Darkness*, reflect the class and gender bias of the author?	In the 1920s, a group of New Critics argued that the interpretation of a work of literature should be based on close examination of the work's imagery and form and that the intentions of the writer and the biases of the reader were not important. These views held sway in U.S. universities until the late 1960s, when they came increasingly under attack by deconstructionists and other postmoderns, who claimed that author intentions and reader's bias were important parts of the work's meaning.

TABLE I	*continued*	
Field	Examples of Current Cutting-Edge Questions	Examples of Historical Controversies
Rhetoric/ Composition	How does hypertext structure and increased attention to visual images in Web-based writing affect the composing processes of writers?	Prior to the 1970s, college writing courses in the United States were typically organized around the rhetorical modes (description, narration, exemplification, comparison and contrast, and so forth). This approach was criticized by the expressivist school associated with the British composition researcher James Britton. Since the 1980s, composition scholars have proposed various alternative strategies for designing and sequencing assignments.
Psychology	What are the underlying causes of gender identification? To what extent are differences between male and female behavior explainable by nature (genetics, body chemistry) versus nurture (social learning)?	In the early 1900s under the influence of Sigmund Freud, psychoanalytic psychologists began explaining human behavior in terms of unconscious drives and mental processes that stemmed from repressed childhood experiences. Later, psychoanalysts were opposed by behaviorists, who rejected the notion of the unconscious and explained behavior as responses to environmental stimuli.

Using Exploratory Writing to Help You Wallow in Complexity

One of the important discoveries of research in rhetoric and composition is the extent to which experienced writers use writing to generate and discover ideas. Not all writing, in other words, is initially intended as a final product for readers. The very act of writing—often without concern for audience, structure, or correctness—can stimulate the mind to produce ideas. Moreover, when you write down your thoughts, you'll have a record of your thinking that you can draw on later. In this section we describe five strategies of exploratory writing and talking: freewriting; focused freewriting; idea mapping; dialectic talk in person, in class discussions, or in electronic discussion boards; and playing the believing and doubting game.

Freewriting *Freewriting*, also sometimes called *nonstop writing* or *silent, sustained writing*, asks you to record your thinking directly. To freewrite, put pen to paper (or sit at your computer screen, perhaps turning *off* the monitor so that you can't see what you are writing) and write rapidly, *nonstop*, for ten to fifteen minutes at a stretch. Don't worry about grammar, spelling, organization, transitions, or other features of edited writing. The object is to think of as many ideas as possible. Some freewriting looks like stream of consciousness. Some is more organized and focused, although it lacks the logical connections and development that would make it suitable for an audience of strangers.

Many freewriters find that their initial reservoir of ideas runs out in three to five minutes. If this happens, force yourself to keep your fingers moving. If you can't think of anything to say, write, "Relax" over and over (or "This is stupid" or "I'm stuck") until new ideas emerge.

What do you write about? The answer varies according to your situation. Often you will freewrite in response to a question or problem posed by your instructor. Sometimes you will pose your own questions and use freewriting to explore possible answers or simply generate ideas.

The following freewrite, by student writer James Gardiner, formed the starting point for his later exploration of issues connected to online social networks such as MySpace.com and Facebook.com. It was written in response to the prompt "What puzzles you about the new digital age?"

JAMES GARDINER'S INITIAL FREEWRITE

Hmm, what puzzles me about the new digital age? Let's see, let's see, OK I'm puzzled by what life used to be like before there was so much technology. I'm amazed by the growing role that technology has on the lives of people my age. It seems that my generation is spending an increasing amount of time surfing the net, talking on cell phones, listening to MP3 players, playing video games, and watching digital television. I wonder what type of effect these new technologies will have on our society as a whole and if the positive aspects that they bring into the lives of their users outweigh the negative aspects. Are kids happier now that they have all this technology? Hmm. What is the effect of text-messaging rather than talking directly to people? Also what about online social networks like Myspace and Facebook? A lot of my friends have a profile on these sites. I've never joined one of these networks or created a profile. What is my reason for avoiding them? Think. Think. OK, for one thing, I have seen how much time people can spend on these sites and I already feel that I spend enough time checking emails and voicemails. Here's another thing—I am a little hesitant to display personal information about myself on a website that can be viewed by anyone in the world. I feel I am a generally private person and there is something about posting personal details of my life in cyberspace that makes me a little uneasy. As these online social networks increase in popularity and membership, I am puzzled by how my generation will be affected by them. Although people use the sites to communicate with one another, they are usually (physically) alone at their computer. I wonder how this new type of online communication will affect other forms of interpersonal communication skills in the "real world." I also question whether young people should be encouraged to limit their time on these networks and what specifically they should use these sites for. [out of time]

Note how this freewrite rambles, moving associatively from one topic or question to the next. Freewrites often have this kind of loose, associative structure. The value of such freewrites is that they help writers discover areas of interest or rudimentary beginnings of ideas. When you read back over one of your freewrites, try to find places that seem worth pursuing. Freewriters call these places "hot spots," "centers of interest," "centers of gravity," or simply "nuggets" or "seeds." Because we believe this technique is of great value to writers, we suggest that you use it to generate ideas for class discussions and essays.

Focused Freewriting Freewriting, as we have just described it, can be quick and associational, like brainstorming aloud on paper. Focused freewriting, in contrast, is less associational and aimed more at developing a line of thought. You wrestle with a specific problem or question, trying to think and write your way into its complexity and multiple points of view. Because the writing is still informal, with the emphasis on your ideas and not on making your writing grammatically or stylistically polished, you don't have to worry about spelling, punctuation, grammar, or organizational structure. Your purpose is to deepen and extend your thinking on the problem. Some instructors will create prompts or give you specific questions to ponder, and they may call this kind of exploratory writing "focused freewriting," "learning log responses," "writer's notebook entries," or "thinking pieces."

Idea Mapping Another good technique for exploring ideas is *idea mapping*, a more visual method than freewriting. To make an idea map, draw a circle in the center of a page and write down your broad topic area (or a triggering question or your thesis) inside the circle. Then record your ideas on branches and subbranches that extend out from the center circle. As long as you pursue one train of thought, keep recording your ideas on subbranches off the main branch. But as soon as that chain of ideas runs dry, go back and start a new branch.

Often your thoughts will jump back and forth between one branch and another. This technique will help you see them as part of an emerging design rather than as strings of unrelated ideas. Additionally, idea mapping establishes at an early stage a sense of hierarchy in your ideas. If you enter an idea on a subbranch, you can see that you are more fully developing a previous idea. If you return to the hub and start a new branch, you can see that you are beginning a new train of thought.

An idea map usually records more ideas than a freewrite, but the ideas are not as fully developed. Writers who practice both techniques report that they can vary the kinds of ideas they generate depending on which technique they choose. Figure 1 shows a student's idea map made while he was exploring issues related to the grading system.

Dialectic Talk Another effective way to explore the complexity of a topic is through face-to-face discussions with others, whether in class, over coffee in the student union, or late at night in bull sessions. Not all discussions are productive; some are too superficial and scattered, others too heated. Good ones are *dialectic*—participants with differing views on a topic try to understand each other and resolve their differences by examining contradictions in each person's position. The key to dialectic conversation is careful listening, which is made possible by an openness to each other's views. A dialectic discussion differs from

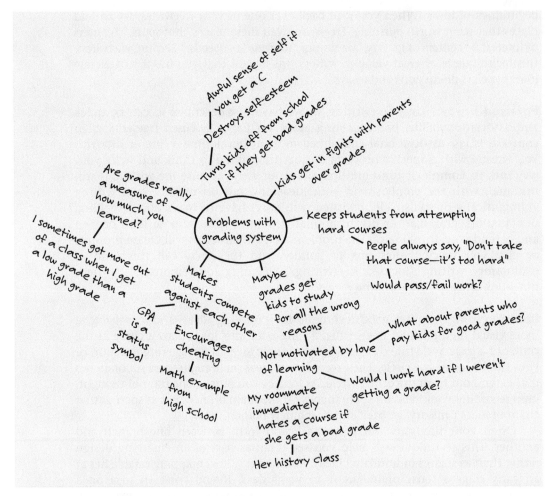

FIGURE 1 Idea Map on Problems with the Grading System

a talk show shouting match or a pro/con debate in which proponents of opposing positions, their views set in stone, attempt to win the argument. In a dialectic discussion, participants assume that each position has strengths and weaknesses and that even the strongest position contains inconsistencies, which should be exposed and examined. When dialectic conversation works well, participants scrutinize their own positions more critically and deeply, and often alter their views. True dialectic conversation implies growth and change, not a hardening of positions.

Dialectic discussion can also take place in electronic discussion boards, chat rooms, blogs, or other digital sites for informal exchange of ideas. If your goal is to generate ideas, your stance should be the exact opposite of the flamer's stance. A flamer's intention is to use brute rhetorical power (sometimes mindlessly obscene or mean, sometimes clever and humorous) to humiliate another writer and shut off further discussion. In contrast, the dialectician's goal is to listen respectfully to other ideas, to test new ways of thinking, to modify ideas in the face of other views, and to see an issue as fully and complexly as possible. If you go on to a discussion board to learn and change, rather than to defend your own position and shut off other views, you will be surprised at how powerful this medium can be.

Playing the Believing and Doubting Game One of the best ways to explore a question is to play what writing theorist Peter Elbow calls the "believing and doubting game." This game helps you appreciate the power of alternative arguments and points of view by urging you to formulate and explore alternative positions. To play the game, you imagine a possible answer to a problematic question and then systematically try first to believe that answer and then to doubt it. The game stimulates your critical thinking, helping you wallow in complexity and resist early closure.

When you play the believing side of this game, you try to become sympathetic to an idea or point of view. You listen carefully to it, opening yourself to the possibility that it is true. You try to appreciate why the idea has force for so many people; you try to accept it by discovering as many reasons as you can for believing it. It is easy to play the believing game with ideas you already believe in, but the game becomes more difficult, sometimes even frightening and dangerous, when you try believing ideas that seem untrue or disturbing.

The doubting game is the opposite of the believing game. It calls for you to be judgmental and critical, to find fault with an idea rather than to accept it. When you doubt a new idea, you try your best to falsify it, to find counterexamples that disprove it, to find flaws in its logic. Again, it is easy to play the doubting game with ideas you don't like, but it, too, can be threatening when you try to doubt ideas that are dear to your heart or central to your own worldview.

Here is how one student played the believing and doubting game with the following assertion from professional writer Paul Theroux that emphasizing sports is harmful to boys.

> Just as high school basketball teaches you how to be a poor loser, the manly attitude towards sports seems to be little more than a recipe for creating bad marriages, social misfits, moral degenerates, sadists, latent rapists and just plain louts. I regard high school sports as a drug far worse than marijuana.

Believing and Doubting Paul Theroux's Negative View of Sports

Believe

1   Although I am a woman I have a hard time believing this because I was a high school basketball player and believe high school sports are *very* important. But here goes. I will try to believe this statement even though I hate it. Let's see. It would seem that I wouldn't have much first-hand experience with how society turns boys

(continued)

into men. I do see though that Theroux is right about some major problems. Through my observations, I've seen many young boys go through humiliating experiences with sports that have left them scarred. For example, a 7-year-old boy, Matt, isn't very athletic and when kids in our neighborhood choose teams, they usually choose girls before they choose Matt. I wonder if he sees himself as a sissy and what this does to him? I have also experienced some first-hand adverse effects of society's methods of turning boys into men. In our family, my dad spent much of his time playing football, basketball, and baseball with my brother. I've loved sports since I was very young so I was eager to play. In order to play with them, I had to play like a boy. Being told you threw or played like a girl was the worst possible insult you could receive. The phrase, "be tough" was something I heard repeatedly while I was growing up. Whenever I got hurt, my dad would say, "Be tough." It didn't matter how badly I was hurt, I always heard the same message. Today, I think, I have a very, very difficult time opening up and letting people get to know me, because for so long I was taught to keep everything inside. Maybe sports does have some bad effects.

Doubt

2   I am glad I get to doubt this too because I have been really mad at all the sports bashing that has been going on in class. I think much of what Theroux says is just a crock. I know that the statement "sports builds character" is a cliché, but I really believe it. It seems to me that the people who lash out at sports clichés are those who never experienced these aspects of athletics and therefore don't understand them. No one can tell me that sports didn't contribute to some of my best and most meaningful friendships and growing experiences. I am convinced that I am a better person because through sports I have had to deal with failure, defeat, frustration, sacrificing individual desires for the benefit of the team, and so on. After my last high school basketball game when after many years of mind games, of hating my coach one minute and the next having deep respect for him, of big games lost on my mistakes, of hours spent alone in the gym, of wondering if the end justifies the means, my coach put his arm around me and told me he was proud. Everything, all the pain, frustration, anxiety, fear, and sacrifice of the past years seemed so worthwhile. You might try to tell me that this story is hackneyed and trite, but I won't listen because it is a part of me, and some thing you will never be able to damage or take away. I think athletes share a special bond. They know what it is like to go through the physical pain of practice time and again. They understand the wide variety of emotions felt (but rarely expressed). They also know what a big role the friendships of teammates and coaches play in an athlete's life.

We admire this writer a great deal—both for the passion with which she defends sports in her doubting section and for the courage of walking in a sports basher's shoes in the believing section. This exercise clearly engaged and stretched her thinking.

Using Exploratory Writing and Talking to Generate Ideas

Background: In our discussion of problem posing, we explain two main ways that you can become gripped by a problem: (1) You can become engaged by a question or issue that is already "out there"—that is, already being examined or debated in some academic or civic community; or (2) you can pose your own question based on your observation of a puzzling phenomenon or artifact. Now in Concept 1, we have shown how exploratory writing and talking can help you learn to wallow in complexity. For this exercise we give you for analysis a poem by e. e. cummings and a pair of historical graphs on life expectancy and causes of death in the twentieth century.

next to of course god america i

"next to of course god america i
love you land of the pilgrims' and so forth oh
say can you see by the dawn's early my
country 'tis of centuries come and go

and are no more what of it we should worry
in every language even deafanddumb
thy sons acclaim your glorious name by gorry
by jingo by gee by gosh by gum
why talk of beauty what could be more beautiful than these heroic happy dead
who rushed like lions to the roaring slaughter
they did not stop to think they died instead
then shall the voice of liberty be mute?"

He spoke. And drank rapidly a glass of water

—*e. e. cummings*

1. *Generating questions using freewriting and discussion*
   Individual task: Read e. e. cummings' poem three or four times, trying to make as much sense of it as you can. Then freewrite for five minutes in response to this prompt: *What do you find puzzling or thought provoking about this poem?* Let the ideas flow through your fingers. You are trying to identify aspects of the poem that you personally find puzzling or thought provoking while also trying to recall memories of conversations already "out there" about issues raised in the poem. While freewriting, you can also explore how you might try to "answer" some of these questions.
   Small-group or whole-class task: Share some of the questions or ideas raised in your freewrites and see how such "dialectic conversation" inspires more ideas.

(continued)

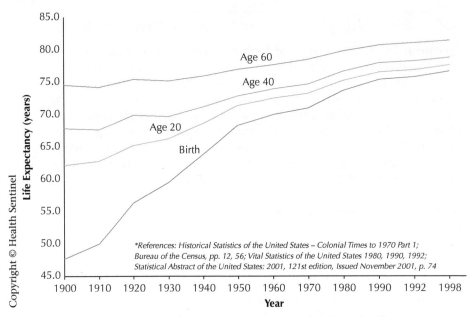

FIGURE 2 U.S. Life Expectancy at Birth, Age 20, Age 40, and Age 60, 1900–1998

2. *Generating questions using idea mapping and discussion*
Repeat the same process, but this time look at the graphs in Figures 2 and 3, and use idea mapping rather than freewriting. Address the question, *What do you find puzzling or thought provoking in these graphs about changes in life expectancy and causes of death in the twentieth century?* On spokes coming out from the center of the idea map, write some questions or ideas raised by

FIGURE 3 U.S. Death Rates for Selected Causes, 1900–2000

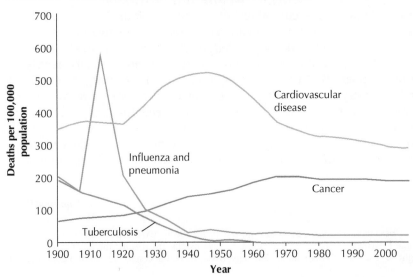

the graphs. Then pursue ideas from each of these spokes so that you begin making a branching map of thoughts. Then share your maps with classmates, using them to spark problem-centered conversations. Finally, discuss which technique works better for you, freewriting or idea mapping. How are they similar or different in the way they stimulate thinking?

3. ***Using freewriting or idea mapping to move from topics to problems***
Another valuable use of exploratory writing and talking is to turn broad topic areas such as "poverty," "music," "globalization," "climate change," "animal rights," or "food" into problematic questions that invite alternative points of view and opportunities for analysis or argument. Using freewriting or idea mapping, start with a broad topic area (either something that interests you or something that your instructor assigns) and explore it in search of questions or problems. Try to recall all the conversations about this topic that you have heard where people expressed confusion or disagreement. Also think of puzzling questions that might emerge from your own personal experiences with the topic area. Your goal is to find a question that interests you and eventually to discover a thesis that gives you an entry into the conversation.

CONCEPT 2 A strong thesis statement surprises readers with something new or challenging.

The strategies for exploring ideas that we offered in the previous section can prepare you to move from posing problems to proposing your own solutions. Your answer to your subject-matter question becomes your **thesis statement**. In this section we show that a good thesis surprises its readers either by bringing something new to the reader or by pushing against other possible ways to answer the writer's question.

Thus a strong thesis usually contains an element of uncertainty, risk, or challenge. A strong thesis implies a naysayer who could disagree with you. According to composition theorist Peter Elbow, a thesis has "got to stick its neck out, not just hedge or wander. [It is] something that can be quarreled with." Elbow's sticking-its-neck-out metaphor is a good one, but we prefer to say that a strong thesis *surprises* the reader with a new, unexpected, different, or challenging view of the writer's topic. By surprise, we intend to connote, first of all, freshness or newness for the reader. Many kinds of closed-form prose don't have a sharply contestable thesis of the sticking-its-neck-out kind highlighted by Elbow. A geology report, for example, may provide readers with desired information about rock strata in an exposed cliff, or a Web page for diabetics may explain how to coordinate meals and insulin injections during a plane trip across time zones. In these cases, the information is surprising because it brings something new and significant to intended readers.

In other kinds of closed-form prose, especially academic or civic prose addressing a problematic question or a disputed issue, surprise requires an argumentative, risky, or contestable thesis. In these cases also, surprise is not inherent in the material but in the intended readers' reception; it comes from the writer's providing an adequate or appropriate response to the readers' presumed question or problem.

In this section, we present two ways of creating a surprising thesis: (1) trying to change your reader's view of your subject; and (2) giving your thesis tension.

Trying to Change Your Reader's View of Your Subject

To change your reader's view of your subject, you must first imagine how the reader would view the subject *before* reading your essay. Then you can articulate how you aim to change that view. A useful exercise is to write out the "before" and "after" views of your imagined readers:

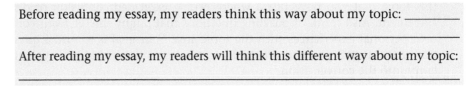

Before reading my essay, my readers think this way about my topic: _____

After reading my essay, my readers will think this different way about my topic:

You can change your reader's view of a subject in several ways.* First, you can enlarge it. Writing that enlarges a view is primarily informational; it provides new ideas and data to add to a reader's store of knowledge about the subject. For example, suppose you are interested in the problem of storing nuclear waste (a highly controversial issue in the United States) and decide to investigate how Japan stores radioactive waste from its nuclear power plants. You could report your findings on this problem in an informative research paper. (Before reading my paper, readers would be uncertain how Japan stores nuclear waste. After reading my paper, my readers would understand the Japanese methods, possibly helping us better understand our options in the United States.)

Second, you can clarify your reader's view of something that was previously fuzzy, tentative, or uncertain. Writing of this kind often explains, analyzes, or interprets. This is the kind of writing you do when analyzing a short story, a painting, an historical document, a set of economic data, or other puzzling phenomena or when speculating on the causes, consequences, purpose, or function of something. Suppose, for example, that you are analyzing the persuasive strategies used in various clothing ads. You are intrigued by a jeans ad that you "read" differently from your classmates. (Before reading my paper, my readers will think that this jeans ad reveals a liberated woman, but after reading my paper they will see that the ad fulfills traditional gender stereotypes.)

Another kind of change occurs when an essay actually restructures a reader's whole view of a subject. Such essays persuade readers to change their minds or make decisions. For example, engineer David Rockwood, in his letter to the editor, wants to change readers' views about

*Our discussion of how writing changes a reader's view of the world is indebted to Richard Young, Alton Becker, and Kenneth Pike, *Rhetoric: Discovery and Change* (New York: Harcourt Brace & Company, 1971).

wind power. (Before reading my letter, readers will believe that wind-generated electricity can solve our energy crisis, but after reading my letter they will see that the hope of wind power is a pipe dream.)

Surprise, then, is the measure of change an essay brings about in a reader. Of course, to bring about such change requires more than just a surprising thesis; the essay itself must persuade the reader that the thesis is sound as well as novel. Later in this chapter (Concept 4), we talk about how writers support a thesis through a network of points and particulars.

Giving Your Thesis Tension through "Surprising Reversal"

Another element of a surprising thesis is tension. By *tension* we mean the reader's sensation of being pulled away from familiar ideas toward new, unfamiliar ones. A strategy for creating this tension—a strategy we call "surprising reversal"—is to contrast your surprising answer to a question with your targeted audience's common answer, creating tension between your own thesis and one or more alternative views. Its basic template is as follows:

> *"Many people believe X (common view), but I am going to show Y (new, surprising view)."*

The concept of surprising reversal spurs the writer to go beyond the commonplace to change the reader's view of a topic.

One of the best ways to employ this strategy is to begin your thesis statement with an "although" clause that summarizes the reader's "before" view or the counterclaim that your essay opposes; the main clause states the surprising view or position that your essay will support. You may choose to omit the *although* clause from your actual essay, but formulating it first will help you achieve focus and surprise in your thesis. The examples that follow illustrate the kinds of tension we have been discussing and show why tension is a key requirement for a good thesis.

Question	What effect has the cell phone had on our culture?
Thesis without Tension	The invention of the cell phone has brought many advantages to our culture.
Thesis with Tension	Although the cell phone has brought many advantages to our culture, it may also have contributed to an increase in risky behavior among boaters and hikers.
Question	Do reservations serve a useful role in contemporary Native American culture?
Thesis without Tension	Reservations have good points and bad points.
Thesis with Tension	Although my friend Wilson Real Bird believes that reservations are necessary for Native Americans to preserve their heritage, the continuation of reservations actually degrades Native American culture.

In the first example, the thesis without tension (cell phones have brought advantages to our culture) is a truism with which everyone would agree and hence lacks surprise. The thesis with tension places this truism (the reader's "before" view) in an *although* clause and goes on to make a surprising or contestable assertion. The idea that the cell phone contributes to risky behavior among outdoor enthusiasts alters our initial, complacent view of the cell phone and gives us new ideas to think about.

In the second example, the thesis without tension may not at first seem tensionless because the writer sets up an opposition between good and bad points. But *almost anything* has good and bad points, so the opposition is not meaningful, and the thesis offers no element of surprise. Substitute virtually any other social institution (marriage, the postal service, the military, prisons), and the statement that it has good and bad points would be equally true. The thesis with tension, in contrast, is risky. It commits the writer to argue that reservations have degraded Native American culture and to oppose the counterthesis that reservations are needed to *preserve* Native American culture. The reader now feels genuine tension between two opposing views.

Tension, then, is a component of surprise. The writer's goal is to surprise the reader in some way, thereby bringing about some kind of change in the reader's view. As you are wallowing in complexity about your subject-matter problem, try the following strategies for bringing something new, surprising, or challenging to your targeted readers:

Strategies for Creating a Thesis with Tension or Surprise

How You Became Gripped with a Problem	Example of a Problem	Your Strategy While You "Wallow in Complexity"	Possible Thesis with Tension or Surprise
The problem is already "out there." *(You enter a conversation already in progress)*			
You don't know where you stand on an issue.	Should health care be rationed?	Look at all sides of the issue, including all the available data, to determine where you stand based on your own examined values.	Although rationing health care at first seems inhumane, it may be the only ethical way to provide affordable health care to all citizens.
You do know where you stand on an issue. *[You need to move from an opinion to an earned thesis.]*	Shanita says that we should build more nuclear power plants to combat global warming, but I say nuclear power is too dangerous.	Research the strengths of the opposing views and the weaknesses of your own view. (*Note: You may change your mind.*)	Although nuclear power poses danger from storage of waste or possible meltdown, the benefits of reducing greenhouse gases and cutting coal pollution outweigh the dangers.

How You Became Gripped with a Problem	Example of a Problem	Your Strategy While You "Wallow in Complexity"	Possible Thesis with Tension or Surprise
Someone gives you a question that you can't yet answer.	Your boss asks you whether the company should enact the proposed marketing plan.	Do the research, critical thinking, and analysis needed to propose the "best solution" to the boss's question.	The marketing team's proposal, despite its creative use of advertising, is too risky to undertake at this time.
You pose the problem yourself. *(You initiate the conversation)*			
You see something puzzling in a natural phenomenon or a cultural activity or artifact.	Why does Merton call rain "meaningless"?	Through critical thinking and research, try to figure out a plausible "best solution" to your question.	Merton's puzzling use of "meaningless" in reference to the rain can perhaps be explained by his admiration for Buddhism.
You discover something inconsistent or contradictory in your own view of the world.	I agree with Merton's argument against consumerism, but I really want a large plasma TV. Is consumerism really bad? Am I a materialist?	Reflect on your own values and beliefs; try to achieve a consistent stand with regard to enduring social or ethical issues.	Although Merton makes me consider the potential shallowness of my desire for a huge plasma TV, I don't think I'm necessarily a materialist.

Developing Thesis Statements Out of Questions

FOR WRITING AND DISCUSSION

It is difficult to create thesis statements on the spot because a writer's thesis grows out of an exploratory struggle with a problem. However, in response to a question one can often propose a claim and treat it as a tentative thesis statement for testing. You may have already done some exploratory talking and writing in response to a problem provided by your instructor or about problems supplied so far in this text: the e. e. cummings poem or the graphs in Figures 2 and 3. Working individually, spend ten minutes considering possible thesis statements that you might make in response to one or more of the questions you have already been thinking about. (Remember that these are tentative thesis statements, done for practice, that you might abandon after doing research or more critical thinking.) Identify a possible audience for your thesis statement,

(continued)

and try to explain why this audience would find your thesis new, surprising, or challenging. Then, working in small groups or as a whole class, share your thesis statements. Select one or two thesis statements that your small group or class thinks are particularly effective and brainstorm the kinds of evidence that would be required to support the thesis.

Alternatively, your instructor might use the following exercises:

1. To what extent should the public support genetically modified foods? (possible audiences: readers of health food magazines; general public concerned about food choices; investors in companies that produce genetically modified seeds)
2. Should the government mandate more fuel-efficient cars? If so, how? (possible audiences: SUV owners; conservative legislators generally in favor of free markets; investors in the automobile industry)

Here is an example:

Problematic question: What can cities do to prevent traffic congestion?

One possible thesis: Although many people think that building light-rail systems won't get people out of their cars, new light-rail systems in many cities have attracted new riders and alleviated traffic problems.

Intended audience: Residents of cities concerned about traffic congestion but skeptical about light-rail

Kinds of evidence needed to support thesis: Examples of cities with successful light-rail systems; evidence that many riders switched from driving cars; evidence that light-rail alleviated traffic problems

CONCEPT 3 In closed-form prose, a typical introduction starts with the problem, not the thesis.

So far we've talked about the importance of finding a good problem and exploring its complexity. Eventually, however, your goal is to contribute to the conversation by stating and supporting your own thesis. First, however, readers need to know what problem your thesis addresses. One of the principles of closed-form prose—which we describe in detail later in this text—is that readers' need to attach new information to old information. In other words, before they can understand an answer, they must first understand the question. One function of the introduction in most closed-form prose is to show your readers what the problem is and to motivate their interest in it. This introduction can be long or short depending on whether your targeted audience is already familiar with the problem or already cares about it. Once readers know what problem you intend to address, they are prepared for your thesis statement.

A Protypical Introduction

To show you how academic writers typically begin by asking a question, we will illustrate with several "prototype" examples.* In the following introduction by student writer Jackie Wyngaard, note how the author first presents a question and then moves, at the end of the introduction, to her thesis statement.

EMP: MUSIC HISTORY OR MUSIC TRIVIA?

Along with other college students new to Seattle, I wanted to see what cultural opportunities the area offers. I especially wanted to see billionaire Paul Allen's controversial Experience Music Project (known as EMP), a huge, bizarre, shiny, multicolored structure that is supposed to resemble a smashed guitar. Brochures say that EMP celebrates the creativity of American popular music, but it has prompted heated discussions among architects, Seattle residents, museum goers, and music lovers, who have questioned its commercialism and the real value of its exhibits. My sister recommended this museum to me because she knows I am a big music lover and a rock and roll fan. Also, as an active choir member since the sixth grade, I have always been intrigued by the history of music. I went to EMP expecting to learn more about music history from exhibits that showed a range of popular musical styles, that traced historical connections and influences, and that enjoyably conveyed useful information. However, as a museum of rock history, EMP is a disappointing failure.

Provides background on EMP

Begins to turn topic area (EMP) into a problem by showing that it has been controversial

Establishes her own purposes and expectations: She expects EMP to teach her about music history.

Implies her question: Is EMP a good place to learn about the history of rock music?

States her thesis

Features of a Good Introduction

Wyngaard's introduction, which shares the structure of many professionally written closed-form introductions, includes the following prototypical features:

- **Background needed to identify the topic area and provide context.** Readers need early on to know the specific topic area of the paper they are about to read—in this case a paper about the Experience Music Project in Seattle rather than, say, shower mold or medieval queenship. Sometimes writers also use a startling scene or statistic as an "attention grabber" as part of the opening background.
- **A direct or implied question.** As soon as possible, readers need to sense the problem, question, or issue that the writer will examine. In this case, Jackie Wyngaard implies her question: Will my expectations about EMP be fulfilled? Note that her question appears directly in her title: "EMP: Music History [her expectations] or Music Trivia [her claim]?"
- **An indication of how the question invites tension or is otherwise problematic.** An effective question or problem supposes the possibility of

---

*A *prototype* is the most typical or generic instance of a class and doesn't constitute a value judgment. For example, a prototype bird might be a robin or blackbird (rather than an ostrich, chicken, hummingbird, or pelican) because these birds seem to exhibit the most typical features of "birdiness." Likewise, a prototype dog would be a medium-sized mutt rather than a St. Bernard or toy poodle.

alternative points of view, different perspectives in tension with each other. In many cases, a writer summarizes alternative arguments sparked by the question or summarizes a particular point of view that the writer intends to oppose. Because Jackie initiates the conversation about EMP's status as a rock museum, she evokes this tension by contrasting her initial expectations with her later disappointment.

- **_An indication of how the question is significant or worth examining._** In order to avoid a "so what?" response, writers must motivate readers' interest in the question. Somebody might say, "Who cares about EMP anyway?" Jackie's strategy is to imagine an audience who shares her interest in rock and roll music and her love of music history. These are the readers who will care whether it is worth big bucks to spend an afternoon in EMP. Readers who identify with Jackie's enthusiasm for rock history will share her engagement with the question. Other strategies for showing a question's significance include pointing to the good or bad consequences of a particular way of answering the question ("If we could understand why the crime rate in New York City dropped dramatically in the 1990s, we could apply these same principles to other cities today") or by showing how an answer to a smaller question might help readers begin to answer a larger question ("If we could better understand the role of the witches in _Macbeth_, we would better understand the ways gender was constructed in Shakespeare's time").

- **_The writer's thesis, which brings something new to the audience._** Once readers are hooked on the writer's question, they are ready for the writer's answer. In this case, Jackie makes the claim that EMP fails as a rock history museum.

- **_[optional] A purpose statement ("The purpose of this paper is ... ") along with a mapping statement forecasting the content and shape of the rest of the article ("First I discuss X, then Y, and finally Z")._** Because her paper is short, Jackie ends the introduction with her thesis. An alternative strategy, common among longer closed-form essays, is to include a purpose statement along with a forecasting passage that maps what is coming. This strategy is used by student writer James Gardiner at the end of his introduction to a paper about the consequences of using online social networks like Facebook. Note how he poses his problematic question and then moves to a purpose statement and mapping statement.

States directly the question his paper will address

Purpose statement

Maps out the argument's structure while motivating readers' interest in question

... While "Facebook Trance" might describe only an occasional and therefore harmless phenomenon, it gives rise to an important question: What are the possible negative consequences of OSNs [online social networks]? What should youthful users be watchful for and guard against? The purpose of this paper is to identify the possible harms of OSNs. I will suggest that overuse of OSNs can be a contributing factor to a decline in grades as well as to other problems such as a superficial view of relationships, an increase in narcissism, and possible future embarrassment.

For a fuller look at the ways a writer can introduce readers to the problem he or she is addressing, consider the following strategies chart:

Strategies for Introducing Your Problem to Targeted Readers	
Situation	**Strategies**
The problem is already "out there" *(You enter a conversation already in progress)*	*If readers are already familiar with the problem and care about it, use a mix of the following strategies:* • Provide background where needed • State the problem directly (often as a grammatical question ending with a question mark) or imply the question through context • Summarize the different points of view on the problem (or) • Summarize the particular point of view you intend to "push against" *If readers are less familiar with the problem:* • Summarize controversy in more depth • Explain why the problem is problematic (show why there are no easy answers to the problem; point out weaknesses in proposed answers; show the history of attempts to solve the problem) *If readers don't already care about the problem:* • Show why the problem is important (answer the "so what?" question) • Show how solving the problem will bring good consequences (or) • Show how answering the question will help us begin to answer a larger question

You pose the problem yourself *(You initiate the conversation)*	• Describe the artifact or phenomenon you are writing about and point to the specific features where you see an inconsistency, gap, or puzzle
	• State the problem directly (often as a grammatical question ending with a question mark)
	• Show how there isn't any immediate, easy answer to the question or problem or how the question can invite controversy/discussion; you can often employ a template such as the following:
	  • Some people might think..., but closer observation shows that....
	  • At first I thought..., but later I saw that....
	  • Part of me thinks..., but another part of me thinks that....
	  • I expected ... ; but what I actually found was....
	• Show why the problem is important (answer the "so what?" question)
	• Show how solving the problem will bring good consequences (or)
	• Show how answering this question will help us begin to answer a larger question

Examining Problem-Thesis Structure of Introductions

Background: Good writing can vary along a continuum from closed to open forms. Although academic essays are typically closed form, they can vary significantly along the continuum. Likewise, the introductions to closed-form essays don't always follow the prototypical structure we just described. But many do. In this exercise, we invite you to analyze additional introductions.

Task: Look at the following introductions. In each case, analyze the extent to which the introduction follows or varies from the prototypical introductions we have described in Concept 3.

1. Paragraphs 1–2 of Ross Taylor's "Paintball: Promoter of Violence or Healthy Fun?"
2. Paragraphs 1–4 of "No to Nukes," a *Los Angeles Times* editorial
3. Paragraphs 1–6 of Shannon King's "How Clean and Green Are Hydrogen Fuel-Cell Cars?"

CONCEPT 4 Thesis statements in closed-form prose are supported hierarchically with points and particulars.

Of course, a surprising thesis is only one aspect of an effective essay. An essay must also persuade the reader that the thesis is believable as well as surprising. Although tabloid newspapers have shocking headlines ("Cloning Produces Three-Headed Sheep"), skepticism quickly replaces surprise when you look inside and find the article's claims unsupported. A strong thesis, then, must both surprise the reader and be supported with convincing particulars.

In fact, the particulars are the flesh and muscle of writing and comprise most of the sentences. In closed-form prose, these particulars are connected clearly to points, and the points precede the particulars. In this section, we explain this principle more fully.

How Points Convert Information to Meaning

When particulars are clearly related to a point, the point gives meaning to the particulars, and the particulars give force and validity to the point. Particulars constitute the evidence, data, details, examples, and subarguments that develop a point and make it convincing. By themselves, particulars are simply information—mere data without meaning.

In the following example, you can see for yourself the difference between information and meaning. Here is a list of information:*

- In almost all species on earth, males are more aggressive than females.
- Male chimpanzees win dominance by brawling.

*The data in this exercise are adapted from Deborah Blum, "The Gender Blur," *Utne Reader* Sept. 1998: 45–48.

- To terrorize rival troops, they kill females and infants.
- The level of aggression among monkeys can be manipulated by adjusting their testosterone levels.
- Among humans, preliminary research suggests that male fetuses are more active in the uterus than female fetuses.
- Little boys play more aggressively than little girls despite parental efforts to teach gentleness to boys and aggression to girls.

To make meaning out of this list of information, the writer needs to state a point—the idea, generalization, or claim—that this information supports. Once the point is stated, a meaningful unit (point with particulars) springs into being:

> Aggression in human males may be a function of biology rather than culture. *Point*
> In almost all species on earth, males are more aggressive than females. Male chimpanzees win dominance by brawling; to terrorize rival troops, they kill females and infants. Researchers have shown that the level of aggression among monkeys can be manipulated by adjusting their testosterone levels. Among humans, preliminary research suggests that male fetuses are more active in the uterus than female fetuses. Also, little boys play more aggressively than little girls despite parental efforts to teach gentleness to boys and aggression to girls.

Particulars

Once the writer states this point, readers familiar with the biology/culture debate about gender differences immediately feel its surprise and tension. This writer believes that biology determines gender identity more than does culture. The writer now uses the details as evidence to support a point.

To appreciate the reader's need for a logical connection between points and particulars, note how readers would get lost if, in the preceding example, the writer included a particular that seemed unrelated to the point ("Males also tend to be taller and heavier than women"—a factual statement, but what does it have to do with aggression?) or if, without explanation, the writer added a particular that seemed to contradict the point ("Fathers play more roughly with baby boys than with baby girls"—another fact, but one that points to culture rather than biology as a determiner of aggression).

Obviously, reasonable people seek some kind of coordination between points and particulars, some sort of weaving back and forth between them. Writing teachers use a number of nearly synonymous terms for expressing this paired relationship: *points/particulars, generalizations/specifics, claims/evidence, ideas/details, interpretations/data, meaning/support.*

How Removing Particulars Creates a Summary

What we have shown, then, is that skilled writers weave back and forth between generalizations and specifics. The generalizations form a network of higher-level and lower-level points that develop the thesis; the particulars (specifics) support each of the points and subpoints in turn. In closed-form prose, the network of points is easily discernible because points are clearly highlighted with transitions, and main points are placed prominently at the heads of paragraphs. (In open-form prose, generalizations are often left unstated, creating gaps where the reader must actively fill in meaning.)

Being able to write summaries and abstracts of articles is an important academic skill.

If you remove most of the particulars from a closed-form essay, leaving only the network of points, you will have written a summary or abstract of the essay. As an example, reread the civil engineer's letter to the editor arguing against the feasibility of wind-generated power. The writer's argument can be summarized in a single sentence:

> Wind-generated power is not a reasonable alternative to other forms of power in the Pacific Northwest because wind power is unreliable, because there are major unsolved problems involved in the design of wind-generation facilities, and because the environmental impact of building thousands of wind towers would be enormous.

What we have done in this summary is remove the particulars, leaving only the high-level points that form the skeleton of the argument. The writer's thesis remains surprising and contains tension, but without the particulars the reader has no idea whether to believe the generalizations or not. The presence of the particulars is thus essential to the success of the argument.

FOR WRITING AND DISCUSSION

Analyzing Supporting Particulars

Compare the civil engineer's original letter with the one-sentence summary just given and then note how the engineer uses specific details to support each point. How do these particulars differ from paragraph to paragraph? How are they chosen to support each point?

How to Use Points and Particulars When You Revise

The lesson to learn here is that in closed-form prose, writers regularly place a point sentence in front of detail sentences. When a writer begins with a point, readers interpret the ensuing particulars not as random data but rather as *evidence* in support of that point. The writer depends on the particulars to make the point credible and persuasive.

This insight may help you understand two of the most common kinds of marginal comments that readers (or teachers) place on writers' early drafts. If your draft has a string of sentences giving data or information unconnected to any stated point, your reader is apt to write in the margin, "What's your point here?" or "Why are you telling me this information?" or "How does this information relate to your thesis?" Conversely, if your draft tries to make a point that isn't developed with particulars, your reader is apt to write marginal comments such as "Evidence?" or "Development?" or "Could you give an example?" or "More details needed."

Don't be put off by these requests; they are a gift. It is common in first drafts for main points to be unstated, buried, or otherwise disconnected from their details and for supporting information to be scattered confusingly throughout the draft or missing entirely. Having to write point sentences obliges you to wrestle with your intended meaning: Just what am I trying to say here? How can I nutshell that in a point? Likewise, having to support your points with particulars causes you to wrestle with the content and shape of your argument: What particulars will make this point convincing? What further research do I need to do to find these particulars?

Chapter Summary

This chapter has introduced you to four concepts that will enable you to think about your subject matter from a rhetorical perspective.

- ***Concept 1: To determine their thesis, writers must often "wallow in complexity."*** What typically initiates the writing process is a problematic question that invites the writer to explore the problem's complexity. To do so, experienced writers often use exploratory techniques such as freewriting, idea mapping, dialectic talk, and the believing and doubting game to generate ideas.
- ***Concept 2: A strong thesis surprises readers with something new or challenging.*** A good thesis tries to change the reader's view of the subject and often creates tension by pushing against alternative views.
- ***Concept 3: In closed-form prose, a typical introduction starts with the problem, not the thesis.*** Readers need to be engaged with the writer's question before they can understand the thesis.
- ***Concept 4: Thesis statements in closed-form prose are supported hierarchically with points and particulars.*** Points give meaning to particulars; particulars make points persuasive. If you remove the particulars from a writer's argument and keep the points, you will have created a summary.

Playing the Believing and Doubting Game

BRIEF WRITING PROJECT

Part 1. The Game. Play the believing and doubting game with one of the assertions listed here (or with another assertion provided by your instructor) by freewriting your believing and doubting responses. Spend ten minutes believing and then ten minutes doubting the assertion, for a total of twenty minutes. When you believe an assertion, you agree, support, illustrate, extend, and apply the idea. When you doubt an assertion, you question, challenge, rebut, and offer counterreasons and counterexamples to the assertion. Note that when students first learn to do exploratory writing, they often run out of ideas quickly and want to stop. But the best ideas often happen when you push through that wall. If you run out of ideas, let your mind follow a tangent. Particularly explore your personal experiences with the subject. Eventually you will get back on track with new ideas.

1. Grades are an effective means of motivating students to do their best work.
2. Facebook is a good way to make new friends.
3. In recent years, advertising has made enormous gains in portraying women as strong, independent, and intelligent.
4. If there is only one kidney available for transplant and two sick persons need it, one in her thirties and one in her sixties, the kidney should go to the younger person.
5. The United States should reinstate the draft.
6. Humans have free will.
7. Fencing at the U.S.–Mexico border is not an effective immigration policy.
8. If students in a large lecture course can listen to a lecture and surf the Web or check e-mail at the same time, then they should be allowed to do so.

Part 2. Reflection. Write a reflective paragraph in which you assess the extent to which the believing and doubting game extended or stretched your thinking. Particularly, answer these questions:

- What was difficult about this writing activity?
- To what extent did it make you take an unfamiliar or uncomfortable stance?
- How can believing and doubting help you wallow in complexity?

 For additional help with writing, reading, and research, go to **www.mycomplab.com.**

THINKING RHETORICALLY ABOUT HOW MESSAGES PERSUADE

A way of seeing is also a way of not seeing.

—Kenneth Burke, Rhetorician

Every time an Indian villager watches the community TV and sees an ad for soap or shampoo, what they notice are not the soap and shampoo but the lifestyle of the people using them, the kind of motorbikes they ride, their dress and their homes.

—Nayan Chanda, Indian-Born Editor of YaleGlobal Online Magazine

In this chapter we expand your understanding of a writer's choices by showing how messages persuade. We'll use the word *message* in its broadest sense to include verbal texts and nonverbal texts such as photographs and paintings or consumer artifacts such as clothing. When you understand how messages achieve their effects, you will be better prepared to analyze and evaluate those messages and to make your own choices about whether to resist them or accede to them.

In this chapter, you will learn three more important rhetorical concepts:

- **CONCEPT 1**   Messages persuade through their angle of vision.
- **CONCEPT 2**   Messages persuade through appeals to *logos*, *ethos*, and *pathos*.
- **CONCEPT 3**   Nonverbal messages persuade through visual strategies that can be analyzed rhetorically.

CONCEPT I Messages persuade through their angle of vision.

One way that messages persuade is through their **angle of vision**, which causes a reader to see a subject from one perspective only—the writer's. Writers create an angle of vision through strategies such as the following:

- Stating point of view directly
- Selecting some details while omitting others
- Choosing words or figures of speech with intended connotations
- Creating emphasis or de-emphasis through sentence structure and organization

The writer's angle of vision—which might also be called a lens, a filter, a perspective, or a point of view—is persuasive because it controls what the reader "sees." Unless readers are rhetorically savvy, they can lose awareness that they are seeing the writer's subject matter through a lens that both reveals and conceals.

A classic illustration of angle of vision is the following thought exercise:

THOUGHT EXERCISE ON ANGLE OF VISION

Suppose you attended a fun party on Saturday night. (You get to choose what constitutes "fun" for you.) Now imagine that two people ask what you did on Saturday night. Person A is a close friend who missed the party. Person B is your parent. How would your descriptions of Saturday night differ?

Clearly there isn't just one way to describe this party. Your description will be influenced by your purpose and audience. You will have to decide:

- What image of myself should I project? (For your friend you might construct yourself as a party animal; for your parent, as a more detached observer.)
- How much emphasis do I give the party? (You might describe the party in detail for your friend while mentioning it only in passing to your parent, emphasizing instead all the homework you did over the weekend.)
- What details should I include or leave out? (Does my parent really need to know that the neighbors called the police?)
- What words should I choose? (The slang you use with your friend might not be appropriate for your parent.)

You'll note that our comments about your rhetorical choices reflect common assumptions about friends and parents. You might actually have a party-loving parent and a geeky friend, in which case your party descriptions would be altered accordingly. In any case, you are in rhetorical control; you choose what your audience "sees" and how they see it.

Recognizing the Angle of Vision in a Text

This thought exercise illustrates a key insight of rhetoric: There is always more than one way to tell a story, and no single way of telling it constitutes the whole truth. By saying that a writer writes from an "angle of vision," we mean that the writer cannot take a godlike stance that allows a universal, unfiltered, totally unbiased or objective way of knowing. Rather, the writer looks at the subject from a certain location, or, to use another metaphor, the writer wears a lens that colors or filters the topic in a certain way. The angle of vision, lens, or filter determines what part of a topic gets "seen" and what remains "unseen," what gets included or excluded, what gets emphasized or de-emphasized, and so forth. It even determines what words get chosen out of an array of options—for example, whether the writer says "panhandler" or "homeless person," "torture" or "enhanced interrogation," "universal health care" or "socialized medicine."

As an illustration of angle of vision, consider the cartoon in Figure 1, which shows different ways that stakeholders "see" sweatshops. For each stakeholder, some aspects of sweatshops surge into view, while other aspects remain unseen or invisible. An alert reader needs to be aware that none of these stakeholders can portray sweatshops in a completely "true" way. Stockholders and corporate leaders emphasize reduced labor costs and enhanced corporate profits and retirement portfolios while de-emphasizing (or omitting entirely) the working conditions in

FIGURE 1 Different Angles of Vision on "Sweatshops"

sweatshops or the plight of American workers whose jobs have been outsourced to developing countries. Consumers enjoy abundant low-cost goods made possible by sweatshops and may not even think about where or how the products are made. Opponents of sweatshops focus on the miserable conditions of sweatshop workers, their low wages, the use of child labor, and the "obscene" profits of corporations. Meanwhile, as the American union worker laments the loss of jobs in the United States, third world workers and their children may welcome sweatshops as a source of income superior to the other harsh alternatives such as scavenging in dumps or prostitution. The multiple angles of vision show how complex the issue of sweatshops is. In fact, most issues are equally complex, and any one view of the issue is controlled by the writer's angle of vision.

To get a hands-on feel for how a writer creates an angle of vision, try doing the following U. R. Riddle activity, which invites you to write a letter of recommendation for a student.

**FOR
WRITING
AND
DISCUSSION**

U. R. Riddle Letter

Background: Suppose that you are a management professor who regularly writes letters of recommendation for former students. One day you receive a letter from a local bank requesting a confidential evaluation of a former student, Uriah Rudy Riddle (U. R. Riddle), who has applied for a job as a management trainee. The bank wants your assessment of Riddle's intelligence, aptitude, dependability, and ability to work with people. You haven't seen U. R. for several years, but you remember him well. Here are the facts and impressions you recall about Riddle:

- Very temperamental student, seemed moody, something of a loner
- Long hair and very sloppy dress—seemed like a misplaced street person; often twitchy and hyperactive
- Absolutely brilliant mind; took lots of liberal arts courses and applied them to business
- Wrote a term paper relating different management styles to modern theories of psychology—the best undergraduate paper you ever received. You gave it an A+ and remember learning a lot from it yourself.
- Had a strong command of language—the paper was very well written
- Good at mathematics; could easily handle all the statistical aspects of the course
- Frequently missed class and once told you that your class was boring
- Didn't show up for the midterm. When he returned to class later, he said only that he had been out of town. You let him make up the midterm, and he got an A.
- Didn't participate in a group project required for your course. He said the other students in his group were idiots.
- You thought at the time that Riddle didn't have a chance of making it in the business world because he had no talent for getting along with people.
- Other professors held similar views of Riddle—brilliant, but rather strange and hard to like; an odd duck.

You are in a dilemma because you want to give Riddle a chance (he's still young and may have had a personality transformation of some sort), but you also don't want to damage your own professional reputation by falsifying your true impressions.

Individual task: Working individually for ten minutes or so, compose a brief letter of recommendation assessing Riddle; use details from the list to support your assessment. Role-play that you have decided to take a gamble with Riddle and give him a chance at this career. Write as strong a recommendation as possible while remaining honest. (To make this exercise more complex, your instructor might ask half the class to role-play a negative angle of vision in which you want to warn the bank against hiring Riddle without hiding his strengths or good points.)

Task for group or whole-class discussion: Working in small groups or as a whole class, share your letters. Then pick representative examples ranging from the most positive to the least positive and discuss how the letters achieve their different rhetorical effects. If your intent is to support Riddle, to what extent does honesty compel you to mention some or all of your negative memories? Is it possible to mention negative items without emphasizing them? How?

Analyzing Angle of Vision

Just as there is more than one way to describe the party you went to on Saturday night or to write about sweatshops, there is more than one way to write a letter of recommendation for U. R. Riddle. The writer's angle of vision determines what is "seen" or "not seen" in a given piece of writing—what gets slanted in a positive or negative direction, what gets highlighted, what gets thrown into the shadows. As rhetorician Kenneth Burke claims in the first epigraph for the chapter, "A way of seeing is also a way of not seeing." Note how the writer controls what the reader "sees." As Riddle's former professor, you might in your mind's eye see Riddle as long-haired and sloppy, but if you don't mention these details in your letter, they remain unseen to the reader. Note too that your own terms "long-haired and sloppy" inter-pret Riddle's appearance through the lens of your own characteristic way of seeing—a way that perhaps values business attire and clean-cut tidiness. Another observer might describe Riddle's appearance quite differently, thus seeing what you don't see.

In an effective piece of writing, the author's angle of vision often works so subtly that unsuspecting readers—unless they learn to think rhetorically—will be drawn into the writer's spell and believe that the writer's prose conveys the "whole picture" of its subject rather than a limited picture filtered through the screen of the writer's perspective.

Contrasting Angles of Vision in Two Texts Consider the differences in what gets seen in the following two descriptions of the Arctic National Wildlife Refuge in Alaska (the ANWR), where proponents of oil exploration are locked in a fierce battle with anti-exploration conservationists. The first passage is from a pro-exploration advocacy group called Arctic Power; the second is from former President Jimmy Carter.

ARCTIC POWER'S DESCRIPTION OF THE ANWR

On the coastal plain [of the ANWR], the Arctic winter lasts for 9 months. It is dark continuously for 56 days in midwinter. Temperatures with the wind chill can reach –110 degrees F. It's not pristine. There are villages, roads, houses, schools, and military installations. It's not a unique Arctic ecosystem. The coastal plain is only a small fraction of the 88,000 square miles that make up the North Slope. The same tundra environment and wildlife can be found throughout the circumpolar Arctic regions. The 1002 Area [the legal term for the plot of coastal plain being contested] is flat. That's why they call it a plain. [...]

Some groups want to make the 1002 Area a wilderness. But a vote for wilderness is a vote against American jobs.

JIMMY CARTER'S DESCRIPTION OF THE ANWR

Rosalynn [Carter's wife] and I always look for opportunities to visit parks and wildlife areas in our travels. But nothing matches the spectacle of wildlife we found on the coastal plain of America's Arctic National Wildlife Refuge in Alaska. To the north lay the Arctic Ocean; to the south rolling foothills rose toward the glaciated peaks of the Brooks Range. At our feet was a mat of low tundra plant life, bursting with new growth, perched atop the permafrost.

As we watched, 80,000 caribou surged across the vast expanse around us. Called by instinct older than history, this Porcupine (River) caribou herd was in the midst of its annual migration. To witness this vast sea of caribou in an uncorrupted wilderness home, and the wolves, ptarmigan, grizzlies, polar bears, musk oxen and millions of migratory birds, was a profoundly humbling experience. We were reminded of our human dependence on the natural world.

Sadly, we were also forced to imagine what we might see if the caribou were replaced by smoke-belching oil rigs, highways and a pipeline that would destroy forever the plain's delicate and precious ecosystem.

How Angle of Vision Persuades To understand more clearly how angle of vision persuades, you can analyze the language strategies at work. Some of these strategies—which writers employ consciously or unconsciously to achieve their intended effects—are described in the following strategies chart.

Strategies for Constructing an Angle of Vision

Strategy	ANWR Example	U. R. Riddle Example
State your intention directly.	• Earlier passages directly state Arctic Powers' pro-drilling and Carter's anti-drilling stances.	• You might say "Riddle would make an excellent manager" or "Riddle doesn't have the personality to be a bank manager."
Select details that support your intentions; omit or de-emphasize others.	• Arctic Power writer (AP) "sees" the cold, barren darkness of the ANWR; Carter sees the beauty.	• A positive view of Riddle would select and emphasize Riddle's good traits and de-emphasize or omit his bad ones.

Jimmy Carter, "Make this national treasure a national monument." The New York Times, December 28, 2000, p. A23. Copyright © 2000, The New York Times. Reprinted by permission of the New York Times Company.

Strategy	ANWR Example	U. R. Riddle Example
	• AP spotlights the people who live on the coastal plain while making the animals invisible; Carter spotlights the caribou while omitting the people. • To AP, drilling means jobs; to Carter it means destructive oil rigs.	• A negative view would take opposite the tack.
Choose words that frame your subject in the desired way or have desired connotations.	• AP frames the ANWR as the dreary "1002 Area"; Carter frames it as a "spectacle of wildlife," a unique "delicate and precious ecosystem." • Arctic Power uses words with negative connotations ("wind chill"); Carter uses words connoting life and growth ("a mat of low tundra plant life").	• "Riddle is an independent thinker who doesn't follow the crowd" (frames him positively in value system that favors individualism). • "Riddle is a loner who thinks egocentrically" (frames him negatively in value system favoring consensus and social skills). • You could say, "Riddle is forthright" or "Riddle is rude"—positive versus negative connotations.
Use figurative language (metaphors, similes, and analogies) that conveys your intended effect.	• AP avoids figurative language, claiming objective presentation of facts. • Carter uses positive metaphors to convey ANWR's vitality (tundra "bursting with new growth") and negative metaphors for drilling ("smoke-belching oil rigs").	• To suggest that Riddle has outgrown his alienating behavior, you could say, "Riddle is a social late bloomer." • To recommend against hiring Riddle while still being positive, you could say, "Riddle's independent spirit would feel caged in by the routine of a bank."
Use sentence structure to emphasize and de-emphasize your ideas. (*Emphasize an idea by placing it at the end of a long sentence, in a short sentence, or in a main clause.*)	• AP uses short sentences to emphasize main points: "It's not pristine." "It's not a unique ecosystem." "That's why they call it a plain." • Carter uses longer sentences for description, with an occasional short sentence to make a point: "We were reminded of our human dependence on the natural world."	Consider the difference between the following: • "Although Riddle had problems relating to other students, he is a brilliant thinker." • "Although Riddle is a brilliant thinker, he had problems relating to other students in the class."

CONCEPT 2 Messages persuade through appeals to *logos*, *ethos*, and *pathos*.

Another way to think about the persuasive power of texts is to examine the strategies writers or speakers use to sway their audiences toward a certain position on an issue. To win people's consideration of their ideas, writers or speakers can appeal to what the classical philosopher Aristotle called *logos*, *ethos*, and *pathos*. Developing the habit of examining how these appeals are functioning in texts and being able to employ these appeals in your own writing will enhance your ability to read and write rhetorically. Let's look briefly at each:

- *Logos* **is the appeal to reason.** It refers to the quality of the message itself—to its internal consistency, to its clarity in asserting a thesis or point, and to the quality of reasons and evidence used to support the point.
- *Ethos* **is the appeal to the character of the speaker/writer.** It refers to the speaker/writer's trustworthiness and credibility. One can often increase one's *ethos* in a message by being knowledgeable about the issue, by appearing thoughtful and fair, by listening well, and by being respectful of alternative points of view. A writer's accuracy and thoroughness in crediting sources and professionalism in caring about the format, grammar, and neat appearance of a document are part of the appeal to *ethos*.
- *Pathos* **is the appeal to the sympathies, values, beliefs, and emotions of the audience.** Appeals to *pathos* can be made in many ways. *Pathos* can often be enhanced through evocative visual images, frequently used in Web sites, posters, and magazine or newspaper articles. In written texts, the same effects can be created through vivid examples and details, through connotative language, and through empathy with the audience's beliefs and values.

To see how these three appeals are interrelated, you can visualize a triangle with points labeled *Message, Audience,* and *Writer* or *Speaker*. Rhetoricians study how effective communicators consider all three points of this *rhetorical triangle*. (See Figure 2.)

We encourage you to ask questions about the appeals to *logos*, *ethos*, and *pathos* every time you examine a text. For example, is the appeal to *logos* weakened by the writer's use of scanty and questionable evidence? Has the writer made a powerful appeal to *ethos* by documenting her sources and showing that she is an authority on the issue? Has the writer relied too heavily on appeals to *pathos* by using numerous heart-wringing examples? Later chapters in this textbook will help you use these appeals competently in your own writing as well as analyze these appeals in others' messages.

CONCEPT 3 Nonverbal messages persuade through visual strategies that can be analyzed rhetorically.

Just as you can think rhetorically about texts, you can think rhetorically about photographs, drawings, and other images as well as artifacts such as clothing or cars.

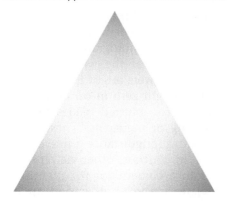

Message
Logos: *How can I make my ideas internally consistent and logical? How can I find the best reasons and support them with the best evidence?*

Audience
Pathos: *How can I make the readers open to my message? How can I best engage my readers' emotions and imaginations? How can I appeal to my readers' values and interests?*

Writer or Speaker
Ethos: *How can I present myself effectively? How can I enhance my credibility and trustworthiness?*

FIGURE 2 Rhetorical Triangle

Visual Rhetoric

Consider, for example, the persuasive power of famous photographs from the war in Iraq. Early in the war, several widely publicized images, particularly the film footage of the toppling of the statue of Saddam Hussein and the "Mission Accomplished" photograph of former President George W. Bush wearing a pilot's flight suit on the deck of the aircraft carrier *Abraham Lincoln*, served to consolidate public support of the war. Later, certain images began eating away at public support. For example, an unauthorized picture of flag-draped coffins filling the freight deck of a military transport plane focused attention on those killed in the war. Particularly devastating for supporters of the war were the images of American guards sexually humiliating Iraqi prisoners in the Abu Ghraib prison. Images like these stick in viewers' memories long after specific texts are forgotten.

What gives images this persuasive power? For one thing, they can be apprehended at a glance, condensing an argument into a memorable scene or symbol that taps deeply into our emotions and values. Images also persuade by appealing to *logos*, *ethos*, and *pathos*. They make implicit arguments (*logos*) while also appealing to our values and emotions (*pathos*) and causing us to respond favorably or unfavorably to the artist or photographer (*ethos*). Like verbal texts, images have an angle of vision, which can be crafted by selecting, manipulating, and often photoshopping images to control what viewers see and thus influence what they think. (Note that "angle of vision" is itself a visual metaphor.) Through the location and angle of the camera, the distance from the subject, and the framing, cropping, and filtering of the image, the photographer steers us toward a particular view of the subject, influencing us to forget, at least momentarily, that there are other ways of seeing the same subject.

Although images can have powerful rhetorical effects, these effects may be less controllable and more audience-dependent than those of verbal texts. Consider, for example, the wind farm photograph at the end of this chapter. In this striking image, the dominance of the whirling turbines could convey several implicit arguments. Some viewers might find that this photo fuels their objections to wind farms. They might zero in on how intrusive, massive, and unattractive wind turbines are. The blurred blades of the gigantic turbines might strike them as frightening or menacing. These same viewers, though, might respond more positively to a longdistance photo of wind turbines against a scarlet sunset over the hills. In contrast, other viewers might interpret these wind turbines in motion as an argument for the plentiful energy that wind farms generate. For these viewers, the photograph's angle of vision, which emphasizes the size and power of these wind towers against a background of barren hills and blue sky, could be used to counter David Rockwood's argument in his letter to the editor that wind power is unreliable and destroys the "pristine wilderness." Instead, to these viewers the photograph suggests that wind farms make productive use of arid or barren land. Interpreted this way, this photo could be seen to use *pathos* to appeal to environmentalists' concerns (preserve beautiful landscape; don't harm wildlife) while evoking positive feelings about technology. In either case, viewers would agree that the photographer is obviously a professional, who uses an upward camera placement to emphasize the technological power of the wind turbines. One's feelings toward the photograph and the photographer may also depend on how much the photograph seems "natural" as opposed to being framed for artistic or political effect. Because images are somewhat open in the way they create visual arguments, writers of texts that include images should anticipate viewers' possible alternative interpretations.

FOR
WRITING
AND
DISCUSSION

Analyzing Visual Messages

The following exercise asks you to think about how rhetorical effects of images can create implicit arguments. Figures 3–6 depict the controversial northernmost part of Alaska—the Arctic National Wildlife Refuge and the North Slope near the Brooks Range that Arctic Power and Jimmy Carter described. This region figures prominently in public debates about the United States' energy independence, climate change, environmental preservation, and unexplored sources of oil. Note that oil drilling has long been established in the North Slope but is currently forbidden in the adjacent ANWR. Working in small groups or as a whole class, explore the rhetorical effect of images by doing the following two tasks.

1. ***Analyzing the Photos.*** Explore the rhetorical effect of these images, noting how the effect may differ from person to person.
   a. In each photograph, on what details has the photographer chosen to focus? How do the details contribute to a dominant impression conveyed by the whole photograph? How does the photograph affect you emotionally? How does it make you feel about the ANWR/North Slope?
   b. Place your impression of the ANWR/North Slope, as conveyed by each of these images, on a continuum from ugly/forbidding to beautiful/fascinating or from barren/empty of animal life to biologically rich.
2. ***Using the Photos.*** Now imagine that you are creating a flyer for each of the following audiences and purposes. Which photo would you use to make the most compelling argument (consider *logos, ethos,* and *pathos*) for each audience? Explain your reasoning. Note that there is no "right answer" for these questions. If you think that none of the photographs would be

FIGURE 3 Caribou Crossing a River in the Arctic National Wildlife Refuge

Tom Walker/Getty

FIGURE 4 Caribou Grazing Near Oil Pipeline in the Arctic North Slope

Accent Alaska/Alamy

FIGURE 5 The ANWR Coastal Plain in Winter

Simon Bruty/Sports Illustrated/Getty

FIGURE 6 Oil-Extraction Plant, North Slope

James Balog/Getty

(*continued*)

appropriate for the designated audience and purpose, what kind of photograph would be more effective?

a. *Audience:* tourists
   Purpose: to invite people to buy tour packages to the Arctic National Wildlife Refuge and the North Slope

b. *Audience*: political leaders and voters
   Purpose: to persuade decision makers to take a pro-environment, anti-business stand on this region

c. *Audience*: political leaders and voters
   Purpose: to persuade decision makers to see this region as remote, empty, and therefore available for oil exploration and business development

d. *Audience*: undecided voters who want both more oil and a preserved environment
   Purpose: to persuade people to see that economic development in the ANWR can be compatible with preserving the region's unique natural beauty and wildlife

The Rhetoric of Clothing and Other Consumer Items

Not only do photographs, paintings, and drawings have rhetorical power, but so do the images projected by many of our consumer choices. Consider, for example, the rhetorical thinking that goes into our choice of clothes. We choose our clothes not only to keep ourselves covered and warm but also to project visually our identification with certain social groups and subcultures. For example, if you want to be identified as a skateboarder, a preppy socialite, a geek, a NASCAR fan, or a junior partner in a corporate law firm, you know how to select clothes and accessories that convey that identification. The way you dress is a code that communicates where you fit (or how you want to be perceived as fitting) within a class and social structure.

How do these symbolic codes get established? They can be set by fashion designers, by advertisers, or by trendy groups or individuals. The key to any new clothing code is to make it look different in some distinctive way from an earlier code or from a code of another group. Sometimes clothing codes develop to show rebellion against the values of parents or authority figures. At other times they develop to show new kinds of group identities.

Clothing codes are played on in conscious ways in fashion advertisements so that consumers become very aware of what identifications are signaled by different styles and brands. This aspect of consumer society is so ubiquitous that one of the marks of growing affluence in third world countries is people's attention to the rhetoric of consumer goods. Consider the second epigraph to this chapter, which indicates that villagers in India watching TV ads notice not only the soap or shampoo being advertised but also the brands of motorbikes and the lifestyles of the people in the ads. Buying a certain kind of consumer good projects a certain kind of status or group or class identity. Our point, from a rhetorical perspective, is that in making a consumer choice, many people are concerned not only with the quality of the item itself but also with its rhetorical symbolism. Note that the same item can send quite different messages to different groups: A Rolex watch might enhance one's credibility at a corporate board meeting while undercutting it at a barbecue for union workers.

Clothing as Visual Arguments

The rhetorical power of clothing especially comes into play in the workplace. This exercise asks to you think about workplace dress codes, which are enforced by peer pressure and peer modeling as well as by company policies. Figures 7 to 10 show four different workplace environments. Working in small groups or as a whole class, consider the rhetoric of workplace clothing by sharing your responses to the following questions:

1. How would you describe the differences in dress codes in each of these environments?
2. If you were employed in one of these workplaces, how much do you think you could vary your style of dress without violating workplace codes?

FIGURE 7 Engineering firm

Jose Luis Pelaez Inc./Blend Images/Corbis

FIGURE 8 Warehouse

Corbis Premium RF/Alamy

FIGURE 9 Associates, Law Firm

Richard G. Bingham II/ Alamy

FIGURE 10 Espresso Bar

Ken Seet Photography/Corbis

(*continued*)

3. Suppose that you are interviewing for a job in one of these workplaces. What clothing would be appropriate for your interview and why? (Note that how you dress for an interview might be different from how you dress once you have the job.) Share your rhetorical thinking about clothing choices aimed at making the best first impression on the people who interview you. Be as specific as possible for all items of clothing including shoes and accessories.
4. To what extent are dress codes for women more complex than those for men?

Chapter Summary

In this chapter we have looked briefly at rhetorical theory in order to explain the persuasive power of both verbal and visual texts.

- *Concept 1: Messages persuade through their angle of vision.* Any text necessarily looks at its subject from a perspective—an angle of vision—that selects and emphasizes some details while omitting or minimizing others. You can analyze writers' angle of vision by considering their direct statements of intention, their selection of details, their word choice, their figures of speech, and their manipulation of sentence structure to control emphasis.
- *Concept 2: Messages persuade through appeals to* **logos**, **ethos**, *and* **pathos.** *Logos* refers to the power of the writer's reasons and evidence; *pathos* to the way the writer connects to the reader's sympathies, emotions, values, and beliefs; and *ethos* to the way the writer portrays himself or herself as trustworthy and credible.
- *Concept 3: Nonverbal messages persuade through visual strategies that can be analyzed rhetorically.* Like verbal texts, visual texts have an angle of vision created by the way the image is framed and by the perspective from which it is viewed. Images also make implicit arguments (*logos*), appeal to the viewer's emotions and values (*pathos*), and suggest the creator's character and trustworthiness (*ethos*). One can also analyze consumer choices (clothing, jewelry, cars) rhetorically because such choices make implicit arguments about the consumer's desired identity.

BRIEF WRITING PROJECT

Analyzing Angle of Vision in Two Passages about Nuclear Energy

Background and Readings

This brief writing project will give you practice at analyzing the angle of vision in different texts. The assignment focuses on two passages about nuclear power plants.

The first passage is from the home page of NuclearPowerNow, a nuclear power advocacy site. It was posted in 2008.

Nuclear Power Now

Nuclear power is the world's largest source of emission-free energy. Nuclear power plants produce no controlled air pollutants, such as sulfur and particulates, or greenhouse gases. The use of nuclear power in place of other energy sources helps to keep the air clean, preserve the Earth's climate, avoid ground-level ozone formation and prevent acid rain.

Nuclear power has important implications for our national security. Inexpensive nuclear power, in combination with fuel cell technology, could significantly reduce our dependency on foreign oil.

Nuclear power plants have experienced an admirable safety record. About 20% of electricity generated in the U.S. comes from nuclear power, and in the last forty years of this production, not one single fatality has occurred as a result of the operation of a civilian nuclear power plant in the United States. In comparison, many people die in coal mining accidents every year and approximately ten thousand Americans die every year from pollution related to coal burning.

The nuclear power industry generates approximately 2,000 tons of solid waste annually in the United States. In comparison, coal fueled power plants produce 100,000,000 tons of ash and sludge annually, and this ash is laced with poisons such as mercury and nitric oxide.

Even this 2,000 tons of nuclear waste is not a technical problem. Reprocessing of nuclear fuel, and the implementation of Integral Fast Reactor technology, will enable us to turn the vast majority of what is currently considered waste into energy.

Unfortunately, the voting public has been victimized by forty years of misinformation regarding the safety of nuclear power. The graphs on nuclear energy showing it to be safe, economical, and in our national interest are countered by anti-nuclear activists using fear tactics to frighten the electorate into inaction.

Until we can successfully educate the American electorate on the real pros and cons of nuclear power, we will not be able to engage in a healthy national discussion on the topic.

The second passage is by Carl Pope, the executive director of the Sierra Club. This brief article was posted in September 2009 on the "Great Debate" blog site hosted by Reuters, a news service focused on business and industry.

Nuclear Power Is Not the Way Forward

Nuclear power is not a responsible choice and makes no sense as part of America's clean energy future. We can meet our energy needs through energy efficiency and renewable energy, and have a clean and healthy world without nuclear power.

There are four insurmountable problems with nuclear power.

First, nuclear power produces highly dangerous radioactive waste. Every nuclear reactor generates about 20 tons of highly radioactive spent nuclear fuel and additional low-level radioactive waste per year. The waste can kill at high doses and cause cancer and birth defects at low doses. Nuclear waste remains dangerous to humans for 200 thousand years.

Worse, we don't know what to do with this waste once it is generated. Some propose dumping nuclear waste in Yucca Mountain, NV; however, the mountain is seismically active. An earthquake in the 1990's caused over $1 million damage to a

Department of Energy (DOE) facility at the site. In addition, a Department of Energy panel of scientists has found that the nuclear material may leak from the containment vessels over time and will contaminate groundwater. On its way to Yucca Mountain, the waste would also pass through thousands of cities and towns and present multiple exposure risks.

Second, nuclear power is prohibitively expensive. The method is not anywhere near cost effective; nuclear plants in the states of Oregon, New York, Maine, Illinois, and Connecticut have been shut down because the owners found it was too expensive to keep them going.

American taxpayers are also subsidizing the nuclear industry. According to the Congressional Research Service, the industry has cost taxpayers tens of billions of dollars in research and development subsidies.

Third, an accident at a coal plant is a problem, but an accident at a nuclear plant can be a disaster. Because human beings operate plants and drive the trucks that transport nuclear waste, accidents can and will happen. The danger with nuclear power is that the stakes in accidents are extremely high. Anyone exposed to radiation leaks or accidents will likely sicken or die from that exposure.

And finally, there is a risk that nuclear material will fall into the wrong hands. Some have recommended that we consider "reprocessing" of spent nuclear fuel, a method that consolidates waste into weapons-usable plutonium. The government has elaborate plans to prevent rogue nations and terrorists from stealing the nuclear fuel or waste to make nuclear bombs. The more nuclear reactors, the more risk of radioactive material being stolen to make bombs.

Nuclear power is not the way forward. America deserves a safer, cleaner, and cheaper energy future.

Your task: Contrast the differences in angle of vision in these two passages by analyzing how they create their different rhetorical effects. Consider factors such as overt statements of meaning, selection/omission of details, connotations of words and figures of speech, and sentence emphasis. To help guide your analysis, review the strategies chart ("Strategies for Constructing an Angle of Vision"). Your goal here is to explain to your readers how these two passages create different impressions of nuclear power.

 For additional help with writing, reading, and research, go to **www.mycomplab.com.**

READING
RHETORICALLY
The Writer as Strong Reader

Many new college students are surprised by the amount, range, and difficulty of reading they have to do in college. Every day they are challenged by reading assignments ranging from scholarly articles and textbooks on complex subject matter to primary sources such as Plato's dialogues or Darwin's *Voyage of the Beagle*.

To interact strongly with challenging texts, you must learn how to read them both with and against the grain. When you read *with the grain* of a text, you see the world through its author's perspective, open yourself to the author's argument, apply the text's insights to new contexts, and connect its ideas to your own experiences and personal knowledge. When you read *against the grain* of a text, you resist it by questioning its points, raising doubts, analyzing the limits of its perspective, or even refuting its argument.

We say that readers read *rhetorically* when they are aware of the effect a text is intended to have on them. Strong rhetorical readers analyze how a text works persuasively and they think critically about whether to enter into or challenge the text's intentions. The two writing projects in this chapter, both of which demand rhetorical reading, introduce you to several of the most common genres of academic writing: the summary, and various kinds of strong response essays, which usually incorporate a summary of the text to which the writer is responding. Thus our goal is to help you become a more powerful reader of academic texts, prepared to take part in the conversations of the disciplines you study.

In this chapter, you will learn to:

- listen carefully to a text, recognize its parts and their functions, and summarize its ideas
- formulate strong responses to texts by interacting with them, either by agreeing with, interrogating, or actively opposing them

Exploring Rhetorical Reading

As an introduction to rhetorical reading, we ask you to imagine that you are investigating different strategies that individual Americans might take to protect the environment. You have come across the 2008 article "Why Bother?" by Michael Pollan in the *New York Times Magazine*. Pollan, a professor of journalism at the

From Chapter 5 of *The Allyn & Bacon Guide to Writing*, Sixth Edition. John D. Ramage, John C. Bean, June Johnson. Copyright © 2012 by Pearson Education, Inc. Published by Pearson Allyn & Bacon. All rights reserved.

University of California Berkeley's Graduate School of Journalism, is known for his popular books on reforming our food-production system for the benefit of humans, animals, and the environment: *The Omnivore's Dilemma: A Natural History of Four Meals* (2007), *In Defense of Food: An Eater's Manifesto* (2009), and *Food Rules* (2010). Before reading Pollan's article, respond to the following opinion survey, using a 1 to 5 scale, with 1 meaning "strongly agree" and 5 meaning "strongly disagree."

Item	Strongly agree	Agree	Neutral	Disagree	Strongly disagree
1. Global warming is a very serious problem.	1	2	3	4	5
2. Going green in my own lifestyle will have no effect on climate change—the magnitude of the problem is too great.	1	2	3	4	5
3. The only way to make a real difference in climate change is through hugely expensive actions taken by governments and businesses.	1	2	3	4	5
4. The best way to combat global warming is for individual Americans to go green in their own consumer choices.	1	2	3	4	5
5. Environmentally conscious people should change the way they eat.	1	2	3	4	5

When you have finished rating your degree of agreement with these statements, read Pollan's article, using whatever note-taking, underlining, or highlighting strategies you normally use when reading for a class. When you have finished reading, complete the exercises that follow.

Michael Pollan
Why Bother?

1   **Why bother?** That really is the big question facing us as individuals hoping to do something about climate change, and it's not an easy one to answer. I don't know about you, but for me the most upsetting moment in *An Inconvenient Truth* came long after Al Gore scared the hell out of me, constructing an utterly convincing case that the very survival of life on earth as we know it is threatened by climate change. No, the really dark moment came during the closing credits, when we are asked to … change our light bulbs. That's when it got really depressing. The immense disproportion

between the magnitude of the problem Gore had described and the puniness of what he was asking us to do about it was enough to sink your heart.

2   But the drop-in-the-bucket issue is not the only problem lurking behind the "why bother" question. Let's say I do bother, big time. I turn my life upside-down, start biking to work, plant a big garden, turn down the thermostat so low I need the Jimmy Carter* signature cardigan, forsake the clothes dryer for a laundry line across the yard, trade in the station wagon for a hybrid, get off the beef, go completely local. I could theoretically do all that, but what would be the point when I know full well that halfway around the world there lives my evil twin, some carbon-footprint *doppelgänger* in Shanghai or Chongqing who has just bought his first car (Chinese car ownership is where ours was back in 1918), is eager to swallow every bite of meat I forswear and who's positively itching to replace every last pound of CO_2 I'm struggling no longer to emit. So what exactly would I have to show for all my trouble?

3   A sense of personal virtue, you might suggest, somewhat sheepishly. But what good is that when virtue itself is quickly becoming a term of derision? And not just on the editorial pages of the *Wall Street Journal* or on the lips of the vice president,* who famously dismissed energy conservation as a "sign of personal virtue." No, even in the pages of the *New York Times* and the *New Yorker,* it seems the epithet "virtuous," when applied to an act of personal environmental responsibility, may be used only ironically. Tell me: How did it come to pass that virtue—a quality that for most of history has generally been deemed, well, a virtue—became a mark of liberal softheadedness? How peculiar, that doing the right thing by the environment—buying the hybrid, eating like a locavore—should now set you up for the Ed Begley Jr.* treatment.

4   And even if in the face of this derision I decide I am going to bother, there arises the whole vexed question of getting it right. Is eating local or walking to work really going to reduce my carbon footprint? According to one analysis, if walking to work increases your appetite and you consume more meat or milk as a result, walking might actually emit more carbon than driving. A handful of studies have recently suggested that in certain cases under certain conditions, produce from places as far away as New Zealand might account for less carbon than comparable domestic products. True, at least one of these studies was co-written by a representative of agribusiness interests in (surprise!) New Zealand, but even so, they make you wonder. If determining the carbon footprint of food is really this complicated, and I've got to consider not only "food miles" but also whether the food came by ship or truck and how lushly the grass grows in New Zealand, then maybe on second thought I'll just buy the imported chops at Costco, at least until the experts get their footprints sorted out.

5   There are so many stories we can tell ourselves to justify doing nothing, but perhaps the most insidious is that, whatever we do manage to do, it will be too little too late. Climate change is upon us, and it has arrived well ahead of schedule.

*Jimmy Carter was the Democratic president (1977–1981) who supported environmental policies, world peace, and human rights.
*Pollan is referring to Dick Cheney who served as George W. Bush's vice president from 2001–2009.
*Ed Begley, Jr., is a prominent television star who has his own green living reality TV show, *Living with Ed*. Begley has explored such topics as tapping the energy produced by people using exercise equipment.

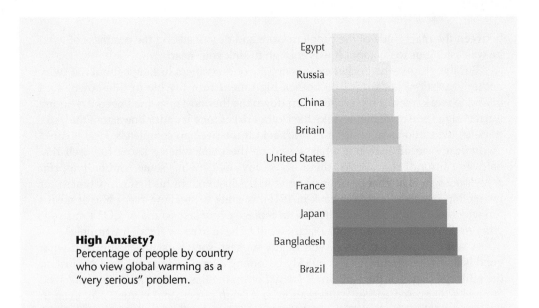

High Anxiety?
Percentage of people by country who view global warming as a "very serious" problem.

Egypt

Russia

China

Britain

United States

France

Japan

Bangladesh

Brazil

Scientists' projections that seemed dire a decade ago turn out to have been unduly optimistic: the warming and the melting is occurring much faster than the models predicted. Now truly terrifying feedback loops threaten to boost the rate of change exponentially, as the shift from white ice to blue water in the Arctic absorbs more sunlight and warming soils everywhere become more biologically active, causing them to release their vast stores of carbon into the air. Have you looked into the eyes 6 of a climate scientist recently? They look really scared.

7   So do you still want to talk about planting gardens?

8   I do.

Whatever we can do as individuals to change the way we live at this suddenly very late date does seem utterly inadequate to the challenge. It's hard to argue with Michael Specter*, in a recent *New Yorker* piece on carbon footprints, when he says: "Personal choices, no matter how virtuous [N.B.!], cannot do enough. It will also take laws and money." So it will. Yet it is no less accurate or hardheaded to say that laws and money cannot do enough, either; that it will also take profound changes in the way we live. Why? Because the climate-change crisis is at its very bottom a crisis of lifestyle—of character, even. The Big Problem is nothing more or less than the sum total of countless little everyday choices, most of them made by us (consumer spending represents 70 percent of our economy), and most of the rest of them made in the 9   name of our needs and desires and preferences.

For us to wait for legislation or technology to solve the problem of how we're living our lives suggests we're not really serious about changing—something our politicians cannot fail to notice. They will not move until we do. Indeed, to look to leaders and experts, to laws and money and grand schemes, to save us from our predicament represents precisely the sort of thinking—passive, delegated, dependent

*Michael Specter is a staff writer for the *New Yorker* and a national science reporter, who has most recently written a book, *Denialism*, about people's refusal to accept scientific evidence.

Graphics by Charles M. Blow, *New York Times Magazine*, April 1, 2008. Copyright © 2008 The New York Times Company, Inc.

for solutions on specialists—that helped get us into this mess in the first place. It's hard to believe that the same sort of thinking could now get us out of it.

10   Thirty years ago, Wendell Berry, the Kentucky farmer and writer, put forward a blunt analysis of precisely this mentality. He argued that the environmental crisis of the 1970s—an era innocent of climate change; what we would give to have back *that* environmental crisis!—was at its heart a crisis of character and would have to be addressed first at that level: at home, as it were. He was impatient with people who wrote checks to environmental organizations while thoughtlessly squandering fossil fuel in their everyday lives—the 1970s equivalent of people buying carbon offsets to atone for their Tahoes and Durangos. Nothing was likely to change until we healed the "split between what we think and what we do." For Berry, the "why bother" question came down to a moral imperative: "Once our personal connection to what is wrong becomes clear, then we have to choose: we can go on as before, recognizing our dishonesty and living with it the best we can, or we can begin the effort to change the way we think and live."

11   For Berry, the deep problem standing behind all the other problems of industrial civilization is "specialization," which he regards as the "disease of the modern character." Our society assigns us a tiny number of roles: we're producers (of one thing) at work, consumers of a great many other things the rest of the time, and then once a year or so we vote as citizens. Virtually all of our needs and desires we delegate to specialists of one kind or another—our meals to agribusiness, health to the doctor, education to the teacher, entertainment to the media, care for the environment to the environmentalist, political action to the politician.

12   As Adam Smith and many others have pointed out, this division of labor has given us many of the blessings of civilization. Specialization is what allows me to sit at a computer thinking about climate change. Yet this same division of labor obscures the lines of connection—and responsibility—linking our everyday acts to their real-world consequences, making it easy for me to overlook the coal-fired power plant that is lighting my screen, or the mountaintop in Kentucky that had to be destroyed to provide the coal to that plant, or the streams running crimson with heavy metals as a result.

13   Of course, what made this sort of specialization possible in the first place was cheap energy. Cheap fossil fuel allows us to pay distant others to process our food for us, to entertain us and to (try to) solve our problems, with the result that there is very little we know how to accomplish for ourselves. Think for a moment of all the things you suddenly need to do for yourself when the power goes out—up to and including entertaining yourself. Think, too, about how a power failure causes your neighbors—your community—to suddenly loom so much larger in your life. Cheap energy allowed us to leapfrog community by making it possible to sell our specialty over great distances as well as summon into our lives the specialties of countless distant others.

14   Here's the point: Cheap energy, which gives us climate change, fosters precisely the mentality that makes dealing with climate change in our own lives seem impossibly difficult. Specialists ourselves, we can no longer imagine anyone but an expert, or anything but a new technology or law, solving our problems. Al Gore asks us to change the light bulbs because he probably can't imagine us doing anything much more challenging, like, say, growing some portion of our own food. We can't imagine it, either, which is probably why we prefer to cross our fingers and talk about the

promise of ethanol and nuclear power—new liquids and electrons to power the same old cars and houses and lives.

15   The "cheap-energy mind," as Wendell Berry called it, is the mind that asks, "Why bother?" because it is helpless to imagine—much less attempt—a different sort of life, one less divided, less reliant. Since the cheap-energy mind translates everything into money, its proxy, it prefers to put its faith in market-based solutions—carbon taxes and pollution-trading schemes. If we could just get the incentives right, it believes, the economy will properly value everything that matters and nudge our self-interest down the proper channels. The best we can hope for is a greener version of the old invisible hand. Visible hands it has no use for.

16   But while some such grand scheme may well be necessary, it's doubtful that it will be sufficient or that it will be politically sustainable before we've demonstrated to ourselves that change is possible. Merely to give, to spend, even to vote, is not to do, and there is so much that needs to be done—without further delay. In the judgment of James Hansen, the NASA climate scientist who began sounding the alarm on global warming 20 years ago, we have only 10 years left to start cutting—not just slowing—the amount of carbon we're emitting or face a "different planet." Hansen said this more than two years ago, however; two years have gone by, and nothing of consequence has been done. So: eight years left to go and a great deal left to do.

17   Which brings us back to the "why bother" question and how we might better answer it. The reasons not to bother are many and compelling, at least to the cheap-energy mind. But let me offer a few admittedly tentative reasons that we might put on the other side of the scale:

18   If you do bother, you will set an example for other people. If enough other people bother, each one influencing yet another in a chain reaction of behavioral change, markets for all manner of green products and alternative technologies will prosper and expand. (Just look at the market for hybrid cars.) Consciousness will be raised, perhaps even changed: new moral imperatives and new taboos might take root in the culture. Driving an S.U.V. or eating a 24-ounce steak or illuminating your McMansion like an airport runway at night might come to be regarded as outrages to human conscience. Not having things might become cooler than having them. And those who did change the way they live would acquire the moral standing to demand changes in behavior from others—from other people, other corporations, even other countries.

19   All of this could, theoretically, happen. What I'm describing (imagining would probably be more accurate) is a process of viral social change, and change of this kind, which is nonlinear, is never something anyone can plan or predict or count on. Who knows, maybe the virus will reach all the way to Chongqing and infect my Chinese evil twin. Or not. Maybe going green will prove a passing fad and will lose steam after a few years, just as it did in the 1980s, when Ronald Reagan took down Jimmy Carter's solar panels from the roof of the White House.

20   Going personally green is a bet, nothing more or less, though it's one we probably all should make, even if the odds of it paying off aren't great. Sometimes you have to act as if acting will make a difference, even when you can't prove that it will. That, after all, was precisely what happened in Communist Czechoslovakia and Poland, when a handful of individuals like Václav Havel and Adam Michnik resolved that they would

simply conduct their lives "as if" they lived in a free society. That improbable bet created a tiny space of liberty that, in time, expanded to take in, and then help take down, the whole of the Eastern bloc.

21   So what would be a comparable bet that the individual might make in the case of the environmental crisis? Havel himself has suggested that people begin to "conduct themselves as if they were to live on this earth forever and be answerable for its condition one day." Fair enough, but let me propose a slightly less abstract and daunting wager. The idea is to find one thing to do in your life that doesn't involve spending or voting, that may or may not virally rock the world but is real and particular (as well as symbolic) and that, come what may, will offer its own rewards. Maybe you decide to give up meat, an act that would reduce your carbon footprint by as much as a quarter. Or you could try this: determine to observe the Sabbath. For one day a week, abstain completely from economic activity: no shopping, no driving, no electronics.

22   But the act I want to talk about is growing some—even just a little—of your own food. Rip out your lawn, if you have one, and if you don't—if you live in a high-rise, or have a yard shrouded in shade—look into getting a plot in a community garden. Measured against the Problem We Face, planting a garden sounds pretty benign, I know, but in fact it's one of the most powerful things an individual can do—to reduce your carbon footprint, sure, but more important, to reduce your sense of dependence and dividedness: to change the cheap-energy mind.

23   A great many things happen when you plant a vegetable garden, some of them directly related to climate change, others indirect but related nevertheless. Growing food, we forget, comprises the original solar technology: calories produced by means of photosynthesis. Years ago the cheap-energy mind discovered that more food could be produced with less effort by replacing sunlight with fossil-fuel fertilizers and pesticides, with a result that the typical calorie of food energy in your diet now requires about 10 calories of fossil-fuel energy to produce. It's estimated that the way we feed ourselves (or rather, allow ourselves to be fed) accounts for about a fifth of the greenhouse gas for which each of us is responsible.

24   Yet the sun still shines down on your yard, and photosynthesis still works so abundantly that in a thoughtfully organized vegetable garden (one planted from seed,

Thomas Hannich/Bransch/NY Times

nourished by compost from the kitchen and involving not too many drives to the garden center), you can grow the proverbial free lunch—CO2-free and dollar-free. This is the most-local food you can possibly eat (not to mention the freshest, tastiest and most nutritious), with a carbon footprint so faint that even the New Zealand lamb council dares not challenge it. And while we're counting carbon, consider too your compost pile, which shrinks the heap of garbage your household needs trucked away even as it feeds your vegetables and sequesters carbon in your soil. What else? Well, you will probably notice that you're getting a pretty good workout there in your garden, burning calories without having to get into the car to drive to the gym. (It is one of the absurdities of the modern division of labor that, having replaced physical labor with fossil fuel, we now have to burn even more fossil fuel to keep our unemployed bodies in shape.) Also, by engaging both body and mind, time spent in the garden is time (and energy) subtracted from electronic forms of entertainment.

25   You begin to see that growing even a little of your own food is, as Wendell Berry pointed out 30 years ago, one of those solutions that, instead of begetting a new set of problems—the way "solutions" like ethanol or nuclear power inevitably do—actually beget other solutions, and not only of the kind that save carbon. Still more valuable are the habits of mind that growing a little of your own food can yield. You quickly learn that you need not be dependent on specialists to provide for yourself—that your body is still good for something and may actually be enlisted in its own support. If the experts are right, if both oil and time are running out, these are skills and habits of mind we're all very soon going to need. We may also need the food. Could gardens provide it? Well, during World War II, victory gardens supplied as much as 40 percent of the produce Americans ate.

26   **But there are sweeter** reasons to plant that garden, to bother. At least in this one corner of your yard and life, you will have begun to heal the split between what you think and what you do, to commingle your identities as consumer and producer and citizen. Chances are, your garden will re-engage you with your neighbors, for you will have produce to give away and the need to borrow their tools. You will have reduced the power of the cheap-energy mind by personally overcoming its most debilitating weakness: its helplessness and the fact that it can't do much of anything that doesn't involve division or subtraction. The garden's season-long transit from seed to ripe fruit—*will you get a load of that zucchini?!*—suggests that the operations of addition and multiplication still obtain, that the abundance of nature is not exhausted. The single greatest lesson the garden teaches is that our relationship to the planet need not be zero-sum, and that as long as the sun still shines and people still can plan and plant, think and do, we can, if we bother to try, find ways to provide for ourselves without diminishing the world.

THINKING CRITICALLY
about "Why Bother?"

1. In three to four sentences, summarize Pollan's main points.

2. Freewrite a response to this question: In what way has Pollan's article caused me to reconsider one or more of my answers to the opinion survey?

3. Working in small groups or as a whole class, compare the note-taking strategies you used while reading this piece. (a) How many people wrote marginal notes? How many underlined or highlighted? (b) Compare the contents of these notes. Did people highlight the same passages or different ones? (c) Individually, look at your annotations and highlights and try to decide why you wrote or marked what you did. Share your reasons for making these annotations. The goal of this exercise is to make you more aware of your thinking processes as you read.

4. Working as a whole class or in small groups, share your responses to the questionnaire and to the postreading questions. What were the most insightful or provocative points in this article? To what extent did this article change people's thinking about the value of individual actions or about the impact of our individual lifestyles on climate change? As a result of Pollan's argument, are you more apt to try growing some of your own vegetables either now or in the future?

Understanding Rhetorical Reading

In this section, we explain why college-level reading is often difficult for new students and offer suggestions for improving your reading process based on the reading strategies of experts.

What Makes College-Level Reading Difficult?

The difficulty of college-level reading stems in part from the complexity of new subject matter. Whatever the subject—from international monetary policies to the intricacies of photosynthesis—you have to wrestle with new and complex materials that might perplex anyone. But in addition to the daunting subject matter, several other factors contribute to the difficulty of college-level reading:

- *Vocabulary.* Many college-level readings contain unfamiliar technical language such as the economic terms *assets, opportunity costs,* or *export subsidy* or the philosophic terms *hermeneutics* or *Neo-Platonism.* Even nontechnical readings and civic writing for the general public can contain unfamiliar terms. For example, in the Pollan article, the literary term *doppelgänger* or the ecological terms *feedback loops* or *pollution-trading systems* may have given you pause. In academia, words often carry specialized meanings that evoke a whole history of conversation and debate that may be inaccessible, even through a specialized dictionary. Good examples might be *postmodernism, string theory,* or *cultural materialism.* You will not fully understand these terms until you are initiated into the disciplinary conversations that gave rise to them.
- *Unfamiliar rhetorical context.* Writers write to an audience for a purpose arising from some motivating occasion. Knowing an author's purpose, occasion, and audience will often clarify confusing parts

of a text. For example, Pollan's article was published in the *New York Times Magazine*, which attracts a liberal, well-educated audience. Pollan assumes that his audience already believes in global warming and takes climate change seriously. In fact, they may be so overwhelmed with the problem that they are ready to give up, shrug, and say, "Why bother?" His purpose is to motivate them to action. A text's internal clues can sometimes help you fill in the rhetorical context, but often you may need to do outside research.

- ***Unfamiliar genre.*** In your college reading, you will encounter a range of genres such as textbooks, trade books, scholarly articles, scientific reports, historical documents, newspaper articles, op-ed pieces, and so forth. Each of these makes different demands on readers and requires a different reading strategy.
- ***Lack of background knowledge.*** Writers necessarily make assumptions about what their readers already know. For example, Pollan makes numerous references to popular culture (Al Gore's *An Inconvenient Truth*; "the Ed Begley Jr. treatment"; "imported chops at Costco") or to general liberal arts knowledge (references to the economist Adam Smith or to the recent history of Communist Czechoslovakia and Poland). The more familiar you are with this cultural background, the more you will understand Pollan's argument on first reading.

FOR WRITING AND DISCUSSION

Appreciating the Importance of Background Knowledge

The importance of background knowledge is easily demonstrated any time you dip into past issues of a newsmagazine or try to read articles about an unfamiliar culture. Consider the following passage from a 1986 *Newsweek* article. How much background knowledge do you need before you can fully comprehend this passage? What cultural knowledge about the United States would a student from Ethiopia or Indonesia need?

> Throughout the NATO countries last week, there were second thoughts about the prospect of a nuclear-free world. For 40 years nuclear weapons have been the backbone of the West's defense. For almost as long American presidents have ritually affirmed their desire to see the world rid of them. Then, suddenly, Ronald Reagan and Mikhail Gorbachev came close to actually doing it. Let's abolish all nuclear ballistic missiles in the next 10 years, Reagan said. Why not all nuclear weapons, countered Gorbachev. OK, the president responded, like a man agreeing to throw in the washer-dryer along with the house.
>
> What if the deal had gone through? On the one hand, Gorbachev would have returned to Moscow a hero. There is a belief in the United States that the Soviets need nuclear arms because nuclear weapons are what make them a superpower. But according to Marxist-Leninist doctrine, capitalism's nuclear capability (unforeseen by Marx and Lenin) is the only thing that can prevent the inevitable triumph of communism. Therefore, an end to nuclear arms would put the engine of history back on its track.
>
> On the other hand, Europeans fear, a nonnuclear United States would be tempted to retreat into neo-isolationism.
>
> —Robert B. Cullen, "Dangers of Disarming," *Newsweek*

Working in small groups or as a class, identify words and passages in this text that depend on background information or knowledge of culture for complete comprehension.

Using the Reading Strategies of Experts

There are parallel differences between the reading processes of experienced and inexperienced readers, especially when they encounter complex materials. In this strategies chart we describe some expert reading strategies that you can begin applying to your reading of any kind of college-level material.

Strategies for Reading Like an Expert		
Strategies	**What to Do**	**Comments**
Reconstruct the rhetorical context.	Ask questions about purpose, audience, genre, and motivating occasion.	If you read an article that has been anthologized (as in the readings in this textbook), note any information you are given about the author, publication, and genre. Try to reconstruct the author's original motivation for writing.
Take notes.	Make extensive marginal notes as you read.	Expert readers seldom use highlighters, which encourage passive, inefficient reading.
Get in the dictionary habit.	Look up words whose meaning you can't get from context.	If you don't want to interrupt your reading, check off words to look up when you are done.
Match your reading speed to your goals.	Speed up when skimming or scanning for information. Slow down for complete comprehension or detailed analysis.	Robert Sternberg, a cognitive psychologist, discovered that novice readers tend to read everything at about the same pace, no matter what their purpose. Experienced readers know when to slow down or speed up.

(continued)

Strategies	What to Do	Comments
Read a complex text in a "multidraft" way.	Read a text two or three times. The first time, read quickly, skimming ahead rapidly, looking at the opening sentences of paragraphs and at any passages that sum up the writer's argument or clarify the argument's structure. Pay particular attention to the conclusion, which often ties the whole argument together.	Rapid "first-draft reading" helps you see the text's main points and structure, thus providing background for a second reading. Often, experienced readers reread a text two or three times. They hold confusing passages in mental suspension, hoping that later parts of the essay will clarify earlier parts.

Reading with the Grain and Against the Grain

The reading and thinking strategies that we have just described enable skilled readers to interact strongly with texts. Your purpose in using these strategies is to read texts both *with the grain* and *against the grain*, a way of reading that is analogous to the believing and doubting game. This concept is so important that we have chosen to highlight it separately here.

When you read with the grain of a text, you practice what psychologist Carl Rogers calls "empathic listening," in which you try to see the world through the author's eyes, role-playing as much as possible the author's intended readers by adopting their beliefs and values and acquiring their background knowledge. Reading with the grain is the main strategy you use when you summarize a text, but it comes into play also when you develop a strong response. When making with-the-grain points, you support the author's thesis with your own arguments and examples, or apply or extend the author's argument in new ways.

When you read against the grain of a text, you question and perhaps even rebut the author's ideas. You are a resistant reader who asks unanticipated questions, pushes back, and reads the text in ways unforeseen by the author. Reading against the grain is a key part of creating a strong response. When you make against-the-grain points, you challenge the author's reasoning, sources, examples, or choices of language. You present alternative lines of reasoning, deny the writer's values, or raise points or specific data that the writer has omitted. Strategies for thinking with the grain and against the grain are shown in the following chart, along with particular occasions when each is helpful.

Strategies for Reading with and Against the Grain	
Reading with the Grain	**Reading Against the Grain**
• Listen to the text, follow the author's reasoning, and withhold judgment.	• Challenge, question, and resist the author's ideas.

Reading with the Grain	Reading Against the Grain
• Try to see the subject and the world from the author's perspective. • Add further support to the author's thesis with your own points and examples. • Apply the author's argument in new ways.	• Point out what the author has left out or overlooked; note what the author has *not* said. • Identify what assumptions, ideas, or facts seem unsupported or inaccurate. • Rebut the author's ideas with counterreasoning and counterexamples.
Occasions When Most Useful	**Occasions When Most Useful**
• In writing summaries, you listen to a text without judgment to identify the main ideas. • In writing analyses, you seek to understand a text to determine points to elaborate on and discuss. • In synthesizing ideas from sources, you determine what ideas to adopt and build on. • In writing arguments, you inhabit an author's viewpoint to deepen your understanding of an issue and to understand alternative views so you can represent them fairly.	• In writing an initial strong response, you determine the ways in which your beliefs, values, and views might be different from the author's. • In writing analyses, you identify limitations in the author's view. • In synthesizing, you determine which ideas to reject, replace, or go beyond. • In writing arguments, you develop refutations and rebuttals to the author's views.

Strong readers develop their ability to read in both ways—with the grain and against the grain. Some readers prefer to separate these approaches by first reading a text with the grain and then rereading it with more against-the-grain resistance. Throughout the rest of this chapter, we show you different ways to apply these strategies in your reading and writing.

Understanding Summary Writing

A **summary** (often called an **abstract**) is a condensed version of a text that extracts and presents main ideas in a way that does justice to the author's intentions. As fairly and objectively as possible, a summary states the main ideas of a longer text, such as an article or even a book. Although the words "summary" and "abstract" are often used interchangeably, the term "abstract" is usually used for a stand-alone summary at the head of a published article. Scholars often present "abstracts" of their own work (that is, a summary of their argument) for publication in a conference program.

Usefulness of Summaries

Students often report later in their academic careers how valuable summary writing skills are. Summary writing fosters a close engagement between you and the text and demonstrates your understanding of it. By forcing you to distinguish between main and subordinate points, summary writing is a valuable tool for improving your reading comprehension. Summary writing is also useful in other ways. For example, summaries at the beginning of articles, in prefaces to books, and on book jackets help readers determine if they want to read the article or book. To participate in conferences, your professors—and perhaps you also—send abstracts of proposed papers to conference committees in hopes of getting the paper accepted for presentation. Engineers and business executives place "executive summaries" at the beginning of proposals of major reports. In the "literature review" section of scientific papers, summaries of previous research are used to demonstrate gaps in knowledge that the present researchers will try to fill. Finally, writing summaries is a particularly important part of research writing, where you often present condensed views of other writers' arguments, either in support of your own view or as alternative views that you are analyzing or responding to.

The Demands that Summary Writing Makes on Writers

Even though summaries are short, they are challenging to write. You must distinguish between the main and subordinate points in a text, and you must provide even coverage of the text. You must also convey clearly the main ideas—ideas that are often complex—in a limited number of words. Often, summaries are written to certain specifications, say, one-tenth of the original article, or 200 words, or 100 words.

One of the biggest challenges of summarizing is framing the summary so that readers can easily tell your own ideas from those of the author you are summarizing. Often, you are incorporating a summary into a piece of writing as a basis of your own analysis or argument, so this distinction is particularly important. You make this distinction by using frequent **attributive tags** (sometimes called "signal phrases") such as "Pollan claims," "according to Pollan," or "Pollan says"; by putting quotation marks around any passages that use the writer's original wording; and by citing the article using the appropriate documentation style. Typically, writers also introduce the summary with appropriate contextual information giving the author's name and perhaps also the title and genre (in research writing, this information is repeated in the "Works Cited" or "References" list). The first sentence of the summary typically presents the main idea or thesis of the entire article. Here is an example summary of the Pollan article using MLA citation and documentation style.

Identification of the article, journal, and author

Gives overview summary of whole article

Summary of "Why Bother?"

In "Why Bother?" published in the *New York Times Magazine*, environmental journalist Michael Pollan asks why, given the magnitude of the climate change problem, any individual should bother to go green, and argues that an individual's actions can bring

multiple rewards for individuals, society, and the environment. Explaining
that "the warming and the melting" (90) are occurring much faster than   *Attributive tag*
earlier models had predicted, Pollan acknowledges the apparent
powerlessness of individuals to make a difference. Not only are we
uncertain what actions to take to preserve the planet, but we realize that
whatever we do will be offset by growing carbon emissions from emerging   *Short quotations*
nations. Our actions will be "too little too late" (89). He asserts that our   *from article, MLA*
                                                                                          documentation
environmental problem is a "crisis of lifestyle"—"the sum total of   *style; number in*
                                                                                          parentheses
countless little everyday choices" (90) made possible by cheap fossil fuel,   *indicates page*
                                                                                          number of original
which has led to our increasingly specialized jobs. Nevertheless, to   *article where*
counteract our practical and moral distance from the environment caused   *quotation is found*
by this specialization, Pollan urges individuals to go green. Although he
concedes that "'laws and money'" (90) are necessary, he still believes that
individual actions may be influential by setting off a "process of viral social
change" (92). A particularly powerful act, he claims, is to convert yards
into vegetable gardens. Growing your own vegetables, he argues, will help
us overcome "specialization," eat locally, reduce carbon emissions, get
healthy exercise, reconnect with neighbors, and restore our relationship
with the earth. (227 words)

Work Cited

Pollan, Michael. "Why Bother?" *New York Times Magazine* 20 Apr. 2008:   *Bibliographic*
                                                                                  citation for
    19+. Rpt. in *The Allyn and Bacon Guide to Writing*. John D.   *Pollan's article*
                                                                                  using MLA style. In
    Ramage, John C. Bean, and June Johnson. 6th ed. New York: *a formal paper, the*
                                                                                  "Works Cited" list
    Pearson, 2012. 88–94. Print.   *begins on a new*
                                                                                  page at the end of
                                                                                  the paper.

Note in this example how the use of attributive tags, quotation marks, and citations makes it easy to tell that the writer is summarizing Pollan's ideas rather than
presenting his own. Note too the writer's attempt to remain neutral and objective
and not to impose his own views. To avoid interjecting your own opinions, you
need to choose your verbs in attributive tags carefully. Consider the difference
between "Smith argues" and "Smith rants" or between "Brown asserts" and
"Brown leaps to the conclusion that. . . . " In each pair, the second verb, by moving
beyond neutrality, reveals the writer's judgment of the author's ideas.

In an academic setting, then, think of summaries as short, tightly written pieces that retain an author's main ideas while eliminating the supporting details. In the writing projects for this chapter, we'll explain the strategies you can use to write a good summary. The following chart lists the criteria for incorporating a summary effectively into your own prose.

CRITERIA FOR AN EFFECTIVE SUMMARY INCORPORATED INTO YOUR OWN PROSE

- Represents the original article accurately and fairly.
- Is direct and concise, using words economically.
- Remains objective and neutral, not revealing the writer's own ideas on the subject, but, rather, only the original author's points.
- Gives the original article balanced and proportional coverage.
- Uses the writer's own words to express the original author's ideas.
- Distinguishes the summary writer's ideas from the original author's ideas by using attributive tags (such as "according to Pollan" or "Pollan argues that").
- Uses quotations sparingly, if at all, to present the original author's key terms or to convey the flavor of the original.
- Is a unified, coherent piece of writing in its own right.
- Cites and documents the text the writer is summarizing and any quotations used according to an appropriate documentation system.

FOR WRITING AND DISCUSSION

Determining What Is a Good Summary

This exercise asks you to work with the "Criteria for an Effective Summary Incorporated into Your Own Prose" (above) as you analyze the strengths and weaknesses of three summaries of the same article: "Protect Workers' Rights" by Bruce Raynor, published in the *Washington Post* on September 1, 2003. Imagine three student writers assigned to summarize this editorial in approximately 200 words. The first of the summaries below we have rated as excellent. Read the excellent summary first and then determine how successful the other summaries are.

SUMMARY 1 (AN EXCELLENT SUMMARY OF THE RAYNOR ARTICLE)

In Bruce Raynor's op-ed article "Protect Workers' Rights," originally published in the *Washington Post* on September 1, 2003, union official Raynor argues that workers everywhere are threatened by the current rules of globalization that allow corporations and governments to seek out the cheapest and least regulated labor around the world. Using the example of the Pillowtex Corporation that recently shut down its plant in Kannapolis, North Carolina, he shows how ending manufacturing that has played a long and major role in the economies of towns leaves workers without severance pay, medical insurance, money to pay taxes and mortgages, and other options for employment. According to Raynor, in the last three years, millions of jobs have been lost in all branches of American manufacturing. While policymakers advise these workers to seek education to retool for white-collar jobs, Raynor points out that fields such as telemarketing and the computer industry are also losing millions of jobs. Furthermore, outsourcing has caused a drop in wages in the United States. The same dynamic of jobs moving to countries with cheaper and less stringent safety and health regulation has recently caused Mexican and Bangladeshi workers to lose their jobs to Chinese workers. Raynor concludes with a call to protect the rights of workers everywhere by rewriting the "rules for the global economy" (A25). (214 words)

Work Cited

Raynor, Bruce. "Protect Workers' Rights." *Washington Post* 1 Sept. 2003: A25. Print.

SUMMARY 2

The closing of the Pillowtex Corporation's factories in the United States represents a loss of sixteen textile plants and about 6,500 jobs, according to Bruce Raynor, president of UNITE, a union of textile workers.

The workers left in Kannapolis, North Carolina, former home of one of the largest Pillowtex plants, are experiencing financial problems as they are unable to buy medical insurance, pay their taxes or mortgages or find other jobs.

Raynor argues that the case of the Pillowtex workers is representative of workers in other industries such as metals, papers, and electronics and that "this is the longest decline since the Great Depression" with about three million jobs gone in the last three years.

He then explains that white-collar jobs are not safe either because millions of jobs in telemarketing, claims adjusting, and even government are predicted to go overseas in the next five years. Furthermore, Raynor states that the possibility of outsourcing jobs leads to lowering of wages within the United States, as "outsourcing has forced down hourly wage rates by 10 percent to 40 percent for many U.S. computer consultants" (A25).

However, according to Raynor, the developing countries like Mexico and Bangladesh that have acquired manufacturing jobs are also threatened by countries like China who can offer employees who are willing to work for even lower wages and under worse conditions.

Raynor concludes that "a prosperous economy requires that workers be able to buy the products that they produce" (A25) and that workers everywhere need to be protected. (251 words)

Work Cited

Raynor, Bruce. "Protect Workers' Rights." *Washington Post* 1 Sept. 2003: A25. Print.

SUMMARY 3

In his article "Protect Workers' Rights," Bruce Raynor, president of UNITE, a textile workers' union, criticizes free trade and globalization for taking away workers' jobs. Using the Pillowtex Corporation's closing of its plant in Kannapolis, North Carolina, as his prime example, Raynor claims that outsourcing has destroyed the economy of this town and harmed workers across the United States. Raynor threatens that millions of white-collar jobs are also being lost and going to be lost in the next five years. Raynor complains that the whole national and global economy is falling apart and is going to get worse. He implies that the only solution is to keep jobs here in the United States. He maintains that workers around the world are also suffering when factories are moved from one developing country to another that has even more favorable conditions for the corporations. Raynor naively fails to factor in the role of consumers and the pressures on corporations into his defense of workers' rights. Clearly, Raynor loves unions and hates corporations; he probably fears that he is going to lose his own job soon. (183 words)

Understanding Strong Response Writing

We have said that the summary or abstract is an important academic genre and that summary writing is an essential academic skill. Equally important is strong response writing in which you identify and probe points in a text, sometimes by examining how a piece is written and often by inserting your own ideas into the text's conversation. "Strong response" is an umbrella term that incorporates a wide variety of ways that you can speak back to a text. In all cases, you are called on to do your own critical thinking by generating and asserting your own responses to the text.

In this section we will explain four different genres of strong response writing:

- Rhetorical critique
- Ideas critique
- Reflection
- Blended version of all three of these

Strong Response as Rhetorical Critique

A strong response as **rhetorical critique** analyzes a text's rhetorical strategies and evaluates how effectively the author achieves his or her intended goals. When writing a rhetorical critique, you discuss how a text is constructed, what rhetorical strategies it employs, and how effectively it appeals to *logos*, *ethos*, and *pathos*. In other words, you closely analyze the text itself, giving it the same close attention that an art critic gives a painting, a football coach gives a game video, or a biologist gives a cell formation. The close attention can be with the grain, noting the effectiveness of the text's rhetorical strategies, or against the grain, discussing what is ineffective or problematic about these strategies. Or an analysis might point out both the strengths and weaknesses of the text's rhetorical strategies.

For example, suppose that you are writing a rhetorical critique of an article from a conservative business journal advocating oil exploration in the Arctic National Wildlife Refuge (ANWR). You might analyze the article's rhetorical strategies by asking questions like these:

- How is the argument shaped to appeal to a conservative, business-oriented audience?
- How has the writer's angle of vision influenced the selection of evidence for his or her argument?
- How does the writer make himself or herself seem credible to this audience?

You would also evaluate the *logos* of the argument:

- How sound is the logic of the argument?
- Is the evidence accurate and current?
- What are the underlying assumptions and beliefs on which the argument is based?

Rhetorical critiques are usually closed-form, thesis-driven essays. The essay has a thesis that captures the writer's overall assessment of the text and maps out the specific points that the writer will develop in the analysis. When you are writing a rhetorical critique, your goal is to find a few rhetorical points that you find particularly intriguing, important, or disturbing to discuss and probe. Typically, your analysis zeroes in on some key features that you, the writer, find noteworthy. In the following strategies chart, we suggest the kinds of questions you can ask about a text to construct a rhetorical critique.

Question-Asking Strategies for Writing a Rhetorical Critique

Ask Questions about Any of the Following:	Examples
Audience and purpose: • Who is the intended audience? • What is the writer's purpose? • How well does the text suit its particular audience and purpose?	Examine how Michael Pollan writes to the well-educated audience of the *New York Times Magazine*, who are aware of climate change debates and most likely concerned about the problems ahead. Consider how Pollan writes to move these readers beyond good intentions to action. Examine how the text's structure, language, and evidence support this purpose.
Influence of genre on the shape of the text: • How has the genre affected the author's style, structure, and use of evidence?	Examine how the genre of the feature editorial for a highbrow magazine accounts for the length, structure, and depth of Pollan's argument. Examine how his references to political and intellectual figures (Al Gore, then Vice President Cheney, Adam Smith, Wendell Berry, and so forth) carry weight in this magazine's investigation of contemporary issues.
Author's style: • How do the author's language choices and sentence length and complexity contribute to the impact of the text?	Examine how Pollan's casual and cordial connections with readers (use of "I," "you," and "we"), his urgency, and his use of questions contribute to the article's effect.
Appeal to *logos*, the logic of the argument: • How well has the author created a reasonable, logically structured argument?	Examine how well Pollan uses logical points to support his claim and make his claim persuasive.

(continued)

Ask Questions about Any of the Following:	Examples
Use of evidence: • How reputable, relevant, current, sufficient, and representative is the evidence?	Examine how Pollan uses references to scientific articles, newspaper accounts, and his own experiences to develop his points.
Appeal to *ethos* and the credibility of the author: • How well does the author persuade readers that he/she is knowledgeable, reliable, credible, and trustworthy?	Examine how Pollan conveys his knowledge of environmentalism, economics, and social trends. Examine the effects of genre and style in creating this *ethos*. Examine whether this *ethos* is effective for readers who are not familiar with Pollan's other writing, are skeptical of climate change, or are less in tune with environmental activism.
Appeal to *pathos*: • How well does the writer appeal to readers' emotions, sympathies, and values?	Examine how Pollan seeks to tap his audience's values and feelings. Consider how he conveys his familiarity with the everyday choices and decisions facing his readers.
Author's angle of vision: • How much does the author's angle of vision or interpretive filter dominate the text, influencing what is emphasized or omitted?	Examine how Pollan's angle of vision shapes his perspective on climate change, his choice of activist solutions, and his development of solutions. Consider how Pollan's reputation as the author of a number of books on food system reform influences his focus in this argument.

For a rhetorical critique, you would probably not choose all of these questions but would instead select three or four to highlight. Your goal is to make insightful observations about how a text works rhetorically and to support your points with examples and short quotations from the text.

Strong Response as Ideas Critique

A second kind of strong response, the **ideas critique,** focuses on the ideas at stake in the text. Rather than treat the text as an artifact to analyze rhetorically (as in a rhetorical critique), you treat it as a voice in a conversation—one perspective on an issue or one solution to a problem or question. Your strong response examines how the ideas of the original author mesh or conflict with your own. Based on your own critical thinking, personal experiences, and research, to what extent do you agree or disagree with the writer's thesis? A with-the-grain reading of a text would support all or some of the text's ideas, while also supplying additional evidence or extending the argument, perhaps applying it in a new context. An against-the-grain reading would challenge the writer's ideas, point out flaws and holes in the writer's thinking, and provide counterexamples and rebuttals. You might agree with some ideas and disagree with others in the text. In any case, in an ideas critique you speak back to the text from your own experience, background, reading, and thoughtful wrestling with the writer's ideas.

As an example, let's return to the article from the conservative business journal on drilling for oil in the ANWR. For an ideas critique, you would give your own views on oil exploration in the ANWR to support or challenge the writer's views, to raise new questions, and otherwise to add your voice to the ANWR conversation.

- You might supply additional reasons and evidence for drilling.
- You might oppose drilling in the ANWR by providing counterreasoning and counterexamples.
- You might propose some kind of synthesis or middle ground, where you would allow drilling in the ANWR but only under certain conditions.

When you write an ideas critique you are thus joining an important conversation about the actual subject matter of a text. Because much academic and professional writing focuses on finding the best solution to complex problems, this kind of strong response is very common. Usually this genre requires closed-form, thesis-governed prose. The following strategies chart suggests questions you can ask about a text to enter into its conversation of ideas.

Question-Asking Strategies for Writing an Ideas Critique

Questions to Ask	Examples
Where do I agree with this author? (with the grain)	Consider how you might amplify or extend Pollan's ideas. Build on his ideas by discussing examples where you or acquaintances have tried to change your lifestyle to lower carbon emissions. Show how these changes might have inspired others to do so.
What new insights has this text given me? (with the grain)	Explore Pollan's ideas that the environmental crisis is at heart a "crisis of lifestyle" or that specialization leads to a disjuncture between our everyday acts and their environmental consequences. Explore Pollan's argument that individual actions may lead to a social revolution. Think of how your eating habits or relationship to gardens has or could contribute to reform.

(continued)

Questions to Ask	Examples
Where do I disagree with this author? (against the grain)	Challenge Pollan's assumptions about the magnitude of the problem. Challenge Pollan's idea that individuals can make a difference. Challenge his assumptions that technological solutions won't work because we still will face a crisis of lifestyle. Challenge the practicality and value of his main solution—growing gardens.
What points has the author overlooked or omitted? (against the grain)	Recognize that Pollan overlooks the constraints that would keep people from gardening. Consider that Pollan chooses not to focus on problems of overpopulation, water shortage, or economic disruption caused by environmentalism.
What new questions or problems has the text raised? (with or against the grain)	Explain how Pollan minimizes the economic impact of environmental action and downplays the role of government and business. Consider how we might need to "change the system" rather than just change ourselves. Consider his apparent lack of interest in technological solutions to the energy crisis.
What are the limitations or consequences of this text? (with or against the grain)	Consider ways that Pollan excludes some of his readers even while reaching out to others. Consider how Pollan, given his books on food and his passion for replacing industrial food production with local food, has written a predictable argument. Consider what new ideas he brings to his readers.

Because critiques of ideas appear in many contexts where writers search for the best solutions to problems, this kind of thinking is essential for academic research. In writing research papers, writers typically follow the template "This other writer has argued A, but I am going to argue B." Often the writer's own view (labeled "B") results from the writer's having wrestled with the views of others.

Strong Response as Reflection

A third kind of strong response is often called a "reflection" or a "reflection paper." (An instructor might say, for example, "Read Michael Pollan's article on climate change and write a reflection about it.") Generally, a **reflection** is an introspective genre; it invites you to connect the reading to your own personal experiences, beliefs, and values. In a reflection paper, the instructor is particularly interested in how the reading has affected you personally—what memories it has triggered, what personal experiences it relates to, what values and beliefs it has challenged, what dilemmas it poses, and so forth. A **reflection paper** is often more exploratory, open-ended, musing, and tentative than a rhetorical critique or an ideas critique, which is usually closed form and thesis governed.

To illustrate, let's consider how you might write a reflection in response to the article in the conservative business journal on drilling for oil in the ANWR. One approach might be to build a reflection around a personal conflict in values by exploring how the reading creates a personal dilemma:

- You might write about your own wilderness experiences, musing about the importance of nature in your own life.
- But at the same time, you might reflect on the extent to which your own life depends on cheap oil and acknowledge your own reluctance to give up owning a car.

In short, you want pristine nature and the benefits of cheap oil at the same time. Another quite different approach might be to reflect on how this article connects to discussions you are having in your other courses, say, the economic cost of individuals' and companies' going green.. Here are some strategies you can use to generate ideas for a reflective strong response:

Question-Asking Strategies for Writing a Reflective Strong Response	
Questions to Ask	Examples
What personal memories or experiences does this text trigger?	Explore how Pollan's article evokes memories of your own frustrations about or successes with "green" living. Have you ever tried to change your habits for environmental reasons? If so, how did you go about doing it? Would your changes have met Berry's and Pollan's criteria for a change of "lifestyle"?
What personal values or beliefs does this text reinforce or challenge?	Explore the extent to which you can or can't identify with Pollan, Al Gore, and others who are proclaiming the seriousness of climate change and advocating changes in lifestyle. To what extent does Pollan as a person of conviction spark your admiration?

(continued)

Questions to Ask	Examples
What questions, dilemmas, or problems does this text raise for me?	Explore how Pollan has challenged readers to take actions that may be difficult for them. For instance, you may have arrived at other solutions or know groups or organizations that are contributing positively in other ways. Perhaps Pollan's level of commitment or his particular approach to living green disturbs you in some way.
What new insights, ideas, or thoughts of my own have been stimulated by this text?	Explore any moments of enlightenment you had while reading Pollan. For example, perhaps his focus on individual action rather than on "laws and money" seems problematic to you. Perhaps there are other causes besides the environment that spur you to concern or to action. Perhaps you are now interested in exploring what inspires people to make major changes in how they live.

As you can tell from these questions, a reflective strong response highlights your own personal experiences and beliefs in conversation with the text. Whereas the focus of a rhetorical critique is on analyzing the way the text works rhetorically and the focus of an ideas critique is on taking a stance on the ideas at stake in the text, a reflective response focuses on the personal dimension of reading the text. Reflections call for a degree of self-disclosure or self-exploration that would be largely absent from the other kinds of strong responses.

Strong Response as a Blend

It should be evident that the boundaries among the rhetorical critique, ideas critique, and reflection overlap and that a strong response could easily blend features of each. In trying to decide how to respond strongly to a text, you often don't have to confine yourself to a pure genre but can mix and match different kinds of responses. You can analyze and critique a text's rhetorical strategies, show how the text challenges your own personal values and beliefs, and also develop your own stance on the text's ideas. In writing a blended response, you can emphasize what is most important to you, while not limiting yourself to only one approach.

Before we turn to the writing project for this chapter, we show you an example of a student's summary/strong response that is a blend of rhetorical critique, ideas critique, and personal reflection. Note that the essay begins by conveying the writer's investment in environmental conservation. It then summarizes Pollan's article. Following the summary, the student writer states his thesis, followed by his strong response, which contains both rhetorical points and points engaging Pollan's ideas.

Kyle Madsen (student)
Can a Green Thumb Save the Planet?
A Response to Michael Pollan

When I was a child, our household had one garbage can, in which my family and I would deposit all of our cardboard, plastic, glass, and paper waste. No one on my block had ever heard of recycling or using energy saving bulbs, and we never considered turning down our thermostats during the frozen winters and ice storms that swept our region from November to March. It wasn't that we didn't care about what we were doing to our environment. We just didn't know any better. However, once I got to college all that changed. My university's policies requested that students separate glass bottles and pizza boxes from plastic candy wrappers and old food containers. Thanks in large part to the chilling success of Al Gore's documentary *An Inconvenient Truth*, many of my old neighbors were starting to catch on as well, and now my home town is as devoted to its recycling as any major metropolitan area. Still, even though we as a country have come a long way in just a few years, there is a long way to go. Environmental journalist Michael Pollan in his article "Why Bother?" for the *New York Times Magazine* examines why working to slow the threat of climate change is such a daunting task.

In "Why Bother?" Michael Pollan explores how we have arrived at our current climate change crisis and argues why and how we should try to change our individual actions. Pollan sums up the recent scientific evidence for rapid climate change and then focuses on people's feeling overwhelmed in the face of this vast environmental problem. He presents his interpretation of how we have contributed to the problem and why we feel powerless. Pollan asserts that the climate-change crisis is "the sum total of countless everyday choices" made by consumers globally and that it is "at its very bottom a crisis of lifestyle—of character, even" (90). Our reliance on "cheap fossil fuel" has contributed to both the problem and to our sense of helplessness. In the final part of his article, Pollan concedes that "laws and money" (90) are necessary to create change, but he still advocates acting on our values and setting an example, which might launch a green social revolution. According to Pollan, "The idea is to find one thing to do in your life that does not involve spending or voting ... that will offer its own rewards" (93). He concludes by encouraging readers to plant gardens in order to reduce carbon emissions, to lessen our "sense of dependence and dividedness" (93)—to empower ourselves to contribute positively to our environment.

Although Pollan has created an argument with strong logical, ethical, and emotional appeals, his very dominant angle of vision—seen in his assumptions, alarmist language, and exclusive focus on garden-growing—may fail to win neutral readers. I also think Pollan's argument loses impact by not discussing more realistic alternatives such as pursuing smart consumerism and better environmental education for children.

Pollan builds a forceful case in his well-argued and knowledgeable interpretation of our climate-change problem as a "crisis of lifestyle—of character, even" (90).

Introduces topic/problem and shows writer's investment in caring for the environment

Identifies Pollan's article and Pollan's purpose

Summary of Pollan's article

Thesis statement focused on rhetorical points

Second part of thesis focused on ideas critique

With-the-grain rhetorical point focused on the logos and ethos of Pollan's argument

His frank confrontation of the problem of how to motivate people is compelling, especially when he admits the contrast between "the magnitude of the problem" and the "puniness" of individual action (89). Pollan both deepens his argument and constructs a positive ethos by drawing on the ideas of environmental ethicist Wendell Berry and classical economist Adam Smith to explain how modern civilization has developed through the division of labor (specialization), which has brought us many advantages but also cut us off from community and environmental responsibility. In this part of his argument, Pollan helps readers understand how our dependence on cheap oil and our lifestyle choices have enhanced our roles as limited, specialized producers and major consumers. Pollan's development of his theory of the "cheap-energy mind" (92) and his reasonable support of this idea are the strongest part of his argument and the most relevant to readers like me. I have thought that we have become small cogs in an overbearing machine of consumption and only larger cogs such as the government can have enough influence on the overall system to make change happen. From time to time, I have wondered what I as one person could really do. This sense of insignificance, which Pollan theorizes, has made me wait until my regular light bulbs burned out before considering replacing them with energy-efficient ones.

Brief reflective comment

With-the-grain rhetorical point focused on the pathos of Pollan's argument

Another strength of Pollan's argument is the way he builds bridges to his audience through his appeals to *pathos*. He understands how overwhelmed the average person can feel when confronted with the climate-change problem. Pollan never criticizes his readers for not being as concerned as he is. Instead he engages them in learning with him. He explores with readers the suggestion of walking to work, a task on par with light bulb changing, when he writes, even if "I decide that I am going to bother, there arises the whole vexed question of getting it right. Is eating local or walking to work really going to reduce my carbon footprint?" (89). By asking questions like these, he speaks as a concerned citizen who tries to create a dialogue with his audience about the problem of climate change and what individuals can do.

Against-the-grain rhetorical point focused on angle of vision

However, despite his outreach to readers, Pollan's angle of vision may be too dominant and intense for some readers. He assumes that his *New York Times Magazine* readers already share his agreement with the most serious views of climate change held by many scientists and environmentalists, people who are focusing on the "truly terrifying feedback loops" (90) in weather and climate. He also assumes that his readers hold similar values about local food and gardening. This intense angle of vision may leave out some readers. For example, I am left wondering why gardening is more effective than, say, converting to solar power. He also tries to shock his readers into action with his occasional alarmist or overly dramatic use of language. For example, he tries to invoke fear: "Have you looked into the eyes of a climate scientist recently? They look really scared" (90). However, how many regular people have run-ins with climate scientists?

Transition to ideas critique, an against-the-grain point critiquing Pollan's ideas—Pollan

In addition, after appearing very in tune with readers in the first part of his argument, in the final part he does not address his readers' practical concerns. He describes in great detail the joys of gardening—specifically how it will connect readers not only to the earth, but to friends and neighbors as well—yet he glosses over the amount of work necessary to grow a garden. He writes, "Photosynthesis still works so abundantly that in a thoughtfully organized vegetable garden (one planted from seed, nourished by compost from the kitchen and involving not too many drives to the gardening center), you can grow the proverbial free lunch" (93–4). However, not everyone has a space for a garden or access to a public one to grow tomatoes themselves, and it takes hours of backbreaking labor to grow a productive vegetable garden—hardly a free lunch. Average Americans work upwards of sixty hours per week, so it is unrealistic to expect them to spend their free time working in a garden. In not addressing readers' objections to gardening or suggesting other ways to mend our cheap oil values, I think Pollan proposes simply another situation for semi-concerned individuals to again say, "Why bother?"

doesn't acknowledge the impracticality of expecting people to grow their own vegetables.

Also, besides gardens, I think Pollan could emphasize other avenues of change such as sustainable consumerism. In different places in the article, he mentions that individuals can use their consumer lifestyles to achieve a more sustainable way of life, but he chooses to insist that gardening be the main means. I would have liked him to discuss how we as consumers could buy more fuel-efficient cars, avoid plastic packaging, drink tap water, and buy products from green industries. This "going green" trend has already taken root in many of America's top industries—at least in their advertising and public relations campaigns. We can't leave a Starbucks without inadvertently learning about what they are doing to offset global warming. But we consumers need to know which industries really are going green in a significant way so that we can spend our shopping dollars there. If Pollan is correct, environmentally conscientious consumers can demand a change from the corporations they rely on, so why not use the same consumerism that got us into this mess to get us out?

Another point critiquing Pollan's ideas. Madsen proposes sustainable consumerism as an alternative to gardening.

Besides sustainable consumerism, I think we should emphasize the promotion of better environmental education for our children. Curriculum in K–12 classrooms presented by teachers rather than information from television or newspapers will shape children's commitment to the environment. A good example is the impact of Recycle Now, an organization aimed at implementing recycling and global awareness in schools. According to Dave Lawrie, a curriculum expert featured on their Web site, "Recycling at school is a hands-on way to show pupils that every single person can help to improve the environment. Everyone in our school has played a part in making a difference." With serious education, kids will learn the habits of respecting the earth, working in gardens, and using energy-saving halogen bulbs, making sustainability and environmental stewardship a way of life.

Another point addressing Pollan's ideas— environmental education in the schools as an alternative to gardening.

While Pollan is correct in pushing us into action now, asking Americans to grow a garden, when changing a light bulb seems daunting, is an unrealistic and limited approach. However, Pollan persuasively addresses the underlying issues in our attitudes toward the climate crisis and works to empower readers to become responsible and involved. Whether it be through gardening, supporting green businesses, or education, I agree with Pollan that the important thing is that you learn to bother for yourself.

Short conclusion bringing closure to the essay.

Works Cited

Lawrie, Dave. "Bringing the Curriculum to Life." School Success Stories. *RecycleNow* 11 Nov. 2009. Web. 28 Feb. 2010.

Pollan, Michael. "Why Bother?" *New York Times Magazine* 20 Apr. 2008: 19+. Rpt. in *The Allyn and Bacon Guide to Writing.* John D. Ramage, John C. Bean, and June Johnson. 6th ed. New York: Pearson, 2012. 88–94. Print.

Citation of works cited in the essay using MLA format

In the student example just shown, Kyle Madsen illustrates a blended strong response that includes both a rhetorical critique of the article and some of his own views. He analyzes Pollan's article rhetorically by pointing out both the persuasive features of the argument and the limiting angle of vision of a worried environmentalist and extremely committed gardening enthusiast. He seconds some of Pollan's points with his own examples, but he also reads Pollan against the grain by suggesting how Pollan's word choice and fixation on gardening as a solution prevent him from developing ideas that might seem more compelling to some readers.

WRITING
PROJECT

A Summary

Write a summary of an article assigned by your instructor for an audience who has not read the article. Write the summary using attributive tags and providing an introductory context as if you were inserting it into your own longer paper (see the model on p. 100). The word count for your summary will be specified by your instructor. Try to follow all the criteria for a successful summary and use MLA documentation style, including a Works Cited entry for the article that you are summarizing. (Note: Instead of an article, your instructor may ask you to summarize a longer text such as a book or a visual-verbal text such as a Web page or an advocacy brochure. We address these special cases at the end of this section.)

Generating Ideas: Reading for Structure and Content

Once you have been assigned an article to summarize, your first task is to read it carefully a number of times to get an accurate understanding of it. Remember that summarizing involves the essential act of reading with the grain as you figure out exactly what the article is saying. In writing a summary, you must focus on both a text's structure and its content. In the following steps, we recommend a process that will help you condense a text's ideas into an accurate summary. As you become a more experienced reader and writer, you'll follow these steps without thinking about them.

Step 1: The first time through, read the text fairly quickly for general meaning. If you get confused, keep going; later parts of the text might clarify earlier parts.

Step 2: Read the text carefully paragraph by paragraph. As you read, write gist statements in the margins for each paragraph. A *gist statement* is a brief indication of a paragraph's function in the text or a brief summary of a paragraph's content. Sometimes it is helpful to think of these two kinds of gist statements as "what it does" statements and "what it says" statements.* A "what

---

*For our treatment of "what it does" and "what it says" statements, we are indebted to Kenneth A. Bruffee, *A Short Course in Writing*, 2nd ed. (Cambridge, MA: Winthrop, 1980).

it does" statement specifies the paragraph's function—for example, "summarizes an opposing view," "introduces another reason," "presents a supporting example," "provides statistical data in support of a point," and so on. A "what it says" statement captures the main idea of a paragraph by summarizing the paragraph's content. The "what it says" statement is the paragraph's main point, in contrast to its supporting ideas and examples.

When you first practice detailed readings of a text, you might find it helpful to write complete *does* and *says* statements on a separate sheet of paper rather than in the margins until you develop the internal habit of appreciating both the function and content of parts of an essay. Here are *does* and *says* statements for selected paragraphs of Michael Pollan's article on climate change activism.

Paragraph 1: *Does*: Introduces the need for environmental action as a current problem that readers know and care about and sets up the argument. ***Says*:** We as individuals often wonder if our small, minor actions are worth doing in light of the magnitude of the climate change problem.

Paragraph 2: *Does*: Explores another reason why individuals may doubt whether individual actions could make a difference. ***Says*:** People willing to change their lifestyles to combat climate change may be discouraged by the increase in a carbon-emissions lifestyle in other parts of the world such as China.

Paragraph 8: *Does*: Expresses an alternative view, partially concedes to it, and asserts a counterview. ***Says*:** Although big money and legislation will be important in reversing climate change, the problem at its heart is a "crisis of lifestyle—of character" (90), and therefore will require the effort of individuals.

Paragraph 18: *Does*: Presents and develops one of Pollan's main reasons that concerned individuals should take personal action to fight climate change. ***Says*:** Setting an example through our own good environmental choices could exert moral influence here and abroad, on individuals and big business.

Writing a *says* statement for a paragraph is sometimes difficult. You might have trouble, for example, deciding what the main idea of a paragraph is, especially if the paragraph doesn't begin with a closed-form topic sentence. One way to respond to this problem is to formulate the question that you think the paragraph answers. If you think of chunks of the text as answers to a logical progression of questions, you can often follow the main ideas more easily. Rather than writing *says* statements in the margins, therefore, some readers prefer writing *says* questions. *Says* questions for the Pollan text may include the following:

- What are some of the biggest obstacles that discourage people from undertaking individual actions to fight climate change?
- Despite our excuses not to act, why is individual action still necessary?
- How is the problem of climate a "crisis of lifestyle"?
- What are the reasons we should "bother"?
- Why is growing one's own vegetable garden a particularly powerful individual act?

No matter which method you use—*says* statements or *says* questions—writing gist statements in the margins is far more effective than underlining or highlighting in helping you recall the text's structure and argument.

Step 3: Locate the article's main divisions or parts. In longer closed-form articles, writers often forecast the shape of their essays in their introductions or use their conclusions to sum up main points. For example, Pollan's article uses some forecasting and transitional statements to direct readers through its parts and main points. The article is divided into several main chunks as follows:

- Introductory paragraphs, which establish the problem to be addressed and describe the reasons that people don't take action to help slow climate change (paragraphs 1–5)
- Two short transitional paragraphs (a one-sentence question and a two-word answer) stating the author's intention to call for individual action in spite of the obstacles. These two paragraphs prepare the move into the second part of the article (paragraphs 6 and 7).
- A paragraph conceding to the need for action beyond the individual (laws and money) followed by a counterclaim that the climate change problem is a "crisis of lifestyle" (paragraph 8)
- Eight paragraphs developing Pollan's "crisis of lifestyle" claim, drawing on Wendell Berry and explaining the concepts of specialization and the "cheap-energy mind" that have led us into both the climate change problem and our feelings of inadequacy to tackle it (paragraphs 9–16)
- A transitional paragraph conceding that reasons against individual action are "many and compelling," but proposing better ways to answer the "why bother" question. (paragraph 17)
- Two paragraphs developing Pollan's reasons for individual action—how individuals will influence each other and broader communities and lead to "viral social change" (paragraphs 18–19)
- Two paragraphs elaborating on the possibility of viral social change based on analogy to the end of Communism in Czechoslovakia and Poland and to various ways individuals might make significant changes in their lifestyles (paragraphs 20–21)
- Five paragraphs detailing Pollan's choice for the best solution for people to reduce their carbon emissions and make a significant environmental statement: grow gardens (paragraphs 22–26)

Instead of listing the sections of your article, you might prefer to make an outline or tree diagram of the article showing its main parts.

Drafting and Revising

Once you have determined the main points and grasped the structure of the article you are summarizing, combine and condense your *says* statements into clear sentences that capture the gist of the article. These shortened versions of your *says* statements will make up most of your summary, although you might mention the structure of the article to help organize the points. For example, you might say, "[Author's name] makes four main points in this article. ... The article concludes with a call to action. … " Because representing an article in your own words in a greatly abbreviated form is a challenge, most writers revise their sentences to find the clearest, most concise way to express the article's ideas accurately. Choose and use your words carefully to stay within your word limit.

The procedures for summarizing articles can work for book-length texts and visual-verbal texts as well. For book-length texts, your *does* and *says* statements may cover chapters or parts of the book. Book introductions and conclusions as well as chapter titles and introductions may provide clues to the author's thesis and subthesis to help you identify the main ideas to include in a book summary. For verbal-visual texts such as a public affairs advocacy ad, product advertisement, Web page, or brochure, examine the parts to see what each contributes to the whole. In your summary, help your readers visualize the images, comprehend the parts, and understand the main points of the text's message.

Plan to create several drafts of all summaries to refine your presentation and wording of ideas. Group work may be helpful in these steps.

Finding Key Points in an Article

FOR WRITING AND DISCUSSION

If the whole class or a group of students is summarizing the same article, brainstorm together and then reach consensus on the main ideas that you think a summary of that article should include to be accurate and complete. Then reread your own summary and check off each idea.

When you revise your summary, consult the criteria on page 102 in this chapter as well as the Questions for Peer Review that follow.

Questions for Peer Review

In addition to the generic peer review questions explained in, Skill 16.4, ask your peer reviewers to address these questions:

1. In what way do the opening sentences provide needed contextual information and then express the overall thesis of the text? What information could be added or more clearly stated?
2. How would you evaluate the writer's representation and coverage of the text's main ideas in terms of accuracy, balance, and proportion? What ideas have been omitted or overemphasized?
3. Has the writer treated the article fairly and neutrally? If judgments have crept in, where could the writer revise?
4. How could the summary use attributive tags more effectively to keep the focus on the original author's ideas?
5. Has the writer used quotations sparingly and cited them accurately? Has the writer translated points into his or her own words? Has the writer included a Works Cited?
6. Where might the writer's choice of words and phrasing of sentences be revised to improve the clarity, conciseness, and coherence of the summary?

A Summary/Strong Response Essay

In response to a text assigned by your instructor, write a "summary/strong response" essay that incorporates a 150–250-word summary of the article. In your strong response to that reading, speak back to its author from your own critical thinking, personal experience, values, and, perhaps, further reading or research. Unless your instructor assigns a specific kind of strong response (rhetorical critique, ideas critique, or reflection), write a blended response in which you are free to consider the author's rhetorical strategies, your own agreement or disagreement with the author's ideas, and your personal response to the text. Think of your response as your analysis of how the text tries to influence its readers rhetorically and how your wrestling with the text has expanded and deepened your thinking about its ideas. As you work with ideas from the text, remember to use attributive tags, quotation marks for any quoted passages, and MLA documentation to distinguish your own points about the text from the author's ideas and language.

Exploring Ideas for Your Strong Response

Earlier in the chapter we presented the kinds of strong responses you may be asked to write in college. We also provided examples of the questions you can ask to generate ideas for different kinds of strong response. Your goal now is to figure out what you want to say. Your first step, of course, is to read your assigned text with the grain, listening to the text so well that you can write a summary of its argument. Use the strategies described in the previous writing project to compose your summary of the assigned text.

After you have written your summary, which demonstrates your full understanding of the text, you are ready to write a strong response. Because your essay cannot discuss every feature of the text or every idea the text has evoked, you will want to focus on a small group of points that enable you to bring readers a new, enlarged, or deepened understanding of the text. You may decide to write a primarily with-the-grain response, praising, building on, or applying the text to a new context, or a primarily against-the-grain response, challenging, questioning, and refuting the text. If your strong response primarily agrees with the text, you must be sure to extend it and apply the ideas rather than simply make your essay one long summary of the article. If your strong response primarily disagrees with the text and criticizes it, you must be sure to be fair and accurate in your criticisms. Here we give you some specific rereading strategies that will stimulate ideas for your strong response, as well as an example of Kyle Madsen's marginal response notes to Pollan's article (Figure 1).

Strategies for Rereading to Stimulate Ideas for a Strong Response

Strategies	What to Do	Comments
Take notes.	Make copious marginal notes while rereading, recording both with-the-grain and against-the-grain responses.	Writing a strong response requires a deep engagement with texts. For example, in Figure 1, observe how Kyle Madsen's notes incorporate with-the-grain and against-the-grain responses and show him truly talking back to and interacting with Pollan's text.
Identify "hot spots" in the text.	Mark all hot spots with marginal notes. After you've finished reading, find these hot spots and freewrite your responses to them in a reading journal.	By "hot spot" we mean a quotation or passage that you notice because you agree or disagree with it or because it triggers memories or other associations. Perhaps the hot spot strikes you as thought provoking. Perhaps it raises a problem or is confusing yet suggestive.
Ask questions.	Write several questions that the text caused you to think about. Then explore your responses to those questions through freewriting, which may trigger more questions.	Almost any text triggers questions as you read. A good way to begin formulating a strong response is to note these questions.
Articulate your difference from the intended audience.	Decide who the writer's intended audience is. If you differ significantly from this audience, use this difference to question the author's underlying assumptions, values, and beliefs.	Your gender, age, class, ethnicity, sexual orientation, political and religious beliefs, interests, values, and so forth, may cause you to feel estranged from the author's imagined audience. If the text seems written for straight people and you are gay, or for Christians and you are a Muslim or an atheist, or for environmentalists and you grew up in a small logging community, you may well resist the text. Sometimes your sense of exclusion from the intended audience makes it difficult to read a text at all.

Michael Pollan

Why Bother?

This idea is very direct and clear.

Why bother? That really is the big question facing us as individuals hoping to do something about climate change, and it's not an easy one to answer. I don't know about you, but for me the most upsetting moment in *An Inconvenient Truth* came long after Al Gore scared the hell out of me, constructing an utterly convincing case that the very survival of life on earth as we know it is threatened by climate change. No, the really dark moment came during the closing credits, when we are asked to . . . change our light bulbs. That's when it got really depressing. The immense disproportion between the magnitude of the problem Gore had described and the puniness of what he was asking us to do about it was enough to sink your heart.

Short sentence sounds casual.

Another very informal statement.

But the drop-in-the-bucket issue is not the only problem lurking behind the "why bother" question. Let's say I do bother, big time. I turn my life upside-down, start biking to work, plant a big garden, turn down the thermostat so low I need the Jimmy Carter signature cardigan, forsake the clothes dryer for a laundry line across the yard, trade in the station wagon for a hybrid, get off the beef, go completely local. I could theoretically do all that, but what would be the point when I know full well that halfway around the world there lives my evil twin, some carbon-footprint *doppelgänger* in Shanghai or Chongqing who has just bought his first car (Chinese car ownership is where ours was back in 1918), is eager to swallow every bite of meat I forswear and who's positively itching to replace every last pound of CO2 I'm struggling no longer to emit. So what exactly would I have to show for all my trouble?

Good word choice? Sounds prejudiced and alarmist.

A sense of personal virtue, you might suggest, somewhat sheepishly. But what good is that when virtue itself is quickly becoming a term of derision? And not just on the editorial pages of the *Wall Street Journal* or on the lips of the vice president, who famously dismissed energy conservation as a "sign of personal virtue." No, even in the pages of the *New York Times* and the *New Yorker*, it seems the epithet "virtuous," when applied to an act of personal environmental responsibility, may be used only ironically. Tell me: How did it come to pass that virtue—a quality that for most of history has generally been deemed, well, a virtue—became a mark of liberal softheadedness? How peculiar, that doing the right thing by the environment—buying the hybrid, eating like a locavore— should now set you up for the Ed Begley Jr.* treatment.

This paragraph shows Pollan's liberal perspective.

Informal speech.

Sounds like Pollan is talking to readers.

How I felt when I saw this film.

Helpful examples.

Look up this word.

Exaggerated statement?

Former Vice President Cheney?

What's the definition of this term?

FIGURE 1 Kyle Madsen's Marginal Response Notes

Practicing Strong Response Reading Strategies

What follows is a short passage by writer Annie Dillard in response to a question about how she chooses to spend her time. This passage often evokes heated responses from our students.

> I don't do housework. Life is too short. ... I let almost all my indoor plants die from neglect while I was writing the book. There are all kinds of ways to live. You can take your choice. You can keep a tidy house, and when St. Peter asks you what you did with your life, you can say, "I kept a tidy house, I made my own cheese balls."

Individual task: Read the passage and then briefly freewrite your reaction to it.

Group task: Working in groups or as a whole class, develop answers to the following questions:

1. What values does Dillard assume her audience holds?
2. What kinds of readers are apt to feel excluded from that audience?
3. If you are not part of the intended audience for this passage, what in the text evokes resistance?

Articulate Your Own Purpose for Reading

Although you usually read a text because you are joining the author's conversation, you might occasionally read a text for an entirely different purpose from what the author intended. For example, you might read the writings of nineteenth-century scientists to figure out what they assumed about nature (or women, or God, or race, or capitalism). Or suppose that you examine a politician's metaphors to see what they reveal about her values, or analyze *National Geographic* for evidence of political bias. Understanding your own purpose will help you read deeply both with and against the grain.

Writing a Thesis for a Strong Response Essay

A thesis for a strong response essay should map out for readers the points that you want to develop and discuss. These points should be risky and contestable; your thesis should surprise your readers with something new or challenging. Your thesis might focus entirely on with-the-grain points or entirely on against-the-grain points, but most likely it will include some of both. Avoid tensionless thesis statements such as "This article has both good and bad points."

Here are some thesis statements that students have written for strong responses in our classes. Note that each thesis includes at least one point about the rhetorical strategies of the text.

EXAMPLES OF SUMMARY/STRONG RESPONSE THESIS STATEMENTS

- In "The Beauty Myth," Naomi Wolf makes a very good case for her idea that the beauty myth prevents women from ever feeling that they are good enough;

however, Wolf's argument is geared too much toward feminists to be persuasive for a general audience, and she neglects to acknowledge the strong social pressures that I and other men feel to live up to male standards of physical perfection.

- Although Naomi Wolf in "The Beauty Myth" uses rhetorical strategies persuasively to argue that the beauty industry oppresses women, I think that she overlooks women's individual resistance and responsibility.
- Although the images and figures of speech that Thoreau uses in his chapter "Where I Lived, and What I Lived For" from *Walden* wonderfully support his argument that nature is spiritually renewing, I disagree with his antitechnology stance and with his extreme emphasis on isolation as a means to self-discovery.
- In "Where I Lived, and What I Lived For" from *Walden*, Thoreau's argument that society is missing spiritual reality through its preoccupation with details and its frantic pace is convincing, especially to twenty-first century audiences; however, Thoreau weakens his message by criticizing his readers and by completely dismissing technological advances.
- Although the booklet *Compassionate Living* by People for the Ethical Treatment of Animals (PETA) uses the design features of layout, color, and image powerfully, its extreme examples, its quick dismissal of alternative views, and its failure to document the sources of its information weaken its appeal to *ethos* and its overall persuasiveness.

FOR WRITING AND DISCUSSION

Examining Thesis Statements for Strong Response Critiques

Working individually or in groups, identify the points in each of the thesis statements in the preceding section and briefly state them. Think in terms of the ideas you are expecting the writers to develop in the body of the essay. As a follow-up to this exercise, you might share in your groups your own thesis statements for your strong response essays. How clearly does each thesis statement lay out points that the writer will probe? As a group, discuss what new, important perspectives each thesis statement promises to bring to readers and how each thesis suits a rhetorical critique, ideas critique, or some combination of these.

Shaping and Drafting

Most strong response essays call for a short contextualizing introduction to set up your analysis. Student writer Kyle Madsen begins by reflecting on personal and societal changes in environmental awareness and then raises the question that Pollan will address: What challenges confront us in changing how we live? Student writer Stephanie Malinowski uses a similar strategy. She begins by tapping into her readers' experiences with outsourcing, and then poses the question that Thomas Friedman addresses in his op-ed piece: Should Americans support or question the practice of outsourcing?

Both student writers introduce the question addressed by the article they are critiquing, and both include a short summary of the article that gives readers a foundation for the critique before they present the points of the article they will address in their strong responses.

Each of the thesis statements in the preceding section as well as Kyle's and Stephanie's thesis statements identifies and maps out two or more points that readers will expect to see developed and explained in the body of the essay. In a closed-form, thesis-driven strong response, readers will also expect the points to follow the order in which they are presented in the thesis. If your strong response is primarily a rhetorical critique, your evidence will come mainly from the text you are analyzing. If your strong response is primarily an ideas critique, your evidence is apt to come from personal knowledge of the issue or from further reading or research. If your strong response is primarily reflective, much of your evidence will be based on your own personal experiences and inner thoughts. A blended response, of course, can combine points from any of these perspectives.

Each point in your thesis calls for a lively discussion, combining general statements and specifics that will encourage readers to see this text your way. Just as you do in your summary, you must use attributive tags to distinguish between the author's ideas and your own points and responses. In addition, you must document all ideas gotten from other sources as well as place all borrowed language in quotation marks or block indentations according to MLA format and include a Works Cited in MLA format. Most strong response essays have short conclusions, just enough commentary to bring closure to the essay.

Revising

In a summary/strong response essay, you may want to work on the summary separately before you incorporate it into your whole essay. Use the peer review questions for summaries for that part of your essay. You will definitely want to get feedback from readers to make your strong response as clear, thorough, and compelling as possible.

Questions for Peer Review

In addition to generic peer review questions, ask your peer reviewers to address these questions:

1. How appealingly do the title and introduction of the essay set up the topic of critique, convey the writer's interest, and lay a foundation for the summary of the article and the writer's thesis?
2. How could the writer's thesis statement be clearer in presenting several focused points about the text's rhetorical strategies and ideas?
3. How could the body of the strong response follow the thesis more closely?
4. Where do you, the reader, need more clarification or support for the writer's points? How could the writer develop with-the-grain or against-the-grain points more appropriately?
5. Where could the writer work on the effectiveness of attributive tags, quotations, and documentation?

Readings

The readings for this chapter address the issue of outsourcing, the practice of moving jobs from developed countries like the United States to developing countries, which have a cheaper workforce. This practice affects available jobs for college graduates and American workers as well as the progress and vitality of the economies of many countries. Outsourcing continues to spark fiery debates about job creation and unemployment in the United States, about the distribution of benefits and harm, and about global economic competition. The readings that follow address these points from multiple perspectives. The questions for analysis have been omitted from all but the student essay by Stephanie Malinowski so that you can do your own independent thinking in preparation for writing your own summary/strong response essay.

Our first reading is an op-ed piece by prominent journalist Thomas L. Friedman, published in the *New York Times* on February 29, 2004. Friedman is known for his pro–free trade enthusiasm and his three books on globalization, *The Lexus and the Olive Tree* (1999), *The World Is Flat: A Brief History of the Twenty-First Century* (2005), and *Hot, Flat, and Crowded* (2008).

Thomas L. Friedman
30 Little Turtles

1   Indians are so hospitable. I got an ovation the other day from a roomful of Indian 20-year-olds just for reading perfectly the following paragraph: "A bottle of bottled water held 30 little turtles. It didn't matter that each turtle had to rattle a metal ladle in order to get a little bit of noodles, a total turtle delicacy. The problem was that there were many turtle battles for less than oodles of noodles."

2   I was sitting in on an "accent neutralization" class at the Indian call center 24/7 Customer. The instructor was teaching the would-be Indian call center operators to suppress their native Indian accents and speak with a Canadian one—she teaches British and U.S. accents as well, but these youths will be serving the Canadian market. Since I'm originally from Minnesota, near Canada, and still speak like someone out of the movie "Fargo," I gave these young Indians an authentic rendition of "30 Little Turtles," which is designed to teach them the proper Canadian pronunciations. Hence the rousing applause.

3   Watching these incredibly enthusiastic young Indians preparing for their call center jobs—earnestly trying to soften their t's and roll their r's—is an uplifting experience, especially when you hear from their friends already working these jobs how they have transformed their lives. Most of them still live at home and turn over part of their salaries to their parents, so the whole family benefits. Many have credit cards and have become real consumers, including of U.S. goods, for the first time. All of them seem to have gained self-confidence and self-worth.

4   A lot of these Indian young men and women have college degrees, but would never get a local job that starts at $200 to $300 a month were it not for the call centers. Some do "outbound" calls, selling things from credit cards to phone services to Americans and Europeans. Others deal with "inbound" calls—everything from tracing lost luggage for U.S. airline passengers to solving computer problems for U.S. customers. The calls are transferred here by satellite or fiber optic cable.

5   I was most taken by a young Indian engineer doing tech support for a U.S. software giant, who spoke with pride about how cool it is to tell his friends that he just spent the day helping Americans navigate their software. A majority of these call center workers are young women, who not only have been liberated by earning a decent local wage (and therefore have more choice in whom they marry), but are using the job to get M.B.A.'s and other degrees on the side.

6   I gathered a group together, and here's what they sound like: M. Dinesh, who does tech support, says his day is made when some American calls in with a problem and is actually happy to hear an Indian voice: "They say you people are really good at what you do. I am glad I reached an Indian." Kiran Menon, when asked who his role model was, shot back: "Bill Gates—[I dream of] starting my own company and making it that big." I asked C. M. Meghna what she got most out of the work: "Self-confidence," she said, "a lot of self-confidence, when people come to you with a problem and you can solve it—and having a lot of independence." Because the call center teams work through India's night—which corresponds to America's day—"your biological clock goes haywire," she added. "Besides that, it's great."

7   There is nothing more positive than the self-confidence, dignity and optimism that comes from a society knowing it is producing wealth by tapping its own brains—men's and women's—as opposed to one just tapping its own oil, let alone one that is so lost it can find dignity only through suicide and "martyrdom."

8   Indeed, listening to these Indian young people, I had a déjà vu. Five months ago, I was in Ramallah, on the West Bank, talking to three young Palestinian men, also in their 20's, one of whom was studying engineering. Their hero was Yasir Arafat. They talked about having no hope, no jobs and no dignity, and they each nodded when one of them said they were all "suicide bombers in waiting."

9   What am I saying here? That it's more important for young Indians to have jobs than Americans? Never. But I am saying that there is more to outsourcing than just economics. There's also geopolitics. It is inevitable in a networked world that our economy is going to shed certain low-wage, low-prestige jobs. To the extent that they go to places like India or Pakistan—where they are viewed as high-wage, high-prestige jobs—we make not only a more prosperous world, but a safer world for our own 20-year-olds.

Our second reading is a summary/strong response essay by student writer Stephanie Malinowski in response to the Friedman article. It follows primarily a "rhetorical critique" strategy for the strong response.

Stephanie Malinowski

Questioning Thomas L. Friedman's Optimism in "30 Little Turtles"

1   You are struggling to fix a problem that arises when you are downloading new computer software on to your computer. You're about to give up on the whole thing when an idea hits you: call the software company itself to ask for assistance. Should

you be surprised when the person who answers the phone to help you is based in India? Should Americans support or question outsourcing?

2   In "30 Little Turtles," an op-ed piece that appeared in the *New York Times* on February 29, 2004, journalist and foreign affairs columnist Thomas L. Friedman argues that outsourcing call center jobs from the Western world to India is transforming the lives of Indian workers and benefiting geopolitics. Friedman supports his argument by detailing his experience visiting a call center in India. He claims that the Indians working to serve Canadian and American markets are happy with how their work has improved their lives. Friedman points out that the working Indian women feel liberated now that they are making a decent wage and can afford such things as a college education. He describes Indian workers' view of their jobs, using words such as "self-confidence" and "independence." At the end of his article, Friedman states that he doesn't favor Indian employment over American employment but that outsourced jobs in countries like India or Pakistan create both prosperity and global security. Although Friedman's article clearly conveys to its audience how some Indian workers are benefiting from outsourcing, his argument relies heavily on personal experience and generalizations. I also think his condescending attitude hurts his argument, and he concludes his article too abruptly, leaving readers with questions.

3   Friedman succeeds in portraying the positive side of outsourcing to his *New York Times* readers who may be questioning the rationale for outsourcing. Friedman interviews the recipients of American jobs to see outsourcing from their perspective and enlightens Americans trying to understand how outsourcing is benefiting workers in other countries. Friedman's opening is vivid and captures the readers' interest by detailing his experience inside an Indian call center. He quotes the Indian workers expressing the joys of working for American and Canadian people. These workers testify to the financial and personal gains these jobs have brought. One woman says that she feels good about her job and herself "when people come to you with a problem and you can solve it" (125). The article is so full of optimism that the reader can't help but empathize with the Indians and feel happy that outsourcing has transformed their lives. Through these emotional appeals, Friedman succeeds in making readers who may have big reservations about outsourcing think about the human dimension of outsourcing.

4   However, Friedman also makes large generalizations based on his few personal experiences, lessening the credibility of his article. The first sentence of the article reads, "Indians are so hospitable." So are *all* Indians "so hospitable"? Friedman seems to make this generalization about national character based on the fact that he was applauded by a room full of Indians after reading a tongue twister paragraph in a perfect Canadian accent. I can see why Friedman appreciates his warm reception, but "feel good" moments can hardly provide evidence for the soundness of global economic policies. Friedman generalizes further about what he sees and hears in the call center room. He talks about the Indian employees in these terms: "All of them seem to have gained self-confidence and self-worth" (124). From this single observation, Friedman makes the assumption that almost every Indian working an outsourcing job must be gaining, and that the overall experience has done wonders for their lives. However, other articles that I have read have mentioned that call center work is basically a

deadend job and that $200 a month is not a big salary. Later in his conclusion, Friedman states that "we make not only a more prosperous world, but a safer world for our own 20-year-olds" (125). Can this conclusion be drawn from one visit to a call center where Indians expressed gratitude for their outsourcing work?

5   An even bigger problem with Friedman's article is the condescending way in which he describes the Indian workers. I think he portrays the culture as being incompetent before the American and Canadian outsourcing jobs came to improve their accents and their lives. One statement that conveys condescension is this remark: "Watching these incredibly enthusiastic young Indians preparing for their call center jobs—earnestly trying to soften their t's and roll their r's—is an uplifting experience … " (124). This passage reminds me of the delight and pride of parents witnessing their children's growth milestones. Friedman is casting the accent neutralization of the Indian workers as overcoming a barrier in order to reach success. Friedman's condescending tone is apparent again when he restates the words of one American caller to an Indian worker, "They say you people are really good at what you do. I am glad I reached an Indian" (125). I see Friedman's reason for including this quote; he wants the reader to know that Indian workers are being valued for their work. However, the words that the American uses, which Friedman deliberately chooses to include in his article, "you people," suggest that Indians are a whole other kind of people different from American workers in their skills. Friedman's condescension also appears when he says that these are "low-wage, low-prestige jobs" (125). This remark is full of problems because it puts down the Indians taking the jobs and the Americans who have lost them, and it misrepresents the outsourcing scene that now includes many highly skilled prestigious jobs.

6   I also think that Friedman weakens his article by concluding abruptly and introducing new ideas to readers that leave them with unanswered questions. Friedman asks the reader, "What am I saying here? That it's more important for young Indians to have jobs than Americans?" (125). This point seems like a relevant question to investigate, but its weakness is that Friedman never even mentions any place in his article the loss that American workers are experiencing. At the end of the article, readers are left with questions. For example, the last sentence reads, "we make not only a more prosperous world, but a safer world for our own 20-year-olds" (125). Although Friedman is implying that outsourcing improves our relationships with other countries and enhances our national safety, nowhere in the article does he substantiate this claim. He seems to have thrown this statement into the conclusion just to end the article on a happy note.

7   Giving a human face to outsourcing is a good idea; however, Friedman does not support his main argument well, and this article comes across as a simplistic, unexplored view of outsourcing. I and other readers are left needing to look for answers to serious questions about outsourcing elsewhere.

Work Cited

Friedman, Thomas L. "30 Little Turtles." *New York Times* 29 Feb. 2004. Rpt. in *The Allyn & Bacon Guide to Writing.* John D. Ramage, John C. Bean, and June Johnson. 6th ed. New York: Pearson, 2012. 124–5. Print.

THINKING CRITICALLY

about "Questioning Thomas L. Friedman's Optimism in '30 Little Turtles'"

1. What rhetorical points has Stephanie Malinowski chosen to analyze in her strong response essay?

2. What examples and quotations from Friedman's article work particularly well as support for her points? Where might she have included more support?

3. Where does Stephanie use attributive tags effectively?

4. If you were to write a rhetorical critique of Friedman's article, what points would you select to analyze?

5. If you were to write an ideas critique, what would you choose to focus on? Where would you agree and disagree with Friedman?

Our third and fourth readings consist of two political cartoons that tell stories about employment and U.S. involvement in outsourcing. As you read these cartoons, identify the characters, the story line, the angle of vision, and the argument each presents.

David Horsey is a two-time Pulitzer Prize winner for editorial cartoons. This cartoon was originally published the *Seattle Post-Intelligencer* on June 4, 2003.

David Horsey
Today's Economic Indicator

David Horsey/2003/Seattle Post Intelligencer

The second cartoon, by Mike Lane, appeared in the *Baltimore Sun* in 2003 and was posted on Cagle Cartoons on August 27, 2003. Lane, a prize-winning and well-known liberal editorial cartoonist, left the Baltimore newspaper in 2004 after thirty-two years.

Mike Lane
Labor Day Blues

Mike Lane

Our fifth reading is an op-ed piece by editorial writer and syndicated columnist Froma Harrop, who writes regularly for the *Providence Journal* and whose columns appear frequently in newspapers around the country. She is known for the articulate, forthright expression of her liberal views on current issues. This piece appeared in the *Seattle Times* on April 17, 2007.

Froma Harrop
New Threat to Skilled U.S. Workers

1   The master plan, it seems, is to move perhaps 40 million high-skill American jobs to other countries. U.S. workers have not been consulted.

2   Princeton economist Alan Blinder predicts that these choice jobs could be lost in a mere decade or two. We speak of computer programming, bookkeeping, graphic design and other careers once thought firmly planted in American soil. For perspective, 40 million is more than twice the total number of people now employed in manufacturing.

3   Blinder was taken aback when, sitting in at the business summit in Davos, Switzerland, he heard U.S. executives talk enthusiastically about all the professional jobs they could outsource to lower-wage countries. And he's a free trader.

4   What America can do to stop this is unclear, but it certainly doesn't have to *speed up* the process through a government program. We refer to the H-1B visa program, which allows educated foreigners to work in the United States, usually for three years. Many in Congress want to nearly double the number of H-1B visas, to 115,000 a year.

5   To the extent that the program helps talented foreign graduates of U.S. universities stay in this country while they await their green cards, it performs a useful service. But for many companies, the visa has become just a tool for transferring American jobs offshore.

6   Ron Hira has studied the dark side of the H-1B program. A professor of public policy at the Rochester Institute of Technology, he notes that the top applicants for visas are outsourcing companies, such as Wipro Technologies of India and Bermuda-based Accenture.

7   The companies bring recruits in from, say, India to learn about American business. After three years here, the workers go home better able to interact with their U.S. customers.

8   In other cases, companies ask their U.S. employees to train H-1B workers who then replace them at lower pay. "This is euphemistically called, 'knowledge transfer,'" Hira says. "I call it 'knowledge extraction.' "

9   Another rap against the program is that it's used to depress the wages of American workers. The program's defenders argue that the law requires companies to pay "the prevailing wage."

10 But "prevailing wage" is a legalism, Hira says. It does not translate into "market wage."

11 The median pay for H-1B computing professionals in fiscal 2005 was $50,000, which means half earn less than that. An American information-technology worker with a bachelor's degree makes more than $50,000 in an entry-level job.

12 Businesses bemoan the alleged shortage of Americans trained to do the work. But wait a second—the law of supply and demand states that a shortage of something causes its price to rise. Wages in information technology have been flat.

13 The companies fret that not enough young Americans are studying science and technology. Well, cutting the pay in those fields isn't much of an incentive, is it?

14   The threat that they will outsource if they can't bring in foreign temps is a hollow one. "There's nothing stopping those companies from working offshore anyway," Hira says. "They're not patriotic."

15   This vision for a competitive America seems to be a few rich U.S. executives commandeering armies of foreign workers. They don't have to train their domestic workforce. They don't have to raise pay to American standards.

16   A provision for revving up the H-1B program is contained in the immigration bill that last year passed the Senate. The co-sponsors, Democrat Ted Kennedy of Massachusetts and Republican John McCain of Arizona, have contended that their legislation requires employers to search for U.S. workers first. It does not.

17   Skilled U.S. workers had better start looking out for their interests. No one else is.

 For additional help with writing, reading, and research, go to **www.mycomplab.com**

WRITING AN AUTOBIOGRAPHICAL NARRATIVE

From Chapter 6 of *The Allyn & Bacon Guide to Writing*, Sixth Edition. John D. Ramage, John C. Bean, June Johnson. Copyright © 2012 by Pearson Education, Inc. Published by Pearson Allyn & Bacon. All rights reserved.

WRITING AN AUTOBIOGRAPHICAL NARRATIVE

This chapter focuses on the rhetorical aim "writing to express or share." Its writing projects ask you to write an autobiographical narrative about something significant in your own life. But rather than state the significance up front in a thesis, you let it unfold in storylike fashion. This narrative structure places autobiographical writing at the open end of the closed-to-open-form continuum, making it more like a nonfiction "short story" than a traditional academic essay.

Autobiographical writing can help us explore, deepen, and complicate our perceptions of the world. In addition to telling stories to convey the complexity and significance of an event, we use stories to reveal something about ourselves. We also use others' stories, particularly during adolescence, to monitor our own growth. Many of us have read the stories of such people as Anne Frank, Maya Angelou, Helen Keller, Malcolm X, and Laura Ingalls Wilder in search of attitudes and behaviors to emulate. Reading their stories becomes a way of critiquing and understanding our own stories.

The writing projects for this chapter address two genres of narrative writing: (1) An **autobiographical narrative** on any significant event or moment in your life that uses the narrative strategies of plot, character, and setting to develop tension, move the story forward, and give it significance, and (2) a **literacy narrative** that uses the same narrative strategies but is centered on the writer's experience with language, reading, writing, school, teachers, or education. Both kinds of narratives draw on the sensibility that you bring to the ordinary as well as the unique events of your life. Good autobiographical narrative does not depend on having an exciting life with highly dramatic moments. On the contrary, some of the most memorable autobiographical and literacy narratives relate ordinary experiences in a vivid manner that shares the writer's humiliations, aspirations, self-discoveries, and revelations. All of us have experienced moments when our world became strange or new—perhaps a first day at a new school or job; a conflict with a parent, teacher, employer, lover, or friend; or an encounter in a lunchroom or on a street corner. Everyone enjoys hearing good writers describe how they coped with and understood these universal situations. It is precisely because readers have experienced these things that they can project themselves easily into the writer's world.

In this chapter, you will learn to:

- find and explore a significant moment in your life and
- write an autobiographical or literacy narrative using literary techniques

Exploring Autobiographical Narrative

Good writing is rooted in the writer's perception of a problem. Problems are at the center not only of thesis-based writing but also of narrative writing. In effective narration, the problem usually takes the form of a *contrary*, two or more things in opposition—ideas, characters, expectations, forces, worldviews, or whatever. Three kinds of contraries that frequently form the plots of autobiographical narratives are the following:

1. ***Old self versus new self.*** The writer perceives changes in himself or herself as a result of some transforming or breakthrough moment or event.
2. ***Old view of person X versus new view of person X.*** The writer's perception of a person (favorite uncle, childhood hero, scary teacher) changes as a result of some revealing moment; the change in the narrator's perception of person X also indicates growth in the narrator's self-perception.
3. ***Old values versus new values that threaten, challenge, or otherwise disrupt the old values.*** The writer confronts an outsider (or a new, unfamiliar situation such as a class or a learning task) that challenges his or her worldview, or the writer undergoes a crisis that creates a conflict in values.

Prior to class discussion, freewrite for ten minutes about episodes in your own life that fit one or more of these typical plots. Then, working in small groups or as a whole class, share your discoveries. Your goal is to begin seeing that each person's life is a rich source of stories.

In considering experiences for a narrative, think of *significant* not as "unusual" or "exciting" but as "revealing" or "conveying an unexpected meaning or insight." Thought of in this way, a significant moment in a story might be a gesture, a remark, a smile, a way of walking or tying a shoe, the wearing of a certain piece of clothing, or the carrying of a certain object in a purse or pocket. Invent a short scene in which a gesture, smile, or brief action reverses one character's feelings about, or understanding of, another character.

1. You thought that Maria had led a sheltered life until _____.
2. You thought Mr. Watson was a racist until _____.
3. Marco (Jillian) seemed the perfect date until _____.

In each case, think of specific details about one revealing moment that reverse your understanding. Here is an example of a scene:

> My dad seemed unforgivingly angry at me until he suddenly smiled, turned my baseball cap backward on my head, and held up his open palm for a high five. "Girl, if you don't change your ways, you're going to be as big a high school screw-up as your old man was."

Understanding Autobiographical Writing

Autobiographical writing may include descriptions of places and people and depictions of events that are more entertaining than enlightening. However, the spine of most autobiographical writing is a key moment or event, or a series of key moments or events, that shapes or reveals the author's emerging character or growth in understanding.

Autobiographical Tension: The Opposition of Contraries

Key events in autobiography are characterized by a clash of opposing values or points of view. These oppositions are typically embodied in conflicts between characters or in divided feelings within the narrator. The contraries in a story can often be summed up in statements such as these:

> My best friend from the eighth grade was suddenly an embarrassment in high school.
> My parents thought I was too young to drive to the movies when in fact I was ready to ride off with Iggy's Motorcycle Maniacs.
> The school I had dreamed of attending turned into a nightmarish prison.
> The subject I had hated most in middle school—science—became my passion in high school.
> The job that bored me and made all my muscles ache rescued me from a hopeless summer.

An autobiographical piece without tension is like an academic piece without a problem or a surprising thesis. No writing is more tedious than a pointless "So what?" narrative that rambles on without tension.

Like the risky thesis statement in closed-form writing, contrariety, or opposition, creates purpose and focus for open-form writing. It functions as an organizing principle, helping the writer determine what to include or omit. It also sets a direction for the writer. When a story is tightly wound and all the details contribute to the story line, the tension moves the plot forward as a mainspring moves the hands of a watch. The tension is typically resolved when the narrator experiences a moment of recognition or insight, vanquishes or is vanquished by a foe, or changes status.

How Literary Elements Work in Autobiographical Narratives

The basic elements of a literary narrative that work together to create a story are plot, character, setting, and theme.

The Importance of Plot By *plot* we mean the basic action of the story, including the selection and sequencing of scenes and events. Often stories don't open with the earliest chronological moment; they may start *in medias res* ("in the middle of things") at a moment of crisis and then flash backward to fill in earlier details that explain the origins of the crisis. What you choose to include in your story and where you place it are concerns of plot. The amount of detail you choose to devote to each scene is also a function of plot. How a writer varies the amount of detail in each scene is referred to as a plot's *pacing*.

Plots typically unfold in the following stages: (a) an arresting opening scene; (b) the introduction of characters and the filling in of background;

(c) the building of tension or conflict through oppositions embedded in a series of events or scenes; (d) the climax or pivotal moment when the tension or conflict comes to a head; and (e) reflection on the events of the plot and their meaning.

To help you recognize story-worthy events in your own life, consider the following list of pivotal moments that have figured in numerous autobiographical narratives:

- Moments of enlightenment or coming to knowledge
- Passages from one realm to the next: from innocence to experience, from outsider to insider or vice versa, from novice to expert, from what you once were to what you now are
- Confrontation with the unknown
- Moments of crisis or critical choice
- Problems maintaining relationships without compromising your own growth or denying your own needs
- Problems accepting limitations and necessities
- Contrasts between common wisdom and your own unique knowledge or experience:

The Importance of Character Which characters from your life will you choose to include in your autobiography? The answer to that question depends on the nature of the tension that moves your story forward. Characters who contribute significantly to that tension or who represent some aspect of that tension with special clarity belong in your story. Whatever the source of tension in a story, a writer typically chooses characters who exemplify the narrator's fears and desires or who forward or frustrate the narrator's growth in a significant way.

Sometimes writers develop characters not through description and sensory detail but through dialogue. Particularly if a story involves conflict between people, dialogue is a powerful means of letting the reader experience that conflict directly. The following piece of dialogue, taken from African-American writer Richard Wright's classic autobiography *Black Boy*, demonstrates how a skilled writer can let dialogue tell the story, without resorting to analysis and abstraction. In the following scene, young Wright approaches a librarian in an attempt to get a book by Baltimore author and journalist H. L. Mencken from a whites-only public library. He has forged a note and borrowed a library card from a sympathetic white coworker and is pretending to borrow the book in his coworker's name.

> "What do you want, boy?"
> As though I did not possess the power of speech, I stepped forward and simply handed her the forged note, not parting my lips.
> "What books by Mencken does he want?" she asked.
> "I don't know ma'am," I said avoiding her eyes.
> "Who gave you this card?"
> "Mr. Falk," I said.
> "Where is he?"

Excerpt from *Black Boy* by Richard Wright. Copyright 1937, 1942, 1944, 1945 by Richard Wright; renewed © 1973 by Ellen Wright. Reprinted by permission of HarperCollins Publishers.

"He's at work, at the M— Optical Company," I said. "I've been in here for him before."

"I remember," the woman said. "But he never wrote notes like this."

Oh, God, she's suspicious. Perhaps she would not let me have the books? If she had turned her back at that moment, I would have ducked out the door and never gone back. Then I thought of a bold idea.

"You can call him up, ma'am," I said, my heart pounding.

"You're not using these books are you?" she asked pointedly.

"Oh no ma'am. I can't read."

"I don't know what he wants by Mencken," she said under her breath.

I knew I had won; she was thinking of other things and the race question had gone out of her mind.

—Richard Wright, *Black Boy*

It's one thing to hear *about* racial prejudice and discrimination; it's another thing to *hear* it directly through dialogue such as this. In just one hundred or so words of conversation, Wright communicates the anguish and humiliation of being a "black boy" in the United States in the 1920s.

Another way to develop a character is to present a sequence of moments or scenes that reveal a variety of behaviors and moods. Imagine taking ten photographs of your character to represent his or her complexity and variety and then arranging them in a collage.

The Importance of Setting Elements of setting are selected as characters are selected, according to how much they help readers understand the conflict or tension that drives the story. When you write about yourself, what you notice in the external world often reflects your inner world. In some moods you are apt to notice the expansive lawn, beautiful flowers, and swimming ducks in the city park; in other moods you might note the litter of paper cups, the blight on the roses, and the scum on the duck pond. The setting typically relates thematically to the other elements of a story. In "No Cats in America?", for example, the author contrasts his parents' parties in the Philippines, replete with music and dancing, firecrackers, a mahjong gambling room, and exotic food and drink such as homemade mango juice and coconut milk, with the American school lunchroom where he opened his Tupperware lunchbox filled with fish and bagoong. The contrast of these settings, especially when the author's American classmates laugh at his lunch, embodies the story's tension.

FOR WRITING AND DISCUSSION

Capturing a Setting

In writing an autobiographical narrative, one of the challenges is to use words to capture scenes so vividly that readers can see in their own minds what you are describing and can share in your experience vicariously. The four photos in Figures 1 through 4 depict four common scenes: a wooded stream, a city street, an elementary school classroom, and an amusement ride at a fair. For this

FIGURE 1 A Wooded Stream

Ken Bube

FIGURE 2 A City Street

Debra McClinton/Taxi/Getty

FIGURE 3 An Elementary School Classroom

Photos Alyson/Getty

FIGURE 4 Amusement Ride at a Fair

Ken Bube

exercise, choose one of these photos, and imagine a scene from your own life that might have taken place there.

Your goal in this exercise is to freewrite a vivid description of a setting, imagining that you are there. Describe the setting fully. What do you see? Hear? Smell? Once you have described the setting, imagine several characters entering this location and what conflict might play out. Try writing a short scene that portrays some tension. Then share your descriptions with your classmates, discussing how your settings might be used in an autobiographical narrative.

The Importance of Theme The word *theme* is difficult to define. Themes, like thesis statements, organize the other elements of the essay. But a theme is seldom stated explicitly and is never proved with reasons and factual evidence. Readers ponder—even argue about—themes, and often different readers are affected very differently by the same theme. Some literary critics view theme as simply a different way of thinking about plot. To use a phrase from critic Northrop Frye, a plot is "what happened" in a story, whereas the theme is "what happens" over and over again in this story and others like it. To illustrate this distinction, we summarize student writer Patrick José's autobiographical narrative "No Cats in America?", one of the essays in the Readings section of this chapter, from a plot perspective and from a theme perspective:

> Plot Perspective It's the story of a Filipino boy who emigrates with his family from the Philippines to the United States when he is in the eighth grade. On the first day of school, he is humiliated when classmates snicker at the lunch his mother packed for him. Feeling more and more alienated each day, he eventually proclaims, "I hate being Filipino!"
>
> Theme Perspective It's the story of how personal identity is threatened when people are suddenly removed from their own cultures and immersed into new ones that don't understand or respect difference. The story reveals the psychic damage of cultural dislocation.

As you can see, the thematic summary goes beyond the events of the story to point toward the larger significance of those events. Although you may choose not to state your theme directly for your readers, you need to understand that theme to organize your story. This understanding usually precedes and guides your decisions about what events and characters to include, what details and dialogue to use, and what elements of setting to describe. But sometimes you need to reverse the process and start out with events and characters that, for whatever reason, force themselves on you, and then figure out your theme after you've written for a while. In other words, theme may be something you discover as you write.

WRITING
PROJECT

Autobiographical Narrative

Write a narrative essay about something significant in your life using the literary strategies of plot, character, and setting. Develop your story through the use of contraries, creating tension that moves the story forward and gives it significance. You can discuss the significance of your story explicitly, perhaps as a revelation, or you can imply it. (The readings at the end of this chapter illustrate different options.) Use specific details and develop contraries that create tension.

This assignment calls for a story. Narrative qualifies as a story only when it depicts a series of connected events that create for the reader a sense of tension or conflict that is resolved through a new understanding or change in status. Your goal for this assignment is to write a story about your life that fulfills these criteria. The suggestions that follow will help you.

Generating and Exploring Ideas

Choosing a Plot

For some of you, identifying a plot—a significant moment or insight arising out of contrariety—will present little problem; perhaps you have already settled on an idea that you generated in one of the class discussion exercises earlier in this chapter. However, if you are still searching for a plot idea, you may find the following list helpful:

- A time when you took some sort of test that conferred new status on you (Red Cross lifesaving exam, driver's test, SAT, important school- or work-related test, entrance exam, team tryout). If you failed, what did you learn from it or how did it shape you? If you succeeded, did the new status turn out to be as important as you had expected it to be?
- A situation in which your normal assumptions about life were challenged (an encounter with a foreign culture, a time when a person you'd stereotyped surprised you).
- A situation in which you didn't fit or fulfill others' expectations of you, or a situation in which you were acknowledged as a leader or exceeded others' expectations of you (call to jury duty, assignment to a new committee, being placed in charge of an unfamiliar project).
- A time when a person who mattered to you (parent, spouse, romantic interest, authority figure) rejected you or let you down, or a time when you rejected or let down someone who cared for you.
- A time when you were irresponsible or violated a principle or law and thereby caused others pain (you shoplifted or drank when underage and were caught, you failed to look after someone entrusted to your care).
- A time when you were criticized unjustly or given a punishment you didn't deserve (you were accused of plagiarizing a paper that you'd written, you were blamed unjustly for a problem at work).

Shaping and Drafting Your Narrative

Once you've identified an event about which you'd like to write, you need to develop ways to show readers what makes that event particularly story-worthy. In thinking about the event, consider the following questions:

HOW TO START

- What are the major contraries or tensions in this story?
- What events and scenes portraying these contraries might you include in your narrative?

- What insights or meaning do you think your story suggests? How would you articulate for yourself the theme of your narrative?
- How might you begin your narrative?

HOW TO THINK ABOUT AND DEVELOP CHARACTERS AND SETTING

- What characters are important in this story?
- How will you portray them—through description, action, dialogue?
- What settings or scenes can you re-create for readers?
- What particulars or physical details will make the setting, characters, and conflicts vivid and memorable?

HOW TO THINK ABOUT AND DEVELOP THE PLOT OF YOUR NARRATIVE

- How might you arrange the scenes in your story?
- What would be the climax, the pivotal moment of decision or insight?

HOW TO CONCLUDE YOUR NARRATIVE

- What resolution can you bring to the tensions and conflicts in your story?
- How can you convey the significance of your story? What will make it something readers can relate to?
- How can the ending of your narrative leave readers thinking about larger human issues and concerns?

When stuck, writers often work their way into a narrative by describing in detail a vividly recalled scene, person, or object. You may not be able to include all the descriptive material, but in the act of writing exhaustively about this one element, the rest of the story may begin to unfold for you, and forgotten items and incidents may resurface. In the course of describing scenes and characters, you will probably also begin reflecting on the significance of what you are saying. Try freewriting answers to such questions as "Why is this important?" and "What am I trying to do here?" Then continue with your rough draft. Remember that it is the storyteller's job to put readers into the story by providing enough detail and context for the readers to see why the event is significant.

Revising

Testing your narrative out on other readers can give you valuable feedback about your effectiveness in grabbing and holding their interest and conveying an insight. Plan to write several drafts of your narrative.

Questions for Peer Review

In addition to generic peer review questions, ask your peer reviewers to address these questions:

OPENING AND PLOT

1. How could the title and opening paragraphs more effectively hook readers' interest and prepare them for the story to follow?
2. How might the writer improve the tension, structure, or pacing of the scenes?
3. How could the writer improve the connections between scenes or use a different organization such as a collage of scenes or flashbacks to enhance the clarity or drama of the narrative?

CHARACTERIZATION

4. Where might the writer provide more information about characters or describe them more fully?
5. Where might the writer use dialogue more effectively to reveal character?

SETTING, THEME, AND LANGUAGE

6. How might the writer make the setting more vivid and connected to the action and significance of the story?
7. What insight or revelation do you get from this story? How could the narrative's thematic significance be made more memorable or powerful?
8. Where do you find examples of specific language? Where could the writer use more concrete language?

Literacy Narrative

WRITING PROJECT

Write an autobiographical narrative that focuses on your experiences with language, reading, writing, or education. You could explore positive or negative experiences in learning to read or write, breakthrough moments in your development as a literate person, or some educational experiences that have shaped your identity as a person or student. Incorporate the literary elements of plot, character, setting, theme, and descriptive language in the telling of your story. Think of your task as finding new significance for yourself in these experiences and sharing your discoveries with your readers in ways that hold their interest and bring them new understanding.

What Is a Literacy Narrative?

A literacy narrative uses the elements of a story to recount a writer's personal experience with language in all its forms—reading and writing, acquiring a second language, being an insider or outsider based on literacy level and cultural context—or with learning how to learn in general through experiences inside and outside of school. The academic and public fascination with literacy narratives has grown out of—and contributed to—contemporary discussions about cultural diversity in the United States and the connections between literacy and cultural power.

Literacy narratives are a frequently encountered and important genre. For example, one of the most famous literacy narratives is by Frederick Douglass, the ex-slave and abolitionist leader who describes learning to read and write as the key to his liberation from slavery. Another well-known literacy narrative is by Zitkala-Ša (Gertrude Bonnin), a Native American woman who exposes the forceful assimilation tactics employed by missionary schools to separate Native American children from their tribes in the late nineteenth and early twentieth centuries. Perhaps the most famous literacy narrative is by Helen Keller, who recounts the moments when an understanding of language broke through the isolation created by her blindness and deafness. More recently, literacy narratives by immigrants from many cultures have explored the role of education in thwarting or encouraging their integration into American society.

Writing a literacy narrative in college classes can help students explore their adjustment to college, link their earlier learning experiences to the literacy demands of college courses, and take ownership of their own education. Thinking about your own literacy experiences compels you to ponder your educational path and your own ideas of the purpose of education. In contemplating the way that ethnic, economic, gender, class, and regional considerations have shaped your own learning to read and write, you will experience the pleasure of self-discovery and cultural insight.

Typical Features of a Literacy Narrative

Literacy narratives resemble other autobiographical narratives in their open-form structure and their inclusion of some or all of these literary features: a plot built on some tensions and presented as well-sequenced scenes, vivid descriptions of settings, well-drawn characters, dialogue, and theme. Like other autobiographical narratives, literacy narratives rely on vivid, concrete language to make settings and dramatic moments come alive for readers. While literacy narratives share many elements with other autobiographical narratives, they differ in their attention to the following features:

DISTINCTIVE FEATURES OF LITERACY NARRATIVES

- A focus on a writer's experience with language, reading, writing, schooling, teachers, or some other important aspect of education.
- A focus on bringing an insight about the significance of learning, language, reading, or writing to readers through an implied theme (although this theme might be explicitly stated, most likely at the end of the narrative).
- A focus on engaging readers and connecting them to an understanding of the writer's educational/learning experience, prompting them to think about their own educational experiences and larger questions about the purpose and value of education.

Analyzing Features of Literacy Narratives

Read the following passages that depict key moments in two students' literacy experiences, and answer the questions about them that direct your attention to specific features.

EXCERPT FROM MEGAN LACY'S LITERACY NARRATIVE

... I was placed in the remedial reading group. Our books had red plastic covers while the other kids had books with yellow covers that looked gold to me. When it was reading time, the rest of the red group and I congregated around a rectangular wood table where Mrs. Hinckley would direct each of us to read a passage from the story aloud. The first time this happened, my stomach dropped. Even the remedial kids were sounding out the words, but I had no idea what those symbols on the page meant.

When my turn came, I muttered meekly, "I can't. ... "

"Don't say 'can't' in my classroom!" Mrs. Hinckley snapped. Then, more gently, she said, "Just sound it out. ... "

I did as she recommended and could hardly believe what was happening. I was reading. I felt superhuman with such a power. After that moment, I read to my mom every night. ...

EXCERPT FROM JEFFREY CAIN'S LITERACY NARRATIVE

In the Walla Walla Public Library, I remember the tomato soup colored carpet, the bad oil paintings of pioneers fording the Columbia River, the musty smell, the oak card catalog with brass knobs, the position of the clock when I first read Jerzi Kosinski's *The Painted Bird*.

"Just read it," my sister-in-law said. "I know you don't read much fiction, but just read this one," she pleaded

Reluctantly, at first, I turned the pages. But each word covertly seduced me; slowly the odyssey of the dark-skinned gypsy affected my spirit like an exotic opiate, until Lehki's painted bird lay pecked to death on the ground. The image haunted my conscience for days. During some of my more restless nights, I was chased like the characters by Nazis through the Black Forest.

Who was this Kosinski? Why did his book affect me this way? How and why did he write like this? Did all writers write like Kosinski?

The novel incited a series of questions that forced me to begin writing notes and summarizing my thoughts. I began a reading journal and my development as a writer shadowed my habits as a reader. ...

1. What literacy experiences have Megan and Jeffrey chosen to focus on?
2. How do Megan and Jeffrey use the narrative elements of plot, setting, and concrete, specific language to involve their readers in their experiences?
3. Based on these excerpts, how would you articulate the theme of each piece?
4. What educational memories of your own are triggered by these excerpts?

Generating and Exploring Ideas

Many of the questions for generating and exploring ideas for the autobiographical narrative apply equally to literacy narratives. To discover ideas that you could fruitfully explore in your literacy narrative, try asking yourself the following questions:

- ***Questions about your experiences with reading and writing*** (obstacles you encountered and perhaps overcame; particularly vivid memories; role of literacy in your self-identity; ways you have changed or grown)
- ***Questions about adjusting to college or educational challenges*** (unexpected problems with reading and writing encountered in college, or earlier in middle school or high school; discovery of holes or weaknesses in your education; educational issues related to your "difference"—ethnic, class, physical/mental, sexual orientation—from the norm)
- ***Questions about your experiences with language*** (issues arising from learning a second language; from being bilingual; from speaking a nonstandard dialect; from having a speech or hearing impairment or a learning disability; from preferring math or art or athletics or video games rather than reading and writing)
- ***Questions about influential (or inhibiting) teachers or mentors*** (influence of people who have helped or hindered your literacy development; people who have changed your view of yourself as a reader or writer)
- ***Questions about literacy and social status or citizenship*** (issues connected to literacy and cultural power or economic success; role of education in preparing you for local, national, or global citizenship).

FOR WRITING AND DISCUSSION

Discovering Experiences with Literacy

Using one or more of the preceding question areas to trigger ideas, freewrite about some of your literacy experiences. Try to identify moments in your life—in the form of scenes that you could describe using the story elements of plot, dialogue, and setting—that might engage readers. What themes about literacy might these scenes uncover? What is at stake?

Shaping and Drafting Your Literacy Narrative

The following questions, which apply the contraries listed earlier in this chapter (old self versus new self, old view of a person versus new view of person, and old values versus new, threatening, or challenging values), can help you shape your narrative in terms of tensions, scenes, and unfolding story.

- Can you portray your literacy experience in terms of a breakthrough or transforming moment that created a new sense of yourself as a reader, writer, or learner?
- Can you depict your literacy experience in terms of your relationship to a teacher or mentor who helped you or hindered you and led to a new view of this person?

- Can you depict your literacy experience as a conflict of values or as a process of change from one way of regarding literacy to another way? What will your readers understand, in terms of what you most value, by reading your literacy narrative?

While some literacy narratives will follow a clear chronological pattern or a tightly connected scene sequence, others may assume the pattern of a collage or a series of snapshots of key moments in your development. Your challenge is to find what pattern best fits the story you want to tell. Note how in her literacy narrative, student writer Stephanie Whipple builds her literacy narrative around two contrasting scenes.

Revising

In writing about experiences that are very close to you, it is particularly important to get responses from readers. Your readers can help you determine how effectively you are capturing and holding their attention and conveying the significance behind your experiences.

Questions for Peer Review

The peer review questions for the autobiographical narrative apply equally well to the literacy narrative. In addition, you can ask your peer reviewers the following questions, which focus specifically on the literacy narrative:

- What insight, revelation, or new understanding about the importance of reading, writing, or education does this narrative offer you?
- How can the narrative's thematic point about literacy be made more memorable or powerful?

Readings

Our first reading is by Kris Saknussemm, a poet and fiction writer. He is the author of the dystopian, futuristic novel Zanesville (2005), and his poems and short stories have appeared in literary magazines around the country, including *The Boston Review, New Letters, The Antioch Review,* and *ZYZZYVA.* This selection is taken from his autobiographical work in progress.

Kris Saknussemm
Phantom Limb Pain

1   When I was thirteen my sole purpose was to shed my baby fat and become the star halfback on our football team. That meant beating out Miller King, the best athlete at my school. He was my neighbor and that mythic kid we all know—the one who's forever better than we are—the person we want to be.

2   Football practice started in September and all summer long I worked out. I ordered a set of barbells that came with complimentary brochures with titles like "How to Develop a He-Man Voice." Every morning before sunrise I lumbered around our neighborhood wearing ankle weights loaded with sand. I taught myself how to do Marine push-ups and carried my football everywhere so I'd learn not to fumble. But that wasn't enough. I performed a ceremony. During a full moon, I burned my favorite NFL trading cards and an Aurora model of the great quarterback Johnny Unitas in the walnut orchard behind our house, where Miller and I'd gotten into a fight when we were seven and I'd burst into tears before he even hit me.

3   Two days after my ceremony, Miller snuck out on his older brother's Suzuki and was struck by a car. He lost his right arm, just below the elbow. I went to see him the day after football practice started—after he'd come back from the hospital. He looked pale and surprised, but he didn't cry. It was hard to look at the stump of limb where his arm had been, so I kept glancing around his room. We only lived about 200 feet away, and yet I'd never been inside his house before. It had never occurred to me that he would also have on his wall a poster of Raquel Welch from *One Million Years* B.C.

4   I went on to break all his records that year. Miller watched the home games from the bench, wearing his jersey with the sleeve pinned shut. We went 10–1 and I was named MVP, but I was haunted by crazy dreams in which I was somehow responsible for the accident—that I'd found the mangled limb when it could've been sewn back on—and kept it in an aquarium full of vodka under my bed.

5   One afternoon several months later, toward the end of basketball season, I was crossing the field to go home and I saw Miller stuck going over the Cyclone fence—which wasn't hard to climb if you had both arms. I guess he'd gotten tired of walking around and hoped no one was looking. Or maybe it was a matter of pride. I'm sure I was the last person in the world he wanted to see—to have to accept assistance from. But even that challenge he accepted. I helped ease him down the fence, one diamond-shaped hole at a time. When we were finally safe on the other side, he said to me, "You know, I didn't tell you this during the season, but you did all right. Thanks for filling in for me."

6   We walked home together, not saying much. But together. Back to our houses 200 feet apart. His words freed me from my bad dreams. I thought to myself, how many things I hadn't told him. How even without an arm he was more of a leader. Damaged but not diminished, he was still ahead of me. I was right to have admired him. I grew bigger and a little more real from that day on.

THINKING CRITICALLY
about "Phantom Limb Pain"

Perhaps the first thing the reader realizes about Saknussemm's narrative is that the climactic event—one boy helping another climb down a Cyclone fence—is a small action; however, it has a big psychological and emotional meaning for the narrator. The events leading to this moment have prepared us to understand the writer's revelation of his new relationship to his rival. Saknussemm's last paragraph comments on the preceding narrative, making connections and pulling out threads of meaning.

1. Saknussemm chooses to leave a lot unsaid, depending on his readers to fill in the gaps. Why do you suppose that he had never been inside Miller King's house before? Why does he feel "somehow responsible for the accident"? What details does Saknussemm use to sketch in Miller's admirable traits?

2. What examples can you find in this narrative of revelatory words, memory-soaked words, and other concrete words low on the ladder of abstraction? Where does Saknussemm use words that *show* what is happening in the narrative instead of simply telling readers?

3. In closed-form prose, writers seldom use sentence fragments. In open-form prose, however, writers frequently use fragments for special effects. Note the two fragments in Saknussemm's final paragraph: "But together. Back to our houses 200 feet apart." Why does Saknussemm use these fragments? What is their rhetorical effect?

4. Part of Saknussemm's style in this narrative is to use understatement and minimalistic language while also using words that resonate with multiple meanings. For example, he lets readers imagine what Miller would look like trying to climb the Cyclone fence with one arm. However, some phrases and words are figurative and symbolic. What does Saknussemm mean by the phrases "grew bigger" and "a little more real" in his final sentence? How do the ideas of size and of reality versus illusion play a role in this narrative and relate to the theme?

For a different approach to narrative, consider student writer Patrick José's "No Cats in America?" Unlike Saknussemm's narrative, José's includes plentiful description. Note also how José creates tension through contrasts in his narrative: between an ideal image of America and a factual image, between life in the Philippines and life in California.

Patrick José (student)
No Cats in America?

1 "There are no cats in America." I remember growing up watching *An American Tail* with my sisters and cousins. Ever since I first saw that movie, I had always wanted to move to America. That one song, "There Are No Cats in America," in which the Mousekewitz family is singing with other immigrating mice, had the most profound effect on me. These were Russian mice going to America to find a better life—a life without cats. At first, I thought America really had no cats. Later, I learned that they meant that America was without any problems at all. I was taught about the American Dream with its promise of happiness and equality. If you wanted a better life, then you better pack up all your belongings and move to America.

2 However, I loved living in the Philippines. My family used to throw the best parties in Angeles City. For a great party, you need some delicious food. Of course there would be lechon, adobo, pancit, sinigang, lumpia, and rice. We eat rice for breakfast, lunch, and dinner, and rice even makes some of the best desserts. (My mom's bibingka and puto are perfect!) And you mustn't forget the drinks. San Miguel and Coke are usually sufficient. But we also had homemade mango juice and coconut milk. And a party wouldn't be a party without entertainment, right? So in one room, we had the gambling room. It's usually outside the house. Everybody would be smoking and drinking while playing mahjong. And sometimes, others would play pepito or pusoy dos. Music and dancing is always a must. And when there are firecrackers, better watch out because the children would go crazy with them.

3 Then one day, a mixed feeling came over me. My dad told us that he had gotten a job … in California. In the span of two months, we had moved to America, found a small apartment, and located a small private Catholic school for the kids. We did not know many people in California that first summer. We only had ourselves to depend on. We would go on car trips, go to the beach, cook, play games. In August, I thought we were living the American Dream.

4 But at the end of summer, school began. I was in the eighth grade. I had my book bag on one shoulder, stuffed with notebooks, folder paper, calculators, a ruler, a pencil box, and my lunch. I still can remember what I had for lunch on the first day of school—rice and tilapia and, in a small container, a mixture of vinegar, tomatoes, and bagoong. My mom placed everything in a big Tupperware box, knowing I eat a lot.

5 When I walked into the classroom, everyone became quiet and looked at me. I was the only Filipino in that room. Everyone was white. We began the day by introducing ourselves. When it got to my turn, I was really nervous. English was one of the courses that I took in the Philippines, and I thought I was pretty proficient at it. But when I first opened my mouth, everyone began to laugh. The teacher told everyone to hush. I sat down, smiling faintly not understanding what was so funny. I knew English, and yet I was laughed at. But it had nothing to do with the language. It was my accent.

6   Some students tried to be nice, especially during lunch. But it didn't last long. I was so hungry for my lunch. I followed a group of students to the cafeteria and sat down at an empty table. Some girls joined me. I didn't really talk to them, but they asked if they could join me. As I opened my Tupperware, I saw their heads turn away. They didn't like the smell of fish and bagoong. The girls left and moved to another table of girls. From the corner of my eye I saw them looking and laughing at me. I tried to ignore it, concentrating on eating my lunch as I heard them laugh. In the Philippines, the only way to eat fish and rice is with your hands. But that was in the Philippines. My manners were primitive here in America. I was embarrassed at the smell, was embarrassed at the way I ate, was embarrassed to be me.

7   When I got home, I lied to my parents. I told them school was great and that I was excited to go back. But deep down, I wanted to go back to the Philippines. When lunch came the next day, I was hungry. In my hand was my lunch. Five feet away was the trash. I stood up, taking my lunch in my hands. Slowly, I walked my way towards the trashcan, opened the lid, and watched as my lunch filled the trashcan. Again, I told my parents I enjoyed school.

8   When my grades began to suffer, the teacher called my parents and scheduled an appointment. The next day, my parents came to the classroom, and when they started talking to the teacher I heard laughter in the background. It humiliated me to have my classmates hear my parents talk.

9   That night, my parents and I had a private discussion. They asked why I lied to them. I told them everything, including my humiliation. They told me not to worry about it, but I pleaded for us to return to the Philippines. My parents said no. "Living here will provide a better future for you and your sisters," they said. Then the unexpected came. I didn't know what I was thinking. I yelled to them with so much anger, "I hate being Filipino!" Silence filled the room. Teardrops rolled down my cheeks. My parents were shocked, and so was I.

10   I went to my room and cried. I didn't mean what I said. But I was tired of the humiliation. Lying on my bed, with my eyes closed, my mind began to wander. I found myself in the boat with the Mousekewitz family singing, "There are no cats in America." If only they knew how wrong they were.

THINKING CRITICALLY
about "No Cats in America?"

Patrick José lets the reader infer his essay's significance from the details of the narrative and from their connection to the framing story of the fictional mice and cats.

1. How do the settings help you understand José's theme at different points in the narrative?

2. What would you say is the narrative's climax or pivotal moment?

3. José's title, first paragraph, and last paragraph are about a children's movie that features the Mousekewitz's song proclaiming that there are no cats in America. How does the "no cats" image function both as part of the underlying tension

of this narrative and as a symbolic vehicle for conveying the theme of José's essay? What is the insight that José has achieved at the end?

4. During a rough draft workshop, José asked his peer reviewers whether he should retain his description of parties in the Philippines, which he thought was perhaps unconnected to the rest of the narrative. His classmates urged him to keep those details. Do you agree with their advice? Why?

5. For Filipinos and Filipinas, the specific names of foods and party games would be rich examples of memory-soaked words. For other readers, however, these names are foreign and strange. Do you agree with José's decision to use these specific ethnic names? Why?

Our final reading, a literacy narrative, is by student writer Stephanie Whipple.

Stephanie Whipple (student)
One Great Book

1   When first asked to remember my earliest experiences with reading, I thought of my favorite books as a young teen, and I was excited to explore how they shaped the person that I am today. However, upon trying to remember the very first books that I ever read as a child, some quite negative and frankly painful memories were brought to the surface.

2   When I was a little girl living in Memphis, Tennessee, I was a well-behaved bright child who never had trouble learning at a good pace or working with other children. In what I am guessing was my first grade class I remember being so excited when I found out that that year I was going to learn to read. My entire life, my mother and both of my older sisters have all reading. I was so excited to be able to read with them and join the big girls' conversations about the books that they were reading.

3   My very first vivid memory of reading was in the playroom of our house in Memphis. I was sitting with my father reading *The Poky Little Puppy* with him, and my younger brother, who had just started kindergarten, was playing with his Nerf gun.

4   "Okay, Steph. Start with this word." My dad points to the first word on the page.

5   "Ff ... i ... fi—"

6   "Five!" My little brother pops his little freckled face over my shoulder.

7   "Stevie, Steph and I are reading this first. You can read it after her" says my father turning to me. "Go ahead Steph."

8   "Five ... li ... lit—"

9   "Little puppies!" yells Stevie from right behind me.

10   I turn away from the book, discouraged.

11   "Stephen!" says our father sternly. "Let Stephanie read. She knows the words; she just has to think about it for a little while. Go play over there and we will read a book when she is done." My Dad turns to me and smiles.

12   "Five little puppies ... d ... dug ... a ... h ... h—"

13 "A hole under the fence!" My brother is behind me again, and I cannot believe that he is smatter than I am. He is only in kindergarten. You're not even supposed to start learning words until the first grade! I drop *The Poky Little Puppy* and run to my mommy, telling myself that reading is stupid, and I don't want to learn how anymore. Drawing and doing other arts and crafts are much more fun anyway, and Stevie can't even draw a bunny!

14 I was by no means a slow learner; Steve was just an exceptionally fast learner when it came to reading. He knew how to read whole chapter books before any of his peers could even read *The Poky Little Puppy.* However, the fact that my little brother could read better than I could made me feel stupid and I lost all of my previous enthusiasm about books.

15 Both of my parents desperately tried to get me to like reading. They were always sure to separate my brother and me when they were helping me with my reading, but I had shut down. My rnom always tried to read to me before bed, but I told her that I hated books. Instead I wanted her to make up stories and tell them to me, or tell me stories about when she was a little girl. I had made up my mind that I hated reading. If I didn't like it, I wouldn't have to be good at it. So, I did just as much reading as my teacher and my parents forced me to do, but that was it. When my brother was reading every word of *Calvin and Hobbes* comics and needing no help from my father, I was coloring Calvin's hair pink and turning Hobbes into a purple tiger with big black sunglasses on.

16 I continued to dislike reading for years. As I got older, I never finished any of the chapter books that I was required to read for school, and I certainly never read the other books that my mother was constantly trying to get me to read. I remember her telling me, "If you just find one book that you really love, you will love reading forever. I promise." My response was always, "Mom, reading is boring. I'm not a nerd." I wanted to spend my spare time playing with my friends and making friendship bracelets, not reading *A Wrinkle in Time* like my dorky little brother.

17 My parents have since told me that my not liking to read broke their hearts. My dad felt like it was his fault for reading with me around my brother. They did not know what to do, and they were convinced that I would go through my entire life without ever enjoying a good book.

18 One rainy summer day when I was about fourteen years old, however, all of this changed. My family and I were at our mountain house in the Poconos and the weather was too bad to go out on the boat or play outside, so I was bored. I approached my mom to ask her to play a game with me while she was sitting on our screened-in porch reading. She told me that she bought me a book that she loved when she was my age, and suggested that she read some of it to me just to see if I might like it. I don't know if it was out of utter boredom, being worn down by my mom constantly nagging me to read, or just out of really wanting to spend time with my mother, but I agreed. The book was about a little girl named Francie who was extremely poor and lived in a city that I was completely unfamiliar with, but I still related to her. I loved Francie, and after my mom finished reading the first chapter to me and left to go to the store, I continued reading the book and didn't put it down

until it was time for dinner. I loved reading! When I was not reading, I was thinking about Francie and hoping that everything would turn out all right for her. The book had opened up a whole new world for me in which a family could be so poor and have almost none of the things that I was accustomed to, but still be happy and full of love and warmth and hope. I spent the whole week reading my book and discussing it with my mom and sisters.

19   I do not remember the next good book or even the next five good books that my mother gave me and I enthusiastically poured myself into. However, to this day whenever anyone mentions *A Tree Grows in Brooklyn*, or I see the movie on TV, or I read about another character named Frances or Francie, I get a warm feeling in my heart, and I thank God for my mother and her persistence. Without my mom, and without that one great book, I might not be the person and the reader that I am today. If anyone ever tells me that they do not like reading, I smile and tell them, "If you just find one book that you really love, you will love reading forever. I promise."

THINKING CRITICALLY
about "One Great Book"

1. In this literacy narrative, how does Stephanie Whipple create tension and establish the main conflicts?

2. In her desire to engage readers with her characters and setting, Stephanie chooses to use the present tense rather than the past tense for her early scene about reading. Do you find this choice effective? (It violates the normal rules about needless shifting of tense.) How else does she try to engage readers in her characters and setting?

3. This piece leads up to a moment of breakthrough and new insight about the significance of reading. How does Stephanie use story elements rather than straight exposition to convey her transformation in her attitude toward literature?

4. In much of this narrative, Stephanie includes words that are specific and descriptive—that is, low on the ladder of abstraction. What passages are vivid and memorable?

5. This piece is fairly straightforward, yet it points to some deeper themes about learning. What new understanding about children and reading does Stephanie want readers to grasp?

 For additional help with writing, reading, and research, go to **www.mycomplab.com**

WRITING AN INFORMATIVE (AND SURPRISING) ESSAY OR REPORT

As a reader, you regularly encounter writing with an informative aim, ranging from the instruction booklet for a smart phone to a newspaper feature story on the South African AIDS crisis. Informative documents include encyclopedias, cookbooks, voters' pamphlets, and various kinds of reports, as well as informative Web sites and magazine articles. In some informative prose, visual representations of information such as diagrams, photographs, maps, tables, and graphs can be as important as the prose itself.

A useful way to begin thinking about informative writing is to classify it according to the reader's motivation for reading. From this perspective, we can place informative prose in two categories.

In the first category, readers are motivated by an immediate need for information (setting the clock on a new microwave) or by curiosity about a subject (the impressionist movement in painting or new developments in rooftop solar panels). Informative writing in this category does not necessarily contain a contestable thesis. Documents are organized effectively, of course, but they often follow a chronological, step-by-step organization (as in a set of instructions) or an "all-about" topic-by-topic organization (as in an encyclopedia article on, say, Pakistan, divided into "Geography," "Climate," "Population," "History," and so forth). The writer provides factual information about a subject without necessarily shaping the information specifically to support a thesis.

In contrast, the second category of informative writing *is* thesis-based and is therefore aligned with other kinds of thesis-based prose. The thesis brings new or surprising information to readers who may not be initially motivated by a need-to-know occasion or by their own curiosity. In fact, readers might not be initially interested in the writer's topic at all, so the writer's first task is to hook readers' interest and motivate their desire to learn something new or surprising about a topic. An excellent strategy for creating this motivation is the technique of "surprising reversal," which we explain later.

In this chapter, you will learn to:

- write an informative report for a targeted audience
- write an informative essay using the surprising-reversal strategy

Exploring Informative (and Surprising) Writing

Let's say that you have just watched an old James Bond movie featuring a tarantula in Bond's bathroom. Curious about tarantulas, you do a quick Web search and retrieve the following short informative pieces. Read each one, and then proceed to the questions that follow.

Our first mini-article comes from the Web site EnchantedLearning.com, a commercial site aimed at providing interesting, fact-filled learning lessons for children.

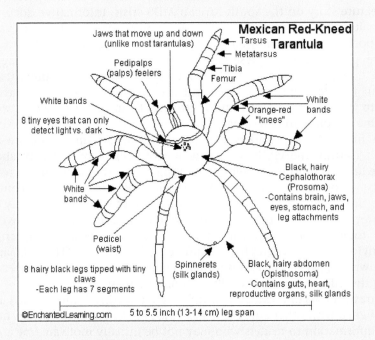

1   Tarantulas are large hairy spiders that live in warm areas around the world, including South America, southern North America, southern Europe, Africa, southern Asia, and Australia. The greatest concentration of tarantulas is in South America. There are about 300 species of tarantulas. The biggest tarantula is *Pseudotherathosa apophysis*, which has a leg span of about 13 inches (33 cm). These arachnids have a very long life span; some species can live over 30 years.

2   **Habitat:** Some tarantulas live in underground burrows; some live on the ground, and others live in trees. They live in rain forests, deserts, and other habitats.

3   **Diet:** Tarantulas are carnivores (meat-eaters). They eat insects (like grasshoppers and beetles), other arachnids, small reptiles (like lizards and snakes), amphibians (like frogs), and some even eat small birds. Tarantulas kill their prey using venomous fangs; they also inject a chemical into the prey that dissolves the flesh. Tarantulas can crush their prey using powerful mouthparts. No person has ever died of a tarantula bite.

4   **Anatomy:** Tarantulas have a hairy two-part body and very strong jaws (with venomous fangs). They have eight hairy legs; each leg has 2 tiny claws at the end and a cushioning pad behind the claws. The hairs on the body and legs are sensitive to touch, temperature, and smell. Tarantulas have a hard exoskeleton and not an internal skeleton. © Copyright EnchantedLearning.com. Used by permission.

The second mini-article comes from the Web site of the University of Washington's Burke Museum. The author of this piece is the curator of arachnids at the Burke Museum.

Rod Crawford
Myths about "Dangerous" Spiders

1   **Myth:** Tarantulas are dangerous or deadly to humans.

2   **Fact:** Outside of southern Europe (where the name is used for a wolf spider, famous in medieval superstition as the alleged cause of "tarantella" dancing), the word tarantula is most often used for the very large, furry spiders of the family Theraphosidae.

3   Hollywood is squarely to blame for these spiders' toxic-to-humans reputation. Tarantulas are large, photogenic and easily handled, and therefore have been very widely used in horror and action-adventure movies. When some "venomous" creature is needed to menace James Bond or Indiana Jones, to invade a small town in enormous numbers, or to grow to gigantic size and prowl the Arizona desert for human prey, the special-effects team calls out the tarantulas!

4   In reality, the venom of these largest-of-all-spiders generally has **very low toxicity to humans**. I myself was once bitten by a Texan species and hardly even felt it. None of the North American species or those commonly kept as pets are considered to pose even a mild bite hazard. There are some reports that a few tropical species may have venom more toxic to vertebrates, but human bite cases haven't been reported, so we can't know for sure.

5   The only health hazard posed by keeping pet tarantulas comes from the irritating chemicals on the hairs of the abdomen, which can cause skin rashes or inflammation of eyes and nasal passages. To prevent such problems, simply keep tarantulas away from your face and wash your hands after handling one.

6   Compared to common pets such as dogs, tarantulas are not dangerous at all. (For more information see the American Tarantula Society.)

European tarantula
Lycosa Tarentula
Southern Europe; body length 2–3 cm
(photo courtesy of Manuel J. Cabrero)
Click image to enlarge

Pink toe tarantula
Avicularia avicularia
Brazil to Trinidad; body length 6–7 cm
(photo courtesy of Ron Taylor)
Click image to enlarge

Both the *European wolf spiders* (**left**) originally called tarantulas, and the *theraphosid spiders* (**right**), often kept as pets and called tarantulas now, have been reputed dangerous to humans. They aren't.

THINKING CRITICALLY
about "Tarantulas" and "Myths about 'Dangerous' Spiders"

1. Why do you think the reading from EnchantedLearning.com uses a diagram of a tarantula while the Burke Museum Web site uses photographs? How is each choice connected to the piece's targeted audience and purpose?

2. How would you describe the difference in organizational strategies for each of the readings?

3. One might suppose that informational writing would be unaffected by the writer's angle of vision—that facts would simply be facts and that informational pieces on the same topic would contain the same basic information. Yet these two short pieces give somewhat different impressions of the tarantula. For example, how do these readings differ in the way they portray the bite of the tarantula? How else do they differ in overall effect?

Understanding Informative Writing

In informative writing, the writer is assumed to have more expertise than the reader on a given subject. The writer's aim is to enlarge the reader's view of the

472

subject by bringing the reader new information. The writer's information can come from a variety of sources:

- From the writer's preexisting expertise in a subject
- From the writer's own personal experiences
- From field research such as observations, interviews, questionnaires, and so forth
- From library or Internet research

We turn now to a closer look at two commonly assigned genres with an informative aim.

Informative Reports

Although the term *report* can have numerous meanings, we will define a **report** as any document that presents the results of a fact-finding or data-gathering investigation. Sometimes report writers limit themselves to presenting newly discovered information, while at other times they go further by analyzing or interpreting the information to explain its implications and significance or to uncover patterns of cause and effect.

Reports of various kinds are among the most common genres that you will read and write as a workplace professional. Often managers have to prepare periodic reports to supervisors on sales, operations, expenses, or team productivity. Equally important are solicited reports, usually assigned by supervisors to individuals or task forces, requesting individuals to investigate a problem, gather crucial information, and report the results.

Characteristics of a Report The text of a report should be concise, with a tightly closed-form structure often broken into sections marked by headings. Individual points might be bulleted. Numeric data are usually displayed in graphs or tables. Long reports usually include a cover page and a table of contents and often begin with an "executive summary" that condenses the main findings into a paragraph.

The Introduction to a Report How you write the introduction to a report depends on the audience you are addressing. In some cases a report is aimed at general readers and published in, say, a popular magazine. In such cases, you must arouse your readers' interest and provide necessary background, just as you would do in most closed-form introductions. Kerri Ann Matsumoto's "How Much Does It Cost to Go Organic?" is a student example of an informative report written for a magazine audience. (Note how Matsumoto "desktop-published" her essay in two-column format to look like a magazine article.)

In other cases, the report is solicited (say, by a supervisor); it is aimed at a specific reader who is already interested in the information and is waiting for you to provide it. In this case, the report is often written as a memorandum. Instead of a title, short reports usually have an informative "subject line" that identifies the report's topic and purpose. The introduction typically creates a brief context for the report, states its purpose, and maps its structure. Here is an example of an introduction:

PROTOTYPE INTRODUCTION FOR A SOLICITED REPORT

To: Ms. Polly Carpenter, Business Manager
From: Ralph Hiner
Subject: Projected costs for the new seed catalog

As you requested, I have researched the projected costs for the new seed catalog. This memo provides background on the marketing plan, itemizes projected expenses, and presents an overall figure for budget planning.

For an example of a short informative report written for a general audience, see "Muslim Americans: Middle Class and Mostly Mainstream."

The following exercise will give you a taste of workplace report writing. Suppose that you are a marketing researcher for a company that designs and produces new video games. One day you receive the following memo from your manager:

To: You
From: Big Boss
Subject: Information about gender differences in video game playing

The marketing team wants to investigate differences in the amount of time male and female college students spend playing video games and in the kinds of video games that each gender enjoys. I want you to conduct appropriate research at local colleges using questionnaires, interviews, and focus groups. Specifically, the marketing team wants to know approximately how many minutes per week an average college male versus a college female spends playing video games. Also investigate whether there is any difference in the kinds of games they enjoy. We need your report by the end of the month.

FOR WRITING AND DISCUSSION

Producing a Solicited Report

1. Assume that your classroom is a "focus group" for your investigation. As a class, create an informal questionnaire to gather the information that you will need for your report.
2. Give the questionnaire to the class and tabulate results.
3. Working individually or in small groups, prepare a memo to Big Boss reporting your results.

Informative Essay Using the Surprising-Reversal Strategy

Another commonly encountered genre is an informative article with surprising information, often found in magazines or newspapers. In this section, we focus on a specific version of this kind of essay—a thesis-based informative article aimed at general audiences. Because readers are assumed to be browsing through the pages of a magazine, the writer's rhetorical challenge is to arouse the reader's curiosity and then to keep the reader reading by providing interesting new information. The writer's first task is to hook the reader on a question and then to provide a surprising thesis that gives shape and purpose to the information. A good way to focus and sharpen the thesis, as we will show, is to use the "surprising-reversal" strategy.

"All-About" Versus "Thesis-Governed" Informative Prose Let's begin by revisiting the difference between an encyclopedic (or "all-about") informative piece and a thesis-based piece. To appreciate this distinction, consider again the difference between the EnchantedLearning.com Web site on tarantulas and the Burke Museum piece "Myths about 'Dangerous' Spiders." The EnchantedLearning.com piece is a short "all-about" report organized under the topic headings "Habitat," "Diet," and "Anatomy." The Web writer may simply have adapted an encyclopedia article on tarantulas into a format for children. In contrast, the Burke Museum piece by Rod Crawford is thesis-based. Crawford wishes to refute the myth that "[t]arantulas are dangerous or deadly to humans." He does so by providing information on the low toxicity of tarantula venom to humans and the relative painlessness of tarantula bites. All of Crawford's data focus on the danger potential of tarantulas. There are no data about habitat, diet, or other aspects of tarantula life—material that would be included if this were an all-about report. Because the piece also includes data about misconceptions of tarantulas, it follows the basic pattern of surprising reversal: "Many people believe that tarantulas are toxic to humans, but I will show that tarantulas are not dangerous at all."

Surprising-Reversal Pattern **Surprising reversal** is our term for a strategy in which the writer's thesis pushes sharply against a counterthesis. This structure automatically creates a thesis with tension focused on a question or problem. Because of its power to hook and sustain readers, surprising-reversal essays can be found in many publications, ranging from easy-reading magazines to scholarly journals. Here, for example, is an abstract of an article from *Atlantic Monthly*.

"REEFER MADNESS" BY ERIC SCHLOSSER

Marijuana has been pushed so far out of the public imagination by other drugs, and its use is so casually taken for granted in some quarters of society, that one might assume it had been effectively decriminalized. In truth, the government has never been tougher on marijuana offenders than it is today. In an era when violent criminals frequently walk free or receive modest jail terms, tens of thousands of people are serving long sentences for breaking marijuana laws.

This article asserts a surprising, new position ("the government has never been tougher on marijuana offenders than it is today") that counters a commonly held view (marijuana laws are no longer enforced). Here are additional examples of the surprising-reversal pattern:

Commonly Held, Narrow, or Inaccurate View	New, Surprising Information
Native Americans used to live in simple harmony with the earth.	Many American Indians used to "control" nature by setting fire to forests to make farming easier or to improve hunting.
Having fathers present in the delivery room helps the mother relax and have an easier birth.	Having fathers present in delivery rooms may reduce the amount of oxytocin produced by the mother and lead to more caesarian sections.

A similar pattern is often found in scholarly academic writing, which typically has the following underlying shape:

Whereas some scholars say X, I am going to argue Y.

Because the purpose of academic research is to advance knowledge, an academic article almost always shows the writer's new view against a background of prevailing views (what other scholars have said). This kind of tension is what often makes thesis-based writing memorable and provocative.

The writer's surprising information can come from personal experience, field research, or library/Internet research. If a college writer bases an informative piece on research sources and documents them according to academic conventions, the magazine genre doubles as an effective college research paper by combining academic citations with a tone and style suitable for general readers. Shannon King's article on hydrogen cars is an example of a student research paper written in magazine article style.

"Surprise" as a Relative Term When using the surprising-reversal strategy, keep in mind that *surprise* is a relative term based on the relationship between you and your intended audience. You don't have to surprise everyone in the world, just those who hold a mistaken or narrow view of your topic. The key is to imagine an audience less informed about your topic than you are. Suppose, as an illustration, that you have just completed an introductory economics course. You are less informed about economics than your professor, but more informed about economics than persons who have never had an econ class. You might therefore bring surprising information to the less informed audience:

The average airplane traveler thinks that the widely varying ticket pricing for the same flight is chaotic and silly, but I can show how this pricing scheme makes perfect sense economically. [written to the "average airplane traveler," who hasn't taken an economics course]

This paper would be surprising to your intended audience, but not to the economics professor. From a different perspective, however, you could also write about economics to your professor because you might know more than your professor about, say, how students struggle with some concepts:

Many economics professors assume that students can easily learn the concept of "elasticity of demand," but I can show why this concept was particularly confusing for me and my classmates. [written to economics professors who aren't aware of student difficulties with particular concepts]

Additionally, your surprising view doesn't necessarily have to be diametrically opposed to the common view. Perhaps you think the common view is *incomplete* or *insufficient* rather than *dead wrong*. Instead of saying, "View X is wrong, whereas my view, Y, is correct," you can say, "View X is correct and good as far as it goes, but my view, Y, adds a new perspective." In other words, you can also create surprise by going a step beyond the common view to show readers something new.

Informative Report

WRITING

PROJECT

Write a short informative report based on data you have gathered from observations, interviews, questionnaires, or library/Internet research. Your report should respond to one of the following scenarios or to a scenario provided by your instructor:

- Your boss runs a chain of health food stores that sell high-nutrition smoothies. Because sales have been flat, she wants to create an advertising campaign to attract more customers to her smoothie bars. She has heard that the boutique coffee drinks sold at coffee shops such as Starbucks are actually high in calories and fat. She has asked you to research the nutritional information on coffee drinks. She would also like you to compare the fat/calorie content of various coffee drinks to that of cheeseburgers, fries, and milkshakes sold at fast-food restaurants. She's hoping that the information you provide will help her launch a campaign to lure customers from coffee shops to her smoothie bars. Write your report in the form of a memorandum to your boss, providing the requested information in a closed-form, crisply presented style.
- You are doing a service-learning project for a health maintenance organization. Your manager is worried about hearing loss in young people, possibly caused by listening to loud music through earbuds plugged into iPods or MP3 players. Your manager asks you to write a short informative article, suitable for publication in the HMO's newsletter, that reports on research on hearing loss due to earbuds. Write your report for a general audience who read the HMO newsletter for helpful health information.

Generating and Exploring Ideas

Your initial goal is to use effective research strategies to find the requested information.

FIGURE 1 Framework for an Informative Report

Title	• For a report addressed to a general audience, an interest-grabbing title • For a solicited report, an informative subject line
Introduction (one to several paragraphs)	• For general audiences, provides background and context and arouses interest • For a solicited report, refers to the request, explains the purpose of the report, and maps its structure
Body section 1 (brief)	• Explains your research process and the sources of your data
Body section 2 (major)	• Provides the information in a logical sequence • Uses closed-form organizational strategies • Displays numeric data in graphs or tables referenced in the text
Conclusion	• Suggests the significance of the information provided

Shaping and Drafting

Although there is no one correct way to organize an informative report, such reports typically have the structure shown in Figure 1. Kerri Ann Matsumoto's essay on the cost of organic food aimed at general audiences, exhibits this typical structure. Her title and introduction announce her research question and engage her readers' interest (how much does it cost to buy organic food versus non-organic food?). The body of the paper then explains her process (she did comparison pricing for a chicken stir-fry for a family of four at an organic and a non-organic store); presents her findings in both words and graphics (organic foods cost more); and suggests the significance of her research (helps readers sort out the advantages of organic foods versus the advantages of spending the extra money in other ways).

Revising

As you revise, make sure that your graphics (if you used them) and your words tell the same story and reinforce each other. As you edit, try to achieve a clear, concise style that allows your intended audience to read quickly. For workplace reports, show your respect for the busy business environment that places many simultaneous demands on managers. When you have a near-final draft, exchange it with a classmate for a peer review.

Questions for Peer Review

In addition to generic peer review questions, ask your peer reviewers to address these questions:

1. If the report is solicited, does the document have a professional appearance (memo format, pleasing use of white space, appropriate use of headings)? Do the subject line and opening overview passage effectively explain the report's occasion, purpose, and structure?
2. If the report is aimed at a general audience, does it follow the manuscript style and document design specified by the instructor? Do the title and introduction provide context and motivate reader interest?
3. Does the writer explain how the research was conducted?
4. Is the report clear, concise, and well organized? How might the presentation of the information be improved?
5. If the report uses graphics, are the graphics referenced in the text? Are they clear, with appropriate titles and labels? How might they be improved?

Informative Essay Using the Surprising-Reversal Strategy

WRITING PROJECT

> Using personal experience, field research, or library/Internet research, write an informative magazine article using a surprising-reversal strategy in a tone and style suitable for general readers. Your task is to arouse your readers' curiosity by posing an interesting question, summarizing a common or expected answer to the question, and then providing new, surprising information that counters or "reverses" the common view. You imagine readers who hold a mistaken or overly narrow view of your topic; your purpose is to give them a new, surprising view.

Depending on the wishes of your instructor, this assignment can draw either on personal experience or on research. Shannon King's "How Clean and Green Are Hydrogen Fuel-Cell Cars?" is an example of a researched essay that enlarges the targeted audience's view of a subject in a surprising way. Although it is an example of a short academic research article, it is written in a relaxed style suitable for magazine publication.

For this assignment, try to avoid issues calling for persuasive rather than informative writing. With persuasive prose, you imagine a resistant reader who may argue back. With informative prose, you imagine a more trusting reader, one willing to learn from your experience or research. Although you hope to enlarge your reader's view of a topic, you aren't necessarily saying that your audience's original view is wrong, nor are you initiating a debate. For example, suppose a writer wanted to develop the following claim: "Many of my friends think that having an alcoholic mother would be the worst thing that could happen to you, but I will show that my mother's disease forced our family closer together." In this case the writer isn't arguing that alcoholic mothers are good or that everyone should have an alcoholic mother. Rather, the writer is simply offering readers a new, unexpected, and expanded view of what it might be like to have an alcoholic mother.

Generating and Exploring Ideas

If you do field research or library/Internet research for your article, start by posing a research question. As you begin doing initial research on your topic area, you will soon know more about your topic than most members of the general public. Ask yourself, "What has surprised me about my research so far? What have I learned that I didn't know before?" Your answers to these questions can suggest possible approaches to your paper. For example, Shannon King began her research believing that fuel-cell technology produced totally pollution-free energy. She didn't realize that one needs to burn fossil fuels in order to produce the hydrogen. This initial surprise shaped her paper. She decided that if this information surprised her, it should surprise others also.

What follows are two exercises you can try to generate ideas for your paper.

Individual Task to Generate Ideas

Here is a template that can help you generate ideas by asking you to think specifically about differences in knowledge levels between you and various audiences.

I know more about X [topic area] than [specific person or persons].

For example, you might say, "I know more about [computer games/gospel music/the energy crisis] than [my roommate/my high school friends/my parents]." This exercise helps you discover subjects about which you already have expertise compared to other audiences. Likewise, you can identify a subject that interests you, do a couple of hours of research on it, and then say: "Based on just this little amount of research, I know more about X than my roommate." Thinking in this way, you might be able to create an intriguing question that you could answer through your research.

Small-Group Task to Generate Ideas

Form small groups. Assign a group recorder to make a two-column list, with the left column titled "Mistaken or Narrow View of X" and the right column titled "Groupmate's Surprising View." Using the surprising-reversal strategy, brainstorm ideas for article topics until every group member has generated at least one entry for the right-hand column. Here are several examples:

Mistaken or Narrow View of X	Groupmate's Surprising View
Being an offensive lineman in football is a no-brain, repetitive job requiring size and strength, but only enough intelligence and athletic ability to push people out of the way.	Jeff can show that being an offensive lineman is a complex job that requires mental smarts as well as size, strength, and athletic ability.
Pawnshops are disreputable places.	Samantha's uncle owns a pawnshop that is a wholesome family business that serves an important social function.
To most straight people, *Frankenstein* is a monster movie about science gone amuck.	Cody can show how to the gay community, *Frankenstein* holds a special and quite different meaning.

To help stimulate ideas, you might consider topic areas such as the following:

- ***People:*** computer programmers, homeless people, cheerleaders, skateboarders, gang members, priests or rabbis, reality show stars, feminists, mentally ill or developmentally disabled persons.
- ***Activities:*** washing dishes, climbing mountains, wrestling, modeling, gardening, living with a chronic disease or disability, owning a certain breed of dog, riding a subway at night, posting status updates on Facebook, entering a dangerous part of a city.
- ***Places:*** particular neighborhoods, specific buildings or parts of buildings, local attractions, junkyards, college campuses, places of entertainment, summer camps.
- ***Other similar categories:*** groups, events, animals and plants, gadgets, and so forth; the list is endless.

Next, go around the room, sharing with the entire class the topics you have generated. Remember that you are not yet committed to writing about any of these topics.

Shaping, Drafting, and Revising

A surprising-reversal informative essay has the features and organization shown in Figure 2.

To create the "surprising-reversal" feel, it's important to delay your thesis until after you have explained your audience's common, expected answer to your opening question. This delay in presenting the thesis creates an open-form feel that readers often find engaging. Shannon King's research paper on hydrogen cars has this surprising-reversal shape.

As a way of helping you generate ideas, we offer the following five questions. Following each question, we speculate about what King might have written if she had used the same questions to help her get started on her essay.

FIGURE 2 Framework for an Informative Essay Using the Surprising-Reversal Strategy

Introduction (one to several paragraphs)	• Engages readers' interest in the writer's question • Provides background and context
Body section 1 (brief)	• Explains the common or popular answer to the writer's question
Body section 2 (major)	• Provides a delayed thesis—the writer's surprising answer to the question • Supports the thesis with information from personal experience or research • Displays numeric data in graphs or tables referenced in the text
Conclusion	• Suggests the significance of the writer's new perspective on the question

1. ***What question does your essay address?*** (King might have asked, "Will hydrogen fuel-cell automobiles solve our nation's energy and pollution crises?")
2. ***What is the common, expected, or popular answer to this question held by your imagined audience?*** (King might have said, "Most people believe that hydrogen fuel-cell cars will solve our country's pollution and energy crises.")
3. ***What examples and details support your audience's view?*** Expand on these views by developing them with supporting examples and details. (King might have noted her research examples praising fuel-cell technology such as the Bush/Cheney National Energy Report or California Governor Arnold Schwarzenegger's desire to build hydrogen fuel stations across the state.)
4. ***What is your own surprising view?*** (King might have said, "Although hydrogen fuel-cell cars are pollution free, getting the hydrogen in the first place requires burning fossil fuels.")
5. ***What examples and details support this view? Why do you hold this view? Why should a reader believe you?*** Writing rapidly, spell out the evidence that supports your point. (King would have done a freewrite about her research discoveries that hydrogen has to be recovered from carbon-based fossils or from electrolysis of water—all of which means continued use of pollution-causing fossil fuels.)

After you finish exploring your responses to these five trigger questions, you will be well on your way to composing a first draft of your article. Now finish writing your draft fairly rapidly without worrying about perfection.

Once you have your first draft on paper, the goal is to make it work better, first for yourself and then for your readers. If you discovered ideas as you wrote, you may need to do some major restructuring. Check to see that the question you are addressing is clear. If you are using the surprising-reversal strategy, make sure that you distinguish between your audience's common view and your own surprising view.

Questions for Peer Review

In addition to the generic peer review questions, ask your peer reviewers to address these questions:

1. What is the question the paper addresses? How effective is the paper at hooking the reader's interest in the question?
2. Where does the writer explain the common or popular view of the topic? Do you agree that this is the common view? How does the writer develop or support this view? What additional supporting examples, illustrations, or details might make the common view more vivid or compelling?
3. What is the writer's surprising view? Were you surprised? What details does the writer use to develop the surprising view? What additional supporting examples, illustrations, or details might help make the surprising view more vivid and compelling?
4. Is the draft clear and easy to follow? Is the draft interesting? How might the writer improve the style, clarity, or interest level of the draft?
5. If the draft includes graphics, are they effective? Do the words and the visuals tell the same story? Are the visuals properly titled and labeled? How might the use of visuals be improved?

Readings

Our first reading, "Muslim Americans: Middle Class and Mostly Mainstream," published in May 2007, illustrates an informative report. Based on field and research data compiled by the Pew Research Center for the People and the Press, this reading is the widely disseminated summary of the Center's longer, more detailed report. The complete report can be read on the Pew Research Center's Web site. This report summary has many features of a workplace document except that it is addressed to a general audience rather than a specific workplace audience.

The Pew Research Center for the People and the Press
Muslim Americans: Middle Class and Mostly Mainstream

1   The first-ever, nationwide, random sample survey of Muslim Americans finds them to be largely assimilated, happy with their lives, and moderate with respect to many of the issues that have divided Muslims and Westerners around the world.

2   The Pew Research Center conducted more than 55,000 interviews to obtain a national sample of 1,050 Muslims living in the United States. Interviews were conducted in English, Arabic, Farsi and Urdu. The resulting study, which draws on Pew's survey research among Muslims around the world, finds that Muslim Americans are a highly diverse population, one largely composed of immigrants. Nonetheless, they are decidedly American in their outlook, values and attitudes. This belief is reflected in Muslim American income and education levels, which generally mirror those of the public.

3   Key findings include:

- Overall, Muslim Americans have a generally positive view of the larger society. Most say their communities are excellent or good places to live.
- A large majority of Muslim Americans believe that hard work pays off in this society. Fully 71% agree that most people who want to get ahead in the U.S. can make it if they are willing to work hard.
- The survey shows that although many Muslims are relative newcomers to the U.S., they are highly assimilated into American society. On balance, they believe that Muslims coming to the U.S. should try and adopt American customs, rather than trying to remain distinct from the larger society. And by nearly two-to-one (63%–32%) Muslim Americans do not see a conflict between being a devout Muslim and living in a modern society.

Muslim Americans: Who Are They?

	Total
Proportion who are …	%
Foreign-born Muslims	**65**
Arab region	24
Pakistan	8
Other South Asia	10
Iran	8
Europe	5
Other Africa	4
Other	6
Native-born Muslims	**35**
African American	20
Other	15
	100
Foreign-born Muslims	**65**
Year immigrated:	
2000–2007	18
1990–1999	21
1980–1989	15
Before 1980	11
Native-born Muslims	**35**
Percent who are …	
Converts to Islam	21
Born Muslim	14

- Roughly two-thirds (65%) of adult Muslims in the U.S. were born elsewhere. A relatively large proportion of Muslim immigrants are from Arab countries, but many also come from Pakistan and other South Asian countries. Among native-born Muslims, roughly half are African American (20% of U.S. Muslims overall), many of whom are converts to Islam.

- Based on data from this survey, along with available Census Bureau data on immigrants' nativity and nationality, the Pew Research Center estimates the total population of Muslims in the United States at 2.35 million.

- Muslim Americans reject Islamic extremism by larger margins than do Muslim minorities in Western European countries. However, there is somewhat more acceptance of Islamic extremism in some segments of the U.S. Muslim public than others. Fewer native-born African American Muslims than others completely condemn al Qaeda. In addition, younger Muslims in the U.S. are much more likely than older Muslim Americans to say that suicide bombing in the defense of Islam can be at least sometimes justified. Nonetheless, absolute levels of support for Islamic extremism among Muslim Americans are quite low, especially when compared with Muslims around the world.

- A majority of Muslim Americans (53%) say it has become more difficult to be a Muslim in the U.S. since the Sept. 11 terrorist attacks. Most also believe that the government "singles out" Muslims for increased surveillance and monitoring.

- Relatively few Muslim Americans believe the U.S.-led war on terror is a sincere effort to reduce terrorism, and many doubt that Arabs were responsible for the 9/11 attacks. Just 40% of Muslim Americans say groups of Arabs carried out those attacks.

U.S. Muslims More Mainstream

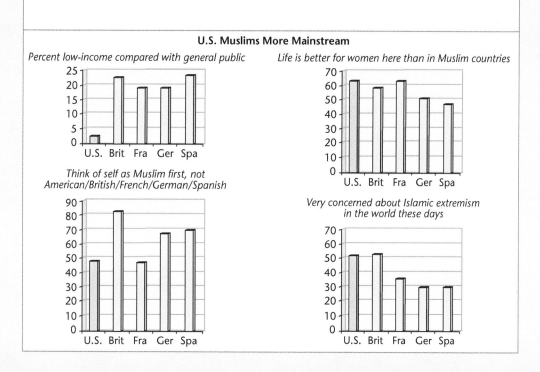

Percent low-income compared with general public

Think of self as Muslim first, not American/British/French/German/Spanish

Life is better for women here than in Muslim countries

Very concerned about Islamic extremism in the world these days

THINKING CRITICALLY

about "Muslim Americans: Middle Class and Mostly Mainstream"

1. Note how this document includes the typical features, with some modifications, of a typical informative report (see Figure 1). Where does the document include the following:
   a. An overview sentence that orients readers to the purpose and content of the document?
   b. An explanation of the writer's research process?
   c. Presentation of the writer's findings using both verbal text and graphics?

2. Typically, informative writing is valuable to the extent that it brings something needed, new, or surprising to the audience and therefore enlarges their view of the topic. What did you find new, surprising, or otherwise worthwhile in this informative report?

Our second reading, by student writer Kerri Ann Matsumoto is formatted to look like a popular magazine article.

THINKING CRITICALLY

about "How Much Does It Cost to Go Organic?"

1. In our teaching, we have discovered that students appreciate the concept of genre more fully if they occasionally "desktop-publish" a manuscript to look like a magazine article, a poster, or a brochure rather than a standard double-spaced academic paper. If Kerri Ann had been an actual freelance writer, she would have submitted this article double-spaced with attached figures, and the magazine publisher would have done the formatting. How does document design itself help signal the document's genre? To what extent has Kerri Ann made this article *sound* like a popular magazine article as well as look like one?

2. Do you think Kerri Ann used graphics effectively in her essay? How might she have revised the graphics or the wording to make the paper more effective?

3. Do you think it is worth the extra money to go organic? How would you make your case in an argument paper with a persuasive aim?

HOW MUCH DOES IT COST TO GO ORGANIC?

Kerri Ann Matsumoto

Organic foods, grown without pesticides, weed killers, or hormone additives, are gaining popularity from small privately owned organic food stores to large corporate markets. With the cost of living rising, how much can a family of four afford to pay for organically grown food before it becomes too expensive?

To find out more information about the cost of organic foods, I went to the Rainbow Market, which is a privately owned organic food store, and to a nearby Safeway. I decided to see what it would cost to create a stir-fry for a family of four. I estimated that the cost of organic vegetables for the stir-fry would cost $3.97. Non-organic vegetables for the same stir-fry, purchased at Safeway, would cost $2.37. If we imagined our family eating the same stir fry every night for a year, it would cost $1,499 for organic and $865 for non-organic for a difference of $584.

After pricing vegetables, I wanted to find out how much it would cost to add to the stir-fry free-range chicken fed only organic feeds, as opposed to non-organic factory farmed chicken. For good quality chicken breasts, the organic chicken was $6.99 per pound and the non-organic was $3.58 per pound. Projected out over a year, the organic chicken would cost $5,103 compared to $2,613 for non-organic chicken.

My research shows that over the course of one year it will cost $6,552 per year to feed our family organic stir-fry and $3,478 for non-organic for a difference of $3,074. If a family chose to eat not only organic dinner, but also all organic meals, the cost of food would sharply increase.

Before going to the Rainbow Market I knew that the price of organic foods was slightly higher than non-organic. However, I did not expect the difference to be so great. Of course, if you did comparison shopping at other stores, you might be able to find cheaper organic chicken and vegetables. But my introductory research suggests that going organic isn't cheap.

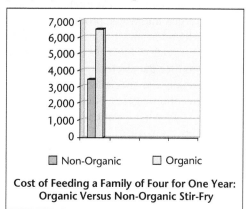

Cost of Feeding a Family of Four for One Year: Organic Versus Non-Organic Stir-Fry

Comparative Cost of Ingredients in an Organic Versus Non-Organic Stir-Fry				
	Vegetables per day	Chicken per day	Total per day	Total per year
Organic	$3.97	$13.98	$17.95	$6552
Non-Organic	$2.37	$7.16	$9.53	$3478

If we add the cost of chicken and vegetables together (see the table and the graph), we can compute how much more it would cost to feed our family of four organic versus non-organic chicken stir-fry for a year.

Is it worth it? Many people today have strong concerns for the safety of the foods that they feed to their family. If you consider that organic vegetables have no pesticides and that the organic chicken has no growth hormone additives, the extra cost may be worth it. Also if you are concerned about cruelty to animals, free-range chickens have a better life than caged chickens. But many families might want to spend the $3,074 difference in other ways. If you put that money toward a college fund, within ten years you could save over $30,000. So how much are you willing to pay for organic foods?

The next reading, by student writer Shannon King, is a short academic research paper using the surprising-reversal strategy. Shannon's paper uses research information to enlarge her readers' understanding of hydrogen fuel-cell vehicles by showing that hydrogen fuel is not as pollution-free as the general public believes.

Shannon King (student)

How Clean and Green Are Hydrogen Fuel-Cell Cars?

1   The United States is embroiled in a controversy over energy and pollution. We are rapidly using up the earth's total supply of fossil fuels, and many experts think that children being born today will experience the end of affordable oil. One energy expert, Paul Roberts, believes that serious oil shortages will start ccurring by 2015 when the world's demand for oil will outstrip the world's capacity for further oil production. An equally serious problem is that the burning of fossil fuels spews carbon dioxide into the atmosphere, which increases the rate of global warming.

2   One hopeful way of addressing these problems is to develop hydrogen fuel cell cars. According to Karim Nice, the author of the fuel cell pages on the *HowStuffWorks* Web site, a fuel cell is "an electrochemical energy conversion device that converts hydrogen and oxygen into water, producing electricity and heat in the process." A hydrogen-fueled car is therefore an electric car, powered by an electric motor. The car's electricity is generated by a stack of fuel cells that act like a battery. In the hydrogen fuel cell, the chemicals that produce the electricity are hydrogen from the car's pressurized fuel tank, oxygen from the air, and special catalysts inside the fuel cell. The fuel cell releases no pollutants or greenhouse gases. The only waste product is pure water.

3   To what extent will these pollution-free fuel cells be our energy salvation? Are they really clean and green?

4   Many people think so. The development of hydrogen fuel cells has caused much excitement. I know people who say we don't need to worry about running out of oil because cars of the future will run on water. One recent *New York Times* advertisement produced by General Motors has as its headline, "Who's driving the hydrogen economy?" The text of the ad begins by saying "The hydrogen economy isn't a pipe dream.... The hydrogen economy is the endgame of a multifaceted strategy General Motors set in motion years ago, with steps that are real, progressive, and well-underway" (General Motors). The Web site for the Hydrogen Fuel Cell Institute includes a picture of a crystal clear blue sky landscape with a large letter headline proclaiming "At long last, a technology too long overlooked promises to transform society." At the bottom of the picture are the words, "Offering clean & abundant power, hydrogen-based fuel cells could soon end our reliance on oil and minimize emissions of pollution and global-warming gases." According to CNN News, the Bush administration proposed devoting 1.7 billion dollars of federal funds to developing hydrogen fuel cells (CNN). The biggest nationally known proponent of hydrogen fuel cells is California Governor Arnold Schwarzenegger, who signed an Executive Order that California's "21 interstate freeways shall be designated as the 'California Hydrogen Highway Network.'" (California). In this executive order, Schwarzenegger envisioned

a network of hydrogen fueling stations along these roadways and in the urban centers that they connect, so that by 2010, every Californian will have access to hydrogen fuel, with a significant and increasing percentage produced from clean, renewable sources. (2)

Schwarzenegger's optimism about the hydrogen highway sums up the common view that hydrogen is a clean alternative energy source that is abundant throughout nature. All we have to do is bottle it up, compress it, and transport it to a network of new "gas stations" where the gas being pumped is hydrogen.

5   But what I discovered in my research is that hydrogen is not as green as most people think. Although hydrogen fuel cells appear to be an environmentally friendly alternative to fossil fuels, the processes for producing hydrogen actually require the use of fossil fuels. The problem is that pure hydrogen doesn't occur naturally on earth. It has to be separated out from chemical compounds containing hydrogen, and that process requires other forms of energy. What I discovered is that there are only two major ways to produce hydrogen. The first is to produce it from fossil fuels by unlocking the hydrogen that is bonded to the carbon in coal, oil, or natural gas. The second is to produce it from water through electrolysis, but the power required for electrolysis would also come mainly from burning fossil fuels. These problems make hydrogen fuel cell cars look less clean and green than they first appear.

6   One approach to creating hydrogen from fossil fuels is to use natural gas. According to Matthew L. Wald, writing in a *New York Times* article, natural gas is converted to hydrogen in a process called "steam reforming." Natural gas (made of hydrogen and carbon atoms) is mixed with steam (which contains hydrogen and oxygen atoms) to cause a chemical reaction that produces pure hydrogen. But it also produces carbon dioxide, which contributes to global warming. According to Wald, if fuel cell cars used hydrogen from steam reforming, they would emit 145 grams of global warming gases per mile compared to 374 grams an ordinary gas-powered car would emit. The good news is that using hydrogen power would cut carbon emissions by more than half. The bad news is that these cars would still contribute to global warming and consume natural gas. Moreover, Wald suggests that the natural gas supply is limited and that natural gas has many better, more efficient uses than converting it to hydrogen.

7   Another method for producing hydrogen would come from coal, which is the cheapest and most abundant source of energy. However, the current method of generating electricity by burning coal is the leading source of carbon dioxide emission. At Ohio University, engineers state we still have enough coal to last us two hundred and fifty years and that we should find some better uses for coal. The engineers have received a 4 million dollar federal grant to investigate the production of hydrogen from coal. They plan on mixing coal with steam, air, and oxygen under high temperatures and pressure to produce hydrogen and carbon monoxide ("Ohio University"). But this too would generate greenhouse gases and is a long way off from producing results.

8   The next likely source of hydrogen is to produce it directly from water using an electrolyzer. Wald explains that the electrolyzer uses an electrical current to break down water molecules into hydrogen and oxygen atoms. Creating hydrogen through electrolysis sounds like a good idea because its only waste product is oxygen. But the

hazardous environmental impact is not in the electrolysis reaction, but in the need to generate electricity to run the electrolyzer. Wald claims that if the electricity to run the electrolyzer came from a typical coal-fired electrical plant, the carbon dioxide emissions for a fuel cell car would be 17 percent worse than for today's gasoline powered cars. One solution would be to run the electrolyzer with wind-generated or nuclear-powered electricity. But wind power would be able to produce only a small fraction of what would be needed, and nuclear power brings with it a whole new set of problems including disposal of nuclear waste.

9   Although there seem to be various methods of producing hydrogen, the current sources being considered do not fulfill the claim that hydrogen fuel cell technology will end the use of fossil fuels or eliminate greenhouse gases. The problem is not with the fuel cells themselves but with the processes needed to produce hydrogen fuel. I am not arguing that research and development should be abandoned, and I hope some day that the hydrogen economy will take off. But what I have discovered in my research is that hydrogen power is not as clean and green as I thought.

Works Cited

California. Executive Dept. "Executive Order S-7-04." 20 Apr. 2004. Web. 24 May 2004.

CNN. "The Issues/George Bush." *CNN.com*. Cable News Network, 2004. Web. 23 May 2004.

General Motors. Advertisement. *New York Times* 28 July 2004: A19. Print.

Hydrogen Fuel Cell Institute. Wilder Foundation, 2001. Web. 27 May 2004.

Nice, Karim, and Jonathan Strickland. "How Fuel Cells Work." *HowStuffWorks.com*. HowStuffWorks, 18 Sept. 2000. Web. 27 May 2004.

"Ohio University Aims to Use Coal to Power Fuel Cells." *Fuel Cell Today*. N.p., 24 Nov. 2003. Web. 3 June 2004.

Roberts, Paul. "Running Out of Oil—and Time." *Los Angeles Times*. Common Dreams News Center, 6 Mar. 2004. Web. 23 Mar. 2004.

Wald, Matthew L. "Will Hydrogen Clear the Air? Maybe Not, Some Say." *New York Times* 12 Nov. 2003: C1. Print.

THINKING CRITICALLY
about "How Clean and Green Are Hydrogen Fuel-Cell Cars?"

1. Explain Shannon King's use of the surprising-reversal strategy. What question does she pose? What is the common answer? What is her surprising answer? How effectively does she use research data to support her surprising answer?

2. The line between information and persuasion is often blurred. Some might argue that Shannon's essay has a persuasive aim that argues against hydrogen fuel-cell cars rather than an informative aim that simply presents surprising information about hydrogen production. To what extent do you agree with our classification of Shannon's aim as primarily informative rather than persuasive? Can it be both?

Our final essay, by syndicated columnist Eugene Robinson, illustrates how an informative article for the general public can be based on data from a major research study—in this case a statistical report by the federal Bureau of Justice. At first glance, the study seems to indicate that no racial profiling occurs at the rate at which white, African-American, and Hispanic drivers are pulled over by police. But in this op-ed piece Robinson pushes deeper into the statistics and presents information showing that "driving while black" is "unsafe at any speed."

Eugene Robinson
You Have the Right to Remain a Target of Racial Profiling

1   Washington—This just in: Driving while black is still unsafe at any speed, even zero miles per hour. The same goes for driving while brown.

2   The federal Bureau of Justice Statistics released a report Sunday showing that white, African-American and Hispanic drivers are equally likely to be pulled over by police for an alleged traffic offense. In 2005, the year covered by the study, black drivers were actually less likely—by a tiny margin—to be stopped by police than drivers belonging to the other groups. You might be tempted to conclude that the constitutional imperative of equal protection had finally been extended to America's streets and highways.

3   But you would be wrong. The study reports that African-American and Hispanic drivers who are stopped by police are more than twice as likely as whites to be subjected to a search. Specifically, police searched only 3.6 percent of white drivers pulled over in a traffic stop, while they searched 9.5 percent of African-Americans who obeyed the flashing lights and 8.8 percent of Hispanics.

4   The report says the "apparent disparities" between racial groups "do not constitute proof that police treat people differently along demographic lines," since there could be "countless other factors and circumstances" that go into the decision of whom to spread-eagle on the hood.

5   All right, those figures alone might not constitute "proof" of bias that would convince a jury beyond a reasonable doubt. They are pretty compelling, though, especially when you also consider that black and Hispanic drivers are much more likely to experience "police use of force" than whites.

6   And besides, the following paragraph in the report pretty effectively demolishes that "move along, folks, nothing to see here" disclaimer about bias:

7   "Police actions taken during a traffic stop were not uniform across racial and ethnic categories. Black drivers (4.5 percent) were twice as likely as white drivers (2.1 percent) to be arrested during a traffic stop, while Hispanic drivers (65 percent) were more likely than white (56.2 percent) or black (55.8 percent) drivers to receive a ticket.

8   "In addition, whites (9.7 percent) were more likely than Hispanics (5.9 percent) to receive a written warning, while whites (18.6 percent) were more likely than blacks (13.7 percent) to be verbally warned by police."

9   African Americans have been putting up with the "driving while black" thing for so long that we've become somewhat cynical. For example, nearly three-quarters of whites and Hispanics who were pulled over for allegedly running a red light or a stop sign were willing to concede that they had been caught dead to rights, while nearly half of African Americans in that situation believed they had committed no infraction. About 90 percent of white drivers detained for some sort of vehicle defect, such as a busted tail-light, thought the stop was legitimate, as opposed to 67 percent of black drivers.

10   Think that's just paranoia? Then try to reconcile the counterintuitive fact that while blacks are much more likely than whites to be arrested in a traffic stop, they are also more likely to be released with no enforcement action, not even a warning. This looks to me like powerful evidence that racial profiling is alive and well. It suggests there was no good reason to stop those people.

11   "About one in 10 searches during a traffic stop uncovered evidence of a possible crime," the report says. What could be wrong with that? Isn't that what police should be doing—enforcing the nation's laws, capturing criminals, making law-abiding Americans that much safer?

12   Of course that's what we pay our police officers to do, but not selectively. Whites, too, drive around with drugs, illegal weapons, open containers of alcohol or other contraband in their cars. The numbers in the report suggest that if white drivers stopped by police were searched at the same rate as blacks or Hispanics, police would uncover evidence of tens of thousands of additional crimes each year, doubtless putting thousands of dangerous people behind bars.

13   But, of course, we don't want a society in which everybody is being patted down by police officers all the time. We don't want a society in which people have to stand by the side of the road, fuming, while police arbitrarily rummage through the stuff in their cars—shopping bags, children's toys, McDonald's wrappers—on the off chance of finding something illegal.

14   If you're black or brown, though, may I see your license and registration, please?

THINKING CRITICALLY
about "You Have the Right to Remain a Target of Racial Profiling"

1. Nationally syndicated African-American columnist Eugene Robinson high-lights statistical data to support his thesis about subtle but pervasive racial discrimination. In doing so, he gives his report a "surprising-reversal struc-ture." What is the common view, seemingly supported by the report, that Robinson believes is mistaken? What is his surprising view? How does he use report data to support his surprising view?

2. What pieces of information from the report do you find most compelling in supporting Robinson's thesis?

3. Analyze this piece from the perspectives of *logos*, *ethos*, and *pathos*.

 For support in learning this chapter's content, follow this path in **MyCompLab**: Resources ⇒ Writing ⇒ Writing Purposes ⇒ Writing to Inform.

ANALYZING IMAGES

This chapter asks you to think about three major kinds of communication through images—documentary or news photos, paintings, and advertisements—to increase your visual literacy skills. By **visual literacy**, we mean your awareness of the importance of visual communication and your ability to interpret or make meaning out of images by examining their context and visual features. We focus on the ways that images influence our conceptual and emotional understanding of a phenomenon and the ways that they validate, reveal, and construct the world.

This chapter invites you to analyze images in order to understand their rhetorical and experiential effects. To **analyze** means to divide or dissolve the whole into its parts, examine these parts carefully, look at the relationships among them, and then use this understanding of the parts to better understand the whole—how it functions, what it means. When you analyze, your goal is to raise interesting questions about the image or object being analyzed—questions that perhaps your reader hasn't thought to ask—and then to provide tentative answers, supported by points and particulars derived from your own close examination.

The ability to analyze visual texts is particularly important because we are surrounded by images from photojournalism, the Internet, billboards, newspapers, television, and magazines. These images, as one critic has stated, "have designs on us." Although glamorous and disturbing images saturate our environment, we do not necessarily have a deep understanding of how they affect us.

> **By writing in a common academic genre—a comparative analysis of two visual texts—in this chapter you will learn to:**
>
> • analyze the persuasive effects of images and how these effects are created
> • respond to visual images as a more informed citizen and perceptive cultural critic

Exploring Image Analysis

To introduce you to image analysis, we provide an exercise that asks you to interact with several news photographs on the issue of immigration reform.

Immigration reform is one of the most complex issues facing the United States today; the problem is particularly acute with respect to immigrants from Mexico

From Chapter 10 of *The Allyn & Bacon Guide to Writing*, Sixth Edition. John D. Ramage, John C. Bean, June Johnson. Copyright © 2012 by Pearson Education, Inc. Published by Pearson Allyn & Bacon. All rights reserved.

and Central America. Immigrants are drawn to the United States by employment opportunities not found in their own countries. U.S. citizens benefit from immigrants' inexpensive labor, which helps keep the prices of services and goods low. In addition to a sizable Mexican-American citizenry, more than ten million illegal immigrants currently live in the United States. All these factors give rise to a number of controversial questions: Should the United States increase border security and focus on building impassable barriers? Should it deport illegal immigrants or explore easier routes to making them citizens? Should it crack down on employers of illegal immigrants or should it implement a guest worker program to legitimize immigrant labor?

Public debate about these issues is particularly susceptible to manipulation by the rhetorical appeal of images. The following exercise asks you to examine the news photos in Figures 1 through 4. Working individually or in groups, consider the rhetorical effect of these photos, first by recording your responses to

FIGURE 1 Wall between Tijuana, Mexico, and the United States

Karen Kasmauski/Corbis

FIGURE 2 Immigrants Crossing the Border Illegally

Guillermo Arias/AP

FIGURE 3 Protestors Marching for Compassionate Treatment of Immigrants

J. Emilio Flores/Corbis

FIGURE 4 Immigrants Saying Their Citizenship Pledge

Carlos Barria/Corbis

them and then by speculating how you might use these images to increase the persuasiveness of different positions on immigration reform.

1. What objects, people, or places stand out in each photo? Does the photo look candid or staged, taken close-up or from a distance? How do the angle of the photo (taken from below or above the subject) and the use of color contribute to the effect?
2. What is the dominant impression conveyed by each photo?
3. Examine how the similarities and differences among the four photos convey different rhetorical impressions of immigrants, Latino culture, or the role of immigrants and ethnic diversity in U.S. culture.
4. Now imagine how you might use these photos to enhance the persuasiveness of particular claims. Choose one or two photos to support or attack each claim below and explain what the photo could contribute to the argument.
   * The United States should seal its border with Mexico by building a wall and increasing border patrols.
   * The United States should offer amnesty and citizenship to immigrants who are currently in the United States illegally.

Understanding Image Analysis: Documentary and News Photographs

Documentary and news photos are aimed at shaping the way we think and feel about an event or cultural/historical phenomenon. For example, consider the newspaper photos, TV news footage, or Internet videos of the billowing clouds of smoke and ash from the collapsing World Trade Center towers on September 11, 2001. Figures 5, 6, and 7 present three well-known documentary images of this event, taken from three different positions and at three slightly different moments as the event unfolded.

Although all three photos convey the severity of the terrorist attack, each has a different impact. Figure 5 records the event shortly before the north tower collapsed and just after the south tower was struck by the second plane, marked in the photo by the red flames. The sheer magnitude and horror of the moment-by-moment action unfolding before our eyes evoked shock, anger, and feelings of helplessness in Americans.

In contrast to the first image, which was taken from a distance below the towers, Figure 6 was taken by a police detective in a helicopter searching for survivors on the roof of the north tower before it collapsed. This photo suggests the apocalyptic explosion and implosion of a contemporary city. The destruction pictured here is too massive to be an ordinary event such as a fire in a major building, and yet the streams of ash and smoke don't reveal exactly what is happening.

Another well-publicized view of this event is that of the firefighters on the ground, seen in Figure 7. Here the firefighters, risking their lives while trying to rescue the people in the towers, have come to symbolize the self-sacrifice, courage, and also vulnerability of the human effort in the face of such colossal

Steven James Silva/Reuters/Landov

FIGURE 5 Terrorist Attack on the World Trade Center

Det. Greg Semendinger/NYPD/AP

FIGURE 6 World Trade Center Attack Seen from the Air

FIGURE 7 Firefighters in the World Trade Center Wreckage

David Turnley/Corbis

destruction. This image also suggests the terror and suspense of a science-fiction-like conflict. All three photos, while memorializing the same event, have different specific subjects, angles of vision, and emotional and mental effects.

The rest of this section introduces you to the ways that photographers think about their use of the camera and the effects they are trying to achieve.

Angle of Vision and Credibility of Photographs

Although the word "documentary" is associated with an objective, transparent, unmediated glimpse of reality, the relationship of documentary photography to its subject matter has always been complex. Historians are now reassessing early documentary photographs, exploring the class and race agendas of the photographers in the kinds of scenes chosen, the photographers' stance toward them, and the wording of the narratives accompanying the photographs. In other words, despite a photograph's appearance of capturing a moment of reality (whose reality?), its effect is always influenced by the photographer's rhetorical angle of vision conveyed through the framing and focusing power of the camera. Perhaps now more than ever, we are aware that the photographer's purpose and techniques actually shape the reality that viewers see. (Think of the multiple cameras tracking a football game and replaying a touchdown from different angles, often creating very different impressions of a particular play.)

The photographer's power to shape reality is enhanced by various strategies for making "unnatural" photographs seem "natural" or "real." For example, photographs can be manipulated or falsified in the following ways:

- staging images (scenes that appear spontaneous but are really posed)
- altering images (airbrushing, reshaping body parts)
- selecting images or parts of images (cropping photographs so that only certain parts are shown)
- mislabeling images (putting a caption on a photograph that misrepresents the image)
- constructing images (putting the head of one person on the body of another)

Research has revealed that many famous photographs were tampered with. As early as the Civil War, composite photos of generals were created by combining heads, bodies, and scenery and inserting figures into scenes. Today this manipulation is also conducted by amateur photographers using photo-editing software. The potential for altering images gives us additional reasons for considering the active role of the photographer and for investigating the credibility and purpose behind images.

How to Analyze a Documentary Photograph

Photographs are always created and interpreted within a social, political, and historical context—the original context in which the photograph was made and viewed and your own context as a current viewer and interpreter. At play are the assumptions, values, and cultural knowledge of the photographer, the original viewers, and the later viewers. Also at play are the sites in which the photograph is viewed—whether in an original news story, a museum, an upscale art exhibit, an expensive coffee-table book, a documentary film, an Internet site, or a text-book. These sites invite us to respond in different ways. For example, one site may call us to social action or deepen our understanding of an event, while another aims to elicit artistic appreciation or to underscore cultural differences.

Examining the Rhetorical Contexts of a Photo A first step in analyzing a documentary photograph is to consider its various rhetorical contexts. The following chart will help you ask illuminating questions.

Strategies for Analyzing the Rhetorical Contexts of Documentary Photographs	
Context	**Questions to Ask**
Photographer's purpose and context in making the photograph	• What was the photographer's original intention/purpose in making the image (to report an event, convey information, persuade viewers to think about the event or people a certain way)? • What was the original historical, cultural, social, and political context in which the photograph was taken?
Original context for displaying the photograph	• Where was the photograph originally viewed (news story, photo essay, scientific report, public exhibit, advocacy Web site)? • How does the original title or caption, if any, reflect the context and shape impressions of the image?
Cultural contexts for interpreting the photograph	• How does the photograph's appearance in a particular place influence your impression of it? • How does your own cultural context differ from that of original viewers? • What assumptions and values do you bring to the context?

Examining the Effects of a Photo on a Viewer In addition to considering the contexts of photographs, we can explore how photographs achieve their effects—that is, how they move us emotionally or intellectually, how they imply arguments and cause us to see the subject in a certain way. An image might soothe us or repel us; it might evoke our sympathies, trigger our fears, or call forth a web of interconnected ideas, memories, and associations.

Before you begin a detailed analysis of a photograph, you will find it helpful to explore the photograph's immediate impact.

- What words come to mind when you view this photograph?
- What is the mood or overall feeling conveyed by the photo?
- Assuming that photographs "have designs on us," what is this photograph trying to get you to feel, think, do, or "see"?

The following chart will help you examine a photograph in detail in order to analyze how it achieves its persuasive effects.*

Strategies for Analyzing the Persuasive Effects of Photographs and Other Images	
What to Examine	**Some Questions to Ask about Rhetorical Effect**
Subject matter: People in portraits Portraits can be formal or informal and can emphasize character or social role. The gaze of the human subjects can imply power through direct eye contact and deference or shyness through lack of eye contact.	Is the emphasis on identity, character, and personality, or representative status (wife of wealthy merchant, king, soldier, etc.), or symbolic (an image of wisdom, daring, etc.)? What do details of clothing and setting (a room's furnishings, for example) reveal about historical period, economic status, national or ethnic identity?
Subject matter: People in scenes Scenes can make a statement about everyday life or capture some aspect of a news event or crisis.	What is the relationship of the people to each other and the scene? Can you re-create the story behind the scene? Does the scene look natural/realistic or staged/aesthetically attractive?
Subject matter: Landscape or nature Scenes can focus on nature or the environment as the dominant subject.	If the setting is outdoors, what are the features of the landscape: urban or rural, mountain or desert? What aspects of nature are shown? If people are in the image, what is the relationship between nature and the human figures? What vision of nature is the artist constructing—majestic, threatening, hospitable, tamed, orderly, wild?

(continued)

*We are indebted to Terry Barrett, Professor Emeritus of Art Education at Ohio State University, for his formulation of questions, "Looking at Photographs, Description and Interpretation," and to Claire Garoutte, Assistant Professor of Photography at Seattle University, for informing our discussion of context in analyzing documentary photographs.

What to Examine	Some Questions to Ask about Rhetorical Effect
Distance from subject: Close-ups tend to increase the intensity of the image and suggest the importance of the subject. Long shots tend to blend the subject into the environment.	Are viewers brought close to the subject or distanced from it? How does the distance from the subject contribute to the effect of the photo or painting?
Angle and orientation: The vantage point from which the photograph was taken and the positioning of the photographer to the subject determine the effect of images. Low angle makes the subject look larger. High angle makes the subject look smaller. A level angle implies equality. Front views tend to emphasize the persons in the image. Rear views often emphasize the scene or setting.	How does the angle influence what you see? Why do you think this angle was chosen? How would the photograph have changed if it had been taken from another angle?
Framing: Framing determines what is inside the image and what is closed off to viewers; it's a device to draw the attention of viewers.	How does the framing of the image direct your attention? What is included and what is excluded from the image? How does what the photo or painting allows you to see and know contribute to its effect? Why do you think this particular frame was chosen?
Light: The direction of the light determines the shadows and affects the contrasts, which can be subtle or strong. Lighting has different effects if it is natural or artificial, bright, soft, or harsh.	How does the light reveal details? What does the direction of the light contribute to the presence of shadows? How do these shadows affect the mood or feeling of the photo?
Focus: Focus refers to what is clearly in focus or in the foreground of the photo versus what is blurry. The range between the nearest and farthest thing in focus in the photo is referred to as the depth of field.	What parts of the image are clearly in focus? Are any parts out of focus? What effect do these choices have on viewers' impression of the image? How great is the depth of field and what effect does that have?
Scale, space, and shape: Size/scale and shape affect prominence and emphasis. Size and scale can be natural, minimized, or exaggerated. Use of space can be shallow, deep, or both.	How do the scale, space, and shape of objects direct viewers' attention and affect a feeling or mood? Are shapes geometric and angular or flowing and organic?

What to Examine	Some Questions to Ask about Rhetorical Effect
Both positive shapes and voids can draw viewers' attention.	Are shapes positive such as objects, or negative such as voids?
Use of repetition, variety, and balance: Repetition of elements can create order, wholeness, and unity. Variety can create interest. Balance can create unity and harmony.	What elements are repeated in this image? What variety is present, say, in shapes? Does the visual weight of the photo seem to be distributed evenly on the sides, top, and bottom? What roles do repetition, variety, and balance play in the impression created by the photo?
Line: Lines can be curved and flowing, straight, or disjointed and angular. Lines can be balanced/symmetrical, stable, and harmonious, or disjointed and agitated.	Does the use of line create structure and convey movement/action or calm/stasis? How does the use of line control how viewers look at the photo or painting?
Color: Choice of black and white can reflect the site of publication, the date of the photo, or an artistic choice. Colors can contribute to the realism and appeal; harmonious colors can be pleasing; clashing or harsh colors can be disturbing.	How many colors are used? What is the relationship of the colors? Which colors dominate? Are the colors warm and vibrant or cool, bright, or dull? How are light and dark used? How does the use of color direct viewers' attention and affect the impression of the image? What emotional response do these colors evoke?

Sample Analysis of a Documentary Photograph

To illustrate how a documentary photograph can work on the viewer's mind and heart, we show you our own analysis of a photo titled *The Fall of the Berlin Wall* (Figure 8), taken by photojournalist Peter Turnley in 1989. At the time, the Berlin Wall, which separated communist East Berlin from democratic West Berlin, symbolized the oppression of communism. In 1987 President Ronald Reagan appealed to Mikhail Gorbachev, president of the Union of Soviet Socialist Republics, saying in a famous speech, "Mr. Gorbachev, tear down this wall." When the border opened in November 1989, marking the end of communist rule in Eastern Europe, East Berliners flooded into West Berlin, sparking weeks of celebration. Peter Turnley is a world-famous American photojournalist whose photos of major world events have appeared on the covers of *Newsweek* as well as international magazines. This photograph appeared in a 1996 exhibit (and later a book) entitled *In Time of War and Peace* at the International Center of Photography in New York.

This documentary photograph of a celebratory scene following the opening of the Berlin Wall in 1989 uses elements of framing, orientation, focus, balance, and color to convey the dominant impression of a life-changing explosion of energy and emotion triggered by this significant event. This distance photo is divided

Peter Turnley/Corbis

FIGURE 8 Fall of the Berlin Wall, 1989, by Peter Turnley

into three horizontal bands—the sky, the wall, and the celebratory crowd—but the focal point is the yelling, triumphant German youth sitting astride the wall, wearing jeans, a studded belt, and a black jacket. The graffiti indicate that the photo was taken from the West Berlin side (East Berliners were not permitted to get close to the wall), and the light post between the two cranes was probably used to illuminate the no-man zone on the communist side.

Every aspect of the photograph suggests energy. In contrast with the mostly homogeneous sky, the wall and the crowd contain many diverse elements. The wall is heavily graffitied in many colors, and the crowd is composed of many people. The wall looks crowded, tattered, and dirty, something to be torn down rather than cleaned up. Most of the graffiti consist of tags, people's response to the ugly obstruction of the wall; West Berliners had no power to destroy the wall, but they could mark it up. The slightly blurred crowd of heads suggests that the people are in motion. At first it is hard to tell if they are angry protesters storming the wall or celebrators cheering on the German youth. The photograph captures this dual emotion—anger and joy—all at once.

At the center of the photograph is the German youth, whose dark jacket makes him stand out against the light blue sky. A few days earlier the wall had fenced him in (at that time, it would have been unthinkable even to approach the wall lest he be shot by border guards). Now he rides the wall like an American cowboy at a rodeo. He has conquered the wall. He has become transformed from prisoner to liberator. His cowboy gesture, reflecting European fascination with American cowboy movies, becomes the symbol of the ideological West, the land of freedom, now the wave of the future for these reunited countries. He holds in his hand a tool (a hammer or chisel?) used to chip away the wall symbolically, but the position of his arm and hand suggests a cowboy with a pistol.

What makes this photograph so powerful is the distance. Had Turnley used a telescopic lens to focus on the German youth up close, the photograph would have been about the youth himself, a personal story. But by placing the youth into a larger frame that includes the crowd, the long expanse of ugly wall, and the cranes and lamppost behind the wall, Turnley suggests both the enormous public and political nature of this event and the implications for individual lives. The youth appears to be the first of the energized crowd to demonstrate the conquering of the powerful barrier that had shaped so many German lives for almost three decades. Thus the composition of this photo packs many layers of meaning and symbolism into its depiction of this historical event.

Exploring a Photograph's Compositional Elements and Rhetorical Effect

In the last five years, documentary photographs have played a key role in persuading audiences that climate change is a serious threat. One recurring image shows mountains with receding or disappearing glaciers. An example is Figure 9, a photo of the Gormer glacier near Zermatt, Switzerland, that was taken by photojournalist Jean-Christophe Bott on August 25, 2009, during the Switzerland Greenpeace Protest. The staging and showing of the photograph were intended to put pressure on national legislation to enact stricter carbon dioxide emission limits and to influence negotiators at the Copenhagen Summit on climate change in September 2009.

1. Working in groups or individually, use the strategies for analyzing the context, composition, and rhetorical effects of photos presented in the strategies charts to describe and interpret this photo. What is the dominant impression conveyed by this photograph?

FIGURE 9 Greenpeace Climate Change Protest in Zermatt, Switzerland

Jean-Christophe Bott/Keystone/AP

503

2. Then using the Internet, search for another photograph that is currently being used in the public discussion of climate change and analyze its context, composition, rhetorical effect, and possible additional uses. What does your photograph contribute to its context?

3. If you were writing to underscore to young voters the importance of climate change, would you use the Greenpeace protest photograph or the one you located? Why?

Understanding Image Analysis: Paintings

When you analyze a painting, many of the strategies used for analyzing documentary photographs still apply. You still look carefully at the subject matter of the painting (the setting, the people or objects in the setting, the arrangement in space, the clothing, the gaze of persons, the implied narrative story, and so forth). Likewise, you consider the painter's distance from the subject, the angle of orientation, the framing, and other features that paintings share with photographs. Additionally, your analysis of paintings will be enriched if you consider, as you did with documentary photographs, the context in which the painting was originally created and originally viewed as well as your own cultural context and place of viewing.

But painters—by means of their choice of paints, their brushstrokes, their artistic vision, and their methods of representation—often do something quite different from photographers. For example, they can paint mythological or imaginary subjects and can achieve nonrepresentational effects not associated with a camera such as a medieval allegorical style or the striking distortions of Cubism. Also, the long history of painting and the ways that historical periods influence painters' choices of subject matter, medium, and style affect what viewers see and feel about paintings. Background on the artist, historical period, and style of paintings (for example, Baroque, Impressionism, Expressionism, and Cubism) can be found in sources such as the Oxford Art Online database. In analyzing paintings, art critics and historians often contrast paintings that have similar subject matter (for example, two portraits of a hero, two paintings of a biblical scene, two landscapes) but that create very different dominant impressions and effects on viewers.

How to Analyze a Painting

Just as with photographs, you should ground your interpretation of a painting in close observation. Many of the elements introduced in the strategies chart for analyzing photographs can apply or be adapted to the analysis of paintings. In addition, you will want to examine the following elements of the paintings you are analyzing.

Strategies for Analyzing the Particular Elements of Paintings

Elements to Analyze	Questions to Ask about Rhetorical Effect
Design and shape of the painting: The width to height, division into parts, and proportional relationship of parts influence the impression of the painting.	What is viewer's impression of the shape of the painting and the relationship of its parts? How does line organize the painting? Is the painting organized along diagonal, horizontal, or vertical lines?
Medium, technique, and brushstrokes: The material with which the painting is made (for example, pen and ink, tempura/water colors, charcoal, oil paints on paper or canvas), and the thickness and style of brushstrokes determine the artistic effect.	In what medium is the artist working? How does the medium contribute to the impression of the painting? Are brushstrokes sharp and distinct or thick, layered, fused? Are they delicate and precise or vigorous? What effect does the awareness or lack of awareness of brushstrokes have on the appearance of the painting?

Sample Analysis of a Painting

As an example of a visual analysis of a painting, we offer an interpretation of a famous painting by Pierre-Auguste Renoir (1841–1919), a French Impressionist painter of the late nineteenth century. The French Impressionists were recognized for their refusal to paint old themes; their embrace of scenes of modern society, especially the city and suburbs; and their experimentation with light and brush-strokes as a way to capture fleeting impressions. Figure 10 shows Renoir's oil paint-ing *La Loge* (The Theater Box), which he painted as his main contribution to the first exhibit of Impressionist paintings in 1874. Impressionist paintings were considered too *avant garde* to be displayed at the conservative state-controlled Salon, which was the official arbiter and channel of the work of established French artists.

Renoir's *La Loge* depicts social life in nineteenth-century urban society as an occasion to act out social roles. This painting of a man and a woman elegantly dressed in a theater box at the opera, a popular social spot of the period, suggests that attending the theater/opera entailed displaying one's wealth, being seen, and inspecting others as much as it did watching a performance. This painting focuses intensely on two members of the audience and specifically on the woman, who catches and holds our gaze. While the man in the background is looking at someone in the audience through his opera glasses, the woman looks directly at viewers and invites their attention.

Renoir has compelled viewers to dwell on this woman by a number of his choices in this painting. He has chosen to paint her in a tightly framed close-up image, which the slightly off-center woman dominates. Her face and eyes convey

Scala/Art Resource, NY

FIGURE 10 Renoir's *La Loge* (1874)

the impression that she and the viewer are staring at each other, while in the shadows the man's eyes are blocked by his opera glasses. Thus this painting combines the woman's portrait with a scene at the opera, even though most of the setting, the theater box, is excluded from the painting. (We know we are at the opera because of the painting's title and the man's and woman's accessories.) There seems to be a story behind the scene: what is the man looking at and why is he not noticing the woman as we, the viewers, are compelled to do? This depiction of a moment seems to be less a shared experience of relationship and more a site for performance: men engaged in looking, women inviting the gaze of others.

Another choice Renoir has made to focus viewers' attention on the woman is his striking use of color. In this painting, the color palette is not large—white, black, brown/gold/sepia, with her red lips and red flowers on her bodice. The white of her face and her upper body is the brightest, suggesting light shining on her. Renoir also highlights the woman with short, thick brushstrokes, which give her shimmering, elegant dress texture and the impression of silk, velvet, and lace. As additional signs of wealth, she wears earrings, a gold bracelet, a flower in her hair, and a flower at her bosom. The stark contrast of the black and white in her dress, the white of her face, and the red of her lips—and the agitated diagonal but converging lines of the stripes of her dress that, along with her arms angled out from her body, shape her into a diamond—all work to direct viewers' eyes to her bosom and most of all to her face. Although the expression of the woman is calm, smiling in mild amusement or subtle emotion, the painting captures intensity, perhaps excitement or anticipation, through the sharp contrast of the red, white, and black. The piece is fairly still and yet we are transfixed by this woman's eyes and lips. With the complex interaction of artistic elements in this painting, Renoir has invited viewers to experience an exciting scene of privileged nineteenth-century urban life.

FOR WRITING AND DISCUSSION

Contrasting the Compositional Features of Two Paintings

This exercise asks you to apply the analysis strategies presented in this chapter to examine the pastel painting *Carousel* by Camille Pissarro shown in Figure 11 and to contrast it with Renoir's painting in Figure 10. Camille Pissarro (1830–1903) was also a French Impressionist who regularly exhibited his works in Impressionist exhibitions. He painted *Carousel* in 1885; the medium is pastel on paper mounted on board.

Your task: Working individually or in groups, analyze Pissarro's painting and then find some striking points of commonality or difference with the Renoir painting that you think merit discussion.

- Begin by applying the strategies for analyzing photographic images and paintings.
- After you have analyzed the visual features of the paintings, consider why Pissarro titled his painting *Carousel*.

FIGURE 11 *Carousel* by Camille Pissarro (1885)

Albright-Knox Art Gallery/Art Resource, NY

• Finally, what are the thematic differences between these two paintings? How do these paintings, both Impressionistic images of well-dressed women at leisure, create similar or different effects on viewers? What view or feeling about life or about the artists' worlds is conveyed in each painting? What way of seeing or thinking are these paintings persuading you to adopt?

Understanding Image Analysis: Advertisements

The images in advertisements are fascinating to analyze. Like other images, they employ the rhetorical strategies we described in the section on documentary photographs. Often, the ad's words (called the "copy") also contribute to its rhetorical effect. Moreover, ads make a more direct and constant demand on us than do documentary photographs and paintings. Advertising, a multibillion-dollar global industry whose business is communicating across a wide range of media to stimulate the purchase of products or services, comes to us in multiple forms: not just as slick, glamorous magazine ads, but also as direct mail, billboards, radio and television commercials, e-advertisements, banners, pop-ups, and spam. Figures 12 and 13, a billboard and a bus ad, illustrate

FIGURE 12 A Billboard Ad

June Johnson

FIGURE 13 Ad on a City Bus

June Johnson

the ordinary ubiquity of ads. Because of advertising's powerful role in shaping our culture and influencing our self-images, we have good reason to analyze the rhetorical strategies of advertisers.

Examining the Appeal of Ads

Think about the images and words in the two car insurance ads in Figures 12 and 13.

1. What do you notice most about the images and copy in these ads?
2. What is the appeal of these ads?
3. How are these ads designed to suit their contexts, a billboard and a bus panel? Why would they be less suitable for a magazine?

How Advertisers Think about Advertising

Although cultural critics frequently focus on ads as manipulative messages that need to be decoded to protect unwary consumers, we confess that we actually enjoy ads, appreciate how they hold down the consumer cost of media, and admire their often-ingenious creativity. (We suspect that others secretly enjoy ads also: Think of how the Super Bowl is popular both for its football and for its ads.) In this section, we take a look at advertising from a marketer's point of view in order to deepen your awareness of an ad's context and the many behind-the-scenes decisions and negotiations that produced it. Whether marketing professionals design an individual ad or a huge marketing campaign, they typically begin by asking questions.

Who Is Our Target Audience? At the outset, marketers identify one or more target audiences for their product or service. They often use sophisticated psychological research to identify segments of the population who share similar values, beliefs, and aspirations and then subdivide these categories according to age, gender, region, income level, ethnicity, and so forth. Think of the different way you'd pitch a product or service to, say, Wal-Mart shoppers versus Neiman Marcus shoppers, steak eaters versus vegans, or skateboarders versus geeks.

How Much Media Landscape Can We Afford? While identifying their target audience, marketers also consider how much terrain they can afford to occupy on the enormous media landscape of billboards, newspapers, magazines, mailing lists, Internet pop-ups, TV and radio commercials, posters, naming rights for sports stadiums, T-shirts, coffee mugs, product placements in films, sandwich boards, or banners carried across the sky by propeller airplanes. Each of these sites has to be rented or purchased, with the price depending on the perceived quality of the location and the timing. For example, a thirty-second TV commercial during the 2010 Super Bowl cost $2.6 million, and a one-time full-page ad in a nationally circulated popular magazine can cost up to $500,000 or more. Overall, advertisers hope to attain the best possible positioning and timing within the media landscape at a price they can afford.

What Are the Best Media for Reaching Our Target Audience? A marketer's goal is to reach the target audience efficiently and with a minimum of overflow—that is, messages sent to people who are not likely buyers. Marketers are keenly aware of both media and timing: Note, for example, how daytime TV is dominated by ads for payday loans, exercise equipment, or technical colleges, while billboards around airports advertise rental cars. Women's fashion magazines advertise lingerie and perfume but not computers or life insurance, while dating services advertise primarily through Internet ads.

Is Our Goal to Stimulate Direct Sales or to Develop Long-Term Branding and Image? Some ads are intended to stimulate retail sales directly: "Buy two, get one free." In some cases, advertisements use information and argument to show how their product or service is superior to that of their competitors. Most advertisements, however, involve parity products such as soft drinks, deodorants, breakfast cereals, or toothpaste. (*Parity products* are roughly equal in quality among competitors and so can't be promoted through any rational or scientific proof of superiority.) In such cases, advertisers' goal is to build brand loyalty based on a long-lasting relationship with consumers. Advertisers, best thought of as creative teams of writers and artists, try to convert a brand name appearing on a cereal box or a pair of jeans to a field of qualities, values, and imagery that lives inside the heads of its targeted consumers. Advertisers don't just want you to buy Nikes rather than Reeboks but also to see yourself as a Nike kind of person, who identifies with the lifestyle or values conveyed in Nike ads.

Mirrors and Windows: The Strategy of an Effective Advertisement

A final behind-the-scenes concept that will help you analyze ads is the marketers' principle of *"mirrors and windows,"* a psychological and motivational strategy to associate a product with a target audience's dreams, hopes, fears, desires, and wishes (often subconscious).

- ***The mirror effect*** refers to the way in which the ad mirrors the target audience's self-image, promoting identification with the ad's message. The target audience has to say, "I am part of the world that this ad speaks to. I have this problem (pimples, boring hair, dandelions, cell phone service without enough bars)."
- ***The window effect*** provides visions of the future, promises of who we will become or what will happen if we align ourselves with this brand. The ad implies a brief narrative, taking you from your ordinary self (mirror) to your new, aspirational self (window).

For example, the acne product Proactiv Solutions uses a very common mirrors/windows strategy. Proactiv infomercials create the mirror effect by featuring regular-looking teenagers with pimples and the window effect by using a gorgeous actress as endorsing spokesperson: If I use Proactiv Solutions, ordinary "me" will look beautiful like Jessica Simpson.

Lars Halbauer/DPA/Landov

FIGURE 14 Geico Gecko Billboard Ad

But the mirrors and windows principle can be used in much more subtle and creative ways. Consider the brilliance of the Geico insurance gecko ads promoting what advertisers call a "a resentful purchase"—that is, something you need to have but that doesn't give you material pleasure like a new pair of shoes or money in a savings account. Insurance, a hassle to buy, is also associated with fear—fear of needing it, fear of not having it, fear of not being able to get it again if you ever use it. In this light, think of the Geico campaign featuring the humorous, big-eyed gecko (friendly, cute) with the distinctive cockney voice (working-class swagger). When this chapter was being written, Geico billboards were sprouting up all over the country (see Figure 14), while large-print ads were appearing in popular magazines along with numerous TV and radio commercials. Here are some of the particular advantages of the gecko for Geico's layered advertising campaign across many media:

- ***"Gecko" sounds like "Geico."*** In fact, this sound-alike feature was the inspiration for the campaign.
- ***The gecko is identifiable by both sight and sound.*** If you see a print ad or a billboard, you remember what the voice sounds like; if you hear a radio ad, you remember what the gecko looks like; on TV or YouTube, you get both sight and sound.
- ***The gecko is cheap.*** The cost of the computer simulations that produce the gecko is minimal in comparison to the royalties paid to celebrities for an advertising endorsement.

- ***The gecko is ethnically/racially neutral.*** Marketers didn't have to decide whether to choose a white versus black versus Asian spokesperson, yet a person of any race or nationality can identify with the little lizard. (Think Kermit the Frog on *Sesame Street*.) Feminist critics, however, might rightly ask why the gecko has to be male.
- ***The gecko is scandal-proof.*** When in 2010 the Tiger Woods imbroglio ruined the golfer's public image, the huge insurance company Accenture, along with TagHauer watches and other companies, had to drop his endorsement ads, forcing them at great expense to create new advertising campaigns and to lose media visibility in the interim.

Yet we must still ask why the gecko is a good advertising device for an insurance company. How does the gecko campaign incorporate mirrors and windows? Let's start with the mirror effect. It is easy to identify with the Geico ads because everyone has to buy insurance and because everyone wants to save money. (The gecko's main sales pitch is that Geico will save you 15 percent.) Moreover, our long cultural history of identifying with animated characters (*Sesame Street, ET*) makes it easy to project our own identities onto the gecko. Additionally, the cockney voice makes the gecko a bit of an outsider, someone breaking into corporate culture through sheer bravado. (Many people think of the gecko's accent as Australian more than cockney, giving the lizard a bit of sexy, macho Crocodile Dundee appeal.)

The ads also create a window effect, which comes from the way the gecko humanizes the insurance company, removing some of the fear and anxiety of buying insurance. You don't think of the gecko as *selling* you the insurance so much as *buying* it for you as your agent, hopping right up on the corporate desk and demanding your rights. Geico becomes a fun company, and you as consumer picture yourself going away with a pile of saved money. Recent ads have added another symbolic feature to the gecko—a pair of glasses—which makes him seem intellectual and responsible, more serious and grown-up. Meanwhile, another Geico campaign, the talking-money ad (see the billboard ad in Figure 12), extends the concept of a humorous, friendly creature, like the gecko, that turns Geico insurance into a savings, not an expense.

FOR WRITING AND DISCUSSION

Designing Ads

This exercise asks you to apply these marketing concepts to designing your own ad. Imagine you are an advertising professional assigned to the Gloopers account. Gloopers is a seaweed (kelp)-based snack treat (a fiction, but pretend it is real) that is very popular under another name in Japan. It was introduced earlier in the American market and failed miserably—what sort of a treat is seaweed? But now, you have laboratory evidence that Gloopers provides crucial nutritional benefits for growing bodies and that it is a healthy alternative to junk food. Many food companies would kill for the endorsement of nutritious content that you now have to work with, but the product is still made out of gunky seaweed. Working in groups or individually, develop a campaign for this product by working out your answers to the following questions:

- Who is your target audience? (Will you seek to appeal to parents as well as children?)
- What is your core message or campaign concept? (Think of a visual approach, including a mirror and window appeal, and perhaps a tagline slogan.)
- What is the best positioning in the media landscape for this campaign?
- How will you build a brand image and brand loyalty?

How to Analyze an Advertisement

In addition to thinking about the decision making behind an ad, when you analyze a print ad you need to ask three overarching questions:

1. How does the ad draw in the target audience by helping them identify with the ad's problematic situation or story (mirror effect)?
2. How does the ad create a field of values, beliefs, and aspirations that serve as windows into a more fulfilled life?
3. How do the ad's images and words work together to create the desired persuasive effects?

For the images in an ad, all the strategies we have already described for documentary photographs and for paintings continue to apply—for example, angle of vision, framing, and so forth. (Review the strategies chart.) With many ads you also have to factor in the creative use of words—puns, connotations, and intertextual references to other ads or cultural artifacts. Note that in professionally created ads, every word, every punctuation mark, and every visual detail down to the props in the photograph or the placement of a model's hands are consciously chosen.

The following strategies chart focuses on questions particularly relevant to print ads.

Strategies for Analyzing the Compositional Features of Print Ads

What to Do	Some Questions to Ask
Examine the settings, furnishings, and all other details.	<ul><li>Is the room formal or informal; neat, lived-in, or messy?</li><li>How is the room furnished and decorated?</li><li>If the setting is outdoors, what are the features of the landscape: urban or rural, mountain or meadow?</li><li>Why are particular animals or birds included? (Think of the differences between using a crow, a hummingbird, or a parrot.)</li></ul>

(continued)

What to Do	Some Questions to Ask
Consider the social meaning of objects.	• What is the emotional effect of the objects in a den: for example, duck decoys and fishing rods versus computers and high-tech printers? • What is the social significance (class, economic status, lifestyle, values) of the objects in the ad? (Think of the meaning of a groomed poodle versus a mutt or a single rose versus a fuchsia in a pot.)
Consider the characters, roles, and actions.	• Who are these people and what are they doing? What story line could you construct behind the image? • Are the models regular-looking people, "beautiful people," or celebrities? • In product advertisements, are female models used instrumentally (depicted as mechanics working on cars or as a consumers buying cars) or are they used decoratively (bikini-clad and lounging on the hood of the latest truck)?
Observe how models are dressed, posed, and accessorized.	• What are the models' facial expressions? • What are their hairstyles and what cultural and social significance do they have? • How well are they dressed and posed?
Observe the relationships among actors and among actors and objects.	• How does the position of the models signal importance and dominance? • Who is looking at whom? • Who is above or below, in the foreground or background?
Consider what social roles are being played out and what values appealed to.	• Are the gender roles traditional or nontraditional? • Are the relationships romantic, erotic, friendly, formal, uncertain? • What are the power relationships among characters?
Consider how document design functions and how the words and images work together.	• What features of document design (variations of font style and size, placement on the page, formal or playful lettering) stand out?

What to Do	Some Questions to Ask
	• How much of the copy is devoted to product information or argument about superiority of the product or service?
	• How much of the copy helps create a field of values, beliefs, aspirations?
	• How do the words contribute to the "story" implied in the visual images?
	• What is the style of the language (for example, connotations, double entendres, puns)?

Sample Analysis of an Advertisement

With an understanding of possible photographic effects and the compositional features of ads, you now have all the background knowledge needed to begin doing your own analysis of ads. To illustrate how an analysis of an ad can reveal the ad's persuasive strategies, we show you our analysis of an ad for Coors Light (Figure 15) that ran in a variety of women's magazines in the mid-1990s. The marketers aimed to attract a new target audience—twenty-something or thirty-something middle-class women—and decided that print ads in magazines constituted the best medium.

This Coors Light ad uses an unusual strategy to target young adult women. Unlike typical beer ads aimed at men, which feature beach girls in bikinis or men bonding together on fishing trips or in sports bars, this Coors Light ad with its "Sam and Me" theme associates beer drinking with the warm friendship of a man and a woman.

Part of the ad's emotional appeal is the totally relaxed "story" shown in the image. The ad reveals a man and a woman, probably in their early- to mid-twenties, in relaxed conversation; they are sitting casually on a tabletop, with their legs resting on chair seats. The woman is wearing casual pants, a summery cotton top, and informal shoes. Her shoulder-length hair has a healthy, mussed appearance, and a braid comes across the front of her shoulder. She is turned away from the man, leans on her knees, and holds a bottle of Coors Light. Her sparkling eyes are looking up, and she smiles happily, as if reliving a pleasant memory. The man is wearing slacks, a cotton shirt with the sleeves rolled up, and scuffed tennis shoes with white socks. He also has a reminiscing smile on his face, and he leans on the woman's shoulder. The words "Coors Light. Just between friends." appear immediately below the picture next to a Coors Light can.

This ad creates its mirror effect by making it easy for women to identify with its story, which includes a good-looking but nonglamorous model and which is told from a woman's point of view (the "me" is the woman in the photograph). The ad's window effect is its opening onto a happy future. It appeals to women's

Sam and Me.

Me and Sam? We're just friends. Best friends, actually, since Mrs. Ainsley's first grade class when I let the hamster loose and Sam took the rap for me. I mean Sam's seen me in braces and I've seen him eat pizza. There's just way too much history here. Sam's my friend. The one I go to when I really need someone to talk to. I bring the Coors Light and Sam brings his shoulder. And sometimes it's Sam bringing the Coors Light and I'm doing the listening. Me and Sam? Together? I've never even thought about it. Okay, so I've thought about it.

Coors Light.
Just between friends.

FIGURE 15 Beer Ad Aimed at Women

desire for close friendships and relationships. Everything about the picture signifies long-established closeness and intimacy—old friends rather than lovers. The way the man leans on the woman shows her strength and independence. Additionally, the way they pose, with the woman slightly forward and sitting up more than the man, results in their taking up equal space in the picture. In many ads featuring male-female couples, the man appears larger and taller than the woman; this picture signifies mutuality and equality.

The words of the ad help interpret the relationship. Sam and the woman have been friends since the first grade, and they are reminiscing about old times. The relationship is thoroughly mutual. Sometimes he brings the Coors Light and sometimes she brings it; sometimes she does the listening and sometimes he does; sometimes she leans on his shoulder and sometimes he leans on hers. Sometimes the ad says, "Sam and me"; sometimes it says, "me and Sam." Even the "bad grammar" of "Sam and me" (rather than "Sam and I") suggests the lazy, relaxed absence of pretense or formality. "Sam" is a "buddy" kind of name rather than a romantic-hero name. But the last three lines of the copy give just a hint of potential romance: "Me and Sam? Together? I've never even thought about it. Okay, so I've thought about it."

Whereas beer ads targeting men portray women as sex objects, this ad appeals to many women's desire for relationships and for romance based on friendship. Its window function is mutuality and love rather than sexual acquisition.

The Coors Light ad was designed to appeal to young adult women. But cultural critics might also point out that the ad reproduces a worldview in which heterosexuality is the norm and in which women find their identities in romance and marriage. From the perspective of cultural criticism, then, advertisements are powerful cultural forces that both reflect cultural values and help construct and reproduce those values, including our sense of what is normal and not normal and our ideas about gender, race, and class. Identifying these cultural values in ads is an important part of ad analysis.

Analyzing Ads from Different Perspectives

FOR WRITING AND DISCUSSION

1. **Credit card campaigns:** Credit card companies have always faced a challenge: persuading consumers to buy with credit cards rather than cash and checks (with the expectation that many customers will not pay off the balance each month and thus pay substantial interest charges). Currently, banks and credit card companies must also overcome consumers' anger and distrust in this age of the banking crisis, overextended consumer debt, and high credit card interest.

   Choose one or more of the magazine ads for credit cards on the next two pages, and analyze them using the ideas presented throughout this section (target audience, choice of medium, brand building, mirror and window strategy, and compositional features).

2. **Cultural Criticism**

   a. Reexamine the same credit card ads from the perspectives of gender, class, and ethnicity. To what extent do these ads break or reinforce traditional notions of gender, race, and class?

FIGURE 16 MasterCharge Ad from the 1970s

b. Locate a gallery of older ads on the Web, and choose several to analyze for perspectives on gender, race, and class. For example, you might analyze the Coppertone sunscreen ad from the 1950s, with its slogan "Don't be a Paleface" and "Tan—Don't Burn." The image of the dog tugging at the little girl's swimsuit bottoms became a national symbol of summertime fun for families. What treatment of race, class, or gender in these older ads, like the Coppertone ad, contributed to making them culturally acceptable at the time and would make them unacceptable now?

Missing the trudge to work: Free

Missing the Monday morning alarm: Free

Missing the British weather: Free

Not missing your nine favourite people: Priceless

Advertising Archives

FIGURE 17 Recent "Priceless: MasterCard" Ad

FIGURE 18 Recent American Express Card Ad

LENNOX

HANDY
IF YOU GET
ROBBED
IN AMERICA.

American Express® has travel offices
in all corners of the globe.
So should you have the misfortune
to be relieved of your moneybelt
we can provide emergency cash
and replace your card, usually within
24 hours. Now who would you rather
have in your corner?

do more

Advertising Archives

Analysis of Two Visual Texts

Choose two documentary/news photographs, two paintings, or two print advertisements to analyze in a closed-form essay. Your two visual texts should have enough in common to facilitate meaningful comparisons. Show these images in your essay, but also describe your two visual texts in detail to highlight what you want viewers to see and to provide a foundation for your analysis. For this closed-form analysis, choose several key points of contrast as the focus. Your thesis statement should make a claim about key differences in the way that your chosen visual texts establish their purposes and achieve their persuasive effects.

Exploring and Generating Ideas for Your Analysis

For the subject of your analysis, your instructor may allow you to choose your own images or may provide them for you. If you choose your own, be sure to follow your instructor's guidelines. In choosing your visual texts, look for some important commonality that will enable you to concentrate on similarities and differences in your analysis:

- *Documentary or news photographs.* Analyze two photographs of an event from magazines with different political biases; two news photographs from articles addressing the same story from different angles of vision; or two images on Web sites presenting different perspectives on a recent controversial issue such as industrial farming or the war against terrorists.
- *Paintings.* Find two paintings with similar subject matter but different dominant impressions or emotional impacts.
- *Print ads.* Look for two ads for the same product (for example, cars, perfume, watches, shampoo) that are aimed at different target audiences or that make appeals to noticeably different value systems.

No matter what type of visual texts you are using, we suggest that you generate ideas and material for your analysis by using the question-asking strategies presented earlier in this chapter.

To help you generate more ideas, go detail by detail through your images, asking how the rhetorical effect would be different if some detail were changed:

- How would this documentary photo have a different effect if the homeless man were lying on the sidewalk instead of leaning against the doorway?
- Why did the artist blur images in the background rather than make them more distinct?
- What if the admakers had chosen a poodle rather than a black Lab? What if this model were a person of color rather than white?

FIGURE 19 Framework for an Analysis of Two Visuals

Introduction	• Hooks readers' interest; • Gives background on the two visual texts you are analyzing; • Sets up the similarities; • Poses the question your paper will address; • Ends with initial mapping in the form of a purpose or thesis statement.
General description of your two visual texts (ads, photographs, paintings)	• Describes each visual text in turn.
Analysis of the two visual texts	• Analyzes and contrasts each text in turn, using the ideas you generated from your observations, question asking, and close examination.
Conclusion	• Returns to the big picture for a sense of closure; • Makes final comments about the significance of your analysis.

Shaping and Drafting Your Analysis

Your closed-form essay should be fairly easy to organize at the big-picture level, but each part will require its own organic organization depending on the main points of your analysis. At the big-picture level, you can generally follow a structure like the one shown in Figure 19.

If you get stuck, we recommend that you write your rough draft rapidly, without worrying about gracefulness or correctness, merely trying to capture your initial ideas. Many people like to begin with the description of the two visual texts and then write the analysis before writing the introduction and conclusion. After you have written your draft, put it aside for a while before you begin revising.

Revising

Most experienced writers make global changes in their drafts when they revise, especially when they are doing analytical writing. The act of writing a rough draft generally leads to the discovery of more ideas. You may also realize that some of your original ideas aren't clearly developed or that the draft feels scattered or disorganized.

We recommend that you ask your classmates for a peer review of your draft early in the revising process to help you enhance the clarity and depth of your analysis.

Questions for Peer Review

In addition to the generic peer review questions, ask your peer reviewers to address these questions:

1. How well do the title, introduction, and thesis set up an academic analysis?
2. Where does the writer capture your interest and provide necessary background information? How might the writer more clearly pose the question to be addressed and map out the analysis?
3. Where could the writer describe the visual texts more clearly so that readers can "see" them?
4. How has the writer established the complexity of the texts and their commonalities and differences?
5. How well has the writer used the questions about angle of vision, artistic techniques, and compositional features presented in this chapter to achieve a detailed and insightful analysis of the texts? Where could the writer add more specific details about settings, props, furniture, posing of characters, facial expressions, manners of dress, and so forth?
6. In what ways could the writer improve this analysis by clarifying, deepening, expanding, or reorganizing the analysis? How has the writer helped you understand something new about these two texts?

Our first two readings argue different perspectives on the ethics of documentary photography, specifically, the photographing of victims of the massive Haiti earthquake of January 2010. The first reading, an op-ed piece by Clark Hoyt, Public Editor of the *New York Times*, appeared on January 23, 2010. For background, you may want to do a Web search of photographs of the Haiti disaster as well as explore the *New York Times'* gallery of photos.

Clark Hoyt
Face to Face with Tragedy

1   It was hard to look at some of the pictures of suffering and death caused by the earthquake in Haiti—and impossible to turn away.

2   The top of one front page in the *Times* was dominated by a woman, her hand to her cheek, as if in shock, walking past partially covered corpses lined up along a dirty curb. The next day, an even larger photograph at the top of page 1 showed a man covered in gray dust, lying alone, dead, statue-like, on a stretcher made from a piece of tattered cardboard spread over a crude ladder. Inside that same paper, the Friday after the disaster, was a gruesome scene from the central morgue in Port-au-Prince: a man mourning the death of his 10-month-old daughter, lying in her diaper atop a pile of bodies.

3   Some readers were offended at these scenes and even more graphic pictures on the paper's Web site, calling them exploitive and sensationalistic. "The numerous photographs printed in the *Times* showing the dead strewn about the streets of Port-au-Prince are unnecessary, unethical, unkind and inhumane," wrote Randy Stebbins of Hammond, La. Christa Robbins of Chicago said, "I feel that the people who have suffered the most are being spectacularized by your blood-and-gore photographs, which do not at all inform me of the relief efforts, the political stability of the region or the extent of damage to families and infrastructure." She spoke for several readers when she added, "If this had happened in California, I cannot imagine a similar depiction of half-clothed bodies splayed out for the camera. What are you thinking?"

4   But other readers were grateful for the shocking pictures, even as they were deeply troubled by them. Mary Louise Thomas of Palatka, Fla., said a different photo of the baby, lying on her dead mother, caused her to cry out, "Oh, my God!" and to sob for an hour. "But run from it? Never," she said. People repelled by such images "should really try staring truth in the face occasionally and try to understand it," she wrote.

5   Mary Claire Carroll of Richmond, Vt., asked, "How else can you motivate or inspire someone like me to donate money" to help out in Haiti? Her son, she added, thinks Americans "are too sheltered and protected from the real world."

6   Every disaster that produces horrific scenes of carnage presents photographers and their editors with the challenge of telling the unsanitized truth without crossing into the offensive and truly exploitive. In 2004, when a giant undersea earthquake unleashed a tsunami that killed tens of thousands along Indian Ocean coastlines, the *Times* ran a dramatic front-page photo of a woman overcome with grief amid rows of dead children, including her own. Some readers protested, but the newspaper's first public editor, Daniel Okrent, concluded that the paper was right to publish the picture. It told the story of the tsunami, he said.

7   I asked Kenneth Irby, leader of the visual journalism group at the Poynter Institute in Florida, for his assessment of the pictures from Haiti. Irby brings unusual perspectives to the task. He is a veteran photojournalist and an ordained minister, the pastor of an African Methodist Episcopal church in Palmetto, Fla. His wife's best friend is Haitian, and her family was still unaccounted for when we talked last week. "I think the *Times* coverage has been raw, truthful and tasteful," he told me, defending even the most graphic images.

8   Irby, who has been in touch with photographers in Haiti, said survivors want the world to see what has happened. "The actual loved ones, the bereaved, implore the journalists to tell their stories," he said.

9   That is exactly what Damon Winter told me. He is the *Times* photographer who took the pictures that elicited most of the protests to me and much praise on the paper's Web site. Winter, who won a Pulitzer Prize last year for his coverage of the Obama presidential campaign, was the first *Times* staff photographer on the scene, flying from New York to the Dominican Republic and then into Haiti aboard a chartered helicopter. He had never been to Haiti or covered a natural disaster.

10   "I have had so many people beg me to come to their home and photograph the bodies of their children, brothers, sisters, mothers, fathers," he said. "There are so many times that I have to apologize and say that I cannot, that I have photographed so many bodies already, and I think it breaks their hearts because they so desperately want people to know what has happened to them, what tremendous pain they are in, and that they desperately need help." Winter said it was important "that I do whatever I can to try and make our readers understand just how dire the situation is here."

11   Jessie De Witt, an international photo editor, said Winter sent the paper 26 pictures on his first day in Haiti, including the picture of the bodies along the curb that wound up on the front page. He sent 65 the next day, including the mourning father and the dead man on the stretcher. De Witt and her colleagues think carefully about photo selections. A picture of a dog eyeing a corpse is out, as are stacks of bodies without context. And they think about juxtaposition: an Armageddon-like scene of people scrambling for supplies from a ruined store was played against a quieter picture of people waiting patiently for medical treatment.

12   Michele McNally, the assistant managing editor in charge of photography, said she was going through all the photos from all sources, and Winter's photos of the single dead man and the grieving father "stopped me in my tracks." Bill Keller, the executive editor, said editors considered both for the front page, but chose the lone body, played big, because it was dramatic and there was "an intimacy that causes people to pause and dwell on the depth of the tragedy." Looking at one person, instead of many, "humanizes it," he said.

13   I asked McNally about Robbins's contention that such pictures would not appear in the paper if the victims were somewhere in the United States. If such pictures existed, she said, she would run them. When Hurricane Katrina hit New Orleans, the *Times* did publish a front-page picture of a body floating near a bridge where a woman was feeding her dog. But despite Katrina's toll, there were relatively few such images in the paper. Irby said that authorities in the United States are generally quick to cordon off disaster scenes.

14　Just as a picture of a grieving mother told the story of the tsunami in 2004, the disturbing images of the last two weeks have been telling the story of Haiti, and the *Times* is right to publish them. As Patricia Lay-Dorsey, a reader from Detroit, put it, Winter's "camera was my eye as much as it was his. And every one of his photos told the truth."

THINKING CRITICALLY
about "Face to Face with Tragedy"

1. According to Clark Hoyt, what are the ethical and rhetorical problems that photojournalists face in photographing disasters like the Haiti earthquake? Who are the different stakeholders in this controversy?

2. We discussed the importance of the photographer's purpose and of the cultural, social, historical and political context of the photograph. What claims does Hoyt make for the purpose and context of the published images of human suffering in Haiti?

3. Research the coverage of the Haiti earthquake in one of the prominent general news commentary sources such as *Newsweek, Time, USA Today* or a leading newspaper's or online news site's archives. What images appear the most often? How did the captions for these images shape your impression of them?

4. What intellectual and emotional impact did these images have on you?

Our second reading, an op-ed piece by Manoucheka Celeste, a doctoral candidate in the Department of Communication at the University of Washington, was published in the *Seattle Times* on January 26, 2010.

Manoucheka Celeste

Disturbing Media Images of Haiti Earthquake Aftermath Tell Only Part of the Story

1　As a Haitian, former journalist and media scholar, [I found] the earthquake in Haiti ... both personally devastating and intellectually challenging.

2　The first earthquake to hit Haiti in more than 200 years was unbelievable, unexpected and unprecedented. The devastation is clear with more than 200,000 lives lost. The damage is real. As we saw, people around the world responded quickly and generously.

3　This catastrophe presented an opportunity for media to respond in an unprecedented way. Some news outlets arrived before relief workers and doctors. We watched the horrors as they happened. I hoped that this was the moment when those of us trained in journalism would do something remarkable: Bring news of an unimaginable event in a way that disrupted the sensational and stereotypical ways that people in the "Third World" are represented.

4   What we got instead was much less humane. Videos of dead bodies, including children and the elderly, filled our television screens. For those of us who tuned in for information about friends and families, it was and is unbearable and despicable. Coverage went from sensational to ridiculous as CNN compared the literacy rates of Haiti and the United States. This was irrelevant as it continued to represent Haiti as a failed state.

5   The focus on poverty, with the repeated tagline "the poorest country in the Western Hemisphere" and references to crime and unrest, make it hard for viewers to imagine any other aspect of life in Haiti. People were called looters for taking food from collapsed buildings after not having eaten for days, framing their survival as a crime. The humanity needed in this moment is clearly missing.

6   Media scholars have long connected media coverage with public opinion, cultivating our attitudes and creating and reinforcing stereotypes. It is predominantly people of color who are shown negatively in news and entertainment. While the images mobilized some to help, they are damaging in the long term as they become ingrained in how we imagine Haitians. For many this is the first and last contact they will have with this population. The images matter as Haitians are shown as less than human. In mass media when images of Haiti and various countries in the African continent are shown, blackness becomes associated with helplessness, danger, poverty and hopelessness.

7   In the most disgusting moment in broadcast history, Pat Robertson proclaimed that Haiti had it coming because of its "deal with the devil," linking Haiti to "godlessness." What Robertson didn't consider was that "godlessness" was used as an excuse to kill and colonize peoples throughout history in the name of God, including Haiti, which, incidentally, is a heavily Christian country.

8   The question that plagues me and hopefully all audiences is: Who is able to die with dignity? In recent media history, there are few, but increasing instances where dead Americans are shown. From Columbine to Sept. 11, we rightfully protect the dead and rarely dare show them on television or in newspapers. Yet, the increasing presence of graphic and emotionally charged images, especially in broadcast media makes it seem normal or desirable.

9   This earthquake, despite the amazing pain that it has caused to so many, presents an unprecedented opportunity. Viewers and readers can demand that in people's darkest hour or once they lose their lives that they are treated with dignity.

10   We want the story without sensationalism and reinforcement of stereotypes. We want the media to value the lives of people who are "not us." As I waited for eight days to hear that my own mother and grandmother in Port-au-Prince are safe, I wanted to hold on to good memories of the person who brought me into the world and the one who taught me to be generous and tenacious. Let's seize the opportunity of this horrific tragedy to demand better from our news sources: dignity for everyone.

THINKING CRITICALLY
about "Disturbing Media Images of Haiti Earthquake Aftermath
Tell Only Part of the Story"

1. In her criticism of the media's use of "graphic and emotionally charged images," how does Manoucheka Celeste argue against the main perspective that Hoyt endorses?

2. Celeste's op-ed piece examines the role of viewers' knowledge, values, and assumptions in interpreting photos in news stories. What historical, political, and racial elements does Celeste underscore?

3. For the photographs of the Haiti disaster that you located and viewed, argue that they either simplified and distorted the issues or pushed them toward complexity and depth. In your mind, what does it mean to treat the human subjects of photographs with "dignity"?

Our final reading is student Lydia Wheeler's analytical essay written for the writing project in this chapter. It analyzes two documentary photos focused on economic hardship and displacement. One photo, taken by photographer Stephen Crowley, accompanied a *New York Times* story about a mother and her daughters in the 2008 recession caused by the collapse of the housing bubble in the United States. The subject, Isabel Bermudez, was subsisting on food stamps at the time of the story, unable to find a job; previously she had supported her daughters with a six-figure salary. Then the market collapsed, she lost her job, and shortly afterward she lost her house. The second photo is a famous image taken in 1936 in Nipoma, California, during the Great Depression. The photo is part of the *Migrant Mother* series by photographer Dorothea Lange. Lydia decided to examine the original newspaper contexts for these photographs and to approach them as depictions of women's experiences of economic crisis.

Lydia Wheeler (student)
Two Photographs Capture Women's Economic Misery

1   During economic crises, the hardship of individuals is often presented to us as statistics and facts: number of bankruptcies, percentage of the population living below the poverty line, and foreclosures or unemployment rates. Although this numerical data can be shocking, it usually remains abstract and impersonal. In contrast, photographers such as Stephen Crowley and Dorothea Lange help us visualize the human suffering involved in the economic conditions, skillfully evoking the emotional, as well as the physical, reality of their subjects. Crowley's color photograph, first published January 2, 2010, in a *New York Times* article titled "Living on Nothing but Food Stamps," is captioned "Isabel Bermudez, who has two daughters and no cash income." Lange's black and white photograph was commissioned by the Resettlement Agency to document Americans living in the Great Depression; she

originally captioned it *Destitute pea pickers in California; a 32 year old mother of seven children. February 1936.* However, in March of the same year, the *San Francisco Times* published Lange's photograph in an article demanding aid for workers like Florence Owens Thompson, the central subject of the picture. Once published, the photograph became famous and was nicknamed *Migrant Mother.* A close look at these two photos shows that through their skillful use of photographic elements such as focus, framing, orientation, and shape, Stephen Crowley and Dorothea Lange capture the unique emotional and physical realities of their subjects, eliciting compassion and admiration, respectively.

2   Stephen Crowley's photograph of a mother sitting in a room, perhaps the dining room of her house, and her young daughter standing and reaching out to comfort her sets up contrasts and tensions that underscore loss and convey grief. The accompanying article explains that Isabel Bermudez, whose income from real estate once amply supported her family, now has no income or prospect for employment and relies entirely on food stamps. A careful examination of Crowley's photograph implies this loss by hinting that Bermudez's wealth is insecure.

3   The framing, distance, and focus of Crowley's photograph emphasize this vanished wealth and the emotional pain. The image is a medium close up with its human subjects to the side, surrounding them with empty space and hints of expensive furnishings. While part of the foreground is sharply focused, the background is blurry and unfocused. There is a suggestion that the room is spacious. Further, the high, decorative backs of the room's chairs, the repetitive design decorating the bookshelf on

Isabel Bermudez, who has two daughters and no cash income, by Stephen Crowley

Stephen Crowley/The New York Times/Redux

Dorothea Lange

Destitute pea pickers in California; a 32 year old mother of seven children
[*Migrant Mother*] by Dorothea Lange

the frame's left, and the houseplant next to the bookshelf show that the room is well furnished, even luxurious. Bermudez and her daughter match their surroundings in being elegantly dressed. Bermudez looks across the room as if absorbed in her troubles; her daughter looks intently at her. Viewers' eyes are drawn to Bermudez's dark dress and her pearl necklace and earrings. However, the ostensible comfort of Bermudez and her surroundings starkly contrasts with her grief.

4   Crowley heightens this contrast and tension through the subjects' orientation and the space between them. The space between Bermudez and her daughter is one of the

photograph's dominant features, but it contains only out-of-focus objects in the background. Neither figure is centered in the photo; neither looks at the camera. Consequently, the viewers' attention moves back and forth between them, creating a sense of uneasiness. The meaning of this photo is focused not on what Bermudez has but on what she has lost.

5   Crowley also evokes sympathy and compassion for his subjects with his choice of angle, scale, and detail. The photograph's slightly high angle makes viewers look down—literally—on Bermudez, making her appear vulnerable and powerless and reinforcing the pathos. The most striking bid for compassion is the tears streaming down Bermudez's well made-up face. The contrast between her tidy appearance and the tear tracks on her face suggest overwhelming sadness. The poignancy of her apparent breakdown is heightened by her somber daughter's attempt to wipe away the tears on her mother's face. Crowley's decisions regarding *Isabel's* composition create an image that is highly disturbing.

6   In contrast to Crowley's photograph, Lange's *Migrant Mother*—through its content, focus, frame, rhythm, and angle—conveys long-standing poverty. Yet through this image of inescapable poverty pressing upon its subjects, it evokes admiration for this mother.

7   Lange's frame and focus generate much of the intensity of *Migrant Mother*. This photo is also a medium close up, but Lange's frame is tight with no open space. The lack of this openness cramps Lange's subjects and creates a claustrophobic feel intensified by the number of subjects shown—four to *Isabel's* two. There is almost no background. The subjects filling the foreground are crowded and sharply focused. The contrast between crowded foreground and empty background exaggerates the former and adds a touch of loneliness to *Migrant Mother*; this mother has no resources besides herself. Additionally, the subjects of *Migrant Mother* almost epitomize poverty: their hair is messy and uncombed, their skin dirt-stained. Even their clothes are worn—from the hem of Thompson's frayed sleeve to the smudges on her baby's blanket, Lange's photograph shows that Thompson can barely afford functional items.

8   *Migrant Mother's* circular lines also create a sense of sameness, stagnation, and hopelessness. Thompson's face draws viewers' eyes as the dominant feature, and Lange has ringed it with several arcs. The parentheses of her standing children's bodies, the angle of her baby in its blanket, and the arc of her dark hair form a ring that hems Thompson in and creates a circular path for the eyes of viewers. Seen with the obvious destitution of Lange's subjects, this repetition is threatening and grimly promises that it will be difficult, if not impossible, for this family to escape its poverty.

9   Like Crowley's *Isabel*, the impact of Lange's *Migrant Mother* derives from both the tragedy of her subjects' situation and their reactions. Lange uses angle and scale to generate sympathy and admiration for Thompson's strength. Once again we see a slightly high angle highlighting the subjects' vulnerability, which Lange reinforces with the slender necks of Thompson's children and a glimpse of her brassiere. However, Lange then contrasts this vulnerability with Thompson's strength, fostering viewers' admiration rather than compassion. *Migrant Mother's* scale, for example, exaggerates rather than diminishes Thompson's size: the photograph's frame focuses viewers' attention on the mother, who looks large, compared to her children. Additionally, Lange's subject

literally supports the bodies of the children surrounding her. Unlike Bermudez, Thompson sits tall as a pillar of strength for her vulnerable children. Even her expression—worried but dry eyed—fosters admiration and respect in viewers. By juxtaposing Thompson's vulnerability with her strength, Lange creates a photograph that conveys both its subjects' poverty and their stoicism in facing the Great Depression.

10   Lange and Crowley guide viewer's reactions to their photographs through careful control of the elements that influence our emotional responses to their work. Though they both show women in economic crises, these artists are able to convey the distinct realities of their subjects' situations and consequently send viewers away in different emotional states: one of compassion, one of admiration. The fame and veneration of Lange's *Migrant Mother* is a testament to her ability to evoke desired emotions. The photograph was exhibited at the Museum of Modern Art in 1941 and again in 1955, and was co-opted by countless movements since it was first published. Whether Crowley's *Isabel* will achieve similar fame for epitomizing this generation's economic crisis remains to be seen, but both photographs certainly succeed in delivering strong, lasting emotional statements.

THINKING CRITICALLY
about "Two Photographs Capture Women's Economic Misery"

1. What photographic elements has Lydia chosen to emphasize in her analysis of each of these photos?

2. What parts of Lydia's analysis help you see and understand these photos with greater insight? Do you agree with her choice of important elements and her analysis of their effects?

3. If you were analyzing these photos, what features would you choose to compare and stress?

my**comp**Lab   For support in learning this chapter's content, follow this path in **MyCompLab**: Resources ⇒ Writing ⇒ Writing and Visuals. Review the Instruction and Multimedia resources, then complete the Exercises and click on Gradebook to measure your progress.

ANALYZING AND SYNTHESIZING IDEAS

In many college courses, you'll be asked to explore connections and contradictions among groups of texts. Distilling main points from more than one text, seeing connections among texts, commenting on meaningful relationships, and showing how the texts have influenced your own thinking on a question are all part of the thinking and writing involved in synthesis.

Synthesis, which is a way of seeing and coming to terms with complexities, is a counterpart to **analysis**. When you analyze something, you break it down into its parts to see the relationships among them. When you synthesize, you take one more step, putting parts together in some new fashion. The cognitive researcher Benjamin Bloom schematized "synthesis" as the fifth of six levels of thinking processes, ranked in order of complexity and challenge: knowledge, comprehension, application, analysis, *synthesis*, and evaluation. Bloom defined synthesis in these terms: "putting together of constituent elements or parts to form a whole requiring original creative thinking."* Synthesis drives those light-bulb moments when you exclaim, "Ah! Now I see how these ideas are related!"

A second useful way to think of synthesis is as a dialectical thinking process. Throughout this text, we have explained that college writing involves posing a significant question that often forces you to encounter clashing or contradictory ideas. Such conflicts intrigued the German philosopher Hegel, who posited that thinking proceeds dialectically when a thesis clashes against an antithesis, leading the thinker to formulate a synthesis encompassing dimensions of both the original thesis and the antithesis. When you write to synthesize ideas, your thinking exemplifies this dialectical process.

Synthesis is an especially important component of academic research writing, where you use synthesis to carve out your own thinking space on a question while sifting through the writings of others. Synthesis, then, is the skill of wrestling with ideas from different texts or sources, trying to forge a new whole out of potentially confusing parts. It is the principal way you enter into a conversation on a social, civic, or scholarly issue.

This chapter introduces you to an important academic genre, the synthesis essay. By writing a synthesis essay, you will learn to:

- interact with a group of texts
- explore their alternative perspectives on an issue
- present a new, enlarged perspective of your own

*Benjamin Bloom, *Taxonomy of Educational Objectives: Handbook I: Cognitive Domain* (New York: David McKay, 1956).

Exploring the Analysis and Synthesis of Ideas

To introduce you to some of the essential thinking moves involved in analyzing and synthesizing, we offer this exercise, which asks you to read two articles on the question, "What effect are cell phones having on our lives as American citizens?" The first reading, "Mobile Phone Tracking Scrutinized" by Nikki Swartz, was published in the *Information Management Journal* for March/April 2006. This journal bills itself as "the leading source of information on topics and issues central to the management of records and information worldwide." The second reading, "Reach Out and Track Someone" by Terry J. Allen, appeared in the May 2006 edition of *In These Times*, a publication "dedicated to informing and analyzing popular movements for social, environmental and economic justice." Read these pieces carefully and then do the exercises that follow.

Nikki Swartz
Mobile Phone Tracking Scrutinized

1   Nearly 200 million Americans have cell phones, but many of them are not aware that wireless technology companies, as well as the U.S. government, track their movements through signals emitted by their handsets.

2   Cellular providers, including Verizon Wireless and Cingular Wireless, know, within about 300 yards, the location of their subscribers whenever a phone is turned on. Even if the phone is not in use, it still communicates with cell tower sites, and the wireless provider keeps track of the phone's position as it travels. These companies are marketing services that turn handsets into even more precise global positioning devices for driving or allowing parents to track the whereabouts of their children.

3   In recent years, law enforcement officials have used cellular technology as a tool for easily and secretly monitoring the movements of suspects. But this kind of surveillance, which investigators have been able to conduct with easily obtained court orders, has now come under tougher legal scrutiny.

4   The *New York Times* reports that, in the last four months of 2005, three federal judges denied prosecutors the right to get cell phone tracking information from wireless companies without first showing "probable cause" that a crime has been or is being committed—the same standard applied to requests for search warrants.

5   The rulings, issued by magistrate judges in New York, Texas, and Maryland, underscore the growing debate over privacy rights and government surveillance in the digital age. Wireless providers keep cell phone location records for varying lengths of time, from several months to years, and have said that they turn over cell location information when presented with a court order to do so.

6   Prosecutors argue that having such data is crucial to finding suspects, corroborating their whereabouts with witness accounts, or helping build a case for a wiretap on the phone. The government has routinely used records of cell phone calls and caller locations to show where a suspect was at a particular time, with access to those records obtainable under a lower legal standard.

7   But it is unclear how often prosecutors have asked courts for the right to obtain cell-tracking data as a suspect is moving. And the government is not required to report publicly when it makes such requests.

8   Prosecutors, while acknowledging that they must get a court order before obtaining real-time cell-site data, argue that a 1994 amendment to the 1986 Stored Communications Act—a standard that calls for the government to show "specific and articulable facts" that demonstrate that the records sought are "relevant and material to an ongoing investigation"—is actually lower than the probable-cause hurdle. In the cell-tracking cases, some legal experts say that the Stored Communications Act refers only to records of where a person has been—historical location data—but does not address live tracking.

9   Prosecutors in the recent cases also unsuccessfully argued that the expanded police powers under the USA PATRIOT Act could be read as allowing cell phone tracking.

10 The magistrate judges, however, ruled that surveillance by cell phone because it acts like an electronic tracking device that can follow people into homes and other personal spaces must meet the same high legal standard required to obtain a search warrant to enter private places.

11 "The distinction between cell site data and information gathered by a tracking device has practically vanished," wrote Stephen W. Smith, a magistrate in Federal District Court in the Southern District of Texas, in his ruling. He added that when a phone is monitored, the process is usually "unknown to the phone users, who may not even be on the phone."

12 In a digital era, the stream of data that carries a telephone conversation or an e-mail message contains a great deal of information, including when and where the communications originated. And that makes it harder for courts to determine whether a certain digital surveillance method invokes Fourth Amendment protections against unreasonable searches.

Terry J. Allen
Reach Out and Track Someone

1   If you are one of the more than 200 million Americans with a cell phone nestled in your pocket, authorities may be able to find you any time day or night—even if you never make or receive a call.

2   You know the Verizon ad where a lockstep crowd personifies the network that accompanies its customer everywhere? Well, within that seemingly friendly horde, a hightech Big Brother is lurking.

3   Most people know that when they make a mobile call—during a 911 emergency, for example—authorities can access phone company technology to pin down their location, sometimes to within a few feet.

4   A lesser-known fact: Cell phone companies can locate you any time you are in range of a tower and your phone is on. Cell phones are designed to work either with

global positioning satellites or through "pings" that allow towers to triangulate and pinpoint signals. Any time your phone "sees" a tower, it pings it.

5   That is what happened last month when a New York City murder highlighted the existence of the built-in capability of phones to locate people even when they aren't making calls.

6   The case of Imette St. Guillen captivated the New York City media as only the murder of a young, attractive, middle-class, white female can. One piece of evidence leading to the arrest of Darryl Littlejohn, the bouncer at the club where St. Guillen was last seen, was what police called "cell phone records." In fact, it was not an actual call that placed Littlejohn at the crime scene. Instead, according to the *New York Daily News*, police traced Littlejohn's route the day of the murder by tracking the "pings" of his cell phone, which were "stored" in a tower and "later retrieved from T-Mobile by cops."

7   Telecom companies and government are not eager to advertise that tracking capability. Nor will companies admit whether they are archiving the breadcrumb trail of pings from a cell phone so that they—or authorities—can trace back, after the fact, where the customer had been at a particular time. "Of course, there is that capability," says Bruce Schneier, chief technical officer with Counterpane Internet Security. "Verizon and the other companies have access to that information and the odds are zero that they wouldn't sell it if it is legal and profitable. This is capitalism after all."

8   But legality can be so tricky to pin down, especially when national security and corporate profits are involved. Communications companies and government have been repeatedly caught collaborating in highly questionable practices. Warrantless wiretapping, now sparking cries for Bush's impeachment, was implemented by the NSA* accessing the "gateway" switches that route calls around the globe. Most of these switches are controlled by AT&T, MCI and Sprint.

9   Recently, the Electronic Frontier Foundation (EFF) said it had internal AT&T documents and a sworn statement by retired AT&T technician Mark Klein showing that the company's use of a "dragnet surveillance" was "diverting Internet traffic into the hands of the NSA wholesale."

10   It is likely that authorities are also accessing cell phone call records and conducting real-time tracing of hapless Palestinians who donated to clinics and liberal activists who dared march for peace. And if the administration's record is a guide, it is interpreting privacy protection laws relating to cell phones in ways that bend and perhaps batter the Constitution.

11   "I think there's a substantial worry that location information about cell phone users is being released without a court order," EFF Staff attorney Kevin Bankston told CNN.

12   Echoing the Bush administration's rationale for warrantless wiretapping, the Justice Department argues that time lost justifying a search warrant can mean dangerous delays. Several judges around the country have disagreed. Citing officials' failure to show probable cause, they have denied government requests for cell phone tracking. According to EFF, a New York magistrate revealed that "the Justice Department had routinely been using a baseless legal argument to get secret authorizations from a number of courts, probably for many years."

*National Security Agency

13   "Justice Department officials countered that courts around the country have granted many such orders in the past without requiring probable cause," the Oct. 28 *Washington Post* reported.

14   Real-time tracking technology also opens disturbing entrepreneurial opportunities. Anyone who provides their kids, spouse or employees with a software-readied cell phone can secretly monitor them on the web. Wherify.com "locates loved ones within feet/meters in about a minute," and allows subscribers to "view location on both street and aerial mapping, to include date/time stamp, lat/long and block address" and "set breadcrumb schedule for periodic locates." Another Internet business promises to sell you the calling records for any phone number you provide. (Note to readers: If you have Karl Rove's number, I'll cough up the $100 fee to get a look.)

15   But as far as invasiveness goes, the ability of the government to secretly track and find you anywhere, anytime, ranks right up with a pelvic exam in Times Square.

INDIVIDUAL TASKS

1. How would you describe each writer's perspective or angle of vision on cell phones? In one or two sentences, summarize each writer's main points in these passages.
2. List ideas that these pieces have in common.
3. List any contradictions or differences you see in these pieces.
4. Freewrite your own response to these readings for five minutes, exploring what questions they raise for you or personal experiences that they might remind you of.

GROUP OR WHOLE-CLASS TASKS

1. Working in small groups or as a whole class, try to reach consensus answers to questions 1, 2, and 3.
2. Share your individual responses to question 4. What are the major questions and issues raised by your group or the whole class? What different views of cell phones in particular and technology in general emerged?

Understanding Analysis and Synthesis

Posing a Synthesis Question

Most academic and professional writing begins with the posing of a problem. Writing a synthesis essay follows the same principle. The need to synthesize ideas usually begins when you pose a problematic question that sends you off on an intellectual journey through a group of texts. The synthesis or focusing question directs you to look for ways that a group of texts are connected and ways that they differ in their approaches to a particular problem or issue. A synthesis question helps you zero in on a problem that these texts address or that you are trying to solve through exploring these texts. Your goal is to achieve your own informed view on that question, a view that reflects your intellectual wrestling with the ideas in your sources and in some way integrates ideas from these sources with your own independent thinking.

Although synthesis writing appears in college courses across the curriculum, how these assignments are set up varies widely. Sometimes instructors will specify the texts and the questions that you are to explore whereas at other times you will be asked to choose your texts and articulate your own synthesis questions. The following examples show typical synthesis assignments that you might encounter in different disciplines, with both the texts and synthesis questions provided in each case.

Environmental Politics Course

Texts to Be Analyzed	Synthesis Questions
Garrett Hardin's essay on overpopulation, "The Tragedy of the Commons," from *Science* (1968)	Are there any common assumptions about the world's environment in these readings?
Kenneth E. Boulding's essay "Economics of the Coming Spaceship Earth" (1966)	What problems and solutions appear in these readings?
A chapter from Ron Bailey's *The True State of the Planet* (1995)	What direction would you take in proposing a solution?
A chapter from Al Gore's *An Inconvenient Truth* (2006)	

American Literature Survey Course

Texts to Be Analyzed	Synthesis Questions
Selections from the *Lowell Offering*, a publication produced in Lowell, Massachusetts, in the 1840s, featuring the writings of young female factory workers	What common questions about changes in women's social roles in the 1800s emerge in these texts?
Historian Gerda Lerner's essay "The Lady and the Mill Girl: Changes in the Status of Women in the Age of Jackson 1800–1840" (1969)	Which text gives you the clearest understanding of the problems with women's changing roles and why?
Herman Melville's short story "The Paradise of Bachelors and the Tartarus of Maids" (1835)	

Synthesis Writing as an Extension of Summary/ Strong Response Writing

You are now familiar with writing summaries of texts and responding strongly to them through critique of their rhetorical strategies and ideas. It is helpful to think of synthesis writing as an extension of those skills. In writing a synthesis essay, you use both with-the-grain and against-the-grain thinking. You listen carefully to texts as you summarize them to determine their main points. You also conduct—at least informally in your exploratory stages—a critique of both the rhetorical features and the ideas of these texts. This analysis builds the platform from which you create a synthesis of ideas—that is, from which you begin your own independent thinking based on the synthesis question that ties your texts together.

A synthesis essay differs from a summary/strong response essay in that a synthesis extends the process to more texts with the aim of bringing them into conversation with each other. A synthesis essay shows how you have taken apart, made sense of, assessed, and recombined the ideas of these texts. A synthesis essay most likely incorporates the following features:

TYPICAL FEATURES OF A SYNTHESIS ESSAY

- A statement of the synthesis question that shows your interest in the texts and presents this question as problematic and significant
- Short summaries of these texts to give your readers a sense of the readings you are working with
- A thesis that indicates how you have analyzed and synthesized the readings to arrive at a new perspective
- Your analysis of key points in these texts, determined in part by the synthesis question
- Your new view, which combines ideas gathered from readings with your own independent ideas

Student Example of a Synthesis Essay

Before we move to the writing project for this chapter—and to the idea-generating strategies of student writers who are analyzing and synthesizing texts—we show you a student example of a synthesis essay. This example, by student writer Kate MacAulay, was written for the writing project for this chapter and addresses the assigned question, "What effect is technology having on humanity and the quality of life in the twenty-first century?" The texts she was asked to analyze and synthesize are these two:

- George Ritzer, "The Irrationality of Rationality: Traffic Jams on Those 'Happy Trails.'" This is a chapter from Ritzer's widely discussed book *The McDonaldization of Society.* New Century Edition (Thousand Oaks, CA: Pine Forge Press, 2000).
- Sherry Turkle, "Who Am We?" published in the magazine *Wired* 4.1 (January 1996): 148–52, 194–99.

We have not reprinted these two lengthy texts; however, later in this chapter, we include students' summaries of both articles and the informal and analytical exploratory pieces of another student writer, Kara Watterson, in order to show you helpful steps in writing synthesis essays.

Kate MacAulay (student)
Technology's Peril and Potential

Recently in English class, we have been focusing on the question, What effect is technology having on humanity and the quality of life in the twenty-first century? We have had heated discussions about the use of cell phones, palm pilots, beepers, e-mail, chat rooms, texting, and the Web. As part of my investigation of this question, I read

two texts: a chapter from George Ritzer's book *The McDonaldization of Society*, entitled "The Irrationality of Rationality: Traffic Jams on Those 'Happy Trails,'" and an article published in the magazine *Wired* entitled "Who Am We?", by Sherry Turkle. In his

chapter, Ritzer, a sociology professor, explains how technology has rationalized businesses and many facets of society following the McDonald's model. He argues that modern technology is causing loss of quality products, time, and relationships. In the McDonaldized system, where everything is designed logically for economy and convenience, things have become more artificial, and our relationships have become more superficial. In her article "Who Am We?", Sherry Turkle, a psychology professor at

MIT, shows how computers and the Internet are transforming our views of ourselves and the way we interact socially. Focusing on computers' capacities for simulation and promoting interaction, Turkle has explored MUDs (multiuser domains), which allow people to create virtual identities. MUDs, Turkle believes, contribute to the formation of postmodern multiple selves and raise new questions about personal iden-

tity and morality. Although both Turkle and Ritzer identify problems in technology's influence and in society's responses to it, Turkle sees more potential and gain where Ritzer sees mostly peril and loss. Both articles made me question how we define our values and morality in this postmodern, technologically advanced world and persuaded me of the need for caution in embracing technology.

Although Ritzer and Turkle both see technology as having some negative effects on human relations and the quality of life, they disagree about exactly where the most interesting and serious problems lie. Ritzer believes that the problems caused by technology are not problems within the individual, but problems imposed on the individual by McDonaldized systems. For example, Ritzer claims that fast-food restaurants

encourage us to eat unhealthy food quickly and also contribute to "the disintegration of the family" (141) by taking away family time. He also believes that rationalized systems create illusions of fun, reality, and friendliness. He talks about the "scripted interactions" (138) that employees are supposed to have with customers, where they are told exactly what to say to every customer, making interactions less real. Further, rationalized systems are dehumanizing in the kinds of jobs they create that "don't offer much in the way of satisfaction or stability" (137), benefiting only stockholders, owners, and employers.

In contrast, Turkle responds to technology's threat by focusing inward on technology's effect on the self and on relationships. While she is clearly intrigued by such Internet capabilities as multiuser domains, she acknowledges that this potential for multiple simultaneous identities threatens the wholeness of individuals, possibly damaging our emotional and psychological selves. Her concern is that people become addicted to these games because in the virtual world it is easy to create better "selves," to be what you wish you were. Turkle shows that people can lose themselves between the real world and the virtual world and be "imprisoned by the screens" (199). Although the virtual world is exciting and fun, she notes that "[o]ur experiences there are serious play" (199). She also examines cases of virtual characters who get into relationships with other characters, including cyber-sex relationships. She ponders the issue of cyber-sex immorality and adultery.

· Despite Turkle and Ritzer's agreement that technology can damage us as a society, they disagree on their overall outlook and on our power to respond positively to technology's influence. I find Ritzer's views almost entirely negative. He believes that we are irreversibly damaged by technological advances because we are completely caught up in the McDonaldized system, with few parts of society left unchanged. Almost all of the family-owned neighborhood restaurants or mom-and-pop grocery stores have been taken over by franchises like Red Robin or Safeway. The costs of these rationalized systems, he says, are "inefficiency, illusions of various types, disenchantment, dehumanization, and homogenization" (124). In this chapter of his book, Ritzer doesn't mention any ways that our lives could be improved by these systems; he gives only examples of the way we are misled and damaged by them.

Turkle's approach strikes me as much more positive and balanced than Ritzer's. Optimistically, she explains that MUDs can give people self-knowledge that they can apply to real life: "[t]he anonymity of MUDs gives people the chance to express multiple and often unexplored aspects of the self, to play with their identity and to try out new ones" (152). Turkle sees an opportunity for us to grow as individuals and to learn to use technology in a positive way: "If we can cultivate awareness of what stands behind our screen personae, we are more likely to succeed in using virtual experience for personal transformation" (199). I think Turkle's views are more complex than Ritzer's. She believes that we have to take responsibility for our own habits and psychological responses to technology. She encourages us to be aware of how we interact with technology and believes that we can grow as individuals using this technology.

After reading these articles, I have realized how the continuing advancement of technology raises new moral questions. In a McDonaldized system, where everything is designed for convenience, there seem to be many places for morals to be left out of the picture. For example, is it okay for us to exchange real human interaction for convenience and saving time? Is there something wrong with our ethics when interesting and fulfilling jobs are eliminated by machines or replaced by dead-end, low-paying Mcjobs? Turkle too shows us how virtual worlds pose new moral questions for us. In MUDs, people can form virtual relationships, even cyber-sex relationships. The people behind the characters are real people, even if they are acting as someone else. If a married person has a cyber-sex relationship on a MUD, is he or she cheating? If a person commits a virtual assault or other crime that has no real-world, physical effects, should he or she feel guilty or sinful for the intention? Ritzer and Turkle have made me see how important these questions are.

Reading the articles made me strongly believe that we must use this technology in moderation in order to preserve individual qualities and our relationships. From our class discussions, I remember what Scott said about the way that the Internet connects people. He said that people like his uncle, who was severely injured on the job, use the

Analytical point: compares and contrasts Ritzer's and Turkle's ideas

Analyzes and elaborates on Ritzer's ideas

Presents writer's independent thinking

Analyzes, contrasts, and elaborates on Turkle's ideas

Presents writer's independent thinking

Transition to writer's synthesis. Synthesis point discusses writer's own view

Elaborates on the connections the writer is making

Synthesis point discusses writer's own view

Internet as a way of "getting out" to meet people and socialize. He pointed out how the Microsoft Gaming Zone has brought his uncle into an ongoing backgammon tournament through which he has made friends. Meanwhile his aunt has gotten a lot of pleasure out of playing and problem solving in the world of MUDs.

Synthesis point discusses writer's own view

But my own experience has left me concerned about the danger we face as emotional, social beings in the face of technology. The other night at a family gathering, one of my cousins, after discussing car buying with some of the relatives, got the urge to research new car prices. He left the room, logged onto the Internet, and spent the rest of the evening looking at cars and prices. We saw him only once the whole evening when he came out to get a slice of pie. My cousin's withdrawal from the conversation made me think about Ritzer's and Turkle's concerns that technology decreases real interactions among people.

Transition and final connections

Conclusion

Ritzer and Turkle offer us a warning that technology can be damaging if we don't recognize and overcome its dangers. I would encourage us not to let ourselves become dominated by technology, not to let it take our full attention just because it is there, and not to overlook the complex moral questions that technology poses. The convenience that technology offers—our e-mail, cell phones, and debit cards—should help us save time that can be spent in nurturing our relationships with other people. The real challenge is to find ways to become even better people because of technology.

Works Cited

Complete citation of articles in MLA format

Ritzer, George. *The McDonaldization of Society*. Thousand Oaks, CA: Pine Forge, 2000. Print.
Turkle, Sherry. "Who Am We?" *Wired* Jan. 1996: 148+. Print.

WRITING PROJECT

A Synthesis Essay

Write a synthesis essay that meets the following criteria:

- Addresses a synthesis question that your instructor provides or that you formulate for yourself
- Summarizes and analyzes the views of at least two writers on this question
- Shows how you have wrestled with different perspectives on the question and have synthesized these ideas to arrive at your own new view of the question.

Ideas for Synthesis Questions and Readings

The writing project for this chapter draws on the kinds of texts you will typically be asked to synthesize in your college courses. This text provides a number of options from which your instructor can choose. Some instructors may assign both the readings and the synthesis questions. Others may assign the readings but invite students to pose their own questions. Still others may leave both the questions and the readings up to the students. The following list of questions and readings found in this text gives you options for subject matter and focus for synthesis essays.

Reading Options for This Assignment

Synthesis Questions	Possible Readings
How have cell phones affected the lives of American citizens?	• Nikki Swartz, "Mobile Phone Tracking Scrutinized." • Terry J. Allen, "Reach Out and Track Someone."
What are the biggest obstacles in managing the problem of undocumented immigrants? What should the United States do to make progress in solving this problem?	Two or more of the excerpts from blogs collected in the Readings section of this chapter.
What should be our attitude toward outsourcing of American jobs? What is the most reasonable approach to solving problems caused by outsourcing?	• Thomas L. Friedman, "30 Little Turtles." • David Horsey, "Today's Economic Indicator" (editorial cartoon). • Mike Lane, "Labor Day Blues" (editorial cartoon). • Froma Harrop, "New Threat to Skilled U.S. Workers."
Should the United States increase its production of electricity by building more nuclear power plants or by pursuing some other form of energy?	• David Rockwood, "A Letter to the Editor." • William Sweet, "Why Uranium Is the New Green." • Stan Eales, "Welcome to Sellafield" (editorial cartoon). • Editorial from the *Los Angeles Times*, "No to Nukes."

Using Learning Logs

In our view, a productive way to generate ideas for your synthesis essay is to break your process into a series of incremental thinking steps that take you gradually from summaries of your chosen texts to an analysis of them and finally to a synthesis of their ideas with your own. The five learning log tasks in the sections that follow will guide you through this process. On several occasions you will have an opportunity to share your learning log explorations with classmates and to use these logs to generate further discussion of ideas. Your instructor will specify whether completion of these learning log tasks will be a requirement for this assignment. In our view, the learning log tasks work best if you keep your writing informal and exploratory with an emphasis on idea generation rather than on corrections and polish.

Exploring Your Texts through Summary Writing

Learning Log Task 1: Write a 200–250-word summary of each of the main texts you will use in your final paper.

As a starting point for grappling with a writer's ideas, writing careful summaries prompts you to read texts with the grain, adopting each text's perspective and walking in each author's shoes. When you summarize a text, you try to achieve an accurate, thorough understanding of it by stating its main ideas in a tightly distilled format.

What follows are student Kara Watterson's summary of the book chapter by Ritzer and student Kate MacAulay's summary of Turkle's article—the two readings they will use in their synthesis essays. Notice how they use attributive tags to show that they are representing Ritzer's and Turkle's ideas as objectively as they can and that these ideas belong to Ritzer or Turkle, not to them.

KARA'S SUMMARY OF RITZER'S CHAPTER

In "The Irrationality of Rationality," the seventh chapter in *The McDonaldization of Society*, sociologist George Ritzer identifies a major sociological and economic problem: in an effort to find the most efficient way to run a business (what Ritzer calls "rationalizing"), more and more companies are following the franchise model pioneered by McDonald's. Although McDonaldization is efficient and economical for the companies, Ritzer argues it can be irrational, inconvenient, inefficient, and costly for consumers who often stand in long lines at fast-food restaurants and supermarkets. Ritzer also claims that McDonaldized systems cause people to forfeit real fun for manufactured fun and illusion. He cites the example of fake international villages at amusement parks and the fake friendliness of the "scripted interactions" (138) that employees are supposed to have with customers. Ritzer explains that our McDonaldized society has begun focusing more on quantity than quality. He believes that McDonaldized systems are dehumanizing: jobs "don't offer much in the way of satisfaction or stability" (137) and families hardly ever eat together any more, a situation that is contributing to the "disintegration of the family" (141). Ritzer also argues that by franchising everywhere, we are losing cultural distinctions. Whether you are in Japan or the United States, products are beginning to look the same. Finally, Ritzer shows that when companies become rationalized, they limit the possibility of connection between human beings. Citing examples from fast-food restaurants to hospitals, he states that there are many serious drawbacks to "our fast-paced and impersonal society" (140).

KATE'S SUMMARY OF TURKLE'S ARTICLE

In her *Wired* article "Who Am We?" psychologist and MIT professor Sherry Turkle explores how computers and the Internet are transforming our views of ourselves and the way we interact socially. Turkle believes that the Internet is moving us toward a "decentered" (149) sense of the self. She says that computers used to be thought of as "calculating machines" (149), but they are increasingly now seen as intelligent objects capable of interaction and simulation. She uses children's interactive computer games to illustrate how some people now think of computers as having personalities and psyches, which make them "fitting partners for dialog and relationship" (150). In the second half of her article, she argues that virtual life raises new moral issues. She uses the example of MUDs (multiuser domains), which allow people to create multiple and often simultaneous virtual identities by playing different characters. She presents examples of the relationships of cyber characters—often cyber-sex—that raise the question of whether cyber-sex is an act of real-life infidelity or adultery. Turkle concludes that it is easy for people to lose themselves between the real world and these virtual worlds. Because we have the ability to create better "selves" in the virtual world, it is possible to become addicted to virtual life and be "imprisoned by the screens" (199). According to Turkle, we are moving toward a "postmodernist culture of simulation" (149), and she cautions that it is more important than ever that we are very self-aware.

Summarizing Your Texts

FOR WRITING AND DISCUSSION

Working in small groups or as a whole class, share your summaries of your two chosen or assigned readings. What important main ideas does your group agree must be included in a summary of each text? What points are secondary and can be left out?

Exploring Your Texts' Rhetorical Strategies

> **Learning Log Task 2:** Analyze the rhetorical strategies used in each of your texts (for example, the way your texts handle purpose; audience; genre; angle of vision; appeals to *logos*, *ethos*, and *pathos*, and use of evidence).

In order to analyze a text and synthesize its ideas, you need to consider the text rhetorically. To whom is the author writing and why? Do you see how the genre of each text influences some of the author's choices about language and structure? What angle of vision shapes each text and accounts for what is included and excluded? Do you share the values of the author or of his or her intended audience?

In the next sections, we show examples of Kara's exploratory thinking. Here is Kara's learning log entry exploring the rhetorical contexts of the Ritzer and Turkle texts:

KARA'S RESPONSE TO LEARNING LOG TASK 2

Although both George Ritzer and Sherry Turkle are scholars, their texts are not really written for scholarly audiences. Both would fall in the category of nonfiction books (articles) written for general audiences and both are written to raise audience awareness of sociological/cultural problems—in this case, the way that technological advances and the fast-food model of business are affecting the quality of life and the way that the Internet is affecting our sense of ourselves and our relationships.

Both Ritzer and Turkle have chosen to write in accessible language so that their ideas can easily be understood by a general audience, and both use many examples to build credibility. Still, because I had no previous personal background with multiuser domains, I found it challenging to imagine some of Turkle's descriptions of the virtual world of MUDs, but I did have previous experience with all of Ritzer's examples so I never felt in over my head while reading his chapters.

From Ritzer's angle of vision, McDonaldization has had a damaging and irreversible effect on the quality of contemporary life, and he is trying to prompt people to slow down this destructive process. His approach is quite one-sided, though. He does admit that "we undoubtedly have gained much from the rationalization of society in general" (132), but he does not develop this idea any further. He refuses to make any further concessions to the rationalization he is fighting. Instead of acknowledging contradicting ideas, Ritzer hammers his point strongly with example after example. By the end of the chapter, the reader is left with a glazed-over feeling, not really taking in the information.

Turkle's angle of vision seems to include curiosity and exploration as well as concern about the way computers are transforming society. She seems to analyze more than argue. She is trying to get across her notion that the Internet lets people adopt many different characters and have multiple selves, for example when they play in MUDs and simulation games. So maybe, in claiming that computers are no longer calculating machines, Turkle, like Ritzer, is only presenting one limited view of her subject, the view that interests her as a psychologist who has written many books and articles on computers, and our changing sense of identity and community.

FOR WRITING AND DISCUSSION

Examining the Rhetorical Strategies of Your Texts

Working in small groups or as a whole class, share what each of you discovered in Learning Log Task 2. Try to reach consensus on the most important rhetorical features of each of the texts you are using for your synthesis essay.

Exploring Main Themes and Similarities and Differences in Your Texts' Ideas

Learning Log Task 3: Identify main issues or themes in your assigned or chosen texts. Then explore the similarities and differences in their ideas.

This learning log task asks you to identify main issues, ideas, or themes that surface in your texts as preparation for looking for similarities and differences among your texts. This process of thinking—comparison and contrast—will help you clarify your understanding of each reading and promote analysis of the underlying values, assumptions, and ideas of each author. Here are some questions that can guide your learning log writing at this stage of your thinking:

QUESTIONS TO HELP YOU GRAPPLE WITH SIMILARITIES AND DIFFERENCES IN YOUR TEXTS

- What main ideas or themes related to your synthesis question do you see in each text?
- What similarities and differences do you see in the way the authors choose to frame the issues they are writing about? How do their theses (either implied or stated) differ?

- What are the main similarities and differences in their angles of vision?
- What commonalities and intersections related to your synthesis question do you see in their ideas? What contradictions and clashes do you see in their ideas?
- What similarities and differences do you see in the authors' underlying values and assumptions?
- What overlap, if any, is there in these authors' examples and uses of terms?
- On the subject of your synthesis question, how would Author A respond to Author B?

Here is an excerpt from Kara's learning log, showing her exploratory analyses of Ritzer's and Turkle's texts. Note how she begins to organize comparisons by points, to make analytical connections among them, and to push herself to think out exactly where these authors agree and differ.

EXCERPT FROM KARA'S RESPONSE TO LEARNING LOG TASK 3

Both Ritzer and Turkle make strong comments about health problems that may be caused by the particular type of technology they are dealing with. For Ritzer, the dangers that arise from McDonaldization can most easily be seen in fast-food restaurants and their fatty, unhealthy foods: "such meals are the last things many Americans need, suffering as they do from obesity, high cholesterol levels, high blood pressure, and perhaps diabetes" (133). He also considers the high level of stress created by our high-speed society that can cause heart attacks, panic attacks, maybe nervous breakdowns. Turkle, too, is concerned about the effects of technology on people's health, but her focus is people's psyches and minds. One person in her research study who creates different identities on the Internet thinks that "MUDding has ultimately made him feel worse about himself" (196). For Turkle, the Internet can be dangerous for what it can do to a person's psyche.

Both authors agree that technological advances are causing a loss of real human connection. McDonaldization fosters fake contact; employees are given guidelines about how to interact with customers and are programmed with what to say and what not to say: "rule Number 17 for Burger King workers is 'Smiles at all times'" (Ritzer 130). Quick sales, not real customer relations, are the main concern. For Turkle too, this loss of human contact is a dilemma. MUDs are not places where you truly get to know a person; they are places where people are acting out characters. These are not real friends that can aid you when you are feeling ill or down. Also, people are spending vast quantities of time logging on, spending time with a computer screen instead of family and friends. . . .

Generating Points about Themes, Shared Ideas, and Differences

FOR WRITING AND DISCUSSION

Working as a whole class or in small groups, share your analyses of similarities and differences in your chosen or assigned texts. Pay close attention to these two overarching questions: How are the texts similar and different? How do each author's assumptions, beliefs, purposes, and values account for these similarities and differences?

Generating Ideas of Your Own

Learning Log Task 4: In light of what you have read and thought about so far, explore your own views on the original synthesis question that has guided your probing of the texts.

One of your biggest challenges in writing a synthesis essay is to move beyond analysis to synthesis. A successful synthesis essay incorporates ideas from your texts and yet represents your own independent thinking, showing evidence of the dialectic process. You need to think about how the differing perspectives of Texts A and B have led you to new realizations that will let you enter the conversation of these texts. As you begin to formulate your synthesis views, you will also need to reassert your personal/intellectual investment in the conversation of the texts. You will need to take ownership of the ideas and to emerge with a clearer sense of your own views. You may also want to consider which text—in your mind—makes the most significant contribution to the question you are exploring. You may want to evaluate the texts to determine which has influenced your thinking the most and why. The following questions should help you use Learning Log Task 4 to generate ideas of your own.

QUESTIONS TO HELP YOU DEVELOP YOUR OWN VIEWS

- What do I agree with and disagree with in the texts I have analyzed?
- How have these texts changed my perception and understanding of an issue, question, or problem? (You might want to use these prompts: "I used to think _____, but now I think _____." "Although these texts have persuaded me that _____, I still have doubts about _____.")
- Related to my synthesis question, what new, significant questions do these texts raise for me?
- What do I now see as the main controversies?
- What is my current view on the focusing question that connects my texts and that all my texts explore?
- How would I position myself in the conversation of the texts?
- If I find one author's perspective more valid, accurate, interesting, or useful than another's, why is that?

To illustrate this learning log task, we show you an excerpt from Kara's exploration.

EXCERPT FROM KARA'S RESPONSE TO LEARNING LOG TASK 4

When I was in Puerto Rico one spring break, I remember how excited my friend and I were to go to a burger place for dinner one night. It was so nice to have American food after days of eating fajitas and enchiladas. At the time, I did not think about how this American restaurant got to Puerto Rico; I was just glad it was there. However, after reading "The Irrationality of Rationality" by George Ritzer, I began to take a closer look at this experience. Both this article and "Who Am We?" have caused me to take a closer look at our society. ... What is it that causes people to surf the Internet for hours on end, to chat with people they have never met? What is this doing to our culture? Are we losing the distinctions evident when you travel from one region to the next, from one country to another? ...

Taking Your Position in the Conversation: Your Synthesis

Learning Log Task 5: Reread your first four learning logs and consider how your own views on the synthesis question have evolved and emerged. Think about the risky, surprising, or new views that you can bring to your readers. In light of your reading and thinking, explore what you want to say in your own voice to show the connections you have made and the new insights you now have.

After you have discovered what you think about the texts you have analyzed—what ideas you accept and reject, what new questions you have formulated, how your ideas have been modified and transformed through your reading experience—you need to find a way to pull your ideas together. Your synthesis view should be the fruit of your intellectual work, a perspective that you have come to after reading the ideas of other writers, pondering them reflectively and keenly. Here are some questions that can help you articulate the points that you want to develop in your essay:

QUESTIONS TO HELP YOU FORMULATE AND DEVELOP YOUR SYNTHESIS VIEWS

- What discoveries have I made after much thought?
- What are the most important insights I have gotten from these readings?
- What is my intellectual or personal investment with the synthesis question at this point?
- Where can I step out on my own, even take a risk, in my thinking about the ideas discussed in these texts?
- What new perspective do I want to share with my readers?

What follows is an excerpt from Kara's learning log. Note how she is beginning to find her stance on the synthesis question of whether technology enriches or dehumanizes our lives.

EXCERPT FROM KARA'S RESPONSE TO LEARNING LOG TASK 5

What is technology doing to our relationships with one another? Both Ritzer and Turkle seem to be urging us away from dependency on technology, and these authors have made me aware of my complacence in accepting technology, but still I see value in technology that these writers don't discuss. ...

I find myself questioning these writers' views. Ritzer seems to believe that families go to McDonald's rather than eat family meals together. He doesn't consider that it is when people are on the road or out already that these restaurants are visited, not when they are sitting at home deciding what is for dinner. Turkle also speaks of the loss of connection that can arise from people constantly at their computers. She raises some very important questions about what technology is doing to our relationships and self-image, but I think she focuses too much on MUDs. How many people actually are doing this MUDding? Also, there are some valid things that come out of relationships on the Internet. I know of several examples of people who have met their future spouses through chat rooms and Online Social Networks. When I left for college, I was not sure whom I would stay in touch with, but because of the Internet, I am able to stay connected to people I would have drifted away from otherwise.

Also, while we note the dangers of technology, I think we need to remember the benefits as well. I agree that cell phones are overused, but how often have cell phones saved people in emergencies or aided people stranded on the road with car problems? I hope to be a doctor. I have great appreciation for the way that cameras can see inside a patient as surgeons are operating and thus reduce the risk of many surgeries. . . .

FOR WRITING AND DISCUSSION

Generating Your Synthesis Points

Prior to the start of this task, work individually to write two or three main points that you want to make in the synthesis portion of your final essay. Working in small groups or as a whole class, share your short list of main points. Briefly explain to your group or to the whole class why these points interest you. Take notes on group ideas.

At this point, you might want to reread Kate MacAulay's synthesis essay, which shows evidence of the ideas discovered in the exploratory thinking she did in her learning logs. You can see how she selected, organized, and developed particular points that probably appeared as kernels in her exploratory writing, just as Kara's learning logs show her emerging ideas.

Shaping and Drafting

Your main project in shaping and drafting your synthesis essay is to move from the kernels of good ideas that you generated in your learning logs to a focused, fully developed, and logically organized discussion of these ideas. Focusing and organizing your ideas for a synthesis essay are both challenging writing tasks. We offer some suggestions for developing the analysis and synthesis sections of your essay and then for formulating a thesis that will direct and hold together your essay.

For the analysis part of your essay, identify the points in Learning Log Tasks 2 and 3 that strike you as the most interesting, lively, profound, or significant. The following strategies will help you focus and develop these ideas.

Strategies for Shaping the Analytical Section of Your Essay

What to Consider in Planning the Analysis Section of Your Essay	Questions and Decisions
• Your analysis section lays the foundation for your synthesis. • The analysis section usually forms about one-half to two-thirds of your essay. • This section discusses several ways that your texts relate to your synthesis question.	• How many analytical points do you want to develop? • What are these points?
• Your analysis section should show that you have wallowed in the complexity of your texts. • It may include points about the rhetorical features of your texts (as in a rhetorical critique), and it may include points about the ideas (as in an ideas critique). • It should map out and explain a number of important similarities and differences in your texts.	Consider developing answers to these questions: • How do your texts frame the problem? How do they present different angles of vision? Where do they intersect in their perspectives and approaches? How do they argue and support their views with evidence? • How rhetorically effective are these texts? • What do the authors do to make their readers think?

For the synthesis part of your essay, use the following strategies to develop points that emerged for you from Learning Log Tasks 4 and 5.

Strategies for Shaping the Synthesis Section of Your Essay

What to Consider in Planning the Synthesis Section of Your Essay	Questions and Decisions
• Your essay should build to your synthesis section. • Typically your synthesis ideas form at least one-third of your essay.	• How can you best show where the texts and their authors promote your own independent thinking? • What synthesis points do you want to explore and discuss?
• The synthesis section of your essay should show your informed, independent thinking. • It should show how you have worked your way to a new understanding.	• What new insights have you developed through studying these texts? • What new perspectives have you gained through the contrast and/or clash of different ideas? • How much or how little have these texts changed your views and why?

Writing a Thesis for a Synthesis Essay

In a synthesis essay, your thesis statement is particularly important and challenging to write. It sets up your readers' expectations, promising an illuminating view of the texts you have worked with. It should reflect earnest intellectual work, promise insights achieved through serious reflection, be your own original connection of ideas, and contain some element of risk and newness. Avoid bland, noncontestable thesis statements such as "These articles have both good and bad points."

You will probably want to work back and forth between formulating your thesis statement and drafting the analysis and synthesis sections of your essay. We recommend that you map out a rough thesis, draft your essay, and then revise and sharpen your thesis. For a synthesis essay, it is sometimes difficult to write a one-sentence, high-level thesis statement that encompasses both your analysis and your synthesis points. In such cases, you can write two lower-level, more specific thesis statements—one for your analysis section and one for your synthesis section—and simply join them together. What is important is that your thesis forecasts your main analysis and synthesis points and creates a map for your reader. The following examples illustrate these different options.

LOW-LEVEL, TWO-SENTENCE THESIS

Lower-level thesis for analysis

Lower-level thesis for synthesis

Whereas Ritzer focuses on the way high-tech society makes us homogeneous and superficial, Turkle focuses on how the Internet unsettles traditional views of the self. Although I agree with Ritzer's argument that McDonaldization is dehumanizing, I think that role-playing in MUDs is actually a healthy way to oppose McDonaldization and expresses human desire to be creative, to develop the self, and to make human connections.

HIGH-LEVEL, ONE-SENTENCE THESIS

Writer chooses high-level, one-sentence thesis rather than two lower-level theses

Ritzer's attack on technological society and Turkle's more optimistic belief that it offers opportunity for growth and discovery have together forced me to consider the superficiality and vulnerability of human relationships in our high-tech society.

Organizing a Synthesis Essay

The biggest organizational decision you have to make in writing a synthesis essay is how much to summarize your texts and how to incorporate these summaries into your essay. Your decision should be guided by your audience's familiarity with the texts you are discussing and the complexity of the points you are making. Two ways of organizing a synthesis essay are shown in Figure 1.

Revising

As you revise your synthesis essay, make sure that you have set up the synthesis question effectively. Then work on clarifying and developing your analytical points while striving for an engaging style. Also consider how to make your synthesis views more clearly reflect your own wrestling with the texts' ideas. Think about finding the most interesting ways to show how these texts have enlarged and deepened your own views.

FIGURE 1 Two Frameworks for a Synthesis Essay

Framework 1

Introduction and summary of both texts (several paragraphs)	• Presents the synthesis question and hooks readers • Summarizes the texts (unless your instructor posits that readers have already read the texts, in which case you can omit the summaries or reduce them to one or two sentences each) • Presents your thesis, which maps out your main analytical and synthesis points (Your thesis might come at the end of the paragraphs with your summaries or in a mini-paragraph of its own.)
Analytical section	• Includes paragraphs discussing and developing your analytical points
Synthesis section	• Includes paragraphs discussing and developing your synthesis points
Concluding paragraph	• Reiterates the values and limitations of the texts you have analyzed • Pulls together your new insights • Leaves readers thinking about your views

Framework 2

Introduction	• Presents the synthesis question and hooks readers • Presents your thesis, which maps out your main analytical and synthesis points
Summary/analysis of first text	• Summarizes the first text • Analyzes the first text
Summary/analysis of second text	• Summarizes the second text • Analyzes the second text
Synthesis section	• Develops several main synthesis points
Concluding paragraph	• Reiterates values and limitations of the texts you have analyzed • Pulls together your new insights • Leaves readers thinking about your views

Questions for Peer Review

In addition to generic peer review questions, ask your peer reviewers to address these questions:

INTRODUCTION, SUMMARIES OF THE TEXT, AND THESIS

1. What works well about the writer's presentation of the synthesis question that connects the texts under examination? How could the writer better show this question's significance and problematic nature?

2. Where could the writer's summaries of the texts be expanded, condensed, or clarified? Where would the summaries be better located in the essay to help readers?
3. How could the thesis be made more focused, risky, and clear in setting up the writer's analytical and synthesis points?

ANALYTICAL SECTION OF THE ESSAY

1. How could the analytical points more clearly compare and contrast the authors' values, assumptions, angles of vision, or rhetorical strategies in addressing the synthesis question?
2. What further textual evidence could the writer add to develop these analytical points and make them more interesting or comprehensive?

SYNTHESIS SECTION OF THE ESSAY

1. How could the writer's synthesis points more clearly demonstrate the writer's thoughtful interaction with these texts?
2. What examples or other specifics could the writer include to develop these synthesis points more effectively?
3. How could the writer conclude this essay more effectively to leave readers with a new perspective on the texts and on the underlying question?

The readings in this chapter immerse you in a network of issues about illegal immigration and immigration reform, which continue to be volatile and contested. These issues cut across political parties and continue to perplex citizens, policymakers, and immigrants. Experts estimate that eleven to twelve million people have illegally crossed the border between the United States and Mexico and are currently living and working in the United States. What caused these persons to risk the dangers of border crossing in order to work in the United States? What questions about human rights and domestic security does this problem raise? What forces are interfering with effective policy discussions and decision making to solve these problems?

For this chapter's readings, we present five blogs on these issues. ("Blog" is an abbreviation for "Web log.") Blogging has become a popular arena for political discourse worldwide as well as for discourse on any subject ranging from hobbies to sports to conspiracy theories. The blogosphere constitutes a new and rapidly evolving rhetorical context open to anyone who desires to create a blogsite or respond to postings on someone else's site. Persons often blog under online pseudonyms. Because a blogger tends to attract persons with similar interests and views, a blogsite serves as a "virtual café" for like-minded people to exchange views. Consequently, blogs often have an uncomfortable "insider feel" for persons trying to enter a blog conversation for the first time. They are also often characterized by informal, colloquial, and occasionally obscene language that wouldn't be encountered in print media. Some widely known and highly influential sites—such as the Daily Kos on the left or MichelleMalkin or Little Green Footballs on the right—are major players in United States political debate. Many people now think that skilled and knowledgeable bloggers play a more important "free press" investigative role in our democracy than do major newspapers dominated by corporate interests.

To avoid influencing your own analysis of these readings, we omit the discussion questions that typically follow. However, as you read each blog, consider the particular blogsite that is hosting this piece (mentioned in the headnote) and also think about these general questions: How does the writer frame the issue? What is the writer's main argument? What types of evidence are included? What is distinctive about the way the writer expresses his or her ideas?

Our first blog is by a Mexican-American woman who identifies herself only as "Dee." According to her blogsite, Dee is a United States citizen with a Hispanic ethnicity. She holds a mid-level management position in a large corporation. Upset by the divisive discourse over immigration, Dee started her own blogsite called "Immigration Talk with a Mexican American: Truth, Honesty, and the American Way." In the blog reprinted below (posted on August 7, 2007), she sums up her placement of blogosphere views of immigration in two categories: the PROs (those who support comprehensive immigration reform) and the ANTIs (those who oppose it). She places herself firmly among the PROs. In this brief blog, her reference to the 12M stands for the estimated twelve million undocumented workers currently in the United States. Her use of abbreviations suggests the insider audience characteristic of blog discourse.

Dee

Comprehensive Immigration Reform: PROs and ANTIs

http://immigrationmexicanamerican.blogspot.com/2007/08/
comprehensive-immigration-reform-pros.html

1   Our country is divided on how to resolve our Immigration issues in our country. Comprehensive Immigration Reform (CIR) is needed. Who is for CIR? PROs. Who is against CIR? ANTIs. What are their perspectives?

2   Pro Profile: There are many, many PRO groups. Each group has a different motivation and they rarely rally together. The largest group is Hispanic Americans. The ethnicities vary and include: Mexican, Central and South American, Cuban, Puerto Rican and more. The majority of PROs who post on the internet are from this group. Other Minority groups include Asian, Southern European, Middle Eastern, African. I only see their posts when I search the international sites. Other PRO groups who also rarely post include: Churches and Humanitarian groups, Businesses that prosper from sales to the 12M (e.g. Banks, Insurance Companies, Retail, etc.), Businesses experiencing Labor Shortages that hire the 12M (e.g. Farming, IT, Construction, Contractors, Retail, etc), Politicians with reasons to support the 12M (e.g. enhance Globalization, running for office, etc). And, of course, the illegal immigrants themselves. The majority of PROs who do post tend to have the following views: They advocate secure borders, sanctioning employers and comprehensive immigration reform (because the current program is broken). The biggest difference between the ANTIs and the PROs is, the PROs advocate a path to citizenship for the 12M, particularly since most of the 12M have worked and contributed to this country for + 5–20 years.

3   ANTI Profile: American. The majority are Anglos. (Anglos = white, Northern European ethnicity). Viewpoint: The majority advocate Deportation (mass or self) of the illegal immigrants in this country. Anything short of Deportation is termed Amnesty by the ANTIs. Many call for a 2000 mile southern border fence. They advocate for restrictive Official English laws even though English is already the National Language. They advocate for changing the 14th amendment and birthright citizenship, hoping to end, what they term "Anchor Babies." There are a few legal immigrants and minorities within their groups, but not many. There are a few politicians that support them, not many. There are hundreds of ANTI websites across the internet. There are hundreds of ANTI radio shows across the country. ANTIs tend to be very angry. They try their darndest to get African Americans to join forces with them citing their uncorroborated claim [that] the 12M drag down the minimum wage. The ANTIs tend to forget the deep alliances between the two ethnic groups which were forged over the previous four decades when they marched together for civil rights. Some of the Worst Terms the ANTIs use: 3rd World Country, Mexifornia, return to American Values.

Our next reading is a blog by Byron Williams, an African-American syndicated columnist. According to his online biography, the Reverend Byron Williams is "a writer, theologian, and activist [who] fuses theology with public policy to bring a fresh social justice perspective to the public arena." He serves as pastor of the Resurrection Community Church in Oakland, California. This blog was posted on The Huffington Post on May 9, 2006.

Byron Williams

Immigration Frenzy Points Out Need for Policy Debate

http://www.huffingtonpost.com/byron-williams/
immigration-frenzy-points_b_20717.html

1   As a child I recall Thanksgiving with mixed emotions. I enjoyed the big family feast with relatives I had not seen since the previous Thanksgiving, but I dreaded the days after. It was turkey ad nauseam. By the sixth day my father would make what he called "Turkey a la King," which was turkey remnants along with whatever else he could find to put in the pot.

2   As emotions flare on both sides of the immigration debate it has morphed into "Immigration a la King." But unlike my father's mysterious concoction, the ingredients are well known. It consists of one part legitimate public policy, one part ethnocentrism, and one part political pandering.

3   There is no doubting we need a legitimate public policy conversation around illegal immigration. The porous nature of America's borders coupled with the post 9/11 climate does warrant national concern.

4   If, however, we remove the legitimate public policy aspect, what's left? What's left is ugly, reactionary fear-based hatred symbolizing America at its worst.

5   With 9/11 approaching its 5th anniversary, why are we just getting around to dealing with immigration? Like a wounded, cornered animal, the Republican-led Congress and the president conveniently fan the flames of one of America's greatest tragedies, resurfacing fear, in order to gain short-term political points.

6   It is hard to embrace the concept that at this late date the administration and Congress are worried about Al Qaeda members coming across the border in man made tunnels or in the back of trucks when you consider the 9/11 attackers entered the country legally.

7   They have successfully created a climate where vigilantes known as the Minutemen—who do a disservice to the brave individuals who fought during the Revolutionary War by embracing the name—are viewed as patriotic by taking the law into their own hands allegedly protecting America's borders.

8   How many poor white southerners willingly accepted a death sentence by fighting for the Confederacy to protect a "southern way of life" in which they did not participate? They were seductively lured, in part, by the notion that all hell would break loose if emancipated African slaves were elevated to their same impoverished status.

9   The ethnocentrism and political pandering has sadly infected parts of the African American community. If one removes the veil of objecting to the comparisons between the civil rights movement and Hispanic immigration demonstrations, which a number of African Americans hide behind, they would discover the same fear that plagues the dominant culture.

---

10   This does not dismiss the obvious concerns about the plight of low-skilled African Americans who find themselves competing with immigrants for certain entry-level employment. But again, this is part of the much needed public policy debate that is submerged under the current political frenzy.

11   Freely throwing around words such [as] "illegal" and "Al Qaeda" opens the door to dehumanization. And once an individual has been dehumanized that individual can be taken advantage of.

12   Even those who compassionately advocate for a guest worker program, forget that the last such program that existed on a large scale in this country was struck down by Abraham Lincoln on September 22, 1863.

13   There are legitimate concerns on both sides of this issue. But history has shown us there is something wrong when marginalized groups are systematically pitted against each other.

14   For all of the cries to protect the borders and the loss of job opportunities for low-skilled Americans, I doubt there would be 11 million undocumented individuals in the country if no one was hiring. There can be no legitimate immigration debate that does not hold the business community equally accountable for hiring undocumented individuals while paying less than a living wage.

15   Each individual must come to his or her decision as to how they feel about immigration. But the only way to have an authentic policy is to have an authentic policy debate—one that does not include the unnecessary ingredients that ultimately lead to dehumanization.

Our third reading, by Victor Davis Hanson, is a posting to Roundup: Historians' Take, a spot for "historians writing about the news," on the History News Network site. Victor Davis Hanson, a former professor of classics and now a Senior Fellow at the Hoover Institution, is known as a military historian, a political essayist, and a regular conservative columnist for the *National Review* and Tribune Media Services. He has published numerous books and his writing has appeared frequently in such well-known newspapers and journals as the *New York Times*, the *Wall Street Journal*, and the *American Spectator*. He also blogs regularly at Pajamas Media. This posting appeared on Wednesday, June 6, 2007.

Victor Davis Hanson

The Global Immigration Problem

http://hnn.us/roundup/entries/39776.html

1   Thousands of aliens crossing our 2,000-mile border from an impoverished Mexico reflect a much larger global one-way traffic problem.

2   In Germany, Turkish workers—both legal and illegal—are desperate to find either permanent residence or citizenship.

3   "Londonstan" is slang for a new London of thousands of unassimilated Pakistani nationals.

4   In France, there were riots in 2005 because many children of North African immigrants are unemployed—and unhappy.

5   Albanians flock to Greece to do farm work, and then are regularly deported for doing so illegally.

6   The list could go on.

7   So why do millions of these border-crossers head to Europe, the United States or elsewhere in the West?

8   Easy. Stable democracies and free markets ensure economic growth, rising standards of living and, thus, lots of jobs, while these countries' birth rates and native populations fall.

9   Employers may console themselves that they pay better than what the immigrants earned back at home. This might be true, but the wages are never enough to allow such newcomers to achieve parity with their hosts.

10   Naturally, immigrants soon get angry. And rather than showing thanks for a ticket out of the slums of Mexico City or Tunis, blatant hypocrisy can follow: the once thankful, but now exhausted, alien may wave the flag of the country he would never return to while shunning the culture of the host county he would never leave.

11   In the second generation—as we see from riots in France or gangs in Los Angeles—things can get even worse.

12   The moment illegal immigrants arrive, a sort of race begins: can these newcomers become legal, speak the host language and get educated before they age, get hurt or lose their job? If so, then they assimilate and their children are held up as models of diversity. If not, the end of the story can be welfare or jail.

13   Hypocrisy abounds on all sides. Free-marketers claim they must have cheap workers to stay competitive. Yet they also count on public subsidies to take care of their former employees when old, sick or in trouble.

14   Governments in countries such as Mexico and Morocco usually care far more about their emigrants once they are long gone. Then these poor are no longer volatile proof of their own failures, but victims of some wealthy foreign government's indifference. And these pawns usually send cash home.

15   The lower middle classes complain most about massive immigration, but then they have to compete with aliens for jobs, often live among them and don't use their services. The wealthier, who hire immigrants for low wages and see them only at work, often think mass immigration, even if illegal, is wonderful.

16   The lasting solution is not the status quo—or even walls, fines, deportation, amnesty or guest-worker programs. Instead, failed societies in Latin America, Africa and much of the Middle East must encourage family planning and get smarter about using their plentiful natural wealth to keep more of their own people home.

17   The remedy for the richer West?

18   It is past time to remember that paying our own poorer laborers more, doing some occasional physical work and obeying the laws—the immigration ones especially—are not icky or a bummer. Rather, this is the more ethical and, in the long run, cheaper approach.

19   There is a final irony. The more Western elites ignore their own laws, allow unassimilated ethnic ghettos and profit from an exploitive labor market, the more their own nations will begin to resemble the very places immigrants fled from.

Our final two pieces focus on disagreements over the "temporary guest worker" program that was part of an immigration reform bill considered (and ultimately rejected) by Congress in 2007. One provision of the bill would have allowed currently illegal immigrants to stay in the United States legally for up to six years as guest workers. In this excerpt from a posting on The Hill Blog, Republican Senator Mike Crapo from Idaho explains why he supported the guest worker provision of the bill, although he eventually voted against the bill for other reasons.

Senator Mike Crapo

Excerpt from "Immigration Policy Must Help Economy While Preserving Ideals"

http://blog.thehill.com/2007/07/07/
immigration-policy-must-help-economy-while-preserving-ideals-sen-mike-crapo/

A robust economy hinges on having a temporary guest worker program to fill jobs that are not filled by American citizens. U.S.-based businesses need economic incentives to keep operations stateside. If they have a dependable labor pool at all skill levels, incentives to move operations overseas are greatly decreased. We appreciate consumer goods and agriculture products "Made in America." We can keep things that way by approaching immigration rationally and sensibly. Whatever the skill level, any temporary guest worker system must be enforceable and reliable for the worker and employer. Once Americans have been given "first right" to jobs, employers such as the agriculture industry must have access to a system that's cost-effective, not bureaucratic, and doesn't carry the risk of prosecution while employers are trying to comply with the law. Congress understands the urgency of reaching a workable solution and is moving in the right direction.

Our last piece is an excerpt from "The Progressive Case Against the Immigration Bill," which appeared in the liberal blog The Daily Kos on June 25, 2007. It gives a different view of the temporary guest worker program than that expressed by Senator Mike Crapo. The author of this piece is "Trapper John," the online identity for Jake McIntyre, who is a contributing editor for The Daily Kos.

Trapper John

Excerpt from "The Progressive Case Against the Immigration Bill"

http://www.dailykos.com/story/2007/6/25/73229/6647

1   This immigration bill is an historically bad bill, one that will undermine wage markets and which will permanently cripple skills training in vital sectors of the

economy. ... [T]he fatal flaw in this bill isn't "amnesty"—it's the euphemistically termed "temporary worker program."

2   The temporary worker program has nothing to do with immigration policy. To the contrary—it is a guaranteed cheap labor program grafted on to an immigration bill. When most people think of "immigration" to the US, they think of people coming to America to build a new life for themselves and their families, just as their ancestors did. But the temporary worker program has nothing to do with building American families and American dreams. Under the program, *400,000–600,000 guest workers would enter the country every year* on two-year visas. Although the visas can be renewed twice, recipients would be denied any path to permanent residency or citizenship. In fact, the guest workers would be precluded from even applying for permanent residency while here on temporary visas.

3   In short, the "temporary workers" will be just that—"temporary," and "workers." Not "immigrants." And they can never be "Americans." Instead, we will have created a permanent caste of non-citizens with no hope of ever becoming citizens. A class of over half-a-million workers without a voice in the political process, here at the sole sufferance of their employers. And those employers won't have to pay their new indentured servants any more than the minimum wage. See, unlike the existing H-2B visa—the visa that governs most "unskilled" temporary workers in the US today—the proposed temporary worker program contains no requirements that employers pay their temporary help the federally determined "prevailing wage" for their occupation and the geographic area. Today, if a contractor can't find a qualified electrician to work on a project in Chicago, the contractor can apply for an H-2B visa. But the contractor is required to pay any foreign electrician entering the US on the H-2B no less than $53.57 per hour, including benefits. That's the prevailing wage for an electrician in Chicago, according to the Department of Labor. And by requiring H-2B sponsors to pay their foreign help the prevailing wage, the H-2B program limits the ability of employers to use guest workers as a tool to undermine wage markets. The proposed temporary worker plan changes all that.

4   Under the proposed plan, there is no wage floor. If the Chicago contractor can't find an electrician in the US to work on his project for $20 per hour, he can import a temporary worker who will. The result will be a swift collapse of wage markets in many industries populated by skilled non-professional workers, like construction. And all of a sudden, we'll be hearing that the work of an electrician is one of those "jobs Americans won't do," like fruit picking. The truth, of course, is that there is no job that an American won't do for the right price. But by creating a steady flow of temporary workers with no ability to stay in the country for more than a couple years, and no practical ability to fight for better wages, the number of jobs that "Americans won't do" will grow dramatically. And they include a host of the jobs that sustain and nourish the middle class. The construction trades. Cosmetology. Culinary arts. These are jobs that take years to master, and consequently pay quite well, because not just anybody can do them. But by busting open the labor markets for these jobs, and opening them with no restrictions to folks from countries with much lower costs of living, we will strangle the middle class lives of the millions of Americans who have proudly earned their paychecks with their skills. ...

5   There's no question that we need immigration reform in this country. We need to find a way to bring the millions of immigrants laboring in the shadows into the light, and into our American family. And to the extent that we have bona fide labor shortages in this country, we need to address them through an expansion of legal immigration. But the price of immigration reform cannot be a temporary worker program that exploits foreign workers, limits real immigration, and guts wages for American workers.

mycomplab   For support in learning this chapter's content, follow this path in **MyCompLab**: Resources ⇒ Writing ⇒ Writing Purposes ⇒ Writing to Analyze. Review the Instruction and Multimedia resources, then complete the Exercises and click on Gradebook to measure your progress.

WRITING A CLASSICAL ARGUMENT

The need for argument arises whenever members of a community disagree on an issue. Classical rhetoricians believed that the art of arguing is essential for good citizenship. If disputes can be resolved through exchange of perspectives, negotiation of differences, and flexible seeking of the best solutions to a problem, then nations won't have to resort to war or individuals to fisticuffs.

The writing project for this chapter introduces you to a classical way of arguing. Your goal is to persuade your audience to adopt your position or at least to regard it more openly or favorably.

In this chapter, you will learn to:

- take a stand on an issue
- offer reasons and evidence in support of your position
- summarize and respond to alternative views

What Is Argument?

The study of argumentation involves two components: truth seeking and persuasion:

- By *truth seeking,* we mean a diligent, open-minded, and responsible search for the best course of action or solution to a problem, taking into account all the available information and alternative points of view.
- By *persuasion,* we mean the art of making a claim* on an issue and justifying it convincingly so that the audience's initial resistance to your position is overcome and they are moved toward your position.

These two components of argument seem paradoxically at odds: Truth seeking asks us to relax our certainties and be willing to change our views; persuasion asks us to be certain, to be committed to our claims, and to get others to change their views. We can overcome this paradox if we dispel two common but misleading views of argument. The most common view is that argument is a fight as in "I just got into a horrible argument with my roommate." This view of argument as a fist-waving, shouting match in which you ridicule anyone who disagrees with you (popularized by radio and television talk shows and the Internet) entirely disregards argument as truth seeking, but it also misrepresents

*By long-standing tradition, the thesis statement of an argument is often called its "claim."

argument as persuasion because it polarizes people, rather than promoting understanding, new ways of seeing, and change.

Another common but misleading view is that argument is a pro/con debate modeled after high school or college debate matches. Although debating can be an excellent way to develop critical thinking skills, it misrepresents argument as a two-sided contest with winners and losers. Because controversial issues involve many different points of view, not just two, reducing an issue to pro/con positions distorts the complexity of the disagreement. Instead of thinking of *both* sides of an issue, we need to think of *all* sides. Equally troublesome, the debate image invites us to ask, "Who won the debate?" rather than "What is the best solution to the question that divides us?" The best solution might be a compromise between the two debaters or an undiscovered third position. The debate image tends to privilege the confident extremes in a controversy rather than the complex and muddled middle.

From our perspective, the best image for understanding argument is neither "fight" nor "debate" but the deliberations of a committee representing a wide spectrum of community voices charged with finding the best solution to a problem. From this perspective, argument is both a *process* and a *product.* As a process, argument is an act of inquiry characterized by fact-finding, information gathering, and consideration of alternative points of view. As a product, it is someone's contribution to the conversation at any one moment—a turn taking in a conversation, a formal speech, or a written position paper such as the one you will write for this chapter. The goal of argument as process is truth seeking; the goal of argument as product is persuasion. When members of a diverse committee are willing to argue persuasively for their respective points of view but are simultaneously willing to listen to other points of view and to change or modify their positions in light of new information or better arguments, then both components of argument are fully in play.

We cannot overemphasize the importance of both truth seeking and persuasion to your professional and civic life. Truth seeking makes you an informed and judicious employee and a citizen who delays decisions until a full range of evidence and alternative views are aired and examined. Persuasion gives you the power to influence the world around you, whether through letters to the editor or blogs on political issues or through convincing position papers for professional life. Whenever an organization needs to make a major decision, those who can think flexibly and write persuasively can wield great influence.

Exploring Classical Argument

An effective way to appreciate argument as both truth seeking and persuasion is to address an issue that is new to you and then watch how your own views evolve. Your initial position will probably reflect what social scientists sometimes call your personal *ideology*—that is, a network of basic values, beliefs, and assumptions that tend to guide your view of the world. However, if you adopt a truth-seeking attitude, your initial position may evolve as the conversation progresses. In fact, the conversation may even cause changes in some of your basic beliefs, since ideologies aren't set in stone and since many of us have unresolved allegiance to competing ideologies that may be logically inconsistent (for example, a belief in freedom of speech combined with a belief that hate speech should be banned). In this exercise we ask you to keep track of how your views change and to note what causes the change.

The case we present for discussion involves ethical treatment of animals.

> Situation: A bunch of starlings build nests in the attic of a family's house, gaining access to the attic through a torn vent screen. Soon the eggs hatch, and every morning at sunrise the family is awakened by the sound of birds squawking and wings beating against rafters as the starlings fly in and out of the house to feed the hatchlings. After losing considerable early morning sleep, the family repairs the screen. Unable to get in and out, the parent birds are unable to feed their young. The birds die within a day. Is this cruelty to animals?

1. Freewrite your initial response to this question. Was the family's act an instance of cruelty to animals (that is, was their act ethically justifiable or not)?
2. Working in small groups or as a whole class, share your freewrites and then try to reach a group consensus on the issue. During this conversation (argument as process), listen carefully to your classmates' views and note places where your own initial views begin to evolve.
3. So far we have framed this issue as an after-the-fact yes/no question: Is the family guilty of cruelty to animals? But we can also frame it as an open-ended, before-the-fact question: "What should the family have done about the starlings in the attic?" Suppose you are a family member discussing the starlings at dinner, prior to the decision to fix the vent screen. Make a list of your family's other options and try to reach class consensus on the two or three best alternative solutions.
4. At the end of the discussion, do another freewrite exploring how your ideas evolved during the discussion. What insights did you get about the twin components of argument, truth seeking and persuasion?

Understanding Classical Argument

Having introduced you to argument as both process and product, we now turn to the details of effective argumentation. To help orient you, we begin by describing the typical stages that mark students' growth as arguers.

Stages of Development: Your Growth as an Arguer

We have found that when we teach argument in our classes, students typically proceed through identifiable stages as their argumentative skills increase. While these stages may or may not describe your own development, they suggest the skills you should strive to acquire.

- *Stage 1: Argument as personal opinion.* At the beginning of instruction in argument, students typically express strong personal opinions but have trouble justifying their opinions with reasons and evidence and often create short, undeveloped arguments that are circular, lacking in evidence, and insulting to those who disagree. The following freewrite, written by a student first confronting the starling case, illustrates this stage:

> The family shouldn't have killed the starlings because that is really wrong! I mean that act was disgusting. It makes me sick to think how so many people are just willing to kill something for no reason at all. How are these parents going to teach their children values if they just go out and kill little birds for no good reason?!! This whole family is what's wrong with America!

This writer's opinion is passionate and heartfelt, but it provides neither reasons nor evidence why someone else should hold the same opinion.

- ***Stage 2: Argument structured as claim supported by one or more reasons.*** This stage represents a quantum leap in argumentative skill because the writer can now produce a rational plan containing point sentences (the reasons) and particulars (the evidence). The writer who produced the previous freewrite later developed a structure like this:

   The family's act constituted cruelty to animals

   - because the starlings were doing minimal harm.
   - because other options were available.
   - because the way they killed the birds caused needless suffering.

- ***Stage 3: Increased attention to truth seeking.*** In stage 3 students become increasingly engaged with the complexity of the issue as they listen to their classmates' views, conduct research, and evaluate alternative perspectives and stances. They are often willing to change their positions when they see the power of other arguments.
- ***Stage 4: Ability to articulate the unstated assumptions underlying their arguments.*** As we show later in this chapter, each reason in a writer's argument is based on an assumption, value, or belief (often unstated) that the audience must accept if the argument is to be persuasive. Often the writer needs to state these assumptions explicitly and support them. At this stage students identify and analyze their own assumptions and those of their intended audiences. Students gain increased skill at accommodating alternative views through refutation or concession.
- ***Stage 5: Ability to link an argument to the values and beliefs of the intended audience.*** In this stage students are increasingly able to link their arguments to their audience's values and beliefs and to adapt structure and tone to the resistance level of their audience. Students also appreciate how delayed-thesis arguments or other psychological strategies can be more effective than closed-form arguments when addressing hostile audiences.

The rest of this chapter helps you progress through these stages. Although you can read the remainder in one sitting, we recommend that you break your reading into sections, going over the material slowly and applying it to your own ideas in progress. Let the chapter's concepts and explanations sink in gradually, and return to them periodically for review. This section on "Understanding Classical Argument" comprises a compact but comprehensive course in argumentation.

Creating an Argument Frame: A Claim with Reasons

Somewhere in the writing process, whether early or late, you need to create a frame for your argument. This frame includes a clear question that focuses the argument, your claim, and one or more supporting reasons. Often your reasons, stated as *because* clauses, can be attached to your claim to provide a working thesis statement.

Finding an Arguable Issue At the heart of any argument is an **issue,** which we can define as a question that invites more than one reasonable answer and thus leads to perplexity or disagreement. This requirement excludes disagreements based on personal tastes, where no shared criteria can be developed ("Baseball is more fun than soccer"). It also excludes purely private questions because issues arise out of disagreements in communities.

Issue questions are often framed as yes/no choices, especially when they appear on ballots or in courtrooms: Should gay marriage be legalized? Should the federal government place a substantial tax on gasoline to elevate its price? Is this defendant guilty of armed robbery? Just as frequently, they can be framed openly, inviting many different possible answers: What should our city do about skateboarders in downtown pedestrian areas? How can we best solve the energy crisis?

It is important to remember that framing an issue as a yes/no question does not mean that all points of view fall neatly into pro/con categories. Although citizens may be forced to vote yes or no on a proposed ballot initiative, they can support or oppose the initiative for a variety of reasons. Some may vote happily for the initiative, others vote for it only by holding their noses, and still others oppose it vehemently but for entirely different reasons. To argue effectively, you need to appreciate the wide range of perspectives from which people approach the yes/no choice.

How you frame your question necessarily affects the scope and shape of your argument itself. In our exploratory exercise we framed the starling question in two ways: (1) Was the family guilty of cruelty to animals? and (2) What should the family have done about the starlings? Framed in the first way, your argument would have to develop criteria for "cruelty to animals" and then argue whether the family's actions met those criteria. Framed in the second way, you could argue for your own solution to the problem, ranging from doing nothing (waiting for the birds to grow up and leave, then fixing the screen) to climbing into the attic and drowning the birds so that their deaths are quick and painless. Or you could word the question in a broader, more philosophical way: When are humans justified in killing animals? Or you could focus on a subissue: When can an animal be labeled a "pest"?

Identifying Arguable Issues

1. Working individually, make a list of several communities that you belong to and then identify one or more questions currently being contested within those communities. (If you have trouble, check your local campus and city newspapers or an organizational newsletter; you'll quickly discover a wealth of contested issues.) Then share your list with classmates.

2. Pick two or three issues of particular interest to you, and try framing them in different ways: as broad or narrow questions, as open-ended or yes/no questions. Place several examples on the chalkboard for class discussion.

Stating a Claim Your **claim** is the position you want to take on the issue. It is your brief, one-sentence answer to your issue question:

> The family was not ethically justified in killing the starlings.
> The city should build skateboarding areas with ramps in all city parks.
> The federal government should substantially increase its taxes on gasoline.

You will appreciate argument as truth seeking if you find that your claim evolves as you think more deeply about your issue and listen to alternative views. Be willing to rephrase your claim to soften it or refocus it or even to reverse it as you progress through the writing process.

Articulating Reasons

Your claim, which is the position you take on an issue, needs to be supported by reasons and evidence. A **reason** (sometimes called a "premise") is a subclaim that supports your main claim. In speaking or writing, a reason is usually linked to the claim with such connecting words as *because, therefore, so, consequently,* and *thus.* In planning your argument, a powerful strategy for developing reasons is to harness the grammatical power of the conjunction *because;* think of your reasons as *because* clauses attached to your claim. Formulating your reasons in this way allows you to create a thesis statement that breaks your argument into smaller parts, each part devoted to one of the reasons.

Suppose, for example, that you are examining the issue "Should the government legalize hard drugs such as heroin and cocaine?" Here are several different points of view on this issue, each expressed as a claim with *because* clauses:

ONE VIEW

Cocaine and heroin should be legalized
- because legalizing drugs will keep the government out of people's private lives.
- because keeping these drugs illegal has the same negative effects on our society that alcohol prohibition did in the 1920s.

Cocaine and heroin should be legalized
- because taking drug sales out of the hands of drug dealers would reduce street violence.
- because decriminalization would cut down on prison overcrowding and free police to concentrate on dangerous crime rather than on finding drug dealers.
- because elimination of underworld profits would change the economic structure of the underclass and promote shifts to socially productive jobs and careers.

STILL ANOTHER VIEW

The government should not legalize heroin and cocaine
- because doing so will lead to an increase in drug users and addicts.
- because doing so will send the message that it is okay to use hard drugs.

Although the yes/no framing of this question seems to reduce the issue to a two-position debate, many different value systems are at work here. The first pro-legalization argument, libertarian in perspective, values maximum individual freedom. The second argument—although it too supports legalization—takes a community perspective valuing the social benefits of eliminating the black market drug-dealing culture. In the same way, individuals could oppose legalization for a variety of reasons.

Generating *Because* Clauses

FOR WRITING AND DISCUSSION

Working in small groups or as a whole class, generate a list of reasons for and against one or more of the following yes/no claims. State your reasons as *because* clauses. Think of as many *because* clauses as possible by imagining a wide variety of perspectives on the issue.

1. The school year for grades 1 through 12 should be lengthened to eleven months.
2. The federal government should place a substantial tax on gasoline.
3. The United States should adopt a single-payer, government-financed health system like that of Canada.
4. Playing violent video games is a harmful influence on teenage boys. [or] Women's fashion and style magazines (such as *Glamour* or *Seventeen*) are harmful influences on teenage girls.
5. The war on terror requires occasional use of "enhanced interrogation techniques" on some detainees.

Articulating Underlying Assumptions

So far, we have focused on the frame of an argument as a claim supported with one or more reasons. Shortly, we will proceed to the flesh and muscle of an argument, which is the evidence you use to support your reasons. But before turning to evidence, we need to look at another crucial part of an argument's frame: its *underlying assumptions.*

What Do We Mean by an Underlying Assumption? Every time you link a claim with a reason, you make a silent assumption that may need to be articulated and examined. Consider this argument:

> The family was justified in killing the starlings because starlings are pests.

To support this argument, the writer would first need to provide evidence that starlings are pests (examples of the damage they do and so forth). But the persuasiveness of the argument rests on the underlying assumption that it is okay to kill pests. If an audience doesn't agree with that assumption, then the argument flounders unless the writer articulates the assumption and defends it. The complete frame of the argument must therefore include the underlying assumption.

Claim: The family was justified in killing the starlings.

Reason: Because starlings are pests.

Underlying assumption: It is ethically justifiable to kill pests.

It is important to examine the underlying assumption that connects any reason to its claim *because you must determine whether your audience will accept that assumption. If not, you need to make it explicit and support it.* Think of the underlying assumption as a general principle, rule, belief, or value that connects the reason to the claim. It answers your reader's question, "Why, if I accept your reason, should I accept your claim?"†

Here are a few more examples:

Claim with reason: Women should be allowed to join combat units because the image of women as combat soldiers would help society overcome gender stereotyping.

Underlying assumption: It is good to overcome gender stereotyping.

Claim with reason: The government should not legalize heroin and cocaine because doing so will lead to an increase in drug users.

Underlying assumption: It is bad to increase the number of drug users.

Claim with reason: The family was guilty of cruelty to animals in the starling case because less drastic means of solving the problem were available.

Underlying assumption: A person should choose the least drastic means to solve a problem.

---

*Our explanation of argument structure is influenced by the work of philosopher Stephen Toulmin, who viewed argument as a dynamic courtroom drama where opposing attorneys exchange arguments and cross-examinations before a judge and jury. Although we use Toulmin's strategies for analyzing an argument structure, we have chosen not to use his specialized terms, which include *warrant* (the underlying assumption connecting a reason to a claim), *grounds* (the evidence that supports the claim), *backing* (the evidence and subarguments that support the warrant), *conditions of rebuttal* (all the ways that skeptics could attack an argument or all the conditions under which the argument wouldn't hold), and finally *qualifier* (an indication of the strength of the claim). However, your instructor may prefer to use these terms and in that case may provide you with more explanation and examples.

Identifying Underlying Assumptions

Identify the underlying assumptions in each of the following claims with reasons.

1. Cocaine and heroin should be legalized because legalizing drugs will keep the government out of people's private lives.
2. The government should raise gasoline taxes because the higher price would substantially reduce gasoline consumption.
3. The government should not raise gasoline taxes because the higher price would place undo hardship on low-income people.
4. The government should not raise gasoline taxes because other means of reducing gasoline consumption would be more effective.
5. The government is justified in detaining suspected terrorists indefinitely without charging them with a crime because doing so may prevent another terrorist attack.

Using Evidence Effectively

Inside your arguments, each of your reasons (as well as any underlying assumptions that you decide to state explicitly and defend) needs to be supported either by subarguments or by evidence. By "evidence" we mean facts, examples, summaries of research articles, statistics, testimony, or other relevant data that will persuade your readers to accept your reasons. Note that evidence always exists within a rhetorical context; as a writer you select and shape the evidence that will best support your position, knowing that skeptics may point to evidence that you did not select. Evidence is thus not the same as "proof"; used ethically, evidence presents the best case for your claim without purporting to be the whole truth.

Evidence can sometimes come from personal experience, but in most cases it comes from your own field or library research. The kinds of evidence most often used in argument are the following:

Factual Data Factual data can provide persuasive support for your arguments. (Keep in mind that writers always select their facts through an angle of vision, so the use of facts doesn't preclude skeptics from bringing in counterfacts.) Here is how evolutionary biologist Olivia Judson used factual data to support her point that malaria-carrying mosquitoes cause unacceptable harm to human lives and wealth.

> Each year, malaria kills at least one million people and causes more than 300 million cases of acute illness. For children worldwide, it's one of the leading causes of death. The economic burden is significant too: malaria costs Africa more than $12 billion in lost growth each year. In the United States, hundreds of millions of dollars are spent every year on mosquito control.

Examples An example from personal experience can often be used to support a reason. Here is how student writer Ross Taylor used personal experience to argue that paintball is safe even though accidents can happen.

I admit that paintball can be dangerous and that accidents do happen. I personally had a friend lose an eye after inadvertently shooting himself in the eye from a very close range. The fact of the matter is that he made a mistake by looking down the barrel of a loaded gun and the trigger malfunctioned. Had he been more careful or worn the proper equipment, he most likely would have been fine. During my first organized paintball experience I was hit in the goggles by a very powerful gun and felt no pain. The only discomfort came from having to clean all the paint off my goggles after the game. When played properly, paintball is an incredibly safe sport.

Besides specific examples like this, writers sometimes invent hypothetical examples, or *scenarios,* to illustrate an issue or hypothesize about the consequences of an event. (Of course, you must tell your reader that the example or scenario is hypothetical.)

Summaries of Research Another common way to support an argument is to summarize research articles. Here is how a student writer, investigating whether menopausal women should use hormone replacement therapy to combat menopausal symptoms, used one of several research articles in her paper. The student began by summarizing research studies showing possible dangers of hormone replacement therapy. She then made the following argument:

> Another reason not to use hormone replacement therapy is that other means are available to ease menopausal symptoms such as hot flashes, irritability, mood changes, and sleep disturbance. One possible alternative treatment is acupuncture. One study (Cohen, Rousseau, and Carey) revealed that a randomly selected group of menopausal women receiving specially designed acupuncture treatment showed substantial decreases in menopausal symptoms as compared to a control group. What was particularly persuasive about this study was that both the experimental group and the control group received acupuncture, but the needle insertion sites for the experimental group were specifically targeted to relieve menopausal symptoms whereas the control group received acupuncture at sites used to promote general well-being. The researchers concluded that "acupuncture may be recommended as a safe and effective therapy for reducing menopausal hot flushes as well as contributing to the reduction in sleep disruptions" (299).*

Statistics Another common form of evidence is statistics. Here is how one writer used statistics to argue that the federal government should raise fuel-efficiency standards placed on auto manufacturers:

> There is very little need for most Americans to drive huge SUVs. One recent survey found that 87 percent of four-wheel-drive SUV owners had never taken their SUVs off-road (Yacobucci). ... By raising fuel-efficiency standards, the government would force vehicle manufacturers to find a way to create more earth-friendly vehicles that would lower vehicle emissions and pollution. An article entitled "Update: What You Should Know Before Purchasing a New Vehicle" states that for

*The examples in this section use the MLA (Modern Language Association) style for documenting sources. The complete bibliographic information for this article would be found in the "Works Cited" pages alphabetized under "Cohen."

every gallon of gasoline used by a vehicle, 20 to 28 pounds of carbon dioxide are released into the environment. This article further states that carbon dioxide emissions from automobiles are responsible for 20 percent of all carbon dioxide released into the atmosphere from human causes.

Just as writers select facts, examples, and research studies according to their angle of vision, so do they select and shape numerical data. In the above example, the writer focuses on the environmental harm caused by vehicles, especially SUVs. But you must always read statistics rhetorically. For example, the same statistical "fact" can be framed in different ways. There is a difference in focus and feel between these two ways of using the same data:

- "20 percent of human-caused CO_2 emissions come from automobiles" [puts automobiles in the foreground]
- "Although cars do cause some pollution, a full 80 percent of human-caused CO_2 emissions come from sources other than cars." [puts automobiles in the background]

Testimony Writers can also use expert testimony to bolster a case. The following passage from a student essay arguing in favor of therapeutic cloning uses testimony from a prominent physician and medical researcher. Part of the paragraph quotes this expert directly; another part paraphrases the expert's argument.

> As Dr. Gerald Fischbach, Executive Vice President for Health and Biomedical Sciences and Dean of Medicine at Columbia University, said in front of a United States Senate subcommittee: "New embryonic stem cell procedures could be vital in solving the persistent problem of a lack of genetically matched, qualified donors of organs and tissues that we face today." Fischbach goes on to say that this type of cloning could also lead to the discovery of cures for diseases such as ALS, Parkinson's disease, Alzheimer's disease, diabetes, heart disease, cancer, and possibly others.

Rather than provide direct research evidence that stem cell cloning might one day lead to cures for diseases, the writer draws on testimony from the dean of a prestigious medical school. Opponents of stem cell research might draw on other experts, selecting those who are skeptical of this claim.

Subarguments Sometimes writers support reasons not directly through data but through sequences of subarguments. Sometimes these subarguments develop a persuasive analogy, hypothesize about consequences, or simply advance the argument through a chain of connected points. In the following passage, taken from a philosophic article justifying torture under certain conditions, the author uses a subargument to support one of his main points—that a terrorist holding victims hostage has no "rights":

> There is an important difference between terrorists and their victims that should mute talk of the terrorist's "rights." The terrorist's victims are at risk unintentionally, not having asked to be endangered. But the terrorist knowingly initiated his actions. Unlike his victims, he volunteered for the risks of his deed. By threatening to kill for profit or idealism, he renounces civilized standards, and he can have no complaint if civilization tries to thwart him by whatever means necessary.

Rather than using direct empirical evidence, the author supports his point with a subargument showing how terrorists differ from victims and thus relinquish their claim to rights.

Evaluating Evidence: The STAR Criteria

To make your arguments as persuasive as possible, apply to your evidence what rhetorician Richard Fulkerson calls the STAR criteria (**S**ufficiency, **T**ypicality, **A**ccuracy, and **R**elevance),* as shown in the chart on this page.

It is often difficult to create arguments in which all your evidence fully meets the STAR criteria. Sometimes you need to proceed on evidence that might not be typical, verifiable, or as up-to-date as you would like. In such cases, you can often increase the effectiveness of your argument by qualifying your claim. Consider the difference between these two claims:

- **Strong claim:** Watching violent TV cartoons increases aggressive play behavior in boys.
- **Qualified claim:** Watching violent TV cartoons can increase aggressive play behavior in some boys.

To be made persuasive, the strong claim requires substantial evidence meeting the STAR criteria. In contrast, the qualified claim requires less rigorous evidence, perhaps only an example or two combined with the results of one study.

The STAR Criteria for Evaluating Evidence

STAR Criteria	Implied Question	Comments
Sufficiency	Is there enough evidence?	If you don't provide enough evidence, skeptical audiences can dismiss your claim as a "hasty generalization." To argue that marijuana is not a harmful drug, you would probably need more evidence than the results of one study or the testimony of a healthy pot smoker.
Typicality	Are the chosen data representative and typical?	If you choose extreme or rare-case examples, rather than typical and representative ones, your audience might accuse you of cherry-picking your data. Testimony from persons whose back pain was cured by yoga may not support the general claim that yoga is good for back pain.
Accuracy	Are the data accurate and up-to-date?	Providing recent, accurate data is essential for your own *ethos* as a writer. Data from 1998 on homelessness or inaccurately gathered data may be ineffective for a current policy argument.
Relevance	Are the data relevant to the claim?	Even though your evidence is accurate, up-to-date, and representative, if it's not pertinent to the claim, it will be ineffective. For example, evidence that nuclear waste is dangerous is not relevant to the issue of whether it can be stored securely in Yucca Mountain.

*Richard Fulkerson, *Teaching the Argument in Writing,* Urbana: National Council of Teachers of English, 1996, pp. 44–53. In this section we are indebted to Fulkerson's discussion.

As you gather evidence, consider also its source and the extent to which your audience will trust that source. While all data must be interpreted and hence are never completely impartial, careful readers are aware of how easily data can be skewed. Newspapers, magazines, blogs, and journals often have political biases and different levels of respectability. Generally, evidence from peer-reviewed scholarly journals is more highly regarded than evidence from secondhand sources. Particularly problematic is information gathered from Internet Web sites, which can vary widely in reliability and degree of bias.

Addressing Objections and Counterarguments

Having looked at the frame of an argument (claim, reasons, and underlying assumptions) and at the kinds of evidence used to flesh out the frame, let's turn now to the important concern of anticipating and responding to objections and counterarguments. In this section, we show you an extended example of a student's anticipating and responding to a reader's objection. We then describe a planning schema that can help you anticipate objections and show you how to respond to counterarguments, either through refutation or concession. Finally, we show how your active imagining of alternative views can lead you to qualify your claim.

Anticipating Objections: An Extended Example In our earlier discussions of the starling case, we saw how readers might object to the argument "The family was justified in killing the starlings because starlings are pests." What rankles these readers is the underlying assumption that it is okay to kill pests. Imagine an objecting reader saying something like this:

> It is *not* okay to get annoyed with a living creature, label it a "pest," and then kill it. This whole use of the term *pest* suggests that humans have the right to dominate nature. We need to have more reverence for nature. The ease with which the family solved their problem by killing living things sets a bad example for children. The family could have waited until fall and then fixed the screen.

Imagining such an objection might lead a writer to modify his or her claim. But if the writer remains committed to that claim, then he or she must develop a response. In the following example in which a student writer argues that it is okay to kill the starlings, note (1) how the writer uses evidence to show that starlings are pests; (2) how he summarizes a possible objection to his underlying assumption that killing pests is morally justified; and (3) how he supports his assumption with further arguments.

STUDENT ARGUMENT DEFENDING REASON AND UNDERLYING ASSUMPTION

The family was justified in killing the starlings because starlings are pests. Starlings are nonindigenous birds that drive out native species and multiply rapidly. When I searched "starlings pests" on Google, I discovered thousands of Web sites dealing with starlings as pests. Starlings are hated by farmers and gardeners because huge flocks of them devour newly planted seeds in spring as well as fruits and berries at harvest. A flock of starlings can devastate a cherry orchard in a few days. As invasive nesters, starlings can also damage attics by tearing up insulation and defecating

Claim with reason

Evidence that starlings are pests

on stored items. Many of the Web site articles focused on ways to kill off starling populations. In killing the starlings, the family was protecting its own property and reducing the population of these pests.

Summary of a possible objection

Many readers might object to my argument, saying that humans should have a reverence for nature and not quickly try to kill off any creature they label a pest. Further, these readers might say that even if starlings are pests, the family could have waited until fall to repair the attic or found some other means of protecting their property without having to kill the baby starlings. I too would have waited until fall if the birds in the attic had been swallows or some other native species without starlings' destructiveness and propensity for unchecked population growth. But starlings should be compared to rats or mice. We set traps for rodents because we know the damage they cause when they nest in walls and attics. We don't get sentimental trying to save the orphaned rat babies. In the same way, we are justified in eliminating starlings as soon as they begin infesting our houses.

Response to the objection

In the preceding example, we see how the writer uses evidence to support his reason and then, anticipating readers' objection to his underlying assumption, summarizes that objection and provides a response to it. One might not be convinced by the argument, but the writer has done a good job of trying to support both his reason (starlings are pests) and his underlying assumption (it is morally justifiable to kill at least some pests).

Using a Planning Schema to Anticipate Objections In the previous example, the student's arguing strategy was triggered by his anticipation of reader objections. Note that a skeptical audience can attack an argument by attacking either a writer's reasons or a writer's underlying assumptions. This knowledge allows us to create a planning schema that can help writers develop a persuasive argument. This schema encourages writers to articulate their argument frame (claim, reason, and underlying assumption) and then to imagine what kinds of evidence or arguments could be used to support both the reason and the underlying assumption. Equally important, the schema encourages writers to anticipate counterarguments by imagining how skeptical readers might object to the writer's reason or underlying assumption or both. To create the schema, simply make a chart with slots for each of these elements. Here is how another student writer used this schema to plan an argument on the starling case:

CLAIM WITH REASON

The family showed cruelty to animals because the way they killed the birds caused needless suffering.

UNDERLYING ASSUMPTION

If it is necessary to kill an animal, then the killing should be done in the least painful way possible.

EVIDENCE TO SUPPORT REASON

First I've got to show how the way of killing the birds (starving them slowly) caused the birds to suffer. I've also got to show that this way of killing was needless since other means were available such as calling an exterminator who would remove the birds and either relocate them or kill them painlessly. If no other alternative was available, someone should have crawled into the attic and found a painless way to kill the birds.

EVIDENCE/ARGUMENTS TO SUPPORT UNDERLYING ASSUMPTIONS

I've got to convince readers it is wrong to make an animal suffer if you don't have to. Humans have a natural antipathy to needless suffering—our feeling of unease if we imagine cattle or chickens caused to suffer for our food rather than being cleanly and quickly killed. If a horse is incurably wounded, we put it to sleep rather then let it suffer. We are morally obligated to cause the least pain possible.

WAYS SKEPTICS MIGHT OBJECT

How could a reader object to my reason? A reader might say that the starlings didn't suffer much (baby birds don't feel pain). A reader might also object to my claim that other means were available: They might say there was no other way to kill the starlings. Poison may cause just as much suffering. Cost of exterminator is prohibitive.

How could a reader object to my underlying assumption? Perhaps the reader would say that my rule to cause the least pain possible does not apply to animal pests. In class, someone said that we shouldn't worry about the baby starlings any more than we would worry about killing baby rats. Laws of nature condemn millions of animals each year to death by starvation or by being eaten alive by other animals. Humans occasionally have to take their place within this tooth-and-claw natural system.

How many of the ideas from this schema would the writer use in her actual paper? That is a judgment call based on the writer's analysis of the audience. If this student's target audience includes classmates who think it is morally okay to kill pests by the most efficient means possible, then she should summarize her classmates' argument fairly and then try to convince them that humans are ethically called to rise above tooth-and-claw nature.

Creating Argument Schemas

FOR
WRITING
AND
DISCUSSION

Working individually or in small groups, create a planning schema for the following arguments. For each claim with reason: (a) imagine the kinds of evidence needed to support the reason; (b) identify the underlying assumption; (c) imagine a strategy for supporting the assumption; and (d) anticipate possible objections to the reason and to the assumption.

1. ***Claim with reason:*** We should buy a hybrid car rather than an SUV with a HEMI engine because doing so will help the world save gasoline. (Imagine this argument aimed at your significant other, who has his or her heart set on a huge HEMI-powered SUV.)
2. ***Claim with reason:*** Gay marriage should be legalized because doing so will promote faithful, monogamous relationships among lesbians and gay men. (Aim this argument at supporters of traditional marriage.)
3. ***Claim with reason:*** The war in Iraq was justified because it rid the world of a hideous and brutal dictator. (Aim this argument at a critic of the war.)

Responding to Objections, Counterarguments, and Alternative Views

We have seen how a writer needs to anticipate alternative views that give rise to objections and counterarguments. Surprisingly, one of the best ways to approach counterarguments is to summarize them fairly. Make your imagined reader's best case against your argument. By resisting the temptation to distort a counterargument, you demonstrate a willingness to consider the issue from all sides. Moreover, summarizing a counterargument reduces your reader's tendency to say, "Yes, but have you thought of ... ?" After you have summarized an objection or counterargument fairly and charitably, you must then decide how to respond to it. Your two main choices are to rebut it or concede to it.

Rebutting Opposing Views When rebutting or refuting an argument, you can question the argument's reasons and supporting evidence or the underlying assumptions or both. In the following student example, the writer summarizes her classmates' objections to abstract art and then analyzes shortcomings in their argument.

> Some of my classmates object to abstract art because it apparently takes no technical drawing talent. They feel that historically artists turned to abstract art because they lacked the technical drafting skills exhibited by Remington, Russell, and Rockwell. Therefore these abstract artists created an art form that anyone was capable of and that was less time consuming, and then they paraded it as artistic progress. But I object to the notion that these artists turned to abstraction because they could not do representative drawing. Many abstract artists, such as Picasso, were excellent draftsmen, and their early pieces show very realistic drawing skill. As his work matured, Picasso became more abstract in order to increase the expressive quality of his work. *Guernica* was meant as a protest against the bombing of that city by the Germans. To express the terror and suffering of the victims more vividly, he distorted the figures and presented them in a black and white journalistic manner. If he had used representational images and color—which he had the skill to do—much of the emotional content would have been lost and the piece probably would not have caused the demand for justice that it did.

Conceding to Opposing Views In some cases, an alternative view can be very strong. If so, don't hide that view from your readers; summarize it and concede to it.

Making concessions to opposing views is not necessarily a sign of weakness; in many cases, a concession simply acknowledges that the issue is complex and that your position is tentative. In turn, a concession can enhance a reader's respect for you and invite the reader to follow your example and weigh the strengths of your own argument charitably. Writers typically concede to opposing views with transitional expressions such as the following:

admittedly	I must admit that	I agree that	granted
even though	I concede that	while it is true that	

After conceding to an opposing view, you should shift to a different field of values where your position is strong and then argue for those new values. For example, adversaries of drug legalization argue plausibly that legalizing drugs would increase the number of users and addicts. If you support legalization, here is how you might deal with this point without fatally damaging your own argument:

> Opponents of legalization claim—and rightly so—that legalization will lead to an increase in drug users and addicts. I wish this weren't so, but it is. Nevertheless, the other benefits of legalizing drugs—eliminating the black market, reducing street crime, and freeing up thousands of police from fighting the war on drugs—more than outweigh the social costs of increased drug use and addiction, especially if tax revenues from drug sales are plowed back into drug education and rehabilitation programs.

The writer concedes that legalization will increase addiction (one reason for opposing legalization) and that drug addiction is bad (the underlying assumption for that reason). But then the writer redeems the case for legalization by shifting the argument to another field of values (the benefits of eliminating the black market, reducing crime, and so forth).

Qualifying Your Claim The need to summarize and respond to alternative views lets the writer see an issue's complexity and appreciate that no one position has a total monopoly on the truth. Consequently, writers often need to qualify their claims—that is, limit the scope or force of a claim to make it less sweeping and therefore less vulnerable. Consider the difference between the sentences "After-school jobs are bad for teenagers" and "After-school jobs are often bad for teenagers." The first claim can be refuted by one counterexample of a teenager who benefited from an after-school job. Because the second claim admits exceptions, it is much harder to refute. Unless your argument is airtight, you will want to limit your claim with qualifiers such as the following:

perhaps	maybe
in many cases	generally
tentatively	sometimes
often	usually
probably	likely
may or might (*rather than* is)	

You can also qualify a claim with an opening *unless* clause ("*Unless* your apartment is well soundproofed, you should not buy such a powerful stereo system").

Seeking Audience-Based Reasons

Much of the advice that we have presented so far can be consolidated into a single principle: Seek "audience-based reasons." By **audience-based reasons**, we mean reasons that depend on underlying assumptions, values, or beliefs that your targeted audience already holds. In such cases, you won't need to state and defend your underlying assumptions because the audience already accepts them. A good illustration comes from civil engineer David Rockwood's argument against wind power. Rockwood's targeted readers are environmentalists who have high hopes for wind-generated electricity. Rockwood's final reason opposing wind power is that constructing thousands of wind towers will damage the pristine mountain environment. To environmentalists, this reason is powerful because its underlying assumption ("Preserving the environment is good") appeals to their values.

When you plan your argument, seek audience-based reasons whenever possible. Suppose, for example, that you are advocating the legalization of heroin and cocaine. If you know that your audience is concerned about street crime, then you can argue that legalization of drugs will make the streets safer.

We should legalize drugs *because doing so will make our streets safer*: It will cut down radically on street criminals seeking drug money, and it will free up narcotics police to focus on other kinds of crime.	Audience-based reason: Underlying assumption is that making our streets safer is a good thing—a value the audience already holds.

For another group of readers—those concerned about improving the quality of life for youths in inner cities—you might argue that legalization of drugs will lead to better lives for people in poor neighborhoods.

We should legalize drugs *because doing so will improve the lives of inner-city youth* by eliminating the lure of drug trafficking that tempts so many inner-city youth into crime.	Audience-based reason: Its underlying assumption is that it is good to improve the lives of inner-city youth.

Or if your audience is concerned about high taxes and government debt, you might say:

We should legalize drugs *because doing so will help us balance federal and state budgets*: It will decrease police and prison costs by decriminalizing narcotics; and it will eliminate the black market in drugs, allowing us to collect taxes on drug sales.	Audience-based reason: Assumes that it is a good thing to balance federal and state budgets.

In contrast, if you oppose legalizing drugs, you could appeal to those concerned about drug addiction and public health by using the following audience-based reason:

We should not legalize drugs *because doing so will increase the number of drug addicts and make drug use seem socially acceptable.*	Audience-based reason: Appeals to the underlying assumption that increasing the number of drug addicts and making drugs socially acceptable are bad things.

In each case, you move people toward your position by connecting your argument to their beliefs and values.

Appealing to *Ethos* and *Pathos*

When the classical rhetoricians examined ways that orators could persuade listeners, they focused on three kinds of proofs: *logos,* the appeal to reason; *ethos,* the appeal to the speaker's character; and *pathos,* the appeal to the emotions and the sympathetic imagination. These appeals are important rhetorical considerations in any kind of writing. Understanding how arguments persuade through *logos, ethos,* and *pathos* is particularly helpful when your aim is persuasion. So far in this chapter we have focused on *logos.* In this section we examine *ethos* and *pathos.*

Appeals to **Ethos** A powerful way to increase the persuasiveness of an argument is to gain your readers' trust. You appeal to *ethos* whenever you present yourself as credible and trustworthy. For most readers to accept your argument, they must perceive you as knowledgeable, trustworthy, and fair. In the following chart, we suggest ways to enhance your argument's *ethos:*

Strategies for Enhancing Your Argument's *Ethos*

What to Do	Explanation
Be knowledgeable by doing your homework.	Your credibility is enhanced when readers are convinced that you know your subject thoroughly.
Use evidence responsibly.	If you cherry-pick your evidence, you may be perceived as a propagandist rather than as a thoughtful arguer who recognizes complexity.
Be fair to alternative views.	If you scorn or misrepresent opposing views, you will win favor only with those who already agree with you. If you are a good listener to others, they will be more apt to listen to you.
Search for values and assumptions you can share with your audience.	You will build bridges toward skeptical readers, rather than alienate them, if you can highlight shared assumptions or values. Use audience-based reasons where possible.
Show that you care about your issue; show also why your readers should care about it.	By showing why the issue matters both to you and your readers, you portray yourself as a person of integrity rather than as someone playing an argumentative game.

Appeals to **Pathos** Besides appealing to *logos* and *ethos,* you might also appeal to what the Greeks called *pathos.* Sometimes *pathos* is interpreted narrowly as an appeal to the emotions and is therefore devalued on the grounds that arguments should be rational rather than emotional. Although appeals to *pathos* can sometimes be irrational and irrelevant ("If you don't give me at least a B in this course, I will lose my scholarship and break my ill grandmother's heart"), they can also arouse audience interest and deepen understanding of an argument's human dimensions. The following chart suggests ways to increase *pathos* in your arguments:

Strategies for Enhancing Your Argument's *Pathos*

What to Do	Explanation	Example
Include storylike anecdotes.	Specific stories often create more emotional appeal than abstract statistics or generalizations.	In promoting health care reform, President Obama often told stories of persons made bankrupt by an illness or deprived of care because of a pre-existing condition. On many occasions, he spoke of his own mother's fight with insurance companies as she lay dying of cancer.
Choose words with emotional or values-laden connotations.	Connotations of words often carry heavy emotional impact.	Opponents of health care reform talked about the Democrats' bill as "being jammed down people's throats"; supporters used words like "safety net," "compassion," or "care for children in poverty."
Where appropriate, use vivid language low on the ladder of abstraction.	Specific words paint pictures that have emotional appeal.	"The homeless man is huddled over the sewer grate, his feet wrapped in newspapers. He blows on his hands, then tucks them under his armpits and lies down on the sidewalk with his shoulders over the grate, his bed for the night." [creates sympathy for the homeless]"Several ratty derelicts drinking wine from a shared sack caused shoppers to avoid going into the store." [creates sympathy for shoppers rather than the homeless]
If the genre permits, include visuals with emotional impact.	Photographs or other visuals, including dramatic graphs or charts, can have a strong emotional appeal.	Articles promoting the environment often include photographs of smoke-belching factories or of endangered animals (often emphasizing their beauty or cuteness); often charts can have emotional appeals—such as a graph portraying dramatic increases in coal-fired electricity plants.

A Brief Primer on Informal Fallacies

We'll conclude our explanation of classical argument with a brief overview of the most common informal fallacies. Informal fallacies are instances of murky reasoning that can cloud an argument and lead to unsound conclusions. Because they can crop up unintentionally in anyone's writing, and because advertisers and hucksters often use them intentionally to deceive, it is a good idea to learn to recognize the more common fallacies.

Post Hoc, Ergo Propter Hoc *("After This, Therefore Because of This")* This fallacy involves mistaking sequence for cause. Just because one event happens before another event doesn't mean the first event caused the second. The connection may be coincidental, or some unknown third event may have caused both of these events.

> **Example**   When the New York police department changed its policing tactics in the early 1990s, the crime rate plummeted. But did the new police tactics cause the decline in crime? (Many experts attributed the decline to other causes.) Persons lauding the police tactics ("Crime declined because the NYPD adopted new tactics") were accused of the *post hoc* fallacy.

Hasty Generalization   Closely related to the *post hoc* fallacy is the hasty generalization, which refers to claims based on insufficient or unrepresentative data. Generally, persuasive evidence should meet the STAR criteria. Because the amount of evidence needed in a given case can vary with the audience's degree of skepticism, it is difficult to draw an exact line between hasty and justified generalizations.

> **Example**   The news frequently carries stories about vicious pit bulls. Therefore all pit bills must be vicious. [or] This experimental drug has been demonstrated safe in numerous clinical trials [based on tests using adult subjects]. Therefore this drug is safe for children.

False Analogy   Arguers often use analogies to support a claim. (We shouldn't go to war in Iraq because doing so will lead us into a Vietnam-like quagmire.) However, analogical arguments are tricky because there are usually significant differences between the two things being compared as well as similarities. (Supporters of the war in Iraq argued that the situation in Iraq in 2002 was very different from that in Vietnam in 1964.) Although it is hard to draw an exact line between a false analogy and an acceptable one, charges of false analogy are frequent when skeptical opponents try to refute arguments based on analogies.

> **Example**   Gun control will work in the United States because it works in England. [or] It's a mistake to force little Johnnie to take piano lessons because you can't turn a reluctant child into a musician any more than you can turn a tulip into a rose.

Either/Or Reasoning This fallacy occurs when a complex, multisided issue is reduced to two positions without acknowledging the possibility of other alternatives.

> **Example**   Either you are pre-choice on abortion or you are against the advancement of women in our culture.

Ad Hominem (*"Against the Person"*) When people can't find fault with an argument, they sometimes attack the arguer, substituting irrelevant assertions about that person's character for an analysis of the argument itself.

> **Example**   We should discount Senator Jones's argument against nuclear power because she has huge holdings in oil stock.

Appeals to False Authority and Bandwagon Appeals These fallacies offer as support the fact that a famous person or "many people" already support it. Unless the supporters are themselves authorities in the field, their support is irrelevant.

> **Example**   Buy Freeble oil because Joe Quarterback always uses it in his fleet of cars. [or] How can abortion be wrong if millions of people support a woman's right to choose?

Non Sequitur (*"It Does Not Follow"*) This fallacy occurs when there is no evident connection between a claim and its reason. Sometimes a *non sequitur* can be repaired by filling in gaps in the reasoning; at other times, the reasoning is simply fallacious.

> **Example**   I don't deserve a B for this course because I am a straight-A student.

Circular Reasoning This fallacy occurs when you state your claim and then, usually after rewording it, you state it again as your reason.

> **Example**   Marijuana is injurious to your health because it harms your body.

Red Herring This fallacy refers to the practice of raising an unrelated or irrelevant point deliberately to throw an audience offtrack. Politicians often employ this fallacy when they field questions from the public or press.

> **Example**   You raise a good question about my support of companies' outsourcing jobs to find cheaper labor. Let me tell you about my admiration for the productivity of the American worker.

Slippery Slope The slippery slope fallacy is based on the fear that one step in a direction we don't like inevitably leads to the next step with no stopping place.

> **Example**   If we allow embryonic stem cells to be used for medical research, we will open the door for full-scale reproductive cloning.

A Classical Argument

Write a position paper that takes a stand on a controversial issue. Your introduction should present your issue, provide background, and state the claim you intend to support. In constructing your claim, strive to develop audience-based reasons. The body of your argument should summarize and respond to opposing views as well as present reasons and evidence in support of your own position. You will need to choose whether to summarize and refute opposing views before or after you have made your own case. Try to end your essay with your strongest arguments. Try also to include appeals to *pathos* and to create a positive, credible *ethos*.

We call this assignment a "classical" argument because it is patterned after the persuasive speeches of ancient Greek and Roman orators. A framework chart showing the generic structure of a classical argument is shown in Figure 1. Although there are many other ways to persuade audiences, the classical approach is a particularly effective introduction to persuasive writing.

FIGURE I Framework for a Classical Argument

INTRODUCTION	• Attention-grabber (often a memorable scene) • Explanation of issue and needed background • Writer's thesis (claim) • Forecasting passage
PRESENTATION OF WRITER'S POSITION	• Main body of essay • Presents and supports each reason in turn • Each reason is tied to a value or belief held by the audience
SUMMARY OF OPPOSING VIEWS	• Summary of views differing from writer's (should be fair and complete)
RESPONSE TO OPPOSING VIEWS	• Refutes or concedes to opposing views • Shows weaknesses in opposing views • May concede to some strengths
CONCLUSION	• Brings essay to closure • Often sums up argument • Leaves strong, lasting impression • Often calls for action or relates topic to a larger context of issues

Generating and Exploring Ideas

The tasks that follow are intended to help you generate ideas for your argument. Our goal is to help you build up a storehouse of possible issues, explore several of these possibilities, and then choose one for deeper exploration before you write your initial draft.

Finding an Issue

If you are having trouble finding an arguable issue for this writing project, consider the following strategies:

Strategies for Finding an Arguable Issue	
What to Do	**Explanation**
Make an inventory of various communities you belong to.	Communities can range from the local (family, dorm, campus) to the state, nation, and world.
Brainstorm contested issues in these communities.	Start off with a fairly large list and then narrow it down according to your personal interest, current knowledge level, and degree of engagement.
On a few of these issues, explore the causes of disagreement.	Ask questions like these: What is at the heart of the disagreement? Disagreement about facts? About beliefs and values? About benefits versus costs?
Then explore your own point of view.	Ask: What is my position on the issue and why? What are alternative points of view? What is at stake?
Determine how much research you'll need to do.	If your issue requires research (check with your instructor), do a bibliographic search and enough skim reading to determine the kinds of arguments surrounding your issue, the kinds of evidence available, and the alternative views that people have taken.
Choose your issue and begin your research.	Your goal is to "wallow in complexity" in order to earn your thesis and create a knowledgeable *ethos*. Note: Some issues allow you to argue from personal experience (see Ross Taylor's argument on paintball). Again, check with your instructor.
Brainstorm claims and reasons on various sides of the issue.	State your own claim and possible *because* clause reasons in support of your claim. Do the same thing for one or more opposing or alternative claims.

Conduct an In-Depth Exploration Prior to Drafting

The following set of tasks is designed to help you explore your issue in depth. Most students take one or two hours to complete these tasks; the time will pay off, however, because most of the ideas that you need for your rough draft will be on paper.

1. Write out the issue your argument will address. Try phrasing your issue in several different ways, perhaps as a yes/no question and as an open-ended question. Try making the question broader, then narrower. Finally, frame the question in the way that most appeals to you.

2. Now write out your tentative answer to the question. This will be your beginning thesis statement or claim. Put a box around this answer. Next, write out one or more different answers to your question. These will be alternative claims that a neutral audience might consider.

3. Why is this a controversial issue? Is there insufficient evidence to resolve the issue, or is the evidence ambiguous or contradictory? Are definitions in dispute? Do the parties disagree about basic values, assumptions, or beliefs?

4. What personal interest do you have in this issue? How does the issue affect you? Why do you care about it? (Knowing why you care about it might help you get your audience to care about it.)

5. What reasons and evidence support your position on this issue? Freewrite everything that comes to mind that might help you support your case. This freewrite will eventually provide the bulk of your argument. For now, freewrite rapidly without worrying whether your argument makes sense. Just get ideas on paper.

6. Imagine all the counterarguments your audience might make. Summarize the main arguments against your position and then freewrite your response to each of the counterarguments. What are the flaws in the alternative points of view?

7. What kinds of appeals to *ethos* and *pathos* might you use to support your argument? How can you increase your audience's perception of your credibility and trustworthiness? How can you tie your argument to your audience's beliefs and values?

8. Why is this an important issue? What are the broader implications and consequences? What other issues does it relate to? Thinking of possible answers to these questions may prove useful when you write your introduction or conclusion.

Shaping and Drafting

Once you have explored your ideas, create a plan. Here is a suggested procedure:

Begin your planning by analyzing your intended audience. You could imagine an audience deeply resistant to your views or a more neutral, undecided audience acting like a jury. In some cases, your audience might be a single person, as when you petition your department chair to waive a requirement in your major. At other times, your audience might be the general readership of a newspaper, church bulletin, or magazine. When the audience is a general readership, you need to imagine from the start the kinds of readers you particularly want to sway. Here are some questions you can ask:

- ***How much does your audience know or care about your issue?*** Will you need to provide background? Will you need to convince them that your issue is important? Do you need to hook their interest? Your answers to these questions will particularly influence your introduction and conclusion.
- ***What is your audience's current attitude toward your issue?*** Are they deeply opposed to your position? If so, why? Are they neutral and undecided? If so, what other views will they be listening to?
- ***How do your audience's values, assumptions, and beliefs differ from your own?*** What aspects of your position will be threatening to your audience? Why? How does your position on the issue challenge your imagined reader's worldview or identity? What objections will your audience raise toward your argument? Your answers to these questions will help determine the content of your argument and alert you to the extra research you may have to do to respond to audience objections.
- ***What values, beliefs, or assumptions about the world do you and your audience share?*** Despite your differences with your audience, where can you find common links? How might you use these links to build bridges to your audience?

Your next step is to plan an audience-based argument by seeking audience-based reasons or reasons whose underlying assumptions you can defend. Here is a process you can use:

1. Create a skeleton, tree diagram, outline, or flowchart for your argument by stating your reasons as one or more *because* clauses attached to your claim. Each *because* clause will become the head of a main section or *line of reasoning* in your argument.
2. Use the planning schema to plan each line of reasoning. If your audience accepts your underlying assumption, you can concentrate on supporting your reason with evidence. However, if your audience is apt to reject the underlying assumption for one of your lines of reasoning, then you'll need to state it directly and argue for it. Try to anticipate audience objections by exploring ways that an audience might question either your reasons or your underlying assumptions.
3. Using the skeleton you created, finish developing an outline or tree diagram for your argument. Although the organization of each part of your argument will grow organically from its content, the main parts of your classical argument should match the framework chart in Figure 1.

This classical model can be modified in numerous ways. A question that often arises is where to summarize and respond to objections and counterarguments. Writers generally have three choices: One option is to handle opposing positions before you present your own argument. The rationale for this approach is that skeptical audiences may be more inclined to listen attentively to your argument if they have been assured that you understand their point of view. A second option is to place this material after you have presented your argument. This approach is effective for neutral audiences who don't start off with strong opposing views. A final option is to intersperse opposing views throughout your argument at appropriate moments. Any of these possibilities, or a combination of all of them, can be effective.

Another question often asked is, "What is the best way to order one's reasons?" A general rule of thumb when ordering your own argument is to put your strongest reason last and your second-strongest reason first. The idea here is to start and end with your most powerful arguments. If you imagine a quite skeptical audience, build bridges to your audience by summarizing alternative views early in the paper and concede to those that are especially strong. If your audience is neutral or undecided, you can summarize and respond to possible objections after you have presented your own case.

Revising

As you revise your argument, you need to attend both to the clarity of your writing and also to the persuasiveness of your argument. As always, peer reviews are valuable, and especially so in argumentation if you ask your peer reviewers to role-play an opposing audience.

Questions for Peer Review

In addition to generic peer review questions, ask your peer reviewers to address these questions:

INTRODUCTION

1. How could the title be improved so that it announces the issue, reveals the writer's claim, or otherwise focuses your expectations and piques interest?
2. What strategies does the writer use to introduce the issue, engage your interest, and convince you that the issue is significant and problematic? What would add clarity and appeal?
3. How could the introduction more effectively forecast the argument and present the writer's claim? What would make the statement of the claim more focused, clear, or risky?

ARGUING FOR THE CLAIM

1. Consider the overall structure: What strategies does the writer use to make the structure of the paper clear and easy to follow? How could the structure of the argument be improved?
2. Consider the support for the reasons: Where could the writer provide better evidence or support for each line of reasoning? Look for the kinds of evidence for each line of reasoning by noting the writer's use of facts, examples,

statistics, testimony, or other evidence. Where could the writer supply more evidence or use existing evidence more effectively?

3. Consider the support for the underlying assumptions: For each line of reasoning, determine the assumptions that the audience needs to grant for the argument to be effective. Are there places where these assumptions need to be stated directly and supported with arguments? How could support for the assumptions be improved?

4. Consider the writer's summary of and response to alternative viewpoints: Where does the writer treat alternative views? Are there additional alternative views that the writer should consider? What strategies does the writer use to respond to alternative views? How could the writer's treatment of alternative views be improved?

CONCLUSION

1. How might the conclusion more effectively bring completeness or closure to the argument?

Our first reading, by student writer Ross Taylor, aims to increase appreciation of paintball as a healthy sport. An avid paintballer, Ross was frustrated by how many of his friends and acquaintances didn't appreciate paintball and had numerous misconceptions about it. The following argument is aimed at those who don't understand the sport or those who condemn it for being dangerous and violent.

Ross Taylor (student)

Paintball:

Promoter of Violence or Healthy Fun?

1 Glancing out from behind some cover, I see an enemy soldier on the move. I level my gun and start pinching off rounds. Hearing the incoming fire, he turns and starts to fire, but it is far too late. His entire body flinches when I land two torso shots, and he falls when I hit his leg. I duck back satisfied with another good kill on my record. I pop up again, this time to scan for more enemy forces. Out of the corner of my eye I see some movement and turn to see two soldiers peeking out from behind a sewer pipe. I move to take cover again, but it's futile. I feel the hits come one by one hitting me three times in the chest and once on the right bicep before I fall behind the cover. I'm hit. It's all over—for me at least. The paintball battle rages on as I carefully leave the field to nurse my welts, which are already showing. Luckily, I watch my three remaining teammates trample the two enemy soldiers who shot me to win the game. This is paintball in all its splendor and glory.

2 Paintball is one of the most misunderstood and generally looked down upon recreational activities. People see it as rewarding violence and lacking the true characteristics of a healthy team sport like ultimate Frisbee, soccer, or pickup basketball. Largely the accusations directed at paintball are false because it is a positive recreational activity. Paintball is a fun, athletic, mentally challenging recreational activity that builds teamwork and releases tension.

3 Paintball was invented in the early 1980s as a casual activity for survival enthusiasts, but it has grown into a several hundred million dollar industry. It is, quite simply, an expanded version of tag. Players use a range of CO_2 powered guns that fire small biodegradable marbles of paint at approximately 250–300 feet per second. The result of a hit is a small splatter of oily paint and a nice dark bruise. Paintball is now played nationwide in indoor and outdoor arenas. Quite often variants are played such as "Capture the Flag" or "Assassination." In "Capture the Flag" the point is to retrieve the heavily guarded flag from the other team and return it to your base. The game of "Assassination" pits one team of "assassins" against the "secret service." The secret service men guard an unarmed player dubbed the "president." Their goal is get from point A to point B without the president's getting tagged. Contrary to popular belief, the games are highly officiated and organized. There is always a referee present. Barrel plugs are required until just before a game begins and must be reinserted as soon as the game ends. No hostages may be taken. A player catching another off guard at close range must first give the player the opportunity to surrender. Most importantly there is no physical contact between players. Punching, pushing, or butt-ending with the gun

is strictly prohibited. The result is an intense game that is relatively safe for all involved.

4   The activity of paintball is athletically challenging. There are numerous sprint and dives to avoid being hit. At the end of a game, typically lasting around 20 minutes, all the players are winded, sweaty, and ultimately exhilarated. The beginning of the game includes a mad dash for cover by both teams with heavy amounts of fire being exchanged. During the game, players execute numerous strategic moves to gain a tactical advantage, often including quick jumps, dives, rolls, and runs. While undercover, players crawl across broad stretches of playing field often still feeling their bruises from previous games. These physical feats culminate in an invigorating and physically challenging activity good for building muscles and coordination.

5   In addition to the athletic challenge, paintball provides strong mental challenge, mainly the need for constant strategizing. There are many strategic positioning methods. For example, the classic pincer move involves your team's outflanking an opponent from each side to eliminate his or her mobility and shelter. In the more sophisticated ladder technique, teammates take turns covering each other as the others move onward from cover to cover. Throughout the game, players' minds are constantly reeling as they calculate their positions and cover, their teammates' positions and cover, and their opponents' positions and strength. Finally, there is the strong competitive pull of the individual. It never fails to amaze me how much thought goes into one game.

6   Teamwork is also involved. Paintball takes a lot of cooperation. You need special hand signals to communicate with your teammates, and you have to coordinate, under rapidly changing situations, who is going to flank left or right, who is going to charge, and who is going to stay back to guard the flag station. The importance of teamwork in paintball explains why more and more businesses are taking their employees for a day of action with the intent of creating a closer knit and smooth-functioning workplace. The value of teamwork is highlighted on the Web site of a British Columbia facility, Action and Adventure Paintball, Ltd, which says that in paintball,

> as in any team sport, the team that communicates best usually wins. It's about thinking, not shooting. This is why Fortune 500 companies around the world take their employees to play paintball together.

An advantage of paintball for building company team spirit is that paintball teams, unlike teams in many other recreational sports, can blend very skilled and totally unskilled players. Women like paintball as much as men, and the game is open to people of any size, body type, and strength level. Since a game usually takes no more than seven to ten minutes, teams can run a series of different games with different players to have lots of different match-ups. Also families like to play paintball together.

7   People who object to paintball criticize its danger and violence. The game's supposed danger gets mentioned a lot. The public seems to have received the impression that paintball guns are simply eye-removing hardware. It is true that paintball can lead to eye injuries. An article by medical writer Cheryl Guttman in a trade magazine for ophthalmologists warns that eye injuries from paintball are on the rise. But the fact is that Guttman's article says that only 102 cases of eye injuries from paintballs were

reported from 1985 to 2000 and that 85 percent of those injured were not wearing the required safety goggles. This is not to say that accidents don't happen. I personally had a friend lose an eye after inadvertently shooting himself in the eye from a very close range. The fact of the matter is that he made a mistake by looking down the barrel of a loaded gun and the trigger malfunctioned. Had he been more careful or worn the proper equipment, he most likely would have been fine. During my first organized paintball experience I was hit in the goggles by a very powerful gun and felt no pain. The only discomfort came from having to clean all the paint off my goggles after the game. When played properly, paintball is an incredibly safe sport.

8   The most powerful argument against paintball is that it is inherently violent and thus unhealthy. Critics claim paintball is simply an accepted form of promoting violence against other people. I have anti-war friends who think that paintball glorifies war. Many new parents today try to keep their kids from playing cops and robbers and won't buy them toy guns. These people see paintball as an upgraded and more violent version of the same antisocial games they don't want their children to play. Some people also point to the connections between paintball and violent video games where participants get their fun from "killing" other people. They link paintball to all the other violent activities that they think lead to such things as gangs or school shootings. But there is no connection between school shootings and paintball. As seen in Michael Moore's *Bowling for Columbine*, the killers involved there went bowling before the massacre; they didn't practice their aim by playing paintball.

9   What I am trying to say is that, yes, paintball is violent to a degree. After all, its whole point is to "kill" each other with guns. But I object to paintball's being considered a promotion of violence. Rather, I feel that it is a healthy release of tension. From my own personal experience, when playing the game, the players aren't focused on hurting the other players; they are focused on winning the game. At the end of the day, players are not full of violent urges, but just the opposite. They want to celebrate together as a team, just as do softball or soccer teams after a game. Therefore I don't think paintball is an unhealthy activity for adults. (The only reason I wouldn't include children is because I believe the pain is too intense for them. I have seen some younger players cry after being shot.) Paintball is simply a game, a sport, that produces intense exhilaration and fun. Admittedly, paintball guns can be used in irresponsible manners. Recently there have been some drive-by paintballings, suggesting that paintball players are irresponsible and violent. However, the percentage of people who do this sort of prank is very small and those are the bad apples of the group. There will always be those who misuse equipment. For example, baseball bats have been used in atrocious beatings, but that doesn't make baseball a violent sport. So despite the bad apples, paintball is still a worthwhile activity when properly practiced.

10   Athletic and mentally challenging, team-building and fun—the game of paintball seems perfectly legitimate to me. It is admittedly violent, but it is not the evil activity that critics portray. Injuries can occur, but usually only when the proper safety equipment is not being used and proper precautions are ignored. As a great recreational activity, paintball deserves the same respect as other sports. It is a great way to get physical exercise, make friends, and have fun.

Thinking Critically
about "Paintball: Promoter of Violence or Healthy Fun?"

1. Before reading this essay, what was your own view of paintball? To what extent did this argument create for you a more positive view of paintball? What aspects of the argument did you find particularly effective or ineffective?

2. How effective are Ross's appeals to *ethos* in this argument? Does he create a persona that you find trustworthy and compelling? How does he do so or fail to do so?

3. How effective are Ross's appeals to *pathos*? How does he appeal to his readers' values, interests, and emotions in trying to make paintball seem like an exhilarating team sport? To what extent does he show empathy with readers when he summarizes objections to paintball?

4. How effective are Ross's appeals to *logos*? How effective are Ross's reasons and evidence in support of his claim? How effective are Ross's responses to opposing views?

5. What are the main strengths and weaknesses of Ross's argument?

Our next three readings focus on the issue of nuclear power—specifically, whether the United States should increase its production of electricity by building more nuclear power plants. The first of these readings, by electrical engineer and science writer William Sweet, appeared in the "Better Planet" section of the science magazine *Discover* in August 2007. Under the title "Why Uranium Is the New Green," it presents arguments in favor of greatly expanding our nuclear-generating capacity. William Sweet, a graduate of the University of Chicago and Princeton University, is the author of *Kicking the Carbon Habit: Global Warming and the Case for Nuclear and Renewable Energy* (Columbia University Press, 2006).

William Sweet
Why Uranium Is the New Green

1   ExxonMobil has thrown in the towel, terminating its campaign to convince the public that global warming is a hoax concocted by some pointy-headed intellectuals. All three major Democratic candidates for president, and some of the top Republican contenders as well, have promised serious action. Leading members of Congress have introduced a half dozen bills that would impose some kind of carbon regulation, and even the president now concedes that climate change is important.

2   Using coal to make electricity accounts for about a third of America's carbon emissions. As a result, tackling emissions from coal-fired power plants represents our best opportunity to make sharp reductions in greenhouse gases.

3   Fortunately, we already have the technology to do that. Unfortunately, right now the United States is addicted to coal, a cheap, abundant power source. Burning coal

produces more than half the country's electricity, despite its immense human and environmental costs. Particulates and other air pollutants from coal-fired power plants cause somewhere between 20,000 and 30,000 premature deaths in the United States *each year*. Fifty tons of mercury—one-third of all domestic mercury emissions—are pumped into the atmosphere annually from coal plants. In addition, the extraction of coal, from West Virginia to Wyoming, devastates the physical environment, and its processing and combustion produce gigantic volumes of waste.

4   For the last decade, coal-burning utilities have been fighting a rearguard action, resisting costly antipollution measures required by environmental legislation. At the same time, they have been holding out the prospect of "clean coal"—in which carbon is captured and stored as coal is burned. But clean-coal technologies have yet to be demonstrated on a large scale commercially, and by the admission of even the president's own climate-technology task force, clean coal doesn't have any prospect of making a big dent in the climate problem in the next 15 to 20 years.

5   By comparison, nuclear and wind power are proven technologies whose environmental risks and costs are thoroughly understood and which can make an immediate difference for the better.

6   The first thing to be appreciated about reactors in the United States is that they are essentially immune to the type of accident that occurred at Chernobyl in April 1986. Put simply, because of fundamental design differences, U.S. reactors cannot experience a sudden and drastic power surge, as happened at Chernobyl's Unit Number 4, causing it to explode and catch fire. In addition, the reliability of U.S. nuclear plants has been constantly improving. In 1980, American nuclear power plants were generating electricity only 56 percent of the time because they frequently needed special maintenance or repair. By 2004, reactor performance had improved to the point of generating electricity over 90 percent of the time.

7   Our regulatory regime, which was enormously strengthened in the wake of the 1979 Three Mile Island accident (during which no one was hurt, by the way), is indisputably much better than the Soviet system, which bred endemic incompetence. Management of U.S. nuclear power plants has improved dramatically since Three Mile Island, and security has been tightened significantly since 9/11 (though more remains to be done). By comparison with other tempting terrorist targets like petrochemical complexes, reactors are well fortified.

8   What about the problem of storing radioactive waste? It is overrated from an engineering standpoint and pales in comparison with the challenges associated with the permanent sequestration of immense quantities of carbon, as required by clean-coal systems. Though the wastes from nuclear power plants are highly toxic, their physical quantity is surprisingly small—barely more than 2,000 tons a year in the United States. The amount of carbon dioxide emitted by our coal plants? Nearly 2 *billion* tons.

9   Let us say it plainly: Today coal-fired power plants routinely kill tens of thousands of people in the United States each year by way of lung cancer, bronchitis, and other ailments; the U.S. nuclear economy kills virtually no one in a normal year.

10   Perhaps the most serious concern about increasing our reliance on nuclear power is whether it might lead to an international proliferation of atomic bombs. Contrary to a stubborn myth, however, countries do not decide to build nuclear weapons because

they happen to get nuclear reactors first; they acquire nuclear reactors because they want to build nuclear weapons. This was true of France and China in the 1950s, of Israel and India in the '60s and '70s, and it's true of Korea and Iran today. Does anybody honestly think that whether Tehran or Pyongyang produces atomic bombs depends on how many reactors the United States decides to build in the next 10 to 20 years?

11   Ultimately, the replacement of old, highly polluting coal-fired power plants by nuclear reactors is essentially no different from deciding, after putting sentimental considerations aside, to replace your inexpensive and reliable—but obsolete—1983 Olds Omega with a 2007 Toyota Camry or BMW 3 Series sedan.

12   All that said, it's important to be clear about nuclear energy's limits. It's likely that the construction of at least one new nuclear power plant will be initiated by the end of this year, ending a two-decade drought in new nuclear plant construction. But by its own estimates, the U.S. nuclear industry can handle only about two new nuclear reactor projects annually at its present-day capacity.

13   Obviously, given these limits, a lot of new wind generation, conservation, and improvements in energy use will also be needed. Wind is especially important because, despite the hopes of many, solar power just isn't going to cut it on a large scale in the foreseeable future. Right now, on a dollar per megawatt basis, solar installations are six or seven times as expensive as wind.

14   Wind turbines already generate electricity almost as inexpensively as fossil fuels. Thanks to a two cents per kiolwatt-hour production incentive from the U.S. government, they are being built at a rate that will increase the amount of wind-generated electricity by nearly three gigawatts a year. Taking into account that wind turbines produce electricity only about a third of the time, that's roughly the equivalent of building one standard one-gigawatt nuclear power plant a year.

15   Currently, nuclear and wind energy (as well as clean coal) are between 25 and 75 percent more expensive than old-fashioned coal at current prices (not including all the hidden health and environmental costs of coal), so it will take a stiff charge on coal to induce rapid replacement of obsolete plants. A tax or equivalent trading scheme that increases the cost of coal-generated electricity by, say, 50 percent would stimulate conservation and adoption of more efficient technologies throughout the economy and prompt replacement of coal by some combination of wind, nuclear, and natural gas. Proceeds from the tax or auctioned credits could (and should) be used to compensate regions and individuals most adversely affected by the higher costs, like the poor.

16   For the last six years, the U.S. government, with well-orchestrated support from industry, has told the American people that we can't afford to attack global warming aggressively. That's nonsense. We're the world's richest country, and we use energy about twice as extravagantly as Europe and Japan. It's no surprise that we account for a quarter of the globe's greenhouse-gas emissions.

17   What the United States needs to do is get in step with the Kyoto Protocol, both to establish its bona fides with the other advanced industrial countries and to give countries like India and China an incentive to accept mandatory carbon limits. That implies cutting U.S. carbon emissions by 25 percent as soon as possible.

18   The United States could do that by simply making the dirtiest and most inefficient coal plants prohibitively expensive by means of the carbon tax or trading systems mentioned above.

19   All we need to move decisively on carbon reduction is a different kind of political leadership at the very top. Surprisingly, it's the muscle-bound action-movie star who runs California who has best captured the spirit of what's needed. Last September, the day Arnold Schwarzenegger signed a bill committing his state to a program of sharp greenhouse-gas reductions, he told an ABC interviewer that climate change kind of "creeps up on you. And then all of a sudden it is too late to do something about it. We don't want to go there."

Thinking Critically
about "Why Uranium Is the New Green"

1. This article includes most of the features typically associated with classical argument—a claim with supporting reasons, a summary of alternative or opposing views, and responses to those views.
   a. What are the chief reasons that Sweet supports nuclear-generated electricity?
   b. What arguments against nuclear-generated electricity does Sweet mention or summarize?
   c. Where and how does he respond to those alternative views or opposing arguments?

2. From the perspective of *logos,* what reasons and evidence in favor of nuclear-generated power do you find most effective in Sweet's argument? Are there weaknesses in his argument? Where and how?

3. How, and to what effect, does Sweet appeal to *pathos* and *ethos*?

4. One of the chief arguments against nuclear power is the problem of storing nuclear waste. How would you analyze rhetorically Sweet's method of responding to that objection? How effective is his response?

Making a case against nuclear power, our next reading is a cartoon by Stan Eales, one of the most prominent cartoonists working in Europe today. Eales was born in 1962 and has a degree in graphic design from Auckland, New Zealand. Sellafield is a famous nuclear power site in England with a long, controversial history. It was the home of the world's first commercial nuclear power plant and is currently a storage site for radioactive waste as well as a major research facility on nuclear power. Sellafield has been the subject of numerous documentaries and protest rallies, including a famous 1992 Greenpeace rally that featured bands such as U2, Public Enemy, and Kraftwerk.

Stan Eales
Welcome to Sellafield

Stan Eales/Cartoon Stock

Thinking Critically
about "Welcome to Sellafield"

1. Translate Eales's cartoon into a verbal argument by finishing this sentence: "Nuclear energy is bad because _____."

2. Cartoons get their power from their ability to encapsulate a complex argument in a striking visual image. In your own words, explain how this cartoon uses *logos, pathos,* and *ethos* to create its persuasive effect.

3. How would William Sweet (previous reading) respond to this cartoon?

Our last nuclear power reading is an editorial appearing in the *Los Angeles Times* on July 23, 2007. It responds to a growing public reassessment of nuclear power as a possible solution to global warming. Its immediate context is the July 2007 earthquake in Japan that damaged a nuclear power plant, causing leakage of a small amount of contaminated water.

Editorial from the *Los Angeles Times*
No to Nukes

1   Japan sees nuclear power as a solution to global warming, but it's paying a price. Last week, a magnitude 6.8 earthquake caused dozens of problems at the world's biggest nuclear plant, leading to releases of radioactive elements into the air and ocean and an indefinite shutdown. Government and company officials initially downplayed the incident and stuck to the official line that the country's nuclear plants are earthquake-proof, but they gave way in the face of overwhelming evidence to the contrary. Japan has a sordid history of serious nuclear accidents or spills followed by cover-ups.

2   It isn't alone. The U.S. government allows nuclear plants to operate under a level of secrecy usually reserved for the national security apparatus. Last year, for example, about nine gallons of highly enriched uranium spilled at a processing plant in Tennessee, forming a puddle a few feet from an elevator shaft. Had it dripped into the shaft, it might have formed a critical mass sufficient for a chain reaction, releasing enough radiation to kill or burn workers nearby. A report on the accident from the Nuclear Regulatory Commission was hidden from the public, and only came to light because one of the commissioners wrote a memo on it that became part of the public record.

3   The dream that nuclear power would turn atomic fission into a force for good rather than destruction unraveled with the Three Mile Island disaster in 1979 and the Chernobyl meltdown in 1986. No U.S. utility has ordered a new nuclear plant since 1978 (that order was later canceled), and until recently it seemed none ever would. But rising natural gas prices and worries about global warming have put the nuclear industry back on track. Many respected academics and environmentalists argue that nuclear power must be part of any solution to climate change because nuclear power plants don't release greenhouse gases.

4   They make a weak case. The enormous cost of building nuclear plants, the reluctance of investors to fund them, community opposition and an endless controversy over what to do with the waste ensure that ramping up the nuclear infrastructure will be a slow process—far too slow to make a difference on global warming. That's just as well, because nuclear power is extremely risky. What's more, there are cleaner, cheaper, faster alternatives that come with none of the risks.

Glowing Pains

5   Modern nuclear plants are much safer than the Soviet-era monstrosity at Chernobyl. But accidents can and frequently do happen. The Union of Concerned Scientists cites 51 cases at 41 U.S. nuclear plants in which reactors have been shut down for more than a year as evidence of serious and widespread safety problems.

6   Nuclear plants are also considered attractive terrorist targets, though that risk too has been reduced. Provisions in the 2005 energy bill required threat assessments at nuclear plants and background checks on workers. What hasn't improved much is the risk of spills or even meltdowns in the event of natural disasters such as earthquakes, making it mystifying why anyone would consider building reactors in seismically unstable places like Japan (or California, which has two, one at San Onofre and the other in Morro Bay).

7   Weapons proliferation is an even more serious concern. The uranium used in nuclear reactors isn't concentrated enough for anything but a dirty bomb, but the same labs that enrich uranium for nuclear fuel can be used to create weapons-grade uranium. Thus any country, such as Iran, that pursues uranium enrichment for nuclear power might also be building a bomb factory. It would be more than a little hypocritical for the U.S. to expand its own nuclear power capacity while forbidding countries it doesn't like from doing the same.

8   The risks increase when spent fuel is recycled. Five countries reprocess their spent nuclear fuel, and the Bush administration is pushing strongly to do the same in the U.S. Reprocessing involves separating plutonium from other materials to create new fuel. Plutonium is an excellent bomb material, and it's much easier to steal than enriched uranium. Spent fuel is so radioactive that it would burn a prospective thief to death, while plutonium could be carried out of a processing center in one's pocket. In Japan, 200 kilograms of plutonium from a waste recycling plant have gone missing; in Britain, 30 kilograms can't be accounted for. These have been officially dismissed as clerical errors, but the nuclear industry has never been noted for its truthfulness or transparency. The bomb dropped on Nagasaki contained six kilograms.

9   Technology might be able to solve the recycling problem, but the question of what to do with the waste defies answers. Even the recycling process leaves behind highly radioactive waste that has to be disposed of. This isn't a temporary issue: Nuclear waste remains hazardous for tens of thousands of years. The only way to get rid of it is to put it in containers and bury it deep underground—and pray that geological shifts or excavations by future generations that have forgotten where it's buried don't unleash it on the surface.

10   No country in the world has yet built a permanent underground waste repository, though Finland has come the closest. In the U.S., Congress has been struggling for decades to build a dump at Yucca Mountain in Nevada but has been unable to overcome fierce local opposition. One can hardly blame the Nevadans. Not many people would want 70,000 metric tons of nuclear waste buried in their neighborhood or transported through it on the way to the dump.

11   The result is that nuclear waste is stored on-site at the power plants, increasing the risk of leaks and the danger to plant workers. Eventually, we'll run out of space for it.

Goin' Fission?

12   Given the drawbacks, it's surprising that anybody would seriously consider a nuclear renaissance. But interest is surging; the NRC expects applications for up to 28 new reactors in the next two years. Even California, which has a 31-year-old ban on construction of nuclear plants, is looking into it. Last month, the state Energy Commission held a hearing on nuclear power, and a group of Fresno businessmen plans a ballot measure to assess voter interest in rescinding the state's ban.

13   Behind all this is a perception that nuclear power is needed to help fight climate change. But there's little chance that nuclear plants could be built quickly enough to make much difference. The existing 104 nuclear plants in the U.S., which supply roughly 20% of the nation's electricity, are old and nearing the end of their useful lives. Just to replace them would require building a new reactor every four or five

months for the next 40 years. To significantly increase the nation's nuclear capacity would require far more.

14   The average nuclear plant is estimated to cost about $4 billion. Because of the risks involved, there is scarce interest among investors in putting up the needed capital. Nor have tax incentives and subsidies been enough to lure them. In part, that's because the regulatory process for new plants is glacially slow. The newest nuclear plant in the U.S. opened in 1996, after having been ordered in 1970—a 26-year gap. Though a carbon tax or carbon trading might someday make the economics of nuclear power more attractive, and the NRC has taken steps to speed its assessments, community opposition remains high, and it could still take more than a decade to get a plant built.

15   Meanwhile, a 2006 study by the Institute for Energy and Environmental Research found that for nuclear power to play a meaningful role in cutting greenhouse gas emissions, the world would need to build a new plant every one to two weeks until mid-century. Even if that were feasible, it would overwhelm the handful of companies that make specialized parts for nuclear plants, sending costs through the roof.

16   The accelerating threat of global warming requires innovation and may demand risk-taking, but there are better options than nuclear power. A combination of energy-efficiency measures, renewable power like wind and solar, and decentralized power generators are already producing more energy worldwide than nuclear power plants. Their use is expanding more quickly, and the decentralized approach they represent is more attractive on several levels. One fast-growing technology allows commercial buildings or complexes, such as schools, hospitals, hotels or offices, to generate their own electricity and hot water with micro-turbines fueled by natural gas or even biofuel, much more efficiently than utilities can do it and with far lower emissions.

17   The potential for wind power alone is nearly limitless and, according to a May report by research firm Standard & Poor's, it's cheaper to produce than nuclear power. Further, the amount of electricity that could be generated simply by making existing non-nuclear power plants more efficient is staggering. On average, coal plants operate at 30% efficiency worldwide, but newer plants operate at 46%. If the world average could be raised to 42%, it would save the same amount of carbon as building 800 nuclear plants.

18   Nevertheless, the U.S. government spends more on nuclear power than it does on renewables and efficiency. Taxpayer subsidies to the nuclear industry amounted to $9 billion in 2006, according to Doug Koplow, a researcher based in Cambridge, Mass., whose Earth Track consultancy monitors energy spending. Renewable power sources, including hydropower but not ethanol, got $6 billion, and $2 billion went toward conservation.

19   That's out of whack. Some countries—notably France, which gets nearly 80% of its power from nuclear plants and has never had a major accident—have made nuclear energy work, but at a high cost. The state-owned French power monopoly is severely indebted, and although France recycles its waste, it is no closer than the U.S. to approving a permanent repository. Tax dollars are better spent on windmills than on cooling towers.

Thinking Critically
about "No to Nukes"

1. This article, like William Sweet's, includes the typical elements associated with classical argument.
   a. What are the editorial writer's chief arguments against nuclear power?
   b. What arguments in favor of nuclear power does this editorial mention or summarize?
   c. How and where does the editorial writer respond to these alternative views?

2. From the perspective of *logos,* what reasons and evidence opposing nuclear-generated power do you find most effective in this editorial? Are there weaknesses in the editorial's arguments? Where and how?

3. In what ways, and with what effectiveness, does the editorial appeal to *pathos* and *ethos*?

4. Both Sweet and the editorial writer have high hopes for wind energy. In fact, the editorial writer concludes by saying, "Tax dollars are better spent on windmills than on cooling towers." How would David Rockwood respond to both writers?

5. Where do you place yourself on the spectrum from "strong support of nuclear power" to "strong opposition to nuclear power"? What new research evidence would be required to persuade you to move in one direction or the other along this spectrum?

Our next reading changes pace, moving from the global issue of nuclear energy to the family issue of how we should discipline our children. "Spare the Rod, Spoil the Parenting" is an op-ed piece by *Miami Herald* columnist Leonard Pitts, Jr. In this editorial, Pitts jumps into the ongoing controversy over corporal punishment, children's rights, childrearing practices, and spanking. Leonard Pitts, one of the nation's foremost African-American opinion writers, won the Pulitzer Prize for commentary in 2004. He is the author of *Becoming Dad: Black Men and the Journey to Fatherhood.*

Leonard Pitts, Jr.
Spare the Rod, Spoil the Parenting

1   I hate to tell you this, but your kid is spoiled. Mine aren't much better.

2   That, in essence, is the finding of a recent Time/CNN poll. Most of us think most of our kids are overindulged, materialistic brats.

3   If you're waiting for me to argue the point, you're in the wrong column.

4   No, I only bring it up as context to talk about a controversial study released late last month. It deals with corporal punishment—spanking—and it has outraged those who oppose the practice while rearming those who support it.

5   It seems that Dr. Diana Baumrind, a psychologist at the University of California at Berkeley, followed 164 middle-class families from the time their children were in preschool until they reached their 20s. She found that most used some form of corporal punishment. She further found that, contrary to what we've been told for years, giving a child a mild spanking (defined as open-handed swats on the backside, arm or legs) does not leave the child scarred for life.

6   Baumrind, by the way, opposes spanking. Still, it's to her credit as an academic that her research draws a distinction other opponents refuse to. That is, a distinction between the minor punishments practiced by most parents who spank and the harsher variants practiced by a tiny minority (shaking and blows to the head or face, for example).

7   Yes, children whose parents treat them that severely are, indeed, more likely to be maladjusted by the time they reach adolescence. And, yes, the parents themselves are teetering dangerously close to child abuse.

8   But does the same hold true in cases where corporal punishment means little more than swatting a misbehaving backside?

9   For years, the official consensus from the nation's child-rearing experts was that it did. Maybe that's about to change. We can only hope.

10 For my money, there was always something spurious about the orthodoxy that assured us all corporal punishment, regardless of severity, was defacto abuse. Nevertheless, we bought into it, with the result being that parents who admitted to spanking were treated as primitive dolts and heaped with scorn. They were encouraged to negotiate with misbehaving children in order to nurture their self-esteem.

11 But the orthodoxy was wrong on several fronts.

12 In the first place, it's plainly ridiculous—and offensive—to equate a child who has been swatted on the butt with one who has been stomped, scalded or punched. In the second, the argument that reasonable corporal punishment leads inevitably to mental instability always seemed insupportable and has just been proven so by Baumrind's study. And in the third, have you ever tried to "negotiate" with a screaming 5-year-old? It may do wonders for the child's self-esteem, but, I promise, it's going to kill yours. Your sanity, too.

13 Don't get me wrong, contrary to what its proponents sometimes claim, corporal punishment is not a panacea for misbehavior. Rearing a child requires not just discipline, but also humor, love and some luck.

14 Yet the very fact that spanking must be exonerated by a university study suggests how far afield we've wandered from what used to be the central tenet of family life: parents in charge. Ultimately, it probably doesn't matter whether that tenet is enforced by spanking or other corrective measures, so long as it is enforced.

15 I've seen too many children behave with too grand a sense of entitlement to believe that it is. Heard too many teachers tell horror stories of dealing with kids from households where parents are not sovereign, adult authority not respected. As a culture, we seem to have forgotten that the family is not a democracy, but a benign dictatorship.

16 Small wonder our kids are brats.

17 So the pertinent question isn't: To spank or not to spank? Rather, it's: Who's in charge here? Who is teaching whom? Who is guiding whom?

18   The answer used to be obvious. It's obvious no more. And is it so difficult to see where that road leads? To understand that it is possible to be poisoned by self-esteem, and that a spoiled child becomes a self-centered adult ill-equipped to deal with the vagaries and reversals of life?

19   Some folks think it's abuse when you swat a child's backside. But maybe, sometimes, it's abuse when you don't.

Thinking Critically
about "Spare the Rod, Spoil the Parenting"

1. In the introductory paragraphs of this op-ed piece, Leonard Pitts, Jr., mentions the rhetorical situation that has called forth his argument. What contemporary research is prompting Pitts's column?

2. Pitts's argument takes a stand on the issue question, "Is spanking a good child-drearing practice?" What claim does he make in this argument? What reasons and evidence does he offer to support this claim?

3. Where does Pitts acknowledge and respond to opposing views?

4. To understand the intensity of the social controversy on this issue, we suggest that you search the keywords "spanking" and "corporal punishment" using an online database and the Web. What different positions do you find represented in articles and by advocacy Web sites such as the site for the Center for Effective Discipline? How would these sources challenge Pitts's position and evidence?

The last reading is by student writer A. J. Chavez, who wrote this paper for the classical argument assignment in this chapter. In proposing the legalization of gay marriage, A. J. Chavez draws on personal knowledge and experience, some Internet research, and information from an anthropology course he was taking simultaneously with first-year composition.

A. J. Chavez (student)
The Case for (Gay) Marriage

1   "What if it was a gay world? And you were straight?" a recent TV spot asks (the ad can be viewed at commercialcloset.org—see "Human Rights Campaign" in Works Cited). The camera pans across a hospital waiting room, filled with gay and lesbian couples. There, a middle-aged man sits, waiting. "Your partner's in a coma. She's not responding," a young male doctor says to him. "Unfortunately, since the state doesn't recognize your marriage, I can't grant you spousal visitation. If she were to wake, or a family member gave consent—I wish there was more I could do. I'm sorry." After that, the camera quickly zooms out from the man's heartbroken face. The scene blurs, and a female voiceover reads the fact that appears on the screen: "hospital visitation: just one

A. J. Chavez, "The Case for (Gay) Marriage, student essay. Reprinted with the permission of the author.

of over 1000 rights granted to a legally married couple." Next, the scene fades into a black screen with a blue rectangle that has a yellow equal sign on it. The female voiceover continues, "Support equality for all Americans. Millionformarriage.org." This spot, sponsored by the Human Rights Campaign, the largest queer political organization in the United States, shows a scenario that undoubtedly happens every day in America, just with the tables turned. According to a report from the United States General Accounting Office, released after the passage of the federal Defense of Marriage Act of 1996, there are at least 1,049 federal laws in the U.S. code that relate to rights specific to marriage (2). Some are obvious, like Social Security or Veterans' Administration benefits upon the death of a spouse for the surviving spouse and children. Others are not so obvious, but equally important, such as the federally guaranteed right of an employee to take time off from work to care for an ill spouse or the so-called "spousal privilege" of not having to testify against a husband or wife in court. Currently, marriage rights are denied to a small, but still significant group in America—gays and lesbians, a group of which I am a part. We are denied the same rights enjoyed by straight people, simply because we are attracted to and love members of our own sex and have chosen to live open, honest lives, instead of closeted ones.

2   In opposition to the current Congressional proposal to amend the Constitution by defining marriage as a union between a man and a woman, I am proposing the nationwide legalization of same-sex marriage. First of all, gay marriage is the easiest way to ensure equality for all. Civil unions can only go part of the way. Secondly, the government must define marriage through a secular framework that respects the spirit of laws already in place, not a religious one that would violate separation between church and state. Third, the costs to taxpayers for legalizing gay marriage would be negligible. Some studies even suggest it would save taxpayer money. Finally, anthropological evidence exists for the existence of what we would refer to today as "gay marriage" across a long time span and wide range of cultures, demonstrating that it is not abnormal or perverted.

3   There are many arguments against gay marriage. Some are definitional, such as "Marriage is between a man and a woman." Other claims against gay marriage stem from concern for the well-being of children raised by gay or lesbian couples from previous straight marriages, adoption, or reproductive assistance. Still others arise out of respect for the Hebrew and Christian scriptures, the moral code from which most of Western civilization has lived by for thousands of years—certain passages in them prohibit homosexual relations. Another objection is that marriage is reserved for procreation, and that gay marriage, obviously, cannot serve this end. Additionally, there is the argument that legal options already exist for gay couples that offer some of the benefits of marriage, such as power of attorney or living will. Some politicians claim that marriage is something that should be left to the states to decide how to define and deal with individually. Furthermore, there is the argument that the legalization of gay marriage will open the doors to the legalization of more radical unions, such as adult-child unions or polygamy. Last, some members of America's queer community oppose gay marriage because they see it as just an attempt to copy and live a hetero lifestyle.

4   My first reason for legalizing gay marriage is that it is the easiest and most effective way to ensure equal rights for all in this country. Currently, sexual minorities receive no explicit protection from federal anti-discrimination acts, such as Title VII from the Civil Rights Act of 1964, which only prohibits discrimination in employment based on "race, color, religion, sex, or national origin." Employers are not required to offer the same benefits to the significant others of gay employees as they do to straight employees. With gay marriage, they would be obliged under laws that protect the rights of married couples to do so. Civil unions relegate gays and lesbians to second-class status. Civil unions or domestic partnerships are offered only by a few states, but can be disregarded by neighboring anti-gay states because of the federal Defense of Marriage Act. Civil unions can guarantee protections only at the state level, and at that, only the state they were issued in. Gay marriage, with its protections, would help prevent discrimination toward sexual minorities from prejudiced individuals. Here, it becomes clear that marriage laws should not just be left to the states, as some politicians who would rather not take a stand on the issue suggest, because if they are, patchwork laws will continue to develop across the nation. Some states will prohibit same-sex marriages and civil unions, while others will provide civil unions, and, perhaps in the future, gay marriage. A clear, federal standard for the inclusion of gay marriage will also prevent possible loopholes in marriage or civil union laws for inappropriate unions between adults and children or among more than two partners.

5   Second, for public policy, marriage, like all other things, needs to be defined through a non-religious, secular framework. The separation of church and state has always been an important tenet in American government. Allowing religious dogma to define marriage violates this tenet, setting up a dangerous precedent for further unification of church and state. If gay marriage were legalized, religions would still be allowed to distinguish what they do and do not see as "marriage." The Human Rights Campaign Web site provides the example of the Catholic church, which does not bless second marriages after divorce. Yet people can still file for divorce and then remarry if they see fit. In this case, the state recognizes a legal marriage that is not officially sanctioned by the church ("I Believe God Meant"). Also, while certain passages of the Bible prohibit sexual relationships between members of the same sex, others condone slavery and polygamy—both practices that would not be approved in American society today. Clearly, appeals to the Bible cannot be used to determine public policy. We would not only violate the important principle of separation between church and state, but by strict Biblical interpretation of morality, we could theoretically have a polygamous, slave-owning society.

6   Another compelling reason for legalizing same-sex marriage is the money that could actually be *saved* in state budgets every year. The FAQ section on marriage on the Human Rights Campaign Web site explains how government savings could add up through increased reliance between gay and lesbian couples on each other, reducing reliance on government assistance programs such as Temporary Assistance to Needy Families (welfare), Supplemental Security Income (disability), food stamps and Medicaid. The Web site cites two economic studies by professors at UCLA and the University of Massachusetts, Amherst, who examined possible savings to state governments in California and New Jersey if domestic benefits were extended to

same-sex couples. According to these studies, the savings were projected to be $10.6 million in California and $61 million in New Jersey ("Won't This Cost"). Additionally, the legalization of gay marriage would provide medical insurance benefits for thousands of currently uninsured children. While gay and lesbian couples obviously cannot conceive children on their own, plenty raise children from previous, heterosexual marriages, adopt children, or use reproductive assistance such as surrogate mothers or assisted insemination to bear their own children. The fact that many gay and lesbian partners are raising children shows the fallacy in claiming that gays should not be allowed to marry because they can't procreate. If we used the logic of procreation in determining whether to grant marriage rights, we would have to ban marriage between elderly couples, between sterile straight couples, and between those who plan to use birth control to prevent pregnancy. Of course, we would never ban such marriages because we recognize the value of having a life partner. Extending marriage benefits to gay partners brings the same benefits to them, with the additional benefit to the states of reducing reliance on state assistance programs and bringing medical insurance to many children.

7   My final reason for the legalization of gay marriage is that same-sex unions have existed across all cultures and times. This is important to recognize, because Judeo-Christian societies like ours tend to discount the legitimacy or even existence of such unions, and of so-called "sexual minorities." Such disregard can be explained by the histories of Judaism and Christianity, says Ted Fortier, Ph.D., a cultural anthropologist at Seattle University. In early Jewish societies, largely due to problems with underpopulation, he notes, any sexual activity without procreative power was considered taboo. Also, in Christian medieval Europe, disease and famine required that the people have all the labor possible to produce food. Again, all nonprocreative sex was labeled taboo. For anthropological purposes, Fortier defines marriage as "a union between a woman and another person." This definition, however, can be quite broad, he says. The "woman" can actually be a man playing a feminine role. He explains that in our culture, we look at gender as a biological concept, instead of a socially determined one. He gives examples of different cultures that distinguish certain men who take on womanly roles as being a third gender, such as that of Tahiti, where every village has a man that takes on the role of a woman, or the Native American *berdache* role, another womanly role played by a man. These men raise children just like the other adults. For the most part, Fortier claims, throughout all societies and cultures marriage has always been about securing resources and property—known as "alliance theory" in anthropology. Looking at our own society with this concept in mind, we see that marriage is utilized in the same way—as a stabilizing combination of tangible and intangible resources that leads to benefits to society, often including the raising of children. Law professor Mark Strasser, in an essay entitled "State Interests in Recognizing Same-Sex Marriage," mentions that "there is no evidence that children will not thrive when raised by same-sex parents and, indeed, some evidence that children may be better off in certain ways when they are raised by same-sex parents than when they are raised by different-sex parents" (37). Strasser refers to the increased tolerance and appreciation of differences that children of gays and lesbians typically have and the innumerable studies over the years that show these children grow up

just as well-adjusted and are no more likely to be homosexual than children living with straight parents. The government, therefore, should recognize and extend marriage protections to same-sex couples as well. While there are some gay/lesbian/ bisexual/transgender people who think gay marriage is just a futile attempt to copy mainstream, straight society, and that the government should not bother legalizing it, entering into any union is based on the mutual choice of two individuals. GLBT persons who find the institution of marriage unsavory would still not be forced by the government to marry if gay marriage were legalized.

8   The case for gay marriage is a strong one indeed, similar to earlier struggles for interracial marriage, which was legalized only relatively recently in American history. Gay marriage will result in an unprecedented addition of formal protections to America's last marginalized minority—the queer community. Studies suggest that it will save individual states millions of dollars in revenue on an annual basis. Gay marriage is not sick or a perversion—it exists across all cultures and times in one form or another and was stigmatized in Judeo-Christian traditions for the practical purpose of achieving as high of a population as possible. It is impossible to turn on a television set or open a newspaper now without seeing a reference to gay marriage. Legalizing gay marriage affirms both the "liberal" ideal of equality and the "conservative" value of community stability and individual rights. It also affirms the dignity of all of mankind.

Works Cited

Fortier, Ted. Personal interview. 26 Feb. 2004.

Human Rights Campaign. Advertisement. *The Commercial Closet*. Commercial Closet Association, 2004. Web. 2 Mar. 2004.

"I Believe God Meant Marriage for Men and Women." *Human Rights Campaign*. Human Rights Campaign, 20 Feb. 2004. Web. 15 Mar. 2004.

Strasser, Mark. "State Interests in Recognizing Same-Sex Marriage." *Marriage and Same Sex Unions: A Debate*. Ed. Lynn D. Wardle et al. Westport: Praeger, 2003. Print.

United States. General Accounting Office. *Categories of Laws Involving Marital Status*. Letter of transmittal. By Barry R. Bedrick. 31 Jan. 1997. Web. 16 Mar. 2004.

"Won't This Cost Taxpayers Too Much Money?" *Human Rights Campaign*. Human Rights Campaign, 2004. Web. 15 Mar. 2004.

Thinking Critically
about "The Case for (Gay) Marriage"

1. In classical arguments there is often an overlap between the reasons used to support one's own claim and the reasons used to rebut opposing views. In such cases the distinction between support and rebuttal can become blurred (not a problem so long as the argument remains clear). In this essay, where does A. J. Chavez summarize the arguments opposing the legalization of gay marriage? How many of these arguments does he respond to as the argument proceeds? Where does he add supporting reasons in favor of gay marriage that aren't initially framed as rebuttals?

2. How effectively does A. J. create appeals to *ethos* in this argument? How would you characterize his persona based on tone, reasonableness, and empathy for opposing views?

3. On the gay marriage issue, opponents of gay marriage can range from conservative audiences with strong religious arguments against same-sex marriage to very liberal gay audiences who believe that gays shouldn't imitate heterosexual relationships. How well does A. J. use appeals to *pathos* to connect with his imagined readers at both ends of this spectrum? How does he appeal to the values, beliefs, and emotions of his audiences? Point out specific passages where you think he is successful or unsuccessful.

4. How would you assess the appeals to *logos* in this argument? Are A. J.'s uses of reasons and evidence persuasive?

5. What do you see as the major strengths and weaknesses of this argument?

PEARSON
mycomplab

For support in learning this chapter's content, follow this path in **MyCompLab**: Resources ⇒ Writing ⇒ Writing Purposes ⇒ Writing to Argue or Persuade. Review the Instruction and Multimedia resources, then complete the Exercises and click on Gradebook to measure your progress.

COMPOSING AND REVISING CLOSED-FORM PROSE

Form is an arousing and fulfillment of desires. A work has form insofar as one part of it leads a reader to anticipate another part, to be gratified by the sequence.

—*Kenneth Burke, Rhetorician*

In this chapter we focus specifically on strategies for composing and revising closed-form prose. To help you avoid information overload, we recommend that you don't try to read this whole chapter in one sitting. The skills taught in this chapter are presented in ten self-contained lessons that can be read comfortably in half an hour or less. You will benefit most from these lessons if you focus on one skill at a time and then return to the lessons periodically as you progress through the term. Each lesson's advice will become increasingly meaningful and relevant as you gain experience as a writer. The first lesson (Skill 1) is intended as a theoretical overview to the rest of the chapter. The remaining lessons can then be assigned and read in any order your instructor desires.

In this chapter, you will learn how these skills can improve your writing:

- **SKILL 1**   Understand reader expectations.
- **SKILL 2**   Convert loose structures into thesis/support structures.
- **SKILL 3**   Plan and visualize your structure.
- **SKILL 4**   Set up reader expectations through effective titles and introductions.
- **SKILLS 5–7**   Keep readers on track through the use of topic sentences, transitions, and the old/new contract.
- **SKILL 8**   Learn four expert moves for organizing and developing ideas.
- **SKILL 9**   Use effective tables, graphs, and charts to present numeric data.
- **SKILL 10**   Write effective conclusions.

Together these lessons will teach you strategies for making your closed-form prose reader-friendly, well structured, clear, and persuasive.

SKILL 1 **Understand reader expectations.**

In this opening lesson, we show you how to think like a reader. Imagine for a moment that your readers have only so much *reader energy*, which they can use either to follow your ideas or to puzzle over confusing passages.* In order to follow your ideas, skilled readers continually make predictions about where a text is heading based on cues provided by the writer. When readers get lost, the writer has often either failed to provide cues or has given misleading cues. "Whoa, you lost me on the turn," a reader might say. "How does this passage relate to what you just said?" In this lesson we explain what readers of closed-form prose expect from writers in order to predict where a text is heading. Specifically we show you that readers expect three things in a closed-form text:

- They expect unity and coherence.
- They expect old information before new information.
- They expect forecasting and fulfillment.

Let's look at each in turn.

Unity and Coherence

Together the terms *unity* and *coherence* are defining characteristics of closed-form prose:

- **Unity** refers to the relationship between each part of an essay and the larger whole.
- **Coherence** refers to the relationship between adjacent sentences, paragraphs, and parts.

The following thought exercise will explore your own expectations for unity and coherence:

THOUGHT EXERCISE 1

Read the following two passages and try to explain why each fails to satisfy your expectations as a reader:

A. Recent research has given us much deeper—and more surprising—insights into the father's role in childrearing. My family is typical of the east side in that we never had much money. Their tongues became black and hung out of their mouths. The back-to-basics movement got a lot of press, fueled as it was by fears of growing illiteracy and cultural demise.

B. Recent research has given us much deeper—and more surprising—insights into the father's role in childrearing. Childrearing is a complex process that is frequently investigated by psychologists. Psychologists have also investigated sleep patterns and dreams. When we are dreaming, psychologists have shown, we are often reviewing recent events in our lives.

*For the useful term *reader energy*, we are indebted to George Gopen and Judith Swan, "The Science of Scientific Writing," *American Scientist* 78 (1990): 550–559. In addition, much of our discussion of writing in this chapter is indebted to the work of Joseph Williams, George Gopen, and Gregory Colomb. See especially Gregory G. Colomb and Joseph M. Williams, "Perceiving Structure in Professional Prose: A Multiply Determined Experience," in Lee Odell and Dixie Goswamie (eds.), *Writing in Nonacademic Settings* (New York: The Guilford Press, 1985), pp. 87–128.

If you are like most readers, Passage A comically frustrates your expectations because it is a string of random sentences. Because the sentences don't relate to each other or to a larger point, Passage A is neither unified nor coherent.

Passage B frustrates expectations in a subtler way. If you aren't paying attention, Passage B may seem to make sense because each sentence is linked to the one before it. But the individual sentences don't develop a larger whole: The topics switch from a father's role in childrearing to psychology to sleep patterns to the function of dreams. This passage has coherence without unity.

To fulfill a reader's expectations, then, a closed-form passage must be both unified and coherent:

> C. (*Unified and coherent*) Recent research has given us much deeper—and more surprising—insights into the father's role in childrearing. It shows that in almost all of their interactions with children, fathers do things a little differently from mothers. What fathers do—their special parenting style—is not only highly complementary to what mothers do but is by all indications important in its own right. [The passage continues by showing the special ways that fathers contribute to childrearing.]

This passage makes a unified point—that fathers have an important role in childrearing. Because all the parts relate to that whole (unity) and because the connections from sentence to sentence are clear (coherence), the passage satisfies our expectations: It makes sense.

Because achieving unity and coherence is a major goal in revising closed-form prose, we'll refer frequently to these concepts in later lessons.

Old before New

One dominant way that readers process information and register ideas is by moving from already known (old) information to new information. In a nutshell, this concept means that new material is meaningful to a reader only if it is linked to old material that is already meaningful. To illustrate this concept, consider the arrangement of names and numbers in a telephone directory. Because we read from left to right, we want people's names in the left column and the telephone numbers in the right column. A person's name is the old, familiar information we already know and the number is the new, unknown information that we seek. If the numbers were in the left column and the names in the right, we would have to read backward.

You can see the same old-before-new principle at work in the following thought exercise:

THOUGHT EXERCISE 2

You are a passenger on an airplane flight into Chicago and need to transfer to Flight 16 to Memphis. As you descend into Chicago, the flight attendant announces transfer gates. Which of the following formats is easier for you to process? Why?

Option A		Option B	
To Atlanta on Flight 29	Gate C12	Gate C12	Flight 29 to Atlanta
To Dallas on Flight 35	Gate C25	Gate C25	Flight 35 to Dallas
To Memphis on Flight 16	Gate B20	Gate B20	Flight 16 to Memphis

If you are like most readers, you prefer Option A, which puts old information before new. In this case, the old/known information is our destination (cities arranged alphabetically) and perhaps our flight number (To Memphis on Flight 16). The new/unknown information is Gate B20. Option B causes us to expend more energy than does Option A because it forces us to hold the number of each gate in memory until we hear its corresponding city and flight number. Whereas Option A allows us to relax until we hear the word "Memphis," Option B forces us to concentrate intensely on each gate number until we find the meaningful one.

Old before New at the Essay Level The principle of old before new has great explanatory power for writers. At the level of the whole essay, this principle helps writers establish the main structural frame and ordering principle of their argument. An argument's frame derives from the writer's purpose to change some aspect of the reader's view of the topic. The reader's original view of the topic—what we might call the common, expected, or ordinary view—constitutes old/known/familiar material. The writer's surprising view constitutes the new/unknown/unfamiliar material. The writer's hope is to move readers from their original view to the writer's new and different view. By understanding what constitutes old/familiar information to readers, the writer can determine how much background to provide, how to anticipate readers' objections, and how to structure material by moving from the old to the new. We treat these matters in more depth in Skill 4, on writing effective titles and introductions.

Old before New at the Sentence Level At the sentence level, the principle of old before new also helps writers create coherence between adjacent parts and sentences. Most sentences in an essay should contain both an old element and a new element. To create coherence, the writer begins with the old material, which links back to something earlier, and then puts the new material at the end of the sentence. (See the discussion of the old/new contract in Skill 7.)

Forecasting and Fulfillment

Finally, readers of closed-form prose expect writers to forecast what is coming and then to fulfill those forecasts. To appreciate what we mean by forecasting and fulfillment, try one more thought exercise:

THOUGHT EXERCISE 3

Although the following paragraph describes a simple procedure in easy-to-follow sentences, most readers still scratch their heads in bewilderment. Why? What makes the passage difficult to understand?

The procedure is actually quite simple. First, you arrange things into different groups. Of course, one pile may be sufficient depending on how much there is to do. If you have to go somewhere else due to lack of facilities, that is the next step; otherwise, you are pretty well set. Next you operate the machines according to the instructions. After the procedure is completed, one arranges the materials into different groups again. Then they can be put in their appropriate places. Eventually, they will be used once more and the whole cycle will have to be repeated. However, that is part of life.

Most readers report being puzzled about the paragraph's topic. Because the opening sentence doesn't provide enough context to tell them what to expect, the paragraph makes no forecast that can be fulfilled. Now try rereading the paragraph, but this time substitute the following opening sentence:

> The procedure for washing clothes is actually quite simple.

With the addition of "for washing clothes," the sentence provides a context that allows you to predict and understand what's coming. In the language of cognitive psychologists, this new opening sentence provides a schema for interpretation. A *schema* is the reader's mental picture of a structure for upcoming material. The new opening sentence allows you as reader to say mentally, "This paragraph will describe a procedure for washing clothes and argue that it is simple." When the schema proves accurate, you experience the pleasure of prediction and fulfillment. In the language of rhetorician Kenneth Burke, the reader's experience of form is "an arousing and fulfillment of desires."

What readers expect from a closed-form text, then, is an ability to predict what is coming as well as regular fulfillment of those predictions. Writers forecast what is coming in a variety of ways:

- by writing effective titles
- by writing effective introductions with forecasting cues
- by placing topic sentences near the beginning of paragraphs
- by creating effective transitions and mapping statements
- by using effective headings and subheadings if appropriate for the genre.

To meet their readers' needs for predictions and fulfillment, closed-form writers start and end with the big picture. They tell readers where they are going before they start the journey, they refer to this big picture at key transition points, and they refocus on the big picture in their conclusion.

SKILL 2 Convert loose structures into thesis/support structures.

In Skill 1 we described readers' expectations for unity and coherence, old information before new, and forecasting and fulfillment. In academic contexts, readers also expect closed-form prose to have a thesis/support structure. Most closed-form academic writing—especially writing with the aim of analysis or persuasion—is governed by a contestable or risky thesis statement. Because developing and supporting a thesis is complex work requiring much critical thought, writers sometimes retreat into loose structures that are easier to compose than a thesis-based argument with points and particulars.

In this lesson we help you better understand thesis-based writing by contrasting it with prose that looks like thesis-based writing but isn't. We show you three common ways in which inexperienced writers give the appearance of writing thesis-based prose while actually retreating from the rigors of making and developing an argument. Avoiding the pitfalls of these loose structures can go a long way toward improving your performance on most college writing assignments.

Avoiding *And Then* Writing, or Chronological Structure

Chronological structure, often called "narrative," is the most common organizing principle of open-form prose. It may also be used selectively in closed-form prose to support a point. But sometimes the writer begins recounting the details of a story and chronological order takes over, driving out the thesis-based structure of points and particulars.

To a large degree, chronological order is the default mode we fall into when we aren't sure how to organize material. For example, if you were asked to analyze a fictional character, you might slip into a plot summary instead. In much the same way, you might substitute historical chronology ("First A happened, then B happened ...") for historical analysis ("B happened because A happened ..."); or you might give a chronological recounting of your research ("First I discovered A, then I discovered B ...") instead of organizing your material into an argument ("I question A's account of this phenomenon on the grounds of my recent discovery of B ...").

The tendency toward loose chronological structure is revealed in the following example from a student's essay on Shakespeare's *The Tempest*. This excerpt is from the introduction of the student's first draft:

PLOT SUMMARY— *AND THEN* WRITING

Prospero cares deeply for his daughter. In the middle of the play Prospero acts like a gruff father and makes Ferdinand carry logs in order to test his love for Miranda and Miranda's love for him. In the end, though, Prospero is a loving father who rejoices in his daughter's marriage to a good man.

Here the student seems simply to retell the play's plot without any apparent thesis. (The body of her rough draft primarily retold the same story in more detail.) However, during an office conference, the instructor discovered that the student regarded her sentence about Prospero's being a loving father as her thesis. In fact, the student had gotten in an argument with a classmate over whether Prospero was a good person or an evil one. The instructor helped her convert her draft into a thesis/support structure:

REVISED INTRODUCTION—THESIS/SUPPORT STRUCTURE

Many persons believe that Prospero is an evil person in the play. They claim that Prospero exhibits a harsh, destructive control over Miranda and also, like Faust, seeks superhuman knowledge through his magic. However, I contend that Prospero is a kind and loving father.

This revised version implies a problem (What kind of father is Prospero?), presents a view that the writer wishes to change (Prospero is harsh and hateful), and asserts a contestable thesis (Prospero is a loving father). The body of her paper can now be converted from plot summary to an argument with reasons and evidence supporting her claim that Prospero is loving.

This student's revision from an *and then* to a thesis/support structure is typical of many writers' experience. Because recounting events chronologically is a natural way to organize, many writers—even very experienced ones—lapse into long stretches of *and then* writing in their rough drafts. However, experienced writers have learned to recognize these *and then* sections in their drafts and to rework this material into a closed-form, thesis-based structure.

Avoiding *All About* Writing, or Encyclopedic Structure

Whereas *and then* writing turns essays into stories by organizing details chronologically, *all about* writing turns essays into encyclopedia articles by piling up details in heaps. When *all about* writing organizes these heaps into categories, it can appear to be well organized: "Having told you everything I learned about educational opportunities in Cleveland, I will now tell you everything I learned about the Rock and Roll Hall of Fame." But the categories do not function as points and particulars in support of a thesis. Rather, like the shelving system in a library, they are simply ways of arranging information for convenient retrieval, not a means of building a hierarchical structure.

An Example of "All About" Structure To illustrate the differences between *all about* writing and thesis-based writing, consider the case of two students choosing to write term papers on the subject of female police officers. One student is asked simply to write "all about" the topic; the other is asked to pose and investigate some problem related to female police officers and to support a thesis addressing that problem. In all likelihood, the first student would produce an initial outline with headings such as the following:

    I. History of women in police roles
       A. Female police or soldiers in ancient times
       B. 19th century (Calamity Jane)
       C. 1900s–1960
       D. 1960–present
    II. How female police officers are selected and trained
   III. A typical day in the life of a female police officer
   IV. Achievements and acts of heroism of female police officers
    V. What the future holds for female police officers

Such a paper is a data dump that places into categories all the information the writer has uncovered. It is riskless, and, except for occasional new information, surpriseless. In contrast, when a student focuses on a significant question—one that grows out of the writer's own interests and demands engagement—the writing can be quite compelling.

Conversion to Problem-Thesis Structure Consider the case of a student, Lynnea, who wrote a research paper entitled "Women Police Officers: Should Size and Strength Be Criteria for Patrol Duty?" Her essay begins with a group of male police officers complaining about being assigned to patrol duty with a new female officer, Connie Jones (not her real name), who is four feet ten inches tall and weighs ninety pounds. Here is the rest of the introduction to Lynnea's essay.

Connie Jones has just completed police academy training and has been assigned to patrol duty in _____. Because she is so small, she has to have a booster seat in her patrol car and has been given a special gun, since she can barely manage to pull the trigger of a standard police-issue .38 revolver. Although she passed the physical requirements at the academy, which involved speed and endurance running, situps, and monkey bar tests, most of the officers in her department doubt her ability to perform competently as a patrol officer. But nevertheless she is on patrol because men and women receive equal assignments in most of today's police forces. But is this a good policy? Can a person who is significantly smaller and weaker than her peers make an effective patrol officer?

Lynnea examined all the evidence she could find—through library and field research (interviewing police officers)—and arrived at the following thesis: "Because concern for public safety overrides all other concerns, police departments should set stringent size and strength requirements for patrol officers, even if these criteria exclude many women." This thesis has plenty of tension because it sets limits on equal rights for women. Because Lynnea considers herself a feminist, it caused her considerable distress to advocate setting these limits and placing public safety ahead of gender equity. The resulting essay was engaging precisely because of the tension it creates and the controversy it engenders.

Avoiding *Engfish* Writing, or Structure without Surprise

Unlike the chronological story and the *all about* paper, the **engfish** essay has a thesis.* But the thesis is a riskless truism supported with predictable reasons—often structured as the three body paragraphs in a traditional five-paragraph theme. It is fill-in-the-blank writing: "The food service is bad for three reasons. First, it is bad because the food is not tasty. Blah, blah, blah about tasteless food. Second, it is bad because it is too expensive. Blah, blah, blah about the expense." And so on. The writer is on autopilot and is not contributing to a real conversation about a real question. In some situations, writers use *engfish* intentionally: bureaucrats and politicians may want to avoid saying something risky; students may want to avoid writing about complex matters that they fear they do not fully understand. In the end, using *engfish* is bad not because what you say is *wrong*, but because what you say couldn't *possibly be* wrong. To avoid *engfish*, stay focused on the need to surprise your reader.

---

*The term *engfish* was coined by the textbook writer Ken Macrorie to describe a fishy kind of canned prose that bright but bored students mechanically produce to please their teachers. See Ken Macrorie, *Telling Writing* (Rochelle Park, NJ: Hayden Press, 1970).

Developing a Thesis/Support Structure

As a class, choose a topic from popular culture such as reality TV shows, Twitter, rap, fad diets, legalizing marijuana, or a topic similar to these.

1. Working as a whole class or in small groups, give examples of how you might write about this topic in an *and then* way, an *all about* way, and an *engfish* way.
2. Then develop one or more questions about the topic that could lead to thesis/support writing. What contestable theses can your class create?

SKILL 3 Plan and visualize your structure.

As we explained in Skill 2, closed-form writing supports a contestable thesis through a hierarchical network of points and particulars. One way to visualize this structure is to outline its skeleton, an exercise that makes visually clear that not all points are on equal levels. The highest-level point is an essay's thesis statement, which is usually supported by several main points that are in turn supported by subpoints and sub-subpoints, all of which are supported by their own particulars. In this lesson we show you how to create such a hierarchical structure for your own papers and how to visualize this structure through an outline, tree diagram, or flowchart.

At the outset, we want to emphasize that structural diagrams are not rigid molds, but flexible planning devices that evolve as your thinking shifts and changes. The structure of your final draft may be substantially different from your initial scratch outline. In fact, we want to show you how your evolving outlines or diagrams can help you generate more ideas and reshape your structure.

With this background, we now proceed to a sequence of steps you can take to plan and visualize a structure.

Making Lists of "Chunks" and a Scratch Outline Early in the Writing Process

Early in the writing process, before you know how to organize your material, you know that you have certain ideas, sections, parts, or "chunks" that you want to include somewhere. Just making a list of these chunks will help you get started. Here is a list of chunks by student writer James Gardiner early in his process of writing a researched argument on online social networks:

CHUNKS THAT I WANT TO INCLUDE SOMEWHERE IN MY PAPER

- Section on the popularity of online social networks (OSNs)
- Tamyra Pierce article that OSNs can lead to bad grades
- Examples of athletes embarrassing team by putting drinking pictures on Facebook
- One of my research article's argument about OSNs and narcissism
- Danah Boyd's argument that OSNs are positive and provide a place to experiment with identity

- Story of college student who posted a revealing picture of herself as Catwoman and was later embarrassed
- The term "Facebook trance"

Once you make a list of chunks, you can begin thinking about which of them are high-level points and which are details in support of a point. Before writing a rough draft, many writers like to make a brief scratch outline to help with planning. Here is James's initial scratch outline.

JAMES'S INITIAL SCRATCH OUTLINE

- Attention-grabber (maybe story of my watching friends use Facebook or some kind of statistic)
- Evidence of popularity of OSNs
- Show the good side of OSNs (Boyd's argument, statements from my friends)
- Then move to bad side (use term "Facebook trance")
  - Narcissism
  - Embarrassing cases (Catwoman, athletes)
  - Lower grades

"Nutshelling" Your Argument as an Aid to Finding a Structure

As you begin drafting, you will find your ideas gradually becoming clearer and more structured. You can accelerate this process through the following short exercise that will help you "nutshell" your argument. The six prompts in this exercise invite you to look at your argument from different perspectives. We recommend that you write your responses to each prompt as a preliminary step in helping you visualize your structure.

EXERCISE FOR NUTSHELLING YOUR ARGUMENT

1. What puzzle or problem initiated your thinking about X?

2. *Template: Many people think X, but I am going to argue Y.*

   Before reading my paper, my readers will think X: [specify what you imagine your readers initially think about your topic] _____.

   But after reading my paper, my readers will think Y: [specify the new or different way readers will think after finishing your paper] _____.

3. The purpose of my paper is _____.

4. My paper addresses the following question: _____.

5. My one-sentence summary answer to this question is this: _____.

6. A tentative title for my paper is this: _____.

   Here are James Gardiner's responses to these prompts:

1. I was initially puzzled why so many students used online social networks. I didn't have a profile on Facebook or MySpace and wondered what the advantages and disadvantages of OSNs might be.

2. Before reading my paper, my readers will believe that OSNs have few detrimental consequences. After reading my paper, my readers will appreciate the potential dangers of OSNs.

3. The purpose of this paper is to point out potential negative consequences of OSNs.
4. What are the possible negative consequences of OSNs?
5. Overuse of OSNs can contribute to a decline in grades, to a superficial view of relationships, to an increase in narcissism, and to possible future embarrassment.
6. Some Dangers of Online Social Networks

Articulating a Working Thesis with Main Points

Once you have nutshelled your argument, you are ready to create a working thesis statement that includes main supporting points. These supporting points help you visualize an emerging structure. Here is James Gardiner's working thesis statement.

> Despite the benefits of online social networks such as MySpace or Facebook, these networks can have negative consequences such as a decline in grades, a superficial view of relationships, an increase in narcissism, and possible future embarrassment.

Using Complete Sentences in Outlines to Convey Meanings

An effective working outline helps you organize *meanings*, not topics. Note that in the outline, tree diagram, and flowchart that follow, James Gardiner uses *complete sentences* rather than phrases in the high-level slots. Because sentences have both subjects and verbs, they can make a point, which asserts a meaning, unlike a phrase, which identifies a topic but doesn't make an assertion about it. Here are examples:

Phrase: Lower grades
Sentence: OSNs can have a negative effect on grades.

Phrase: OSNs and narcissism
Sentence: OSNs may contribute to a rise in narcissism among today's young people.

Any point—whether a thesis, a main point, or a subpoint—is a contestable assertion that requires its own particulars for support. By using complete sentences rather than phrases in an outline, the writer is forced to articulate the point of each section of the emerging argument.

Sketching Your Structure Using an Outline, Tree Diagram, or Flowchart

Once you have created a working thesis statement, you can sketch your structure to show how points, subpoints, and particulars can be arranged to support your thesis. We offer you three different ways to visualize your argument: outlines, tree diagrams, and flowcharts. Use whichever strategy best fits your way of thinking and perceiving.

Outlines The most common way of visualizing structure is the traditional outline, which uses letters and numerals to indicate levels of points, subpoints, and particulars. If you prefer outlines, we recommend that you use the outlining feature of your word processing program, which allows you to move and insert material and change heading levels with great flexibility.

Figure 1 shows the first half of James Gardiner's detailed outline for his argument. Note that, except in the introduction, James uses complete sentences rather than phrases for each level.

FIGURE 1 James Gardiner's Outline for First Half of Paper

Thesis: Despite the benefits of online social networks like MySpace or Facebook, these networks can have negative consequences such as a decline in grades, a superficial view of relationships, an increase in narcissism, and possible future embarrassment.

I Introduction
 A Attenion-grabber about walking into any computer lab
 B Media evidence shows a large increase in the popularity of OSNs among young people.
 C The term "Facebook Trance" indicates possible harms of OSNs.
 D Thesis paragraph

II Admittedly, OSNs have positive benefits.
 A They provide a way to stay in close contact with friends and family.
 B Researcher Danah Boyd says that OSNs give young people a place to experiment with identities and voices.
 C They provide a way to get quick additional information about someone you've met in class or at a party.

III Despite these benefits, OSNs have potential negative consequences.
 A They can have a negative effect on grades.
  1 Researcher Tamyra Pierce found that high school students with MySpace accounts were more likely to report a decline in grades than those without accounts.
  2 Her data show heavy use of OSNs among as many as 59 percent of students, taking time away from school, work, and sleep.
  3 Other writers apply the high school study to college.
 B OSNs have a tendency to promote superficial relationships.
  1 A study by Chou, Condron, and Belland shows that for some users, online relationships can result in problems with real-life interpersonal relationships.
  2 Another researcher, Matsuba, found that online relationships might hinder some people from developing an adult identity.
  3 A possible contributing factor to the superficiality of online relationships might be the absence of nonverbal communication.
 C OSNs might also contribute to a rise in narci

Tree Diagrams A tree diagram displays a hierarchical structure visually, using horizontal and vertical space instead of letters and numbers. Figure 2 shows James's argument as a tree diagram. His thesis is at the top of the tree. His main reasons, written as point sentences, appear as branches beneath his claim. Supporting evidence and arguments are subbranches beneath each reason.

Unlike outlines, tree diagrams allow us to *see* the hierarchical relationship of points and particulars. When you develop a point with subpoints or particulars, you move down the tree. When you switch to a new point, you move across the tree to make a new branch. Our own teaching experience suggests that for many writers, this visual/spatial technique produces fuller, more detailed, and more logical arguments than does a traditional outline.

Flowcharts A flowchart presents the sequence of sections as separate boxes, inside which (or next to which) the writer notes the material needed to fill each box. A flowchart of James's essay is shown in Figure 3.

FIGURE 2 James's Tree Diagram

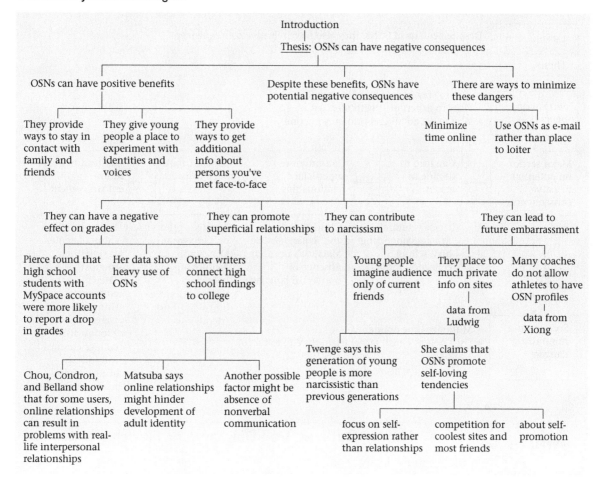

Letting the Structure Evolve

Once you have sketched out an initial structural diagram, use it to generate ideas. Tree diagrams are particularly helpful because they invite you to place question marks on branches to "hold open" spots for new points or supporting particulars. If you have only two main points, for example, you could draw a third main branch and place a question mark under it to encourage you to think of another supporting idea. Likewise, if a branch has few supporting particulars, add question marks beneath it. The trick is to think of your structural diagrams as evolving sketches rather than rigid blueprints. As your ideas grow and change, revise your structural diagram, adding or removing points, consolidating and refocusing sections, moving parts around, or filling in details.

FIGURE 3 James's Flowchart

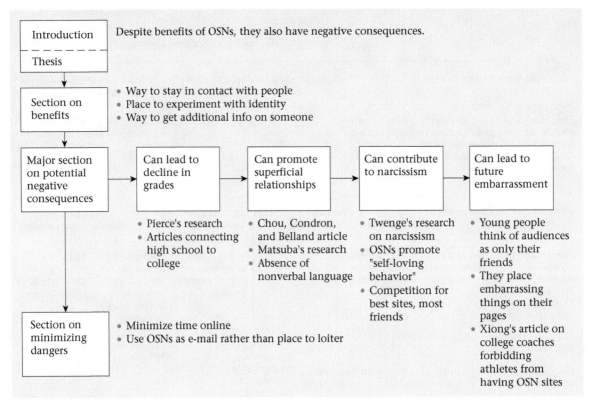

FOR
WRITING
AND
DISCUSSION

Making Outlines, Tree Diagrams, or Flowcharts

Working individually, complete the outline or the tree diagram for James Gardiner's researched argument. Use complete sentences in the outline. Then convene in small groups to compare your outlines. Finally, share points of view on which method of representing structure—outlines, tree diagrams, or flowcharts—works best for different members of the class.

SKILL 4 Set up reader expectations through effective titles and introductions.

Because effective titles and introductions give readers a big-picture overview of a paper's argument, writers often can't compose them until they have finished one or more drafts. But as soon as you know your essay's big picture, you'll find that writing titles and introductions follows some general principles that are easy to learn.

Avoiding the "Topic Title" and the "Funnel Introduction"

Some students have been taught an opening strategy, sometimes called the "funnel," that encourages students to start with broad generalizations and then narrow down to their topics. This strategy often leads to a "topic title" (which names the topic area but doesn't forecast the problem being addressed or the surprise the writer will bring to readers) and vapid generalizations in the opening of the introduction, as the following example shows:

B. F. SKINNER

Since time immemorial people have pondered the question of freedom. The great philosophers of Greece and Rome asked what it means to be free, and the question has echoed through the ages up until the present day. One modern psychologist who asked this question was B. F. Skinner, who wanted to study whether humans had free will or were programmed by their environment to act the way they did. ...

Here the writer eventually gets to his subject, B. F. Skinner, but so far presents no sense of what the point of the essay will be or why the reader should be interested. A better approach is to hook your readers immediately with an effective title and a problem-posing introduction.

Hooking Your Reader with an Effective Title

Good titles follow the principle of old before new information that we introduced in Skill 1. A good title needs to have something old (a word or phrase that hooks into a reader's existing interests) and something new (a word or phrase that forecasts the writer's problematic question, thesis, or purpose). Here are examples of effective titles from two student essays:

"Why Facebook Might Not Be Good for You"
"Paintball: Promoter of Violence or Healthy Fun?"

The old information in these titles ("Facebook" and "Paintball") ties into readers' preexisting knowledge or interests. But the titles also indicate each essay's direction or purpose—the new information that promises to expand or challenge the readers' views. The first writer will argue that Facebook might be harmful in some way; the second writer will explore the problem of violence versus fun in paintball.

As these examples show, your title should provide a brief overview of what your paper is about. Academic titles are typically longer and more detailed than are titles in popular magazines. There are three basic approaches that academic writers take, as shown in the following strategies chart.

Strategies for Writing Titles of Academic Papers	
What to Do	Examples
State or imply the question that your essay addresses.	Will Patriarchal Management Survive Beyond the Decade?
	The Impact of Cell Phones on Motor Vehicle Fatalities [Implied question: What is the impact ... ?]
	(continued)

What to Do	Examples
State or imply, often in abbreviated form, your essay's thesis.	The Writer's Audience Is Always a Fiction How Foreign Aid Can Foster Democratization in Authoritarian Regimes
Use a two-part title separated by a colon: • On the left, present key words from your essay's issue or problem or a "mystery phrase" that arouses interest. • On the right, place the essay's question, thesis, or summary of purpose.	Deep Play: Notes on a Balinese Cockfight Coping with Hurricane Katrina: Psychological Stress and Resilience among African-American Evacuees

Such titles might seem overly formal to you, but they indicate how much an academic writer wishes to preview an article's big picture. Although the titles in popular magazines may be more informal, they often use these same strategies. Here are some titles from popular magazines such as *Redbook* and *Forbes*:

"Is the Coffee Bar Trend About to Peak?" (question)
"A Man *Can* Take Maternity Leave—And Love It" (abbreviated thesis)
"Feed Your Face: Why Your Complexion Needs Vitamins" (two parts linked by colon)

Composing a title for your essay can help you find your focus when you get bogged down in the middle of a draft. Thinking about your title forces you to *nutshell* your ideas by seeing your project's big picture. It causes you to reconsider your purpose and to think about what's old and what's new for your audience.

From Old to New: The General Principle of Closed-Form Introductions

Just as effective titles present something old and something new, so do dynamic and powerful introductions. Old information is something your readers already know and find interesting before they start reading your essay. New information is the surprise of your argument, the unfamiliar material that you add to your readers' understanding.

Because the writer's thesis statement forecasts the new information the paper will present, a thesis statement for a closed-form essay typically comes *at the end of the introduction*. What precedes the thesis is typically the problem or question that the thesis addresses—the old information that the reader needs in order to understand the conversation that the thesis joins. A typical closed-form introduction has the following shape:

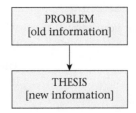

PROBLEM
[old information]

THESIS
[new information]

The length and complexity of your introduction is a function of how much your reader already knows and cares about the question or problem your paper addresses. The function of an introduction is to capture the reader's interest in the first few sentences, to identify and explain the question or problem that the essay addresses, to provide any needed background information, and to present the thesis. You can leave out any of the first three elements if the reader is already hooked on your topic and already knows the question you are addressing. For example, in an essay exam you can usually start with your thesis statement because you can assume the instructor already knows the question and finds it interesting.

To illustrate how an effective closed-form introduction takes the reader from the question to the thesis, consider how the following student writer revised his introduction to a paper on Napster.com:

ORIGINAL INTRODUCTION (CONFUSING)

Napster is all about sharing, not stealing, as record companies and some musicians would like us to think. Napster is an online program that was released in October of '99. Napster lets users easily search for and trade mp3s—compressed, high-quality music files that can be produced from a CD. Napster is the leading file sharing community; it allows users to locate and share music. It also provides instant messaging, chat rooms, an outlet for fans to identify new artists, and a forum to communicate their interests.

Thesis statement

Background on Napster

Most readers find this introduction confusing. The writer begins with his thesis statement before the reader is introduced to the question that the thesis addresses. He seems to assume that his reader is already a part of the Napster conversation, and yet in the next sentences, he gives background on Napster. If the reader needs background on Napster, then the reader also needs background on the Napster controversy. In rethinking his assumptions about old-versus-new information for his audience, this writer decided he wants to reach general newspaper readers who may have heard about a lawsuit against Napster and are interested in the issue but aren't sure of what Napster is or how it works. Here is his revised introduction:

REVISED INTRODUCTION (CLEARER)

Several months ago the rock band Metallica filed a lawsuit against Napster.com, an online program that lets users easily search for and trade mp3s—compressed, high-quality music files that can be produced from a CD. Napster.com has been wildly popular among music lovers because it creates a virtual community where users can locate and share music. It also provides instant messaging, chat rooms, an outlet for fans to identify new artists, and a forum to communicate their interests. But big-name bands like Metallica, alarmed at what they see as lost revenues, claim that Napster.com is stealing their royalties. However, Napster is all about sharing, not stealing, as some musicians would like us to think.

Triggers readers' memory of lawsuit

Background on Napster

Clarification of problem (Implied question: Should Napster be shut down?)

Thesis

This revised introduction fills in the old information the reader needs in order to recall and understand the problem; then it presents the thesis.

Typical Elements of a Closed-Form Introduction

Now that you understand the general principle of closed-form introductions, let's look more closely at its four typical features or elements:

1. *An opening attention-grabber.* If you aren't sure that your reader is already interested in your problem, you can begin with an attention-grabber (what journalists call the "hook" or "lead"), which is typically a dramatic vignette, a startling fact or statistic, an arresting quotation, an interesting scene, or something else that taps into your reader's interests. Attention-grabbers are uncommon in academic prose (where you assume your reader will be initially engaged by the problem itself) but frequently used in popular prose.

2. *Explanation of the question to be investigated.* If your reader already knows about the problem and cares about it, then you need merely to summarize it. This problem or question is the starting point of your argument. If you aren't sure whether your audience fully understands the question or fully cares about it, then you need to explain it in more detail, showing why it is both problematic and significant.

3. *Background information.* In order to understand the conversation you are joining, readers sometimes need background information such as a definition of key terms, a summary of events leading up to the problem, factual details needed for explaining the context of the problem, and so forth. In academic papers, this background often includes a review of what other scholars have said about the problem.

4. *A preview of where your paper is heading.* The final element of a closed-form introduction sketches the big picture of your essay by previewing the kind of surprise or challenge readers can expect and giving them a sense of the whole. This preview is initially new information for your readers (this is why it comes at the end of the introduction). Once stated, however, it becomes old information that readers will use to locate their position in their journey through your argument. By predicting what's coming, this preview initiates the pleasurable process of forecasting/fulfillment that we discussed in Skill 1. Writers typically forecast the whole by stating their thesis, but they can also use a purpose statement or a blueprint statement to accomplish the same end. These strategies are the subject of the next section.

Forecasting the Whole with a Thesis Statement, Purpose Statement, or Blueprint Statement

The most succinct way to forecast the whole is to state your thesis directly. Student writers often ask how detailed their thesis statements should be and whether it is permissible, sometimes, to delay revealing the thesis until the conclusion—an open-form move that gives papers a more exploratory, mystery-novel feel. It is useful, then, to outline briefly some of your choices as a writer. To illustrate a writer's options for forecasting the whole, we use James Gardiner's research paper on online social networks.

Strategies for Forecasting the Whole Paper

Options	What to Do	Examples
Short thesis	State claim without summarizing your supporting argument or forecasting your structure.	Online social networks can have negative consequences.
Detailed thesis	Summarize whole argument; may begin with an *although* clause that summarizes the view you are trying to change.	Despite the benefits of online social networks like MySpace or Facebook, these networks can have negative consequences such as a decline in grades, a superficial view of relationships, an increase in narcissism, and possible future embarrassment.
Purpose statement	State your purpose or intention without summarizing the argument. A purpose statement typically begins with a phrase such as "My purpose is to …" or "In the following paragraphs I wish to …"	My purpose in this essay is to show the potential negative consequences of online social networks.
Blueprint or mapping statement	Describe the structure of your essay by announcing the number of main parts and describing the function or purpose of each one.	After discussing briefly the positive benefits of online social networks, I will describe four potential negative consequences. Finally I will suggest ways to avoid these consequences by using OSNs wisely.
Combination of elements	Include two or more of these elements. In long essays, academic writers sometimes have a purpose statement followed by a detailed thesis and blueprint statement.	[James's essay is not long enough nor complex enough to need an extensive multisentence overview.]
Thesis question only *[Implies a reflective or exploratory paper rather than an argument]*	State the question only, without initially implying your answer. This open-form strategy invites the reader to join the writer in a mutual search.	Although online social networks are widely popular, something about them makes me feel uncomfortable. I am wondering if there are unappreciated risks as well as benefits associated with OSNs.

Which of these options should a writer choose? There are no firm rules to help you answer this question. How much you forecast in the introduction and where you reveal your thesis is a function of your purpose, audience, and genre. The more you forecast, the clearer your argument is and the easier it is to read quickly. You minimize the demands on readers' time by giving them the gist of your argument in the introduction, making it easier to skim your essay if they don't have time for a thorough reading. The less you forecast, the more demands you make on readers' time: You invite them, in effect, to accompany you through the twists and turns of your own thinking process, and you risk losing them if they become confused, lost, or bored. For these reasons, academic writing is generally closed form and aims at maximum clarity. In many rhetorical contexts, however, more open forms are appropriate.

If you choose a closed-form structure, we can offer some advice on how much to forecast. Readers sometimes feel insulted by too much forecasting, so include only what is needed for clarity. For short papers, readers usually don't need to have the complete supporting argument forecast in the introduction. In longer papers, however, or in especially complex ones, readers appreciate having the whole argument forecast at the outset. Academic writing in particular tends to favor explicit and often detailed forecasting.

Revising a Title and Introduction

Individual task: Choose an essay you are currently working on or have recently completed and examine your title and introduction. Ask yourself these questions:

- What audience am I imagining? What do I assume are my readers' initial interests that will lead them to read my essay (the old information I must hook into)? What is new in my essay?
- Do I have an attention-grabber? Why or why not?
- Where do I state or imply the question or problem that my essay addresses?
- Do I explain why the question is problematic and significant? Why or why not?
- For my audience to understand the problem, do I provide too much background information, not enough, or just the right amount?
- What strategies do I use to forecast the whole?

Based on your analysis of your present title and introduction, revise as appropriate.

Group task: Working with a partner or in small groups, share the changes you made in your title or introduction and explain why you made the changes.

SKILL 5 Create effective topic sentences for paragraphs.

In our lesson on outlining (Skill 3) we suggested that you write complete sentences rather than phrases for the high-level slots of the outline in order to articulate the *meaning* or *point* of each section of your argument. In this lesson we show you how to place these points where readers expect them: near the beginning of the sections or paragraphs they govern.

When you place points before particulars, you follow the same principle illustrated in our old-before-new exercise (Skill 1) with the flight attendant announcing the name of the city before the departure gate (the city is the old information, the departure gate the new information). When you first state the point, it is the new information that the next paragraph or section will develop. Once you have stated it, it becomes old information that helps readers understand the meaning of the particulars that follow. If you withhold the point until later, the reader has to keep all the particulars in short-term memory until you finally reveal the point that the particulars are supposed to support or develop.

Placing Topic Sentences at the Beginning of Paragraphs

Readers of closed-form prose need to have point sentences (usually called "topic sentences") at the beginnings of paragraphs. However, writers of rough drafts often don't fulfill this need because drafting is an exploratory process in which writers are often still searching for their points as they compose. Consequently, in their rough drafts writers often omit topic sentences entirely or place them at the ends of paragraphs, or they write topic sentences that misrepresent what the paragraphs actually say. During revision, then, you should check your body paragraphs carefully to be sure you have placed accurate topic sentences near the beginning.

What follow are examples of the kinds of revisions writers typically make. We have annotated the examples to explain the changes the writer has made to make the paragraphs unified and clear to readers. The first example is from a later draft of the essay on the dorm room carpets.

Revision–Topic Sentence First

Another reason for the university not to buy carpets is the cost.

 ^ According to Rachel Jones, Assistant Director of Housing Services, the   *Topic sentence placed first*

initial purchase and installation of carpeting would cost $300 per room.

Considering the number of rooms in the three residence halls, carpeting amounts

to a substantial investment. Additionally, once the carpets are installed, the

university would need to maintain them through the purchase of more vacuum

cleaners and shampoo machines. This money would be better spent on other

dorm improvements that would benefit more residents, such as expanded kitchen

facilities and improved recreational space. ~~Thus carpets would be too expensive.~~

In the original draft, the writer states the point at the end of the paragraph. In his revision he states the point in an opening topic sentence that links back to the thesis statement, which promises "several reasons" that the university should not buy carpets for the dorms. The words "Another reason" thus link the topic sentence to the argument's big picture.

Revising Paragraphs for Unity

In addition to placing topic sentences at the heads of paragraphs, writers often need to revise topic sentences to better match what the paragraph actually says, or revise the paragraph to better match the topic sentence. Paragraphs have unity when all their sentences develop the point stated in the topic sentence. Paragraphs in rough drafts are often not unified because they reflect the writer's shifting, evolving, thinking-while-writing process. Consider the following paragraph from an early draft of an argument against euthanasia by student writer Dao Do. Her peer reviewer labeled it "confusing." What makes it confusing?

We look at more examples from Dao's essay later in this chapter.

Early Draft–Confusing

First, euthanasia is wrong because no one has the right to take the life of another person. Some people say that euthanasia or suicide will end suffering and pain. But what proofs do they have for such a claim? Death is still mysterious to us; therefore, we do not know whether death will end suffering and pain or not. What seems to be the real claim is that death to those with illnesses will end *our* pain. Such pain involves worrying over them, paying their medical bills, and giving up so much of our time. Their deaths end our pain rather than theirs. And for that reason, euthanasia is a selfish act, for the outcome of euthanasia benefits us, the nonsufferers, more. Once the sufferers pass away, we can go back to our normal lives.

The paragraph opens with an apparent topic sentence: "Euthanasia is wrong because no one has the right to take the life of another person." But the rest of the paragraph doesn't focus on that point. Instead, it focuses on how euthanasia benefits the survivors more than the sick person. Dao had two choices: to revise the paragraph to fit the topic sentence or to revise the topic sentence to fit the paragraph. Here is her revision, which includes a different topic sentence and an additional sentence midparagraph to keep particulars focused on the opening point. Dao unifies this paragraph by keeping all its parts focused on her main point: "Euthanasia ... benefits the survivors more than the sick person."

Revision for Unity

Revised topic sentence better forecasts focus of paragraph

Keeps focus on "sick person"

First, euthanasia is wrong because it benefits the survivors more than the sick person.
~~First, euthanasia is wrong because no one has the right to take the life of another person.~~ Some people say that euthanasia or suicide will end suffering and pain. But what proofs do they have for such a claim? Death is still

mysterious to us; therefore, we do not know whether death will end suffering and
Moreover, modern pain killers can relieve most of the pain a sick person has to endure. ◄───
pain or not. What seems to be the real claim is that death to those with illnesses

will end *our* pain. Such pain involves worrying over them, paying their medical

bills, and giving up so much of our time. Their deaths end our pain rather than

theirs. And for that reason, euthanasia is a selfish act, for the outcome of

euthanasia benefits us, the nonsufferers, more. Once the sufferers pass away,

we can go back to our normal lives.

Concludes subpoint about sick person

Supports subpoint about how euthanasia benefits survivors

A paragraph may lack unity for a variety of reasons. It may shift to a new direction in the middle, or one or two sentences may simply be irrelevant to the point. The key is to make sure that all the sentences in the paragraph fulfill the reader's expectations based on the topic sentence.

Adding Particulars to Support Points

Just as writers of rough drafts often omit point sentences from paragraphs, they also sometimes leave out the particulars needed to support a point. In such cases, the writer needs to add particulars such as facts, statistics, quotations, research summaries, examples, or further subpoints. Consider how adding additional particulars to the following draft paragraph strengthens a student writer's argument opposing the logging of old-growth forests.

DRAFT PARAGRAPH: PARTICULARS MISSING

One reason that it is not necessary to log old-growth forests is that the timber industry can supply the world's lumber needs without doing so. For example, we have plenty of new-growth forest from which timber can be taken (Sagoff 89). We could also reduce the amount of trees used for paper products by using other materials besides wood for paper pulp. In light of the fact that we have plenty of trees and ways of reducing our wood demands, there is no need to harvest old-growth forests.

REVISED PARAGRAPH: PARTICULARS ADDED

One reason that it is not necessary to log old-growth forests is that the timber industry can supply the world's lumber needs without doing so. For example, we have plenty of new-growth forest from which timber can be taken as a result of major reforestation efforts all over the United States (Sagoff 89). In the Northwest, for instance, Oregon law requires every acre of timber harvested to be replanted. According to Robert Sedjo, a forestry expert, the world's demand for industrial wood could be met by a widely implemented tree farming system (Sagoff 90). We could also reduce the amount of trees used for paper products by using a promising new innovation called Kenaf, a fast-growing annual herb which is fifteen feet tall and is native to Africa. It has been used for making rope for many years, but recently it was found to work just as well for paper pulp. In light of the fact that we have plenty of trees and ways of reducing our wood demands, there is no need to harvest old-growth forests.

Added particulars support subpoint that we have plenty of new-growth forest

Added particulars support second subpoint that wood alternatives are available

Revising Paragraphs for Points-First Structure

Individual task: Bring to class a draft-in-progress for a closed-form essay. Pick out several paragraphs in the body of your essay and analyze them for "points-first" structure. For each paragraph, ask the following questions:

- Does my paragraph have a topic sentence near the beginning?
- If so, does my topic sentence accurately forecast what the paragraph says?
- Does my topic sentence link to my thesis statement or to a higher-order point that my paragraph develops?
- Does my paragraph have enough particulars to develop and support my topic sentence?

Group task: Then exchange your draft with a partner and do a similar analysis of your partner's selected paragraphs. Discuss your analyses of each other's paragraphs and then help each other plan appropriate revision strategies. If time permits, revise your paragraphs and show your results to your partner. [Note: Sometimes you can revise simply by adding a topic sentence to a paragraph, rewording a topic sentence, or making other kinds of local revisions. At other times, you may need to cross out whole paragraphs and start over, rewriting from scratch after you rethink your ideas.]

SKILL 6 Guide your reader with transitions and other signposts.

As we have explained, when readers read closed-form prose, they expect each new sentence, paragraph, and section to link clearly to what they have already read. They need a well-marked trail with signposts signaling the twists and turns along the way. They also need resting spots at major junctions where they can review where they've been and survey what's coming. In this lesson, we show you how transition words as well as summary and forecasting passages can keep your readers securely on the trail.

Using Common Transition Words to Signal Relationships

Transitions are like signposts that signal where the road is turning and limit the possible directions that an unfolding argument might take. Consider how the use of "therefore" and "nevertheless" limits the range of possibilities in the following examples:

> While on vacation, Suzie caught the chicken pox. Therefore, _____.
> While on vacation, Suzie caught the chicken pox. Nevertheless, _____.

"Therefore" signals to the reader that what follows is a consequence. Most readers will imagine a sentence similar to this one:

> Therefore, she spent her vacation lying in bed itchy, feverish, and miserable.

In contrast, "nevertheless" signals an unexpected or denied consequence, so the reader might anticipate a sentence such as this:

> Nevertheless, she enjoyed her two weeks off, thanks to a couple of bottles of calamine lotion, some good books, and a big easy chair overlooking the ocean.

Here is a list of the most common transition words and phrases and what they signal to the reader:*

Words or Phrases	What They Signal
first, second, third, next, finally, earlier, later, meanwhile, afterward	*sequence*—First we went to dinner; then we went to the movies.
that is, in other words, to put it another way, — (dash), : (colon)	*restatement*—He's so hypocritical that you can't trust a word he says. To put it another way, he's a complete phony.
rather, instead	*replacement*—We shouldn't use the money to buy opera tickets; rather, we should use it for a nice gift.
for example, for instance, a case in point	*example*—Mr. Carlyle is very generous. For example, he gave the janitors a special holiday gift.
because, since, for	*reason*—Taxes on cigarettes are unfair because they place a higher tax burden on the working class.
therefore, hence, so, consequently, thus, then, as a result, accordingly, as a consequence	*consequence*—I failed to turn in the essay; therefore I flunked the course.
still, nevertheless	*denied consequence*—The teacher always seemed grumpy in class; nevertheless, I really enjoyed the course.
although, even though, granted that (*with* still)	*concession*—Even though the teacher was always grumpy, I still enjoyed the course.
in comparison, likewise, similarly	*similarity*—Teaching engineering takes a lot of patience. Likewise, so does teaching accounting.
however, in contrast, conversely, on the other hand, but	*contrast*—I disliked my old backpack immensely; however, I really like this new one.
in addition, also, too, moreover, furthermore	*addition*—Today's cars are much safer than those of ten years ago. In addition, they get better gas mileage.
in brief, in sum, in conclusion, finally, to sum up, to conclude	*conclusion or summary*—In sum, the plan presented by Mary is the best choice.

Using Transitions

FOR
WRITING
AND
DISCUSSION

This exercise is designed to show you how transition words govern relationships between ideas. Working in groups or on your own, finish each of the following statements using ideas of your own invention. Make sure what you add fits the logic of the transition word.

1. Writing is difficult; therefore _____.
2. Writing is difficult; however, _____.

(continued)

*Although all the words on the list serve as transitions or connectives, grammatically they are not all equivalent, nor are they all punctuated the same way.

3. Writing is difficult because _____.
4. Writing is difficult. For example, _____.
5. Writing is difficult. To put it another way, _____.
6. Writing is difficult. Likewise, _____.
7. Although writing is difficult, _____.

In the following paragraph, various kinds of linking devices have been omitted. Fill in the blanks with words or phrases that would make the paragraph coherent. Clues are provided in brackets.

Writing an essay is a difficult process for most people. _____ [contrast] the process can be made easier if you learn to practice three simple techniques. _____ [sequence] learn the technique of nonstop writing. When you are first trying to think of ideas for an essay, put your pen to your paper and write nonstop for ten or fifteen minutes without letting your pen leave the paper. Stay loose and free. Let your pen follow the waves of thought. Don't worry about grammar or spelling. _____ [concession] this technique won't work for everyone, it helps many people get a good cache of ideas to draw on. A _____ [sequence] technique is to write your rough draft rapidly without worrying about being perfect. Too many writers try to get their drafts right the first time. _____ [contrast] by learning to live with imperfection, you will save yourself headaches and a wastepaper basket full of crumpled paper. Think of your first rough draft as a path hacked out of the jungle—as part of an exploration, not as a completed highway. As a _____ [sequence] technique, try printing out a triple-spaced copy to allow space for revision. Many beginning writers don't leave enough space to revise. _____ [consequence] these writers never get in the habit of crossing out chunks of their rough draft and writing revisions in the blank spaces. After you have revised your rough draft until it is too messy to work from anymore, you can _____ [sequence] enter your changes into your word processor and print out a fresh draft, again setting your text on triple-space. The resulting blank space invites you to revise.

Writing Major Transitions between Parts

In long closed-form pieces, writers often put *resting places* between major parts—transitional passages that allow readers to shift their attention momentarily away from the matter at hand to get a sense of where they've been and where they're going. Often such passages sum up the preceding major section, refer back to the essay's thesis statement or opening blueprint plan, and then preview the next major section. Here are three typical examples:

So far I have looked at a number of techniques that can help people identify debilitating assumptions that block their self-growth. In the next section, I examine ways to question and overcome these assumptions.

Now that the difficulty of the problem is fully apparent, our next step is to examine some of the solutions that have been proposed.

These, then, are the major theories explaining why Hamlet delays. But let's see what happens to Hamlet if we ask the question in a slightly different way. In this next section, we shift our critical focus, looking not at Hamlet's actions, but at his language.

Signaling Major Transitions with Headings

In many genres, particularly scientific and technical reports, government documents, business proposals, textbooks, and long articles in magazines or scholarly journals, writers conventionally break up long stretches of text with headings and subheadings. Headings are often set in different type sizes and fonts and mark transition points between major parts and subparts of the argument.

SKILL 7 Bind sentences together by placing old information before new information.

The previous skill focused on marking the reader's trail with transitions. This skill will enable you to build a smooth trail without potholes or washed-out bridges.

The Old/New Contract in Sentences

A powerful way to prevent gaps is to follow the old/new contract—a writing strategy derived from the principle of old before new that we explained and illustrated in Skill 1. Simply put, the old/new contract asks writers to begin sentences with something old—something that links to what has gone before—and then to end sentences with new information.

To understand the old/new contract more fully, try the following thought exercise. We'll show you two passages, both of which explain the old/new contract. One of them, however, follows the principle it describes; the other violates it.

THOUGHT EXERCISE

Which of these passages follows the old/new contract?

VERSION 1

The old/new contract is another principle for writing clear closed-form prose. Beginning your sentences with something old—something that links to what has gone before—and then ending your sentences with new information that advances the argument is what the old/new contract asks writers to do. An effect called *coherence*, which is closely related to *unity*, is created by following this principle. Whereas the clear relationship between the topic sentence and the body of the paragraph and between the parts and the whole is what *unity* refers to, the clear relationship between one sentence and the next is what *coherence* relates to.

VERSION 2

Another principle for writing clear closed-form prose is the old/new contract. The old/new contract asks writers to begin sentences with something old—something that links to what has gone before—and then to end sentences with new information that advances the argument. Following this principle creates an effect called *coherence*, which is closely related to unity. Whereas *unity* refers to the clear relationship between the body of a paragraph and its topic sentence and between the parts and the whole, *coherence* refers to the clear relationship between one sentence and the next, between part and part.

If you are like most readers, you have to concentrate much harder to understand Version 1 than Version 2 because Version 1 violates the old-before-new way that our minds normally process information. When a writer doesn't begin a sentence with old material, readers have to hold the new material in suspension until they have figured out how it connects to what has gone before. They can stay on the trail, but they have to keep jumping over the potholes between sentences.

To follow the old/new contract, place old information near the beginning of sentences in what we call the **topic position** and place new information that advances the argument in the predicate or **stress position** at the end of the sentence. We associate topics with the beginnings of sentences simply because in the standard English sentence, the topic (or subject) comes before the predicate— hence the notion of a "contract" by which we agree not to fool or frustrate our readers by breaking with the "normal" order of things. The contract says that the old, backward-linking material comes at the beginning of the sentence and that the new, argument-advancing material comes at the end.

FOR WRITING AND DISCUSSION

Practicing the Old/New Contract

Here are two more passages, one of which obeys the old/new contract while the other violates it. Working in small groups or as a whole class, reach consensus on which of these passages follows the old/new contract. Explain your reasoning by showing how the beginning of each sentence links to something old.

PASSAGE A

Play is an often-overlooked dimension of fathering. From the time a child is born until its adolescence, fathers emphasize caretaking less than play. Egalitarian feminists may be troubled by this, and spending more time in caretaking may be wise for fathers. There seems to be unusual significance in the father's style of play. Physical excitement and stimulation are likely to be part of it. With older children more physical games and teamwork that require the competitive testing of physical and mental skills are also what it involves. Resemblance to an apprenticeship or teaching relationship is also a characteristic of fathers' play: Come on, let me show you how.

PASSAGE B

An often-overlooked dimension of fathering is play. From their children's birth through adolescence, fathers tend to emphasize play more than caretaking. This emphasis may be troubling to egalitarian feminists, and it would indeed be wise for most fathers to spend more time in caretaking. Yet the fathers' style of play seems to have unusual significance. It is likely to be both physically stimulating and exciting. With older children it involves more physical games and teamwork that require the competitive testing of physical and mental skills. It frequently resembles an apprenticeship or teaching relationship: Come on, let me show you how.

How to Make Links to the "Old"

To understand how to link to "old information," you need to understand more fully what we mean by "old" or "familiar." In the context of sentence-level coherence, we mean everything in the text that the reader has read so far. Any upcoming sentence is new information, but once the reader has read it, it becomes old information. For example, when a reader is halfway through a text, everything previously read—the title, the introduction, half the body—is old information to which you can link to meet your readers' expectations for unity and coherence.

In making these backward links, writers have three targets:

1. They can link to a key word or concept in the immediately preceding sentence (creating coherence).
2. They can link to a key word or concept in a preceding point sentence (creating unity).
3. They can link to a preceding forecasting statement about structure (helping readers map their location in the text).

Writers have a number of textual strategies for making these links. In Figure 4 our annotations show how a professional writer links to old

FIGURE 4 How a Professional Writer Follows the Old/New Contract

Recent research has given us much deeper—and more surprising—insights into the father's role in childrearing. It shows that in almost all of their interactions with children, fathers do things a little differently from mothers. What fathers do—their special parenting style—is not only highly complementary to what mothers do but is by all indications important in its own right.

For example, an often-overlooked dimension of fathering is play. From their children's birth through adolescence, fathers tend to emphasize play more than caretaking. This may be troubling to egalitarian feminists, and it would indeed be wise for most fathers to spend more time in caretaking.

Yet the fathers' style of play seems to have unusual significance. It is likely to be both physically stimulating and exciting. With older children it involves more physical games and teamwork that require the competitive testing of physical and mental skills. It frequently resembles an apprenticeship or teaching relationship: Come on, let me show you how.

David Popenoe, "Where's Papa?" from *Life Without Father: Compelling New Evidence that Fatherhood and Marriage Are Indispensable for the Good of Children and Society.*

Annotations (left): Refers to "fathers" in previous sentence • Transition tells us new paragraph will be an example of previous concept • Refers to "fathers" • New information that becomes topic of this paragraph • Repeats words "father" and "play" from the topic sentence of the preceding paragraph

Annotations (right): Refers to "research" in previous sentence • Rephrases idea of "childrearing" • Repeats "fathers" from previous sentence • Rephrases concept in previous paragraph • Pronoun sums up previous concept • "It" refers to fathers' style of play information within the first five or six words of each sentence. What follows is a compendium of these strategies:

Strategies for Linking to the "Old"

What to Do	Example Shown in Figure 4
Repeat a key word from the preceding sentence or an earlier point sentence.	Note the number of sentences that open with "father," "father's," or "fathering." Note also the frequent repetitions of "play."
Use a pronoun to substitute for a key word.	In our example, the second sentence opens with the pronouns "It," referring to "research," and "their," referring to "fathers." The last three sentences open with the pronoun "It," referring to "father's style of play."
Summarize, rephrase, or restate earlier concepts.	In the second sentence, "interactions with children" restates the concept of childrearing. Similarly, the phrase "an often-overlooked dimension" sums up a concept implied in the preceding paragraph—that recent research reveals something significant and not widely known about a father's role in childrearing. Finally, note that the pronoun "This" in the second paragraph sums up the main concept of the previous two sentences. (But see our warning on the next page about the overuse of "this" as a pronoun.)
Use a transition word such as *first ...*, *second ...*, *third ...*, or *therefore* or *however* to cue the reader about the logical relationship between an upcoming sentence and the preceding ones.	Note how the second paragraph opens with "For example," indicating that the upcoming paragraph will illustrate the concept identified in the preceding paragraph.

These strategies give you a powerful way to check and revise your prose. Comb your drafts for gaps between sentences where you have violated the old/new contract. If the opening of a new sentence doesn't refer back to an earlier word, phrase, or concept, your readers could derail, so use what you have learned to repair the tracks.

FOR WRITING AND DISCUSSION

Applying the Old/New Contract to Your Own Draft

Individual task: Bring to class a draft-in-progress for a closed-form essay. On a selected page, examine the opening of each sentence. Place a vertical slash in front of any sentence that doesn't contain near the beginning some backward-looking element that links to old, familiar material. Then revise these sentences to follow the old/new contract.

> **Group task:** Working with a partner, share the changes you each made on your drafts. Then on each other's pages, work together to identify the kinds of links made at the beginning of each sentence. (For example, does the opening of a sentence repeat a key word, use a pronoun to substitute for a key word, rephrase or restate an earlier concept, or use a transition word?)

As we discussed in Skill 1, the principle of old before new has great explanatory power in helping writers understand their choices when they compose. In this last section, we give you some further insights into the old/new contract.

Avoiding Ambiguous Use of "This" to Fulfill the Old/New Contract

Some writers try to fulfill the old/new contract by frequent use of the pronoun *this* to sum up a preceding concept. Occasionally such usage is effective, as in our example passage on fathers' style of play when the writer says: "*This* may be troubling to egalitarian feminists." But frequent use of *this* as a pronoun creates lazy and often ambiguous prose. Consider how our example passage might read if many of the explicit links were replaced by *this*:

LAZY USE OF *THIS* AS PRONOUN

Recent research has given us much deeper—and more surprising—insights into **this.** It shows that in doing **this,** fathers do things a little differently from mothers. **This** is not only highly complementary to what mothers do but is by all indications important in its own right.

For example, an often-overlooked dimension of **this** is play.

Perhaps this passage helps you see why we refer to *this* (used by itself as a pronoun) as "the lazy person's all-purpose noun-slot filler."*

SKILL 8 Learn four expert moves for organizing and developing ideas.

Writers of closed-form prose often employ a conventional set of moves to organize parts of an essay. In using the term *moves*, we are making an analogy with the "set moves" or "set plays" in such sports as basketball, volleyball, and soccer. For example, a common set move in basketball is the "pick," in which an offensive player without the ball stands motionless in order to block the path of a defensive player who is guarding the dribbler. Similarly, certain organizational patterns in writing occur frequently enough to act as set plays for writers. These patterns set

---

*It's acceptable to use *this* as an adjective, as in "this usage"; we refer here only to *this* used by itself as a pronoun.

up expectations in the reader's mind about the shape of an upcoming stretch of prose, anything from a few sentences to a paragraph to a large block of paragraphs. As you will see, these moves also stimulate the invention of ideas. Next, we describe four of the most powerful set plays.*

The *For Example* Move

Perhaps the most common set play occurs when a writer makes an assertion and then illustrates it with one or more examples, often signaling the move explicitly with transitions such as *for example, for instance*, or *a case in point is ...* . Here is how student writer Dao Do used the *for example* move to support her third reason for opposing euthanasia:

FOR EXAMPLE MOVE

Topic sentence →

Transition signaling the move →

Extended example supporting point

My third objection to euthanasia is that it fails to see the value in suffering. Suffering is a part of life. We see the value of suffering only if we look deeply within our suffering. For example, I never thought my crippled uncle from Vietnam was a blessing to my grandmother until I talked to her. My mother's little brother was born prematurely. As a result of oxygen and nutrition deficiency, he was born crippled. His tiny arms and legs were twisted around his body, preventing him from any normal movements such as walking, picking up things, and lying down. He could only sit. Therefore, his world was very limited, for it consisted of his own room and the garden viewed through his window. Because of his disabilities, my grandmother had to wash him, feed him, and watch him constantly. It was hard, but she managed to care for him for forty-three years. He passed away after the death of my grandfather in 1982. Bringing this situation out of Vietnam and into Western society shows the difference between Vietnamese and Western views. In the West, my uncle might have been euthanized as a baby. Supporters of euthanasia would have said he wouldn't have any quality of life and that he would have been a great burden. But he was not a burden on my grandmother. She enjoyed taking care of him, and he was always her company after her other children got married and moved away. Neither one of them saw his defect as meaningless suffering because it brought them closer together.

This passage uses a single, extended example to support a point. You could also use several shorter examples or other kinds of illustrating evidence such as facts or statistics. In all cases the *for example* move creates a pattern of expectation and fulfillment. This pattern drives the invention of ideas in one of two ways: It urges the writer either to find examples to develop a generalization or to formulate a generalization that shows the point of an example.

---

*You might find it helpful to follow the set plays we used to write this section. This last sentence is the opening move of a play we call "division into parallel parts." It sets up the expectation that we will develop four set plays in order. Watch for the way we chunk them and signal transitions between them.

Practicing the *For Example* Move

Working individually or in groups, develop a plan for supporting one or more of the following generalizations using the *for example* move:

1. Another objection to state sales taxes is that they are so annoying.
2. Although assertiveness training has definite benefits, it can sometimes get you into real trouble.
3. Sometimes effective leaders are indecisive.

The *Summary/However* Move

This move occurs whenever a writer sums up another person's viewpoint in order to qualify or contradict it or to introduce an opposing view. Typically, writers use transition words such as *but, however, in contrast,* or *on the other hand* between the parts of this move. This move is particularly common in academic writing, which often contrasts the writer's new view with prevailing views. Here is how Dao uses a *summary/however* move in the introduction of her essay opposing euthanasia:

SUMMARY/HOWEVER MOVE

Should euthanasia be legalized? My classmate Martha and her family think it should be. Martha's aunt was blind from diabetes. For three years she was constantly in and out of the hospital, but then her kidneys shut down and she became a victim of life support. After three months of suffering, she finally gave up. Martha believes this three-month period was unnecessary, for her aunt didn't have to go through all of that suffering. If euthanasia were legalized, her family would have put her to sleep the minute her condition worsened. Then, she wouldn't have had to feel pain, and she would have died in peace and with dignity. However, despite Martha's strong argument for legalizing euthanasia, I find it wrong.

Issue over which there is disagreement

Summary of opposing viewpoint

Transition to writer's viewpoint

Statement of writer's view

The first sentence of this introduction poses the question that the essay addresses. The main body of the paragraph summarizes Martha's opposing view on euthanasia, and the final sentence, introduced by the transition "However," presents Dao's thesis.

Practicing the *Summary/However* Move

For this exercise, assume that you favor development of wind-generated electricity. Use the *summary/however* move to acknowledge the view of civil engineer David Rockwood's letter opposing wind-generated electricity. Assume that you are writing the opening paragraph of your own essay. Follow the pattern of Dao's introduction: (a) begin with a one-sentence issue or question; (b) summarize Rockwood's view in approximately one hundred words; and (c) state your own view, using *however* or *in contrast* as a transition. Write out your paragraph on your own, or work in groups to write a consensus paragraph. Then share and critique your paragraphs.

The *Division-into-Parallel-Parts* Move

Among the most frequently encountered and powerful of the set plays is the *division-into-parallel-parts* move. To initiate the move, a writer begins with an umbrella sentence that forecasts the structure and creates a framework. (For example, "Freud's theory differs from Jung's in three essential ways" or "The decline of the U.S. space program can be attributed to several factors.") Typical overview sentences either specify the number of parts that follow by using phrases such as "two ways," "three differences," or "five kinds," or they leave the number unspecified, using words such as *several, a few,* or *many.* Alternatively, the writer may ask a rhetorical question that implies the framework: "What are some main differences, then, between Freud's theory and Jung's? One difference is. ... "

To signal transitions from one part to the next, writers use two kinds of signposts in tandem. The first is a series of transition words or bullets to introduce each of the parallel parts. Here are typical series of transition words:

> First ... Second ... Third ... Finally ...
> First ... Another ... Still another ... Finally ...
> One ... In addition ... Furthermore ... Also ...

The second kind of signpost, usually used in conjunction with transitions, is an echolike repetition of the same grammatical structure to begin each parallel part.

> I learned several things from this course. First, *I learned that* [development]. Second, *I learned that* [development]. Finally, *I learned that* [development].

The *division-into-parallel-parts* move can be used within a single paragraph, or it can control larger stretches of text in which a dozen or more paragraphs may work together to complete a parallel series of parts. (For example, you are currently in the third part of a parallel series introduced by the mapping sentence: "Next, we describe four of the most powerful set plays.") Here is an example of a student paragraph organized by the *division-into-parallel-parts* move.

DIVISION-INTO-PARALLEL-PARTS MOVE

Mapping statement forecasts "move"

Transition to first parallel part

Transition to second parallel part

Transition to third parallel part

Final transition completes "move"

In this paper I will argue that political solutions to homelessness must take into account four categories of homeless people. A first category is persons who are out of work and seek new jobs. Persons in this category may have been recently laid off, unable to meet their rental payments, and forced temporarily to live out of a car or van. They might quickly leave the ranks of the homeless if they can find new jobs. A second category includes the physically disabled or mentally ill. Providing housing addresses only part of their problems since they also need medical care and medication. For many, finding or keeping a job might be impossible. A third category is the street alcoholic or drug addict. These persons need addiction treatment as well as clothing and shelter and will not become productive citizens until they become sober or drug free. The final category includes those who, like the old railroad "hobo," choose homelessness as a way of life.

Instead of transition words, writers can also use bullets followed by indented text:

USE OF BULLETS TO SIGNAL PARALLEL PARTS

The Wolf Recovery Program is rigidly opposed by a vociferous group of ranchers who pose three main objections to increasing wolf populations:

- They perceive wolves as a threat to livestock. [development]
- They fear the wolves will attack humans. [development]
- They believe ranchers will not be compensated by the government for their loss of profits. [development]

FOR WRITING AND DISCUSSION

Practicing the *Division-into-Parallel-Parts* Move

Working individually or in small groups, use the *division-into-parallel-parts* move to create, organize, and develop ideas to support one or more of the following point sentences.

1. To study for an exam effectively, a student should follow these [specify a number] steps.
2. Why do U.S. schoolchildren lag so far behind European and Asian children on standardized tests of mathematics and science? One possible cause is ... [continue].
3. Constant dieting is unhealthy for several reasons.

The *Comparison/Contrast* Move

A common variation on the *division-into-parallel-parts* move is the *comparison/ contrast* move. To compare or contrast two items, you must first decide on the points of comparison (or contrast). If you are contrasting the political views of two presidential candidates, you might choose to focus on four points of comparison: differences in their foreign policy, differences in economic policy, differences in social policy, and differences in judicial philosophy. You then have two choices for organizing the parts: the *side-by-side pattern,* in which you discuss all of candidate A's views and then all of candidate B's views; or the *back-and-forth pattern,* in which you discuss foreign policy, contrasting A's views with B's views, then move on to economic policy, then social policy, and then judicial philosophy. Figure 5 shows how these two patterns would appear on a tree diagram.

There are no cut-and-dried rules that dictate when to use the *side-by-side pattern* or the *back-and-forth pattern.* However, for lengthy comparisons, the *back-and-forth pattern* is often more effective because the reader doesn't have to store great amounts of information in memory. The *side-by-side pattern* requires readers to remember all the material about A when they get to B, and it is sometimes difficult to keep all the points of comparison clearly in mind.

FIGURE 5 Two Ways to Structure a Comparison or Contrast

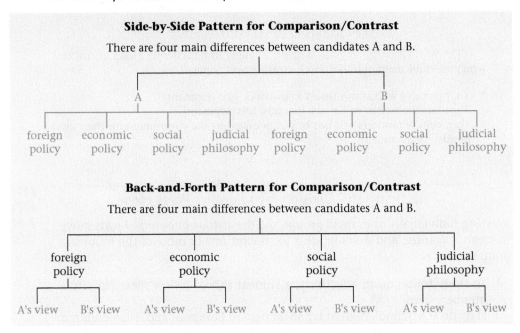

Practicing the *Comparison/Contrast* Move

Working individually or in groups, create tree diagrams for stretches of text based on one or more of the following point sentences, all of which call for the *comparison/contrast* move. Make at least one diagram follow the *back-and-forth pattern* and at least one diagram follow the *side-by-side pattern*.

1. To understand U.S. politics, an outsider needs to appreciate some basic differences between Republicans and Democrats.
2. Although they are obviously different on the surface, there are many similarities between the Boy Scouts and a street gang.
3. There are several important differences between closed-form and open-form writing.

SKILL 9 Use effective tables, graphs, and charts to present numeric data.

In contemporary analyses and arguments, writers often draw on quantitative data to support their points. Writers can make numbers speak powerfully by means of reader-effective graphics including tables, graphs, and charts. Generally, quantitative data displayed in tables invite the reader to tease out many different stories that the numbers might tell. In contrast, line graphs, bar graphs, or pie charts focus vividly on one story.

How Tables Tell Many Stories

Data displayed in tables usually have their origins in raw numbers collected from surveys, questionnaires, observational studies, scientific experiments, and so forth. These numbers are then consolidated and arranged in tables where they can be analyzed for potentially meaningful patterns. Consider, for example, Table 1, produced by the National Center for Education Statistics. It shows the number of postsecondary degrees earned by men and women from 1960 to 2007.

Reading a Table Tables are read in two directions: from top to bottom and from left to right. To read a table efficiently, begin with the title, *which always includes elements from both the vertical and horizontal dimensions of the table.* Note how this rule applies to Table 1.

- The table's horizontal dimension is indicated in the first part of the title: "Earned Degrees Conferred by Level and Sex." Reading horizontally, we see the names of the degrees (associate's, bachelor's, and so forth) with subcategories indicating male and female.
- The table's vertical dimension is indicated in the second part of the title: "1960 to 2007." Reading vertically, we see selected years between 1960 and 2007.

Beneath the title are further instructions: Numbers represent thousands except for one column labeled "percent."

We are now prepared to read specific information from the table. In 1994, for example, colleges and universities in the United States conferred 2,206,000 degrees, of which 45.1 percent were earned by men. In that same year, 532,000 men and 637,000 women earned bachelors's degrees while 27,000 men and 17,000 women earned doctoral degrees.

Discovering Stories in the Data You need to peruse the table carefully before interesting patterns begin to emerge. Among the stories the table tells are these:

- The percent of women receiving postsecondary degrees rose substantially between 1960 and 2007 (with a corresponding fall for men).
- This increased percentage of degrees given to women is more dramatic for associate's and bachelor's degrees than it is for master's, first professional, or doctoral degrees.

As we show in the next section, these two stories, which must be teased out of this table, can be told more dramatically with graphs.

Using a Graphic to Tell a Story

Whereas tables can embed many stories and invite detailed examination of the numbers, a graph or chart makes one selected story immediately visible.

Line Graph A line graph converts numerical data to a series of points on a grid and connects them to create flat, rising, or falling lines. The result gives us a picture of the relationship between the variables represented on the horizontal and vertical axes.

TABLE 1 Earned Degrees Conferred by Level and Sex: 1960 to 2007

[In thousands (477 represents 477,000), except percent. Based on survey]

Year ending	All degrees Total	All degrees Percent male	Associate's Male	Associate's Female	Bachelor's Male	Bachelor's Female	Master's Male	Master's Female	First professional Male	First professional Female	Doctoral Male	Doctoral Female
1960[1]	477	65.8	(NA)	(NA)	254	138	51	24	(NA)	(NA)	9	1
1970	1,271	59.2	117	89	451	341	126	83	33	2	26	4
1975	1,666	56.0	191	169	505	418	162	131	49	7	27	7
1980	1,731	51.1	184	217	474	456	151	147	53	17	23	10
1985	1,828	49.3	203	252	483	497	143	143	50	25	22	11
1990	1,940	46.6	191	264	492	560	154	171	44	27	24	14
1991	2,025	45.8	199	283	504	590	156	181	44	28	25	15
1992	2,108	45.6	207	297	521	616	162	191	45	29	26	15
1993	2,167	45.5	212	303	533	632	169	200	45	30	26	16
1994	2,206	45.1	215	315	532	637	176	211	45	31	27	17
1995	2,218	44.9	218	321	526	634	179	219	45	31	27	18
1996[2]	2,248	44.2	220	336	522	642	179	227	45	32	27	18
1997[2]	2,288	43.6	224	347	521	652	181	238	46	33	27	19
1998[2]	2,298	43.2	218	341	520	664	184	246	45	34	27	19
1999[2]	2,323	42.7	218	342	519	682	186	254	44	34	25	19
2000[2]	2,385	42.6	225	340	530	708	192	265	44	36	25	20
2001[2]	2,416	42.4	232	347	532	712	194	274	43	37	25	20
2002[2]	2,494	42.2	238	357	550	742	199	283	43	38	24	20
2003[2]	2,621	42.1	253	380	573	775	211	301	42	39	24	22
2004[2]	2,755	41.8	260	405	595	804	230	329	42	41	25	23
2005[2]	2,850	41.6	268	429	613	826	234	341	44	43	27	26
2006[2]	2,936	41.3	270	443	631	855	238	356	44	44	29	27
2007[2]	3,007	41.2	275	453	650	875	238	366	45	45	30	30

NA Not available.
[1] First-professional degrees are included with bachelor's degrees.
[2] Beginning 1996, data reflect the new classification of institutions.

Source: U.S. National Center for Education Statistics, *Digest of Education Statistics*, annual.

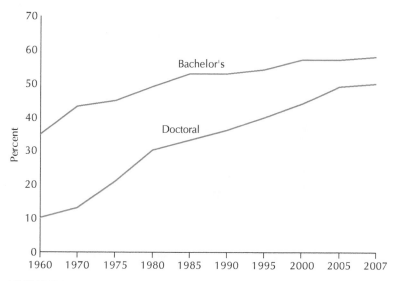

FIGURE 6 Percentage of Bachelor's and Doctoral Degrees Conferred on Females: 1960–2007

Suppose you wanted to tell the story of the increasing percentage of women receiving bachelor's and doctoral degrees from 1960 to 2007. Using Table 1 you can calculate these percentages yourself and display them in a line graph as shown in Figure 6. To determine what a graph tells you, you need to clarify what's represented on the two axes. By convention, the horizontal axis of a graph contains the predictable, known variable that has no surprises, such as time or some other sequence—in this case, the years 1960 to 2007 in predictable chronological order. The vertical axis contains the unpredictable variable that tells the graph's story—in this case, the percent of degrees conferred on women in each year on the graph. The ascending lines tell the stories at a glance.

Bar Graph Bar graphs use bars of varying lengths, extending either horizontally or vertically, to contrast two or more quantities. To make the story of women's progress in earning doctoral degrees particularly vivid (the same story told in the "doctoral" line in Figure 6), you could use a bar graph as shown in Figure 7. To read a bar graph, note carefully the title and the axes to see what is compared to what. Bars are typically distinguished from each other by use of different colors, shades, or patterns of cross-hatching. The special power of bar graphs is that they can help you make quick comparisons. Figure 7 tells you at a glance that in 1960, women received far fewer doctoral degrees than men but that in 2007 they received an equal percentage.

Pie Chart A pie chart, also called a circle graph, depicts the different percentages of a total (the pie) represented by variously sized slices. Suppose you wanted to know the most popular undergraduate majors in American colleges and universities. These statistics, which are available in table format from the National Center for Education Statistics, can be quickly converted into a pie chart as

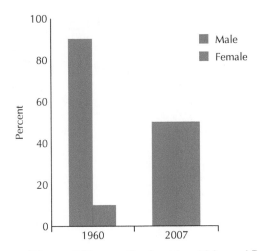

FIGURE 7 Percentage of Doctoral Degrees Conferred on Males and Females: 1960 and 2007

shown in Figure 8. As you can see, a pie chart shows at a glance how the whole of something is divided into segments. In 2007, for example, 7 percent of graduating seniors majored in education while 22 percent majored in business. The effectiveness of pie charts diminishes as you add more slices. In most cases, you begin to confuse readers if you include more than five or six slices.

Incorporating a Graphic into Your Essay

Today, most word processing programs, often integrated with a spreadsheet, easily allow you to create a graphic and insert it into your document. In some cases,

FIGURE 8 Distribution of Bachelor's Degrees by Majors, 2007

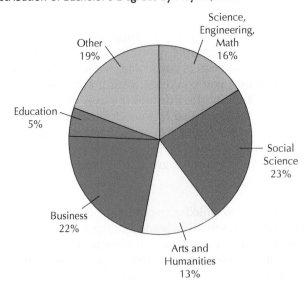

your instructor may give you permission to make a graphic with pen or pencil and paste it into your document.

Designing Your Graphic In academic manuscripts, graphics are designed conservatively without bells and whistles such as three-dimensional effects or special fonts and patterns. Keep the graphic as simple and uncluttered as possible. Also in academic manuscripts, do not wrap text around the graphic. In contrast, in popular published work, writers often use flashy fonts, three dimensions, text wrapping, and other effects that would undermine your *ethos* in an academic setting.

Numbering, Labeling, and Titling the Graphic In newspapers and popular magazines, writers often include graphics in boxes or sidebars without specifically referring to them in the text. However, in academic manuscripts or scholarly works, graphics are always labeled, numbered, titled, and referred to in the text. Tables are listed as "Tables," while line graphs, bar graphs, pie charts, or any other kinds of drawings or photographs are labeled as "Figures." By convention, the title for tables goes above the table, while the title for figures goes below.

Referencing the Graphic in Your Text Academic and professional writers follow a referencing convention called independent redundancy. The graphic should be understandable without the text; the text should be understandable without the graphic. In other words, the text should tell in words the same story that the graphic displays visually. An example is shown in Figure 9.

FIGURE 9 Example of a Student Text with a Referenced Graph

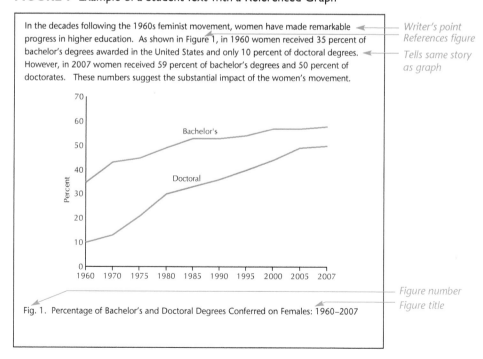

In the decades following the 1960s feminist movement, women have made remarkable ◄—— *Writer's point* ——— *References figure* progress in higher education. As shown in Figure 1, in 1960 women received 35 percent of bachelor's degrees awarded in the United States and only 10 percent of doctoral degrees. ◄—— *Tells same story as graph* However, in 2007 women received 59 percent of bachelor's degrees and 50 percent of doctorates. These numbers suggest the substantial impact of the women's movement.

Figure number
Figure title

Fig. 1. Percentage of Bachelor's and Doctoral Degrees Conferred on Females: 1960–2007

SKILL 10 Write effective conclusions.

Conclusions can best be understood as complements to introductions. In both the introduction and the conclusion, writers are concerned with the essay as a whole more than with any given part. In a conclusion, the writer attempts to bring a sense of completeness and closure to the profusion of points and particulars laid out in the body of the essay. The writer is particularly concerned with helping the reader move from the parts back to the big picture and to understand the importance or significance of the essay.

Because many writers find conclusions challenging to write, we offer six possible strategies for ending an essay.

Strategies for Concluding an Essay		
Strategies	**What to Do**	**Comments**
Simple summary conclusion	Recap what you have said.	This approach is useful in a long or complex essay or in an instructional text that focuses on concepts. However, in a short, easy-to-follow essay, a summary conclusion can be dull and even annoying to readers. A brief summary followed by a more artful concluding strategy can sometimes be effective.
Larger significance conclusion	Draw the reader's attention to the importance or the applications of your argument.	The conclusion is a good place to elaborate on the significance of your problem by showing how your proposed solution to a question leads to understanding a larger, more significant question or brings practical benefits to individuals or society. If you posed a question about values or about the interpretation of a confusing text or phenomenon, you might show how your argument could be applied to related questions, texts, or phenomena.
Proposal conclusion	Call for action.	Often used in analyses and arguments, a *proposal* conclusion states the action that needs to be taken and briefly

Strategies	What to Do	Comments
		explains its advantages over alternative actions or describes its beneficial consequences. If your paper analyzes the negative consequences of shifting from a graduated to a flat-rate income tax, your conclusion may recommend an action such as modifying or opposing the flat tax.
	Call for future study.	A *call-for-future-study* conclusion indicates what else needs to be known or resolved before a proposal can be offered. Such conclusions are especially common in scientific writing.
***Scenic* or *anecdotal* conclusion**	Use a scene or brief story to illustrate the theme without stating it explicitly.	Often used in popular writing, a scene or anecdote can help the reader experience the emotional significance of the topic. For example, a paper favoring public housing for the homeless may end by describing an itinerant homeless person collecting bottles in a park.
***Hook and return* conclusion**	Return to something mentioned at the beginning of the essay.	If the essay begins with a vivid illustration of a problem, the conclusion can return to the same scene or story but with some variation to indicate the significance of the essay.
***Delayed-thesis* conclusion**	State the thesis for the first time at the end of the essay.	This strategy is effective when you are writing about complex or divisive issues and you don't want to take a stand until you have presented all sides. The introduction of the essay merely states the problem, giving the essay an exploratory feel.

FOR WRITING AND DISCUSSION

Writing Conclusions

Choose a paper you have just written and write an alternative conclusion using one of the strategies discussed in this lesson. Then share your original and revised conclusions in groups. Have group members discuss which one they consider most effective and why.

PEARSON mycomplab For support in learning this chapter's content, follow this path in MyCompLab: Resources ⇒ Writing ⇒ Writing Process ⇒ Planning and Drafting. Review the Instruction and Multimedia resources about planning and drafting, and then complete the Exercises and click on Gradebook to measure your progress.

COMPOSING AND REVISING OPEN-FORM PROSE

Good writing is supposed to evoke sensation in the reader—not the fact that it's raining, but the feel of being rained upon.

—*E. L. Doctorow, Novelist*

Although much of this text focuses on closed-form prose, there are many kinds of good writing, and we probably all share the desire at times to write in ways other than points-first, thesis-governed prose. In our epigraph, novelist E. L. Doctorow suggests another way to think of "good writing": Writing that evokes sensations, that triggers in the reader's imagination the very feel of the rain.

In this chapter, we shift our attention to open-form writing, which, because it uses literary strategies such as story, plot, characterization, setting, and theme, is often called *literary nonfiction*. Of course, it should be remembered that writing exists on a continuum from closed to open forms and that many features of open-form prose can appear in primarily closed-form texts. In fact, many of the example essays in this book combine elements of both open and closed styles. At the extremes of the continuum, closed- and open-form writing are markedly different, but the styles can be blended in pleasing combinations.

Our goal in this chapter is to give you some practical lessons on how to write effective open-form prose. But we need to acknowledge at the outset that, whereas closed-form prose is governed by a few widely accepted conventions, one of the main features of open-form prose is its freedom to play with conventions in a bewildering variety of ways. Consequently, our discussion of open-form writing seeks more to introduce you to guiding principles rather than to treat open-form writing exhaustively.

In this chapter, you will learn these skills for open-form writing:

- **SKILL 1**   Make your narrative a story, not an *and then* chronology.
- **SKILL 2**   Write low on the ladder of abstraction.
- **SKILL 3**   Disrupt your reader's desire for direction and clarity.
- **SKILL 4**   Tap the power of figurative language.
- **SKILL 5**   Expand your repertoire of styles.
- **SKILL 6**   Use open-form elements to create "voice" in closed-form prose.

From Chapter 18 of *The Allyn & Bacon Guide to Writing*, Sixth Edition. John D. Ramage, John C. Bean, June Johnson. Copyright © 2012 by Pearson Education, Inc. Published by Pearson Allyn & Bacon. All rights reserved.

Key Features of Open-Form Prose

Writing at the closed end of the spectrum seeks to be efficient and reader-friendly. By forecasting what's coming, placing points first, and putting old information before new, closed-form writers try to convey complex ideas in as clear a way as possible, enabling readers to grasp ideas quickly. In contrast, open-form writers, by violating or simply stretching those same conventions, set up a different kind of relationship with readers. They often provide more pleasure in reading, but just as often demand more patience, more tolerance of ambiguity, and more openness to a range of meanings and nuance. They are likely to take readers backstage to share the process of their thinking. They often cast themselves in the role of narrators or characters reporting all the coincidences, disappointments, and confusion they experienced during their quest for understanding. In this process of sharing, they make readers codiscoverers of ideas and insights.

Open-form prose is also characterized by its emphasis on an aesthetic use of language—that is, language used to please and entertain. Without the benefit of a thesis or points appearing first to convey meaning, open-form prose depends on the very specificity of words—the ability of words to create mental pictures, to appeal to readers' senses and emotions, and to conjure up memories.

SKILL 1 Make your narrative a story, not an *and then* chronology.

We have said that open-form prose is narrative based and uses the strategies of a story. In this first section we want you to think more deeply about the concept of a story—particularly how a story differs from an *and then* chronology. Both a story and an *and then* chronology depict events happening in time. But there are important differences between them. In the following exercise, we'd like you to try your own hand at articulating the differences between a story and an *and then* chronology.

FOR WRITING AND DISCUSSION

And Then Chronology Versus Story

Individual task:

1. Read the student autobiographical narrative "No Cats in America?" by Patrick José.
2. Then read the following autobiographical narrative entitled "The Stolen Watch," which was submitted by a student as a draft for an assignment on narrative writing.

THE STOLEN WATCH

Last fall and winter I was living in Spokane with my brother, who during this time had a platonic girlfriend come over from Seattle and stay for a weekend. Her

---

name was Karen, and we became interested in each other and I went over to see her at the first of the year. She then invited me to, supposedly, the biggest party of the year, called the Aristocrats' Ball. I said sure and made my way back to Seattle in February. It started out bad on Friday, the day my brother and I left Spokane. We left town an hour late, but what's new. Then my brother had to stop along the way and pick up some parts; we stayed there for an hour trying to find this guy. It all started out bad because we arrived in Seattle and I forgot to call Karen. We were staying at her brother's house and after we brought all our things in, we decided to go to a few bars. Later that night we ran into Karen in one of the bars, and needless to say she was not happy with me. When I got up the next morning I knew I should have stayed in Spokane, because I felt bad vibes. Karen made it over about an hour before the party. By the time we reached the party, which drove me crazy, she wound up with another guy, so her friends and I decided to go to a few bars. The next morning when I was packing, I could not find my watch and decided that someone had to have taken it. We decided that it had to have been the goon that Karen had wound up with the night before, because she was at her brother's house with him before she went home. So how was I going to get my watch back?

We decided the direct and honest approach to the problem would work out the best. We got in contact and confronted him. This turned out to be quite a chore. It turned out that he was visiting some of his family during that weekend and lived in Little Harbor, California. It turned out that Karen knew his half brother and got some information on him, which was not pretty. He had just been released by the army and was trained in a special forces unit, in the field of Martial Arts. He was a trained killer! This information did not help matters at all, but the next bit of information was just as bad if not worse. Believe it or not, he was up on charges of attempted murder and breaking and entering. In a way, it turned out lucky for me, because he was in enough trouble with the police and did not need any more. Karen got in contact with him and threatened him that I would bring him up on charges if he did not return the watch. His mother decided that he was in enough trouble and sent me the watch. I was astounded, it was still working and looked fine. The moral of the story is don't drive 400 miles to see a girl you hardly know, and whatever you do, don't leave your valuables out in the open.

Group task: Share your responses to the following questions:

1. How does your experience of reading "No Cats in America?" differ from your experience of reading "The Stolen Watch"? Try to articulate the different ways you reacted to the two pieces while in the process of reading them.
2. Based on the differences between these two pieces, how would you define a "story"? Begin by brainstorming all the ways that the two pieces differ. Then try to identify the essential differences that make one a "story" and the other an *and then* chronology.

Now that you have tried to define a story for yourselves, we would like to explain our own four criteria for a story: (1) depiction of events through time, (2) connectedness, (3) tension, and (4) resolution. If we combine these criteria into a sentence, it would read like this: A story depicts events that are connected causally or thematically to create a sense of tension that is resolved through action, insight, or understanding. These four criteria occurring together turn a chronology into a story.

Depiction of Events through Time

The essence of storytelling is the depiction of events through time. Whereas thesis-based writing descends from problem to thesis to supporting reasons and evidence, stories unfold linearly, temporally, from event to event. You may start in the middle of the action and then jump backward and forward, but you always encounter some sequence of events happening in time. This temporal focus creates a sense of "onceness." Things that happen at a point in time happen only once, as the classic fairy-tale opening "Once upon a time" suggests. When you compose and revise a narrative, you want to try to capture the "onceness" of that experience. As the essayist E. B. White once advised a young writer, "Don't write about Man but about a man."

Consider how Val Plumwood, a professor of women's studies and author of the book *Feminism and the Mastery of Nature*, depicts the events leading up to a disturbing encounter with a crocodile. (Later in the story, the reader sees how this encounter shapes her understanding of humans' place in the food chain and the need for a respectful, rather than a dominating, attitude toward other animals.)

> In the early wet season, Kakadu's paper-bark wetlands are especially stunning, as the water lilies weave white, pink, and blue patterns of dreamlike beauty over the shining thunderclouds reflected in their still waters. Yesterday, the water lilies and the wonderful bird life had enticed me into a joyous afternoon's idyll as I ventured onto the East Alligator Lagoon for the first time in a canoe lent by the park service. "You can play about on the backwaters," the ranger had said, "but don't go onto the main river channel. The current's too swift, and if you get into trouble, there are the crocodiles. Lots of them along the river!" I followed his advice and glutted myself on the magical beauty and bird life of the lily lagoons, untroubled by crocodiles.
>
> Today, I wanted to repeat the experience despite the drizzle beginning to fall as I neared the canoe launch site. I set off on a day trip in search of an Aboriginal rock art site across the lagoon and up a side channel. The drizzle turned to a warm rain within a few hours, and the magic was lost. The birds were invisible, the water lilies were sparser, and the lagoon seemed even a little menacing. I noticed now how low the 14-foot canoe sat in the water, just a few inches of fiberglass between me and the great saurian, close relatives of the ancient dinosaurs. ...
>
> After hours of searching the maze of shallow channels in the swamp, I had not found the clear channel leading to the rock art site, as shown on the ranger's sketch map. When I pulled my canoe over in driving rain to a rock outcrop for a hasty, sodden lunch, I experienced the unfamiliar sensation of being watched. Having never been one for timidity, in philosophy or in life, I decided, rather than return defeated to my sticky trailer, to explore a clear, deep channel closer to the river I had traveled the previous day.
>
> The rain and wind grew more severe, and several times I pulled over to tip water from the canoe. The channel soon developed steep mud banks and snags. Farther on, the channel opened up and was eventually blocked by a large sandy

bar. I pushed the canoe toward the bank, looking around carefully before getting out of the shallow and pulling the canoe up. I would be safe from crocodiles in the canoe—I had been told—but swimming and standing or wading at the water's edge were dangerous. Edges are one of the crocodile's favorite food-capturing places. I saw nothing, but the feeling of unease that had been with me all day intensified.

In this example of literary nonfiction, Plumwood persuades readers to appreciate the beauties of the exotic Australian rain forest as well as its dangers. Note how her method includes the depicting of events that happen once in time—her wondrous first day of exploration, the ranger's warning to stay away from the main river, her second day's unsuccessful search by canoe for a site of Aboriginal rock art, and then her emerging discovery that in the increasing intensity of the rainstorm, she had reached the junction with the main river. Plumwood's powerful narrative becomes the basis for a profound concluding reflection on what she calls humans' "ecological identity."

Connectedness

The events of a story must also be connected, not merely spatially or sequentially, but causally or thematically. When discussing "The Stolen Watch" in the previous exercise, you might have asked yourselves, "What does all that stuff about forgetting to call Karen and stopping for parts, etc., have to do with the stolen watch? Is this story about the watch or about confronting a potential killer?" If so, you instinctively understood the concept of connectedness. Stories are more than just chronicles of events. Novelist E. M. Forster offered the simplest definition of a story when he rejected "The king dies and then the queen died," but accepted "The king died and then the queen died ... of grief." The words "of grief" connect the two events to each other in a causal relationship, converting a series of events into a patterned, meaningfully related sequence of events. Now examine this passage to see the connections the writer establishes between the scenes.

THEMATIC AND CAUSAL CONNECTEDNESS

I have been so totally erased from nature lately, like a blackboard before school starts, that yesterday when I was in the Japanese section of San Francisco, Japantown, I saw the sidewalk littered with chocolate wrappers.

There were hundreds of them. Who in the hell has been eating all these chocolates? I thought. A convention of Japanese chocolate eaters must have passed this way.

Then I noticed some plum trees on the street. Then I noticed that it was autumn. Then I noticed that the leaves were falling as they will and as they must every year. Where had I gone wrong?

—Richard Brautigan, "Leaves"

Brautigan's narrative becomes a story only when you realize that the "chocolate wrappers" are really plum leaves; the two images are connected by the writer's changed perception, which illuminates the thematic question raised at the beginning and end: Why has he become "so totally erased from nature"? As you write, connect the elements of your narrative causally and thematically.

Tension or Conflict

The third criterion for a story—tension or conflict—creates the anticipation and potential significance that keep the reader reading. In whodunit stories, the tension follows from attempts to identify the murderer or to prevent the murderer from doing in yet another victim. In many comic works, the tension is generated by confusion or misunderstanding that drives a wedge between people who would normally be close. Tension always involves contraries, such as those between one belief and another, between opposing values, between the individual and the environment or the social order, between where I am now and where I want to be or used to be. In the following passage, notice how the contraries create dramatic tension that engages readers.

DRAMATIC TENSIONS

Straddling the top of the world, one foot in China and the other in Nepal, I cleared the ice from my oxygen mask, hunched a shoulder against the wind, and stared absently down at the vastness of Tibet. I understood on some dim, detached level that the sweep of earth beneath my feet was a spectacular sight. I'd been fantasizing about this moment, and the release of emotion that would accompany it, for many months. But now that I was finally here, actually standing on the summit of Mount Everest, I just couldn't summon the energy to care.

It was early in the afternoon of May 10, 1996. I hadn't slept in fifty-seven hours. The only food I'd been able to force down over the preceding three days was a bowl of ramen soup and a handful of peanut M&M's. Weeks of violent coughing had left me with two separated ribs that made ordinary breathing an excruciating trial. At 29,028 feet up in the troposphere, so little oxygen was reaching my brain that my mental capacity was that of a slow child. Under the circumstances, I was incapable of feeling much of anything except cold and tired.

—Jon Krakauer, *Into Thin Air*

Notice how this passage presents several contraries or conflicts: the opposition between the narrator's expectation of what it would be like to stand on the top of Mount Everest and the actuality once he's there; and the opposition between the physical strength and stamina of the climber and the extreme danger of climbing this mountain. The reader wonders how Krakauer reached the summit with no sleep, almost no food, and a violent and agonizing cough; more important, the reader wonders why he kept on climbing. We can ask this important query of any narrative: What conflicts and tensions are prompting readers' ongoing questions and holding their interest?

Resolution, Recognition, or Retrospective Interpretation

The final criterion for a story is the resolution or retrospective interpretation of events. The resolution may be stated explicitly or implied. Fables typically sum up the story's significance with an explicit moral at the end. In contrast, the interpretation of events in poetry is almost always implicit. Note how the following haiku collapses events and resolution.

RESOLUTION

A strange old man
stops me,
Looking out of my deep mirror.

—Hitomaro, *One Hundred Poems from the Japanese*

In this tiny story, two things happen simultaneously. The narrator is stopped by a "strange old man" and the narrator looks into a mirror. The narrator's *recognition* is that he is that same old man. This recognition—"That's me in the mirror; when I wasn't looking, I grew old!"—in turn ties the singular event of the story back to more universal concerns and the reader's world.

The typical direction of a story, from singular event(s) to general conclusion, reverses the usual points-first direction of closed-form essays. Stories force readers to read inductively, gathering information and looking for a pattern that's confirmed or unconfirmed by the story's resolution. This resolution is the point *toward* which readers read. It often drives home the significance of the narrative. Typically, a reader's satisfaction or dissatisfaction with a story hinges on how well the resolution manages to explain or justify the events that precede it. Writers need to ask: How does my resolution grow out of my narrative and fit with the resolution the reader has been forming?

Identifying Criteria for "Story"

FOR WRITING AND DISCUSSION

1. Working as a whole class or in small groups, return to Patrick José's essay "No Cats in America?" and explain how it qualifies as a story rather than an *and then* chronology. How does it meet all four of the criteria: depiction of events through time, connectedness, tension, and resolution?
2. Consider again "The Stolen Watch." It seems to meet the criterion of "depiction of events through time," but it is weak in connectedness, tension, and resolution. How could the writer revise the chronology to make it a story? Brainstorm several different ways that this potentially exciting early draft could be rewritten.
3. If you are working on your own open-form narrative, exchange drafts with a classmate. Discuss each other's draft in light of this lesson's focus on story. To what extent do your drafts exhibit the features of a story rather than those of an *and then* chronology? Working together, develop revision plans that might increase the story elements in your narratives.

SKILL 2 Write low on the ladder of abstraction.

The concept of "ladder of abstraction" describes the way in which words can be arranged from the very abstract (living creatures, clothing) down to the very specific (our dog Charley with the floppy ears; my hippie Birkenstocks with the saltwater stains). In this lesson we show why and how open-form writers stay low on the ladder of abstraction through their use of concrete words, revelatory words, and memory-soaked words.

Concrete Words Evoke Images and Sensations

To appreciate the impact of specific, concrete language, look again at the opening sentence of Val Plumwood's narrative about her encounter with crocodiles:

> In the early wet season, Kakadu's paper-bark wetlands are especially stunning, as the water lilies weave white, pink, and blue patterns of dreamlike beauty over the shining thunderclouds reflected in their still waters.

Here is how that same passage might sound if rewritten a level higher on the ladder of abstraction:

> In the early wet season the Kakadu landscape is especially stunning, as the water plants weave their colorful patterns of dreamlike beauty over the clouds reflected in the water's surface.

This is still quite a nice sentence. But something is lost when you say "landscape" rather than "paper-bark wetlands," "clouds" rather than "thunderclouds," or "colorful" rather than "white, pink, and blue." The lower you write on the ladder of abstraction, the more you tap into your readers' storehouse of particular memories and images.

The power of concrete words has been analyzed by writer John McPhee in a widely quoted and cited interview. When asked why he wrote the sentence "Old white oaks are rare because they had a tendency to become bowsprits, barrel staves, and queen-post trusses" instead of a more generic sentence such as, "Old white oaks are rare because they were used as lumber," he responded in a way that reveals his love of the particular:

> There isn't much life in [the alternative version of the sentence]. If you can find a specific, firm, and correct image, it's always going to be better than a generality, and hence I tend, for example, to put in trade names and company names and, in an instance like this, the names of wood products instead of a general term like "lumber." You'd say "Sony" instead of "tape recorder" if the context made it clear you meant to say tape recorder. It's not because you're on the take from Sony, it's because the image, at least to this writer or reader, strikes a clearer note.

Some readers might complain that the particulars "bowsprits, barrel staves, and queen-post trusses" don't help readers' understanding, as do particulars in closed-form prose, but instead give most readers a moment's pause. Today most barrel staves and bowsprits are made of metal, not oak, and few contemporary readers encounter them on a regular basis no matter what they're made of. Furthermore, few readers at any time could readily identify "queen-post trusses," a technical term from the building trade. Instead of smoothly completing the reader's understanding of a point, McPhee's particulars tend to arrest and even sidetrack, sending the reader in pursuit of a dictionary.

But if McPhee's examples momentarily puzzle, it's the sort of puzzlement that can lead to greater understanding. Precisely because they are exotic terms, these words arouse the reader's curiosity and imagination. "Exotic language is of value," says McPhee. "A queen-post truss is great just because of the sound of the words and what they call to mind. The 'queen,' the 'truss'—the ramifications in everything."

For McPhee, the fact that these words trip up the reader is a point in their favor. If McPhee had said that old white oaks are rare these days because they became parts of "ships, barrels, and roofs," no one would blink or notice. If you were to visualize the items, you'd probably call up some ready-made pictures that leave little trace in your mind. You also wouldn't hear the sounds of the words. (In this regard, notice McPhee's emphasis on images sounding "a clearer note.") Your forward progress toward the point would be unimpeded, but what would be lost? A new glimpse into a lost time when oak trees were used to make exotic items that today exist mostly in old books and memories.

Another quality also recommends words that readers trip over, words such as *bowsprit, barrel stave,* and *queen-post truss:* their power to persuade the reader to believe in the world being described. Tripping over things, whether they're made of steel or words, forces the reader to acknowledge their independence, the reality of a world outside the reader's own head. For this reason, writers of formula fiction—thrillers, westerns, romances, and the like—will load their texts with lots of little details and bits of technical information from the time and place they describe. Because their stories are otherwise implausible (e.g., the description of the Evil Empire's doomsday machine), they need all the help they can get from their details (the size of the toggle bolts used to keep the machine in place while it's blasting out intergalactic death rays) to convince readers that the story is real.

Using Revelatory Words and Memory-Soaked Words

As we have seen, concrete language, low on the ladder of abstraction, can evoke imaginative experiences for readers. Two particularly powerful kinds of concrete language are revelatory words and memory-soaked words. By *revelatory* words we mean specific details that reveal the social status, lifestyle, beliefs, and values of people. According to writer Tom Wolfe, carefully chosen details can reveal a person's *status life*—"the entire pattern of behavior and possessions through which people express their position in the world or what they think it is or hope it to be." Wolfe favors writing that records "everyday gestures, habits, manners, customs, styles of furniture, clothing, decoration, styles of traveling, eating, keeping house, modes of behaving toward children, servants, superiors, inferiors, peers, plus the various looks, glances, poses, styles of walking and other symbolic details that might exist within a scene." Thus subtle differences in a person's status life might be revealed in details about fast food (a Big Mac versus a Subway turkey wrap), body piercing (pierced ears versus pierced tongue), a watch (a Timex versus a Rolex), or music (Kenny Chesney versus Busta Rhymes).

Another way to create powerful concrete language is through *memory-soaked* words. Such words trigger a whole complex of ideas, emotions, and sensations in readers who share memories from a particular era. People who grew up in the 1950s, for example, might have deep associations with 45-rpm records, the *Ed Sullivan Show,* or the words "duck tail" or "tail fins." For Vietnam veterans, Nancy

Sinatra's "These Boots Were Made for Walking" or the whirr of helicopter blades might evoke strong memories. Persons growing up in the 1970s or 1980s might remember "Cookie Monster," "Pez guns," or 8-track tapes. In recent years, our students have come up with these memory-soaked words from their own childhoods: American Girl dolls, Power Rangers, Ghostbuster action figures, Super Nintendo, Pokeman, *American Idol,* and The Sims.

FOR
WRITING
AND
DISCUSSION

Working Low on the Ladder of Abstraction

1. Working in small groups or as a whole class, try your own hand at using revelatory words to reveal status life. Create a list of specific details that you might associate with each of the following: middle school girls at a slumber party; friends at a tailgate party before a football game; the kitchen of an upscale urban apartment of a two-profession couple who subscribe to *Gourmet* magazine; the kitchen of a middle-class, middle America family with three kids and a collection of *Good Housekeeping* magazines; the kitchen of an apartment shared by college students. (If you are describing kitchens, for example, consider the different *status life* signaled by ketchup versus stone-ground mustard or by an iceberg lettuce salad with ranch dressing versus an almond mandarin salad.)

2. Also try your hand at finding memory-soaked words. Make a list of specific words and names associated with your childhood that you now rarely hear or see. Share your list with others in your group and identify the items that have the strongest associations.

3. If you are working on your own open-form narrative, exchange drafts with a classmate and, working together, find specific examples where each of you has successfully used concrete, revelatory, or memory-soaked words. Then find passages that could be profitably revised by moving down a rung on the ladder of abstraction or by adding concrete details that follow the advice in this lesson.

SKILL 3 Disrupt your reader's desire for direction and clarity.

The epigraph by the philosopher Kenneth Burke speaks about form as "an arousing and fulfillment of desires." In closed-form prose, we can easily see this process at work: The writer previews what he or she is going to say, arousing the reader's desire to see the general outline fleshed out with specifics, and then fulfills that desire speedily through a presentation of pertinent points and particulars.

In more open-form prose, the fulfillment of desire follows a less straightforward path. Writers offer fewer overviews and clues, leaving readers less sure of where they're headed; or writers mention an idea and then put it aside for a while as they pursue some other point whose relevance may seem tenuous to the reader. Rather than establish the direction or point of their prose, writers suspend that direction, waiting until later in the prose to show how the ideas are meaningfully related. In other words, the period of arousal is longer and more drawn out; the fulfillment of desire is delayed until the end, when the reader finally sees how the pieces fit together.

Open-form prose gives you the opportunity to overlay your narrative core with other patterns of ideas—to move associatively from idea to idea, to weave a complex pattern of meaning in which the complete picture emerges later. Often the way you achieve these surprising twists and turns of structure and meaning is by playing with the conventions of closed-form prose. For example, in the autobiographical narrative "No Cats in America?", Patrick José breaks the cardinal closed-form rule that titles should forecast the essay's thesis: If José's essay were closed form, it should be about some kind of surprising decline of cats in America. However, José's title is metaphoric, and the reader doesn't completely comprehend its significance until the last lines of the essay. This delaying of meaning—requiring the reader to help cocreate the meaning—is typical of open-form prose. Here in this section we describe some of your open-form options for surprising your readers and delaying their fulfillment of desires.

Disrupting Predictions and Making Odd Juxtapositions

Open-form writers frequently violate the principle of forecasting and mapping. Consider the following introduction to an essay:

PASSAGE WITH DISRUPTED PREDICTIONS AND ODD JUXTAPOSITIONS

I suppose their little bones have years ago been lost among the stones and winds of those high glacial pastures. I suppose their feathers blew eventually into the piles of tumbleweed beneath the straggling cattle fences and rotted there in the mountain snows, along with dead steers and all the other things that drift to an end in the corners of the wire. I do not quite know why I should be thinking of birds over the *New York Times* at breakfast, particularly the birds of my youth half a continent away. It is a funny thing what the brain will do with memories and how it will treasure them and finally bring them into odd juxtapositions with other things, as though it wanted to make a design, or get some meaning out of them, whether you want it or not, or even see it.

Whose bones? What feathers?

Birds? What birds?

What do birds have to do with how the brain works? Where is this writer going?

—Loren Eisley, "The Bird and the Machine"

Note the sequence of ideas from bones to birds to breakfast over the *New York Times* to comments about the workings of the brain. In fact, in this essay it takes Eisley six full paragraphs in which he discusses mechanical inventions to return to the birds with the line: "... or those birds, I'll never forget those birds. ... "

Throughout these paragraphs, what drives the reader forward is curiosity to discover the connections between the parts and to understand the meaning of the essay's title, "The Bird and the Machine." Actually, Eisley's comment about the brain's "odd juxtapositions" of memories with "other things, as though it wanted to make a design, or get some meaning out of them" could be a description of this open-form technique we've called "disrupting predictions and making odd juxtapositions." Open-form writers can choose when "odd juxtapositions" are an appropriate strategy for inviting the reader to accompany the discovering, reflecting writer on a journey toward meaning.

Leaving Gaps

An important convention of closed-form prose is the old/new contract, which specifies that the opening of every sentence should link in some way to what has gone before. Open-form prose often violates this convention, leaving *gaps* in the text, forcing the reader to puzzle over the connection between one part and the next.

The following passage clearly violates the old/new contract. This example recounts the writer's thoughts after startling a weasel in the woods and exchanging glances with it.

Gap caused by unexplained or unpredicted shift from weasel to philosophic musing

What goes on in [a weasel's brain] the rest of the time? What does a weasel think about? He won't say. His journal is tracks in clay, a spray of feathers, mouse blood and bone: uncollected, unconnected, loose-leaf, and blown.

I would like to learn, or remember, how to live. I come to Hollins Pond not so much to learn how to live as, frankly, to forget about it.

—Annie Dillard, "Living Like Weasels"

Dillard suddenly switches, without transition, from musing about the mental life of a weasel to asserting that she would like to learn how to live. What is the connection between her encounter with the weasel and her own search for how to live? Dillard's open-form techniques leave these gaps for readers to ponder and fill in, inviting us to participate in the process of arriving at meaning. Just as open-form writers can deliberately avoid predicting or mapping statements, they also have the liberty to leave gaps in a text when it suits their purpose.

Disrupting Reader Expectations

If you are currently working on an open-form narrative, exchange drafts with a classmate. Discuss in what way the strategies explained in this lesson might be appropriate for your purposes. Where might you currently "explain too much" and benefit by juxtaposing scenes without explanatory filler? Where might you use other strategies from this lesson?

SKILL 4 Tap the power of figurative language.

Open-form writers often use figurative language in situations in which closed-form writers would use literal language. In this brief section, we show you some of the power of figurative language.

When journalist Nicholas Tomalin describes a captured Vietnamese prisoner as young and slight, the reader understands him in a literal way, but when, a moment later, he compares the prisoner to "a tiny, fine-boned wild animal," the reader understands him in a different way; the reader understands not only what the subject looks like—his general physical attributes—but how that particular boy appears in that moment to those around him—fierce, frightened, trapped.

Metaphors abound when literal words fail. When writers encounter eccentric people or are overwhelmed by the strangeness of their experiences, they use *figurative language*—imaginative comparisons—to explain their situation and their reactions to it. Figurative language—similes, metaphors, and personifications—enables the writer to describe an unfamiliar thing in terms of different, more familiar things. The surprise of yoking two very unlike things evokes from the reader a perception, insight, or emotional experience that could not otherwise be communicated. The originality and vividness of the imaginative comparison frequently resonates with meaning for readers and sticks in their minds long afterward.

In the following passage, Isak Dinesen describes an experience that most of us have not had—seeing iguanas in the jungle and shooting one. After reading this passage, however, we have a striking picture in our minds of what she saw and a strong understanding of what she felt and realized.

PASSAGE USING FIGURATIVE LANGUAGE

In the Reserve I have sometimes come upon the Iguana, the big lizards, as they were sunning themselves upon a flat stone in a riverbed. They are not pretty in shape, but nothing can be imagined more beautiful than their coloring. They shine like a heap of precious stones or like a pane cut out of an old church window. When, as you approach, they swish away, there is a flash of azure, green and purple over the stones, the color seems to be standing behind them in the air, like a comet's luminous tail. *(Similes heaped up)* *(Simile)*

Once I shot an Iguana. I thought that I should be able to make some pretty things from his skin. A strange thing happened then, that I have never afterwards forgotten. As I went up to him, where he was lying dead upon his stone, and actually while I was walking a few steps, he faded and grew pale, all color died out of him as in one long sigh, and by the time that I touched him he was gray and dull like a lump of concrete. It was the live impetuous blood pulsating within the animal, which had radiated out all that glow and splendor. Now that the flame was put out, and the soul had flown, the Iguana was as dead as a sandbag. *(Metaphor of dying applied to color)* *(Simile)* *(Metaphor)* *(Simile)*

—Isak Dinesen, "The Iguana"

The figurative language in this passage enables readers to share Dinesen's experience. It also compacts a large amount of information into sharp, memorable images.

Using Figurative Language

FOR WRITING AND DISCUSSION

1. Figurative language can fall flat when it takes the form of clichés ("I stood transfixed like a bump on a log") or mixed metaphors ("Exposed like a caterpillar on a leaf, he wolfed down his lunch before taking flight"). But when used effectively, figurative language adds powerfully compressed and meaningful images to a passage. Working individually or in small groups, find examples of figurative language in one or more of the example

passages in this chapter. See if you can reach consensus on what makes a particular instance of figurative language effective or ineffective.

2. If you are currently working on an open-form narrative, exchange drafts with a classmate. See if you can find instances of figurative language in your current drafts and analyze their effectiveness. Perhaps you can also discover places where figurative language could be profitably added to the text.

SKILL 5 Expand your repertoire of styles.

Style is a combination of sentence structure, word choice, and rhythm that allows writers to vary their emphasis and tone in a variety of ways. In this section, we show you how to expand your repertoire of styles through a classic method of teaching in which you try to imitate other writers' styles. This rhetorical practice—called "creative imitation"—has a long history beginning with the rhetoricians of classical Greece and Rome. When you do creative imitation, you examine a passage from an expert stylist and try to emulate it. You substitute your own subject matter, but you try to imitate the exact grammatical structures, lengths and rhythms of the sentences, and the tones of the original passage. The long-range effect of creative imitation is to expand your stylistic choices; the more immediate effect is to increase your skill at analyzing a writer's style. Most practitioners find that creative imitation encourages surprising insights into their own subject matter (when seen through the lens of the original writer's style) as well as a new understanding of how a particular piece of writing creates its special effects.

You begin a creative imitation by asking questions such as these: What is distinctive about the sentences in this passage of writing? How do choices about sentence length and complexity, kinds of words, figures of speech, and so forth create a writer's voice? After close examination of the passage, you then think of your own subject matter that could be appropriately adapted to this writer's style.

To help you understand creative imitation, we provide the following example. In this passage, the writer, Victoria Register-Freeman, is exploring how relations between young men and women today threaten to undo some of the twentieth century's progress toward gender equality. In the section of her article that precedes this passage, Register-Freeman explains how she, as a single mother, taught her boys to cook, sew, do laundry, and "carry their weight domestically." But then, as she explains in this passage, teenage girls undid her attempts at creating gender equality:

REGISTER-FREEMAN PASSAGE

Then came puberty and hunkhood. Over the last few years, the boys' domestic skills have atrophied because handmaidens have appeared en masse. The damsels have driven by, beeped, phoned and faxed. Some appeared so frequently outside the front door they began to remind me of the suction-footed Garfields spread-eagled on car windows. While the girls varied according to height, hair color and basic body type, they shared one characteristic. They were ever eager to help the guys out.

—Victoria Register-Freeman, "My Turn: Hunks and Handmaidens"

Register-Freeman's voice projects the image of a concerned mother and feminist social critic. Her tone includes a range of attitudes: serious, personal, factual, ironic, frustrated. Note how this passage begins and ends with short, clipped sentences. The second sentence states a problem that the next three sentences develop with various kinds of details. The third sentence includes a series of colorful verbs; the fourth uses a metaphor (the ever-present girls compared to Garfields on car windows). The fifth sentence builds to the point in the sixth sentence, which is delivered bluntly and simply.

Here is one writer's attempt at a creative imitation:

CREATIVE IMITATION OF REGISTER-FREEMAN

Then came prosperity and popularity. Over the last ten years, Seattle's special charms have faded because expansion has occurred too rapidly. Traffic has multiplied, thickened, amplified, and slowed. Traffic jams appeared so often on the freeways and arterials they began to remind me of ants swarming over spilled syrup. While the congestion varied according to time, seasons, and weather conditions, it had one dominant effect. It increasingly threatened to spoil the city's beauty.

Practicing Style through Creative Imitation

FOR WRITING AND DISCUSSION

1. Do your own creative imitation of the passage from Register-Freeman.
2. Choose one or both of the following passages for creative imitation. Begin by jotting down all the specific observations you can make about the stylistic features of the passage. Then choose a topic that matches the topic of the original in its degree of lightness or seriousness and its depth. Explore your topic by presenting it using the sentence structures and kinds of words used in the original. Try to imitate the original phrase by phrase and sentence by sentence. You may find it helpful to use a dictionary and thesaurus.
   a. Africa is mystic; it is wild; it is a sweltering inferno; it is a photographer's paradise, a hunter's Valhalla, an escapist's Utopia. It is what you will, and it withstands all interpretations. It is the last vestige of a dead world or the cradle of a shiny new one. To a lot of people, as to myself, it is just "home." It is all of these things but one thing—it is never dull.

      —Beryl Markham, "Flying Elsewhere," *West with the Night*

   b. The disease was bubonic plague, present in two forms: one that infected the bloodstream, causing the buboes and internal bleeding, and was spread by contact; and a second, more virulent pneumonic type that infected the lungs and was spread by respiratory infection. The presence of both at once caused the high mortality and speed of contagion. So lethal was the disease that cases were known of persons going to bed well and dying before they woke, of doctors catching the illness at bedside and dying before the patient.

      —Barbara Tuchman, "This Is the End of the World," *A Distant Mirror*

SKILL 6 Use open-form elements to create "voice" in closed-form prose.

So far we have been talking about features of open-form prose in its purer forms. Sometimes, however, writers wish simply to loosen basically closed-form prose by combining it with some features of open-form prose. If, for example, an academic wanted to share new developments in a field with a popular audience, he or she would be well-advised to leaven his or her prose with some elements of open-form writing. In this final section, we offer several pieces of advice for loosening up closed-form prose.

Introducing Some Humor

Humor is rare in tightly closed prose because humor is nonfunctional—it doesn't *have* to be there for a writer to make a point—and closed-form prose values efficiency, saying what you have to say in the most economical fashion.

Humor is particularly valuable in that it can make imposing subjects more manageable for readers. Formal, abstract language can put readers off, estranging them from the subject; humor has the power to "de-strange" a subject, to allow the audience to look at it long enough to understand it. Many popular books on science and many of the best instructional books on car repair, cooking, money management, and others of life's drearier necessities use a humorous style to help their phobic readers get on with life.

To appreciate the effect of humor, consider the following passages from two different instructional books on how to operate the database program Paradox. The first passage, from *Windows in 21 Days*, uses a clear, humor-free, closed-form style.

> In this book, you learn by following detailed step-by-step exercises based on real-world problems in database application design. Every exercise leads you further into the power of "Paradox for Windows" as you develop the components of an automated application. This section does the following: explains the assumptions and conventions used in this book; lists the hardware and software requirements and setup needed to run Paradox for Windows and use this book efficiently; and offers some suggestions for strategies to get the most from this book. The step-by-step exercises make it easy.

Now note the different effect produced by the following passage from one of the hugely popular *For Dummies* books:

> Welcome to *Paradox for Windows for Dummies*, a book that's not afraid to ask the tough questions like "When's lunch?" and "Who finished the cookie dough ice cream?" If you're more interested in food (or Australian Wombats, for that matter) than you are in Paradox for Windows, this book is for you. If you're more interested in Paradox for Windows, please get some professional help before going out into society again.
>
> My goal is to help you get things done despite the fact that you're using Paradox. Whether you're at home, in your office, or at home in your office (or even if you just *feel* like you live at work) *Paradox for Windows for Dummies* is your all-in-one guidebook through the treacherous, frustrating, and appallingly technical world of the relational database.

Thinking about Humor

1. Which of these two instructional books would you prefer to read?
2. The second passage says that the world of relational databases is "treacherous, frustrating, and appallingly technical," whereas the first stresses that the "step-by-step exercises [in the book] make it easy." Why do you suppose the humorous passage stresses the difficulty of databases whereas the humorless passage stresses the ease of a step-by-step approach? Is it good strategy for the humorous writer to stress the difficulty of Paradox?
3. Under what rhetorical circumstances are humorous instructions better than strictly serious instructions? When is a strictly serious approach better?

Using Techniques from Popular Magazines

Writers who publish regularly for popular audiences develop a vigorous, easy-reading style that differs from the style of much academic writing. The effect of this difference is illustrated by the results of a famous research study conducted by Michael Graves and Wayne Slater at the University of Michigan. For this study, teams of writers revised passages from a high school history textbook.* One team consisted of linguists and technical writers trained in producing closed-form texts using the strategies of forecasting structure, putting points first, following the old/new contract and using transitions. A second team consisted of two *Time-Life* book editors.

Whereas the linguists aimed at making the passages clearer, the *Time-Life* writers were more concerned with making them livelier. The result? One hundred eleventh-grade students found the *Time-Life* editors' version both more comprehensible and more memorable. The problem with the original textbook wasn't lack of clarity but rather dryness. According to the researchers, the *Time-Life* editors did not limit themselves

> to making the passages lucid, well-organized, coherent, and easy to read. Their revisions went beyond such matters and were intended to make the texts interesting, exciting, vivid, rich in human drama, and filled with colorful language.

To see how they achieved this effect, let's look at their revision. Here is a passage about the Vietnam War taken from the original history text:

ORIGINAL HISTORY TEXT

> The most serious threat to world peace developed in Southeast Asia. Communist guerrillas threatened the independence of the countries carved out of French Indo-China by the Geneva conference of 1954. In South Vietnam, Communist guerrillas (the Viet Cong) were aided by forces from Communist North Vietnam in a struggle to overthrow the American-supported government. ...

*The study involved three teams, but for purposes of simplification we limit our discussion to two.

671

Shortly after the election of 1964, Communist gains prompted President Johnson to alter his policy concerning Vietnam. American military forces in Vietnam were increased from about 20,000 men in 1964 to more than 500,000 by 1968. Even so, North Vietnamese troops and supplies continued to pour into South Vietnam.

Here is the *Time-Life* editors' revision:

HISTORY PRESENTED IN POPULAR MAGAZINE STYLE

In the early 1960s the greatest threat to world peace was just a small splotch of color on Kennedy's map, one of the fledgling nations sculpted out of French Indo-China by the Geneva peacemakers of 1954. It was a country so tiny and remote that most Americans had never uttered its name: South Vietnam. ...

Aided by Communist North Vietnam, the Viet Cong guerrillas were eroding the ground beneath South Vietnam's American-backed government. Village by village, road by road, these jungle-wise rebels were waging a war of ambush and mining: They darted out of tunnels to head off patrols, buried exploding booby traps beneath the mud floors of huts, and hid razor-sharp bamboo sticks in holes. ...

No sooner had Johnson won the election than Communist gains prompted Johnson to go back on his campaign promise. The number of American soldiers in Vietnam skyrocketed from 20,000 in 1964 to more than 500,000 by 1968. But in spite of GI patrols, leech-infested jungles, swarms of buzzing insects, and flash floods that made men cling to trees to escape being washed away— North Vietnamese troops streamed southward without letup along the Ho Chi Minh Trail.

What can this revision teach you about invigorating closed-form prose? What specifically are the editors doing here?

First, notice how far the level of abstraction drops in the revision. The original is barren of sensory words; the revision is alive with them ("South Vietnam" becomes a "small splotch of color on Kennedy's map"; "a struggle to overthrow the American-supported government" becomes "[They] buried exploding booby traps beneath the mud floors of huts, and hid razor-sharp bamboo sticks in holes").

Second, notice how much more dramatic the revision is. Actual scenes, including a vision of men clinging to trees to escape being washed away by flash floods, replace a chronological account of the war's general progress. According to the editors, such scenes, or "nuggets"—vivid events that encapsulate complex processes or principles—are the lifeblood of *Time-Life* prose.

Finally, notice how the revision tends to delay critical information for dramatic effect, moving information you would normally expect to find early on into a later position. In the first paragraph, the *Time-Life* writers talk about "the greatest threat to world peace" in the early 1960s for four lines before revealing the identity of that threat—South Vietnam.

Enlivening Closed-Form Prose with Open-Form Elements

Here is a passage from a student argument opposing women's serving on submarines. Working individually or in small groups, enliven this passage by using some of the techniques of the *Time-Life* writers.

> Not only would it be very expensive to refit submarines for women personnel, but having women on submarines would hurt the morale of the sailors. In order for a crew to work effectively, they must have good morale or their discontent begins to show through in their performance. This is especially crucial on submarines, where if any problem occurs, it affects the safety of the whole ship. Women would hurt morale by creating sexual tension. Sexual tension can take many forms. One form is couples' working and living in a close space with all of the crew. When a problem occurs within the relationship, it could affect the morale of those directly involved and in the workplace. This would create an environment that is not conducive to good productivity. Tension would also occur if one of the women became pregnant or if there were complaints of sexual harassment. It would be easier to deal with these problems on a surface ship, but in the small confines of a submarine these problems would cause more trouble.

 For additional help with writing, go to **www.mycomplab.com.**

ASKING QUESTIONS, FINDING SOURCES

ur goal is to explain the skills you'll need for successful college-level research papers. In this chapter, we help you start on the right track as a college researcher.

In this chapter, you will learn these skills:

- **SKILL 1**   Argue your own thesis in response to a research question.
- **SKILL 2**   Understand differences among kinds of sources.
- **SKILL 3**   Use purposeful strategies for searching libraries, databases, and Web sites.

An Overview of Research Writing

Although the research paper is a common writing assignment in college, students are often baffled by their professor's expectations. Many students think of research writing as finding information on a topic or as finding quotations to support a thesis rather than as wrestling with a question or problem. One of our colleagues calls these sorts of papers "data dumps": The student dumps a bucket of data on the professor's desk and says, "Here's what I found out about sweatshops, Professor Jones. Enjoy!" Another colleague calls papers full of long quotations "choo-choo train papers": big boxcars of indented block quotations coupled with little patches of a student's own writing.

Characteristics of a Good Research Paper

But a research paper shouldn't be a data dump or a train of boxcar quotations. Instead, it should follow these principles of writing:

- A research paper should pose an interesting and significant problem.
- A research paper should respond to the problem with a contestable thesis.
- In a research paper, sources should be used purposefully and ethically.

An Effective Approach to Research

How does a writer develop a research paper with these characteristics? Early on, your goal is to develop a research question and, through your research process, to begin "wallowing in complexity." You become immersed in alternative points of view, clashing values, different kinds of evidence (often conflicting), and unresolved questions arising from gaps in current knowledge. Relying on your own critical thinking, you eventually refine your research question and begin to formulate your own thesis. In your completed research paper, some of your sources provide background information, others supply supporting evidence, and still others present alternative points of view that you are pushing against. Throughout, your research data should come from credible sources that are documented in a formal, academic style.

The Role of Documentation in College Research

Much of the writing you encounter in popular magazines or online journalism has the characteristics of a research paper—a thesis and support—but not the documentation that college professors expect. By **documentation**, we mean the in-text citations and accompanying bibliography that allow readers to identify and locate your sources for themselves. Such documentation makes all the difference because new knowledge is inevitably built on the work of others. In academic culture, authors who hope to gain acceptance for new findings and ideas must explain the roots of their work as well as show how they reached their conclusions. By documenting their sources according to appropriate conventions, research writers establish a credible *ethos* and provide a valuable resource for others who wish to locate the same sources.

Many of the writing projects in this text invite your use of research sources. As you study this material, keep in mind your twofold purpose in reading research sources:

1. To develop your own answer to your research question (your thesis) by bringing your critical thinking to bear on your research sources
2. To position yourself in a conversation with others who have addressed the same question

Throughout, you need to use your research sources responsibly in order to avoid plagiarism and to present yourself as an ethical apprentice scholar joining the academic community. As you begin your research project, make sure that you know your institution's and your teachers' policies on plagiarism and academic honesty.

SKILL 1 Argue your own thesis in response to a research question.

The best way to produce effective, engaged, and ethically responsible research papers is to begin with a good research question. A good question keeps you in charge of your writing. It reminds you that your task is to forge an answer to this question yourself, in your own voice, through your own critical thinking. This approach helps you avoid the wrong paths of data dumping, strung-together quotations, and uncertainties about why and how you are using sources.

Topic Focus Versus Question Focus

To see the difference between a topic focus and a problem focus, suppose a friend asks you what your research paper is about. Consider differences in the following responses:

> Topic Focus: I am doing a paper on eating disorders.
> Question Focus: I'm trying to sort out what the experts say is the best way to treat severe anorexia nervosa. Is inpatient or outpatient treatment more effective?

> Topic Focus: I am doing my paper on gender-specific toys for children.
> Question Focus: I am puzzled about some of the effects of gender-specific toys. Do boys' toys, such as video games, toy weapons, and construction sets, develop intellectual and physical skills more than girls' toys do?

As these scenarios suggest, a topic focus invites you to collect information without a clear purpose—a sure road toward data dumping. In contrast, a question focus requires you to be a critical thinker who must assess and weigh data and understand multiple points of view. A topic focus encourages passive collection of information. A question focus encourages active construction of meaning. The more active your thinking, the more likely you will write in your own voice with no worries about purposeless uses of sources or possible plagiarism.

Formulating a Research Question

How do you arrive at a research question? Good research questions can emerge from puzzles that you pose for yourself or from controversial questions already "out there" that are being actively debated by others. In most cases your initial research question will evolve as you do your research. You may make it broader or narrower, or refocus it on a newly discovered aspect of your original problem.

You can test the initial feasibility of your research question by considering the following prompts:

- Are you personally interested in this question?
- Is the question both problematic and significant?
- Is the question limited enough for the intended length of your paper?
- Is there a reasonable possibility of finding information on this question based on the time and resources you have available?
- Is the question appropriate for your level of expertise?

Establishing Your Role as a Researcher

After you have formulated your research question, you need to consider the possible roles you might play as a researcher. Your role is connected to the aim or purpose of your paper—to explore, to inform, to analyze, or to persuade. To appreciate your options, consider the following strategies based on typical roles researchers can play:

Strategies for Establishing Your Role as a Researcher		
Aims and Roles	**What to Do**	**Examples of Research Questions**
Reporter of information that fills a knowledge gap	Find, synthesize, and report data related to an information question.	• How do Japan and France dispose of nuclear waste from nuclear power plants? • What attitude do elementary math teachers have toward the University of Chicago's *Everyday Math* curriculum?
Reporter of the current best thinking on a problem	Research the current thinking of experts on some important problem and report what the experts think.	• What are the views of experts on the causes of homosexuality? • What do researchers consider the possible dangers of online social networks?
Conductor of original field research in response to an empirical question	Pose a problem that requires field research, conduct the research, and present results in a scientific report. Often, include a "review of the literature" section.	• To what extent do pictures of party drinking appear on our students' Facebook profiles? • How do the study habits of humanities majors differ from those of science and engineering majors?
Reviewer of a controversy (primarily an informative aim)	Investigate and report differing arguments on various sides of a controversy.	• What are the arguments for and against granting amnesty and eventual U.S. citizenship to illegal immigrants? • What policy approaches have been proposed to the U.S. government for increasing fuel economy of automobiles?

Aims and Roles	What to Do	Examples of Research Questions
Advocate for a position in a controversy (primarily an analytic and persuasive aim)	Assert a position using research data for background, for support, or for alternative views.	• Should the United States grant amnesty and eventual citizenship to illegal immigrants? (Writer argues yes or no.) • What is the best way for the U.S. government to ensure that cars achieve higher fuel economy? (Writer argues for a specific approach.)
Analyzer of an interpretive or evaluative question who also positions himself or herself within a critical conversation	Do your own original analysis of a text, phenomenon, or data source, but also relate your views to what others have said about the same or similar questions.	• To what extent does the film *Avatar* present a Christian worldview? • How effective is microlending at alleviating poverty in third world countries?

Using Research Roles to Generate Research Questions

FOR WRITING AND DISCUSSION

Working individually or in small groups, develop research questions on a general topic such as music, health, sports, use of fossil fuels, a literary work, or some other topic specified by your instructor. Develop research questions that would be appropriate for each of the following roles:

1. Reporter of information to fill a knowledge gap
2. Reporter of the current best thinking of experts on a problem
3. Original field or laboratory researcher
4. Reviewer of a controversy
5. Advocate in a controversy
6. Critical thinker about an interpretive or evaluatve question in conversation with other thinkers
7. Miscellaneous (good questions that don't fit neatly into any of these other roles)

A Case Study: James Gardiner's Research on Online Social Networks

To illustrate how a student writer poses a research question and argues his own thesis, let's return to James Gardiner's investigation of online social networks (OSNs).

James's original problem was his uncertainty about why OSNs are so popular and why he himself had chosen not to have a Facebook profile. In his original freewrite, he said, "I am a little hesitant to display personal information about myself on a website that can be viewed by anyone in the world." He also was afraid that joining an OSN would take up too much time.

Later in the course he decided to investigate OSNs for a major research project. As he began reading articles about OSNs, he noted that many researchers were highly favorable of OSNs, arguing that they provide new ways for teenagers to maintain relationships with friends, to explore their own self-images, and to practice constructing online identities. However, James remained somewhat skeptical of OSNs and, late in his initial research, he encountered the term "Facebook trance" and located an article on Internet addictions. He became more and more interested in exploring the negative aspects of OSNs. At the conclusion of his exploratory essay, James sums up the direction he would like to move in further research:

> As I continue with my research, I am not sure what thesis I will assert for my final project. I still want to do more research on the negative effects of OSNs. For example, I haven't found studies that explore the possible phoniness of Facebook relationships. I remember a passage from Copeland where one user labels Facebook interaction as "communication lean." According to this student, "It's all a little fake—the 'friends'; the profiles that can be tailored to what others find appealing; the 'groups' that exist only in cyberspace." I'm still thinking about that quotation. Do OSNs contribute to deeper, more meaningful relationships or do they promote a superficial phoniness? I hope to explore this issue further before writing my major paper.

James's exploratory research gave him a solid background on OSNs, enabling him to bring his own critical thinking to bear on his research sources. In order to convert his exploratory narrative into a closed-form research paper, he eventually created a thesis statement focused on potential dangers of OSNs.

FOR WRITING AND DISCUSSION

Following James Gardiner's Research Process

Working individually, read James's exploratory paper and his final research paper. Then, working in small groups or as a whole class, try to reach consensus answers to the following questions:

1. Trace the steps in James's thinking from the time he first becomes interested in OSNs until he finally settles on their possible negative effects. What were the key moments that shaped his thinking? How did his thinking evolve?
2. We have used James's story as an example of a student in charge of his own writing. Where do you see James doing active critical thinking? Where do you see instances of what we have called "rhetorical reading"—that is, places where James asks questions about an author's purpose, angle of vision, and selection of evidence?
3. How is James's final paper different from a data dump or a choo-choo train paper? How does it demonstrate ethical use of sources?

SKILL 2 **Understand differences among kinds of sources.**

To be an effective researcher, you need to understand the differences among the many kinds of sources that you might use while doing your research. These can be classified in different ways, such as primary versus secondary sources (a scheme that focuses on how you'll use the source in your final paper) or as print versus Web sources (a scheme based on its medium of publication). In this section we'll explain a variety of ways to distinguish among different kinds of sources. Your payoff will be an increased ability to read sources rhetorically and to use them purposefully in your research writing.

Primary and Secondary Sources

Researchers often distinguish between primary and secondary sources. **Primary sources** are the original documents, artifacts, or data that you are actively analyzing; **secondary sources** are works by other people who have analyzed the same documents, artifacts, or data. In short, secondary sources comment upon or analyze primary sources. Table 1 presents some examples.

The distinction between primary and secondary sources is sometimes slippery and depends on context. In the media studies example from Table 1, the parenting Web site is a secondary source if your research question focuses on *South Park*. But if you are investigating the political biases of parenting Web sites, then this site becomes a primary source.

Some research projects use primary sources extensively, while others mainly or exclusively involve secondary sources. You may be asked, for example, to bring your critical thinking to bear on specific primary sources—for example, gender stereotypes in children's birthday cards, political views expressed in old *Archie*

TABLE I	**Examples of Primary and Secondary Sources**	
Field	Examples of Primary Sources	Examples of Secondary Sources
History	Diaries, speeches, newspaper accounts, letters, manuscripts, official records, old photographs, old news reels, archeological sites	• Scholarly book on European fascism in the 1930s • 1970s film about the rise of the Nazis in Germany
Media studies	Rap lyrics, advertisements, graffiti, episodes of *South Park*, bumper stickers, documentary photographs	• Scholarly journal article analyzing racism in *South Park* • Parenting Web site objecting to *South Park*
Nursing	Patient records, direct observation of patients, research findings on transmission of AIDS virus; public health data on swine flu	• Popular magazine article about nurses working in third world hospital • Blog site focusing on nursing issues

comic books, or legal requirements for "proof" in transcripts from witchcraft trials. In these cases, your secondary research would focus on what other scholars have said about these issues in scholarly books or articles. Modern libraries together with the Internet now make available a wealth of primary sources—government documents, historical archives, slide collections, population or ethnographic data, maps, health data, and so forth.

For other kinds of research projects, particularly those connected to civic issues, students often need to work mainly or exclusively with secondary sources. In trying to decide where you stand, say, on nuclear power plants, on a single-payer medical system, or on immigration policy, you will need to enter the civic conversation about these issues carried on in secondary sources. You'll also need to pay attention to what these secondary sources use as evidence in support of their arguments. Were they able to use primary sources for their evidence? Or does their evidence come from other secondary sources? In trying to evaluate each of these secondary sources, you'll need to employ all your rhetorical skills, as we begin to show in the next section.

Reading Secondary Sources Rhetorically

When you look at a secondary source—whether in stable print form or in often unstable Web form—you need to think rhetorically about the kind of source you are perusing and the original author's purpose in producing the source. In this section we'll look specifically at print sources, which are commonly classified either as books or as periodicals (magazines, newspapers, scholarly journals, and so forth), and contrast them with Web sources.

Table 2 shows how these sources can be analyzed according to genre, publisher, author credentials, and angle of vision. The last column in Table 2 identifies contextual clues that will help you recognize what category each of these sources belongs to. We suggest that you take a few moments now to peruse the information in these tables so that you can begin to appreciate the distinctions we are making among types of sources.

Print Sources Versus Web-Only Sources New researchers need to appreciate the differences in stability and reliability between print sources and Web-only sources. Print sources (books, journals, magazines, newspapers) are stable in contrast to materials published on Web sites, which might change hourly. If you work from print sources, you can be sure that others will be able to track down your sources for their own projects. Furthermore, print publications generally go through an editorial review process that helps ensure accuracy and reputability. In contrast, Web-only documents from individuals or small organizations may be unedited and thus unreliable. Because the cost of producing, distributing, and storing print materials is high, books and periodicals are now often published in electronic formats, complicating the distinction between print and Web sources.

TABLE 2 A Rhetorical Overview of Print Books and Periodicals

Genre and Publisher	Author and Angle of Vision	How to Recognize Them
Books		
SCHOLARLY BOOKS • University/academic presses • Nonprofit • Selected through peer review	**Author:** Professors, researchers **Angle of vision:** Scholarly advancement of knowledge	• University press on title page • Specialized academic style • Documentation and bibliography • Sometimes available as e-books
TRADE BOOKS (NONFICTION) • Commercial publishers (for example, Penguin Putnam) • Selected for profit potential	**Author:** Journalists, freelancers, scholars aiming at popular audience **Angle of vision:** Varies from informative to persuasive; often well researched and respected, but sometimes shoddy and aimed for quick sale	• Covers designed for marketing appeal • Popular style • Usually documented in an informal rather than an academic style • Sometimes available as e-books
REFERENCE BOOKS • Publishers specializing in reference material • For-profit through library sales	**Author:** Commissioned scholars **Angle of vision:** Balanced, factual overview	• Titles containing words such as *encyclopedia, dictionary,* or *guide* • Found in reference section of library or online through library Web site
Periodicals		
SCHOLARLY JOURNALS • University/academic presses • Nonprofit • Articles chosen through peer review • Examples: *Journal of Abnormal Psychology, Review of Metaphysics*	**Author:** Professors, researchers, independent scholars **Angle of vision:** Scholarly advancement of knowledge; presentation of research findings; development of new theories and applications	• Not sold on magazine racks • No commercial advertising • Specialized academic style • Documentation and bibliography • Cover often has table of contents • Often can be found in online databases
PUBLIC AFFAIRS MAGAZINES • Commercial, "for-profit" presses • Manuscripts reviewed by editors • Examples: *Harper's, Commonweal, National Review*	**Author:** Staff writers, freelancers, scholars for general audiences **Angle of vision:** Aims to deepen public understanding of issues; magazines often have political bias of left, center, or right	• Long, well-researched articles • Ads aimed at upscale professionals • Often has reviews of books, theater, film, and the arts • Often can be found in online databases or on the Web

(continued)

TABLE 2 *continued*

Genre and Publisher	Author and Angle of Vision	How to Recognize Them
Periodicals (*continued*)		
TRADE MAGAZINES • Commercial, "for-profit" presses • Focused on a profession or trade • Examples: *Advertising Age, Automotive Rebuilder, Farm Journal*	**Author:** Staff writers, industry specialists **Angle of vision:** Informative articles for practitioners; advocacy for the profession or trade	• Title indicating trade or profession • Articles on practical job concerns • Ads geared toward a particular trade or profession
NEWSMAGAZINES AND NEWSPAPERS • Newspaper chains and publishers • Examples: *Time, Newsweek, Washington Post, Los Angeles Times*	**Author:** Staff writers and journalists; occasional freelance pieces **Angle of vision:** News reports aimed at balance and objectivity; editorial pages reflect perspective of editors; op-ed pieces reflect different perspectives	• Readily familiar by name, distinctive cover style • Widely available on newsstands, by subscription, and on the Web • Ads aimed at broad, general audience
POPULAR NICHE MAGAZINES • Large conglomerates or small presses with clear target audience • Focused on special interests of target audience • Examples: *Seventeen, People, TV Guide, Car and Driver, Golf Digest*	**Author:** Staff or freelance writers **Angle of vision:** Varies—in some cases content and point of view are dictated by advertisers or the politics of the publisher	• Glossy paper, extensive ads, lots of visuals • Popular, often distinctive style • Short, undocumented articles • Credentials of writer often not mentioned

These changes mean that when evaluating and citing sources, researchers must now pay attention to whether a source retrieved electronically was originally a print source made available electronically (by being posted to a Web site or contained in a database) or is in fact a Web-only source. You'll need to know this information in order to read the source rhetorically, evaluate its trustworthiness, and cite it properly. When you retrieve print sources electronically, be aware that you may lose important contextual clues about the author's purpose and angle of vision—clues that would be immediately apparent in the original print source. These clues come from such things as statements of editorial policy, other articles in the same magazine or journal, or advertisements targeting specific audiences. (The increasing availability of *.pdf* or *portable document format* files, which reproduce the appearance of the original print page, makes understanding publication contexts much easier. When .pdf format is available, take advantage of it.)

Scholarly Books and Journal Articles Versus Trade Books and Magazines

Note in Table 2 the distinction between scholarly books or journal articles, which are peer-reviewed and published by nonprofit academic presses, and trade books or magazines, which are published by for-profit presses. By **peer review**, which is a highly prized concept in academia, we mean the selection process by which scholarly manuscripts get chosen for publication. When manuscripts are submitted to an academic publisher, the editor sends them for independent review to experienced scholars who judge the rigor and accuracy of the research and the significance and value of the argument. The process is highly competitive and weeds out much shoddy or trivial work.

In contrast, trade books and magazines are not peer-reviewed by independent scholars. Instead, they are selected for publication by editors whose business is to make a profit. Fortunately, it can be profitable for popular presses to publish superbly researched and argued material because college-educated people, as lifelong learners, create a demand for intellectually satisfying trade books or magazines written for the general reader rather than for the highly specialized reader. These can be excellent sources for undergraduate research, but you need to separate the trash from the treasure. Trade books and magazines are aimed at many different audiences and market segments and can include sloppy, unreliable, and heavily biased material.

Encyclopedias, Wikipedia, and Other Reference Books and Wikis

Another kind of source is an encyclopedia or other kind of reference work. These are sometimes called "tertiary sources" because they provide distilled background information derived from primary and secondary sources. Encyclopedias and reference works are excellent starting places at the beginning of a research project. New researchers, however, should be aware of the difference between a commissioned encyclopedia article and an article in the online source *Wikipedia*. Professional encyclopedia companies such as *Encyclopedia Britannica* commission highly regarded scholars with particular expertise in a subject to write that subject's encyclopedia entry. Usually the entry is signed so that the author can be identified. In contrast, all forms of wikis—including *Wikipedia*—are communal projects using collaborative wiki software. *Wikipedia, the Free Encyclopedia* (its official name) is written communally by volunteers; anyone who follows the site's procedures can edit an entry. The entry's accuracy and angle of vision depend on collective revisions by interested readers.

Wikipedia is a fascinating cultural product that provides rapid overview information, but it is not a reliable academic source. It is often accused of inaccurate information, editorial bias, and shifting content because of constant revisions by readers. Most instructors will not accept *Wikipedia* as a factual or informative source.

Identifying Types of Sources

Your instructor will bring to class a variety of sources—different kinds of books, scholarly journals, magazines, and downloaded material. Working individually or in small groups, try to decide which category in Table 2 each piece belongs to. Be prepared to justify your decisions on the basis of the cues you used to make your decision.

SKILL 3 Use purposeful strategies for searching libraries, databases, and Web sites.

In the previous section, we explained differences among the kinds of sources you may encounter in a research project. In this section, we explain how to find these sources by using your campus library's own collection, library-leased electronic databases, and Web search engines for finding material on the World Wide Web.

Checking Your Library's Home Page

We begin by focusing on the specialized resources provided by your campus library. Your starting place and best initial research tool will be your campus library's home page. This portal will lead you to two important resources: (1) the library's online catalog and (2) direct links to the periodicals and reference databases leased by the library. Here you will find indexes to a wide range of articles in journals and magazines and direct access to frequently used reference materials, including statistical abstracts, biographies, dictionaries, and encyclopedias. Furthermore, many academic library sites post lists of good research starting points, organized by discipline, including Web sites librarians have screened.

In addition to checking your library's home page, make a personal visit to your library to learn its features and especially to note the location of a researcher's best friend and resource: the reference desk. Make use of reference librarians—they are there to help you.

Searching Efficiently: Subject Searches Versus Keyword Searches At the start of a research project, researchers typically search an online catalog or database by subject or by keywords. Your own research process will be speedier if you understand the difference between these kinds of searches.

- *Subject searches.* Subject searches use predetermined categories published in the reference work *Library of Congress Subject Headings*. This work informs you that, for example, material on "street people" would be classified under the heading "homeless persons." If the words you use for a subject search don't yield results, seek help from a librarian, who can show you how to use the subject heading guide to find the best word or phrase.
- *Keyword searches.* Keyword searches are not based on predetermined subject categories. Rather, the computer locates the keywords you provide in titles,

abstracts, introductions, and sometimes bodies of text. Keyword searches in online catalogs are usually limited to finding words and phrases in titles. We explain more about keyword searches in the upcoming section on using licensed databases, whose search engines look for keywords in bodies of text as well as in titles.

Finding Print Articles: Searching a Licensed Database

For many research projects, useful sources are print articles immediately available in your library's periodical collection. You find these articles by searching licensed databases leased by your library.

What Is a Licensed Database? Electronic databases of periodical sources are produced by for-profit companies that index articles in thousands of periodicals and construct engines that can search the database by author, title, subject, keyword, date, genre, and other characteristics. In most cases the database contains an abstract of each article, and in many cases it contains the complete text of the article, which you can download and print. These databases are referred to by several different generic names: "licensed databases" (our preferred term), "periodicals databases," or "subscription services." Because access to these databases is restricted to fee-paying customers, they can't be searched through Web engines like Google. Most university libraries allow students to access these databases from a remote computer by using a password. You can therefore use the Internet to connect your computer to licensed databases as well as to the World Wide Web (see Figure 1).

Although the methods of accessing licensed databases vary from institution to institution, we can offer some widely applicable guidelines. Most likely your library has online one or more of the following databases:

- **EBSCOhost:** Includes citations and abstracts from journals in most disciplines as well as many full-text articles from thousands of journals.
- **ProQuest:** Gives access to full text of articles from magazines and journals in many subject areas; may include full-text articles from newspapers.

FIGURE I Licensed Database Versus Free-Access Portions of Internet

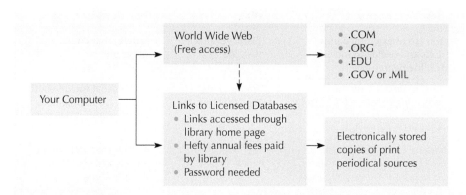

- *FirstSearch Databases:* Incorporates multiple specialized databases in many subject areas, including WorldCat, which contains records of books, periodicals, and multimedia formats from libraries worldwide.
- *Lexis-Nexis Academic Universe:* Is primarily a full-text database covering current events, business, and financial news; includes company profiles and legal, medical, and reference information.
- *JSTOR:* Offers full text of scholarly journal articles across many disciplines; you can limit searches to specific disciplines.

Given the variability of these and many other resources, we once again refer you to your campus library's Web site and the librarians at the reference desk (who often answer questions by e-mail). There you will find the best advice about where to look for what. Then, when you decide to use a specific source for your research project, be sure to include in your notes the names of both the database and the database company because you will need to include that information when you cite your sources.

More on Keyword Searching To use an online database, you need to be adept at keyword searching. When you type a word or phrase into a search box, the computer will find sources that contain the same words or phrases. If you want the computer to search for a phrase, put it in quotation marks. Thus if you type *"street people"* using quotation marks, the computer will search for those two words occurring together. If you type in *street people* without quotation marks, the computer will look for the word *street* and the word *people* occurring in the same document but not necessarily together. Use your imagination to try a number of related terms. If you are researching gendered toys and you get too many hits using the keyword *toys,* try *gender toys, Barbie, G.I. Joe, girl toys, boy toys, toys psychology,* and so forth. You can increase the flexibility of your searches by using Boolean terms to expand, narrow, or limit your search (see Table 3 for an explanation of Boolean searches).

TABLE 3   Boolean Search Commands

Command and Function	Research Example	What to Type	Search Result
X OR Y (Expands your search)	You are researching Barbie dolls and decide to include G.I. Joe figures.	"Barbie doll" OR "G.I. Joe"	Articles that contain either phrase
X AND Y (Narrows your search)	You are researching the psychological effects of Barbie dolls and are getting too many hits under *Barbie dolls.*	"Barbie dolls" AND psychology	Articles that include both the phrase "Barbie dolls" and the word *psychology*
X NOT Y (Limits your search)	You are researching girls' toys and are tired of reading about Barbie dolls. You want to look at other popular girls' toys.	"girl toys" NOT Barbie	Articles that include the phrase "girl toys" but exclude *Barbie*

Illustration of a Database Search

As an illustration of a database search, we'll use student writer James Gardiner's research on online social networks. Figure 2 shows the results from James's search using the keywords *online relationships* and *loneliness* on the database EBSCOhost. As the figure shows, EBSCOhost returned three articles from scholarly journals that deal in some way with online relationships and loneliness. The first article, "Searching for Self and Relationships Online," comes from an academic journal (*CyberPsychology & Behavior*) and a full text of the article is available online in .pdf format. To get more information, James clicked on the name of the article. The resulting screen gives an abstract of the article as well as complete data about when and where the article was published in print. Based on the abstract, James downloaded the .pdf file and

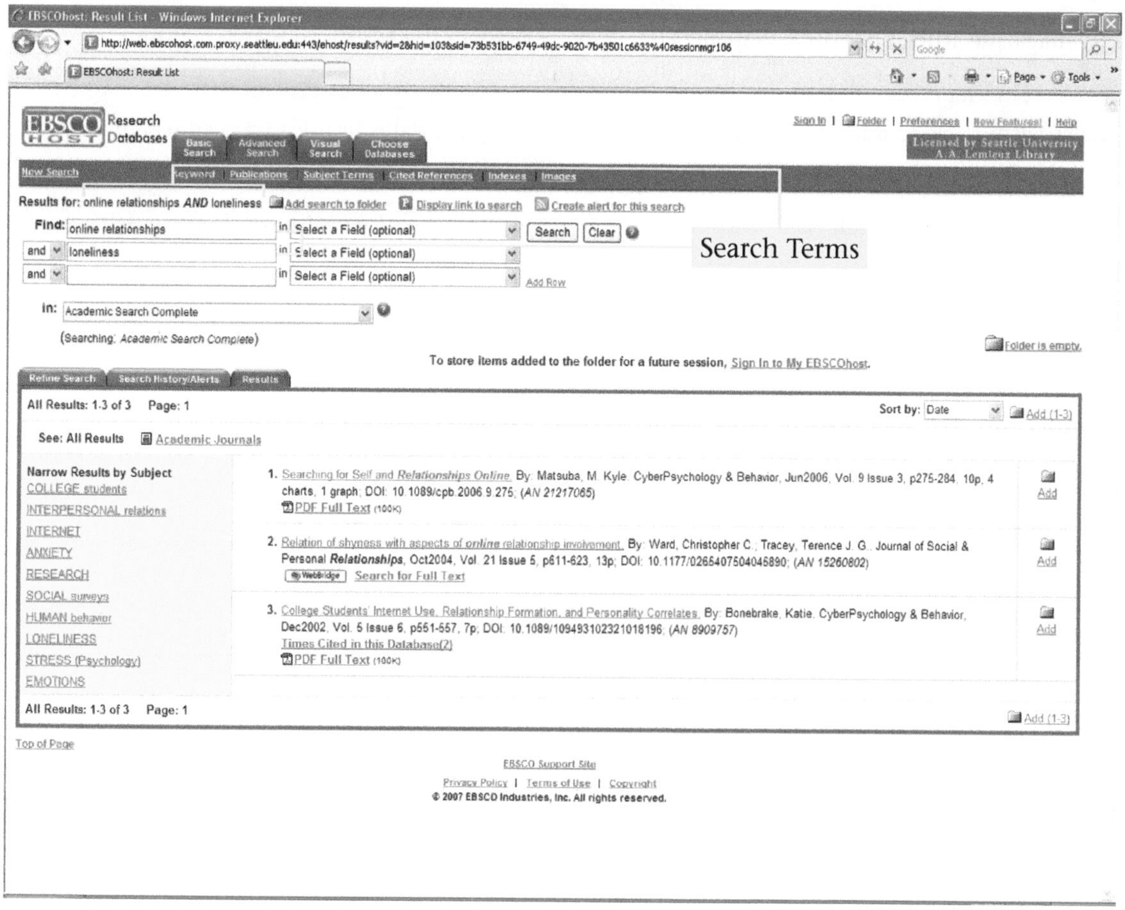

FIGURE 2 Sample Results List from a Search Using EBSCOhost

eventually used this article in his final research paper.

A particularly valuable feature of databases is the way that you can limit or expand your searches in a variety of useful ways. Here are some strategies for focusing, narrowing, or expanding your list of sources:

Strategies for Narrowing or Expanding Your Searches on Licensed Databases	
What You Want	**What to Do**
Only scholarly articles in peer-reviewed journals	Check the box for "peer-reviewed" articles in the database search box (different databases have different procedures—ask a librarian).
Only short articles (or only long articles)	Specify length of articles you want in the advanced search feature.
Only magazine articles or only newspaper articles	Specify in the advanced search feature.
Articles within a certain range of dates	Specify the dates in the advanced search feature.
Only articles for which "full text" is available	Check the box for "full text" in the database search box.
Only articles from periodicals carried by your library	Check method used by database. (Most databases accessed through your library will indicate whether your library carries the magazine or journal.)
All articles	Don't check any of the limiting boxes.
To narrow (or expand) the focus of the search	• Experiment with different keywords. • Use Boolean techniques: *online relationships* AND *friendship*; *online relationships* OR *MySpace* (see Table 3). • Try different databases. • Ask your reference librarian for help.

After you've identified articles you'd like to read, locate physically all those available in your library's periodical collection. (This way you won't lose important contextual cues for reading them rhetorically.) For those unavailable in your library, print them from the database (if full text is provided), or order them through interlibrary loan.

Finding Cyberspace Sources: Searching the World Wide Web

Another valuable resource is the World Wide Web. To understand the logic of Web search engines, you need to know that the Internet is divided into restricted sections open only to those with special access rights and a "free-access" section. Web engines such as Google search only the free-access portion of the Internet. When you type keywords into a Web search engine, it searches for matches in material made available on the Web by all the users of the world's network of computers—government agencies, corporations, advocacy groups, information services, individuals with their own Web sites, and many others.

The following example will quickly show you the difference between a licensed database search and a Web search. When we entered the keywords *online relationships* and *loneliness* into EBSCOhost, we received three hits from scholarly journals (see Figure 2). In contrast, when we typed *online relationships loneliness* into Google, we received "about 1,670,000" hits. The first screen for this search is shown in Figure 3.

FIGURE 3 First Few Hits from Google

Comparing a Licensed Database Search and a Web Search

Working in small groups or as a whole class, see if you can reach consensus on the following questions:

1. How does a licensed database search differ from a Web search? Explain what is being searched in each case.
2. There is no way that James or any other researcher could scroll through more than a million hits. However, just the first five hits on Google (see Figure 3) offer interesting possibilities for James's research. Which of these sites might be worth exploring and why? As you look at each hit, pay attention to the URL, as well as to the description, to see if you can predict the kind of organization that sponsors the site.

Using Web Search Engines Different search engines search the Web in different ways, so it is important that you try a variety of search engines when you look for information. For example, a service offered by Google is "Google Scholar," with which you can limit a Web search to academic or scholarly sources. (But you will still need to turn to your library's collection or licensed databases for a full text of the source.) On campus, reference librarians and disciplinary experts can give you good advice about what has worked well in the past for particular kinds of searches. On the Web, an additional resource is NoodleTools.com, which offers lots of good advice for choosing the best search engine.

Determining Where You Are on the Web As you browse the Web looking for resources, clicking from link to link, try to figure out what site you are actually in at any given moment. This information is crucial, both for properly documenting a Web source and for reading the source rhetorically.

To know where you are on the Web, begin by identifying the home page, which is the material to the left of the first single slash in the URL (universal resource locator). The generic structure of a typical URL looks like this: http://www.servername.domain/directory/subdirectory/filename.filetype

Here is a specific example, the URL for the NINDS (National Institute of Neurological Disorders and Stroke) Cerebral Aneurysm Information Page:

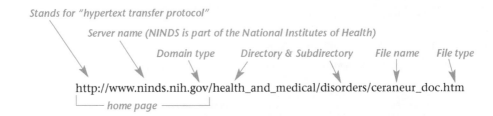

Stands for "hypertext transfer protocol"

Server name (NINDS is part of the National Institutes of Health)

Domain type   Directory & Subdirectory   File name   File type

http://www.ninds.nih.gov/health_and_medical/disorders/ceraneur_doc.htm

home page

When you click on a link in one site, you may be sent to a totally different site. To determine the home page of this new site, simply note the root URL immediately following the "www."* To view the home page directly, delete the codes to the right of the initial home page URL in your computer's location window and hit Enter. You will then be linked directly to the site's home page, where you may be able to find an "About" link through which you can gather information about the purpose and sponsors of the page. Being able to examine a site's home page helps you read the site rhetorically and document it properly.

PEARSON mycomplab ▌ For support in learning this chapter's content, follow this path in MyCompLab: Resources ⇒ Research ⇒ The Research Assignment ⇒ Finding Sources. Review the Instruction and Multimedia resources about finding sources, and then complete the Exercises and click on Gradebook to measure your progress.

---

*Not all URLs begin with "www" after the first set of double slashes. Our description doesn't include variations of the most typical URL types. You can generally find the home page of a site by eliminating all codes to the right of the first slash mark after the domain or country name.

EVALUATING SOURCES

From Chapter 20 of *The Allyn & Bacon Guide to Writing*, Sixth Edition. John D. Ramage, John C. Bean, June Johnson. Copyright © 2012 by Pearson Education, Inc. Published by Pearson Allyn & Bacon.

EVALUATING SOURCES

In this chapter, you will learn these research skills:

- **SKILL 1**   Read sources rhetorically and take purposeful notes.
- **SKILL 2**   Evaluate sources for reliability, credibility, angle of vision, and degree of advocacy.
- **SKILL 3**   Use your rhetorical knowledge to evaluate Web sources.

SKILL 1   Read sources rhetorically and take purposeful notes.

Once you've located a stack of books and magazine or journal articles, it's easy to feel overwhelmed. How do you begin reading all this material? There is no one right answer to this question. At times you need to read slowly with analytical closeness. At other times you can skim a source, looking only for its gist or for a needed piece of information. In this section, we offer some advice on how to read your sources with rhetorical savvy and take notes that will help you write your final paper.

Reading with Your Own Goals in Mind

How you read a source depends to a certain extent on where you are in the research process. Early in the process, when you are in the thesis-seeking, exploratory stage, your goal is to achieve a basic understanding of your research area. You need to become aware of different points of view, learn what is unknown or controversial about your research question, see what values or assumptions are in conflict, and build up your store of background knowledge. As we saw in the case of James Gardiner, one's initial research question often evolves as one's knowledge increases and interests shift.

Given these goals, at the early stages of research you should select "overview" kinds of sources to get you into the conversation. In some cases, even an encyclopedia or specialized reference work can be a good start for getting general background.

As you get deeper into your research, your questions become more focused, and the sources you seek out become more specialized. Once you formulate a thesis and plan a structure for your paper, you can determine more clearly the sources you need. For example, after James Gardiner decided to focus on the negative aspects of online social networks, he began following up leads on Internet addiction, on OSNs as sites for narcissistic display, and on the possible superficiality of online relationships. At the same time he remained open-minded about the psychological and social benefits of OSNs.

Reading Your Sources Rhetorically

To read your sources rhetorically, you should keep two basic questions in mind:

1. What was the source author's purpose in writing this piece?
2. What might be my purpose in using this piece?

Let's begin with the first question. The following chart sums up the strategies you can use to read your sources rhetorically, along with research tips for answering some of the questions you've posed.

Strategies for Reading Your Sources Rhetorically

Questions to Ask	What to Do	Results
• Who is this author? • What are his or her credentials and affiliations?	• Look for the author's credentials at the end of the article or in the contributors' page. • Google the author's name. • In a database results list, click on the author's name for a list of other articles he/she has written.	• Helps you assess author's *ethos* and credibility. • Helps you establish author's angle of vision.
• What is this source's genre? • Who is the intended audience?	• If the source is downloaded, identify the original publication information. • If the source comes from a periodical, look at the print copy for clues about the audience (titles of other articles, ads, document design). • If a Web-only source, see Skill 3.	• Helps you further determine the author's angle of vision as well as the source's reliability and credibility. • Helps explain rhetorical features of the source.

(continued)

Questions to Ask	What to Do	Results
• What is this author's purpose? • How is this author trying to change his/her audience's view of the topic?	• Determine whether the piece is primarily expressive, informational, analytical, or persuasive. • If the source comes from the Web, who is the site's sponsor? Read the "About us" material on the site's home page. • If it is a print source, determine the reputation and bias of the journal, magazine, or press (see Table 1).	• Helps you evaluate the source for angle of vision and degree of advocacy. • Helps you decide how you might use the source in your own argument.
• What is this author's angle of vision or bias? • What facts, data, and other evidence does this author cite and what are the sources for the data? • What are this author's underlying values, assumptions, and beliefs? • What is omitted or censored from this text?	• Apply the rhetorical reading strategies. • Evaluate the source for reliability, credibility, angle of vision, and degree of advocacy as explained in Skill 2. • If a Web source, evaluate it using strategies explained in Skill 3.	• Helps you bring your own critical thinking to bear on your sources. • Keeps your paper intellectually honest and interesting.

This chart reinforces a point we've made throughout this text: All writing is produced from an angle of vision that privileges some ways of seeing and filters out other ways. You should guard against reading your sources as if they present hard, undisputed facts or universal truths. For example, if one of your sources says that "Saint-John's-wort [an herb] has been shown to be an effective treatment for depression," some of your readers might accept that statement as fact; but many wouldn't. Skeptical readers would want to know who the author is, where his views have been published, and what he uses for evidence. Let's say the author is someone named Samuel Jones. Skeptical readers would ask whether Jones is relying on published research, and if so, whether the studies have been peer-reviewed in reputable, scholarly journals and whether the research has been replicated by other scientists. They would also want to know whether Jones has financial connections to companies that produce herbal remedies and supplements. Rather than settling the question about Saint-John's-wort as a treatment for depression, a quotation from Jones might open up a heated controversy about medical research.

Reading rhetorically is thus a way of thinking critically about your sources. It influences the way you take notes, evaluate sources, and shape your argument.

Taking Purposeful Notes

Many beginning researchers opt not to take notes—a serious mistake, in our view. Instead, they simply photocopy or printout articles, perhaps using a highlighter to mark passages. This practice, which experienced researchers almost never use, reduces your ability to engage the ideas in a source, to synthesize different sources, and to find your own voice in a conversation. When you begin drafting your paper, you'll have no bibliographic information, no notes to refer to, no record of your thinking-in-progress. Your only recourse is to revisit all your sources, thumbing through them one at a time—a practice that leads to passive cutting and pasting (and possible plagiarism).

Recording Bibliographic Information To take good research notes, begin by making a bibliographic entry for the source, following the documentation format assigned by your instructor—usually MLA (Modern Language Association) or APA (American Psychological Association). Although you may be tempted to put off doing this mechanical task ("Hey, boring, I can do this documentation stuff later"), there are two reasons to do it immediately:

- Doing it now, while the source is in front of you, will save you time in the long run. Otherwise, you'll have to try to retrieve the source, in a late-night panic, just before the paper is due.
- Doing it now will make you look at the source rhetorically. Is this a peer-reviewed journal article? A magazine article? An op-ed piece? A blog? Making the bibliographic entry forces you to identify the source's genre.

Recording Ideas and Information and Responding to Each Source To take good research notes, follow the habits for "strong reading" by weaving back and forth between two modes of writing:

- ***Your informational notes on each source:*** Summarize each source's argument and record useful information. To avoid the risk of plagiarizing later, make sure that you put quotation marks around any passages that you copy word for word (be sure to copy *exactly*). When you summarize or paraphrase passages, be sure to put the ideas entirely into your own words.
- ***Your own exploratory notes as you think of ideas:*** Write down your own ideas as they occur to you. Record your thinking-in-progress as you mull over and speak back to your sources.

An approach that encourages both modes of writing is to keep a dialectic or double-entry journal. Divide a page in half; enter your informational notes on one side and your exploratory writing on the other. If you use a computer, you can put your informational notes in one font and your own exploratory writing in another.

Taking effective notes is different from the mechanical process of copying out passages or simply listing facts and information. Rather, make your notes purposeful by imagining how you might use a given source in your research paper. The following chart shows the different functions that research sources might play in your argument and highlights appropriate note-taking strategies for each function.

Strategies for Taking Notes According to Purpose

Function that Source Might Play in Your Argument	Strategies for Informational Notes	Strategies for Exploratory Notes
Provides background about your problem or issue	• Summarize the information. • Record specific facts and figures useful for background.	• Speculate on how much background your readers will need.
Gives an alternative view that you will mention briefly	• Summarize the source's argument in a couple of sentences; note its bias and perspective. • Identify brief quotations that sum up the source's perspective.	• Jot down ideas on how and why different sources disagree. • Begin making an idea map of alternative views.
Provides an alternative or opposing view that you might summarize fully and respond to	• Summarize the article fully and fairly. • Note the kinds of evidence used.	• Speculate about why you disagree with the source and whether you can refute the argument, concede to it, or compromise with it. • Explore what research you'll need to support your own argument.
Provides information or testimony that you might use as evidence	• Record the data or information. • If using authorities for testimony, quote short passages. • Note the credentials of the writer or person quoted.	• Record new ideas as they occur to you. • Continue to think purposefully about additional research you'll need.

Function that Source Might Play in Your Argument	Strategies for Informational Notes	Strategies for Exploratory Notes
Mentions information or testimony that counters your position or raises doubts about your argument	• Note counterevidence. • Note authorities who disagree with you.	• Speculate how you might respond to counterevidence.
Provides a theory or method that influences your approach to the issue	• Note credentials of the author. • Note passages that sparked ideas.	• Freewrite about how the source influences your method or approach.

SKILL 2 Evaluate sources for reliability, credibility, angle of vision, and degree of advocacy.

When you read sources for your research project, you need to evaluate them as you go along. As you read each potential source, ask yourself questions about the author's reliability, credibility, angle of vision, and degree of advocacy.

Reliability

"Reliability" refers to the accuracy of factual data in a source. If you check a writer's "facts" against other sources, do you find that the facts are correct? Does the writer distort facts, take them out of context, or otherwise use them unreasonably? In some controversies, key data are highly disputed—for example, the frequency of date rape or the risk factors for many diseases. A reliable writer acknowledges these controversies and doesn't treat disputed data as fact. Furthermore, if you check out the sources used by a reliable writer, they'll reveal accurate and careful research—respected primary sources rather than hearsay or secondhand reports. Journalists of reputable newspapers (not tabloids) pride themselves on meticulously checking out their facts, as do editors of serious popular magazines. Editing is often minimal for Web sources, however, and they can be notoriously unreliable. As you gain knowledge of your research question, you'll develop a good ear for writers who play fast and loose with data.

Credibility

"Credibility" is similar to "reliability" but is based on internal rather than external factors. It refers to the reader's trust in the writer's honesty, goodwill, and trustworthiness and is apparent in the writer's tone, reasonableness, fairness in summarizing opposing views, and respect for different perspectives. Audiences differ in how much credibility they will grant to certain authors. Nevertheless, a writer can achieve a reputation for credibility, even among bitter political opponents, by applying to issues a sense of moral courage, integrity, and consistency of principle.

Angle of Vision and Political Stance

By "angle of vision," we mean the way that a piece of writing is shaped by the underlying values, assumptions, and beliefs of its author, resulting in a text that reflects a certain perspective, worldview, or belief system. Of paramount importance are the underlying values or beliefs that the writer assumes his or her readers will share. You can get useful clues about a writer's angle of vision and intended audience by doing some quick research into the politics and reputation of the author on the Internet or by analyzing the genre, market niche, and political reputation of the publication in which the material appears.

Determining Political Stance Your awareness of angle of vision and political stance is especially important if you are doing research on contemporary cultural or political issues. In Table 1, we have categorized some well-known political commentators, publications, policy research institutes (commonly known as *think tanks*), and blogs across the political spectrum from left/liberal to right/conservative.

TABLE I   Angles of Vision in U.S. Media and Think Tanks: A Sampling Across the Political Spectrum[1]

Commentators

Left	Left Center	Center	Right Center	Right
Barbara Ehrenreich	E. J. Dionne	David Ignatius	David Brooks	Charles Krauthammer
Bob Herbert	Leonard Pitts	Thomas Friedman	Peggy Noonan	Cal Thomas
Michael Moore (film-maker)	Eugene Robinson	Kathleen Hall Jamieson	Jonah Goldberg	Glenn Beck (radio/TV)
Bill Moyers (television)	Nicholas Kristof	Kevin Phillips	Andrew Sullivan	Rush Limbaugh (radio/TV)
Paul Krugman	Maureen Dowd	David Broder	George Will	Bill O'Reilly (radio/TV)
Thom Hartman (radio)	Mark Shields	William Saletan	Ruben Navarrette, Jr.	Kathleen Parker
Rachel Maddow (radio)	Frank Rich	Mary Sanchez		Thomas Sowell

Newspapers and Magazines[2]

Left/Liberal	Center	Right/Conservative
The American Prospect	*Atlantic Monthly*	*American Spectator*
Harper's	*Business Week*	*Fortune*
Los Angeles Times	*Commentary*	*National Review*
Mother Jones	*Commonweal*	*Reader's Digest*
The Nation	*Foreign Affairs*	*Reason*
New York Times	*New Republic*	*Wall Street Journal*
New Yorker	*Slate*	*Washington Times*
Salon	*Washington Post*	*Weekly Standard*
Sojourners		

TABLE I *continued*

Blogs

Liberal/Left	Center	Right/Conservative
americablog.com	donklephant.com	conservativeblogger.com
atrios.blogspot.com	newmoderate.blogspot.com	drudgereport.com
crooksandliars.com	politics-central.blogspot.com	instapundit.com
dailykos.com	rantingbaldhippie.com	littlegreenfootballs.com
digbysblog.blogspot.com	stevesilver.net	michellemalkin.com
firedoglake.com	themoderatevoice.com	polipundit.com
huffingtonpost.com	washingtonindependent.com	powerlineblog.com
mediamatters.com	watchingwashington.blogspot.com	sistertoldjah.com
talkingpointsmemo.com		redstate.com
wonkette.com		townhall.com

Think Tanks

Left/Liberal	Center	Right/Conservative
Center for American Progress	The Brookings Institution	American Enterprise Institute
Center for Media and Democracy (sponsors Disinfopedia.org)	Carnegie Endowment for International Peace	Cato Institute (Libertarian)
Institute for Policy Studies	Council on Foreign Relations	Center for Strategic and International Studies
Open Society Institute (Soros Foundation)	Jamestown Foundation	Heritage Foundation (sponsors Townhall.com)
Progressive Policy Institute	National Bureau of Economic Research	Project for the New American Century
Urban Institute		

[1] *For further information about the political leanings of publications or think tanks, ask your librarian about* Gale Directory of Publications and Broadcast Media *or* NIRA World Directory of Think Tanks.

[2] *Newspapers are categorized according to positions they take on their editorial page; any reputable newspaper strives for objectivity in news reporting and includes a variety of views on its op-ed pages. Magazines do not claim and are not expected to present similar breadth and objectivity.*

Although the terms *liberal* and *conservative* or *left* and *right* often have fuzzy meanings, they provide convenient shorthand for signaling a person's overall views about the proper role of government in relation to the economy and social values. Liberals, tending to sympathize with those potentially harmed by unfettered free markets (workers, consumers, plaintiffs, endangered species), are typically comfortable with government regulation of economic matters while conservatives, who tend to sympathize with business interests, typically assert faith in free markets and favor a limited regulatory role for government. On social issues, conservatives tend to espouse traditional family values and advocate laws that would maintain these values (for example, promoting a Constitutional amendment limiting marriage to a bond between a man and a woman). Liberals, on the other hand, tend to espouse individual choice regarding marital partnerships and a wide range of other issues. Some persons identify themselves as economic conservatives but social liberals; others side with workers' interests on economic issues but are conservative on social issues.

Finally, many persons regard themselves as "centrists." In Table 1 the column labeled "Center" includes commentators who seek out common ground between the left and the right and who often believe that the best civic decisions are compromises between opposing views. Likewise, centrist publications and institutes often approach issues from multiple points of view, looking for the most workable solutions.

Degree of Advocacy

By "degree of advocacy" we mean the extent to which an author unabashedly takes a persuasive stance on a contested position as opposed to adopting a more neutral, objective, or exploratory stance. For example, publications affiliated with advocacy organizations (the Sierra Club, the National Rifle Association) will have a clear editorial bias. When a writer has an ax to grind, you need to weigh carefully the writer's selection of evidence, interpretation of data, and fairness to opposing views. Although no one can be completely neutral, it is always useful to seek out authors who offer a balanced assessment of the evidence. Evidence from a more detached and neutral writer may be more trusted by your readers than the arguments of a committed advocate. For example, if you want to persuade corporate executives on the dangers of global warming, evidence from scholarly journals may be more persuasive than evidence from an environmentalist Web site or from a freelance writer for a leftist popular magazine such as *Mother Jones*.

SKILL 3 Use your rhetorical knowledge to evaluate Web sources.

In the previous section we focused on reading sources rhetorically by asking questions about a source's reliability, credibility, angle of vision, and degree of advocacy. In this section we focus on evaluating sources from the World Wide Web.

The Web as a Unique Rhetorical Environment

In addition to familiar entertainment and commercial sites, the Web can provide access to highly specialized data banks, historical archives, government documents, blogosphere commentary, scholarly portals useful for academic researchers, and much more. The Web is also a great vehicle for democracy, giving voice to the otherwise voiceless. Anyone with a cause and a rudimentary knowledge of Web design can create a site. The result is a rhetorical medium that differs in significant ways from print.

Consider, for example, the difference in the way writers attract readers. Magazines displayed on racks attract readers through interest-grabbing covers and teaser headlines inviting readers to look inside. Web sites, however, can't begin attracting readers until the readers have found them through links from another site or through a "hit" from a Web search. Research suggests that Web surfers stay connected to a site for no more than thirty seconds unless something immediately attracts their interest; moreover, they seldom scroll down to see the bottom of a page. The design of a home page—the arrangement and size of the print, the use of images and colors, the locations and labels of navigational buttons—must hook readers immediately and send a clear message about the purpose and contents of the site. If the home page is a confused jumble or simply a long, printed text, the average surfer will take one look and move on.

The biggest difference between the Web and print is the Web's hypertext structure. Users click from link to link rather than read linearly down the page. Users often "read" a Web page as a configuration of images and strategically arranged text that is interspersed with bullets, boxes, and hot links. Long stretches of linear text are usually found only deep within a site, usually through links to .pdf files or other archived or posted documents.

Criteria for Evaluating a Web Source

When you evaluate a Web source, we suggest that you ask five different kinds of questions about the site in which the source appeared, as shown in Table 2. These questions, developed by scholars and librarians as points to consider when

TABLE 2	Criteria for Evaluating Web Sites
Criteria	Questions to Ask
1. Authority	• Is the document author or site sponsor clearly identified? • Does the site identify the occupation, position, education, experience, or other credentials of the author? • Does the home page or a clear link from the home page reveal the author's or sponsor's motivation for establishing the site? • Does the site provide contact information for the author or sponsor such as an e-mail or organization address?
2. Objectivity or Clear Disclosure of Advocacy	• Is the site's purpose clear (for example, to inform, entertain, or persuade)? • Is the site explicit about declaring its point of view? • Does the site indicate whether the author is affiliated with a specific organization, institution, or association? • Does the site indicate whether it is directed toward a specific audience?
3. Coverage	• Are the topics covered by the site clear? • Does the site exhibit a suitable depth and comprehensiveness for its purpose? • Is sufficient evidence provided to support the ideas and opinions presented?
4. Accuracy	• Are the sources of information stated? • Do the facts appear to be accurate? • Can you verify this information by comparing this source with other sources in the field?
5. Currency	• Are dates included in the Web site? • Do the dates apply to the material itself, to its placement on the Web, or to the time the site was last revised and updated? • Is the information current, or at least still relevant, for the site's purpose? For your purpose?

you are evaluating Web sites, will help you determine the usefulness of a site or source for your own purposes.

As a researcher, the first question you should ask about a potentially useful Web source should be, Who placed this piece on the Web and why? You can begin answering this question by analyzing the site's home page, where you will often find navigational buttons linking to "Mission," "About Us," or other identifying information about the site's sponsors. You can also get hints about the site's purpose by asking, What kind of Web site is it? Different kinds of Web sites have different purposes, often revealed by the domain identifier following the server name:

- *.com sites:* These are commercial sites designed to promote a business's image, attract customers, market products and services, and provide customer service. Their angle of vision is to promote the view of the corporation or business. Often material has no identified author. (The sponsoring company is often cited as the author.)

- *.org sites:* These are sites for nonprofit organizations or advocacy groups. Some sites provide accurate, balanced information related to the organization's mission work (Red Cross, World Vision), while others promote political views (Heritage Foundation) or advocate a cause (Persons for the Ethical Treatment of Animals).

- *.edu sites:* These sites are associated with a college or university. Home pages aim to attract prospective students and donors and provide a portal into the site. Numerous subsites are devoted to research, pedagogy, libraries, and so forth. The angle of vision can vary from strong advocacy on issues (a student paper, an on-campus advocacy group) to the objective and scholarly (a university research site).

- *.gov or .mil sites:* These sites are sponsored by a government agency or military units. They can provide a range of basic data about government policy, bills in Congress, economic forecasts, census data, and so forth. Their angle of vision varies from objective informational sites to sites that promote the agency's agenda.

Analyzing Your Own Purposes for Using a Web Source

Besides analyzing a sponsor's purpose for establishing a Web site, you also need to analyze your own purpose for using the site. To illustrate strategies for evaluating a Web site, we'll use as examples two hypothetical student researchers who are interested in the civic controversy over gun control. In both cases, the students are particularly interested in women's concerns about gun control.

Our first student researcher asked the question, "How are women represented and involved in the public controversy over gun control?" She did an initial Google search using "women gun control" as keywords and found dozens of pro-gun and anti-gun sites sponsored by women or by women's organizations. The home page of one such site, sponsored by the organization Women Against Gun Control, is shown at the end of this chapter. Fascinated by the Annie Oakley–like image (gun-toting cowgirl) on this home page, our researcher decided to focus her project on the ways that women depict themselves on pro-gun and anti-gun sites and on the kinds of arguments they make. These Web sites thus became primary sources for this student's project.

Our second researcher was more directly interested in determining her own stance in the gun control debate. She was trying to decide, from a woman's perspective, whether to advocate for gun control laws or to oppose gun control—whether even to join the National Rifle Association (NRA) and perhaps buy a gun and learn to shoot. As a researcher, her dilemma was how much she could use data about guns, crime, firearm accidents, and violence against women obtained from these sites. The sites for her were mostly secondary rather than primary sources.*

Let's look at each student's research process in turn.

Researcher 1: Using Women and Guns Web Sites for Rhetorical Analysis Our first student quickly found herself immersed in a vigorous national conversation on gun control by women's groups and by traditionally male-dominated groups seeking support or membership from women. Her research goal was to analyze these sites rhetorically to understand the ways that women frame their interests and represent themselves. She discovered that the angle of vision of each kind of site—whether pro-gun or anti-gun—led to the filtering of evidence in distinctive ways. For example, anti-gun women's groups emphasized accidental deaths from guns (particularly of children), suicides from easy access to guns, domestic violence turned deadly, guns in schools, and gun-related crime (particularly juvenile crime). In contrast, pro-gun women's groups emphasized armed resistance to assaults and rapes, inadequate police responses to crime, the right of individuals to protect themselves and their families, and the Second Amendment right to keep and bear arms. (Women's pro-gun sites often framed the gun control issue as pro-self-defense versus anti-self-defense.) She also noted that most of these sites made powerful use of visual elements—icons, colors (bright pink in particular), and well-known symbols—to enhance their emotional appeals. For instance, pro-gun sites often had patriotic themes with images of waving American flags, stern-eyed eagles, and colonial patriots with muskets. Anti-gun sites often had pictures of young children, with an emphasis on innocence, childhood fun, and family.

Researcher 1 noted that many of these sites tailored their appeals directly to women. The most well-known of the anti-gun sites is the Million Mom March Organization, which describes itself (on the "About us" link) as "the nation's largest, non-partisan, grassroots organization leading the fight to prevent gun violence. ..." Its mission statement ends with these words; "With one loud voice, we will continue to cry out that we love our children more than the gun lobby loves its guns." In Figure 1, we have reproduced some images, text boxes for anecdotes, and "fact statements" from this site's home page.

---

*The terms *primary* and *secondary* sources are relative terms often used by researchers to differentiate between original data (primary sources) and data filtered through another researcher's perspective (secondary sources). Thus the Women Against Gun Control site is a primary source for someone doing a rhetorical analysis of gun Web sites, but it is a secondary source for statistical data about gun violence.

What started as one of the largest marches on Washington is now a national network of 75 Million Mom March Chapters that work locally in the fight against gun violence and the devastation it causes.

contact your local chapter

why i march

I march for my son, Chad, who was an innocent victim of gun violence.

- *Rita*

Read Rita's story.
Read stories from other moms

Other anecdotes cycle through this box

fact file

Other "facts" that cycle into "Fact File" every five seconds

15,000 kids were killed by firearms in the last five years

MillionMomMarch.org

- One child or a teen is killed by firearms every 3 hours
- A person is killed by a gun every 17 minutes in America
- More than 176 Americans go to an ER with a firearm injury every day
- 34 percent of America's children live in a home with at least one firearm
- On average, more than a thousand kids commit suicide with a firearm every year

FIGURE I Images, Anecdotes, and Fact Statements from the Million Mom March Home Page (www.millionmommarch.org)

For Researcher 1, it is evident that both this site and the Women Against Gun Control site, as well as other pro-gun or anti-gun sites, are useful and relevant for her purpose of analyzing rhetorically how women are portrayed in the Second Amendment debate.

Analyzing the Rhetorical Elements of Two Home Pages

FOR WRITING AND DISCUSSION

Working in small groups or as a whole class, try to reach consensus answers to the following questions about how Web sites seek to draw in readers.

1. How are the images of women in the Women Against Gun Control site different from those on the Million Mom March page? How do pieces of text (such as "Ladies of High-Caliber" on the Women Against Gun Control site or one of the "facts" on the Million Mom March site) contribute to the visual-verbal effects of the home pages?
2. In the Women Against Gun Control (WAGC) page, what seems to be the Web designer's intention in the use of color, curved background lines, and images?
3. How does the home page for each site use *logos, ethos,* and *pathos* to sway readers toward its point of view?

Researcher 2: Using Women and Guns Web Sites for Data on Guns and Gun Violence Researcher 2 intends to create her own research-based argument on whether women should support or oppose gun control. Her dilemma is this: To what extent can she use "facts" appearing on these sites (such as the statement on the Women Against Gun Control site that "guns are used defensively 2.5 million times per year")?

She frequently encountered equivalent kinds of pithy statistical statements. In her initial Web search, she found an article entitled "Women Are the Real Victims of Handgun Control" by Kelly Ann Connolly, who was identified as the director of the Nevada State Rifle and Pistol Association. The site, www.armedandsafe.com, included a biographical note identifying Connolly as a public school teacher with a master's degree.

Connolly argues that a woman can walk confidently down any street in America if she is carrying a concealed weapon and is skilled in using it. She offers as support anecdotes of women who fought off rapists and cites numerous statistics, attributing the sources to "Bureau of Justice Statistics (1999)." Here are some examples from her article:

- 3 out of 4 American women will be a victim of violent crime at least once in their lifetime.
- 2 million women are raped each year, one every 15 seconds.
- Rapists know they have only a 1 in 605 chance of being caught, charged, convicted, and sentenced to serving time.

The purpose of these statistics is to increase women's anxiety about the prevalence of rape and other violent crimes and to reduce women's confidence in the police or justice system to protect them. The implied solution is to buy a pistol and learn how to use it.

How should our second researcher proceed in evaluating such an article for her own research purposes? Her first step is to evaluate the site itself. She found the home page by deleting extensions from the URL and looking directly at the home page (www.armedandsafe.com), which turned out to be the commercial site for a firing range that provided lessons in the use of rifles, pistols, and machine guns. The site obviously advocated Second Amendment rights and promoted gun ownership as a means of domestic and personal security. The images on the home page, showing a fierce eagle emerging from a collage of the American flag, the burning World Trade Center towers, and an aircraft carrier, were meant to reflect the patriotic sentiments that tend to dominate pro-gun Web sites. Researcher 2 could easily evaluate this site against the five criteria:

1. **Authority:** She could clearly tell that this was the commercial site of a firing range.
2. **Advocacy:** The site clearly advocated Second Amendment rights and gun ownership.
3. **Coverage:** The site did not cover gun-control issues in a complex way. Every aspect of the site was filtered to support its pro-gun vision.
4. **Accuracy:** At this point she was unable to check the accuracy of the site's data against other sources, but she assumed that all data would be rhetorically filtered and selected to promote the site's angle of vision.
5. **Currency:** Both anecdotal and statistical data were dated, taken primarily from the 1990s.

Based on this analysis, how might Researcher 2 use Connolly's article from this site? Our view is that the article could be very useful as one perspective on the gun-control controversy. It is a fairly representative example of the argument that guns can increase a woman's sense of confidence and well-being, and it clearly shows the kinds of rhetorical strategies such articles use—statistics on rape, descriptions of guns as equalizers in empowering women, and so forth. A summary of this article's argument could therefore be effective for presenting the pro-gun point of view.

As a source of factual data, however, the article is unusable. It would be irresponsible for her to claim that "3 out of 4 American women will be a victim of violent crime at least once in their lifetime" and to cite Connolly's article as an authoritative source. (Similarly, she would be irresponsible to claim that "a person is killed by a gun every 17 minutes in America" and give the Million Mom March site as a source.) Researcher 2 should instead look at primary data on crime statistics and guns compiled by trustworthy sources such as the Department of Justice, the FBI, state police departments, or peer-reviewed research by scholars (government statistics are all easily available from the Web). One purpose of reading sources rhetorically is to appreciate how much advocates for a given position will filter data. Trying to find the original data and to interpret it for yourself are two of the challenges of responsible research.

Unpacking Factoids in Advocacy Web Sites

Consider the following two "factoids" from the sites we have just discussed:

Factoid 1: "3 out of 4 American women will be a victim of violent crime at least once in their lifetime." [from the Connolly article "Women Are the Real Victims of Handgun Control"]

Factoid 2: "A person is killed by a gun every 17 minutes in America." [from the Million Mom March home page]

Working individually or in small groups, try to reach consensus on the following questions. (When doing your own back-of-the-envelope calculations, consider the population of the United States to be 300 million people, with half of those being women.)

1. Based on the two primary sources shown here below, try to determine
   a. how these factoids were computed.
   b. how accurate they seem to be.

SOURCE 1: DATA ON VIOLENT CRIME RATES BY GENDER OF VICTIM, 1973–2003

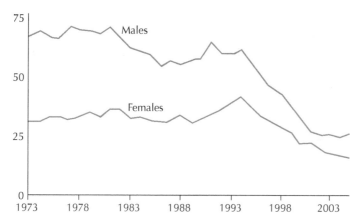

Adjusted victimization rate per 1,000 persons age 12 and over.

The violent crimes included are rape, robbery, aggravated and simple assault, and homicide.

Source: Bureau of Justice Statistics, Department of Justice (http://ojp.usdoj.gov/bjs/glance/vsx2.htm).

SOURCE 2: DATA ON DEATH BY FIREARMS

Firearm—In 2003, 30,136 persons died from firearm injuries in the United States (...), accounting for 18.4 percent of all injury deaths in 2003. Firearm suicide and homicide, the two major component causes, accounted for 56.1 and 39.6 percent, respectively, of all firearm injury deaths in 2003. In 2003, the age-adjusted death rate for firearm injuries was 10.3 deaths per 100,000 U.S. standard population. Males had an age-adjusted rate that was 6.8 times that for females,

(continued)

the black population had a rate that was 2.1 times that of the white population, and the non-Hispanic population had a rate that was 1.3 times that of the Hispanic population (...). The decrease between 2002 and 2003 in the age-adjusted death rate for firearm injuries was not statistically significant (...).

Source: Centers for Disease Control and Prevention. "Deaths: Final Data for 2003." *National Vital Statistics Reports* 54.13 (2006). 2 Sept. 2007 <http://www.cdc.gov/nchs/data/nvsr54/nvsr54_13.pdf>.

2. Why do the factoids on each site have a different rhetorical impact than the original data displayed in statistical graphs and tables would? How do the factoids spin raw data in favor of a certain angle of vision?
3. Why do we say that Researcher 2 would be irresponsible if she used either the Connolly article or the Million Mom March Web site as a source of data on gun issues?
4. Note in the graph on violent crime (Source 1 above) how sharply crime rates fell from 1993 to 2003. Scholars have debated extensively the causes of this decline. How does this graph suggest the importance of "currency" when evaluating evidence?

In this chapter we have focused on evaluating sources, particularly on reading sources rhetorically and taking purposeful notes; on evaluating sources for reliability, credibility, angle of vision, and degree of advocacy; and on using your rhetorical knowledge to evaluate Web sources.

Women Against Gun Control

"The Second Amendment IS the Equal

Click here to sign and read our new forum board!

WAGC sends amicus brief to the U.S. Supreme Court!
Click Here (Opens New Window)
Click here to read a press release regarding this hearing.

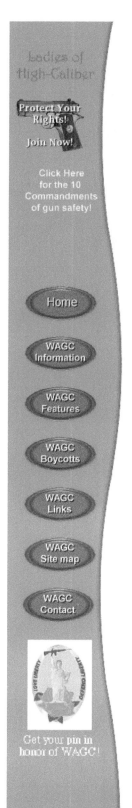

Ladies of
High-Caliber

Protect Your
Rights!

Join Now!

Click Here
for the 10
Commandments
of gun safety!

Home

WAGC
Information

WAGC
Features

WAGC
Boycotts

WAGC
Links

WAGC
Site map

WAGC
Contact

Get your pin in
honor of WAGC!

Click here
for a
special
message
from
WAGC
President,
Janalee
Tobias

Contact Us

Postal Address

- WAGC

  PO Box 95357
  South Jordan, UT
  84095

Telephone

- 801-328-9660

E-Mail

- info@wagc.com
- State and Local Chapters
- webmaster

It's a Fact:

RECENT RESEARCH INDICATES THAT GUNS ARE USED DEFENSIVELY 2.5 MILLION TIMES PER YEAR.

It's not surprising then, that more women than ever want to keep their rights to own and carry a gun.
The reason is simple: Women **are** concerned about becoming victims of crime. Guns give women a fighting chance against crime.

Join Women Against Gun Control. Take the Women Against Gun Control Pledge and you qualify for a membership in Women Against Gun Control, a grass roots volunteer organization dedicated to preserving our gun rights.

Join thousands of women (and men) in sending a powerful message throughout the world.

"Guns **SAVE** Lives. We do **NOT** support gun control. Gun Control does **NOT** control crime!"

2nd Amendment
A well regulated Militia being necessary to the security of a free State, the right of the people to keep and bear Arms shall not be infringed.

"The Second Amendment IS Homeland Security."

Special Article
Have gun, will not fear it anymore

Rosie
O' Donnel

Hillary
Clinton

Janet
Reno

Diane
Feinstein

Want Americans
to believe all
women support
gun control...

Let's BLOW
HOLES
in this MYTH!

If women are
disarmed, a
rapist will
never hear...

"STOP OR
I'LL
SHOOT!"

Looking for
Pro-Second
Amendment and
Pro-Freedom
Books? Check
Out These Book
Reviews and
Help Support
This Site!

THE UTAH
G.I.R.A.F.F.E. SOCIETY

Support WAGC
Efforts with the
Utah GIRAFFE
Society!

INCORPORATING SOURCES INTO YOUR OWN WRITING

So far, we have covered strategies for finding and evaluating sources. Now we focus on the skills needed for incorporating sources into your own writing.

In this chapter, you will learn the following skills:

- **SKILL 1**   Let your own argument determine your use of sources.
- **SKILL 2**   Know when and how to use summary, paraphrase, and quotation.
- **SKILL 3**   Use attributive tags to distinguish your ideas from a source's.
- **SKILL 4**   Punctuate quotations correctly.
- **SKILL 5**   Avoid plagiarism by following academic conventions for ethical use of sources.

Many of the examples in this chapter will be based on the following short article about violence in the Old West. This chapter will be most useful to you if you read the article first.

Roger D. McGrath
The Myth of Violence in the Old West*

1   It is commonly assumed that violence is part of our frontier heritage. But the historical record shows that frontier violence was very different from violence today. Robbery and burglary, two of our most common crimes, were of no great significance in the frontier towns of the Old West, and rape was seemingly nonexistent.

2   Bodie, one of the principal towns on the trans-Sierra frontier, illustrates the point. Nestled high in the mountains of eastern California, Bodie, which boomed in the late 1870s and early 1880s, ranked among the most notorious frontier towns of the Old West. It was, as one prospector put it, the last of the old-time mining camps.

*From Roger D. McGrath, "The Myth of Violence in the Old West," *Gunfighters, Highwaymen, and Vigilantes: Violence on the Frontier.* Regents of the University of California, 1984.

3   Like the trans-Sierra frontier in general, Bodie was indisputably violent and law-less, yet most people were not affected. Fistfights and gunfights among willing combatants—gamblers, miners, and the like—were regular events, and stagecoach holdups were not unusual. But the old, the young, the weak, and the female—so often the victims of crime today—were generally not harmed.

4   Robbery was more often aimed at stagecoaches than at individuals. Highwaymen usually took only the express box and left the passengers alone. There were eleven stagecoach robberies in Bodie between 1878 and 1882, and in only two instances were passengers robbed. (In one instance, the highwaymen later apologized for their conduct.)

5   There were only ten robberies and three attempted robberies of individuals in Bodie during its boom years, and in nearly every case the circumstances were the same: the victim had spent the evening in a gambling den, saloon, or brothel; he had revealed that he had on his person a significant sum of money; and he was staggering home drunk when the attack occurred.

6   Bodie's total of twenty-one robberies—eleven of stages and ten of individuals—over a five-year period converts to a rate of eighty-four robberies per 100,000 inhabitants per year. On this scale—the same scale used by the FBI to index crime—New York City's robbery rate in 1980 was 1,140, Miami's was 995, and Los Angeles's was 628. The rate for the United States as a whole was 243. Thus Bodie's robbery rate was significantly below the national average in 1980.

7   Perhaps the greatest deterrent to crime in Bodie was the fact that so many people were armed. Armed guards prevented bank robberies and holdups of stagecoaches carrying shipments of bullion, and armed homeowners and merchants discouraged burglary. Between 1878 and 1882, there were only thirty-two burglaries—seventeen of homes and fifteen of businesses—in Bodie. At least a half-dozen burglaries were thwarted by the presence of armed citizens. The newspapers regularly advocated shooting burglars on sight, and several burglars were, in fact, shot at.

8   Using the FBI scale, Bodie's burglary rate for those five years was 128. Miami's rate in 1980 was 3,282, New York's was 2,661, and Los Angeles's was 2,602. The rate of the United States as a whole was 1,668, thirteen times that of Bodie.

9   Bodie's law enforcement institutions were certainly not responsible for these low rates. Rarely were robbers or burglars arrested, and even less often were they convicted. Moreover, many law enforcement officers operated on both sides of the law.

10   It was the armed citizens themselves who were the most potent—though not the only—deterrent to larcenous crime. Another was the threat of vigilantism. Highwaymen, for example, understood that while they could take the express box from a stagecoach without arousing the citizens, they risked inciting the entire populace to action if they robbed the passengers.

11   There is considerable evidence that women in Bodie were rarely the victims of crime. Between 1878 and 1882 only one woman, a prostitute, was robbed, and there were no reported cases of rape. (There is no evidence that rapes occurred but were not reported.)

12   Finally, juvenile crime, which accounts for a significant portion of the violent crime in the United States today, was limited in Bodie to pranks and malicious mischief.

13　　If robbery, burglary, crimes against women, and juvenile crime were relatively rare on the trans-Sierra frontier, homicide was not: thirty-one Bodieites were shot, stabbed, or beaten to death during the boom years, for a homicide rate of 116. No U.S. city today comes close to this rate. In 1980, Miami led the nation with a homicide rate of 32.7; Las Vegas was a distant second at 23.4. A half-dozen cities had rates of zero. The rate for the United States as a whole in that year was a mere 10.2.

14　　Several factors contributed to Bodie's high homicide rate. A majority of the town's residents were young, adventurous, single males who adhered to a code of conduct that frequently required them to fight even if, or perhaps especially if, it could mean death. Courage was admired above all else. Alcohol also played a major role in fostering the settlement of disputes by violence.

15　　If the men's code of conduct and their consumption of alcohol made fighting inevitable, their sidearms often made it fatal. While the carrying of guns probably reduced the incidence of robbery and burglary, it undoubtedly increased the number of homicides.

16　　For the most part, the citizens of Bodie were not troubled by the great number of killings; nor were they troubled that only one man was ever convicted of murder. They accepted the killings and the lack of convictions because most of those killed had been willing combatants.

17　　Thus the violence and lawlessness of the trans-Sierra frontier bear little relation to the violence and lawlessness that pervade American society today. If Bodie is at all representative of frontier towns, there is little justification for blaming contemporary American violence on our frontier heritage.

SKILL I　Let your own argument determine your use of sources.

For effective college-level research, your own argument should govern your use of sources. How you incorporate a research source into your own paper—whether, for example, you summarize it fully or simply draw a few pieces of factual information from it—depends on your own purpose. As an illustration, consider how three hypothetical writers might use Roger D. McGrath's article "The Myth of Violence in the Old West." In each case, the writer's goal is not to reproduce McGrath's article but to use the article in support of the writer's own argument.

Writer I: An Analytical Paper on Causes of Violence in Contemporary Society

The first writer is analyzing the causes of violence in contemporary U.S. society. She wants to reject one possible cause—that contemporary violence is a direct outgrowth of our violent past. To make this point, she summarizes McGrath's argument that the Old West was not as violent as most people think. This summary then becomes evidence for her own argument.

Identification of source

Many people believe that our Wild West heritage is one of the causes of contemporary violence. But Roger McGrath, in his article "The Myth of Violence in the Old West," shows that today's violence is much different from frontier violence.

Summary of McGrath's argument

He explains that in a typical frontier town, violence involved gunslingers who were "willing combatants," whereas today's typical victims—"the old, the young, the weak,

Page number of original material

and the female"—were unaffected by crime (554). Because the presence of an armed populace deterred robbery and burglary, theft was much less common in the Old West than today. On the other hand, McGrath explains, killings were fueled by guns, alcohol, and a code of conduct that invited fighting, so murders were much more frequent than in any U.S. city today (555). Thus, according to McGrath, there is little resemblance between violence on the frontier and violence in today's cities,

Writer 1's own argument

so we cannot blame current violence on a tumultuous frontier past.

In this passage the author summarizes McGrath's argument in order to refute the violent frontier theory about the causes of contemporary violence. This author will proceed to other causes of violence and will not return to McGrath.

Writer 2: A Persuasive Paper Supporting Gun Control

In our next case, the writer uses McGrath's article to argue in favor of gun control. The writer wants to refute the popular pro-gun argument that law-abiding citizens need to be armed to protect themselves against criminals.

Identification of source

Opponents of gun control often argue that guns benefit society by providing protection against intruders. But such protection is deadly, as Roger McGrath shows in his

Data from McGrath's article

study of violence in the frontier town of Bodie, California. Although guns reduced theft, as seen in the low rate of theft in the well-armed town of Bodie, the presence of guns also led to a homicide rate far above that of the most violent city in the U.S. today. The homicide rate in the frontier town of Bodie, California, for example, was

Page number in original

116 per 100,000, compared to the current national average of 10.2 per 100,000 (555). True, Bodie citizens reduced the theft rate by being heavily armed, but at a cost of a homicide rate more than ten times the current national average. To protect our

Writer 2's own analysis of the data and his argument

consumer goods at the cost of so much human life is counter to the values of most Americans.

McGrath's article contains data (low rate of crimes against property, high homicide rate) that can be used on either side of the gun control debate. This writer acknowledges the evidence from Bodie showing that gun possession reduces theft and then works that potentially damaging information into an argument for gun control. How might you use the McGrath article to oppose gun control?

Writer 3: An Informative Paper Showing Shifting Definitions of Crime

The third writer summarizes part of McGrath's article to support her thesis that a community's definition of crime is constantly shifting.

> Our notion of criminal activity shifts over time. For example, only a short time ago on the American frontier, murder was often ignored by law enforcement. Roger McGrath, in his discussion of violence in the frontier town of Bodie, California, during the 1870s and 1880s, showed that the townspeople accepted homicides as long as both the murderer and the victim were "willing combatants" who freely participated in gunfights (554). These young males who were the "willing combatants" in Bodie share many characteristics with modern gang members in that they were encouraged to fight by a "code of conduct." According to McGrath, "A majority of the town's residents were young, adventurous, single males who adhered to a code of conduct that frequently required them to fight even if ... it could mean death" (555). Today's gang members also follow a code of conduct that requires violence—often in the form of vengeance. Although joining a gang certainly makes youths "willing combatants," that status doesn't prevent prosecution in court. Today's "willing combatants" are criminals, but yesterday's "willing combatants" were not.

Identification of source

Partial summary of McGrath's article

Page number

Writer draws comparisons with modern criminals.

Quotation from McGrath's article

Writer extends her comparison.

This writer uses McGrath's article to make a point completely different from McGrath's. But by extending and applying information from McGrath's article to a new context, the writer gathers fuel for her own argument about shifting definitions of the word *criminal*.

Using Sources for a Purpose

FOR WRITING AND DISCUSSION

Each of the hypothetical writers uses McGrath's article for a different purpose. Working individually or in groups, answer the following questions.

1. What are the differences in the ways the writers use the original article?
2. How are these differences related to differences in each writer's purpose?

SKILL 2 Know when and how to use summary, paraphrase, and quotation.

As a research writer, you need to incorporate sources gracefully into your own prose so that you stay focused on your own argument. Depending on your purpose, you might (1) summarize all or part of a source author's argument, (2) paraphrase a relevant portion of a source, or (3) quote small passages from the source directly. Whenever you use a source, you need to avoid plagiarism by referencing the source with an in-text citation, by putting paraphrases and summaries entirely in your own words, and by placing quotation marks around quoted passages. The following strategies chart gives you an overview of summary, paraphrase, and quotation as ways of incorporating sources into your own prose.

Strategies for Incorporating Sources into Your Own Prose		
Strategies	What to Do	When to Use These Strategies
Summarize the source.	Condense a source writer's argument by keeping main ideas and omitting details.	• When the source writer's whole argument is relevant to your purpose • When the source writer presents an alternative or opposing view that you want to push against • When the source writer's argument can be used in support of your own
Paraphrase the source.	Reproduce an idea from a source writer but translate the idea entirely into your own words; a paraphrase should be approximately the same length as the original.	• When you want to incorporate factual information from a source or to use one specific idea from a source • When the source passage is overly complex or technical for your targeted audience • When you want to incorporate a source's point in your own voice without interrupting the flow of your argument

Strategies	What to Do	When to Use These Strategies
Quote short passages from the source using quotation marks.	Work brief quotations from the source smoothly into the grammar of your own sentences (see Skill 4 on the mechanics of quoting).	• When you need testimony from an authority (state the authority's credentials in an attributive tag—see Skill 3) • In summaries, when you want to reproduce a source's voice, particularly if the language is striking or memorable • In lieu of paraphrase when the source language is memorable
Quote long passages from the source using the block method.	Results in a page with noticeably lengthy block quotations (see Skill 4)	• When you intend to analyze or critique the quotation—the quotation is followed by your detailed analysis of its ideas or rhetorical features • When the flavor and language of testimonial evidence is important

With practice, you'll be able to use all these strategies smoothly and effectively.

Summarizing

Summaries can be as short as a single sentence or as long as a paragraph. Make the summary as concise as possible so that you don't distract the reader from your own argument. Writer 1's summary of the McGrath article is a good example of a graceful summary used in support of the writer's own thesis.

Paraphrasing

Unlike a summary, which is a condensation of a source's whole argument, a **paraphrase** translates a short passage from a source's words into the writer's own words. Writers often choose to paraphrase when the details of a source passage are particularly important or when the source is overly technical and needs to be simplified for the intended audience. When you paraphrase, be careful to avoid reproducing the original writer's grammatical structure and syntax. If you mirror the original sentence structure while replacing occasional words with synonyms or small structural changes, you will be doing what composition specialists call

"patchwriting"—that is, patching some of your language into someone else's writing.* Patchwriting is a form of academic dishonesty because you aren't fully composing your own sentences and thus misrepresent both your own work and that of the source writer. An acceptable paraphrase needs to be entirely in your own words. To understand patchwriting more fully, track the differences between unacceptable patchwriting and acceptable paraphrase in the following example.

ORIGINAL

There is considerable evidence that women in Bodie were rarely the victims of crime. Between 1878 and 1882 only one woman, a prostitute, was robbed, and there were no reported cases of rape. (There is no evidence that rapes occurred but were not reported.)

Finally, juvenile crime, which accounts for a significant portion of the violent crime in the United States today, was limited in Bodie to pranks and malicious mischief.

UNACCEPTABLE PATCHWRITING

Note phrases taken word for word from original.

According to McGrath, much evidence exists that women in Bodie were rarely the victims of crime. Between 1878 and 1882 only one woman was robbed, and she was a prostitute. There were no reported cases of rape and no evidence that unreported rapes occurred. Also juvenile crime, which occurs frequently in the United States today, was limited in Bodie to pranks and mischief.

ACCEPTABLE PARAPHRASE

Only one word-for-word phrase

Quotation marks around exact phrase

Page number of original

Violence in Bodie was different from violence today. According to McGrath, women in Bodie seldom suffered at the hands of criminals. No reported rapes occurred in Bodie between 1878 and 1882, and the only female robbery victim was a prostitute. Another difference, as McGrath points out, is that juvenile crime was rare except for occasional "pranks and malicious mischief" (554).

Both the patchwriting example and the acceptable paraphrase reproduce the same ideas as the original in approximately the same number of words. But the writer of the paraphrase has been more careful to change the sentence structure substantially and to focus more clearly on his own argument (differences between Bodie and the present). In the acceptable paraphrase, one unquoted phrase still mirrors the original: "between 1878 and 1882." But this phrase is short and carries little of the passage's meaning. The longer mirrored phrase is quoted exactly. In contrast, the patchwritten version contains longer strings of borrowed language without quotation marks.

*We are indebted to the work of Rebecca Moore Howard and others who have led composition researchers to reexamine the use of sources and plagiarism from a cultural and rhetorical perspective. See especially Rebecca Moore Howard, *Standing in the Shadow of Giants: Plagiarists, Authors, Collaborators.* Stamford, CT: Ablex Pub., 1999.

Among novice writers, the use of Web sources can particularly lead to patch-writing. It is all too easy to copy and paste a Web-based passage into your own draft and then attempt to revise it by changing some of the words. In contrast, patchwriting almost never occurs if you are generating your own language—that is, if you are converting information from a source into your own words in order to make your own argument.

When you first practice paraphrasing, you might try paraphrasing a passage twice to avoid patchwriting and achieve an acceptable paraphrase.

- The first time, read the passage carefully and put it into your own words, looking at the source as little as possible.
- The second time, paraphrase your own paraphrase. Then recheck your final version against the original to make sure you have eliminated similar sentence structure and word-for-word strings.

We'll return to the problem of patchwriting in our discussion of plagiarism (Skill 5).

Quoting

Besides summary and paraphrase, writers often choose to quote directly in order to give the reader the flavor and style of the source author's prose or to make a memorable point in the source author's own voice. Our previous example of an acceptable paraphrase includes such a quotation in the last sentence. Be careful not to quote a passage that you don't fully understand. (Sometimes novice writers quote a passage because it sounds impressive.) When you quote, you must reproduce the source author's original words exactly, without any changes, unless you indicate changes with ellipses or brackets. Also be careful to represent the author's intentions and meaning fairly; don't change the author's meaning by taking quotations out of context. Because the mechanics of quoting offers its own difficulties, we devote a separate section to it later in this chapter (Skill 4).

SKILL 3 Use attributive tags to distinguish your ideas from a source's.

Whenever you use sources in your writing, you need to signal to your reader which words and ideas come from your source and which are your own. There are generally two ways of doing so:

- ***State source author's name in an attributive tag.*** You can identify the source by using a short phrase (called an **attributive tag** or sometimes a **signal phrase** or **signal tag**) such as "according to McGrath," "McGrath says," "in McGrath's view," and so on. In the humanities, the source author's full name is commonly used the first time the author is mentioned. If the tag refs to a specific passage or quotation in the source, then a page number is placed in parentheses at the end of the quotation.

Attributive tag

> According to Roger D. McGrath, violence was not as common in the Wild West as most people think.

Attributive tag

Page number of quotation.

> McGrath explains that "frontier violence was very different from violence today" (553).

- **State source author's name in a parenthetical citation.** You can identify a source by placing the author's name in parentheses at the end of the material taken from the source (called a **parenthetical citation**).

Source identified in parentheses

> Violence was not as common in the Wild West as most people think (McGrath).

Page number of quotation.

> "Frontier violence was very different from violence today" (McGrath 553).

Of these two methods, attributive tags are generally preferred, especially when you are writing for general rather than specialist audiences. The attributive tag method has three advantages:

- It signals where borrowed material starts and ends.
- It avoids ambiguities about what is "fact" and what is filtered through a source's angle of vision.
- It allows the writer to frame the borrowed material rhetorically.

Let's look at each of these in turn.

Attributive Tags Mark Where Source Material Starts and Ends

The parenthetical method requires readers to wait until the end of the writer's use of source material before the source is identified. Attributive tags, in contrast, identify the source from the moment it is first used. Here are excerpts from Writer 1's summary of McGrath, in which we have highlighted the attributive tags. Note the frequency with which the writer informs the reader that this material comes from McGrath.

USE OF ATTRIBUTIVE TAGS IN WRITER 1'S SUMMARY

Many people believe that our Wild West heritage is one of the causes of contemporary violence. But Roger McGrath, in his article "The Myth of Violence in the Old West," shows that today's violence is much different from frontier violence. He explains that. ... On the other hand, McGrath explains, killings were fueled. ... Thus, according to McGrath, there is little resemblance between violence on the frontier and violence in today's cities. ...

Here the attributive tags signal the use of McGrath's ideas throughout the summary. The reader is never confused about which words and ideas come from McGrath.

Attributive Tags Avoid Ambiguities that Can Arise with the Parenthetical Citations

Not only does the parenthetical method fail to mark where the source material begins, it also tends to imply that the source material is a "fact" rather than the view of the source author. In contrast, attributive tags always call attention to the source's angle of vision. Note this ambiguity in the following passage, where parenthetical citations are used without attributive tags:

AMBIGUOUS ATTRIBUTION

There are many arguments in favor of preserving old-growth forests. First, it is simply unnecessary to log these forests to supply the world's lumber. We have plenty of new-growth forest from which lumber can be taken (Sagoff 89–90). Recently there have been major reforestation efforts all over the United States, and it is common practice now for loggers to replant every tree that is harvested. These new-growth forests, combined with extensive planting of tree farms, provide more than enough wood for the world's needs. Tree farms alone can supply the world's demand for industrial lumber (Sedjo 90).

When confronted with this passage, skeptical readers might ask, "Who are Sagoff and Sedjo? I've never heard of them." It is also difficult to tell how much of the passage is the writer's own argument and how much is borrowed from Sagoff and Sedjo. Is this whole passage a paraphrase? Finally, the writer tends to treat Sagoff's and Sedjo's assertions as uncontested facts rather than as professional opinions. Compare the preceding version with this one, in which attributive tags are added:

CLEAR ATTRIBUTION

There are many arguments in favor of preserving old-growth forests. First, it is simply unnecessary to log these forests to supply the world's lumber. According to environmentalist Carl Sagoff, we have plenty of new-growth forest from which lumber can be taken (89–90). Recently there have been major reforestation efforts all over the United States, and it is common practice now for loggers to replant every tree that is harvested. These new-growth forests, combined with extensive planting of tree farms, provide more than enough wood for the world's needs. According to forestry expert Robert Sedjo, tree farms alone can supply the world's demand for industrial lumber (90).

We can now see that most of the paragraph is the writer's own argument, into which she has inserted the expert testimony of Sagoff and Sedjo, whose views are treated not as indisputable facts but as the opinions of authorities in this field.

Attributive Tags Frame the Source Material Rhetorically

When you introduce a source for the first time, you can use the attributive tag not only to introduce the source but also to shape your readers' attitudes toward the source. In the previous example, the writer wants readers to respect Sagoff and Sedjo, so she identifies Sagoff as an "environmentalist" and Sedjo as a "forestry expert." If the writer favored logging old-growth forests and supported the logging industry's desire to create more jobs, she might have used different tags: "Carl Sagoff, an outspoken advocate for spotted owls over people," or "Robert Sedjo, a forester with limited knowledge of world lumber markets."

When you compose an initial tag, you can add to it any combination of the following kinds of information, depending on your purpose, your audience's values, and your sense of what the audience already knows or doesn't know about the source:

Strategies for Modifying Attributive Tags to Shape Reader Response	
Add to Attributive Tags	**Examples**
Author's credentials or relevant specialty (enhances credibility)	Civil engineer David Rockwood, a noted authority on stream flow in rivers
Author's lack of credentials (decreases credibility)	City Council member Dilbert Weasel, a local politician with no expertise in international affairs
Author's political or social views	Left-wing columnist Alexander Cockburn [has negative feeling]; Alexander Cockburn, a longtime champion of labor [has positive feeling]
Title of source if it provides context	In her book *Fasting Girls: The History of Anorexia Nervosa*, Joan Jacobs Brumberg shows that [establishes credentials for comments on eating disorders]
Publisher of source if it adds prestige or otherwise shapes audience response	Dr. Carl Patrona, in an article published in the prestigious *New England Journal of Medicine*
Historical or cultural information about a source that provides context or background	In his 1960s book popularizing the hippie movement, Charles Reich claims that
Indication of source's purpose or angle of vision	Feminist author Naomi Wolfe, writing a blistering attack on the beauty industry, argues that

Our point here is that you can use attributive tags rhetorically to help your readers understand the significance and context of a source when you first introduce it and to guide your readers' attitudes toward the source.

Evaluating Different Ways to Use and Cite a Source

What follow are four different ways that a writer can use the same passage from a source to support a point about the greenhouse effect. Working in groups or as a whole class, rank the four methods from "most effective" to "least effective." Assume that you are writing a researched argument addressed to your college classmates.

1. ***Quotation with parenthetical citation***
   The greenhouse effect will have a devastating effect on the earth's environment: "Potential impacts include increased mortality and illness due to heat stress and worsened air pollution, as in the 1995 Chicago heat wave that killed hundreds of people. ... Infants, children and other vulnerable populations—especially in already-stressed regions of the world—would likely suffer disproportionately from these impacts" (Hall 19).

2. ***Quotation with attributive tag***
   The greenhouse effect will have a devastating effect on the earth's environment. David C. Hall, president of Physicians for Social Responsibility, claims the following: "Potential impacts include increased mortality and illness due to heat stress and worsened air pollution, as in the 1995 Chicago heat wave that killed hundreds of people. ... Infants, children and other vulnerable populations—especially in already-stressed regions of the world—would likely suffer disproportionately from these impacts" (19).

3. ***Paraphrase with parenthetical citation***
   The greenhouse effect will have a devastating effect on the earth's environment. One of the most frightening effects is the threat of diseases stemming from increased air pollution and heat stress. Infants and children would be most at risk (Hall 19).

4. ***Paraphrase with attributive tag***
   The greenhouse effect will have a devastating effect on the earth's environment. One of the most frightening effects, according to David C. Hall, president of Physicians for Social Responsibility, is the threat of diseases stemming from increased air pollution and heat stress. Infants and children would be most at risk (19).

SKILL 4 Punctuate quotations correctly.

In Skill 2, we explained your options for incorporating a source into your own paper—summary, paraphrase, and quotation. Whenever you quote, you must make nuts-and-bolts decisions about punctuation such as when and how to use quotation marks, commas, colons, brackets, and ellipses. When you learn these skills, you will know how to punctuate any quotation correctly, including how to make slight changes in the quotation to fit the grammar of your own sentence. This section answers the following mechanical question about quotations:

- How do I quote a complete sentence from my source?
- How do I insert quoted words and phrases into my own sentences?
- How do I indicate my own modifications to a quotation?
- How do I indicate that I have left something out of a quotation?
- How do I quote something that already has quotation marks in it?
- What if I want to use a long quotation?

These explanations will cover the big picture about the mechanics of quoting. Additional explanations covering variations and specific cases can be found in any good handbook.

Quoting a Complete Sentence

In some cases, you will want to quote a complete sentence from your source. Typically, you will include an attributive tag that tells the reader who is being quoted. At the end of the quotation, you usually indicate its page number in parentheses.

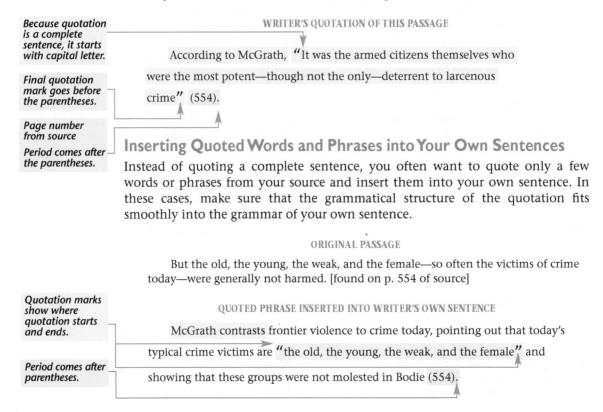

ORIGINAL PASSAGE

It was the armed citizens themselves who were the most potent—though not the only—deterrent to larcenous crime. [found on p. 554 of source]

Because quotation is a complete sentence, it starts with capital letter.

WRITER'S QUOTATION OF THIS PASSAGE

According to McGrath, "It was the armed citizens themselves who were the most potent—though not the only—deterrent to larcenous crime" (554).

Final quotation mark goes before the parentheses.

Page number from source

Period comes after the parentheses.

Inserting Quoted Words and Phrases into Your Own Sentences

Instead of quoting a complete sentence, you often want to quote only a few words or phrases from your source and insert them into your own sentence. In these cases, make sure that the grammatical structure of the quotation fits smoothly into the grammar of your own sentence.

ORIGINAL PASSAGE

But the old, the young, the weak, and the female—so often the victims of crime today—were generally not harmed. [found on p. 554 of source]

Quotation marks show where quotation starts and ends.

QUOTED PHRASE INSERTED INTO WRITER'S OWN SENTENCE

McGrath contrasts frontier violence to crime today, pointing out that today's typical crime victims are "the old, the young, the weak, and the female" and showing that these groups were not molested in Bodie (554).

Period comes after parentheses.

Modifying a Quotation

Occasionally you may need to alter a quotation to make it fit your own context. Sometimes the grammar of a desired quotation doesn't match the grammar of your own sentence. At other times, the meaning of a quoted word is unclear because it is removed from its original context. In these cases, use brackets to modify the quotation's grammar or to add a clarifying explanation. Place your changes or additions in brackets to indicate that the bracketed material is not part of the original wording. You should also use brackets to show a change in capitalization.

ORIGINAL PASSAGES

The newspapers regularly advocated shooting burglars on sight, and several burglars were, in fact, shot at. [found on p. 554 of source]

Highwaymen, for example, understood that while they could take the express box from a stagecoach without arousing the citizens, they risked inciting the entire populace to action if they robbed the passengers. [found on p. 554 of source]

QUOTATIONS MODIFIED WITH BRACKETS

By "regularly advocat[ing] shooting burglars on sight," newspapers in Bodie helped an armed citizenry deter crime (McGrath 554).

Brackets show change in quotation to fit grammar of writer's sentence.

Parenthetical method of identifying source

Public sentiment influenced what laws were likely to be broken. According to McGrath, "[W]hile they [highwaymen] could take the express box from a stagecoach without arousing the citizens, they risked inciting the entire populace to action if they robbed the passengers" (554).

Attributive tag

Brackets show a lowercase letter changed to a capital letter.

Brackets show that writer has added a word to explain what "they" stands for.

Omitting Something from a Quoted Passage

Another way that writers modify quotations is to leave words out of the quoted passage. To indicate an omission, use three spaced periods called an **ellipsis** (. . .). Placement of the ellipsis depends on where the omission of material occurs. In the middle of a sentence, each of the periods should be preceded and followed by a space. When your ellipsis comes at the boundary between sentences, use an additional period to mark the end of the first sentence. When a parenthetical page number must follow the ellipsis, insert it before the final (fourth) period in the sequence.

ORIGINAL PASSAGES

Finally, juvenile crime, which accounts for a significant portion of the violent crime in the United States today, was limited in Bodie to pranks and malicious mischief. [found on p. 554 of source]

Bodie's law enforcement institutions were certainly not responsible for these low rates. Rarely were robbers or burglars arrested, and even less often were they convicted. Moreover, many law enforcement officers operated on both sides of the law. [found on p. 554 of source]

Three spaced periods mark omitted words in middle of sentence.

According to McGrath, "juvenile crime . . . was limited in Bodie to pranks and malicious mischief" (554).

This period ends the sentence.

These three periods form the ellipsis.

"Bodie's law enforcement institutions were certainly not responsible for these low rates. . . . Moreover, many law enforcement officers operated on both sides of the law" (McGrath 554).

Ellipsis marks omitted words before the end of the sentence.

Quotation mark shows where quotation ends.

"Bodie's law enforcement institutions were certainly not responsible for these low rates. Rarely were robbers or burglars arrested . . ."

This period ends the sentence.

(McGrath 554).

Quoting Something That Already Contains a Quotation

Occasionally a passage that you wish to quote will already contain quotation marks. If you insert the passage within your own quotation marks, change the original double marks (") into single marks (') to indicate the quotation within the quotation. The same procedure works whether the quotation marks are used for quoted words or for a title. Make sure that your attributive tag signals who is being quoted. Because the McGrath article contains no internal quotation marks, we will use a different example to illustrate quotations within quotations.

And finally, we tend to stereotype because it helps us make sense out of a highly confusing world, a world which William James once described as "one great, blooming, buzzing confusion." [Passage from an article by Robert Heilbroner, who here quotes William James]

Regular quotation marks indicate the material quoted from Heilbroner.

Robert Heilbroner explains that people create stereotypes "because it helps us make sense out of a highly confusing world, a world which William James once described as 'one great, blooming, buzzing confusion'."

Heilbroner's own attributive tag notes William James.

Single quotation marks indicate the material quoted from James.

Using a Block Quotation for a Long Passage

If your quoted passage uses more than four lines in your own paper, use the block indentation method rather than quotation marks. Block quotations are generally introduced with an attributive tag followed by a colon. The indented block of text, rather than quotation marks, signals that the material is a direct quotation. Block quotations occur rarely in scholarly writing and are used primarily in cases where the writer intends to analyze the text being quoted. If you overuse block quotations, you produce a "choo-choo train" paper that is simply a collage of other people's voices.

ORIGINAL PASSAGE

Fistfights and gunfights among willing combatants—gamblers, miners, and the like—were regular events, and stagecoach holdups were not unusual. But the old, the young, the weak, and the female—so often the victims of crime today—were generally not harmed.

BLOCK QUOTATION

McGrath describes the people most affected by violence in the frontier town of Bodie: ◄

> Fistfights and gunfights among willing combatants—gamblers, miners, and the like—were regular events, and stagecoach holdups were not unusual. But the old, the young, the weak, and the female—so often the victims of crime today—were generally not harmed. (554) ◄

Block quotation introduced with a colon

No quotation marks

Block indented 1 inch on left.

Period and mark end of sentence.

Page number in parentheses after the closing period and space.

SKILL 5 Avoid plagiarism by following academic conventions for ethical use of sources.

Unethical use of sources—called **plagiarism**—is a major concern not only for writing teachers but for teachers in all disciplines. To combat plagiarism, many instructors across the curriculum use plagiarism-detection software like turnitin.com. Their purpose, of course, is to discourage students from cheating. But sometimes students who have no intention of cheating can fall into producing papers that look like cheating. That is, they produce papers that might be accused of plagiarism even though the students had no intention of deceiving their readers.* Our goal in this section is to explain the concept of plagiarism more fully and to sum up the strategies needed to avoid it.

Why Some Kinds of Plagiarism May Occur Unwittingly

To understand how unwitting plagiarism might occur, consider Table 1, where the middle column—"Misuse of Sources"—shows common mistakes of novice writers. Everyone agrees that the behaviors in the "Fraud" column constitute deliberate cheating and deserve appropriate punishment. Everyone also agrees that good scholarly work meets the criteria in the "Ethical Use of Sources" column. Novice researchers, however, may find themselves unwittingly in the middle column until they learn the academic community's conventions for using research sources.

*See Rebecca Moore Howard, *Standing in the Shadow of Giants: Plagiarists, Authors, Collaborators.* Stamford, CT: Ablex Pub., 1999.

TABLE 1   **Plagiarism and the Ethical Use of Sources**

Plagiarism		Ethical Use of Sources
Fraud	**Misuse of Sources** *(Common Mistakes Made by New Researchers)*	
The writer • buys paper from a paper mill • submits someone else's work as his own • copies chunks of text from sources with obvious intention of not being detected • fabricates data or makes up evidence • intends to deceive	The writer • copies passages directly from a source, references the source with an in-text citation, but fails to use quotation marks or block indentation • in attempting to paraphrase a source, makes some changes, but follows too closely the wording of the original ("patchwriting") • fails to indicate the sources of some ideas or data (often is unsure what needs to be cited or has lost track of sources through poor note taking) • in general, misunderstands the conventions for using sources in academic writing	The writer • writes paper entirely in her own words or uses exact quotations from sources • indicates all quotations with quotation marks or block indentation • indicates her use of all sources through attribution, in-text citation, and an end-of-paper list of works cited

You might appreciate these conventions more fully if you recognize how they have evolved from Western notions of intellectual property and patent law associated with the rise of modern science in the seventeenth and eighteenth centuries. A person not only could own a house or a horse, but also could own an idea and the words used to express that idea. You can see these cultural conventions at work—in the form of laws or professional codes of ethics—whenever a book author is disgraced for lifting words or ideas from another author or whenever an artist or entrepreneur is sued for stealing song lyrics, publishing another person's photographs without permission, or infringing on some inventor's patent.

This understanding of plagiarism may seem odd in some non-Western cultures where collectivism is valued more than individualism. In these cultures, words written or spoken by ancestors, elders, or other authority figures may be regarded with reverence and shared with others without attribution. Also in these cultures, it might be disrespectful to paraphrase certain passages or to document them in a way that would suggest the audience didn't recognize the ancient wisdom.

However, such collectivist conventions won't work in research communities committed to building new knowledge. In the academic world, the conventions separating ethical from unethical use of sources are essential if research findings are to win the community's confidence. Effective research can occur only within ethical and responsible research communities where people do not fabricate data and where current researchers respect and acknowledge the work of those who have gone before them.

Strategies for Avoiding Plagiarism

The following chart will help you review the strategies for using source material ethically and avoiding plagiarism.

Strategies for Avoiding Plagiarism or the Appearance of Plagiarism		
What to Do	**Why to Do It**	**Where to Find More Information**
At the beginning		
Read your college's policy on plagiarism as well as statements from your teachers in class or on course syllabi.	Understanding policies on plagiarism and academic integrity will help you research and write ethically.	
Pose a research question rather than a topic area.	Arguing your own thesis gives you a voice, establishes your *ethos*, and urges you to write ethically.	
At the note-taking stage		
Create a bibliographic entry for each source.	This action makes it easy to create an end-of-paper bibliography and encourages rhetorical reading	
When you copy a passage into your notes, copy word for word and enclose it with in quotation marks.	It is important to distinguish a source's words from your own words.	
When you enter summaries or paraphrases into your notes, avoid patchwriting.	If your notes contain any strings of a source's original wording, you might later assume that these words are your own.	Skill 2
Distinguish your informational notes from your personal exploratory notes	Keeping these kinds of notes separate will help you identify borrowed ideas when it's time to incorporate the source material into your paper.	

(continued)

What to Do	Why to Do It	Where to Find More Information
When writing your draft		
Except for exact quotations, write the paper entirely in your own words.	This strategy keeps you from patchwriting when you summarize or paraphrase.	Skill 2
Indicate all quotations with quotation marks or block indentation. Use ellipses or brackets to make changes to fit your own grammar.	Be careful to represent the author fairly; don't change meaning by taking quotations out of context.	Skills 2 and 4
When you summarize or paraphrase, avoid patchwriting.	Word-for-word strings from a source must either be avoided or placed in quotation marks. Also avoid mirroring the source's grammatical structure.	Skill 2
Never cut and paste a Web passage directly into your draft. Paste it into a separate note file and put quotation marks around it.	Pasted passages are direct invitations to patchwrite.	Skill 2
Inside your text, use attributive tags or parenthetical citations to identify all sources. List all sources alphabetically in a concluding works cited or references list.	This strategy makes it easy for readers to know when you are using a source and where to find it.	Skill 3
Cite with attributive tags or parenthetical citations all quotations, paraphrases, summaries, and any other references to specific sources.	These are the most common in-text citations in a research paper.	
Use in-text citations to indicate sources for all visuals and media such as graphs, maps, photographs, films, videos, broadcasts, and recordings.	The rules for citing words and ideas apply equally to visuals and media cited in your paper.	
Use in-text citations for all ideas and facts that are not common knowledge.	Although you don't need to cite widely accepted and noncontroversial facts and information, it is better to cite them if you are unsure.	

Avoiding Plagiarism

Read the passage below. Unlike the ethical summary of McGrath's article produced by Writer 1, the writer of the following passage would likely be accused of plagiarism.

SUMMARY OF McGRATH'S ARTICLE (AN EXAMPLE OF PLAGIARISM)

It is commonly assumed that violence is part of our Wild West heritage. But Roger McGrath, in his article "The Myth of Violence in the Old West," shows that frontier violence was very different from violence today. He explains that in a typical frontier town, violence involved gunslingers who were "willing combatants," whereas today's typical victims—the old, the young, the weak, and the female—were unaffected by crime (554). The greatest deterrent to crime in Bodie was the fact that so many people were armed. Armed guards prevented bank robberies and stagecoach holdups, and armed citizens stopped burglary. On the other hand, McGrath explains, Bodie had a high homicide rate. Most of the town's residents were young single males who adhered to a code of conduct that frequently required them to fight. Alcohol also played a major role. Therefore murders were much more frequent than in any U.S. city today (554). Thus, according to McGrath, there is little resemblance between violence on the frontier and violence in today's cities, so we cannot blame current violence on our tumultuous frontier past.

Working in small groups or as a whole class, respond to the following questions.

1. How does this passage cross the line into plagiarism? (You'll need to compare the passage to Writer 1's ethical summary.)
2. The writer of this passage might say, "How can this be plagiarism? I cited my source and gave page numbers." How would you explain the problem to this writer?
3. Psychologically or cognitively, what may have caused this writer to misuse the source? How might this writer's note-taking process or composing process have differed from that of Writer 1? In other words, what happened that got this writer into trouble?

mycomplab | For support in learning this chapter's content, follow this path in MyCompLab: Resources ⇒ Research ⇒ The Research Assignment ⇒ Integrating Sources. Review the Instruction and Multimedia resources about integrating sources, then complete the Exercises and click on Gradebook to measure your progress.

CITING AND DOCUMENTING SOURCES

From Chapter 22 of *The Allyn & Bacon Guide to Writing*, Sixth Edition. John D. Ramage, John C. Bean, June Johnson. Copyright © 2012 by Pearson Education, Inc. Published by Pearson Allyn & Bacon. All rights reserved.

CITING AND DOCUMENTING SOURCES

In this chapter we focus on the nuts and bolts of documenting sources in a way appropriate to your purpose, audience, and genre, using the systems of the Modern Language Association (MLA) and the American Psychological Association (APA).* Accurate documentation not only helps other researchers locate your sources but also contributes substantially to your own *ethos* as a writer.

Specifically, in this chapter you will learn the following skills:

- **SKILL 1**   Know what needs to be cited and what doesn't.
- **SKILL 2**   Understand the connection between in-text citations and the end-of-paper list of cited works.
- **SKILL 3**   Cite and document sources using MLA style.
- **SKILL 4**   Cite and document sources using APA style.

SKILL 1 Know what needs to be cited and what doesn't.

Beginning researchers are often confused about what needs to be cited and what doesn't. Table 1 will help you make this determination. If you are in doubt, it is better to cite than not to cite.

It is often difficult to determine when a given piece of information falls into the "common knowledge" column of Table 1. The answer depends both on your target audience's background knowledge and on your own ability to speak as an authority. Consider the statement "Twitter and Facebook are forms of social networking." That information is noncontroversial and well known and so doesn't require citation. But if you added, "Twitter is more popular with middle-aged adults than with teenagers," you would need to cite your source (some newspaper article or poll?) unless you are a teenager speaking with authority from your own experience, in which case you would provide personal-experience examples. If you are uncertain, our best advice is this: When in doubt, cite.

---

*Our discussion of MLA style is based on the *MLA Handbook for Writers of Research Papers*, 7th ed. (2009). Our discussion of APA style is based on the *Publication Manual of the American Psychological Association*, 6th ed. (2010).

TABLE 1	Determining What Needs to Be Cited	
What Needs to Be Cited		**What Does Not Need to Be Cited**

You must cite all references to your research sources as well as any information that is not commonly known by your targeted audience:

- Any quotation
- Any passage that you paraphrase
- Any passage or source that you summarize or otherwise refer to
- Any image, photograph, map, drawing, graph, chart, or other visual that you download from the Web (or find elsewhere) and include in your paper
- Any sound or video file that you use in a multimedia project
- Any idea, fact, statistic, or other information that you find from a source and that is not commonly known by your targeted audience

You do not need to cite commonly shared, widely known knowledge that will be considered factual and noncontroversial to your targeted audience:

- Commonly known facts (Water freezes at 32 degrees Fahrenheit.)
- Commonly known dates (Terrorists flew airplanes into New York's World Trade Center on September 11, 2001.)
- Commonly known events (Barack Obama defeated John McCain for the presidency.)
- Commonly known historical or cultural knowledge (Twitter and Facebook are forms of social networking.)

SKILL 2 Understand the connection between in-text citations and the end-of-paper list of cited works.

The most common forms of documentation use what are called in-text citations that match an end-of-paper list of cited works (as opposed to footnotes or endnotes). An ***in-text citation*** identifies a source in the body of the paper at the point where it is summarized, paraphrased, quoted, inserted, or otherwise referred to. At the end of your paper you include a list—alphabetized by author (or by title if there is no named author)—of all the works you cited. Both the Modern Language Association (MLA) system, used primarily in the humanities, and the American Psychological Association (APA) system, used primarily in the social sciences, follow this procedure. In MLA, your end-of-paper list is called **Works Cited.** In APA it is called **References.**

Whenever you place an in-text citation in the body of your paper, your reader knows to turn to the Works Cited or References list at the end of the paper to get the full bibliographic information. The key to the system's logic is this:

- Every source in Works Cited or References must be mentioned in the body of the paper.
- Conversely, every source mentioned in the body of the paper must be included in the end-of-paper list.
- The first word in each entry of the Works Cited or References list (usually an author's last name) must also appear in the in-text citation. In other words, there must be a one-to-one correspondence between the first word in each entry in the end-of-paper list and the name used to identify the source in the body of the paper.

739

Suppose a reader sees this phrase in your paper: "According to Debra Goldstein. ..." The reader should be able to turn to your Works Cited list and find an alphabetized entry beginning with "Goldstein, Debra." Similarly, suppose that in looking over your Works Cited list, your reader sees an article by "Guillen, Manuel." This means that the name "Guillen" has to appear in your paper in one of two ways:

- As an attributive tag: Economics professor Manuel Guillen argues that....
- As a parenthetical citation, often following a quotation: "...changes in fiscal policy" (Guillen 49).

Because this one-to-one correspondence is so important, let's illustrate it with some complete examples using the MLA formatting style:

If the body of your paper has this:	Then the Works Cited list must have this:
According to linguist Deborah Tannen, political debate in America leaves out the complex middle ground where most solutions must be developed.	Tannen, Deborah. *The Argument Culture: Moving from Debate to Dialogue*. New York: Random, 1998. Print.
In the 1980s, cigarette advertising revealed a noticeable pattern of racial stereotyping (Pollay, Lee, and Carter-Whitney).	Pollay, Richard W., Jung S. Lee, and David Carter-Whitney. "Separate, but Not Equal: Racial Segmentation in Cigarette Advertising." *Journal of Advertising* 21.1 (1992): 45–57. Print.
On its Web site, the National Men's Resource Center offers advice to parents on how to talk with children about alcohol and drugs ("Talking").	"Talking with Kids about Alcohol and Drugs." *Menstuff*. National Men's Resource Center, 1 Mar. 2007. Web. 26 June 2007.

How to format an MLA in-text citation and a Works Cited list entry is the subject of the next section. The APA system is similar except that it emphasizes the date of publication in both the in-text citation and the References entry. APA formatting is the subject of Skill 4.

SKILL 3 Cite and document sources using MLA style.

An in-text citation and its corresponding Works Cited entry are linked in a chicken-and-egg system: You can't cite a source in the text without first knowing how the source's entry will be alphabetized in the Works Cited list. However, since most Works Cited entries are alphabetized by the first author's last name, for convenience we start with in-text citations.

In-Text Citations in MLA Style

A typical in-text citation contains two elements: (1) the last name of the author and (2) the page number of the quoted or paraphrased passage. However, in some cases a work is identified by something other than an author's last name, and sometimes no page number is required. Let's begin with the most common cases.

Typically, an in-text citation uses one of these two methods:

- **_Parenthetical method._** Place the author's last name and the page number in parentheses immediately after the material being cited.

    The Spanish tried to reduce the status of Filipina, women who had been able to

    do business, get divorced, and sometimes become village chiefs (Karnow 41).

- **_Attributive tag method._** Place the author's name in an attributive tag at the beginning of the source material and the page number in parentheses at the end.

    According to Karnow, the Spanish tried to reduce the status of Filipina women,

    who had been able to do business, get divorced, and sometimes become village

    chiefs (41).

Once you have cited an author and it is clear that the same author's material is being used, you need cite only the page numbers in parentheses in subsequent citations. A reader who wishes to look up the source will find the bibliographic information in the Works Cited section by looking for the entry under "Karnow."

Let's now turn to the variations. Table 2 identifies the typical variations and shows again the one-to-one connection between the in-text citation and the Works Cited list.

TABLE 2   In-Text Citations in MLA Style

Type of Source	Works Cited Entry at End of Paper (Construct the entry while taking notes on each source.)	In-Text Citation in Body of Paper (Use the first word of the Works Cited entry in parentheses or an attributive tag; add page number at end of quoted or paraphrased passage.)
One author	Pollan, Michael. *The Omnivore's Dilemma: A Natural History of Four Meals*. New York: Penguin, 2006. Print.	…(Pollan 256). OR According to Pollan,…(256).
More than one author	Pollay, Richard W., Jung S. Lee, and David Carter-Whitney. "Separate, but Not Equal: Racial Segmentation in Cigarette Advertising." *Journal of Advertising* 21.1 (1992): 45–57. Print.	…race" (Pollay, Lee, and Carter-Whitney 52). OR Pollay, Lee, and Carter-Whitney have argued that "advertisers…race" (52). *For the in-text citation, cite the specific page number rather than the whole range of pages given in the Works Cited entry.*

(continued)

TABLE 2 *continued*

Type of Source	Works Cited Entry at End of Paper	In-Text Citation in Body of Paper (*Use the first word of the Works Cited entry in parentheses or an attributive tag; add page number at end of quoted or paraphrased passage.*)
Author has more than one work in Works Cited list	Dombrowski, Daniel A. *Babies and Beasts: The Argument from Marginal Cases*. Urbana: U of Illinois P, 1997. Print. ---. *The Philosophy of Vegetarianism*. Amherst: U of Massachusetts P, 1984. Print.	…(Dombrowski, *Babies* 207). …(Dombrowski, *Philosophy* 328). OR According to Dombrowski,…(*Babies* 207). Dombrowski claims that… (*Philosophy* 328). *Because author has more than one work in Works Cited, include a short version of title to distinguish between entries.*
Corporate author	American Red Cross. *Standard First Aid*. St. Louis: Mosby Lifeline, 1993. Print.	…(American Red Cross 102). OR Snake bite instructions from the American Red Cross show that… (102).
No named author (Work is therefore alphabetized by title.)	"Ouch! Body Piercing." *Menstuff*. National Men's Resource Center, 1 Feb. 2001. Web. 17 July 2004.	…("Ouch!"). According to the National Men's Resource Center,…("Ouch!"). • *Add "Ouch!" in parentheses to show that work is alphabetized under "Ouch!" not "National."* • *No page numbers are shown because Web site pages aren't stable.*
Indirect citation of a source that you found in another source *Suppose you want to use a quotation from Peter Singer that you found in a book by Daniel Dombrowski. Include Dombrowski but not Singer in Works Cited.*	Dombrowski, Daniel A. *Babies and Beasts: The Argument from Marginal Cases*. Urbana: U of Illinois P, 1997. Print.	Animal rights activist Peter Singer argues that…(qtd. in Dombrowski 429). • *Singer is used for the attributive tag, but the in-text citation is to Dombrowski.* • *"qtd. in" stands for "quoted in."*

When to Use Page Numbers in In-Text Citations When the materials you are citing are available in print or in .pdf format, you can provide accurate page numbers for parenthetical citations. If you are working with Web sources or HTML files, however, do not use the page numbers obtained from a printout because they will not be consistent from printer to printer. If the item has numbered paragraphs, cite them with the abbreviation *par.* or *pars.*—for example,

"(Jones, pars. 22–24)." In the absence of reliable page numbers for the original material, MLA says to omit page references from the parenthetical citation. The following chart summarizes the use of page numbers in in-text citations.

Include a page number in the in-text citation:	Do not include a page number:
If the source has stable page numbers (print source or .pdf version of print source): • If you quote something • If you paraphrase a specific passage • If you refer to data or details from a specific page or range of pages in the source	• If you are referring to the argument of the whole source instead of a specific page or passage • If the source does not have stable page numbers (articles on Web sites, HTML text, and so forth)

Works Cited List in MLA Style

In the MLA system, you place a complete Works Cited list at the end of the paper. The list includes all the sources that you mention in your paper. However, it does *not* include works you read but did not use. Entries in the Works Cited list follow these general guidelines:

- Entries are arranged alphabetically by author, or by title if there is no author.
- Each entry includes the medium of publication of the source you consulted— for example, *Print, Web, DVD, Performance, Oil on canvas,* and so on.
- If there is more than one entry per author, the works are arranged alphabetically by title. For the second and all additional entries, type three hyphens and a period in place of the author's name.

> Dombrowski, Daniel A. *Babies and Beasts: The Argument from Marginal Cases.*
> Urbana: U of Illinois P, 1997. Print.
>
> ---. *The Philosophy of Vegetarianism.* Amherst: U of Massachusetts P, 1984. Print.

You can see a complete, properly formatted Works Cited list on the last pages of James Gardiner's paper.

The remaining pages in this section show examples of MLA citation formats for different kinds of sources and provide explanations and illustrations as needed.

MLA Citation Models

Print Articles in Scholarly Journals

General Format for Print Article in Scholarly Journal

Author. "Article Title." *Journal Title* volume number.issue number (year): page

numbers. Print.

Note that all scholarly journal entries include both volume number and issue number, regardless of how the journal is paginated. For articles published in a scholarly Web journal or scholarly journal articles retrieved from an online database the specific listings later in this chapter.

One author

Herrera-Sobek, Maria. "Border Aesthetics: The Politics of Mexican Immigration in Film
and Art." *Western Humanities Review* 60.2 (2006): 60–71. Print.

Two or three authors

Pollay, Richard W., Jung S. Lee, and David Carter-Whitney. "Separate, but Not Equal:
Racial Segmentation in Cigarette Advertising." *Journal of Advertising* 21.1 (1992):
45–57. Print.

Four or more authors

Either list all the authors in the order in which they appear, or use "et al." (meaning "and others") to replace all but the first author.

Buck, Gayle A., et al. "Examining the Cognitive Processes Used by Adolescent Girls and
Women Scientists in Identifying Science Role Models: A Feminist Approach."
Science Education 92.4 (2008): 688–707. Print.

Print Articles in Magazines and Newspapers

If no author is identified, begin the entry with the title or headline. Distinguish
between news stories and editorials by putting the word "Editorial" after the title.
If a magazine comes out weekly or biweekly, include the complete date ("27 Sept.
2010"). If it comes out monthly, then state the month only ("Sept. 2010").

General Format for Magazines and Newspapers

Author. "Article Title." *Magazine Title* day Month year: page numbers. Print.

Note: If the article continues in another part of the magazine or newspaper,
add "+" to the number of the first page to indicate the nonsequential pages.

Magazine article with named author

Snyder, Rachel L. "A Daughter of Cambodia Remembers: Loung Ung's Journey." *Ms.*
Aug.–Sept. 2001: 62–67. Print.

Magazine article without named author

"Daddy, Daddy." *New Republic* 30 July 2001: 2–13. Print.

Review of book, film, or performance

Schwarz, Benjamin. "A Bit of Bunting: A New History of the British Empire Elevates
Expediency to Principle." Rev. of *Ornamentalism: How the British Saw Their Empire*,
by David Cannadine. *Atlantic Monthly* Nov. 2001: 126–35. Print.

Kaufman, Stanley. "Polishing a Gem." Rev. of *The Blue Angel*, dir. Josef von Sternberg.
New Republic 30 July 2001: 28–29. Print.

Lahr, John. "Nobody's Darling: Fascism and the Drama of Human Connection in *Ashes to Ashes*." Rev. of *Ashes to Ashes*, by Harold Pinter. The Roundabout Theater Co. Gramercy Theater, New York. *New Yorker* 22 Feb. 1999: 182–83. Print.

Newspaper article

Henriques, Diana B. "Hero's Fall Teaches Wall Street a Lesson." *Seattle Times* 27 Sept. 1998: A1+. Print.

Page numbers in newspapers are typically indicated by a section letter or number as well as a page number. The "+" indicates that the article continues on one or more pages later in the newspaper.

Newspaper editorial

"Dr. Frankenstein on the Hill." Editorial. *New York Times* 18 May 2002, natl. ed.: A22. Print.

Letter to the editor of a magazine or newspaper

Tomsovic, Kevin. Letter. *New Yorker* 13 July 1998: 7. Print.

Print Books

General Format for Print Books

Author. *Title*. City of publication: Publisher, year of publication. Print.

One author

Pollan, Michael. *The Omnivore's Dilemma: A Natural History of Four Meals*. New York: Penguin, 2006. Print.

Two or more authors

Dombrowski, Daniel A., and Robert J. Deltete. *A Brief, Liberal, Catholic Defense of Abortion*. Urbana: U of Illinois P, 2000. Print.

Belenky, Mary, et al. *Women's Ways of Knowing: The Development of Self, Voice, and Mind*. New York: Basic, 1986. Print.

If there are four or more authors, you have the choice of listing all the authors in the order in which they appear on the title page or using "et al." (meaning "and others") to replace all but the first author. Your Works Cited entry and the parenthetical citation should match.

Second, later, or revised edition

Montagu, Ashley. *Touching: The Human Significance of the Skin*. 3rd ed. New York: Perennial, 1986. Print.

In place of "3rd ed.," you can include abbreviations for other kinds of editions: "Rev. ed." (for "Revised edition") or "Abr. ed." (for "Abridged edition").

Republished book (for example, a paperback published after the original hardback edition or a modern edition of an older work)

Hill, Christopher. *The World Turned Upside Down: Radical Ideas During the English Revolution*. 1972. London: Penguin, 1991. Print.

Wollstonecraft, Mary. *The Vindication of the Rights of Woman, with Strictures on Political and Moral Subjects*. 1792. Rutland: Tuttle, 1995. Print.

The date immediately following the title is the original publication date of the work.

Multivolume work

Churchill, Winston S. *A History of the English-Speaking Peoples*. 4 vols. New York: Dodd, 1956–58. Print.

Churchill, Winston S. *The Great Democracies*. New York: Dodd, 1957. Print. Vol. 4 of *A History of the English-Speaking Peoples*. 4 vols. 1956–58.

Use the first method when you cite the whole work; use the second method when you cite one individually titled volume of the work.

Article in familiar reference work

"Mau Mau." *The New Encyclopaedia Britannica*. 15th ed. 2002. Print.

Article in less familiar reference work

Ling, Trevor O. "Buddhism in Burma." *Dictionary of Comparative Religion*. Ed. S. G. F. Brandon. New York: Scribner's, 1970. Print.

Translation

De Beauvoir, Simone. *The Second Sex*. 1949. Trans. H. M. Parshley. New York: Bantam, 1961. Print.

Illustrated book

Jacques, Brian. *The Great Redwall Feast*. Illus. Christopher Denise. New York: Philomel, 1996. Print.

Graphic novel

Miyazaki, Hayao. *Nausicaa of the Valley of Wind*. 4 vols. San Francisco: Viz, 1995–97. Print.

Corporate author (a commission, committee, or other group)

American Red Cross. *Standard First Aid*. St. Louis: Mosby Lifeline, 1993. Print.

No author listed

The New Yorker Cartoon Album: 1975–1985. New York: Penguin, 1987. Print.

Whole anthology

O'Connell, David F., and Charles N. Alexander, eds. *Self Recovery: Treating Addictions Using Transcendental Meditation and Maharishi Ayur-Veda*. New York: Haworth, 1994. Print.

Anthology article

Royer, Ann. "The Role of the Transcendental Meditation Technique in Promoting
   Smoking Cessation: A Longitudinal Study." *Self Recovery: Treating Addictions
   Using Transcendental Meditation and Maharishi Ayur-Veda*. Ed. David F.
   O'Connell and Charles N. Alexander. New York: Haworth, 1994.
   221–39. Print.

When you cite an individual article, give the inclusive page numbers for the article at the end of the citation, before the medium of publication.

Articles or Books from an Online Database

General Format for Material from Online Databases

Author. "Title." *Periodical Name* Print publication data including date and volume/
   issue numbers: pagination. *Database*. Web. Date of access.

Journal article from online database

Matsuba, M. Kyle. "Searching for Self and Relationships Online." *CyberPsychology and
   Behavior* 9.3 (2006): 275–84. *Academic Search Complete*. Web. 14 Apr. 2007.

To see where each element in this citation was found, see Figure 1, which shows the online database screen from which the Matsuba article was accessed. For articles in databases, follow the formats for print newspapers, magazines, or scholarly journals, as relevant. When the database text provides only the starting page number of a multipage article, insert a plus sign after the number, before the period.

Broadcast transcript from online database

Conan, Neal. "Arab Media." *Talk of the Nation*. With Shibley Telhami. 4 May 2004.
   Transcript. *LexisNexis*. Web. 31 July 2004.

The label "Transcript" after the broadcast date indicates a text (not audio) version.

E-book from online database

Hanley, Wayne. *The Genesis of Napoleonic Propaganda, 1796–1799*. New York: Columbia
   UP, 2002. *Gutenberg-e*. Web. 31 July 2010.

Machiavelli, Niccolo. *Prince*. 1513. *Bibliomania*. Web. 31 July 2009.

Information about the original print version, including a translator if relevant and available, should be provided.

Other Internet Sources

General Format for Web Sources Since Web sources are often unstable, MLA recommends that you download or printout your Web sources. The goal in

FIGURE 1 Article Downloaded from an Online Database, with Elements Identified for an MLA-Style Citation

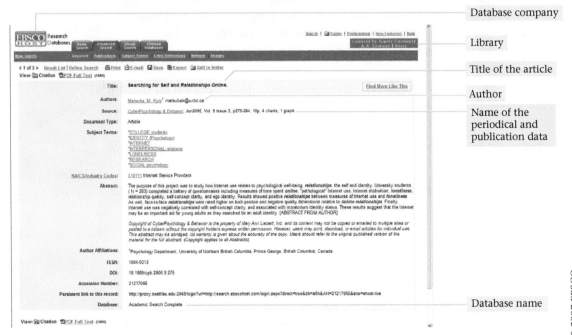

Matsuba, M. Kyle. "Searching for Self and Relationships Online." *CyberPsychology and Behavior* 9.3 (2006): 275–84. *Academic Search Complete*. Web. 14 Apr. 2007.

citing these sources is to enable readers to locate the material. To that end, use the basic citation model and adapt it as necessary.

Author, editor, director, narrator, performer, compiler, or producer of the work, if available. *Title of a long work, italicized.* OR "Title of page or document that is part of a larger work, in quotation marks. *Title of the overall site, usually taken from the home page, if this is different from the title of the work.* Publisher or sponsor of the site (if none, use N.p.), day Month year of publication online or last update of the site (if not available, use n.d.). Web. day Month year you accessed the site.

Saucedo, Robert. "A Bad Idea for a Movie." *theeagle.com.* Bryan College Station Eagle, 1 July 2010. Web. 7 July 2010.

To see where each element of the Saucedo citation comes from, see the Web article in Figure 2.

FIGURE 2 An Article Published on the Web, with Elements Identified for an MLA-Style Citation

Site title

Date posted

Article title

Author of the article

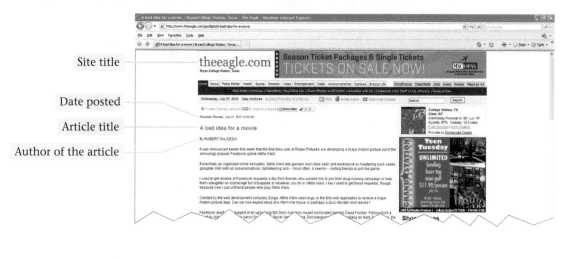

Site sponsor

Saucedo, Robert. "A Bad Idea for a Movie." *theeagle.com*. Bryan College Station Eagle, 1 July 2010. Web. 7 July 2010.

MLA assumes that readers will use a search engine to locate a Web source, so do not include a URL *unless* the item would be hard to locate without it. If you do include a URL, it goes at the end of the citation, after the access date. Enclose it in angle brackets < > followed by a period. If you need to break the URL from one line to the next, divide it only after a slash. Do not hyphenate a URL. See the home page entries on the next page for examples of citations with URLs.

Entire Web site

BlogPulse. Intelliseek, n.d. Web. 24 July 2010.

Padgett, John B., ed. *William Faulkner on the Web*. U of Mississippi, 26 Mar. 2007. Web. 25 June 2009.

Documents within a Web site

Marks, John. "Overview: Letter from the President." *Search for Common Ground*. Search for Common Ground, n.d. Web. 25 June 2007.

Gourlay, Alexander S. "Glossary." *The William Blake Archive*. Lib. of Cong., 2005. Web. 21 Jan. 2009.

"Ouch! Body Piercing." *Menstuff*. National Men's Resource Center, 1 Feb. 2001. Web. 17 July 2004. <http://www.menstuff.org/issues/byissue/fathersgeneral.html#bodypiercing>.

Citing and Documenting Sources

Article from a newspaper or newswire site

Bounds, Amy. "Thinking Like Scientists." *Daily Camera* [Boulder]. Scripps Interactive
   Newspaper Group, 26 June 2007. Web. 26 June 2007.

"Great Lakes: Rwanda Backed Dissident Troops in DRC-UN Panel." *IRIN*. UN Office for
   the Coordination of Humanitarian Affairs, 21 July 2004. Web. 31 July 2004.

Article from a scholarly e-journal

Welch, John R., and Ramon Riley. "Reclaiming Land and Spirit in the Western Apache
   Homeland." *American Indian Quarterly* 25.4 (2001): 5–14. Web. 19 Dec. 2001.

Broadcast transcript from a Web site

Woodruff, Judy, Richard Garnett, and Walter Dellinger. "Experts Analyze Supreme
   Court Free Speech Rulings." Transcript: background and discussion. *Online
   NewsHour*. PBS, 25 June 2007. Web. 26 June 2007.

Blog posting

Dyer, Bob, and Ella Barnes. "The 'Greening' of the Arctic." *Greenversations*. U.S.
   Environmental Protection Agency, 7 Oct. 2008. Web. 11 Oct. 2010.
   <http://blog.epa.gov/blog/2008/10/07/the-greening-of-the-artic/>.

To see where each element of this citation comes from, refer to Figure 3.

Podcast

"The Long and Winding Road: DNA Evidence for Human Migration." *Science Talk*.
   Scientific American, 7 July 2008. Web. 21 July 2010.

Web video

Beck, Roy. "Immigration Gumballs." *YouTube*. YouTube, 2 Nov. 2006. Web. 23 July 2009.

For films and DVDs, see page 588.

Home Pages

Agatucci, Cora. *Culture and Literature of Africa*. Course home page. Humanities Dept.,
   Central Oregon Community College, Jan. 2007–May 2007. Web. 31 July 2007.
   <http://web.cocc.edu/cagatucci/classes/hum211/>.

African Studies Program. Home page. School of Advanced International Study, Johns
   Hopkins U, n.d. Web. 31 July 2007.

Sharpe, William F. Home page. May 2004. Web. 31 July 2004.
   <http://www.stanford.edu/~wfsharpe/>.

E-mail

Daffinrud, Sue. "Scoring Guide for Class Participation." Message to the author. 12 Dec.
   2001. E-mail.

Use the subject line as the title of the e-mail. Use "E-mail" as the medium of publication and omit your access date.

FIGURE 3 A Blog Posting from the Web, with Citation Elements Identified

URL

Site sponsor

Name of blog

Title of posting

Date of posting

Blog author

Dyer, Bob, and Ella Barnes. "The 'Greening' of the Arctic." *Greenversations*. U.S. Environmental Protection Agency,

7 Oct. 2008. Web. 11 Oct. 2008. <http://blog.epa.gov/blog/2008/10/07/the-greening-of-the-arctic/>.

Miscellaneous Sources

Television or radio program
Begin with the episode name, if any, in quotation marks, followed by the program name, italicized. Use "Television" or "Radio" as the medium of publication.

"Lie Like a Rug." *NYPD Blue*. Dir. Steven Bochco and David Milch. ABC. KOMO, Seattle.

6 Nov. 2001. Television.

If you accessed a program on the Web, give the basic citation information without the original medium of publication; then include the Web publication information with an access date.

Ashbrook, Tom. "Turf Wars and the American Lawn." *On Point*. Natl. Public Radio,

22 July 2008. Web. 23 July 2009.

For podcasts, see the previous page.

Film or video recording

Shakespeare in Love. Dir. John Madden. Perf. Joseph Fiennes and Gwyneth Paltrow.

     Screenplay by Marc Norman and Tom Stoppard. Universal Miramax, 1998. Film.

Use "DVD" or "Videocassette" rather than "Film" as the medium of publication if that is the medium you consulted. If you accessed a film or video on the Web, omit the original medium of publication, include the Web site or database name (italicized), the sponsor and posting date, "Web" as medium of publication, and the date of access.

Shakespeare in Love. Dir. John Madden. Perf. Joseph Fiennes and Gwyneth Paltrow.

     Screenplay by Marc Norman and Tom Stoppard. Universal Miramax, 1998.

     Netflix. Netflix, n.d. Web. 9 Mar. 2010.

For videos published originally on the Web, see two pages previous.

Sound recording

Begin the entry with what your paper emphasizes—for example, the artist's, composer's, or conductor's name—and adjust the elements accordingly. List the medium—CD, LP, Audiocassette—last.

Dylan, Bob. "Rainy Day Women #12." *Blonde on Blonde*. Columbia, 1966. LP.

If you accessed the recording on the Web, drop the original medium of publication and include the Web site or database name (italicized), "Web" as the medium of publication, and the access date.

Dylan, Bob. "Rainy Day Women #12." *Blonde on Blonde*. Columbia, 1966. *Lala*. La La

     Media, n.d. Web. 10 Mar. 2010.

Cartoon or advertisement

Trudeau, Garry. "Doonesbury." Comic strip. *Seattle Times* 19 Nov. 2001: B4. Print.

Banana Republic. Advertisement. *Details* Oct. 2001: 37. Print.

Interview

Castellucci, Marion. Personal interview. 7 Oct. 2010.

Lecture, speech, or conference presentation

Sharples, Mike. "Authors of the Future." Conference of European Teachers of Academic

     Writing. U of Groningen. Groningen, Neth. 20 June 2001. Lecture.

Government publications

In general, follow these guidelines:

- Usually cite as author the government agency that produced the document. Begin with the highest level and then branch down to the specific agency:

       United States. Dept. of Justice. FBI.

       Idaho. Dept. of Motor Vehicles.

- Follow this with the title of the document, italicized.
- If a specific person is clearly identified as the author, you may begin the citation with that person's name, or you may list the author (preceded by the word "By") after the title of the document.
- Follow standard procedures for citing publication information for print sources or Web sources.

> United States. Dept. of Justice. FBI. *The School Shooter: A Threat Assessment Perspective.* By Mary Ellen O'Toole. 2000. Web. 16 Aug. 2001.

James Gardiner (student), "Why *Facebook* Might Not Be Good for You" (MLA-Style Research Paper)

As an illustration of a student research paper written in MLA style, we present James Gardiner's paper on online social networks.

Gardiner 1

James Gardiner

Professor Johnson

Writing Seminar: Inquiry and Argument

15 May 2007

Why *Facebook* Might Not Be Good for You:

Some Dangers of Online Social Networks

Walk into any computer lab located at any college campus across the country and you'll see dozens of students logged onto an online social network (OSN). In the last few years, the use of these networks has skyrocketed among Internet users, especially young adults. These new virtual communities are significantly influencing the way young people communicate and interact with one another. A report titled "E-Expectations: The Class of 2007" went so far as to label upcoming college freshmen "the Social-Networking Generation" (qtd. in Joly).

In late 2006, the Pew Internet Project, a nonpartisan, nonprofit research group that examines the social impact of the Internet, reported that 55 percent of online teens have created a personal profile on OSNs and that 48 percent of teens visit social networking Web sites daily, with 22 percent visiting several times a day (Lenhart and Madden 2). The two most popular OSNs are *MySpace* and *Facebook*. *MySpace* is a general networking site that allows anyone to join, develop a profile, and display personal information. In less than four years of existence, *MySpace* has exploded to become the third most visited Web site on the Internet behind only *Google* and *Yahoo* ("Top Sites") with more than 100 million members (Joly). *Facebook* is geared more toward college students (until recently it required that a person attend a university to join the network) and is the number-one site accessed by 18- to 24-year-olds. According to research studies cited in an article in the *Toronto Star*, 90 percent of all undergraduates log on to *Facebook* and

Gardiner 2

60 percent log on daily (George-Cosh W1). *Facebook* has also experienced unprecedented growth in its relatively short existence and now ranks as the seventh most visited site on the Internet ("Top Sites") and has a member base of more than 19 million (Joly).

With the use of OSNs increasing among young people, the term "Facebook trance" has emerged to describe a person who loses all track of time and stares at the screen for hours (Copeland). While "Facebook trance" might describe only an occasional and therefore harmless phenomenon, it gives rise to important questions: What are the possible negative consequences of OSNs? What should youthful users be watchful for and guard against? The purpose of this paper is to identify the possible harms of OSNs. I will suggest that overuse of OSNs can be a contributing factor to a decline in grades as well as to other problems such as a superficial view of relationships, an increase in narcissism, and possible future embarrassment.

I don't mean to deny that OSNs have positive consequences for young people. For one thing, they provide a "virtual hangout" that acts as a convenient and cost-effective way to stay in close contact with friends and family. According to the Pew survey, 91 percent of users use OSNs to keep in touch with their regularly seen friends, while 82 percent use the sites to stay in touch with distant friends (Lenhart and Madden). OSNs let young people regularly view their friends' profiles, leave short messages or comments, and share personal information. OSN researcher Danah Boyd also claims that these sites give young people a platform on which to experiment with identities, voice their opinions, and practice how they present themselves through personal data, pictures, and music placed in their profiles (Bowley). OSNs also assist them in learning more about people they've met offline. Used as an investigative tool, OSNs offer quick ways to get additional background information on someone. For example, a student could use an OSN to decide whom to partner with for

Gardiner 3

a class project, to learn more about a new roommate, or to find out more about someone he or she just met at a party, all by browsing classmates' profiles.

Despite these benefits, OSNs have a downside. One potential harm is that OSNs could have a negative effect on grades. One study shows a direct connection between the amount of time spent on the networks and declining grades in school. A college newspaper article entitled "Research Links *MySpace* Use to Drop in Grades" reports a survey of high school students conducted by Fresno State University professor Tamyra Pierce. Pierce found that students with *MySpace* accounts were significantly more likely than students without *MySpace* accounts to report a decline in grades since the previous year. According to Pierce, "We can't know for sure that *MySpace* caused the lower grades, but when compared to other after-school activities (work, sports, video games, etc.), only *MySpace* showed significance" (qtd. in "Research Links"). Pierce's research also revealed that 42 percent of polled students said they often had *MySpace* open while doing homework, and 34 percent stated that they would delay homework to spend time on social networking sites. Pierce adds that 59 percent of students reported spending "between 30 minutes and six hours daily on *MySpace*." Such heavy usage significantly takes time away from school work, extracurricular activities, and sleep. Although this specific study focused on high school students, it would be safe to assume that the results would be generally similar for college students. In fact, the results of the Fresno State study were reported in other college newspapers (Scrabis; Jimenez); the writers for these college newspapers usually included anecdotes from their own campuses about college students obsessed with OSNs. One Penn State student said of *MySpace*, "I keep getting rid of it and then getting it back again because I'm addicted. It's like cocaine" (qtd. in Scrabis).

Another potential problem with OSNs is their tendency to promote superficial or unsatisfying relationships. According to Chou, Condron, and

Use quotation marks for article titles.

Use "qtd. in" for a source quoted in another source.

756

Gardiner 4

Belland, for some users "over-dependence on online relationships may result in significant problems with real-life interpersonal and occupational functioning" (381). When logged on to the network, students may believe that they are "in touch" with people, when actually they are physically alone with their computers. In a controversial 1998 article cited by Matsuba, Kraut and his colleagues suggested that extensive Internet use "was associated with declines in participants' communication with family members in the household, declines in the size of their social circle, and increases in their depression and loneliness" (qtd. in Matsuba 275). Matsuba conducted an extensive study to test Kraut's conclusions. Matsuba found that persons who scored high on measures of loneliness spent more time on the Internet than persons who scored low on the loneliness measures. In another facet of his study, Matsuba found that for persons who established online friendships, these friendships did not seem "as rich and diverse in quality compared to face-to-face friendships" (283). Matsuba concludes that while online communication can be used to enhance relationships, it can become a problem when it begins to replace offline interaction. He found that face-to-face friendships scored higher for both positive and negative aspects of relationships than did online friendships. He then speculates, "While it is possible that the internet is helping [lonely] people in their search, the possibility remains that the internet is hindering them in facing life in the 'real' world and thus preventing them from developing an adult identity" (283).

Matsuba's finding that face-to-face friendships are more "rich and diverse in quality" than online friendships has led me to speculate that a possible problem with OSNs is the complete lack of nonverbal communication exchanged between users. According to communications professor Julia T. Woods, "Scholars estimate that nonverbal behaviors account for 65 percent to 93 percent of the total meaning of communication" (132). Since the people

Gardiner 5

interacting on OSNs are unable to view each other, they are unable to gauge the other's subtle body language, facial expressions, and voice tones that are such vital ingredients of effective communication. Part of achieving the "adult identity" called for by Matsuba is learning to communicate nonverbally as well as verbally in an environment requiring real contact.

For me, a particularly interesting yet subtle danger of OSNs is their contribution to a rise in narcissism. In an article with the subtitle "Study Says Many Students Are Narcissists," journalist E. Hoover reports on the unpublished research of Jean M. Twenge, a psychology professor at San Diego State University, who says that new technologies such as OSNs have "stoked the self-loving tendencies of modern students" (qtd. in Hoover). Twenge's recent research shows that college kids today are more narcissistic than college kids were in the 1980s; she labels the current generation of youth as "the most narcissistic in recent history" (Hoover). According to Hoover, Twenge defines narcissism as "excessive vanity and a sense of entitlement." Narcissists, Hoover reports, "tend to lack empathy for others, behave aggressively when insulted, and ignore the needs of those around them."

According to Twenge, narcissism finds expression on OSNs in the way that young people on *MySpace* and *Facebook* compete with each other to be heard. In another article reporting Twenge's research, Melissa Ludwig states that OSNs have "gone beyond touching base with friends to an arena where people vie for the most digital friends, the best videos, the coolest sites, and the biggest audience" (A15). She then quotes Twenge: "Now it all becomes a competition, seeking attention and seeking status rather than a true connection between people, or a meaningful connection." The work of Twenge and others suggests that the popularity of OSNs is partly the result of young people's finding an online way to express their narcissistic tendencies. The sites may contribute to self-expression more than to connection and friendship.

Gardiner 6

A final danger of OSNs is that persons will place on their sites material that they will later regret. Young people tend to think that their audiences are only their like-minded friends and classmates. They often don't imagine their professors, their potential employers, or even their parents reading their sites. One journalist describes a *MySpace* profile in which a college student has posted photos of herself in "a skin-tight black leather Catwoman costume, two triangles of vinyl struggling to cover her silicone-enhanced breasts" (Ludwig A15). Ludwig continues:

> Much of the stuff floating around in cyberspace is tame, mundane even. But there also is plenty that's racy, embarrassing or squeamishly intimate. Bad or good, Generation Next is living out loud and doing it online, before a global audience, in a medium where digital archives may linger for a long, long time.... [Generation Nexters] still are too young to fully grasp the permanence of their online actions, and the possible consequences down the road. (A15)

One indication of this danger has already surfaced in the case of some sports teams. The University of Minnesota Duluth recently barred all athletes from creating profiles on *MySpace*, *Facebook*, and similar sites, a policy that, according to journalist Chao Xiong, aims to shield students and the school from bad press that might occur from the posting of inappropriate material. Xiong reports that athletic departments across the country are considering similar bans. One coach at the UM-Duluth campus said, "It was amazing to me how revealing people are with their lives on the Internet" (qtd. in Xiong 1A). (This coach had established her own *Facebook* profile in order to police the activities of her team members.) Xiong reports that across the country athletes have embarrassed their programs by posting pictures of themselves drinking blindfolded at parties or making disparaging comments about coaches or teammates. It is unclear

Indent longer quotations 10 spaces or 1 inch.

Use ellipsis to show omitted words.

Use brackets when inserting explanatory words in quotation.

Cite page number after period.

whether coaches have the legal right to forbid their team members to place profiles on OSNs (some students are claiming violation of free speech rights). However, the fact that athletic programs are concerned about the impact of these social networks shows the potential negative consequence of posting embarrassing material on OSNs.

Although I don't support the banning of *Facebook* or *MySpace* profiles for athletes or other students, I do think that young people should be aware of some of the problems associated with them. Two of the problems I have noted here—decline in grades and narcissistic competition for the coolest sites—could be avoided by students' simply limiting their time online. Knowing that OSNs can promote a superficial view of friendships might encourage people to use OSNs to stay in touch face-to-face with friends rather than try to find online substitutes for real friendships. Finally, young people should be aware that the materials they post on their profiles might one day come back to haunt them. To gain the maximum benefits of online social networks and avoid the pitfalls associated with them, my advice to today's students would be to use them as an advanced e-mail-type communication tool rather than as a place to loiter and waste valuable hours that they will never get back.

Gardiner 8

Works Cited

Bowley, Graham. "The High Priestess of Internet Friendship." *Financial*
    Times Weekend Magazine 27 Oct. 2006. *LexisNexis Academic.*
    Web. 22 Feb. 2007.

Chou, Chien, Linda Condron, and John C. Belland. "A Review of the Research on
    Internet Addiction." *Educational Psychology Review* 17.4 (2005): 363–89.
    Academic Search Complete. Web. 22 Feb. 2007.

Copeland, Libby. "Click Clique: *Facebook's* Online College Community."
    Washingtonpost.com. Washington Post, 28 Dec. 2004. Web. 24 Feb. 2007.

George-Cosh, David. "Social Net: Thousands of Local Students Build
    Friendships on *Facebook.*" *TheStar.com.* Toronto Star, 20 Jan. 2007.
    Web. 15 Apr. 2007.

Hoover, E. "Here's You Looking at You, Kid: Study Says Many Students Are
    Narcissists." *Chronicle of Higher Education* 53.29 (9 Mar. 2007): A41.
    Academic Search Complete. Web. 14 Apr. 2007.

Jimenez, Eddie. "*MySpace* Adds to Overload for Teens." *Fresno Bee* 9 Mar. 2007.
    Newspaper Source. Web. 14 Apr. 2007.

Joly, Karine. "*Facebook, MySpace*, and Co." *University Business*. Professional
    Media Group, Apr. 2007. Web. 5 May 2007.

Lenhart, Amanda, and Mary Madden. "Social Networking Websites and Teens:
    An Overview." *Pew Internet and American Life Project*. Pew Research
    Center, 3 Jan. 2007. Web. 19 Feb. 2007.

Ludwig, Melissa. "LOOK@ME: Generation Next Is Living Out Loud and
    Online." *MySanAntonio.com.* San Antonio Express News, 15 Mar. 2007.
    Web. 15 Apr. 2007.

Matsuba, M. Kyle. "Searching for Self and Relationships Online."
    CyberPsychology and Behavior 9.3 (2006): 275–84. *Academic Search*
    Complete. Web. 14 Apr. 2007.

MLA Style

Start Works Cited list on a new page.

Center heading.

List sources alphabetically.

Use day-month-year format for dates.

Italicize database names.

Italicize periodical titles.

Use quotation marks for article titles.

Gardiner 9

"Research Links *MySpace* Use to Drop in Grades." *FresnoStateNews.com*.

California State U, 9 Mar. 2007. Web. 2 May 2007.

Scrabis, J. "*MySpace* Usage May Lower Grades in Both High School, College

Students." *Daily Collegian*. Pennsylvania State U, 23 Mar. 2007.

Web. 15 Apr. 2007.

"Top Sites for United States." *alexia.com*. N.p., n.d. Web. 2 May 2007.

<http://www.alexia.com/site/ds/

top_sites?cc=US&ts_mode=country&lang=none>.

Woods, Julia T. *Interpersonal Communication*: *Everyday Encounters*.

5th ed. New York: Wadsworth, 2007. Print.

Xiong, Chao. "Not Their Space." *Minneapolis Star Tribune* 16 Apr. 2007.

LexisNexis. Web. 2 May 2007.

Put URLs in angle brackets.

Italicize book titles.

Check that everything cited in paper is in Works Cited list.

SKILL 4 Cite and document sources using APA style.

In many respects, the APA style and the MLA style are similar and the basic logic is the same. In the APA system, the list where readers can find full bibliographic information is titled "References"; as in MLA format, it includes only the sources cited in the body of the paper. The distinguishing features of APA citation style are highlighted in the following sections.

In-Text Citations in APA Style

A typical APA-style in-text citation contains three elements: (1) the last name of the author, (2) the date of the publication, and (3) the page number of the quoted or paraphrased passage. Table 3 identifies some typical variations and shows again the one-to-one connection between the in-text citation and the References list.

TABLE 3 In-Text Citations in APA Style

Type of Source	References Entry at End of Paper	In-Text Citation in Body of Paper
One author	Pollan, M. (2006). *The omnivore's dilemma: A natural history of four meals*. New York, NY: Penguin.	…(Pollan, 2006, p. 256). OR According to Pollan (2006), … (p. 256).
Two authors	Kwon, O., & Wen, Y. (2010). An empirical study of the factors affecting social network service use. *Computers in Human Behavior, 26*, 254–263. doi:10.1016 /j.chb.2009.04.011	…(Kwon & Wen, 2010, p. 262). OR Kwon and Wen (2010) claim that…(p. 262).
Three to five authors	Pollay, R. W., Lee, J. S., & Carter-Whitney, D. (1992). Separate, but not equal: Racial segmentation in cigarette advertising. *Journal of Advertising, 21*(1), 45–57.	…race" (Pollay, Lee, & Carter-Whitney, 1992, p. 52). OR Pollay, Lee, and Carter-Whitney have argued that "advertisers… race" (1992, p. 52). *For subsequent citations, use Pollay et al. For a quotation, use the specific page number, not the whole range of pages.*

(*continued*)

APA Style

TABLE 3   *continued*

Type of Source	References Entry at End of Paper	In-Text Citation in Body of Paper
Author has more than one work in References list	Dombrowski, D. A. (1984). *The philosophy of vegetarianism.* Amherst, MA: University of Massachusetts Press. Dombrowski, D. A. (1997). *Babies and beasts: The argument from marginal cases.* Urbana: University of Illinois Press.	…(Dombrowski, 1984, p. 207). …(Dombrowski, 1997, p. 328). OR Dombrowski (1984) claims that…(p. 207). According to Dombrowski (1997),…(p. 328).
Indirect citation of a source that you found in another source *You use a quotation from Peter Singer from a book by Dombrowski. Include Dombrowski, not Singer, in References.*	Dombrowski, D. A. (1997). *Babies and beasts: The argument from marginal cases.* Urbana: University of Illinois Press.	Animal rights activist Peter Singer argues that…(as cited in Dombrowski, 1997, p. 429). *Singer is used for the attributive tag, but the in-text citation is to Dombrowski.*

References List in APA Style

The APA References list at the end of a paper presents entries alphabetically. If you cite more than one item for an author, repeat the author's name each time and arrange the items in chronological order, beginning with the earliest. In cases where two works by an author appeared in the same year, arrange them in the list alphabetically by title, and then add a lowercase "a" or "b" (etc.) after the date so that you can distinguish between them in the in-text citations:

Smith, R. (1999a). *Body image in non-Western cultures, 1750–present.* London, England: Bonanza Press.

Smith, R. (1999b). Eating disorders reconsidered. *Journal of Appetite Studies, 45,* 295–300.

APA Citation Models

Print Articles in Scholarly Journals

General Format for Print Article in Scholarly Journal

Author. (Year of Publication). Article title. *Journal Title, volume number,* page numbers. doi: xx.xxxx/x.xxxx.xx

If there is one, include the **DOI** (digital object identifier), a number that is uniquely assigned to many journal articles. Note the style for capitalizing article titles and for italicizing the volume number.

One author

Herrera-Sobek, M. (2006). Border aesthetics: The politics of Mexican immigration in film and art. *Western Humanities Review, 60,* 60–71. doi:10.1016/j.chb.2009.04.011

Two to seven authors

Kwon, O., & Wen, Y. (2010). An empirical study of the factors affecting social network service use. *Computers in Human Behavior, 26,* 254–263.

When a source has more than seven authors, list the first six and the last one by name. Use ellipses (...) to indicate the authors whose names have been omitted.

Scholarly journal that restarts page numbering with each issue

Pollay, R. W., Lee, J. S., & Carter-Whitney, D. (1992). Separate, but not equal: Racial segmentation in cigarette advertising. *Journal of Advertising, 21*(1), 45–57.

Note that the issue number and the parentheses are *not* italicized.

Print Articles in Magazines and Newspapers

General Format for Print Article in Magazine or Newspaper

Author. (Year, Month Day). Article title. *Periodical Title, volume number,* page numbers.

If page numbers are discontinuous, identify every page, separating numbers with a comma.

Magazine article with named author

Hall, S. S. (2001, March 11). Prescription for profit. *The New York Times Magazine,* 40–45, 59, 91–92, 100.

Magazine article without named author

Daddy, daddy. (2001, July 30). *New Republic, 225,* 12–13.

Review of book or film

Schwarz, B. (2001, November). A bit of bunting: A new history of the British empire elevates expediency to principle [Review of the book *Ornamentalism: How the British saw their empire*]. *Atlantic Monthly, 288,* 126–135.

Kaufman, S. (2001, July 30). Polishing a gem [Review of the motion picture *The blue angel*]. *New Republic, 225,* 28–29.

Newspaper article

Henriques, D. B. (1998, September 27). Hero's fall teaches Wall Street a lesson. *Seattle Times,* pp. A1, A24.

Newspaper editorial

Dr. Frankenstein on the hill [Editorial]. (2002, May 18). *The New York Times,* p. A22.

Letter to the editor of a magazine or newspaper

Tomsovic, K. (1998, July 13). Culture clash [Letter to the editor]. The New Yorker, 7.

Print Books

General Format for Print Books

Author. (Year of publication). *Book title: Subtitle.* City, State [abbreviated]: Name of
Publisher.

Brumberg, J. J. (1997). *The body project: An intimate history of American girls.* New York,
NY: Vintage.

If the publisher's name indicates the state in which it is located, list the city but
omit the state.

Reid, H., & Taylor, B. (2010). *Recovering the commons: Democracy, place, and global justice.*
Champaign: University of Illinois Press.

Second, later, or revised edition

Montagu, A. (1986). *Touching: The human significance of the skin* (3rd ed.). New York, NY:
Perennial Press.

*Republished book (for example, a paperback published after the original hardback
edition or a modern edition of an older work)*

Wollstonecraft, M. (1995). *The vindication of the rights of woman, with strictures on
political and moral subjects.* Rutland, VT: Tuttle. (Original work published 1792)

The in-text citation should read: (Wollstonecraft, 1792/1995).

Multivolume work

Churchill, W. S. (1956–1958). *A history of the English-speaking peoples* (Vols. 1–4). New
York, NY: Dodd, Mead.

Citation for all the volumes together. The in-text citation should read: (Churchill,
1956–1958).

Churchill, W. S. (1957). *A history of the English-speaking peoples: Vol. 4. The great
democracies.* New York, NY: Dodd, Mead.

Citation for a specific volume. The in-text citation should read: (Churchill, 1957).

Article in reference work

Ling, T. O. (1970). Buddhism in Burma. In S. G. F. Brandon (Ed.), *Dictionary of
comparative religion.* New York, NY: Scribner's.

Translation

De Beauvoir, S. (1961). *The second sex* (H. M. Parshley, Trans.). New York, NY: Bantam
Books. (Original work published 1949)

The in-text citation should read: (De Beauvoir, 1949/1961).

Corporate author (a commission, committee, or other group)

American Red Cross. (1993). *Standard first aid*. St. Louis, MO: Mosby Lifeline.

Anonymous author

The New Yorker cartoon album: 1975–1985. (1987). New York, NY: Penguin Books.
The in-text citation is (*New Yorker*, 1987).

Whole anthology

O'Connell, D. F., & Alexander, C. N. (Eds.). (1994). *Self recovery: Treating addictions using transcendental meditation and Maharishi Ayur-Veda*. New York, NY: Haworth Press.

Anthology article

Royer, A. (1994). The role of the transcendental meditation technique in promoting smoking cessation: A longitudinal study. In D. F. O'Connell & C. N. Alexander (Eds.), *Self recovery: Treating addictions using transcendental meditation and Maharishi Ayur-Veda* (pp. 221–239). New York, NY: Haworth Press.

Articles or Books from an Online Database

Article from database with digital object identifier (DOI)

Scharrer, E., Daniel, K. D., Lin, K.-M., & Liu, Z. (2006). Working hard or hardly working? Gender, humor, and the performance of domestic chores in television commercials. *Mass Communication and Society, 9*(2), 215–238. doi:10.1207/s15327825mcs0902_5

Omit the database name. If an article or other document has been assigned a digital object identifier (DOI), include the DOI at the end. To see where the information in the Scharrer citation came from, refer to Figure 4.

Article from database without DOI

Highland, R. A., & Dabney, D. A. (2009). Using Adlerian theory to shed light on drug dealer motivations. *Applied Psychology in Criminal Justice, 5*(2), 109–138. Retrieved from http://www.apcj.org

Omit the database name. Instead, use a search engine to locate the publication's home page, and cite that URL. If you need to break a URL at the end of a line, do not use a hyphen. Instead, break it *before* a punctuation mark or *after* http://.

Other Internet Sources

General Format for Web Documents

Author, editor, director, narrator, performer, compiler, or producer of the work, if available. (Year, Month Day of posting). *Title of web document, italicized.* Retrieved from Name of website if different from author or title: URL of home page

Barrett, J. (2007, January 17). *MySpace is a natural monopoly*. Retrieved from ECommerce Times website: http://www.ecommercetimes.com

FIGURE 4 Scholarly Journal Article with a Digital Object Identifier (DOI) with Elements Identified for an APA-Style Citation

Scharrer, E., Daniel, K. D., Lin, K.-M., & Liu, Z. (2006). Working hard or hardly working?

Gender, humor, and the performance of domestic chores in television commericals.

Mass Communication and Society, 9(2), 215–238. doi:10.1207/s15327825mcs0902_5

To see where each element of the Barrett citation comes from, refer to Figure 2. If there is no posting date for the document you cite, use *n.d.* (for "no date").

Marks, J. (n.d.). "Overview: Letter from the president." Retrieved June 3, 2010, from the Search for Common Ground website: http://www.sfcg.org

Entire Web site

BlogPulse. (n.d.). Retrieved September 3, 2010, from the Intelliseek website: http://www.intelliseek.com

Article from a newspaper site

Bounds, A. (2007, June 26). Thinking like scientists. *Daily Camera* [Boulder]. Retrieved from http://www.dailycamera.com

Article from a scholarly e-journal

Welch, J. R., & Riley, R. (2001). Reclaiming land and spirit in the western Apache homeland. *American Indian Quarterly, 25*, 5–14. Retrieved from http://muse.jhu.edu/journals/american_indian_quarterly

Reference material

Cicada. (2004). In *Encyclopaedia Britannica*. Retrieved from http://www.britannica.com

E-book

Hoffman, F. W. (1981). *The literature of rock: 1954–1978*. Retrieved from
    http://www.netlibrary.com

E-mail, interviews, and personal correspondence

Cite personal correspondence in the body of your text, but not in the References
list: "Daffinrud (personal communication, December 12, 2001) claims that...."

Blog Posting

Dyer, B., & Barnes, E. (2008, October 7). The "greening" of the Arctic [Web log post].
    Retrieved from http://blog.epa.gov/blog/2008/10/07/the-greening-of-the-arctic

To see where each element of this citation comes from, refer to Figure 3.

Web video

Beck, R. (2006, November 2). Immigration gumballs [Video file]. Retrieved from
    http://www.youtube.com/watch?v=n7WJeqxuOfQ

Podcast

Funke, E. (Host). (2007, June 26). *ArtScene* [Audio podcast]. National Public Radio.
    Retrieved from http://www.npr.org

Miscellaneous Sources

Television program

Bochco, S., & Milch, D. (Directors). (2001, November 6). Lie like a rug [Television series
    episode]. In *NYPD blue*. New York, NY: American Broadcasting Company.

Film

Madden, J. (Director). (1998). *Shakespeare in love* [Motion picture]. United States:
    Universal Miramax.

Sound recording

Dylan, B. (1966). Rainy day women #12. On *Blonde on blonde* [Record]. New York, NY:
    Columbia.

Government publications

O'Toole, M. (2000). *The school shooter: A threat assessment perspective*. Washington,
    DC: U.S. Federal Bureau of Investigation. Retrieved from http://www.fbi.gov/
    publications/school/school2.pdf

Index